Human Olfactory Displays and Interfaces:

Odor Sensing and Presentation

Takamichi Nakamoto
Tokyo Institute of Technology, Japan

Information Science
REFERENCE

Managing Director:	Lindsay Johnston
Editorial Director:	Joel Gamon
Book Production Manager:	Jennifer Romanchak
Publishing Systems Analyst:	Adrienne Freeland
Development Editor:	Myla Merkel
Assistant Acquisitions Editor:	Kayla Wolfe
Typesetter:	Lisandro Gonzalez
Cover Design:	Nick Newcomer

Published in the United States of America by
Information Science Reference (an imprint of IGI Global)
701 E. Chocolate Avenue
Hershey PA 17033
Tel: 717-533-8845
Fax: 717-533-8661
E-mail: cust@igi-global.com
Web site: http://www.igi-global.com

Copyright © 2013 by IGI Global. All rights reserved. No part of this publication may be reproduced, stored or distributed in any form or by any means, electronic or mechanical, including photocopying, without written permission from the publisher. Product or company names used in this set are for identification purposes only. Inclusion of the names of the products or companies does not indicate a claim of ownership by IGI Global of the trademark or registered trademark.

Library of Congress Cataloging-in-Publication Data

Human olfactory displays and interfaces: odor sensing and presentation / Takamichi Nakamoto, editor.
    p. cm.
 Includes bibliographical references and index.
 Summary: "This book provides the opportunity to learn about olfactory displays and their odor reproduction, offering the fundamental and latest research of sensors and sensing systems as well as presentation technique"-- Provided by publisher.
 ISBN 978-1-4666-2521-1 (hardcover) -- ISBN 978-1-4666-2522-8 (ebook) -- ISBN 978-1-4666-2523-5 (print & perpetual access) 1. Olfactory sensors. 2. Olfactometry. 3. Biosensors. 4. Smell--Threshold. I. Nakamoto, Takamichi, 1959-
 QP458.H85 2013
 612.8'6--dc23
                                    2012023342

British Cataloguing in Publication Data
A Cataloguing in Publication record for this book is available from the British Library.

All work contributed to this book is new, previously-unpublished material. The views expressed in this book are those of the authors, but not necessarily of the publisher.

Editorial Advisory Board

Kenshi Hayashi, *Kyushu University, Japan*
Junichi Ide, *T. Hasegawa Co Ltd., Japan*
Krinshna C. Persaud, *University of Manchester, UK*
Takao Yamanaka, *Sophia University, Japan*
Yasuyuki Yanagida, *Meijo Univiersity, Japan*

List of Reviewers

Yuuichi Bannai, *Kanagawa Institute of Technology, Japan*
Hyung-Gi Byun, *Kangwon National University, Korea*
Julian W. Gardner, *University of Warwick, UK*
Gheorghita Ghinea, *Brunel University, UK*
Ricardo Gutierrez-Osuna, *Texas A&M University, USA*
Masataka Imura, *Osaka University, Japan*
Hiroshi Ishida, *Tokyo University of Agriculture and Technology, Japan*
Dong Wook Kim, *National Institute of Information and Communications Technology, Japan*
Mutsumi Kimura, *Shinshu University, Japan*
Yoshihiko Kuwana, *National Institute of Agrobiological Sciences, Japan*
Santiago Marco, *University of Barcelona, Spain*
Takashi Mihara, *Olympus Corporation, Japan*
Yuji Miyahara, *Tokyo Medical and Dental University, Japan*
Toshiaki Nagakura, *Osaka Electro-Communication University, Japan*
Akio Nakamura, *T. Hasegawa Co., Ltd., Japan*
Noritaka Nakaso, *Toppan Printing Co., Ltd., Japan*
Chica Ohshima, *Saga University, Japan*
Atsushi Saito, *Shibaura Institute of Technology, Japan*
Giorgio Sberveglieri, *University of Brescia, Italy*
Michiko Seyama, *NTT Microsystem Integration Laboratories, Japan*
Abhijit V. Shevade, *Jet Propulsion Laboratory (JPL), California Institute of Technology, USA*
Mana Sriyudthsak, *Chulalongkorn University, Thailand*
Iwao Sugimoto, *Tokyo University of Technology, Japan*
Yoshinori Takei, *Kanazawa Institute of Technology, Japan*

Akira Tomono, *Tokai University, Japan*

Mitsuo Tonoike, *Aino University, Japan*

Alex Vergara, *University of California, San Diego, USA*

Bartosz Wyszynski, *Tokyo Institute of Technology, Japan*

Masaki Yamaguchi, *Iwate University, Japan*

Table of Contents

Section 1
Fundamentals

Detailed Table of Contents

Section 1
Fundamentals

This chapter provides the introduction to olfaction from a physiological aspect. The basic anatomical organization of the olfactory system, physiology of olfactory transduction including an olfactory receptor, odor signal processing in an olfactory bulb, are explained.

The mechanism of odor perception is described. Basic characteristics such as olfactory acuity, threshold, adaptation, and Weber-Fechner's law are explained. Then, the non-invasive measurements of olfactory responses in the brain using Electroencephalography (EEG), Magnetoencephalography (MEG), and functional Magnetic Resonance Imaging (f-MRI) are described.

This chapter shows fundamentals of the olfactory display, such as scent generation, scent delivery, and the evaluation method of smell presentation. Scent generation is the production of scented air with specified components and concentrations. Scent delivery is the conveyance of the scented air from its generator to a human nose. It enables spatio-temporal control of olfactory stimuli essential for virtual reality. A variety of techniques for olfactory display are introduced in this chapter.

This chapter shows the interaction of olfaction with vision and gustation. By using cross-modal interaction between olfaction and vision, olfactory sensation different from the actual smell is obtained. Moreover, a pseudo gustatory experience is provided utilizing interaction among olfaction, gestation, and vision. Those effects were confirmed by the questionnaire surveys.

Chapter 5

This chapter introduces various aspects of odor analysis. First, sensory tests followed by their application are explained. Then, gas analysis methods, such as preconcentrator, gas chromatography, etc., are shown. The combination of Gas Chromatography with Olfactometry (GC-O) method is often used for Aroma Extraction Dilution Analysis (AEDA). Gas sensing devices in an odor sensing system are described. Principles of metal oxide gas sensors, Quartz Crystal Microbalance (QCM) gas sensors, organic semiconductors, carbon black composites, electrochemical sensors, and plasmonic sensors are introduced. Finally, pattern recognition techniques for discrimination among odors using an array of gas sensors are explained. Bayesian classification, maximum-likelihood classification, and neural networks are reviewed.

An odor recorder is a gadget to record smells as well as reproduce them. This chapter shows the fundamental techniques, such as methods to quantify mixture composition, research trend of an odor recorder, and various types of odor recorders. Then, a mixture quantification technique using a huge number of odor-component candidates and exploration methods to extract odor components are explained.

Section 2
Latest Studies

Quartz crystal microbalance coated with radio-frequency sputtered organic film is described. Chiral vapor discrimination, aroma sensing of tea leaves, the effect of surface water on aliphatic acetate sensing, and ionic-liquid added sputtered sensing film are explained.

The design of materials for sensing films coated over quartz crystal microbalances is described. Materials include typical polymers, polymers with nanobrushes, and nanostructured macromolecular metal complexes. Their sensitivities to volatile organic compounds are thoroughly investigated.

Microcantilevers coated with several polymers together with a preconcentrator detect Volatile Organic Compounds (VOCs). The theory, the control circuit, and the experimental result are presented. The estimated detection limit is sub-ppb levels for toluene and p-xylene after the vapor accumulation for 5 minutes at the preconcentrator.

A spherical surface acoustic wave device has an Interdigital Transducer (IDT) attached to a piezoelectric ball where an excited surface acoustic wave propagates many roundtrips. It works as an odor-sensing device when an organic sensing film is appropriately coated. Although various coating techniques are introduced, the ball-SAW device is coated using the self-assembling technique, employing chemisorptions of mixed synthetic-lipids with lipopolymers, followed by physisorption of amphipihilic GC materials show high sensitivity under various humidity levels.

Yasuaki Takada, Hitachi, Ltd., Japan
Yuichiro Hashimoto, Hitachi, Ltd., Japan
Hisashi Nagano, Hitachi, Ltd., Japan
Masuyuki Sugiyama, Hitachi, Ltd., Japan
Masuyoshi Yamada, Hitachi, Ltd., Japan
Minoru Sakairi, Hitachi, Ltd., Japan

Although mass spectrometry is typically an off-line measurement method, on-line measurement using mass spectrometry without any pretreatment of the analyte is presented. It can be applied to the detection of environmental pollutants and explosives. High-throughput detection of an explosive is demonstrated.

Julian W. Gardner, University of Warwick, UK
James A. Covington, University of Warwick, UK
Fauzan Khairi Che Harun, Universiti Teknologi Malaysia, Malaysia

An electronic mucosa is proposed mimicking a mucous layer within a nasal cavity which causes chromatographic effect. It consists of large-scale spatially distributed sensors and microcolumns and provides spatio-temporal signals with rich information for odor discrimination. The signal processing method based on the convolution function, which is being developed for the electronic mucosa, is also explained.

Abhijit V. Shevade, Jet Propulsion Laboratory (JPL), California Institute of Technology, USA
Margie L. Homer, Jet Propulsion Laboratory (JPL), California Institute of Technology, USA
Adam K. Kisor, Jet Propulsion Laboratory (JPL), California Institute of Technology, USA
Shiao-Ping S. Yen, Jet Propulsion Laboratory (JPL), California Institute of Technology, USA
Liana M. Lara, Jet Propulsion Laboratory (JPL), California Institute of Technology, USA
Hanying Zhou, Jet Propulsion Laboratory (JPL), California Institute of Technology, USA
Kenneth S. Manatt, Jet Propulsion Laboratory (JPL), California Institute of Technology, USA
Scott Gluck, Jet Propulsion Laboratory (JPL), California Institute of Technology, USA
Margaret A. Ryan, Jet Propulsion Laboratory (JPL), California Institute of Technology, USA

This chapter shows the application of an electronic nose to the International Space Station (ISS). The electronic nose composed of an array of chemiresistive sensors is used for monitoring targeted chemical species, such as leaks or spills. Ammonia, mercury, sulphur dioxide, and organic compounds were aimed to be quantified. The monitoring data on ISS for seven months show the short-term presence of alcohols, octafluoropropane, formaldehyde, etc.

The electronic nose often encounters the problem of sensor drift. Although the problem is related to a sensor device, it is possible to enhance the robustness using multivariate signal processing. The correction of unwanted variance and three-way data arrangement technique and a method based on principal component analysis are described.

Visualization and initial evaluation of the odor-sensing data are indispensable for an odor measurement. Exploratory data analysis is used to check the data quality, calculate the statistics, and produce the plots. This chapter introduces the visualization and data mining tools for both raw and preprocessed data including principal component analysis, cluster analysis, and cluster validity. Several case studies are demonstrated.

Gas sensors have the problem of selectivity, and background odor interferes with target odor. This chapter shows a signal processing technique for background suppression. A perceptron neural network with anti-Hebbian learning is used for the adaptation to the background gas. This algorithm is implemented into a FPGA digital circuit for real-time sensing of the target gas.

A salivary biosensor enables the measurement of the sedative state, which indicates a measure of comfort or relaxation, induced by a fragrance. The handheld SAA (Salivary Amylase Activity) monitor was developed by the authors and was applied to measure the psychological state of a subject after inhalation of the fragrance. It was found that this sensor provides a useful indicator of relaxation or refreshment of the subject.

Neocortial responses to odors were investigated using Near-Infrared Spectroscopy (NIRS). It is possible to observe the adaptation to sugar using NIRS. Since the degree of the cross adaptation reveals the similarity of an artificial sweetener to actual sugar, it might be an important indicator for screening effective flavoring to obtain delicious taste.

An aroma chip is an olfactory display using a chemical container made of a functional polymer. Its aroma release is controlled by a reversible phase transition of the functional polymer between sol and gel accompanied with temperature change. Its temperature is controlled using a Peltier device. This approach enables a soundless olfactory display and is expected to be a simple and easy-to-use device.

An odor pulse ejection technique using an inkjet device is described. It is possible to emit a scent for a short time using an inkjet device and switch smells rapidly. The pulse ejection technique reduces the quantity of scent, and thus, the problems of olfactory adaptation and smell lingering in the air are almost solved.

Since spatio-temporal control is important in virtual reality, the concentration of the scent generated by an olfactory display is determined by the simulation of Computational Fluid Dynamics (CFD) under a given environment of a virtual space. It enables realistic change in the odor concentration with time and space. Result of sensory tests for CFD-based odor presentation at the virtual environment is described.

Display technology to present images with scents and its sensory evaluation are described. The display using an air cannon and a projector screen and that using an LED panel and an air blower are presented. The evaluation methods, such as subjective assessment, measurement of oculo-pupillary reflex, and skin conductance change, are also explained.

The influence of olfaction in multimedia for entertaining people was investigated using a questionnaire survey. The information assimilation of the video with smell was better than that of the video without the presence of olfactory media. Moreover, subjects generally perceived more enjoyment of the olfaction-enhanced multimedia. However, further research is required to investigate the impact of olfaction on information recall.

Chapter 24

Odor receptors recognize not whole chemical structures of odorants but their partial structures. It can be said that a combination of activated olfactory receptors is determined by the combination of molecular partial structures. Such combinatorial molecular information is odor code. Odor reproduction based upon odor code sensing is described.

Foreword

Olfaction and taste are two truly chemical senses in which the interaction of the molecule and/or group of molecules with olfactory receptors triggers a chain of complex physiological events, which end in a cognitively interpreted "sensation." In humans, such sensation can be articulated and can lead to various descriptions that can be anything from general, e.g. "pleasant/unpleasant," to highly specific, such as chlorine, ammonia, or cinnamon. For most vertebrates, smell is existentially important because it pre-defines actions as diverse as "to run" or "to mate." It could be argued that some animals are biological machines whose sole purpose in life is to reproduce and olfaction is one of the key enabling functions. For many years, engineers and scientists have been fascinated with the idea of explaining olfaction and constructing artificial olfactory machines that do just that. Thus, biology has once more inspired creative activity that has resulted in hundreds of worthwhile and also some questionable publications. It has even received recognition at the Nobel Prize level. The present book belongs to this enormously fertile, but complex area of scientific endeavor.

My own entry into it was a NATO Workshop held in Reykjavik in 1991, to which I was invited by Julian Gardner, one of the contributors to this book. At that workshop there was also a demonstration of a very real olfactory situation. Professor Toyosaka Moriizumi opened a bottle of 12-year-old Suntory whiskey and asked the audience to report on the progressive spreading of a pleasant odour plume through the lecture room. At that point, I decided to intensify our own research in gas sensors. Needless to say that "Toyo" Moriizumi and I became life-long friends, until his untimely passing in 2010. On the paper that he presented, one of the co-authors was his student, Takamichi Nakamoto—the editor of this volume. Over the years, I became closely involved with the outstanding work of the group at the Tokyo Institute of Technology, which is truly a "hotbed of artificial olfactory" research.

The volume that Takamichi Nakamoto assembled does not answer or pretend to answer all the open questions related to olfaction. It is a compilation of highly relevant chapters that can be broadly divided to three groups: physiology and fundamentals of olfaction (1-4, 16-18), hardware and analytical aspects (5-13, 19), and information processing (14-15, 20-23).

Because it is a multi-authored book, there is an inevitable overlap between some chapters. For that reason alone, a crosscutting index is an essential feature of this volume. The fact that the book is multi-authored is an asset because it brings multiple viewpoints on issues that are far from being completely understood. There are several topics, which are notable for their absence. Two important sensing platforms are not covered: work function-based sensors and large optical sensing arrays. In addition, the chemical and material aspects of sensing materials are covered rather thinly. Nonetheless, overall, the book is an invaluable source of information and ideas about topics that spans areas as diverse as physiology, chemistry, physics, engineering, and informatics.

Jiri Janata
Georgia Institute of Technology, USA

Jiri Janata *is Georgia Research Alliance Eminent Scholar in the School of Chemistry and Biochemistry, Georgia Institute of Science and Technology. Between 1991 and 1997, he was an Associate Director of Environmental Molecular Sciences Laboratory, Pacific Northwest National Laboratory, in Richland, Washington. Prior to that appointment, he was Professor of Materials Science and Professor of Bioengineering at the University of Utah for 17 years. He was born in Czechoslovakia, where he received his Ph.D. degree in Analytical Chemistry from the Charles University (Prague) in 1965. His current interests include interfacial chemistry, chemical sensors, and electroanalytical chemistry with particular emphasis on development of chemical sensors for environmental and security applications.*

Preface

Although a human interface for vision and audio has been already been developed, an olfactory interface has not. However, people are becoming interested in olfaction as the next-generation human interface. A human interface for olfaction is composed of an olfactory display and an odor sensing system called an electronic nose. An olfactory display is an output of a machine, whereas the odor sensing system is its input. These are important to realize a human olfactory interface. Since an odor sensing system has been studied for last two decades, the researcher population is relatively large. An international conference of machine olfaction is held every two years. However, there are not many olfactory-display researchers, since the olfactory display only recently evolved in virtual reality. Although both fields have been studied separately, it is indispensable to see and understand both the olfactory display and the odor sensing system for developing human olfactory interfaces and their applications.

This is the first book to describe the entire human olfactory interface, including the olfactory display. This book introduces a new interface to researchers and developers in the area of human interface as well as researchers in the sensor field. It may also offer resources to developers in industries such as consumer electronics, electronic instruments, communications, virtual realities, foods, beverages, fragrances, chemicals, medicals, advertisements, amusements, and games. Final year undergraduates and graduates in the fields related to those above may read this book as an accessible starting point to understanding human olfactory interface.

This book is divided into two sections. The first section is composed of six chapters and provides the fundamental knowledge. Beginners can start learning human olfactory interfaces through this section. Even experts can update their knowledge, since this new field is progressing rapidly. People can use this section like a bible of human olfactory interface.

The second section is composed of 18 chapters and shows a variety of the latest studies in human olfactory interfaces, such as the technologies for both odor sensing and its presentation. People can learn the latest technologies through many case studies. This section describes materials and devices for sensing technologies, signal processing techniques, their application, and the evaluation techniques of human perception. Then, devices for olfactory display, evaluation techniques of olfactory display, and odor reproduction are explained. People can learn a variety of aspects of human olfactory interfaces through this section. Each chapter is briefly introduced below.

Chapter one is a very nice introduction of the physiological aspect of engineering. It describes olfactory receptors and the first stage of signal processing in the brain, the olfactory bulb. Chapter two then describes the basic characteristics of human olfaction, such as olfactory acuity, threshold, adaptation, and olfactory disorders. Moreover, it shows new non-invasive measurement techniques of brain activities related to olfaction.

Chapter three introduces the fundamentals of olfactory display, such as scent generation, scent delivery, and evaluation of olfactory display. Much information for olfactory-display beginners is available in this chapter. Chapter four shows multimodal interaction of olfaction with other senses, such as vision and gustation. The cross-modal interaction between olfaction and vision can expand the range of scents using a small number of actual odors. Furthermore, the olfactory stimulus enables the pseudo-gustatory experience.

Chapter five introduces the fundamentals of the odor analysis method, such as sensory evaluation, gas analysis instruments, devices for odor sensing systems, and pattern recognition techniques. This chapter is a good introduction for beginners in olfactory display as well as those of sensing systems. Chapter six shows the combination of odor sensing system with an olfactory display called an odor recorder. Since a variety of odors can be expressed using the mixture composition of odor components, it shows the overview of the mixture quantification techniques, followed by the case studies of odor recording.

Then, individual studies are described in section 2. Chapters 7 and 8 show sensing materials coated with quartz crystal microbalance. Radio frequency sputtered organic films in chapter seven and polymeric nanomaterials in chapter eight have interesting sensing properties. Chapter nine describes the microcantilever array combined with a preconcentrator. The theory, the experimental setup, and the experimental result are shown in this chapter. Chapter ten introduces a spherical surface acoustic wave sensor coated with organic film. The device enables a long propagation path compared with conventional surface acoustic wave sensors in spite of its compact size. Chapter eleven shows the technique of real-time mass spectrometry. High-throughput detection of explosives has been successfully demonstrated.

Chapters 12 and 13 explain the system of electronic noses. The electronic mucosa in chapter twelve utilizes signals in spatio-temporal domain to raise the sensing capability. Chapter thirteen shows the application of an electronic nose to the environmental monitoring at the International Space Station for seven months.

Chapters 14 to 16 study the issues of data analysis in the odor sensing system. Chapter fourteen shows the mathematical method to increase the robustness against sensor drift. Chapter fifteen provides the method of exploratory data analysis to check the data quality, to calculate the statics, and to obtain the data structure easily. Chapter sixteen shows the method to suppress the influence of background smells mimicking the biological adaptation characteristics.

Then, objective evaluation methods of human perception are described in chapters 17 and 18. Chapter seventeen shows the salivary biosensor to detect the sedative state induced by fragrance. Chapter eighteen explains near-infrared spectroscopy to monitor cortical response to flavoring. The adaptation of cortical responses is used to measure the similarity between the flavors.

Chapters 19 to 23 are related to an olfactory display. Chapter nineteen describes a scent generation device called an aroma chip. The surface of a chemical container is composed of a functional polymer gel for controlling release of a scent utilizing its phase transition between sol and gel. Chapter twenty shows an olfactory display based upon an inkjet printer mechanism. Since it enables the emission of scent pulse for a short time, various olfactory characteristics can be measured. Chapter twenty-one shows the combination of the fluid dynamics simulation with olfactory display. The scent with concentration, at any point in virtual space, calculated by the simulator is emitted using an olfactory display.

Chapter twenty-two shows the interaction of image with olfaction and its evaluation. The method of scent emission through the display screen and the psychological effect evaluated by point-of-gaze measurement are described. Chapter twenty-three explains the empirical study focusing on the influence of olfaction to augment multimedia application.

Chapter 24 describes odor reproduction using odor code extracted from molecular informatics. The concept of odor reproduction using the odor code is discussed.

Plenty of topics from various aspects, such as physiology, odor perception, cross-modal interaction, devices and signal processing methods of odor sensing systems, and devices and evaluation of olfactory display are provided. Readers can learn almost all the issues in the human olfactory interface. Since this is the first book to cover the whole human olfactory interface, it is expected to become a distinguished reference in this field.

Takamichi Nakamoto
Tokyo Institute of Technology, Japan

Acknowledgment

I would like to thank all of the contributors to this book. First, I would like to thank the chapter authors. Second, I would like to thank the referees, who provided constructive feedback to the authors. The readability of each chapter was improved after the revision according to the reviewers' comments. Finally, I would like to thank the staff at IGI Global.

Artificial olfaction, the major part of this book, was pioneered by the late Prof. Toyosaka Moriizumi, as mentioned by Prof. Jiri Janata in the Foreword. Although he passed away in 2010, the research on artificial olfaction has progressed because of his contribution. Much of this book is based upon his tremendous works.

Takamichi Nakamoto
Tokyo Institute of Technology, Japan

Section 1
Fundamentals

Chapter 1
Introduction to Olfaction:
Physiology

Graeme Lowe
Monell Chemical Senses Center, USA

ABSTRACT

This chapter introduces the basic anatomy and physiology of the neural systems involved in the detection and identification of odors by vertebrate animals. It describes the cellular architecture and function of these systems, tracing the path of sensory signals from the initial steps of sniffing and chemical stimulus transduction in the nose, through to the synaptic processing pathways in the circuits of the olfactory bulb and major areas of olfactory cortex. Included are reviews of the latest research findings and hypotheses shaping our fundamental understanding of olfactory mechanisms, with particular emphasis on mammalian olfaction.

INTRODUCTION

The sense of smell is both ancient and ubiquitous. Olfactory sensory systems have evolved in the simplest and the most complex animals to acquire and interpret information about chemical signals in the environment, a basic need shared by all motile organisms. Many essential biological functions are served by olfaction. The scent of a predator or smoke from a fire can alert an animal to impending danger, triggering life saving avoidance or escape responses. Odor cues may be critical for navigation and the location of food

or mates, and for social communication between members of the same species. The olfactory system of humans can also serve these basic biological functions. However, modern man is more reliant on the advanced senses of vision and hearing in daily life. Thus, our media and computer interfaces are universally engineered for visual display and sound, but have not routinely incorporated odor devices. For humans, olfaction seems to be a more primeval sense that nonetheless can significantly enrich our lives in important ways. It adds a flavor dimension to food and enhances the meaning and memory of our experiences through association with odors. This chapter deals with the physiology of olfaction, focusing on vertebrate animals

DOI: 10.4018/978-1-4666-2521-1.ch001

Copyright © 2013, IGI Global. Copying or distributing in print or electronic forms without written permission of IGI Global is prohibited.

and particularly mammals, which have been well studied. We will review how the nose detects odorants and how this sensory information is relayed to the brain. We will discuss current views about how central neural circuits may process this information to enable us to perceive odors.

In seeking to understand the design and workings of any system, it is helpful to specify its operational capabilities. Different species of animals have optimized their olfactory systems to function in different ecological contexts. However, we can list some key capabilities that would dictate the design of these systems: (1) detection of small organic molecules (*odorants*), either in aqueous phase (for aquatic species) or vapor phase (for air-breathing species); (2) wide range of detection sensitivity for odorants: psychophysical studies on vertebrates have reported airborne detection thresholds ranging over $\sim 2 \cdot 10^{-18}\,\mathrm{M} - 10^{-4}\,\mathrm{M}$; (3) wide diversity of odorants, with many hundreds or thousands of different compounds detected and discriminated; (4) fast detection and recognition of odorants; in rodents, detection and discrimination is possible after a single brief sniff lasting < 200 ms; (5) adaptation or habituation to background odorants; (6) shifts in perceived odor quality with changing odorant concentration; (7) identification of new odors in the presence of background odorants; (8) ability to discriminate between very similar odorants; (9) perception of odorant mixtures either as component odors ('elemental'), or as holistic objects ('configural'); (10) dependence of odor perception on prior olfactory experience, context and association with other sensory inputs. Here we will review some of the neural systems and physiological mechanisms that help to accomplish these tasks.

ANATOMICAL ORGANIZATION OF THE OLFACTORY SYSTEM

The structures that make up vertebrate olfactory systems can be divided into peripheral and central components (Allison, 1953). In the periphery, the nasal cavities enclose an *olfactory epithelium* (OE) that is responsible for sampling and detecting chemical cues in the environment. This information is then relayed to central systems by the *Olfactory Nerve* (ON), the first of twelve cranial nerves that interface the brain with the external world. In fish, lamellar folds of the olfactory sensory epithelium occupy a capsule that communicates with the external aqueous medium through a pair of openings or *nares*. In air breathing vertebrates, the olfactory epithelium resides on a series of convoluted shelves of bony cartilage, the nasal *turbinates*, that are housed in a nasal cavity positioned between the oral cavity and the brain (Figures 1a, 2a). The olfactory epithelium is a specialized sensory area of mucus-lined nasal tissues (*nasal mucosa*) (Graziadei, 1971). It contains several million *Olfactory Sensory Neurons* (OSNs), which are specialized neurons with a bipolar morphology (Figures 2b–d, 3c). Each OSN cell body (or *soma*) extends a long *dendrite* to the epithelial surface, where an apical *knob* sprouts fine *cilia* containing the odorant detection apparatus. A thin cable or *axon* extends basally from each OSN cell body (Figure 2c), and axons bundle together to form the olfactory nerve which enters the skull through fine perforations of the bony *cribriform plate* separating the nasal cavity from the brain. The OSNs are embedded in a matrix of *sustentacular cells*, which are positioned between the OSN dendrites.

The olfactory nerve axons project to a superficial layer of the *olfactory bulb*, which is the first major brain center dedicated to processing of odor signals arriving from the nose (Shepherd, 1972). Here, olfactory nerve terminals are organized into hundreds or thousands of discrete ball-like structures, the *glomeruli*, where they make synaptic contact with dendrites of a variety of olfactory bulb neurons (Figure 1b). As its name suggests, the olfactory bulb has an ellipsoidal shape, and its internal construction is laminated like the layers of an onion. The layers are arranged as follows

Figure 1. Basic anatomical organization of the mammalian olfactory system. a) Diagram of parasagittal section through a rodent head showing the location of major structures in the peripheral olfactory pathway. Airborne odorant molecules are transported by inhalation (sniffing) through the nostrils into the nasal cavity, where they contact a specialized sensory epithelium on the olfactory turbinates (airflow pattern shown approximately by arrows). The turbinates are separated from the olfactory bulb by a thin, finely perforated layer of bone, the cribriform plate. b) The olfactory epithelium contains millions of olfactory sensory neurons (OSNs). Each OSN chooses to express one unique olfactory receptor (OR) out of hundreds or thousands available in the genome, and all OSNs expressing the same receptor (e.g. OR1) send their axonal projections to a few discrete glomeruli on the surface of the olfactory bulb. Different receptors (e.g. OR2) send axonal projections to different glomeruli. c) The olfactory bulb (OB) directs its output to various higher level processing centers, collectively termed olfactory cortex. These include anterior olfactory nucleus (AON), olfactory tubercle (OT), piriform cortex (PC), amygdala (AM), and entorhinal cortex (EC). d) The convergent projections of ORs to bulb glomeruli make it possible to directly visualize the coding of odorant stimuli by olfactory receptors in real time. A highly sensitive, cooled, charge-coupled device (CCD) camera is used to inspect the surgically exposed dorsal surface of the olfactory bulb. Changes in light scattering or in the fluorescence of reporter molecules (i.e. activity-sensitive dyes or proteins) are associated with increases in glomerular physiological activity. Since each glomerulus represents input from one specific OR, this kind of imaging reveals dynamic maps of ORs binding, recognizing and responding to specific molecular structures. Different odorant stimuli evoke unique patterns of glomerular activation (illustrated here as dark spots). Since these patterns may include overlapping subsets of glomeruli, the brain is presented with a potentially combinatorial code of stimulus intensity or identity.

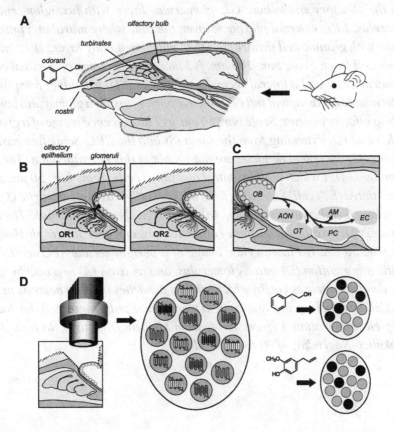

Figure 2. Anatomy of the brain and neurons of the mouse olfactory system. a) Sagittal section of a mouse head showing location of olfactory system components relative to other parts of the brain. Arrows show path of air flow as odorants are sampled by sniffing, enter the nares (NA) and are delivered to the olfactory epithelium (OE). Olfactory sensory neurons (OSNs) in the OE send axons to the olfactory bulb (OB), which sends output to multiple areas of olfactory cortex, including anterior olfactory nucleus (AON). The piriform cortex is located lateral to the AON and is not visible here. Other marked brain areas are: CC, cerebral cortex; TH, thalamus; HT, hypothalamus; CE, cerebellum; PO, pons; ME, medulla. Scale bar: 5 mm. b) Olfactory sensory neurons (OSNs) in the olfactory epithelium. This is a fluorescence image of a slice of OE taken from a transgenic mouse in which all mature OSNs are tagged by enhanced green fluorescent protein (EGFP), coexpressed with olfactory marker protein (OMP). The cell bodies or somata (S) extend a dendrite (D) which terminates in a small swelling or knob (K) on the apical surface of the epithelium where odorants arrive and are detected. Scale bar: 20 μm. c) Wider view of olfactory sensory neurons in the olfactory epithelium. This fluorescence image of a slice of OE from the transgenic mouse in Fig 4B, shows the dense packing of OSNs and their axons (A) which course through the base of the epithelium and coalesce into nerve bundles projecting to the olfactory bulb. Scale bar: 40 μm. d) Solitary olfactory sensory neuron. This cell was dissociated from the tissue of the OE, and its dendrite has contracted and partially merged with the soma (S). A crown of olfactory cilia (C) containing the molecular apparatus of odorant detection is visible sprouting from the knob on apical end of the cell. The cell is visualized by fluorescence of EGFP coexpressed with the I7 olfactory receptor. Scale bar: 5 μm. e) Cell layers of the olfactory bulb. This thin section (20 μm) was imaged under differential interference contrast to reveal cellular processes such as dendrites, and cell bodies were further highlighted by fluorescent staining of cell membranes (Alexa Fluor 594). ONL, olfactory nerve layer, where OSN axons arrive from the olfactory epithelium; GL, glomerular layer, with juxtaglomerular cells packed around each glomerulus; EPL, external plexiform layer, the zone where mitral and tufted cell dendrites synaptically interact with granule cell dendrites; MCL, mitral cell body layer; IPL, internal plexiform layer; GCL, granule cell layer. Scale bar: 100 μm. f) Fluorescence image of a mitral cell, showing the apical primary dendrite (PD) and a lateral secondary dendrite (SD) extending from the soma (S). The primary dendrite terminates in an apical tuft (T) which arborizes inside a glomerulus; an axon (A) sends bulb output signals to olfactory cortex. Scale bar: 50 μm. g) Fluorescence image of a granule cell, showing a fine apical dendrite (D) extending from the soma (S) into the EPL. Some fine basal dendrites are also visible, but spines on the apical dendrite are not visible at this magnification. The apical dendrite releases the transmitter GABA which inhibits mitral and tufted cells. Scale bar: 50 μm. h) Fluorescence image of an external tufted (ET) cell. Extending from the soma (S) is a single dendrite (D) which projects into a glomerulus where it elaborates a tuft (T). An axon (A) leads out of the bulb. The tuft releases the transmitter glutamate, which excites dendrites of other neurons and coordinates rhythmic activity of the glomerulus. Scale bar: 50 μm. i) Fluorescence image of a periglomerular (PG) cell. The small soma (S) sends a dendritic arborization (D) into a glomerulus, and an axon (A) to a nearby target in the glomerular layer. The dendrite releases GABA which inhibits dendrites of other neurons in the glomerulus. Scale bar: 50 μm. Cell morphology in Figures 4f–4i were visualized by intracellular loading of the dye Alexa Fluor 594 by electroporation. Figures 4b–4c from Michele Dibattista, 4d from Anna Boccaccio, 4e from Luba Dankulich-Nagrudny, 4f–4i from Jie Ma.

continued on following page

Figure 2. Continued

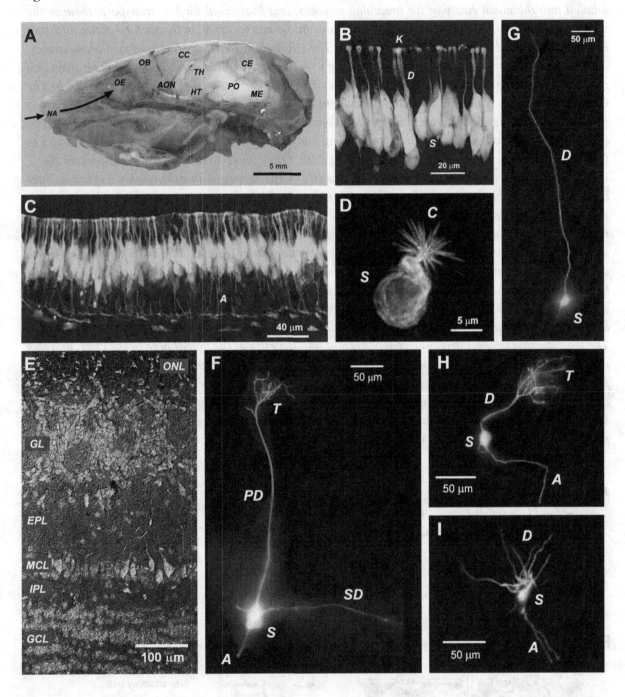

(from outermost to innermost) (Figures 2e, 4): (1) the Olfactory Nerve Layer (ONL) contains the olfactory nerve axons; (2) the *Glomerular Layer* (GL) includes a 2-dimensional array of glomeruli with associated *juxtaglomerular cells*;

(3) the *External Plexiform Layer* (EPL) is a broad layer filled with branching dendrites of many neurons and includes the bodies of *tufted cells*, a class of neurons that send output signals from the bulb; (4) the *mitral cell layer* is a thin layer con-

Figure 3. Physiology of vertebrate olfactory transduction. a) During sniffing, airborne odorants are inhaled into the nasal cavity of air breathing animals, and intranasal airflow transports them to the olfactory turbinates. Volatile odorants then dissolve into a mucus layer on the surface of the olfactory epithelium and bind to olfactory receptors (ORs). The ORs belong to a large family of membrane associated receptors with 7 transmembrane domains, of which 3 are hypervariable (shown in dark gray) and probably determine each receptors molecular specificity (or molecular receptive range, MRR). b) The ORs reside in cilia, which are long, thin extensions of the distal dendrite of olfactory sensory neurons (OSNs). Cilia are several hundred microns long and only 200 nm in diameter, which greatly increases the cell surface area available for odorant binding and detection. The binding of odorant molecules to ORs triggers a cascade of biochemical events in cilia. ORs couple to and activate a G-protein (G$_{olf}$), which in turn activates the enzyme adenylyl cyclase III (ACIII), up-regulating the synthesis of intraciliary cAMP. The cAMP binds to and opens CNG channels, which allows positively charged calcium ions to enter the cilia, initiating the depolarization of the cell. This calcium binds to and opens chloride channels (ANO2), and the efflux of chloride anions may further assist in depolarizing the cell and converting a chemical (odorant) signal into an electrical (membrane voltage) signal. Termination of the response occurs when calcium binds to and activates calmodulin (CaM) which desensitizes the CNG channels to cAMP. A phosphodiesterase enzyme (PDE1C) brings cAMP back down to a basal level. Restoration of the ionic balance of cilia after transduction depends on several ion exchangers driven by ionic gradients: NKCX4 removes calcium ions, and NKCC1 and SLC4A1 replenish chloride ions in the cilia. c) The transduction process drives electrical current into the cilia at the apical pole of the OSN, and this passes charge down the long dendrite to the cell body (soma). The current loop is completed by charge flowing out of the soma via the resting potassium conductance. This slow 'generator current' is measurable as the EOG (electro-olfactogram), a voltage signal recorded by electrodes placed on the mucosal surface. It depolarizes the soma and triggers the firing of trains of action potentials or spikes. The spikes propagate along the axon in the olfactory nerve, to glomeruli in the olfactory bulb.

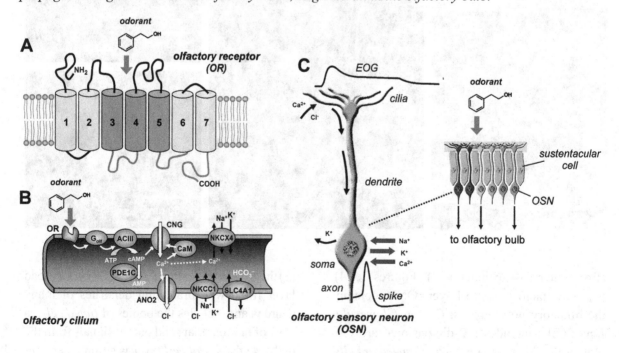

Figure 4. Odor signal processing by synaptic networks in the olfactory bulb. Odorants activate multiple kinds of olfactory receptors (OR) in olfactory sensory neurons (OSN) of the olfactory epithelium (OE) in the nose. The OSN axons transmit combinatorial patterns of inputs to multiple glomeruli in the outer glomerular layer (GL) of the olfactory bulb. Each glomerulus contains a complex circuit of interconnected dendrites from surrounding juxtaglomerular cells, including external tufted (ET), periglomerular (PG) and short axon (SA) cells. The OSN axon terminals excite ET cells which in turn drive the bulb output circuitry by exciting (via intraglomerular glutamate release) the principal neurons: mitral cells (MC) in the mitral cell layer (MCL), and tufted cells (TC) in the external plexiform layer (EPL). Some OSN excitation may also directly drive MC/TC dendrites. The strength and dynamics (timing) of the MC/TC spiking output is regulated by feed-forward and feedback inhibition from GL interneurons, the PG cells. Interactions between glomerular circuits of different ORs arise from lateral inhibitory connections of local interneurons: SA cells in the glomerular layer, and granule cells (GC) in the EPL. It is surmised that these horizontal pathways either selectively suppress some glomerular outputs, or couple them to generate collective spike timing codes transmitted across wide assemblies of cells. In the granule cell layer (GCL), deep short axon cells (dSAC) are excited by MC/TC axon collaterals routed through the internal plexiform layer (IPL), and they send inhibitory feedback vertically back up to interneurons in the EPL and glomerular layer. Output from the olfactory bulb networks is relayed to olfactory cortex through the lateral olfactory tract (LOT). Dark gray arrows: excitatory synaptic pathways releasing the transmitter glutamate; light gray arrows: inhibitory synaptic pathways releasing the transmitter GABA.

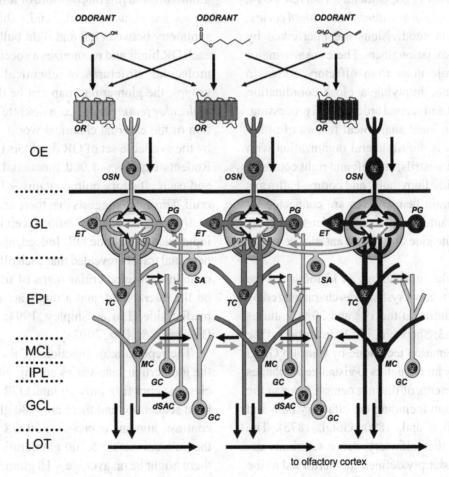

taining densely packed cell bodies of mitral cells, another major class of bulb output neurons; (5) the *Internal Plexiform Layer* (IPL) is a narrow layer containing axon collaterals of mitral and tufted cells, and centrifugal fibers coming into the bulb from other brain regions; (6) the *granule cell layer* (GCL) contains cell bodies of granule cells, local interneurons that inhibit the mitral and tufted cells; (7) in the core of the olfactory bulb, axon fibers of mitral and tufted cells are routed through the *Lateral Olfactory Tract* (LOT), which relays output signals from the bulb to *olfactory cortex* (Figure 1c). The olfactory cortex is a heterogenous collection of areas which probably serve a variety of different functions related to higher level olfactory processing (Wilson, Kadohisa, & Fletcher, 2006). Some of the main subdivisions are: *Anterior Olfactory Nucleus* (AON), *Piriform Cortex* (PC), *Olfactory Tubercle* (OT), *cortical amygdala,* and *lateral entorhinal cortex.* These cortical subdivisions are interlinked by extensive association fibers. There are also major feedback projections from olfactory cortex to olfactory bulb, implying a close coordination between first and second order central processing. Another prominent anatomical feature of olfactory systems is their bilateral organization with left and right nostrils, and left and right copies of olfactory epithelium, bulb, and cortex. Pathways in the two brain hemispheres are connected by fibers of the anterior olfactory nucleus that cross to the opposite side through an anterior commissure.

The cellular morphology or histology of the peripheral olfactory system was characterized by numerous studies in the 19th and 20th Centuries (Allison, 1953; Shepherd, 1972). Invention of the silver impregnation technique by Camillo Golgi enabled early investigators to visualize the shapes and arrangements of distinct neuron types in the nervous system including the olfactory bulb and its glomeruli (Cajal, 1890; Golgi, 1875). The observation that olfactory nerve terminals assemble into sharply defined glomeruli led to the suggestion that "there are different types of olfactory receptor which are differentially susceptible to various forms of olfactory stimulus, and that impulses from several categories of receptor become segregated and conveyed to different glomeruli of corresponding categories" (Le Gros Clark, 1951). This far-sighted hypothesis was finally confirmed by a major breakthrough many decades later, when powerful molecular tools allowed the cloning and identification of a large family ($\sim 10^2 - 10^3$) of *Olfactory Receptors* (ORs) in the mouse (Buck & Axel, 1991). By genetically labeling olfactory sensory neurons expressing a unique receptor, it was possible to directly visualize the targeting of their axons to unique glomeruli (Mombaerts, et al., 1996). The pattern of OR projections forms a stereotypic map of receptor identity over the 2-dimensional array of glomeruli, and this map is more or less conserved across individual animals, and exhibits mirror symmetry between left and right bulbs. Because each OR binds and recognizes a specific range of molecular structures or chemical functional groups, the glomerular map can be thought of a *molecular feature* map, i.e. a discrete representation of the external chemical world as analyzed by the available set of OR detectors (Figure 1d). Rodents express $\sim$ 1,000 functional OR genes, and each olfactory bulb contains $\sim$ 1,800 glomeruli. This ratio suggests that there are two glomeruli in each olfactory bulb, receiving sensory input encoded by one OR. Indeed, application of neuronal tracers revealed that each olfactory bulb contains two glomerular maps of the ORs, one on the lateral side, and a duplicate map on the medial side (Liu & Shipley, 1994; Lodovichi, Belluscio, & Katz, 2003).

The repertoire of functional ORs and size of the glomerular map varies among different species. In zebra fish, only 50 intact OR genes have been sequenced and there are $\sim$ 80 glomeruli. In contrast, humans express $\sim$ 350 OR genes, and the bulb contains > 5,500 glomeruli, suggesting there might be on average $\sim$ 16 glomeruli receiving information encoded by each OR (Maresh, Rodriguez, Whitman, & Greer, 2008). Although there is about a 3-fold difference between the number of ORs expressed in mice vs. humans, OR gene sequences can be clustered into similar phylogenetic trees (Godfrey, Malnic, & Buck, 2004; Malnic, Godfrey, & Buck, 2004; Zhang & Firestein, 2002), and odor response profiles of mouse OSNs cluster in a similar way to human perceived odor qualities (Furudono, Sone, Takizawa, Hirono, & Sato, 2009). Thus, there might be some basic similarities in olfactory stimulus representation of different mammalian species.

In addition to the large, diverse family of ORs, a much smaller group of distinctive receptors (15 in mouse, 6 in human) known as *Trace-Amine Associated Receptors* (TAARs) has also been identified in the olfactory epithelium. These receptors bind volatile amines and may be useful for detecting pheromone or kairomone signals in urine (Liberles & Buck, 2006). Pheromones are chemical signals emitted by an animal that are detected by a member of the same species and utilized for social or reproductive communication. Kairomones mediate communication between different species, usually to the advantage of the receiver; for example, mice can be alerted to the presence of predators by detecting specific odorants in predator urine. Pheromone detection in many mammals also depends heavily on another major chemosensory pathway composed of the *vomeronasal organ* and *accessory olfactory bulb*, which operates in parallel with the main olfactory system (Brennan & Keverne, 2004; Dulac & Wagner, 2006).

ODORANT SAMPLING

In order to be detected, odorant molecules in the environment must reach and bind to ORs. The olfactory epithelium of vertebrates lies protected inside a nasal cavity or chamber, and active transport is needed to bring chemicals from the external environment into contact with receptors. In fish, the olfactory chamber is ventilated by beating cilia or pumping actions of connected accessory sacs that may be driven indirectly by respiratory movements of jawbones (Cox, 2008). In air-breathing vertebrates, the olfactory epithelium is strategically located in the peripheral airflow path of the respiratory system. Thus, the same motor system that controls respiration is also available for voluntary sniffing as a means to actively sample airborne chemicals.

In normal breathing, nasal airflow rates in humans are ~ 150 ml/s per nostril, and only 5–10% of inhaled air is delivered to the olfactory epithelium. This low basal delivery of odorants to sensory receptors can be increased by sniffing. Human sniffing consists of one or more ~ 1.6 s inhalations of elevated flow rate (300 – 1,000 ml/s per nostril), which computational models show can increase the absorption of odorants by the nasal mucosa (Zhao, Dalton, Yang, & Scherer, 2006). Rodents can either sniff at low frequencies (~ 1 – 3 Hz), or engage in bouts of rhythmic high frequency sniffing (4 – 12 Hz). Rapid sniffing can increase the rate of sampling of odorants from the environment (Wesson, Verhagen, & Wachowiak, 2009), and may also temporarily attenuate signal transfer from ORs to glomeruli in the olfactory bulb, which might permit adaptation to background odorants and facilitate detection of newly encountered odorants (Verhagen, Wesson, Netoff, White, & Wachowiak, 2007). Although repetitive sniffing may enhance performance of difficult odor-guided tasks, just a single sniff (lasting < 200 ms in mouse) is sufficient for basic odor discrimination (Uchida & Mainen, 2003).

The act of sniffing is a motor activity under neural control, which allows it to be closely coordinated with neural processing of odor signals in the brain (Mainland & Sobel, 2006). Mechanical stimulation of nasal tissues by airflow appears to be required to perceive odors delivered indirectly by the bloodstream to the olfactory epithelium (Bocca, Antonelli, & Mosciaro, 1965), and sniffing even odorless air will drive the activity of central neurons in olfactory bulb and olfactory cortex. This central neural activity is oscillatory and the oscillations occur in several frequency ranges: a low frequency range (*theta* frequencies of $\sim 3 - 10$ Hz) in concert with the extrinsic sniff rhythm; and higher frequency bands (*beta* frequencies of $\sim 10 - 30$ Hz, and *gamma* frequencies of $\sim 30 - 100$ Hz) generated when intrinsic biophysical and synaptic mechanisms of bulb or cortical circuits synchronize the firing of specific populations of neurons during odor coding. Periodic sniffing can entrain the theta frequency firing of short sequences of spikes (high frequency *bursts*) by neurons in olfactory bulb glomeruli, organizing the activity of bulb circuits into discrete computational cycles (Wachowiak & Shipley, 2006). There appear to be brain feedback loops that dynamically regulate sniffing to optimize levels of sensory input, e.g. sniff vigor and flow rate is reduced for strong or unpleasant stimuli, and increased for weak or pleasant stimuli (Teghtsoonian, Teghtsoonian, Berglund, & Berglund, 1978). It is thought that this *olfactomotor* response is an integral part of odor perception, just as saccadic eye movements are an integral part of visual perception.

The interplay between perceived odor quality, intensity and sniffing is related to the anatomical organization of peripheral olfactory structures. Different odorants with different aqueous solubilities have different sorption rates into the nasal mucosa, with faster retention of more polar compounds and slower retention of more hydrophobic compounds (Mozell & Jagodowicz, 1973). This results in a chromatographic partitioning (*imposed pattern*) of odorants into different zones of sensory epithelium. Thus, in rodents, more polar odorants tend to be captured immediately by dorso-medial areas of the turbinates where inhaled air is initially directed (Figure 1a), while the sorption of more hydrophobic odorants extends into ventro-lateral areas which are positioned downstream in the airflow path (Schoenfeld & Cleland, 2006; Yang, Scherer, Zhao, & Mozell, 2007). The differential spatial partitioning depends on airflow rate, which is actively controlled by sniffing. One might predict an impact of flow rate on patterns of sensory input to glomeruli, and this has been observed (Oka, Takai, & Touhara, 2009). Spatial partitioning is also correlated with differential spatial expression (*inherent pattern*) of different types of ORs in zones across the turbinates (Ressler, Sullivan, & Buck, 1993). Phylogenetic analysis of olfactory receptor gene sequences reveals two broad OR families, 'Class I' and 'Class II' (Zhang & Firestein, 2002). Fishes express only the Class I genes, indicating that they encode ORs detecting more polar, water-soluble odorants. Air-breathing vertebrates express both Class I and Class II receptors, and in rodents Class I ORs are concentrated in the dorso-medial nasal mucosa. The dorso-medial zone could be optimized to detect more polar compounds that are preferentially deposited in this part of the nose.

OLFACTORY TRANSDUCTION

Once odorants in the inhaled airstream reach the nasal turbinates, they dissolve into the watery mucus layer overlying the surface of the olfactory epithelium. This initial step can contribute a significant amplification of the chemical signal, increasing the molar concentration of odorants by a factor of $\sim 10^2 - 10^4$. Examples of air-water partition coefficients (K_{aw} = concentration in water/ concentration in air) of commonly studied odorants are: $K_{aw} = 83$ for 5α-androst-16-en-3-one, a hydrophobic odorant, and $K_{aw} = 30,000$ for isovaleric acid, a polar odorant. This might be a consideration in reconciling the low behavioral detection thresholds in air, with relatively high concentrations of odorants in aqueous phase needed to activate ORs *in vitro* ($EC_{50} \sim 10^{-6} - 10^{-3}$ M) (Abaffy, Matsunami, & Luetje, 2006). After partitioning into mucus, odorants may interact with Odorant Binding Proteins (OBPs) before or after they interact with ORs on the cilia of receptor cells. OBPs have been suggested to play a role in solubilizing or transporting odorants to receptors (Borysik, Briand, Taylor, & Scott, 2010; Ko, Lee, Oh, & Park, 2010). They belong to the lipocalin family of low molecular weight (~ 15–20 kDa) soluble proteins that serve as carriers of hydrophobic ligands, including pheromones. However, their exact biological role has yet to be fully defined. In the epithelium, the sustentacular cells and acinar cells of *Bowman's glands* are responsible for secreting the molecular components of the mucus, and regulating its ionic and protein composition. Enzymes secreted into the mucus may transform or degrade odorants, influencing the dynamics of receptor activation and the kinds of ligands present. For example, aldehydes are enzymatically converted into alcohols and acids, leading to measurable changes in patterns of glomerular activation in the olfactory bulb (Nagashima & Touhara, 2010). Further detoxification and removal of odorants may be performed inside sustentacular cells expressing biotransformation enzymes, including olfactory-specific isoforms of cytochrome P-450, UDP-glucuronosyltransferase and glutathione S-transferase (Chen, Getchell, Ding, & Getchell, 1992; Ben Arie, Khen, & Lancet, 1993). The P-450 enzyme CYP2A13 is expressed in human olfactory mucosa (Su, et al., 2000), and is able to convert an odorant with mixed woody/ fruity/ raspberry qualities into one with a strong raspberry odor (Schilling, Kaiser, Natsch, & Gautschi, 2010). Since the olfactory epithelium is in direct contact with the external environment, such biochemical mechanisms are useful adaptations to shield cells from injury by reactive or toxic volatile chemicals, or infectious microbial agents (Harkema, Carey, & Wagner, 2006). Cells that do die are continually replaced by a process of ongoing neurogenesis, in which progenitor cells in the basal layer of the epithelium divide and differentiate into mature OSNs with a turnover rate of ~ 30 days (Graziadei & Monti-Graziadei, 1978).

Olfactory transduction involves the detection and conversion of a chemical signal (i.e. an odorant) into an intracellular voltage signal that is ultimately translated into sequences of brief (millisecond) electrical impulses (*action potentials* or *spikes*) which are the universal language of neurons. This conversion is achieved by a chain of biochemical reactions in the cilia of OSNs, catalyzed by membrane bound enzymes. The first transduction event is the binding of an odorant molecule to an Olfactory Receptor (OR) located in the ciliary membrane. An OR is encoded by a gene ~ 1 kilobase long, and the translated protein with ~ 300 amino acids (molecular weight ~ 60 – 80 kDa) folds into seven alpha-helical transmembrane domains forming the characteristic conformation of a *G-Protein Coupled Receptor* (GPCR) (Figure 3a). There are three hypervariable domains, which presumably form an odorant binding pocket that recognizes specific odorants. Sequence diversity in the hypervariable domains generates a large repertoire of ORs capable of recognizing a great many odorants. Properties of OR binding are matched to functional properties of olfaction: (1) a relatively low binding affinity and short dwell time (~ 1 ms) means that odorants can be bound and released quickly at higher concentrations (Bhandawat, Reisert, & Yau, 2005), essential for fast signal termination so that the cell may respond quickly to changing stimuli; (2) a relatively low ligand specificity means that individual receptors have relatively broad tuning and respond to a range of odorants with similar molecular features (Araneda, Kini, & Firestein, 2000), enabling a large expansion of coding capacity by combinatorial schemes representing stimuli with multiple parallel channels of input encoded by multiple receptors (Malnic, Hirono, Sato, & Buck, 1999).

Upon binding an odorant molecule, an OR triggers a cascade of intracellular reactions (Figure 3b). First, the OR undergoes a conformational transition that favors the binding of one of its intracellular loop domains by G_{olf}, a Guanosine 5'-Triphosphate (GTP) -binding protein (G-protein) that is localized to and highly enriched in olfactory cilia (Belluscio, Gold, Nemes, & Axel, 1998; Jones & Reed, 1989). An inactive G-protein is composed of 3 subunits (α, β and γ), with Guanosine 5'-Diphosphate (GDP) bound to the α subunit. When G_{olf} binds to an OR, the α subunit releases GDP, binds GTP, and dissociates from β and γ. The α-GTP subunit then binds to an enzyme, type III Adenylyl Cyclase (ACIII), which is also highly enriched in the cilia of OSNs (Bakalyar & Reed, 1990; Wong, et al., 2000). This association switches ACIII into an active state which catalyzes the conversion of Adenosine-5'-Triphosphate (ATP) molecules into 3'-5'-cyclic adenosine monophosphate or cyclic AMP (= cAMP). The synthesized cAMP functions as a diffusible intracellular messenger inside the olfactory cilia. It binds to and opens *Cyclic Nucleotide-Gated* (CNG) ion channels in the ciliary membrane (half activation at $\sim 2 - 20$ µM cAMP), causing an influx of Na^+ and Ca^{2+} cations (Nakamura & Gold, 1987). The CNG channels are composed of three subunits, CNGA2, CNGA4 and CNGB1b which assemble into a channel with a high permeability for Ca^{2+} ions. If the Ca^{2+} concentration of the surrounding mucus is in the millimolar range, much of the cation influx through CNG channels is carried by Ca^{2+} ions (Frings, Seifert, Godde, & Kaupp, 1995). This flood of Ca^{2+} into the cilia activates a second type of ion channel, Anoctamin 2 (ANO2), that conducts chloride (Cl^-) anions across the membrane (Kleene, 1993; Stephan, et al., 2009). The function of the chloride channel depends on physiological adaptations of OSNs to regulate their internal ciliary Cl^- to an elevated level of $\sim 55 - 80$ mM (Kaneko, Putzier, Frings, Kaupp, & Gensch, 2004; Kaneko, Nakamura, & Lindemann, 2001), compared to an estimated ~ 50 mM in the external mucus (Reuter, Zierold, Schroder & Frings, 1998). Thus, when odorants trigger the series of enzymatic reactions eventually leading to opening of the Cl^- channel, a

Cl^- efflux from the cilia increases net internal positive charge and depolarizes the OSN from its negative resting potential. The activation by odorants of two ion channels in series (CNG and ANO2) has been theorized to serve several functions: (1) near threshold, the response becomes a non-linear, cooperative function of the degree of OR activation, allowing selective amplification of signals versus noise (Lowe & Gold, 1995); (2) extra depolarizing current from the Cl^- channel can contribute to and amplify the OSN electrical response under certain extracellular ionic conditions (Lowe & Gold, 1993; Kurahashi & Yau, 1993); (3) the Cl^- channel provides an alternative source of depolarizing current if lowered mucus cation concentrations reduce the current carried by CNG channels; this would be beneficial to animals like fish or amphibians whose mucosa is exposed to an aquatic environment (Kurahashi & Yau, 1994). Interestingly, it was recently reported that basic odorant discrimination performance in mice was not adversely affected when the gene encoding ANO2 was knocked out, suggesting that the CNG channel alone is sufficient to support olfactory transduction (Billig, Pal, Fidzinski, & Jentsch, 2011).

Olfactory transduction of vertebrates can be compared and contrasted to known mechanisms of invertebrates, which evolved independent solutions to the problem of odor detection. In the nematode worm, *Caenorhabditis elegans*, a large family of $\sim 500 - 1000$ GPCRs, including several hundred ORs detecting volatile organic compounds, are expressed in only 32 OSNs, so each neuron expresses and integrates inputs from multiple receptors (Bargmann, 2006). Excitatory responses of OSNs may be triggered when the receptors couple to guanylyl cyclase, which synthesizes cGMP to activate a CNG channel, or to lipid signaling pathways to activate a TRPV channel. In the insects, OSNs reside in sensory hairs deployed externally over the antennae and maxillary palps, and they express a smaller repertoire of ORs (e.g. 62 ORs in the fruit fly,

Drosophila melanogaster (Robertson, et al., 2003); 131 ORs in the mosquito *Aedes aegypti* (Bohbot, et al., 2007)). Although insect ORs are also composed of 7 transmembrane segments, they are not homologous to other GPCRs. Compared to vertebrate ORs and other GPCRs, insect ORs exhibit a reverse transmembrane topology, with the amino terminus intracellular and the carboxy terminus extracellular. Function of insect ORs requires assembly of a heteromeric complex composed of a variable OR, and a conserved co-receptor belonging to the Or83b or ORCO family (Voshall & Hansson, 2011). The two subunits form an odorant-gated non-selective cation channel with high calcium permeabillty (Sato, et al., 2008). Compared to the slower second messenger system of vertebrates, a channel directly gated by odorous ligands provides faster OSN depolarization (latency < 30 ms), which may enable antennae to track rapid stimulus fluctuations encountered by insects flying through filamentous odor plumes. Some evidence suggests a role for cyclic AMP second messenger signaling in insect olfactory transduction, and the ORCO subunit has been hypothesized to serve as a CNG channel (Wicher, et al., 2008). However, this issue is controversial (Kaupp, 2010), and second messengers may actually serve a modulatory role in insect olfaction (Nakagawa & Vosshall, 2009).

The strong calcium and chloride gradients across the vertebrate OSN ciliary membrane make up the electrochemical 'battery' driving olfactory signal amplification. The electrochemical gradient depends on membrane transporter proteins: a cotransporter NKCC1, that uses influx of Na^+ and K^+ to drive Cl^- anions into the cilia, and an exchanger SLC4A1, that uses efflux of HCO_3^- anions to drive Cl^- anions into the cilia (Hengl, et al., 2010). Maintenance of the Ca^{2+} gradient depends on movement of Ca^{2+} out of the cilia by an ATP-driven calcium pump (Antolin, Reisert, & Matthews, 2010), and an exchanger, NCKX4, coupling Na^+ and K^+ influx to Ca^{2+} efflux (Stephan, et al., 2009). These various transporters restore

the ionic balance of the cilia after odorant stimulation, helping to terminate the cellular response (Figure 3b). Other elements contributing to negative regulation of the transduction pathway are the *phosphodiesterase* enzymes that break down cAMP. The enzyme PDE1C is located in the cilia where it opposes and balances cAMP synthesis by ACIII, and the enzyme PDE4A is located outside the cilia in the dendrite and cell body where it can act to restrict cAMP signaling to the cilia (Yan, et al., 1995; Cygnar & Zhao, 2009).

Adaptation is the proportional decrease in responses to stimuli in the presence of a maintained background stimulus, and is a general property of sensory systems, including olfaction. The underlying cellular bases of adaptation can be observed in the desensitization of the responses of neurons in sensory pathways to tonic stimulation, and the attenuation of their responses to repeated stimuli (also called 'paired-pulse adaptation'). At least two calcium-dependent feedback pathways have been identified in olfactory cilia that have been hypothesized to play a role in adaptation by immediately attenuating transduction output. These are mediated by the binding of Ca^{2+} to calmodulin (CaM), a universal regulatory protein: (1) CaM reduces the sensitivity of the CNG channel to cAMP (Chen & Yau, 1994); and (2) CaM activates CaM-dependent protein kinase II which phosphorylates and attenuates the activity of ACIII (Wei, et al., 1998; Leinders-Zufall, Ma, & Zufall, 1999). However, recent research indicates that CaM regulation of the CNG channel contributes to response termination, not paired-pulse adaptation, and CaM regulation of PDE1C is not a determinant of response termination, although it may be a minor contributor to paired-pulse adaptation (Cygnar & Zhao, 2009; Song, et al., 2008). The actual roles of the two CaM feedback pathways in OSN adaptation is still not settled.

The inward transduction current in the cilia produces a relatively slow, graded depolarizing potential in OSNs lasting from tens to hundreds of milliseconds. This can be measured directly by intracellular electrical recording from a single OSN, or indirectly by placing an electrode on the mucosal surface of the olfactory epithelium to record an extracellular voltage signal, the *Electro-olfactogram* (EOG) (Figure 3c). The slow charging time of the OSN membrane (~ 50–100 ms) limits the speed of the response, but the small size of OSNs (~ 10 μm diameter) and correspondingly high input impedance (> 5 – 40 GΩ) increases their sensitivity to small depolarizing currents. The slow voltage transient is relayed from the distal cilia of an OSN, down a long dendrite to the cell body (soma) where it activates membrane conductances responsible for generating spikes (Figure 3c). The firing of spikes is required for information transmission by OSN axons over longer distances to glomeruli in the olfactory bulb. Only a small current of ~ 1 – 2 pA, corresponding to ~ 35 odorant molecular binding events in frog or ~ 20 events in mouse, is sufficient to bring an OSN to spike firing threshold (Bhandawat, Reisert, & Yau, 2010; Ben Chaim, Cheng, & Yau, 2011).

As in other neurons, the firing of spikes in OSNs depends on the opening and closing of voltage-gated Na^+ and K^+ channels (Narusuye, Kawai, & Miyachi, 2003). In addition, firing rate can be modulated or shaped by Ca^{2+} channels. For example, in newt OSNs a low threshold T-type Ca^{2+} current was found to substantially amplify the voltage-gated current by contributing up to ~ 30% of the total current (Kawai & Miyachi, 2001). Calcium entry into the cell body *via* high-voltage activated Ca^{2+} channels can activate Ca^{2+}-dependent K^+ channels, which then oppose the transduction current and slow down the rate of spiking. Thus, spike signaling from nose to brain is controlled by a combination of membrane biophysics at the OSN cell body, and transduction kinetics in the OSN cilia. The signals that are relayed by OSNs to the olfactory bulb consist of time varying sequences of spikes, and these dynamic signals could be useful for *temporal coding* of sensory information. A simple case of temporal coding is representation of stimulus intensity by

spike firing rate. The OSN firing rate increases monotonically, up to 200 – 300 Hz, with increasing transduction current, and increasing odorant concentration (Reisert & Matthews, 2001; Tomaru & Kurahashi, 2005). A higher frequency spike train could in theory encode, by frequency modulation, temporal fluctuations in odorant concentrations at lower frequencies of < 10 Hz. For example, externally located olfactory receptors on insect antennae track choppy plumes of airborne odorants and control flight behavior (Vickers, 2006). For the intranasally located ORs of mammals, odorant dynamics at theta frequencies of ~ 2 –10 Hz are determined by active sniffing and the physics of mucosal deposition. Fast timing properties of spikes in OSNs sent to olfactory bulb neurons could be useful for odorant coding purposes, rather than for keeping track of environmental fluctuations of chemo-signals. For example, different spike timing in OSNs expressing different ORs might arise from an interaction between imposed patterns of odorant deposition, and the inherent zonation of OR expression on the nasal turbinates (Schoenfeld & Cleland, 2006). This could mean that certain ORs, and corresponding olfactory glomeruli, are activated sooner than others. Thus, a *spatial* or *identity* code distributed across parallel OR/glomerular data lines could be multiplexed with temporal information.

Although the majority of OSNs in the mammalian olfactory epithelium respond to odorants through the cAMP transduction pathway, a minority of them lack this mechanism. Instead, they employ an alternative transduction pathway with 3', 5'-cyclic guanosine monophosphate or cyclic GMP (= cGMP) as an intracellular signal. Their cilia contain a membrane bound guanylyl cyclase enzyme, GC-D, which functions both as a receptor for odorants, and as an enzyme catalyzing the synthesis of cGMP from guanosine 5'-triphosphate or GTP. During transduction, cGMP opens a different CNG channel composed of a distinct subunit, CNGA3, leading to cell depolarization. A phosphodiesterase, PDE2, breaks down cGMP and terminates the signal. The GC-D receptors are activated by urine peptides, uroguanylin and guanylin (Leinders-Zufall, et al., 2007), or low levels of carbon dioxide (CO_2) (Hu, et al., 2007). In rodents, the GC-D neurons project their olfactory nerve axons to a subset of glomeruli located in a ring around the posterior region of the olfactory bulb (and hence are termed 'necklace glomeruli').

The highly precise organization in which individual OSNs express one unique OR, TAAR or GC-D type of receptor and send axons to defined glomeruli, might suggest that olfactory signals are peripherally segregated and signal processing can only occur in central neural circuits. However, some phenomena in the olfactory epithelium suggest that peripheral processing is also important. Olfactory stimuli in the real world usually contain mixtures of different odorants, and one odorant could indirectly interfere with the OR binding of another odorant. These *mixture interactions* may alter responses of OSNs to pure monomolecular stimuli (Duchamp-Viret, Duchamp, & Chaput, 2003). Different odorants can be competitive agonists or antagonists at the ligand binding pocket of ORs, e.g. citral isomers geranial and neral exert different suppression on octanal responses of the rat I7 receptor (Araneda, Peterlin, Zhang, Chesler, & Firestein, 2004) and responses of the mouse mOR-EG receptor to eugenol are inhibited by structurally related compounds (Oka, Omura, Kataoka, & Touhara, 2004). Spiking responses of rat OSNs to structurally diverse odorants show evidence of competitive and non-competitive mixture interactions (Rospars, Lansky, Chaput, & Duchamp-Viret, 2008). Odorants by their very nature are hydrophobic with an affinity for membranes, and could therefore interact with a variety of proteins in the lipid bilayer. Thus, odorants can suppress currents conducted by CNG channels in olfactory cilia (Takeuchi, Ishida, Hikichi, & Kurahashi, 2009; Kurahashi, Lowe, & Gold, 1994), and by voltage-gated channels in OSN

cell bodies (Kawai, Kurahashi, & Kaneko, 1997; Kawai, 1999a; Kawai, 1999b).

ODOR SIGNAL PROCESSING IN THE OLFACTORY BULB (AS SHOWN IN FIGURE 4)

Signal flow into the olfactory bulb starts when OSN nerve terminals release the excitatory transmitter glutamate onto neuronal dendrites inside glomeruli. This excites the principal neurons of each activated glomerulus – External Tufted (ET), mitral, and tufted cells – causing them to discharge spikes. At this first synapse, there is a massive convergence of OR-encoded sensory signals at this primary input stage (~ $10^2 - 10^3$ OSNs per glomerulus) which is theorized to provide a large amplification of signal over noise (Duchamp-Viret, Duchamp, & Vigouroux, 1989; van Drongelen, Holley, & Doving, 1978). In mammals, each mitral or tufted cell connects through an apical *primary dendrite* to one glomerulus encoding input from one olfactory receptor (Figure 2f). Because of this one-to-one connectivity, one might expect that these bulb output neurons would just copy to olfactory cortex essentially the same basic patterns of sensory inputs that they receive from the glomerular array. However, patterns of mitral and tufted cell activity are strongly modified by inhibition from interneurons in the glomerular and granule cell layers, which synthesize and release the inhibitory neurotransmitter γ-amino butyric acid (GABA) (Figure 4). Some of these interneurons enable cells associated with different glomeruli to inhibit each other in a process known as *lateral inhibition*.

The strategic location of juxtaglomerular cells at the first central synapse receiving OSN inputs has earned them the title of 'gatekeepers' of the olfactory system. They are heterogeneous and include at least two major classes of GABA-releasing interneurons, *periglomerular cells* (PG cells) (Figure 2i), and *Short Axon cells* (SA cells). At least some of the PG cells are unusual neurons in that they lack axons and rely exclusively on dendrodendritic synapses to receive inputs and send outputs (Kosaka & Kosaka, 2011). Each PG cell extends its dendrite into one glomerulus to regulate the activity of the principal cells (ET, mitral and tufted cells) connected to that glomerulus. They act as an inhibitory brake on the excitation of principal cells. Some of them ('Type 1' PG) are activated by direct OSN input, and others ('Type 2' PG) are activated by glutamate released from dendrites of principal cells. Dendrites of PG cells have numerous tiny knob-like extensions (*spines* or 'gemmules') that make contact with dendrites of principal cells through specialized dendrodendritic synapses. These are two-way *reciprocal synapses* forming a negative feedback loop: glutamate released from principal cell dendrites excites PG cells via fast ionotropic glutamate receptors (glutamate-gated cation channels, the AMPA and NMDA types), and GABA released from PG cell dendrites inhibits principal cells via fast ionotropic $GABA_A$ receptors. The Type 1 PG cells can implement a gating operation through feedforward inhibition, that prevents principal cells from being activated to firing threshold by weaker OSN inputs (Gire & Schoppa, 2009). It has been theorized that this is used to filter out weakly stimulated glomeruli from the odor code (Cleland & Sethupathy, 2006). Another role of PG cells is to regulate the strength of olfactory sensory input by tonic presynaptic inhibition of OSN terminals mediated by slow metabotropic $GABA_B$ receptors (Pirez & Wachowiak, 2008). In contrast to PG cells, the SA cells extend dendrites or axonal projections into multiple glomeruli over both short and long distances, and could therefore mediate lateral inhibition between glomeruli (Kosaka & Kosaka, 2011; Kiyokage, et al., 2010). As these projections may travel hundreds of microns in the glomerular layer, the name 'short axon' may not be an accurate description. Interglomerular lateral inhibition might begin with an ET cell of

one glomerulus exciting an SA cell, which would inhibit mitral and tufted cells in another glomerulus, perhaps by an indirect polysynaptic pathway involving ET and PG cells in the second glomerulus (Aungst, et al., 2003). Collective inhibition of ensembles of glomeruli through SA cells could be used as a mechanism to scale and normalize glomerular patterns of output. The SA cells are also known to synthesize dopamine (as indicated by the marker *Tyrosine Hydroxylase* (TH), the rate limiting biosynthetic enzyme), although its physiological role as a transmitter or modulator in odor signal processing is not yet known.

Another major class of inhibitory interneurons are the *granule cells*. These possess small cell bodies residing in densely packed strata in deeper layers of the olfactory bulb, under the sharply demarcated mitral cell body layer. Because they lack axons to transmit long-range outputs, granule cells communicate locally, solely through their dendrites. They have short basal dendrites, which receive feedback projections from olfactory cortex and modulatory inputs from subcortical brain nuclei. They also have a long apical dendrite extending up past the mitral cell bodies into the *External Plexiform Layer* (EPL) (Figure 2g). Their apical dendrites bear numerous spines that make reciprocal synaptic contacts with lateral *secondary dendrites* of mitral and tufted cells. The EPL is filled with an enormous number of these dendrodendritic synapses having an ultrastructure similar to the reciprocal synapses of PG cells. Mitral and tufted cell dendrites release glutamate that excites granule cells by activating AMPA and NMDA type glutamate receptors on spines, and granule cell spines release GABA to inhibit mitral and tufted cells (Isaacson & Strowbridge, 1998). Using this efficient circuit design, mitral or tufted cells of any glomerulus could in principle inhibit mitral or tufted cells of any other glomerulus. Lateral inhibition might begin with mitral cells (MC1) of one glomerulus exciting a group of granule cells that share synaptic connections with mitral cells (MC2) of a second glomerulus. Those granule cells would release GABA onto MC2 dendrites, inhibiting output from the second glomerulus. The intrinsic membrane properties of both mitral and granule dendrites seem well adapted for this type of processing: (1) spikes triggered in mitral cell bodies can actively propagate long distances in secondary dendrites, exciting granule cells associated with faraway glomeruli (Lowe, 2002; Xiong & Chen, 2002); (2) granule cell apical dendrites have nonlinear active membranes able to cooperatively integrate excitation received by multiple spines (Zelles, Boyd, Hardy, & Delaney, 2006; Egger, Svoboda, & Mainen, 2005).

The outputs of mitral and tufted cells are further shaped by *negative feedback* inhibition from interneurons. Negative feedback is a consequence of the reciprocal character of dendrodendritic synapses, which allows the numerous PG and granule cells to send robust inhibition back to the same mitral or tufted cells that excite them. The *deep Short Axon Cells* (dSACs) located below the mitral cell layer, are another large class of GABAergic interneurons likely to influence the dynamics of mitral/ tufted outputs. The dSACs are excited by mitral/ tufted cells, and many of them send major back-projections to the glomerular layer where they likely inhibit PG cells (Eyre, Antal, & Nusser, 2008). This second layer of feedback should turn off PG inhibition and disinhibit mitral/ tufted cells, and thus facilitate their reexcitation from one sniff to the next. Two other kinds of dSACs project to the EPL, and to the granule cell layer, although their targets have not been characterized (Eyre et al., 2008). The latter kind also sends axons to olfactory cortical areas, and thus comprises another class of bulb output neurons.

COMPUTATIONS PERFORMED BY OLFACTORY BULB CIRCUITS

As the first brain center receiving olfactory input, the olfactory bulb has been studied intensively over the past decade. However, the neural computations performed by the bulb, and their significance for odor detection and perception, are still debated. Theories about olfactory bulb function have been based on the stereotypic projections OSN axons and ORs to discrete glomeruli arranged in a 2-dimensional array. Because different odorants activate different subsets of ORs, each odorant stimulus activates a unique 2-dimensional pattern of glomeruli. These spatial representations can be directly visualized by metabolic mapping using uptake of radio-labeled 2-deoxyglucose (Johnson, Woo, & Leon, 1998; Stewart, Kauer, & Shepherd, 1979), or by optical imaging techniques (Meister & Bonhoeffer, 2001; Wachowiak & Cohen, 2001; Rubin & Katz, 1999). The activity patterns have been considered as 'odor images,' in analogy to the 2-dimensional image of visual space projected by the lens of the eye onto the retina. Parallels were drawn between the olfactory bulb and the retina which applies center-surround inhibitory mechanisms to enhance the contrast of visual scenes by lateral inhibition between ganglion cells of the retina (Kuffler, 1953; Luo & Katz, 2001). By analogy, spatial patterns of bulb input were thought to be 'sharpened' by lateral inhibitory pathways which suppress output from mitral and tufted cells of weakly responsive glomeruli. The output neurons would relay to higher cortical centers a filtered pattern of activity emphasizing more strongly responsive glomeruli. The extensive network of inhibitory synaptic connections in the bulb could support such filtering functions.

The simple model of spatial image processing of olfactory input patterns by center-surround inhibition has been challenged by recent findings. The model presumes that odorant stimuli are mapped smoothly onto the 2-dimensional glomerular sheet, like picture elements of a visual scene. However, the high dimensional space of odorant molecular configurations is fragmented into discontinous domains when projected into 2 dimensions (Cleland & Sethupathy, 2006). Functional mapping of activity patterns by radio-labeled 2-deoxyglucose uptake, or optical imaging, has revealed that odorants with various functional groups are represented by glomeruli segregated in broad spatial domains or clusters (Johnson & Leon, 2007; Mori, Takahashi, Igarashi, & Yamaguchi, 2006; Uchida, Takahashi, Tanifuji, & Mori, 2000), which might be related to zonal partitioning of odorants and ORs in the olfactory epithelium. However, this coarse *chemotopic* order breaks down when examined more closely at length scales finer than ~ 5 glomerular spacings, and neighboring glomeruli can exhibit widely divergent odorant tuning curves (Soucy, Albeanu, Fantana, Murthy, & Meister, 2009). Another premise of the center-surround model is that PG or granule cell inhibition between glomeruli is homogenous and isotropic across the olfactory bulb. However, the connections of mitral cells to surrounding glomeruli is sparse and selective (Fantana, Soucy, & Meister, 2008). Tracing of synaptic connections by pseudorabies virus has uncovered linkages between specific columns of glomerular circuits, indicating a heterogeneity of functional connections of inhibitory interneurons (Willhite, et al., 2006). Therefore, the connection matrix between olfactory glomeruli is probably not uniform and invariant, and specific ensembles of linked glomeruli could be working together to code and process specific olfactory stimuli. Lateral inhibition might still be useful to sharpen the stimulus tuning of mitral cells to a range of different odorants (Yokoi, Mori, & Nakanishi, 1995), but its operation would depend on membership of glomeruli in linked ensembles. Such ensembles might be either 'hardwired' as genetically programmed networks, or 'soft-wired' by synaptic connectivity that reflects a memory of recent odor experiences. The latter possibility is suggested by the fact that odor experience and learning is correlated with clear changes in mitral cell responses to odorants (Doucette & Restrepo, 2008), and by increases in granule cell activation (Mandairon, Didier, & Linster, 2008). Several potential cellular substrates of odor memory have been described in the bulb: (1) adult neurogenesis in which new inhibitory interneurons derived from stem cells of the subventricular zone are added to bulbar circuits (Moreno, et al., 2009; Lazarini & Lledo, 2011); these new cells enter the bulb from the *rostral migratory stream*; (2) *Long Term Potentiation* (LTP) of the dendrodendritic synapses between mitral and granule cells (Zhang, et al., 2010); and (3) LTP of the strength of glutamatergic excitatory synapses on granule cell basal dendrites (Gao & Strowbridge, 2009; Nissant, Bardy, Katagiri, Murray, & Lledo, 2009); these synapses are made by feedback projections from olfactory cortex, and they might enable odor memories stored in the cortex to influence the filtering of odor inputs by bulb circuits.

Another possibility that has received considerable attention is the potential role of *temporal coding* in odor representations (Laurent, 2002). The spatial code of OR activation has been shown to be multiplexed with variations in the timing of sensory input that could arise from interactions between odorants and ORs in the olfactory epithelium. In the mouse, there are clear differences between glomeruli in the latencies and rise times of OSN input signals encoded by different ORs (Carey, Verhagen, Wesson, Pirez, & Wachowiak, 2009; Spors, Wachowiak, Cohen, & Friedrich, 2006). The timing variation is ~ 100 – 300 ms, which can be encompassed by the time frame of a single sniff that is sufficient to achieve odor discrimination (Uchida & Mainen, 2003). Networks of neurons in glomeruli are tuned to respond rhythmically at the lower theta frequencies of sniffing (Hayar, Karnup, Ennis, & Shipley, 2004), and the intrinsic burst spiking of ET cells is important for coordinating such activity (Liu & Shipley, 2008). Excitation by incoming OSN terminals triggers a cascade of synaptic transmission inside a glomerulus: (1) ET cells are excited and entrained to burst in synchronous rhythm (Hayar, Karnup, Shipley, & Ennis, 2004); (2) ET cell dendrites release glutamate, which excites mitral and tufted cell dendrites (De Saint, Hirnet,

Westbrook, & Charpak, 2009); (3) responses of the principal neurons are amplified by positive feedback through glutamate autoreceptors (Ma & Lowe, 2007; Schoppa & Westbrook, 2002; Salin, Lledo, Vincent, & Charpak, 2001); (4) glutamate transmission between principal neuron dendrites synchronizes their slow depolarization (known as *'Long-Lasting Depolarization'* or LLD) (Carlson, Shipley, & Keller, 2000); and electrical coupling by gap junctions (Connexin 36) synchronizes their fast spiking (Christie, et al., 2005; Ma & Lowe, 2010). The end result of this glomerular processing is the transformation of OSN synaptic inputs into coordinated or synchronous firing of spike trains by mitral and tufted cells, relayed to olfactory cortex. Temporal coding is present at this output stage, because individual mitral or tufted cells respond to different odorants with differently timed firing patterns over a single sniff period (Cury & Uchida, 2010; Shusterman, Smear, Koulakov, & Rinberg, 2011). These differences could originate from variations in OSN input timing, and from differential lateral inhibition by interneurons (i.e. the SA, PG, and granule cells). Recently, direct evidence for temporal coding was obtained from mice whose OSNs have been made light-sensitive by the expression of channelrhodopsin-2 (Smear, Shusterman, O'Connor, Bozza, & Rinberg, 2011). These mice could be trained to discriminate variations in the timing of light-triggered OSN inputs as short as 10 ms, relative to the phase of the sniff cycle.

Synchronization of spiking with millisecond accuracy has been observed in both mitral and tufted cells belonging to the same glomerulus (Schoppa & Westbrook, 2002; Ma & Lowe, 2010). In rodents, synchronization can finely coordinate the activities of ~ 50 mitral or tufted cells connected to each glomerulus. Such temporal correlation can be a mechanism for 'binding' together the many output signals of a glomerulus, for collective information transfer to downstream cortical networks. Precisely synchronized spikes can be picked out by *coincidence detection* in the downstream neurons. When spikes arrive at two excitatory presynaptic terminals on a neuron, coming from two different presynaptic neurons, they trigger release of glutamate which depolarizes the postsynaptic membrane via AMPA receptors. These *Excitatory Postsynaptic Potentials* (EPSPs) are brief voltage pulses, lasting a few tens of milliseconds. During coincidence detection, EPSPs summate and drive the postsynaptic cell to fire spikes only when they overlap closely in time.

Spike synchrony may also serve to temporally bind the outputs of *different* glomeruli. This would enable the bulb to integrate the molecular features encoded by several ORs into a single group for relay to olfactory cortex. Whereas synchronization of mitral and tufted cells in the same glomerulus relies on direct electrical communication through gap junction contacts between dendrites, cells from different glomeruli are synchronized by time-correlated GABAergic inhibition received from shared granule cell connections (Schoppa, 2006; Galan, Fourcaud-Trocme, Ermentrout, & Urban, 2006). The process depends on a natural resonant oscillation generated by intrinsic conductances of the mitral/tufted membrane (Desmaisons, Vincent, & Lledo, 1999). Spike timing is locked to the oscillation over the gamma frequency range (~ 40–100 Hz) characteristic of mitral cell activity, and synchronous spiking is promoted by *Inhibitory Postsynaptic Potentials* (IPSPs) which reset the phase of oscillation. Another possible function of synchronizing mitral cell activity between glomeruli is for induction of *Long Term Potentiation* (LTP) of synaptic connections between coactive neurons, to strengthen assemblies of interlinked glomerular circuits. Stimulation of populations of mitral cells by high frequency spike trains (100 Hz 'tetanic' stimulus) has been reported to induce LTP of mitral-granule dendrodendritic synapses (Zhang, et al., 2010). Experience-dependent modifications of the matrix of synaptic connections between glomerular columns could be used to store odor memories in the olfactory bulb networks. Odor-evoked synchronous activity of subpopulations of bulb neurons in the beta (10 – 30 Hz) and gamma (40 – 100 Hz) frequency ranges is detectable as a massed oscillatory signal – the extracellular Local Field Potential (LFP), measurable by inserted electrodes or Electroencephalogram (EEG) electrodes on the bulb surface (Freeman & Baird, 1987; Adrian, 1950).

The synchronization of spike outputs from mitral or tufted cells connected to the same glomerulus (i.e. *sister* mitral/ tufted cells) is consistent with the classical concept of a glomerulus as a fundamental, irreducible unit of interconnected neurons cooperating to process and relay sensory information encoded by a unique OR (Chen & Shepherd, 2005). However, synchronization between cells is not 100%. In spike trains recorded from pairs of sister cells, many spikes in one cell may not coincide precisely with spikes in the other cell. Synchrony is significant if the number of coincident spikes statistically exceeds the number expected from purely random overlap. This means that spike synchrony codes can coexist with other modes of information coding. Indeed, recent findings from mice indicate that the ~ 50 mitral and tufted cells connected to the same glomerulus relay correlated but not identical signals to olfactory cortex. Among sister mitral/ tufted cells receiving input from the I7 OR (with heptanal as a ligand), there is concentration-dependent variability in response tuning curves across a panel of 69 sampled odorants (Tan, Savigner, Ma, & Luo, 2010). A wider survey of mitral/ tufted cells receiving inputs from other ORs discovered that sister pairs can differ in the timing of their spiking responses relative to the phase of sniffing (Dhawale, Hagiwara, Bhalla, Murthy, & Albeanu, 2010). Intriguingly, the degree of synchronization of these pairs decreased rather than increased during an odorant response. Spike synchrony could be set up as an internal state of the glomerular network, and used as a 'carrier' signal to be modulated by external odor stimuli.

The different responses of sister mitral/ tufted cells can be due to differential connections to different sets of inhibitory interneurons. In the particular case of mitral vs. tufted cells, differences between their locations in the bulb (with mitral cells positioned more deeply) and the lengths of the secondary dendrites (longer in mitral cells), can lead to different interactions with granule cells. Compared to mitral cells, the tufted cells respond to odors with more robust firing, broader tuning, and less lateral inhibition (Nagayama, Takahashi, Yoshihara & Mori, 2004). Functional diversity is also suggested by neurochemical diversity. For example, a population of *superficial tufted cells* in the outer EPL, just below the glomerular layer, is distinguished by synthesis of the peptide, Cholecystokinin (CCK). These tufted cells appear to serve a specialized purpose as an *intrabulbar association system*, to link and coordinate *isofunctional glomeruli* on opposite sides of the bulb that receive inputs from OSNs expressing the same OR (Schoenfeld, Marchand, & Macrides, 1985; Lodovichi, et al., 2003).

The computational significance of the dynamic, time-varying spike activity patterns generated in populations of mitral/ tufted cells remains a fundamental question for further investigation. In output neurons of the insect antennal lobe (the analog of the olfactory bulb), oscillatory patterns evolving over periods of hundreds of milliseconds after an odorant stimulus have been suggested to serve as a substrate for temporal coding, using time as an extra dimension to restructure the representations of sensory data (Wehr & Laurent, 1996). In the fish olfactory bulb, population patterns of mitral/ tufted cell activity change over time so as to reduce the overlap of patterns that are similar at the level of glomerular input. This process can be considered as *sparsening* and *decorrelating* the representations, which could make it easier for higher brain centers (e.g. olfactory cortex) to process, interpret, and discriminate different odor stimuli (Friedrich, Yaksi, Judkewitz, & Wiechert, 2009).

MODULATION OF ODOR SIGNAL PROCESSING IN THE OLFACTORY BULB

During odor signal processing, various populations of neurons in the olfactory bulb with distinctive biophysical properties interact with each other through networks of fast synaptic transmission (on time scales of ~ 1 – 100 ms) supported by ionotropic receptors at glutamatergic and GABAergic synapses, as well as by electrical synapses. Basic odor encoding activity patterns are generated through these synaptic interactions. These patterns can be modulated by diverse neurochemical signals typically operating on slower time scales (~ 100 ms – 10 s, or longer). Neuromodulation can be classified into two types – intrinsic and extrinsic. In the case of *intrinsic neuromodulation*, the modulator signals come from local neurons within the bulb. They may be useful for regulating excitability and for slow coordination of network activity, enriching patterns of neural response over time. An example of intrinsic modulation is the action of glutamate not only on fast ionotropic receptors, but also on slow *metabotropic glutamate receptors* (mGluRs) coupled to intracellular second messenger pathways. Of eight known mGluRs belonging to 3 groups, the group I receptors (mGluR1, mGluR5) are found in mitral, ET, granule and PG cells. Mitral cells express high levels of mGluR1, and when glutamate is released in the glomerulus during odor stimulation (either from OSN terminals or ET/ mitral/ tufted cell dendrites), the subsequent activation of mGluR1 receptors can enhance the excitation of mitral cells and increase calcium entry into the mitral cell apical dendrites (Heinbockel, Heyward, Conquet, & Ennis, 2004; Yuan & Knopfel, 2006). This process depends on upregulation of low voltage-activated (T-type) Ca^{2+} channels in apical dendrites (Johnston & Delaney, 2010). Since Ca^{2+} is the signal for neurotransmitter release, elevated internal Ca^{2+} is expected to accelerate glutamate release from mitral cell dendrites, adding another

positive feedback loop for driving the LLD that controls mitral cell bursting. The ET cells also contain group I mGluRs whose activation can strengthen their slow, rhythmic bursting activity and hence their control of mitral cells in the intraglomerular network (Dong, et al., 2009). These excitatory modulations of principal cells are counterbalanced by group I mGluRs on PG and granule cells (Dong, Hayar, & Ennis, 2007), which increase GABA release and amplify inhibition. This probably helps to terminate a mitral cell burst, in preparation for its response to the next odor sniff. In addition to these slow modulatory effects of glutamate, the fast inhibitory transmitter GABA can also be considered a slow intrinsic modulator that applies tonic, presynaptic inhibition to OSN terminals through the metabotropic $GABA_B$ receptor.

Other neurochemicals secreted by cells in the olfactory bulb may also function as intrinsic neuromodulators, although their physiological effects are not yet fully elucidated. The gaseous free radical signaling molecule, *Nitric Oxide* (NO), is likely to have a prominent modulatory role in olfaction, based on the heavy expression its synthetic enzyme, neuronal *Nitric Oxide Synthase* (nNOS), and metalloprotein NO receptor, *soluble Guanylyl Cyclase* (sGC), in certain neurons in the bulb (Gutierrez-Mecinas, et al., 2005; Kosaka & Kosaka, 2007). In glomeruli, mutually exclusive subpopulations of ET or PG cells contain either nNOS or sGC, suggesting that NO synthesized by one subpopulation acts on receptors on the other subpopulation. The ability of NO to diffuse freely across cell membranes distinguishes it from conventional transmitters, and makes it a useful signal for broadcasting messages through the dense plexus of dendrites and OSN terminals inside a glomerulus: (1) NO would be released from nNOS-expressing ET or PG cells when they fire spikes, opening voltage-gated Ca^{2+} channels; (2) calcium entering the cell binds and activates calmodulin, and Ca^{2+}-CaM then activates nNOS; (3) the activated nNOS catalyzes formation of NO from the amino acid L-arginine; (4) in target ET and PG cells expressing sGC, a heme group of sGC binds NO, activating sGC which then synthesizes cGMP; (5) the cGMP is an intracellular messenger that could alter target cell physiology either by directly regulating ion channels, or by instructing enzymes (kinases) to phosphorylate proteins. Mitral cells can also express sGC, and they might be sensitive to NO released by granule cells. One study showed that NO is required for formation of specific olfactory memories in which sheep learn to recognize the odor of newborn lambs (Kendrick, et al., 1997). It was suggested that this comes about through a long lasting change in the mitral-granule dendrodendritic synapse.

Various other neuroactive substances synthesized by olfactory bulb neurons have the potential to function as intrinsic neuromodulators. About 10% of juxtaglomerular cells are specialized Short Axon (SA) cells that synthesize *dopamine*, and OSN terminals can be presynaptically inhibited by dopamine through D_2 receptors (Ennis, et al., 2001). Since these SA cells are connected to multiple glomeruli, the dopamine that is released from their dendrites could be responsible for collective feedback inhibition of olfactory sensory inputs received from groups of ORs. Activation of D_2 receptors in the bulb can reduce odor discrimination performance in rats (Escanilla, Yuhas, Marzan, & Linster, 2009). Several kinds of neuropeptide are synthesized and secreted by olfactory bulb neurons, and their cellular distributions can vary among different species of animals. In rats and mice, *somatostatin* is present in deep Short Axon Cells (dSACs) in the granule cell layer, and in mice it is also present in the *Van Gehuchten interneurons* in the inner EPL, outside the mitral cell layer (Lepousez, et al., 2010). In mice, somatostatin modulates mitral cells through the sst2 receptor. This increases gamma oscillations, which are a signature of temporal coding by synchronized activity, and improves odor discrimination performance (Lepousez, Mouret, Loudes, Epelbaum, & Viollet, 2010). The physiological functions

of other peptide modulators in the bulb, such as neuropeptide Y and cholecystokinin, have yet to be defined.

In the case of *extrinsic neuromodulation*, odor signal processing by bulb neurons is modulated by external factors, including physiological status and behavioral context. The profound influence of extrinsic factors is suggested by large differences between odor-evoked spike activities recorded from mitral cells in anesthetized and awake mice (Rinberg, Koulakov, & Gelperin, 2006). Extrinsic factors exert their influences through a rich innervation by centrifugal fibers projecting diffusely to the bulb from other brain centers. Major fiber projections of subcortical origin include those containing three extrinsic modulators – *noradrenalin* (NA), *acetylcholine* (ACh), and *serotonin* (5-hydroxytryptamine, or 5-HT). Noradrenergic fibers from the locus coeruleus (LC) mostly terminate in the granule cell layer, with some innervation of the EPL. Granule cells play vital roles in the inhibitory gating or temporal shaping of mitral/tufted cell spike output, and in the organization of synchronized assemblies of mitral/tufted cells. Modulation of granule cell physiology is therefore a powerful locus of control to regulate odor signal processing in the bulb. The NA released by the LC axon terminals exerts dual actions on granule cells: at low NA concentrations, mitral cell odorant responses may be amplified by disinhibition through the NA suppression of granule cells via α2 adrenergic receptors; at higher NA concentrations, activation of α1 and β adrenergic receptors excites granule cells, leading to greater inhibition of mitral cells. The level of activity of LC neurons is governed by vigilance or attention during learning of odor discrimination tasks, and differing behavioral states can modulate mitral/tufted cell signal processing. Activation of α1 receptors makes rats more sensitive to low odorant concentrations (Escanilla, Arrellanos, Karnow, Ennis, & Linster, 2010), and block of α and β receptors in the bulb can interfere with the ability of mice to discriminate similar odors

(Doucette, Milder, & Restrepo, 2007). In mice, habituation to repeated presentations of an odorant is prevented by chemical lesions destroying the LC and its NA fibers, and is restored by NA infusions into the bulb (Guerin, Peace, Didier, Linster, & Cleland, 2008). This suggests that NA modulation of bulb circuits is required for odor habituation. Intrabulbar drug infusion showed that NMDA-type glutamate receptors, which control granule cell excitation, are required for odor habituation (Chaudhury, et al., 2010). The disinhibition of mitral/ tufted cells by α2 adrenergic modulation causes prolonged enhancement of synchronous oscillatory activity (Pandipati, Gire, & Schoppa, 2010), which could promote synaptic plasticity.

Cholinergic fibers from the basal forebrain (horizontal limb of the diagonal band of Broca, or HDB) terminate in glomerular, mitral cell, and granule cell layers. The acetylcholine (ACh) that they release can activate nicotinic receptors in the glomerular and mitral cell layers, or muscarinic receptors in the granule cell layer. The main targets of ACh appear to be interneurons. When ACh binds muscarinic receptors on granule cells, it increases granule cell excitability through a Ca^{2+}-dependent pathway that regulates a cation channel (Pressler, Inoue, & Strowbridge, 2007), and this will accentuate mitral cell inhibition. However, ACh may also decrease the excitability of some granule cells (Castillo, Carleton, Vincent & Lledo, 1999). Nicotinic ACh receptors also seem to have dual effects on the circuit, exciting PG cells, but also increasing mitral cell activity. The net effect of ACh modulation is thought to be a refining or sharpening of representations of odorants by spatial or temporal patterns of mitral and tufted cell activity. Indeed, there is a stronger control of the dendrodendritic inhibition of mitral cells by granule cells in awake states with higher cholinergic regulation, compared to weaker control in anesthetized or slow wave sleep states with lower cholinergic regulation (Tsuno, Kashiwadani, & Mori, 2008). Behavioral and pharmacological experiments further demonstrate that ACh modu-

lation of bulb networks does enhance olfactory discrimination performance (Mandairon, et al., 2006; Chaudhury, Escanilla, & Linster, 2009).

Serotonergic fibers from the dorsal and medial raphe nuclei of the brainstem terminate in the glomerular layer of the olfactory bulb, where they contact dendrites of both GABAergic interneurons and principal neurons (Gracia-Llanes, et al., 2010). Serotonin depolarizes some PG cells (via 5HT2C receptors) and mitral cells (via 5HT2A receptors), and inhibits other mitral cells through activation of interneurons (Hardy, Palouzier-Paulignan, Duchamp, Royet, & Duchamp-Viret, 2005). By exciting PG cells, it indirectly down-regulates the gain of OSN inputs to glomeruli by elevating the release of GABA, which leads to presynaptic inhibition of OSN terminals via the metabotropic $GABA_B$ receptor (Petzold, Hagiwara, & Murthy, 2009). The serotonin pathway is active when animals are awake, alert, and investigating their environment by sniffing. Decreasing the gain of OSN synaptic transmission would help the olfactory bulb adjust to the stronger sensory stimulation in these circumstances.

ODOR ENCODING IN OLFACTORY CORTEX

Olfactory cortex includes a heterogenous collection of areas in the brain that receive and process signals conveyed from the olfactory bulb by mitral and tufted cells. Based on differences in anatomy and physiology, various olfactory cortical areas are considered to be specialized for different olfactory tasks. Our understanding of their functions is still preliminary. A major component of olfactory cortex that has been a focus of much study is the *Piriform Cortex* (PC) (Haberly, 2001; Wilson, et al., 2006). The PC is subdivided into *anterior Piriform Cortex* (aPC), and *posterior Piriform Cortex* (pPC), and the two subdivisions differ in connectivity and organization. Mitral and tufted cell axons are bundled in the *Lateral Olfactory*

Tract (LOT) which extends over the aPC and supplies it with strong, fast synaptic input. The pPC is situated posterior to the aPC and LOT, and it is innervated by LOT axon collateral branches, and hence receives weaker, less direct input from the bulb. The aPC also sends heavier back-projections to granule cells of bulb than does the pPC, so there is more feedback and tighter coupling between aPC and bulb circuits. Neural circuitry in the PC conforms to a laminar layout typical of cortical structures in the brain. Compared to the six layers of neocortex, the PC is simpler, with three layers: layer I is the most superficial and contains LOT axons and apical dendrites of *pyramidal neurons* (the glutamatergic principal neurons of the PC); layer II contains bodies of pyramidal and *semilunar* pyramidal neurons; layer III is deepest and contains basal dendrites of pyramidal neurons, and bodies of *deep pyramidal neurons*. Layer I is further separable into layer Ia in which LOT fibers contact the distal portions of pyramidal neuron dendrites, and layer Ib in which excitatory *association fibers* contact the proximal portions of pyramidal neuron dendrites. The association fibers are an extensive web of branching axons arising from the whole population of pyramidal neurons throughout the PC. The other major elements of the PC circuitry are several types of local GABAergic interneurons, which provide inhibitory control of the pyramidal neurons.

How is odor information encoded by pyramidal neurons in PC? Are there discrete sensory maps similar to glomerular patterns representing odor quality in the olfactory bulb? Earlier studies using neural tracers indicated that olfactory bulb output neurons make diffuse overlapping projections to the PC without clear spatial order (Luskin & Price, 1982; Haberly & Price, 1977; Scott, McBride, & Schneider, 1980) (Figure 5). This was confirmed more recently by precise microinjection of tracer dye into single glomeruli, which revealed broad projections of mitral cell axons distributed throughout the PC (Nagayama, et al., 2010), and by reverse tracing with trans-synaptic

rabies virus, which revealed that many glomeruli send convergent projections to local areas of the PC (Miyamichi, et al., 2010). In contrast to the patterns of activated glomeruli representing odors in the olfactory bulb, odor-evoked patterns of neural activity in the PC are widely distributed and there is no clear spatial patterning that can be correlated with the chemical identity of the odorant stimulus (Stettler & Axel, 2009). Different odorants activate ~ 3 – 20% of the pyramidal neurons, in different but overlapping ensembles. The broadly overlapped mapping of sensory inputs to the PC is significant when considering the widespread association fibers between the pyramidal neurons (Figure 5). Each neuron sends excitatory contacts to many thousands of other neurons. It is estimated that one pyramidal neuron receives recurrent excitatory input from ~ 2,000 other pyramidal neurons, and afferent (sensory) excitation from ~ 200 mitral/ tufted cells in the olfactory bulb (Franks et al., 2011). This suggests that PC neural networks may be working to synthesize holistic representations of odor objects (i.e. odor 'gestalt') by combining multiple *molecular features*—the physicochemical properties of odorant molecules—recognized by multiple ORs. Indeed, psychophysics shows that olfaction is a synthetic sense whereby the brain perceives high-level odor constructs, rather than low-level chemical information of molecular features. For example, it is difficult or impossible for people to identify components in a large blend of many odorants, e.g. the aroma of coffee with hundreds of volatile compounds (Jinks & Laing, 2001). Integration and synthesis of odor objects by pyramidal neurons in the PC may not be a uniform process. A recent study of odor responses in aPC pyramidal neurons of awake, behaving mice found that not all cells displayed broad odorant tuning (Zhan & Luo, 2010). Only ~ 25% were broadly tuned and excited by most compounds of a test panel of 24 odorants. The rest were narrowly tuned and responded to a few or none of the test odorants. Thus, the cell ensembles recruited to

Figure 5. Odor signal processing by synaptic networks in the piriform cortex. This simplified schematic shows how ensembles of mitral and tufted cells (MC/ TC) convey parallel data streams from different glomeruli (encoding information about different molecular structural features detected by various ORs) to the piriform cortex (PC) via the lateral olfactory tract (LOT). In the outer layer (Ia) of PC, the LOT fibers make excitatory synaptic contacts with apical dendrites of pyramidal neurons (PN). The projections from bulb to PC are diffuse and widely distributed: MC/ TCs of individual glomeruli send fibers to many thousands of PNs in anterior and posterior piriform cortex; and conversely, each PN receives and integrates inputs from MC/ TCs of multiple glomeruli. The activity of PNs during odorant stimulation is regulated by early inhibition from feed-forward interneurons (FF-IN) in layer Ia, and by widespread late, recurrent inhibition from fast-spiking interneurons (FS-IN) in layer II/ III. An extensive web of excitatory association fibers in layer Ib interconnects thousands of PNs. Plasticity in these synapses is thought to be important for synthesis and storage of odor object memory in the piriform network. Also illustrated here is the direct feedback from PNs to granule cells of the olfactory bulb, which could provide a mechanism for activity in the PC to coordinate with and modulate the inhibitory filtering of odor representations in the bulb. Dark gray synapses: excitatory pathways releasing the transmitter glutamate; light gray synapses: inhibitory pathways releasing the transmitter GABA.

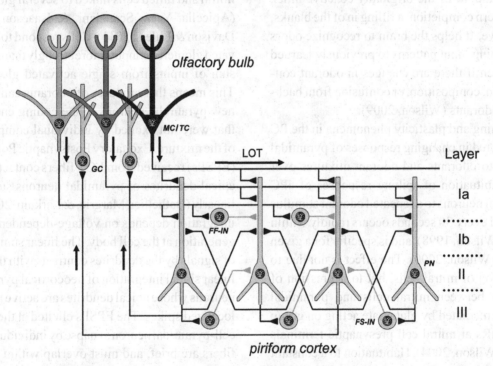

encode odor objects could include both shared and unique elements.

The PC may not only synthesize, but also store odor objects as memories. Its densely interconnected wiring scheme is reminiscent of theoretical neural networks constructed as models of associative memory (Hopfield & Tank, 1986;

McNaughton & Morris, 1987). It is hypothesized that odor memories are stored as particular patterns of synaptic weights between pyramidal neurons. A memory would be learned and stored when certain sub-networks of pyramidal neurons are coactivated by strong bursting activation of odorant-specific patterns of mitral/ tufted cell input. A *Hebbian* mechanism for strengthening association fiber synapses between coactive neurons would induce LTP in this sub-network. Later 'recall' of the odor memory would involve re-excitation of this coactivated sub-network by the same pattern of mitral/ tufted cell inputs. According to this theory, perception and discrimination of odors is closely tied to odor learning and memory because input patterns are recognized by comparing them with a library of odor objects accumulated in the PC from previous olfactory experiences (Wilson & Stevenson, 2003a, 2003b). Strengthened excitatory synaptic connections between pyramidal neurons would allow reexcitation by a slightly different input pattern that did not activate all of the originally coactive units. This pattern completion, a filling in of the blanks, is adaptive. It helps the brain to recognize odors by matching input patterns to previously learned odors even if there are changes in odorant concentration, composition, or confusion from background odorants (Wilson, 2009).

Learning and plasticity phenomena in the PC are reflected in changing responses of pyramidal neurons to odorants and odorant mixtures over time. Habituation of spiking responses of aPC pyramidal neurons to a repeated odorant stimulus delivered every 30 seconds occurs rapidly within 4 trials (Wilson, 1998), and is specific for a given odorant (Wilson, 2000). The effect is not due to habituation of mitral cells, but to depression of synapses between mitral cells and pyramidal neurons, mediated by glutamate acting on group III mGluRs at mitral cell presynaptic terminals (Best & Wilson, 2004). Habituation to a constant stimulus is useful when novel odorant stimuli need to be discriminated from background odorants. It has been found that habituation to a novel odorant mixture leads to habituation to the components of the mixture. This means that the PC encodes the mixture as a collection of separate components. However, such cross-habituation between mixtures and components is reduced if animals have had prior experience with the mixture (Wilson,

2003). Experience has induced the synthesis and storage of the mixture as a distinct odor object, which can be discriminated from mixture components. The memory storage process depends on acetylcholine acting through muscarinic ACh receptors (Wilson, 2001), which suppress and control pyramidal neuron excitation by the association fiber synapses (Barkai & Hasselmo, 1997).

The synaptic and dendritic properties of PC pyramidal neurons appear to be well adapted for the purpose of olfactory signal integration and representation of odors by distributed cell ensembles. The wide, overlapping projections from the olfactory bulb to the PC allows pyramidal neurons to integrate convergent synaptic inputs from multiple mitral and tufted cells linked to several glomeruli (Apicella, Yuan, Scanziani, & Isaacson, 2010; Davison & Ehlers, 2011). Cells respond to coactivated glomerular inputs more strongly than a linear sum of inputs from single activated glomeruli. This means that mixtures of odorants can recruit new pyramidal neurons to the coding ensemble that were not excited by individual components of the mixture. Excitatory Postsynaptic Potentials (EPSPs) received from LOT fibers contacting the apical dendrites of pyramidal neurons summate linearly (Bathellier, Margrie, & Larkum, 2009), so integration depends on voltage-dependent spike generation at the cell body. The linear summation of signals by the dendrites contrasts with the non-linear signal integration of neocortical pyramidal neurons whose apical dendrites are active and fire localized spikes. The EPSPs elicited at the mitral cell-pyramidal neuron synapse by individual LOT fibers are brief, and must overlap within a short time window ($\sim$ 10 ms) to summate and generate a response. This defines the coincidence detection window for integrating input signals conveyed by synchronized assemblies of spiking mitral and tufted cells (Franks & Isaacson, 2006).

Computations in the PC are assisted by several classes of inhibitory interneurons regulating the excitation of pyramidal neurons. In layer Ia, interneurons receive direct synaptic input from mitral and tufted cell axons in the LOT, so they are excited in parallel with the pyramidal neuron distal dendrites. When odorant stimuli elicit a series of spikes in LOT fibers, layer Ia interneurons respond quickly but momentarily to inhibit pyramidal dendrites and delay the pyramidal neuron response (Stokes & Isaacson, 2010). This early *feedforward inhibition* is most effective for weak LOT inputs with few spikes, and it could force a later timing of integration of LOT inputs by the pyramidal neuron cell body. It can be overcome by strong, bursting LOT activity, which would enable the PC to selectively process olfactory bulb signals encoded by mitral and tufted cell bursting. Spike input from the LOT fibers also excites a type of cortical interneuron known as 'fast spiking' (FS) interneurons (so named because they generate discharges of high-frequency spikes) in deeper Layer III. This occurs after a longer delay, resulting in later inhibition of pyramidal neurons. The FS interneurons are activated by pyramidal neuron axon collateral branches, and they send *recurrent inhibition* to cell bodies of other pyramidal neurons. Due to their wide connectivity, their inhibition should balance the excitation of the pyramidal neuron network by widespread association fibers. Indeed, it was shown that long range recurrent inhibition is stronger than recurrent excitation, and it scales with excitation strength (Franks, et al., 2011). This inhibition works to restrict amplification of sensory inputs by association fibers to a brief time window of ~ 100 ms after LOT activation. Thus, PC inhibitory interneurons are expected to have important functions in regulating the dynamics and temporal aspects of synthetic odor coding and memory formation.

The diffuse mapping of olfactory receptor inputs to the PC contrasts with projections to some other cortical centers. For example, the *Anterior Olfactory Nucleus* (AON), a separate cortical structure located anterior to the PC, is a complex nucleus with several subdivisions. One subdivision, the *Anterior Olfactory Nucleus pars Externa* (AONpE), has a special relationship with left and right olfactory bulbs. Pyramidal neurons in AONpE receive inputs from mitral or tufted cells in the ipsilateral olfactory bulb (on the same side), and they send their axons through the anterior commissure to granule cells in the contralateral olfactory bulb (on the opposite side). The projection from olfactory bulb to AONpE preserves the precise topographic representation of ORs. Interhemispheric connections of AONpE establish synaptic linkages between isofunctional glomerular circuits of the left and right bulbs that process sensory input encoded by the same ORs (Yan, et al., 2008). Together with the intrabulbar association system of superficial tufted cells, this *interbulbar association system* furnishes the neural pathways necessary for coordination of all OR-coded signal processing by both olfactory bulbs.

The *amygdala* is a heterogeneous assemblage of brain nuclei in the limbic system (Swanson & Petrovich, 1998) that includes systems important in emotional learning and memory, including fear and appetitive conditioning. Emotional contexts are linked to sensory inputs, and the sense of smell is well known to provoke particularly strong emotional recall of memories (Herz & Cupchik, 1995). The *anterior cortical nucleus* of the amygdala receives inputs from aPC pyramidal neurons (Haberly & Price, 1978), giving it access to associative odor memories assumed to be stored in PC networks. There is also a direct projection from the olfactory bulb to the *posterolateral cortical nucleus* of the amygdala. Using dye-tracing methods to follow mitral and tufted cell axons from single glomeruli, it was found that OR-encoded projections to this part of the amygdala are organized into spatially distinct, invariant regions in the posterolateral cortical nucleus (Sosulski, Lissitsyna, Cutforth, Axel, & Datta, 2011). This is another case of olfactory cortical connections that differ from the diffuse associative-memory architecture of the PC. It implies that different ORs can activate segregated local circuits in the amygdala, which may underlie different innate, odor-guided behaviors. In fact, it has been found that the amygdala receives a greater degree of input from the dorsal part of the olfactory bulb (Miyamichi, et al., 2010), and when the dorsal bulb of mice is ablated by genetic manipulation, they lose their innate avoidance of odors signaling the presence of predators or spoiled foods (Kobayakawa, et al., 2007).

CONCLUSION

We have introduced and described the basic morphology and physiology of structures comprising the first three stages of olfactory sensory processing in vertebrates—the olfactory epithelium, olfactory bulb, and olfactory cortex. A range of recent research has also been described to provide an up-to-date review of our evolving understanding of mechanisms and design principles underlying the sense of smell. Because olfaction is among the oldest of sensory modalities, its inner workings display an elegance and economy of design honed by a long history of evolution and adaptation. We can now understand how olfactory systems may perform the duties we listed in the Introduction. The detection and discrimination of a wide diversity of small organic molecules is made possible by the remarkable genetic expansion of the Olfactory Receptor proteins (ORs) into families with hundreds to thousands of independent chemical detector channels. The broad tuning, low affinity and brief ligand binding of most ORs allows for combinatorial coding and fast tracking of dynamic odorant stimuli. Quick detection and discrimination is possible because ORs can activate a transduction cascade in tens of milliseconds, and sensory input encoded by combinations of many ORs is processed rapidly by the olfactory bulb in a massively parallel circuit. The glomerular patterned encoding predicts that the number of activated OR channels can increase at higher odorant concentrations, explaining shifts in odor quality with intensity. Odorant detection sensitivity is boosted by convergence of OSNs to glomeruli which amplifies the signal-to-noise ratio

for second order neurons in the olfactory bulb. The precise mapping of OR detector channels to discrete glomerular units facilitates the wiring of inhibitory circuits in the bulb. Inhibition filters sensory input patterns and synchronizes spike output signals to communicate with cortical areas. Adaptation or habituation to odors could be mediated by a hierarchy of mechanisms operating on different timescales: desensitization of transduction in the olfactory cilia, modulation of olfactory bulb processing by noradrenergic input to granule cells, or modulation of pyramidal neuron excitation in piriform cortex. Discrimination between new odors and background odors is achieved by habituation processes, and discrimination between similar odorants involves adaptive learning and odor object synthesis in piriform cortical networks. Storage of odor objects as memories in cortex can alter mixture perceptions from 'elemental' to 'configural,' and this storage could be modulated so as to link odor memories with other non-olfactory memories.

ACKNOWLEDGMENT

Supported by National Institute on Deafness and Other Communication Disorders (NIDCD) grant R01DC04208. Thanks to Johannes Reisert for critical review of the manuscript, and to Michele Dibattista, Anna Boccaccio, Luba Dankulich-Nagrudny, and Jie Ma for images of olfactory sensory neurons and olfactory bulb.

REFERENCES

Abaffy, T., Matsunami, H., & Luetje, C. W. (2006). Functional analysis of a mammalian odorant receptor subfamily. *Journal of Neurochemistry, 97*, 1506–1518. doi:10.1111/j.1471-4159.2006.03859.x

Adrian, E. D. (1950). The electrical activity of the mammalian olfactory bulb. *Electroencephalography and Clinical Neurophysiology, 2,* 377–388. doi:10.1016/0013-4694(50)90075-7

Allison, A. C. (1953). The morphology of the olfactory system of vertebrates. *Biological Reviews of the Cambridge Philosophical Society, 28,* 195–244. doi:10.1111/j.1469-185X.1953. tb01376.x

Antolin, S., Reisert, J., & Matthews, H. R. (2010). Olfactory response termination involves Ca^{2+}-ATPase in vertebrate olfactory receptor neuron cilia. *The Journal of General Physiology, 135,* 367–378. doi:10.1085/jgp.200910337

Apicella, A., Yuan, Q., Scanziani, M., & Isaacson, J. S. (2010). Pyramidal cells in piriform cortex receive convergent input from distinct olfactory bulb glomeruli. *The Journal of Neuroscience, 30,* 14255–14260. doi:10.1523/JNEUROSCI.2747-10.2010

Araneda, R. C., Kini, A. D., & Firestein, S. (2000). The molecular receptive range of an odorant receptor. *Nature Neuroscience, 3,* 1248–1255. doi:10.1038/81774

Araneda, R. C., Peterlin, Z., Zhang, X., Chesler, A., & Firestein, S. (2004). A pharmacological profile of the aldehyde receptor repertoire in rat olfactory epithelium. *The Journal of Physiology, 555,* 743–756. doi:10.1113/jphysiol.2003.058040

Aungst, J. L., Heyward, P. M., Puche, A. C., Karnup, S. V., Hayar, A., & Szabo, G. (2003). Centre-surround inhibition among olfactory bulb glomeruli. *Nature, 426,* 623–629. doi:10.1038/nature02185

Bakalyar, H. A., & Reed, R. R. (1990). Identification of a specialized adenylyl cyclase that may mediate odorant detection. *Science, 250,* 1403–1406. doi:10.1126/science.2255909

Bargmann, C. I. (2006). Chemosensation in C. elegans. *WormBook.* Retrieved from http://www.wormbook.org

Barkai, E., & Hasselmo, M. H. (1997). Acetylcholine and associative memory in the piriform cortex. *Molecular Neurobiology, 15,* 17–29. doi:10.1007/BF02740613

Bathellier, B., Margrie, T. W., & Larkum, M. E. (2009). Properties of piriform cortex pyramidal cell dendrites: Implications for olfactory circuit design. *The Journal of Neuroscience, 29,* 12641–12652. doi:10.1523/JNEUROSCI.1124-09.2009

Belluscio, L., Gold, G. H., Nemes, A., & Axel, R. (1998). Mice deficient in G_{olf} are anosmic. *Neuron, 20,* 69–81. doi:10.1016/S0896-6273(00)80435-3

Ben Arie, N., Khen, M., & Lancet, D. (1993). Glutathione S-transferases in rat olfactory epithelium: Purification, molecular properties and odorant biotransformation. *Biochemical Journal, 292*(2), 379–384.

Ben Chaim, Y., Cheng, M. M., & Yau, K. W. (2011). Unitary response of mouse olfactory receptor neurons. *Proceedings of the National Academy of Sciences of the United States of America, 108,* 822–827. doi:10.1073/pnas.1017983108

Best, A. R., & Wilson, D. A. (2004). Coordinate synaptic mechanisms contributing to olfactory cortical adaptation. *The Journal of Neuroscience, 24,* 652–660. doi:10.1523/JNEUROSCI.4220-03.2004

Bhandawat, V., Reisert, J., & Yau, K. W. (2005). Elementary response of olfactory receptor neurons to odorants. *Science, 308,* 1931–1934. doi:10.1126/science.1109886

Bhandawat, V., Reisert, J., & Yau, K. W. (2010). Signaling by olfactory receptor neurons near threshold. *Proceedings of the National Academy of Sciences of the United States of America, 107,* 18682–18687. doi:10.1073/pnas.1004571107

Billig, G. M., Pal, B., Fidzinski, P., & Jentsch, T. J. (2011). Ca^{2+}-activated Cl^- currents are dispensable for olfaction. *Nature Neuroscience, 14*(6), 763–769. doi:10.1038/nn.2821

Bocca, E., Antonelli, A. R., & Mosciaro, O. (1965). Mechanical co-factors in olfactory stimulation. *Acta Oto-Laryngologica, 59,* 243–247. doi:10.3109/00016486509124558

Bohbot, J., Pitts, R. J., Kwon, H. W., Rützler, M., Robertson, H. M., & Zwiebel, L. J. (2007). Molecular characterization of the Aedes aegypti odorant receptor gene family. *Insect Molecular Biology, 16,* 525–537.

Borysik, A. J., Briand, L., Taylor, A. J., & Scott, D. J. (2010). Rapid odorant release in mammalian odour binding proteins facilitates their temporal coupling to odorant signals. *Journal of Molecular Biology, 404,* 372–380. doi:10.1016/j.jmb.2010.09.019

Brennan, P. A., & Keverne, E. B. (2004). Something in the air? New insights into mammalian pheromones. *Current Biology, 14,* R81–R89. doi:10.1016/j.cub.2003.12.052

Buck, L., & Axel, R. (1991). A novel multigene family may encode odorant receptors: A molecular basis for odor recognition. *Cell, 65,* 175–187. doi:10.1016/0092-8674(91)90418-X

Cajal, S. R. Y. (1890). Origen y terminación de las fibras nerviosas olfatorias. *Gaceta Sanitaria de Barcelona, 3,* 133–139, 174–181, 206–212.

Carey, R. M., Verhagen, J. V., Wesson, D. W., Pirez, N., & Wachowiak, M. (2009). Temporal structure of receptor neuron input to the olfactory bulb imaged in behaving rats. *Journal of Neurophysiology, 101,* 1073–1088. doi:10.1152/jn.90902.2008

Carlson, G. C., Shipley, M. T., & Keller, A. (2000). Long-lasting depolarizations in mitral cells of the rat olfactory bulb. *The Journal of Neuroscience, 20,* 2011–2021.

Castillo, P. E., Carleton, A., Vincent, J. D., & Lledo, P. M. (1999). Multiple and opposing roles of cholinergic transmission in the main olfactory bulb. *The Journal of Neuroscience, 19,* 9180–9191.

Chaudhury, D., Escanilla, O., & Linster, C. (2009). Bulbar acetylcholine enhances neural and perceptual odor discrimination. *The Journal of Neuroscience, 29,* 52–60. doi:10.1523/JNEUROSCI.4036-08.2009

Chaudhury, D., Manella, L., Arellanos, A., Escanilla, O., Cleland, T. A., & Linster, C. (2010). Olfactory bulb habituation to odor stimuli. *Behavioral Neuroscience, 124,* 490–499. doi:10.1037/a0020293

Chen, T. Y., & Yau, K. W. (1994). Direct modulation by Ca²⁺-calmodulin of cyclic nucleotide–activated channel of rat olfactory receptor neurons. *Nature, 368,* 545–548. doi:10.1038/368545a0

Chen, W. R., & Shepherd, G. M. (2005). The olfactory glomerulus: a cortical module with specific functions. *Journal of Neurocytology, 34,* 353–360. doi:10.1007/s11068-005-8362-0

Chen, Y., Getchell, M. L., Ding, X., & Getchell, T. V. (1992). Immunolocalization of two cytochrome P450 isozymes in rat nasal chemosensory tissue. *Neuroreport, 3,* 749–752. doi:10.1097/00001756-199209000-00007

Christie, J. M., Bark, C., Hormuzdi, S. G., Helbig, I., Monyer, H., & Westbrook, G. L. (2005). Connexin36 mediates spike synchrony in olfactory bulb glomeruli. *Neuron, 46,* 761–772. doi:10.1016/j.neuron.2005.04.030

Cleland, T. A., & Sethupathy, P. (2006). Non–topographical contrast enhancement in the olfactory bulb. *BMC Neuroscience, 7,* 7. doi:10.1186/1471-2202-7-7

Cox, J. P. (2008). Hydrodynamic aspects of fish olfaction. *Journal of the Royal Society, Interface, 5,* 575–593. doi:10.1098/rsif.2007.1281

Cury, K. M., & Uchida, N. (2010). Robust odor coding via inhalation-coupled transient activity in the mammalian olfactory bulb. *Neuron, 68,* 570–585. doi:10.1016/j.neuron.2010.09.040

Cygnar, K. D., & Zhao, H. (2009). Phosphodiesterase 1C is dispensable for rapid response termination of olfactory sensory neurons. *Nature Neuroscience, 12,* 454–462. doi:10.1038/nn.2289

Davison, I. G., & Ehlers, M. D. (2011). Neural circuit mechanisms for pattern detection and feature combination in olfactory cortex. *Neuron, 70,* 82–94. doi:10.1016/j.neuron.2011.02.047

De Saint, J. D., Hirnet, D., Westbrook, G. L., & Charpak, S. (2009). External tufted cells drive the output of olfactory bulb glomeruli. *The Journal of Neuroscience, 29,* 2043–2052. doi:10.1523/JNEUROSCI.5317-08.2009

Desmaisons, D., Vincent, J. D., & Lledo, P. M. (1999). Control of action potential timing by intrinsic subthreshold oscillations in olfactory bulb output neurons. *The Journal of Neuroscience, 19,* 10727–10737.

Dhawale, A. K., Hagiwara, A., Bhalla, U. S., Murthy, V. N., & Albeanu, D. F. (2010). Non-redundant odor coding by sister mitral cells revealed by light addressable glomeruli in the mouse. *Nature Neuroscience, 13,* 1404–1412. doi:10.1038/nn.2673

Dong, H. W., Hayar, A., Callaway, J., Yang, X. H., Nai, Q., & Ennis, M. (2009). Group I mGluR activation enhances Ca²⁺-dependent nonselective cation currents and rhythmic bursting in main olfactory bulb external tufted cells. *The Journal of Neuroscience, 29,* 11943–11953. doi:10.1523/JNEUROSCI.0206-09.2009

Dong, H. W., Hayar, A., & Ennis, M. (2007). Activation of group I metabotropic glutamate receptors on main olfactory bulb granule cells and periglomerular cells enhances synaptic inhibition of mitral cells. *The Journal of Neuroscience, 27,* 5654–5663. doi:10.1523/JNEUROSCI.5495-06.2007

Doucette, W., Milder, J., & Restrepo, D. (2007). Adrenergic modulation of olfactory bulb circuitry affects odor discrimination. *Learning & Memory (Cold Spring Harbor, N.Y.), 14,* 539–547. doi:10.1101/lm.606407

Doucette, W., & Restrepo, D. (2008). Profound context-dependent plasticity of mitral cell responses in olfactory bulb. *PLoS Biology, 6,* e258. doi:10.1371/journal.pbio.0060258

Duchamp–Viret, P., Duchamp, A., & Chaput, M. A. (2003). Single olfactory sensory neurons simultaneously integrate the components of an odour mixture. *The European Journal of Neuroscience, 18,* 2690–2696. doi:10.1111/j.1460-9568.2003.03001.x

Duchamp-Viret, P., Duchamp, A., & Vigouroux, M. (1989). Amplifying role of convergence in olfactory system a comparative study of receptor cell and second-order neuron sensitivities. *Journal of Neurophysiology, 61,* 1085–1094.

Dulac, C., & Wagner, S. (2006). Genetic analysis of brain circuits underlying pheromone signaling. *Annual Review of Genetics, 40,* 449–467. doi:10.1146/annurev.genet.39.073003.093937

Egger, V., Svoboda, K., & Mainen, Z. F. (2005). Dendrodendritic synaptic signals in olfactory bulb granule cells: Local spine boost and global low-threshold spike. *The Journal of Neuroscience, 25,* 3521–3530. doi:10.1523/JNEUROSCI.4746-04.2005

Ennis, M., Zhou, F. M., Ciombor, K. J., Aroniadou–Anderjaska, V., Hayar, A., & Borrelli, E. (2001). Dopamine D2 receptor-mediated presynaptic inhibition of olfactory nerve terminals. *Journal of Neurophysiology, 86,* 2986–2997.

Escanilla, O., Arrellanos, A., Karnow, A., Ennis, M., & Linster, C. (2010). Noradrenergic modulation of behavioral odor detection and discrimination thresholds in the olfactory bulb. *The European Journal of Neuroscience, 32,* 458–468. doi:10.1111/j.1460-9568.2010.07297.x

Escanilla, O., Yuhas, C., Marzan, D., & Linster, C. (2009). Dopaminergic modulation of olfactory bulb processing affects odor discrimination learning in rats. *Behavioral Neuroscience, 123,* 828–833. doi:10.1037/a0015855

Eyre, M. D., Antal, M., & Nusser, Z. (2008). Distinct deep short-axon cell subtypes of the main olfactory bulb provide novel intrabulbar and extrabulbar GABAergic connections. *The Journal of Neuroscience, 28,* 8217–8229. doi:10.1523/JNEUROSCI.2490-08.2008

Fantana, A. L., Soucy, E. R., & Meister, M. (2008). Rat olfactory bulb mitral cells receive sparse glomerular inputs. *Neuron, 59,* 802–814. doi:10.1016/j.neuron.2008.07.039

Franks, K. M., & Isaacson, J. S. (2006). Strong single-fiber sensory inputs to olfactory cortex: Implications for olfactory coding. *Neuron, 49,* 357–363. doi:10.1016/j.neuron.2005.12.026

Franks, K. M., Russo, M. J., Sosulski, D. L., Mulligan, A. A., Siegelbaum, S. A., & Axel, R. (2011). Recurrent circuitry dynamically shapes the activation of piriform cortex. *Neuron, 72,* 49–56. doi:10.1016/j.neuron.2011.08.020

Freeman, W. J., & Baird, B. (1987). Relation of olfactory EEG to behavior: Spatial analysis. *Behavioral Neuroscience, 101,* 393–408. doi:10.1037/0735-7044.101.3.393

Friedrich, R. W., Yaksi, E., Judkewitz, B., & Wiechert, M. T. (2009). Processing of odor representations by neuronal circuits in the olfactory bulb. *Annals of the New York Academy of Sciences, 1170,* 293–297. doi:10.1111/j.1749-6632.2009.04010.x

Frings, S., Seifert, R., Godde, M., & Kaupp, U. B. (1995). Profoundly different calcium permeation and blockage determine the specific function of distinct cyclic nucleotide-gated channels. *Neuron, 15,* 169–179. doi:10.1016/0896-6273(95)90074-8

Furudono, Y., Sone, Y., Takizawa, K., Hirono, J., & Sato, T. (2009). Relationship between peripheral receptor code and perceived odor quality. *Chemical Senses, 34,* 151–158. doi:10.1093/chemse/bjn071

Galan, R. F., Fourcaud–Trocme, N., Ermentrout, G. B., & Urban, N. N. (2006). Correlation-induced synchronization of oscillations in olfactory bulb neurons. *The Journal of Neuroscience, 26,* 3646–3655. doi:10.1523/JNEUROSCI.4605-05.2006

Gao, Y., & Strowbridge, B. W. (2009). Long–term plasticity of excitatory inputs to granule cells in the rat olfactory bulb. *Nature Neuroscience, 12,* 731–733. doi:10.1038/nn.2319

Gire, D. H., & Schoppa, N. E. (2009). Control of on/off glomerular signaling by a local GABAergic microcircuit in the olfactory bulb. *The Journal of Neuroscience, 29,* 13454–13464. doi:10.1523/JNEUROSCI.2368-09.2009

Godfrey, P. A., Malnic, B., & Buck, L. B. (2004). The mouse olfactory receptor gene family. *Proceedings of the National Academy of Sciences of the United States of America, 101,* 2156–2161. doi:10.1073/pnas.0308051100

Golgi, C. (1875). Sulla fina struttura dei bulbi olfactorii. *Rivista Sperimentale di Freniatria e Medicina Legale, 1,* 405–425.

Gracia–Llanes, F. J., Blasco–Ibanez, J. M., Nacher, J., Varea, E., Liberia, T., & Martinez, P. (2010). Synaptic connectivity of serotonergic axons in the olfactory glomeruli of the rat olfactory bulb. *Neuroscience, 169,* 770–780. doi:10.1016/j.neuroscience.2010.05.034

Graziadei, P. P. (1971). The olfactory mucosa of vertebrates. In L. M. Beidler (Ed.), *Handbook of Sensory Physiology: Vol 4: Chemical Senses: 1 – Olfaction,* (pp. 27–58). New York, NY: Springer–Verlag.

Graziadei, P. P., & Monti–Graziadei, A. G. (1978). Continuous nerve cell renewal in the olfactory system. In M. Jacobson (Ed.), *Handbook of Sensory Physiology: Vol 9: Development of Sensory Systems,* (pp. 55–83). New York, NY: Springer–Verlag.

Guerin, D., Peace, S. T., Didier, A., Linster, C., & Cleland, T. A. (2008). Noradrenergic neuromodulation in the olfactory bulb modulates odor habituation and spontaneous discrimination. *Behavioral Neuroscience, 122,* 816–826. doi:10.1037/a0012522

Gutierrez–Mecinas, M., Crespo, C., Blasco–Ibanez, J. M., Gracia–Llanes, F. J., Marques–Mari, A. I., & Martinez–Guijarro, F. J. (2005). Soluble guanylyl cyclase appears in a specific subset of periglomerular cells in the olfactory bulb. *The European Journal of Neuroscience, 21,* 1443–1448. doi:10.1111/j.1460-9568.2005.03960.x

Haberly, L. B. (2001). Parallel-distributed processing in olfactory cortex: New insights from morphological and physiological analysis of neuronal circuitry. *Chemical Senses, 26,* 551–576. doi:10.1093/chemse/26.5.551

Haberly, L. B., & Price, J. L. (1977). The axonal projection patterns of the mitral and tufted cells of the olfactory bulb in the rat. *Brain Research, 129,* 152–157. doi:10.1016/0006-8993(77)90978-7

Haberly, L. B., & Price, J. L. (1978). Association and commissural fiber systems of the olfactory cortex of the rat. *The Journal of Comparative Neurology, 178,* 711–740. doi:10.1002/cne.901780408

Hardy, A., Palouzier–Paulignan, B., Duchamp, A., Royet, J. P., & Duchamp–Viret, P. (2005). 5-Hydroxytryptamine action in the rat olfactory bulb: In vitro electrophysiological patch–clamp recordings of juxtaglomerular and mitral cells. *Neuroscience, 131,* 717–731. doi:10.1016/j.neuroscience.2004.10.034

Harkema, J. R., Carey, S. A., & Wagner, J. G. (2006). The nose revisited: A brief review of the comparative structure, function, and toxicologic pathology of the nasal epithelium. *Toxicologic Pathology, 34,* 252–269. doi:10.1080/01926230600713475

Hayar, A., Karnup, S., Ennis, M., & Shipley, M. T. (2004). External tufted cells: A major excitatory element that coordinates glomerular activity. *The Journal of Neuroscience, 24,* 6676–6685. doi:10.1523/JNEUROSCI.1367-04.2004

Hayar, A., Karnup, S., Shipley, M. T., & Ennis, M. (2004). Olfactory bulb glomeruli: external tufted cells intrinsically burst at theta frequency and are entrained by patterned olfactory input. *The Journal of Neuroscience, 24,* 1190–1199. doi:10.1523/JNEUROSCI.4714-03.2004

Heinbockel, T., Heyward, P., Conquet, F., & Ennis, M. (2004). Regulation of main olfactory bulb mitral cell excitability by metabotropic glutamate receptor mGluR1. *Journal of Neurophysiology, 92,* 3085–3096. doi:10.1152/jn.00349.2004

Hengl, T., Kaneko, H., Dauner, K., Vocke, K., Frings, S., & Mohrlen, F. (2010). Molecular components of signal amplification in olfactory sensory cilia. *Proceedings of the National Academy of Sciences of the United States of America, 107,* 6052–6057. doi:10.1073/pnas.0909032107

Herz, R. S., & Cupchik, G. C. (1995). The emotional distinctiveness of odor–evoked memories. *Chemical Senses, 20,* 517–528. doi:10.1093/chemse/20.5.517

Hopfield, J. J., & Tank, D. W. (1986). Computing with neural circuits: A model. *Science, 233,* 625–633. doi:10.1126/science.3755256

Hu, J., Zhong, C., Ding, C., Chi, Q., Walz, A., & Mombaerts, P. (2007). Detection of near-atmospheric concentrations of CO_2 by an olfactory subsystem in the mouse. *Science, 317,* 953–957. doi:10.1126/science.1144233

Isaacson, J. S., & Strowbridge, B. W. (1998). Olfactory reciprocal synapses: Dendritic signaling in the CNS. *Neuron, 20,* 749–761. doi:10.1016/S0896-6273(00)81013-2

Jinks, A., & Laing, D. G. (2001). The analysis of odor mixtures by humans: Evidence for a configurational process. *Physiology & Behavior, 72,* 51–63. doi:10.1016/S0031-9384(00)00407-8

Johnson, B. A., & Leon, M. (2007). Chemotopic odorant coding in a mammalian olfactory system. *The Journal of Comparative Neurology, 503,* 1–34. doi:10.1002/cne.21396

Johnson, B. A., Woo, C. C., & Leon, M. (1998). Spatial coding of odorant features in the glomerular layer of the rat olfactory bulb. *The Journal of Comparative Neurology, 393,* 457–471. doi:10.1002/(SICI)1096-9861(19980420)393:4<457::AID-CNE5>3.0.CO;2-#

Johnston, J., & Delaney, K. R. (2010). Synaptic activation of T-type Ca^{2+} channels via mGluR activation in the primary dendrite of mitral cells. *Journal of Neurophysiology, 103,* 2557–2569. doi:10.1152/jn.00796.2009

Jones, D. T., & Reed, R. R. (1989). G_{olf}: An olfactory neuron specific-G protein involved in odorant signal transduction. *Science, 244,* 790–795. doi:10.1126/science.2499043

Kaneko, H., Nakamura, T., & Lindemann, B. (2001). Noninvasive measurement of chloride concentration in rat olfactory receptor cells with use of a fluorescent dye. *American Journal of Physiology. Cell Physiology, 280,* C1387–C1393.

Kaneko, H., Putzier, I., Frings, S., Kaupp, U. B., & Gensch, T. (2004). Chloride accumulation in mammalian olfactory sensory neurons. *The Journal of Neuroscience, 24,* 7931–7938. doi:10.1523/JNEUROSCI.2115-04.2004

Kaupp, U. B. (2011). Olfactory signalling in vertebrates and insects: differences and commonalities. *Nature Reviews. Neuroscience, 11,* 188–200.

Kawai, F. (1999a). Odorant suppression of delayed rectifier potassium current in newt olfactory receptor cells. *Neuroscience Letters, 269,* 45–48. doi:10.1016/S0304-3940(99)00424-3

Kawai, F. (1999b). Odorants suppress T- and L-type Ca^{2+} currents in olfactory receptor cells by shifting their inactivation curves to a negative voltage. *Neuroscience Research, 35,* 253–263. doi:10.1016/S0168-0102(99)00091-7

Kawai, F., Kurahashi, T., & Kaneko, A. (1997). Nonselective suppression of voltage–gated currents by odorants in the newt olfactory receptor cells. *The Journal of General Physiology, 109,* 265–272. doi:10.1085/jgp.109.2.265

Kawai, F., & Miyachi, E. (2001). Enhancement by T-type Ca^{2+} currents of odor sensitivity in olfactory receptor cells. *The Journal of Neuroscience, 21,* RC144.

Kendrick, K. M., Guevara–Guzman, R., Zorrilla, J., Hinton, M. R., Broad, K. D., & Mimmack, M. (1997). Formation of olfactory memories mediated by nitric oxide. *Nature, 388,* 670–674. doi:10.1038/41765

Kiyokage, E., Pan, Y. Z., Shao, Z., Kobayashi, K., Szabo, G., & Yanagawa, Y. (2010). Molecular identity of periglomerular and short axon cells. *The Journal of Neuroscience, 30,* 1185–1196. doi:10.1523/JNEUROSCI.3497-09.2010

Kleene, S. J. (1993). Origin of the chloride current in olfactory transduction. *Neuron, 11,* 123–132. doi:10.1016/0896-6273(93)90276-W

Ko, H. J., Lee, S. H., Oh, E. H., & Park, T. H. (2010). Specificity of odorant-binding proteins: A factor influencing the sensitivity of olfactory receptor-based biosensors. *Bioprocess and Biosystems Engineering*, *33*, 55–62. doi:10.1007/s00449-009-0348-3

Kobayakawa, K., Kobayakawa, R., Matsumoto, H., Oka, Y., Imai, T., & Ikawa, M. (2007). Innate versus learned odour processing in the mouse olfactory bulb. *Nature*, *450*, 503–508. doi:10.1038/nature06281

Kosaka, T., & Kosaka, K. (2007). Heterogeneity of nitric oxide synthase-containing neurons in the mouse main olfactory bulb. *Neuroscience Research*, *57*, 165–178. doi:10.1016/j.neures.2006.10.005

Kosaka, T., & Kosaka, K. (2011). "Interneurons" in the olfactory bulb revisited. *Neuroscience Research*, *69*, 93–99. doi:10.1016/j.neures.2010.10.002

Kuffler, S. W. (1953). Discharge patterns and functional organization of the mammalian retina. *Journal of Neurophysiology*, *16*, 37–68.

Kurahashi, T., Lowe, G., & Gold, G. H. (1994). Suppression of odorant responses by odorants in olfactory receptor cells. *Science*, *265*, 118–120. doi:10.1126/science.8016645

Kurahashi, T., & Yau, K. W. (1993). Co-existence of cationic and chloride components in odorant–induced current of vertebrate olfactory receptor cells. *Nature*, *363*, 71–74. doi:10.1038/363071a0

Kurahashi, T., & Yau, K. W. (1994). Olfactory transduction: Tale of an unusual chloride current. *Current Biology*, *4*, 256–258. doi:10.1016/S0960-9822(00)00058-0

Laurent, G. (2002). Olfactory network dynamics and the coding of multidimensional signals. *Nature Reviews. Neuroscience*, *3*, 884–895. doi:10.1038/nrn964

Lazarini, F., & Lledo, P. M. (2011). Is adult neurogenesis essential for olfaction? *Trends in Neurosciences*, *34*, 20–30. doi:10.1016/j.tins.2010.09.006

Le Gros Clark, W. E. (1951). The projection of the olfactory epithelium on the olfactory bulb in the rabbit. *Journal of Neurology, Neurosurgery, and Psychiatry*, *14*, 1–10. doi:10.1136/jnnp.14.1.1

Leinders–Zufall, T., Cockerham, R. E., Michalakis, S., Biel, M., Garbers, D. L., & Reed, R. R. (2007). Contribution of the receptor guanylyl cyclase GC-D to chemosensory function in the olfactory epithelium. *Proceedings of the National Academy of Sciences of the United States of America*, *104*, 14507–14512. doi:10.1073/pnas.0704965104

Leinders–Zufall, T., Ma, M., & Zufall, F. (1999). Impaired odor adaptation in olfactory receptor neurons after inhibition of Ca^{2+}/calmodulin kinase II. *The Journal of Neuroscience*, *19*, RC19.

Lepousez, G., Csaba, Z., Bernard, V., Loudes, C., Videau, C., & Lacombe, J. (2010). Somatostatin interneurons delineate the inner part of the external plexiform layer in the mouse main olfactory bulb. *The Journal of Comparative Neurology*, *518*, 1976–1994. doi:10.1002/cne.22317

Lepousez, G., Mouret, A., Loudes, C., Epelbaum, J., & Viollet, C. (2010). Somatostatin contributes to in vivo gamma oscillation modulation and odor discrimination in the olfactory bulb. *The Journal of Neuroscience*, *30*, 870–875. doi:10.1523/JNEUROSCI.4958-09.2010

Liberles, S. D., & Buck, L. B. (2006). A second class of chemosensory receptors in the olfactory epithelium. *Nature*, *442*, 645–650. doi:10.1038/nature05066

Liu, S., & Shipley, M. T. (2008). Multiple conductances cooperatively regulate spontaneous bursting in mouse olfactory bulb external tufted cells. *The Journal of Neuroscience*, *28*, 1625–1639. doi:10.1523/JNEUROSCI.3906-07.2008

Liu, W. L., & Shipley, M. T. (1994). Intrabulbar associational system in the rat olfactory bulb comprises cholecystokinin-containing tufted cells that synapse onto the dendrites of GABAergic granule cells. *The Journal of Comparative Neurology, 346,* 541–558. doi:10.1002/cne.903460407

Lodovichi, C., Belluscio, L., & Katz, L. C. (2003). Functional topography of connections linking mirror–symmetric maps in the mouse olfactory bulb. *Neuron, 38,* 265–276. doi:10.1016/S0896-6273(03)00194-6

Lowe, G. (2002). Inhibition of backpropagating action potentials in mitral cell secondary dendrites. *Journal of Neurophysiology, 88,* 64–85.

Lowe, G., & Gold, G. H. (1993). Nonlinear amplification by calcium-dependent chloride channels in olfactory receptor cells. *Nature, 366,* 283–286. doi:10.1038/366283a0

Lowe, G., & Gold, G. H. (1995). Olfactory transduction is intrinsically noisy. *Proceedings of the National Academy of Sciences of the United States of America, 92,* 7864–7868. doi:10.1073/pnas.92.17.7864

Luo, M., & Katz, L. C. (2001). Response correlation maps of neurons in the Mammalian olfactory bulb. *Neuron, 32,* 1165–1179. doi:10.1016/S0896-6273(01)00537-2

Luskin, M. B., & Price, J. L. (1982). The distribution of axon collaterals from the olfactory bulb and the nucleus of the horizontal limb of the diagonal band to the olfactory cortex, demonstrated by double retrograde labeling techniques. *The Journal of Comparative Neurology, 209,* 249–263. doi:10.1002/cne.902090304

Ma, J., & Lowe, G. (2007). Calcium permeable AMPA receptors and autoreceptors in external tufted cells of rat olfactory bulb. *Neuroscience, 144,* 1094–1108. doi:10.1016/j.neuroscience.2006.10.041

Ma, J., & Lowe, G. (2010). Correlated firing in tufted cells of mouse olfactory bulb. *Neuroscience, 169,* 1715–1738. doi:10.1016/j.neuroscience.2010.06.033

Mainland, J., & Sobel, N. (2006). The sniff is part of the olfactory percept. *Chemical Senses, 31,* 181–196. doi:10.1093/chemse/bjj012

Malnic, B., Godfrey, P. A., & Buck, L. B. (2004). The human olfactory receptor gene family. *Proceedings of the National Academy of Sciences of the United States of America, 101,* 2584–2589. doi:10.1073/pnas.0307882100

Malnic, B., Hirono, J., Sato, T., & Buck, L. B. (1999). Combinatorial receptor codes for odors. *Cell, 96,* 713–723. doi:10.1016/S0092-8674(00)80581-4

Mandairon, N., Didier, A., & Linster, C. (2008). Odor enrichment increases interneurons responsiveness in spatially defined regions of the olfactory bulb correlated with perception. *Neurobiology of Learning and Memory, 90,* 178–184. doi:10.1016/j.nlm.2008.02.008

Mandairon, N., Ferretti, C. J., Stack, C. M., Rubin, D. B., Cleland, T. A., & Linster, C. (2006). Cholinergic modulation in the olfactory bulb influences spontaneous olfactory discrimination in adult rats. *The European Journal of Neuroscience, 24,* 3234–3244. doi:10.1111/j.1460-9568.2006.05212.x

Maresh, A., Rodriguez, G. D., Whitman, M. C., & Greer, C. A. (2008). Principles of glomerular organization in the human olfactory bulb - Implications for odor processing. *PLoS ONE, 3,* e2640. doi:10.1371/journal.pone.0002640

McNaughton, B. L., & Morris, R. G. M. (1987). Hippocampal synaptic enhancement and information storage within a distributed memory system. *Trends in Neurosciences, 10,* 408–415. doi:10.1016/0166-2236(87)90011-7

Meister, M., & Bonhoeffer, T. (2001). Tuning and topography in an odor map on the rat olfactory bulb. *The Journal of Neuroscience, 21,* 1351–1360.

Miyamichi, K., Amat, F., Moussavi, F., Wang, C., Wickersham, I., & Wall, N. R. (2010). Cortical representations of olfactory input by trans-synaptic tracing. *Nature, 472,* 191–196. doi:10.1038/nature09714

Mombaerts, P., Wang, F., Dulac, C., Chao, S. K., Nemes, A., & Mendelsohn, M. (1996). Visualizing an olfactory sensory map. *Cell, 87,* 675–686. doi:10.1016/S0092-8674(00)81387-2

Moreno, M. M., Linster, C., Escanilla, O., Sacquet, J., Didier, A., & Mandairon, N. (2009). Olfactory perceptual learning requires adult neurogenesis. *Proceedings of the National Academy of Sciences of the United States of America, 106,* 17980–17985. doi:10.1073/pnas.0907063106

Mori, K., Takahashi, Y. K., Igarashi, K. M., & Yamaguchi, M. (2006). Maps of odorant molecular features in the mammalian olfactory bulb. *Physiological Reviews, 86,* 409–433. doi:10.1152/physrev.00021.2005

Mozell, M. M., & Jagodowicz, M. (1973). Chromatographic separation of odorants by the nose: Retention times measured across in vivo olfactory mucosa. *Science, 181,* 1247–1249. doi:10.1126/science.181.4106.1247

Nagashima, A., & Touhara, K. (2010). Enzymatic conversion of odorants in nasal mucus affects olfactory glomerular activation patterns and odor perception. *The Journal of Neuroscience, 30,* 16391–16398. doi:10.1523/JNEUROSCI.2527-10.2010

Nagayama, S., Enerva, A., Fletcher, M. L., Masurkar, A. V., Igarashi, K. M., & Mori, K. (2010). Differential axonal projection of mitral and tufted cells in the mouse main olfactory system. *Frontiers in Neural Circuits, 4,* 1–8. doi:10.3389/fncir.2010.00120

Nagayama, S., Takahashi, Y. K., Yoshihara, Y., & Mori, K. (2004). Mitral and tufted cells differ in the decoding manner of odor maps in the rat olfactory bulb. *Journal of Neurophysiology, 91,* 2532–2540. doi:10.1152/jn.01266.2003

Nakagawa, T., & Voshall, L. B. (2009). Controversy and consensus: noncanonical signaling mechanisms in the insect olfactory system: Noncanonical signaling mechanisms in the insect olfactory system. *Current Opinion in Neurobiology, 19,* 284–292. doi:10.1016/j.conb.2009.07.015

Nakamura, T., & Gold, G. H. (1987). A cyclic nucleotide-gated conductance in olfactory receptor cilia. *Nature, 325,* 442–444. doi:10.1038/325442a0

Narusuye, K., Kawai, F., & Miyachi, E. (2003). Spike encoding of olfactory receptor cells. *Neuroscience Research, 46,* 407–413. doi:10.1016/S0168-0102(03)00131-7

Nissant, A., Bardy, C., Katagiri, H., Murray, K., & Lledo, P. M. (2009). Adult neurogenesis promotes synaptic plasticity in the olfactory bulb. *Nature Neuroscience, 12,* 728–730. doi:10.1038/nn.2298

Oka, Y., Omura, M., Kataoka, H., & Touhara, K. (2004). Olfactory receptor antagonism between odorants. *The EMBO Journal, 23,* 120–126. doi:10.1038/sj.emboj.7600032

Oka, Y., Takai, Y., & Touhara, K. (2009). Nasal airflow rate affects the sensitivity and pattern of glomerular odorant responses in the mouse olfactory bulb. *The Journal of Neuroscience, 29,* 12070–12078. doi:10.1523/JNEUROSCI.1415-09.2009

Pandipati, S., Gire, D. H., & Schoppa, N. E. (2010). Adrenergic receptor–mediated disinhibition of mitral cells triggers long-term enhancement of synchronized oscillations in the olfactory bulb. *Journal of Neurophysiology, 104*, 665–674. doi:10.1152/jn.00328.2010

Petzold, G. C., Hagiwara, A., & Murthy, V. N. (2009). Serotonergic modulation of odor input to the mammalian olfactory bulb. *Nature Neuroscience, 12*, 784–791. doi:10.1038/nn.2335

Pirez, N., & Wachowiak, M. (2008). In vivo modulation of sensory input to the olfactory bulb by tonic and activity-dependent presynaptic inhibition of receptor neurons. *The Journal of Neuroscience, 28*, 6360–6371. doi:10.1523/JNEUROSCI.0793-08.2008

Pressler, R. T., Inoue, T., & Strowbridge, B. W. (2007). Muscarinic receptor activation modulates granule cell excitability and potentiates inhibition onto mitral cells in the rat olfactory bulb. *The Journal of Neuroscience, 27*, 10969–10981. doi:10.1523/JNEUROSCI.2961-07.2007

Reisert, J., & Matthews, H. R. (2001). Response properties of isolated mouse olfactory receptor cells. *The Journal of Physiology, 530*, 113–122. doi:10.1111/j.1469-7793.2001.0113m.x

Ressler, K. J., Sullivan, S. L., & Buck, L. B. (1993). A zonal organization of odorant receptor gene expression in the olfactory epithelium. *Cell, 73*, 597–609. doi:10.1016/0092-8674(93)90145-G

Reuter, D., Zierold, K., Schroder, W. H., & Frings, S. (1998). A depolarizing chloride current contributes to chemoelectrical transduction in olfactory sensory neurons in situ. *The Journal of Neuroscience, 18*, 6623–6630.

Rinberg, D., Koulakov, A., & Gelperin, A. (2006). Sparse odor coding in awake behaving mice. *The Journal of Neuroscience, 26*, 8857–8865. doi:10.1523/JNEUROSCI.0884-06.2006

Robertson, H. M., Warr, C. G., & Carlson, J. R. (2003). Molecular evolution of the insect chemoreceptor gene superfamily in Drosophila melanogaster. *Proceedings of the National Academy of Sciences of the United States of America, 100*(2), 14537–14542. doi:10.1073/pnas.2335847100

Rospars, J. P., Lansky, P., Chaput, M., & Duchamp–Viret, P. (2008). Competitive and noncompetitive odorant interactions in the early neural coding of odorant mixtures. *The Journal of Neuroscience, 28*, 2659–2666. doi:10.1523/JNEUROSCI.4670-07.2008

Rubin, B. D., & Katz, L. C. (1999). Optical imaging of odorant representations in the mammalian olfactory bulb. *Neuron, 23*, 499–511. doi:10.1016/S0896-6273(00)80803-X

Salin, P. A., Lledo, P. M., Vincent, J. D., & Charpak, S. (2001). Dendritic glutamate autoreceptors modulate signal processing in rat mitral cells. *Journal of Neurophysiology, 85*, 1275–1282.

Sato, K., Pellegrino, M., Nakagawa, T., Nakagawa, T., Vosshall, L. B., & Touhara, K. (2008). Insect olfactory receptors are heteromeric ligand–gated ion channels. *Nature, 452*, 1002–1006. doi:10.1038/nature06850

Schilling, B., Kaiser, R., Natsch, A., & Gautschi, M. (2010). Investigation of odors in the fragrance industry. *Chemoecology, 20*, 135–147. doi:10.1007/s00049-009-0035-5

Schoenfeld, T. A., & Cleland, T. A. (2006). Anatomical contributions to odorant sampling and representation in rodents: Zoning in on sniffing behavior. *Chemical Senses, 31*, 131–144. doi:10.1093/chemse/bjj015

Schoenfeld, T. A., Marchand, J. E., & Macrides, F. (1985). Topographic organization of tufted cell axonal projections in the hamster main olfactory bulb: An intrabulbar associational system. *The Journal of Comparative Neurology, 235*, 503–518. doi:10.1002/cne.902350408

Schoppa, N. E. (2006). Synchronization of olfactory bulb mitral cells by precisely timed inhibitory inputs. *Neuron, 49*, 271–283. doi:10.1016/j.neuron.2005.11.038

Schoppa, N. E., & Westbrook, G. L. (2002). AMPA autoreceptors drive correlated spiking in olfactory bulb glomeruli. *Nature Neuroscience, 5*, 1194–1202. doi:10.1038/nn953

Scott, J. W., McBride, R. L., & Schneider, S. P. (1980). The organization of projections from the olfactory bulb to the piriform cortex and olfactory tubercle in the rat. *The Journal of Comparative Neurology, 194*, 519–534. doi:10.1002/cne.901940304

Shepherd, G. M. (1972). Synaptic organization of the mammalian olfactory bulb. *Physiological Reviews, 52*, 864–917.

Shusterman, R., Smear, M. C., Koulakov, A. A., & Rinberg, D. (2011). Precise olfactory responses tile the sniff cycle. *Nature Neuroscience, 14*, 1039–1044. doi:10.1038/nn.2877

Smear, M., Shusterman, R., O'Connor, R., Bozza, T., & Rinberg, D. (2011). Perception of sniff phase in mouse olfaction. *Nature, 479*, 397–400. doi:10.1038/nature10521

Song, Y., Cygnar, K. D., Sagdullaev, B., Valley, M., Hirsh, S., & Stephan, A. (2008). Olfactory CNG channel desensitization by Ca^{2+}/CaM via the B1b subunit affects response termination but not sensitivity to recurring stimulation. *Neuron, 58*, 374–386. doi:10.1016/j.neuron.2008.02.029

Sosulski, D. L., Lissitsyna, B. M., Cutforth, T., Axel, R., & Datta, S. R. (2011). Distinct representations of olfactory information in different cortical centres. *Nature, 472*(7342), 213–216. doi:10.1038/nature09868

Soucy, E. R., Albeanu, D. F., Fantana, A. L., Murthy, V. N., & Meister, M. (2009). Precision and diversity in an odor map on the olfactory bulb. *Nature Neuroscience, 12*, 210–220. doi:10.1038/nn.2262

Spors, H., Wachowiak, M., Cohen, L. B., & Friedrich, R. W. (2006). Temporal dynamics and latency patterns of receptor neuron input to the olfactory bulb. *The Journal of Neuroscience, 26*, 1247–1259. doi:10.1523/JNEUROSCI.3100-05.2006

Stephan, A. B., Shum, E. Y., Hirsh, S., Cygnar, K. D., Reisert, J., & Zhao, H. (2009). ANO2 is the cilial calcium-activated chloride channel that may mediate olfactory amplification. *Proceedings of the National Academy of Sciences of the United States of America, 106*, 11776–11781. doi:10.1073/pnas.0903304106

Stettler, D. D., & Axel, R. (2009). Representations of odor in the piriform cortex. *Neuron, 63*, 854–864. doi:10.1016/j.neuron.2009.09.005

Stewart, W. B., Kauer, J. S., & Shepherd, G. M. (1979). Functional organization of rat olfactory bulb analysed by the 2-deoxyglucose method. *The Journal of Comparative Neurology, 185*, 715–734. doi:10.1002/cne.901850407

Stokes, C. C., & Isaacson, J. S. (2010). From dendrite to soma: dynamic routing of inhibition by complementary interneuron microcircuits in olfactory cortex. *Neuron, 67*, 452–465. doi:10.1016/j.neuron.2010.06.029

Su, T., Bao, Z., Zhang, Q. Y., Smith, T. J., Hong, J. Y., & Ding, X. (2000). Human cytochrome P450 CYP2A13: Predominant expression in the respiratory tract and its high efficiency metabolic activation of a tobacco–specific carcinogen, 4-(methylnitrosamino)-1-(3-pyridyl)-1-butanone. *Cancer Research, 60*, 5074–5079.

Swanson, L. W., & Petrovich, G. D. (1998). What is the amygdala? *Trends in Neurosciences, 21*, 323–331. doi:10.1016/S0166-2236(98)01265-X

Takeuchi, H., Ishida, H., Hikichi, S., & Kurahashi, T. (2009). Mechanism of olfactory masking in the sensory cilia. *The Journal of General Physiology, 133*, 583–601. doi:10.1085/jgp.200810085

Tan, J., Savigner, A., Ma, M., & Luo, M. (2010). Odor information processing by the olfactory bulb analyzed in gene–targeted mice. *Neuron, 65*, 912–926. doi:10.1016/j.neuron.2010.02.011

Teghtsoonian, R., Teghtsoonian, M., Berglund, B., & Berglund, U. (1978). Invariance of odor strength with sniff vigor: An olfactory analogue to size constancy. *Journal of Experimental Psychology. Human Perception and Performance, 4*, 144–152. doi:10.1037/0096-1523.4.1.144

Tomaru, A., & Kurahashi, T. (2005). Mechanisms determining the dynamic range of the bullfrog olfactory receptor cell. *Journal of Neurophysiology, 93*, 1880–1888. doi:10.1152/jn.00303.2004

Tsuno, Y., Kashiwadani, H., & Mori, K. (2008). Behavioral state regulation of dendrodendritic synaptic inhibition in the olfactory bulb. *The Journal of Neuroscience, 28*, 9227–9238. doi:10.1523/JNEUROSCI.1576-08.2008

Uchida, N., & Mainen, Z. F. (2003). Speed and accuracy of olfactory discrimination in the rat. *Nature Neuroscience, 6*, 1224–1229. doi:10.1038/nn1142

Uchida, N., Takahashi, Y. K., Tanifuji, M., & Mori, K. (2000). Odor maps in the mammalian olfactory bulb: Domain organization and odorant structural features. *Nature Neuroscience, 3*, 1035–1043. doi:10.1038/79857

van Drongelen, W., Holley, A., & Doving, K. B. (1978). Convergence in the olfactory system: Quantitative aspects of odour sensitivity. *Journal of Theoretical Biology, 71*, 39–48. doi:10.1016/0022-5193(78)90212-6

Verhagen, J. V., Wesson, D. W., Netoff, T. I., White, J. A., & Wachowiak, M. (2007). Sniffing controls an adaptive filter of sensory input to the olfactory bulb. *Nature Neuroscience, 10*, 631–639. doi:10.1038/nn1892

Vickers, N. J. (2006). Winging it: Moth flight behavior and responses of olfactory neurons are shaped by pheromone plume dynamics. *Chemical Senses, 31*, 155–166. doi:10.1093/chemse/bjj011

Vosshall, L. B., & Hansson, B. S. (2011). A unified nomenclature system for the insect olfactory coreceptor. *Chemical Senses, 36*, 497–498. doi:10.1093/chemse/bjr022

Wachowiak, M., & Cohen, L. B. (2001). Representation of odorants by receptor neuron input to the mouse olfactory bulb. *Neuron, 32*, 723–735. doi:10.1016/S0896-6273(01)00506-2

Wachowiak, M., & Shipley, M. T. (2006). Coding and synaptic processing of sensory information in the glomerular layer of the olfactory bulb. *Seminars in Cell & Developmental Biology, 17*, 411–423. doi:10.1016/j.semcdb.2006.04.007

Wehr, M., & Laurent, G. (1996). Odour encoding by temporal sequences of firing in oscillating neural assemblies. *Nature, 384*, 162–166. doi:10.1038/384162a0

Wei, J., Zhao, A. Z., Chan, G. C., Baker, L. P., Impey, S., & Beavo, J. A. (1998). Phosphorylation and inhibition of olfactory adenylyl cyclase by CaM kinase II in Neurons: A mechanism for attenuation of olfactory signals. *Neuron, 21*, 495–504. doi:10.1016/S0896-6273(00)80561-9

Wesson, D. W., Verhagen, J. V., & Wachowiak, M. (2009). Why sniff fast? The relationship between sniff frequency, odor discrimination, and receptor neuron activation in the rat. *Journal of Neurophysiology, 101*, 1089–1102. doi:10.1152/jn.90981.2008

Wicher, D., Schäfer, R., Bauernfeind, R., Stensmyr, M. C., Heller, R., Heinemann, S. H., & Hansson, B. S. (2008). Drosophila odorant receptors are both ligand–gated and cyclic–nucleotide-activated cation channels. *Nature, 452*, 1007–1011. doi:10.1038/nature06861

Willhite, D. C., Nguyen, K. T., Masurkar, A. V., Greer, C. A., Shepherd, G. M., & Chen, W. R. (2006). Viral tracing identifies distributed columnar organization in the olfactory bulb. *Proceedings of the National Academy of Sciences of the United States of America, 103*, 12592–12597. doi:10.1073/pnas.0602032103

Wilson, D. A. (1998). Habituation of odor responses in the rat anterior piriform cortex. *Journal of Neurophysiology, 79*, 1425–1440.

Wilson, D. A. (2000). Odor specificity of habituation in the rat anterior piriform cortex. *Journal of Neurophysiology, 83*, 139–145.

Wilson, D. A. (2001). Scopolamine enhances generalization between odor representations in rat olfactory cortex. *Learning & Memory (Cold Spring Harbor, N.Y.), 8*, 279–285. doi:10.1101/lm.42601

Wilson, D. A. (2003). Rapid, experience-induced enhancement in odorant discrimination by anterior piriform cortex neurons. *Journal of Neurophysiology, 90*, 65–72. doi:10.1152/jn.00133.2003

Wilson, D. A. (2009). Pattern separation and completion in olfaction. *Annals of the New York Academy of Sciences, 1170*, 306–312. doi:10.1111/j.1749-6632.2009.04017.x

Wilson, D. A., Kadohisa, M., & Fletcher, M. L. (2006). Cortical contributions to olfaction: Plasticity and perception. *Seminars in Cell & Developmental Biology, 17*, 462–470. doi:10.1016/j.semcdb.2006.04.008

Wilson, D. A., & Stevenson, R. J. (2003a). Olfactory perceptual learning: The critical role of memory in odor discrimination. *Neuroscience and Biobehavioral Reviews, 27*, 307–328. doi:10.1016/S0149-7634(03)00050-2

Wilson, D. A., & Stevenson, R. J. (2003b). The fundamental role of memory in olfactory perception. *Trends in Neurosciences, 26*, 243–247. doi:10.1016/S0166-2236(03)00076-6

Wong, S. T., Trinh, K., Hacker, B., Chan, G. C., Lowe, G., & Gaggar, A. (2000). Disruption of the type III adenylyl cyclase gene leads to peripheral and behavioral anosmia in transgenic mice. *Neuron, 27*, 487–497. doi:10.1016/S0896-6273(00)00060-X

Xiong, W., & Chen, W. R. (2002). Dynamic gating of spike propagation in the mitral cell lateral dendrites. *Neuron, 34*, 115–126. doi:10.1016/S0896-6273(02)00628-1

Yan, C., Zhao, A. Z., Bentley, J. K., Loughney, K., Ferguson, K., & Beavo, J. A. (1995). Molecular cloning and characterization of a calmodulin–dependent phosphodiesterase enriched in olfactory sensory neurons. *Proceedings of the National Academy of Sciences of the United States of America, 92*, 9677–9681. doi:10.1073/pnas.92.21.9677

Yan, Z., Tan, J., Qin, C., Lu, Y., Ding, C., & Luo, M. (2008). Precise circuitry links bilaterally symmetric olfactory maps. *Neuron, 58*, 613–624. doi:10.1016/j.neuron.2008.03.012

Yang, G. C., Scherer, P. W., Zhao, K., & Mozell, M. M. (2007). Numerical modeling of odorant uptake in the rat nasal cavity. *Chemical Senses, 32*, 273–284. doi:10.1093/chemse/bjl056

Yokoi, M., Mori, K., & Nakanishi, S. (1995). Refinement of odor molecule tuning by dendro-dendritic synaptic inhibition in the olfactory bulb. *Proceedings of the National Academy of Sciences of the United States of America, 92*, 3371–3375. doi:10.1073/pnas.92.8.3371

Yuan, Q., & Knopfel, T. (2006). Olfactory nerve stimulation-evoked mGluR1 slow potentials, oscillations, and calcium signaling in mouse olfactory bulb mitral cells. *Journal of Neurophysiology, 95*, 3097–3104. doi:10.1152/jn.00001.2006

Zelles, T., Boyd, J. D., Hardy, A. B., & Delaney, K. R. (2006). Branch-specific Ca²⁺ influx from Na+-dependent dendritic spikes in olfactory granule cells. *The Journal of Neuroscience, 26,* 30–40. doi:10.1523/JNEUROSCI.1419-05.2006

Zhan, C., & Luo, M. (2010). Diverse patterns of odor representation by neurons in the anterior piriform cortex of awake mice. *The Journal of Neuroscience, 30,* 16662–16672. doi:10.1523/JNEUROSCI.4400-10.2010

Zhang, J. J., Okutani, F., Huang, G. Z., Taniguchi, M., Murata, Y., & Kaba, H. (2010). Common properties between synaptic plasticity in the main olfactory bulb and olfactory learning in young rats. *Neuroscience, 170,* 259–267. doi:10.1016/j.neuroscience.2010.06.002

Zhang, X., & Firestein, S. (2002). The olfactory receptor gene superfamily of the mouse. *Nature Neuroscience, 5,* 124–133.

Zhao, K., Dalton, P., Yang, G. C., & Scherer, P. W. (2006). Numerical modeling of turbulent and laminar airflow and odorant transport during sniffing in the human and rat nose. *Chemical Senses, 31,* 107–118. doi:10.1093/chemse/bjj008

ADDITIONAL READING

Akers, K. G., Sakaguchi, M., & Arruda–Carvalho, M. (2010). Functional contribution of adult–generated olfactory bulb interneurons: odor discrimination versus odor memory. *The Journal of Neuroscience, 30,* 4523–4525. doi:10.1523/JNEUROSCI.0443-10.2010

Cleland, T. A. (2010). Early transformations in odor representation. *Trends in Neurosciences, 33,* 130–139. doi:10.1016/j.tins.2009.12.004

Fleischer, J., Breer, H., & Strotmann, J. (2009). Mammalian olfactory receptors. *Frontiers in Cellular Neuroscience, 3,* 9. doi:10.3389/neuro.03.009.2009

Gottfried, J. A. (2010). Central mechanisms of odour object perception. *Nature Reviews. Neuroscience, 11,* 628–641. doi:10.1038/nrn2883

Kato, A., & Touhara, K. (2009). Mammalian olfactory receptors: pharmacology, G protein coupling and desensitization. *Cellular and Molecular Life Sciences, 66,* 3743–3753. doi:10.1007/s00018-009-0111-6

Katz, D. B., Matsunami, H., Rinberg, D., Scott, K., Wachowiak, M., & Wilson, R. I. (2008). Receptors, circuits, and behaviors: New directions in chemical senses. *The Journal of Neuroscience, 28,* 11802–11805. doi:10.1523/JNEUROSCI.3613-08.2008

Khan, A. G., Parthasarathy, K., & Bhalla, U. S. (2010). Odor representations in the mammalian olfactory bulb. *Wiley Interdisciplinary Reviews: Systems Biology and Medicine, 2,* 603–611. doi:10.1002/wsbm.85

Linster, C., Nai, Q., & Ennis, M. (2011). Nonlinear effects of noradrenergic modulation of olfactory bulb function in adult rodents. *Journal of Neurophysiology, 105,* 1432–1443. doi:10.1152/jn.00960.2010

Lledo, P. M., Gheusi, G., & Vincent, J. D. (2005). Information processing in the mammalian olfactory system. *Physiological Reviews, 85,* 281–317. doi:10.1152/physrev.00008.2004

Mandairon, N., & Linster, C. (2009). Odor perception and olfactory bulb plasticity in adult mammals. *Journal of Neurophysiology, 101,* 2204–2209. doi:10.1152/jn.00076.2009

Mombaerts, P. (2004). Genes and ligands for odorant, vomeronasal and taste receptors. *Nature Reviews. Neuroscience, 5,* 263–278. doi:10.1038/nrn1365

Schoenfeld, T. A., & Cleland, T. A. (2005). The anatomical logic of smell. *Trends in Neurosciences, 28*, 620–627. doi:10.1016/j.tins.2005.09.005

Urban, N. N., & Arevian, A. C. (2009). Computing with dendrodendritic synapses in the olfactory bulb. *Annals of the New York Academy of Sciences, 1170*, 264–269. doi:10.1111/j.1749-6632.2009.03899.x

Wachowiak, M., & Shipley, M. T. (2006). Coding and synaptic processing of sensory information in the glomerular layer of the olfactory bulb. *Seminars in Cell & Developmental Biology, 17*, 411–423. doi:10.1016/j.semcdb.2006.04.007

Wilson, D. A., & Linster, C. (2008). Neurobiology of a simple memory. *Journal of Neurophysiology, 100*, 2–7. doi:10.1152/jn.90479.2008

Wilson, D. A., & Stevenson, R. J. (2006). *Learning to smell: Olfactory perception from neurobiology to behavior*. Baltimore, MD: Johns Hopkins University Press.

Wilson, R. I., & Mainen, Z. F. (2006). Early events in olfactory processing. *Annual Review of Neuroscience, 29*, 163–201. doi:10.1146/annurev.neuro.29.051605.112950

Zufall, F., & Munger, S. D. (2010). Receptor guanylyl cyclases in mammalian olfactory function. *Molecular and Cellular Biochemistry, 334*, 191–197. doi:10.1007/s11010-009-0325-9

Chapter 2
Odor Perception:
The Mechanism of How Odor is Perceived

Mitsuo Tonoike
Aino University, Japan

ABSTRACT

Though olfaction is one of the necessary senses and indispensable for the maintenance of the life of the animal, the mechanism of olfaction had not yet been understood well compared with other sensory systems such as vision and audition. However, recently, the most basic principle of "signal transduction on the reception and transmission for the odor" has been clarified. Therefore, the important next problem is how the information of odors about is processed in the Central Nervous System (CNS) and how odor is perceived in the human brain. In this chapter, the basic olfactory systems in animal and human are described and examples such as "olfactory acuity, threshold, adaptation, and olfactory disorders" are discussed. The mechanism of olfactory information processing is described under the results obtained by using a few new non-invasive measuring methods. In addition, from a few recent studies, it is shown that olfactory neurophysiological information is passing through some deep central regions of the brain before finally being processed in the orbito-frontal areas.

INTRODUCTION

Olfaction is a sense that is indispensable for life. Because olfaction is an important sense in daily life, it is necessary to understand the characteristics of olfaction, such as how odors are evaluated correctly. Moreover, it is important to know the mechanisms by which odors are perceived.

Until quite recently, the mechanism of olfactory reception had not yet been well described or understood compared to other sensory systems,

such as vision and audition. However, the mechanisms of most basic signal transduction on the odor reception of the olfactory cell and signal transmission have recently been clarified.

At the second stage of olfactory processing, the signals from the olfactory cells are transmitted to the Olfactory Bulb (OB). To understand this process, it is necessary to clarify the mechanisms of processing of olfactory information and the relationship between the odor and the OB. An "odor map" in the OB was first proposed after several

DOI: 10.4018/978-1-4666-2521-1.ch002

Copyright © 2013, IGI Global. Copying or distributing in print or electronic forms without written permission of IGI Global is prohibited.

pioneering studies. After the processing stage in the OB, olfactory information is transmitted to the Central Nervous System (CNS).

In this report, I will first review what is known about olfactory systems in humans and other animals. I will describe the characteristics of olfaction, including olfactory acuity, threshold, adaptation, and olfactory disorders. The mechanism of olfactory information processing in the human brain will be described under the results obtained using new non-invasive measurement methods such as Electroencephalography (EEG), Magnetoencephalography (MEG), and functional Magnetic Resonance Imaging (f-MRI). The neurophysiological properties of olfactory-related neurons in the human brain will also be described. Olfactory information is finally processed in the orbito-frontal areas of the cortex.

OLFACTORY SYSTEM AND CHARACTERISTICS OF OLFACTION

Olfactory Acuity

One characteristic of human olfaction is a very high acuity for odor identification.

Minimum concentrations for the identification of different odors have been defined as "olfactory thresholds" for each odor. Now, gas chromatographs are usually used to detect and evaluate the concentration of an odor. However, this method remains inferior to On the other hand, human olfaction for most odors. In general, olfactory acuity in other animals is considered to be superior to human olfaction; for example, dogs have a high sensitivity and a high acuity for odors. Table 1 (Takagi, 1999) compares the threshold concentrations for detection of various odorants among humans, dogs, and fishes.

The dog's olfaction shows the threshold of Acetic acid, Butyric acid, and Valeric acid is

Table 1. Comparison of the threshold concentration for detection of various odorants among human, dogs, and fishes (Takagi, 1999)

Odorant	Man, Dog, Fish	Number of molecules in 1 cm³ of water or air
Acetic acid	Man	5.0×10^{13}
	Dog	5.0×10^{5}
Butyric acid	Man	7.0×10^{9}
	Dog	9.0×10^{3}
Valeric acid	Man	6.0×10^{10}
	Dog	3.5×10^{4}
β-Phenyl ethyl alcohol	Eel	1.77×10^{3}
	Minnow	2.17×10^{14}
	Rainbow trout	5.1×10^{11}
Eugenol	Eel	3.0×10^{5}
	Minnow	3.0×10^{14}

superior to our human by a factor of about 10⁻⁶. The thresholds in some fish are also shown for comparison. On the other hand, the olfactory threshold to β-phenyl ethyl alcohol of the eel may be equivalent to that of the dog.

Olfactory Fatigue and Adaptation

Other important characteristics of olfaction are olfactory fatigue and adaptation.

If we keep sniffing one odor continually, soon we can no longer perceive the odor. Olfactory fatigue results from accommodation of the olfactory receptor cells.

Kurahashi(Kurahashi & Yau, 1993; Kurahashi & Menini, 1997)found out that olfactory fatigue on the olfactory receptor cells was regulated by co-existance of Ca^{2+} current induced into the membrane of olfactory cilia, CNG channel, and Cl^- channel activated by Ca^{2+}. He explains the olfactory fatigue has the mechanism expanding the dynamic range of olfactory sensory cells. Figure 1 shows olfactory fatigue phenomenon of the so-called S-type function in relation with "dose-response relation." In the non-fatigue state (solid line S-type function), a little difference between A and B was not discriminated. However, in the fatigue state, S-type function moved parallel for the more stronger intensity level (dashed line S-type function) in Figure 1.

Thus, olfactory cells can respond to the stimulus intensity in the various wide range.

In contrast, olfactory adaptation is analyzed by a negative feedback mechanism in the OB. If we fail to smell one odor due to olfactory fatigue, we can generally still smell other odors. This phenomenon of olfaction is called "selective fatigue."

Relationship between Stimulus Intensity and Strength of Sensation

Human olfaction is here represented by Weber-Fechner's law, same as other senses.

Figure 1. The mechanism of olfactory fatigue on receptor cells (solid line = under non-fatigue state, dashed line = under fatigue state)

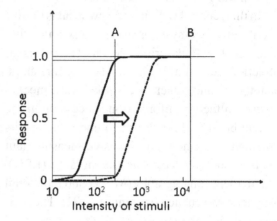

Weber-Fechner's law expresses a relationship between the intensity of the stimulus, S, and the strength of the sensation, R:

$$R = K \log S$$

(where K is a constant)

This law means the response of sensation R is in proportion to the logarithms of the intensity of stimulus S. However, this law often consists at the usual concentration level as shown in Figure 2(a).

In contrast, for a larger range of odor concentrations, Steven's law is usually used and is typically a better fit to the data as shown in Figure 2(b).

$$R = K S^n$$

(where K is a constant and n is a numerical for odor)

Odors have another special characteristic. When concentration of an odor is increased, its quality becomes different. For example, though indol is a famous bad odor, it becomes the pleasant flower odor in very weak concentration. All kind of odors become bad odors when their concentrations are highly raised. In contrast, bad odors become less unpleasant and some can become even pleasant, when their concentrations are lowered.

Figure 2. Comparison with Weber-Fechner's law and Steven's law

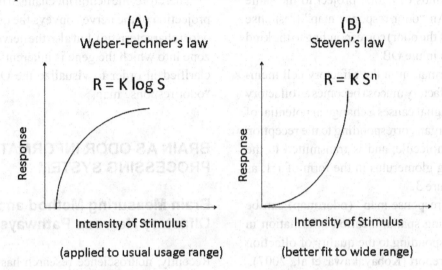

Changing Quality and Preference for Odors

Another important characteristic of odor perception is that odor quality changes when odor concentration is increased. These changes in quality are said to occur with extremely small amounts of contamination in the odorant substances. Another notable characteristic of olfaction is that smells are often accompanied by pleasant or unpleasant sensations. Preference for odors varies markedly among individuals. Odor preferences are thought to be particularly different between men and women, and are also are known to vary by age.

It is well known that an odor having smelled usually as an experience in his childhood is often strongly memorized and he would become to like its odor even grown-up age.

Reception and Transduction Mechanisms of Odor

It has been shown that olfactory receptor cells have reception proteins for odors. Their gene families were cloned in 2004 by Buck and Axel (1991) so reception and transduction mechanisms of odor perception have now been clarified. The gene family groups clarified the existence of about

1000 kinds in all animals and of about 300 kinds in humans by making good use of the PCR method.

The basic principle of the odor reception mechanism in the olfactory cell membrane was clarified by this genetic research, and this breakthrough will enable us to produce an artificial odorant sensor in the near future, if the transduction mechanisms of odor reception and the signaling algorithms can be imitated. Recently, new odorant sensors and odor identification devices using previously described odor reception principles have been developed (Yamanaka, et al., 2003).

Neural Mechanism and Odor Response Map in the OB

Recently, a certain odor receptor protein in the odorant gene families has been identified. The principle of the neural mechanism—that the olfactory nerves expand from the same olfactory cells and are projected selectively to only one glomerulus in the OB—was also clarified.

First, each olfactory cell receptor represents only one odorant for some kinds of odors. Second, the olfactory nerve projects to only one glomerulus (Mori, et al., 1992) corresponding to the odor information in the OB. Thus, the nerves from the olfactory cell, which have similar responses to the same kinds of odors, project to the same glomerulus. An "odor response map" (response distribution of the odor) corresponding to the kind of odor exists in the OB.

Odor information in the olfactory cell membrane in the olfactory mucosa becomes an olfactory signal. This signal causes a change in potential of the receptor organ corresponding to the reception of the odor molecule, and is transmitted to the corresponding glomerulus in the form of 1:1, as shown in Figure 3.

An "odor response map" (odor map) can be developed using spatial location information in the OB corresponding to the quality of olfaction of each odor report (Kobayakawa, et al., 2007).

Third, additional studies have continued to provide evidence for the existence of a spatial "odor response map" in the OB (Kobayakawa, et al., 2007). This structure was built in as a gene odor of an inherent natural enemy, and the nerve projection to generate the action of the evasion reaction existed in the zone on mouse's back smelling in the side of olfactory bulb. Kobayakawa et al. reported that the fox odor (2, 4, 5-trimethylthiazoline; TMT) caused mice to take evasive action, and showed that olfactory activity in the mice was localized in the back side of the OB.

Therefore, the neural mechanism by which the projection of the nerve conveys the quality of the odor (characteristic), but also the nerve projection zone into which the gene is inherently built, was clarified in order to visualize the OB using an "odor response map."

BRAIN AS ODOR INFORMATION PROCESSING SYSTEM

Brain Measuring Method and Olfactory Nervous Pathways to Odor

Recently, neuroscience research has undergone tremendous technological improvements for measuring brain activity non-invasively.

Activation of specific peripheral receptors that activate different parts of the human brain while careful measurements of brain activity are being carried out is now common practice. Research using imaging techniques has become increasingly sophisticated.

For instance, Electroencephalography (EEG) can, in real time, measure changes in the set potential from the potential of the synapse by the

Figure 3. Neural connections to the olfactory bulb from olfactory cells

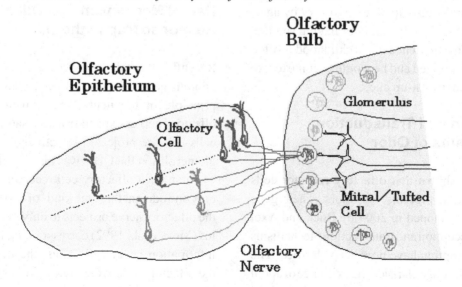

group of nerve cells in a limited part of the brain using two or more electrodes fixed to the scalp.

However, the problem with this method is the influence of electrolytic distortion, as electrical resistance during EEG measurement varies according to the location in the brain. Therefore, because the error margin assumes the location of the signal source in the brain based on the brain wave measurement data, correction of electrolytic distortion becomes an important problem.

Figure 4 shows example data of the responding waves on the olfactory evoked potentials in human. We estimated that the main peak of the evoked potential with about 350 ms latency was the olfactory factor evoked by odor stimulation.

Figure 5 shows the topographical time pattern's map drawn by amplitude values of olfactory evoked potentials responding to odor stimulation. Each circle shows the distribution of amplitude potential values on the scalp of the head at each latency time from odor stimulation time (over

Figure 4. Wave form of olfactory evoked potentials (OEP); odor: odorant pulses stimulation with 100 ms duration (Amyl-acetate); we can obtain the peak changing of OEP on the dose rate response

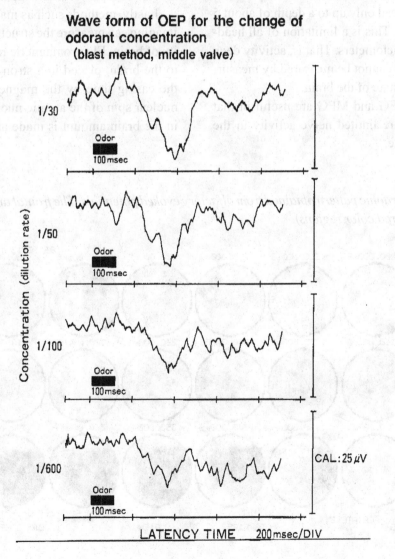

Wave form of OEP for the change of odorant concentration
(blast method, middle valve)

view of the head: upper parts in a circle are the frontal regions of the nose side). Red color shows the activated positive potential and blue color shows negative potential of the response on the scalp. Therefore, Figure 5 shows the clear topographical changing patterns (red color regions are activated) at the frontal lobe side of the head.

On the other hand, one merit of brain wave measurement is that it is not influenced by electrolytic distortion using Magnetoencephalography (MEG). MEG uses two or more super-conducting interference devices (SQUID) elements. The accuracy of estimating the signal source location in the brain, however, is more limited, because it is only possible to measure it from the epidermal surface of the head only up to a depth of about 5 cm in the brain. This is a limitation of all head-type neuromagnetometers. That is, activity deep within the brain cannot be measured by measuring the current state of the brain.

However, EEG and MEG are useful in that they can measure limited nerve activity in the brain in real time.

In contrast, there are various methods for measurement of brain activity. For example, there are measurement methods of brain cell biochemistry. Metabolic state measures of brain activity can reveal areas of local activation. A mildly invasive imaging method is positron radiation measures, where an isotope-tracer is introduced into the body before scanning.

In Positron Emission Tomography (PET) measurement, a short radioisotope (isotope) is injected into the brain, and the amount penetrated with gamma rays generated when the discharged positron disappears by the coincidence method and for a biochemical amount of metabolizing of the brain part to make the image.

Lastly, methods such as magnetic resonance imaging can measure the structure and the activity of brain. Electromagnetic radiation is added to the brain, placed in a strong magnetic field, the easing time by the magnetic resonance of nuclear spin of the atomic nucleus of hydrogen in the brain amount is made an image, and the

Figure 5. Topographic pattern obtained from olfactory evoked potentials. The frontal areas are activated at 220-300 ms (red color regions).

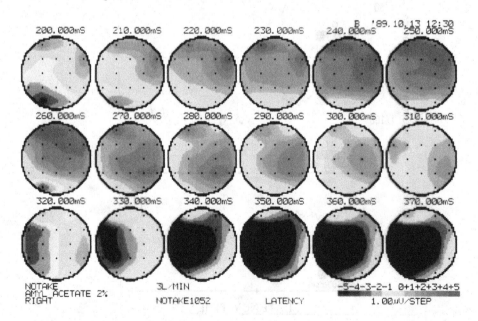

dislocation imaging of brain's structure is made as the Magnetic Resonance Imaging (MRI).

In particular, it is possible to observe hemoglobin corresponding to the consumption of oxygen in blood by making the image, and showing the statistic of the difference of the magnetic susceptibility with the hemoglobin, and making the amount of blood flow of the part in the activated brain an image in functional MRI (f-MRI) method.

The advantage of the measurement using EEG and MEG is good resolution time, but this is not an advantage of PET and MRI measurements.

An advanced Near Infrared Spectroscopy (NIRS) method is a measurement in which near-infrared rays irradiate from the outside of the head in the brain, penetrating into the brainpan and meninges. However, NIRS method has no high sensitivity because it uses the diffuse skylight that can be reflected on the surface layer in the brain.

On the other hand, it has a noteworthy merit of a large degree of freedom for the head movement, even if the body of subject moves in the measuring.

Two Olfactory Nervous Pathways and Frontal Lobe as Olfactory Centers in the Brain

Important neurophysiological research has been conducted on olfaction in rhesus monkeys and the olfactory nervous pathways from OB to the olfactory center in the brain were found by Takagi et al. (1999).

Two olfactory nervous pathways were greatly clarified as a result of this research. The existence of an olfactory nervous pathway to OB in rhesus monkeys was clarified.

One pathway projected to the back of the posterior-central part of the orbito-frontal area (CPOF) via a mediodorsal of the thalamus. In another of these two olfactory nervous pathways, which was identified by Tanabe et al. (1975) a pathway projected to back of the lateral-posterior outside of the orbito-frontal area (LPOF) via the

outer portion of the hypothalamus, and another nerve pathway was found by Yarita et al. (1980).

Figure 6 shows these two olfactory nervous pathways. In addition to the anesthetized rhesus monkey odor electrophysiology experiment mentioned above, it was proven that perception and identification of the odor was done in the central part of LPOF of the frontal lobe.

On the other hand, the selection characteristic of the kind of odor showed the response to occur in the central part of CPOF of the frontal lobe according to Yarita (1980). Thus, this is not an analytical activity like the identification of odor. The possibility of the processing of odorant information on integrated function was suggested in the central part of CPOF.

The olfactory nervous pathway in humans is similar to the olfactory nervous pathway in monkeys, and the existence of a sense of odorant center in humans is clear from research on human olfaction using MEG and fMRI. Many researches on the human olfaction using fMRI method have been also conducted by Rolls (1996).

PROCESSING OF HIGHER-ORDER INFORMATION IN BRAIN ON HUMAN OLFACTION

Mechanism of Perception and Recognition of Odor

Both usual perception and identification of an odor and the recognition of the odor are the result of the processing of information in the brain. In general, we do not distinguish recognition, perception, and identification of odors.

However, when the sense of odor identification inspection is precisely executed, for example, when using a "T & T Olfactometer" which was invented in Japan, it is clarified that two thresholds exist: a detection threshold and a cognitive threshold. It is clear that odor threshold is another function in the brain, and in the threshold measurement of an odor, it reports a perception

Figure 6. Two olfactory pathways and two olfactory centers in the monkey brain (Takagi, 1999)

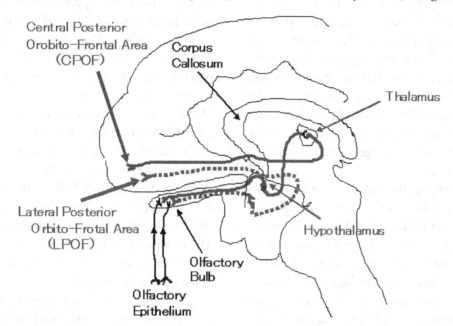

function and a recognition function more plainly for patients with the cognitive threshold problem. Many examples of the unbridgeable gulf syndrome are reported to be a detection threshold and a cognitive threshold problem.

The perception function part of olfaction is likely accomplished by a part of the brain devoted to perception, whereas the recognition function in olfaction is probably done by a different part of the brain specific to the recognition function. The relationship between perception and recognition could only be distinguished as a result of experiments defining areas of the olfactory pathway active at different times using MEG.

Figure 7 shows the results of an experiment identifying brain response measurements by MEG when odorant gas was administered into the right and left nostrils and the localization of activation in the brain was monitored (Tonoike, et al., 1996).

The upper-left figure in Figure 7 shows the responding MEG evoked waves measured by 122-ch SQUID sensors (over view: upper is the frontal side on the head). We can see the MEG wave responses changing in about 350 ms latency at the right and left frontal areas. The upper-right figure in Figure 7 shows the contour map pattern of the magnetic fields on the sensor helmet over the head obtained by the calculation from 122-SQUID responding data and two arrows (in the right and left frontal side areas) show the Equivalent Current Dipoles (ECDs) estimated by using the two-dipole source estimation method. Using these MEG experimental data and the calculation of magnetic fields we obtained the lower-figure in Figure 7 which showed two olfactory centers (circle: ipsi-lateral side, triangle: contra-lateral side) at the orbito-frontal areas estimated in the real human brain.

In the experiment, the brain magnetic field response to odorant stimulation was measured after stimuli were delivered to the right and left nostrils. The signal sources of the obtained olfactory center parts were localized to the right and left symmetrical brain areas by the two dipole method in six subjects. Evidence for the existence of the olfactory nervous center was obtained from the results, illustrating a clear area of activation in the right and left orbito-frontal parts.

Moreover, the brain side activated after olfactory stimulation was on the same side as the

Figure 7. Olfactory centers identified by MEG experiments in human

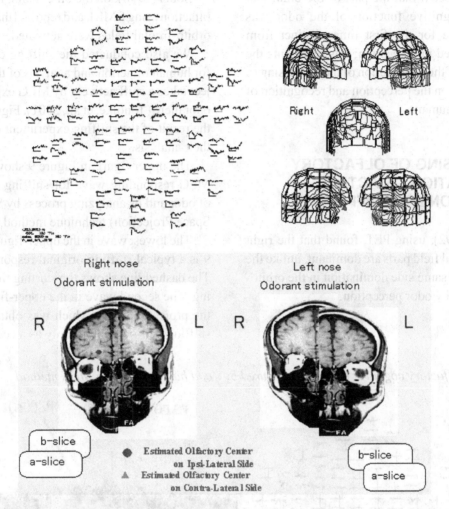

nostril where the odor was delivered, showing an ipsilateral connection structure (Tonoike, 2011). The part with a slightly different orbito-frontal field of a right and left brain in two places was activated, and the possibility that the nostril on the odor stimulation side and the brain side of the same side are dominant was suggested in the perception of the odor in the subject.

On the other hand, we conducted an MEG experiment using an "odd ball task" experimental design that uses two different odors, and measured the brain response to cognitive function of the odor (Tonoike, et al., 2004). Odor stimuli were frequently delivered to the nose at random at a presentation probability such as 1:3, and in this experiment, the target odor is concentrated one's attention on the odor uncommonly presented, and the subject is required to count the number of odor that stimulated the nose less frequently as shown in Figure 8.

As a result, a wavy peak of magnetic field response reaction (P300m) of the brain activity that responds only to the odor stimulation uncommonly presented as shown in Figure 8 is measured with latency time that about 500ms is slow, and this response element clarifies that it is a so-called cognitive response element for the first time (Tonoike, et al., 2003).

It is expected that the part of the brain that controls cognitive function of the odor was made visible for the first time, distinct from parts involved in perception; this represents the beginning of the clarification of the processing of information on the perception and recognition of the odor in humans.

PROCESSING OF OLFACTORY INFORMATION ON ACTIVE OLFACTION BY "SNIFFING"

Zatorre (1992), using PET, found that the right orbito-frontal field parts are dominant, unlike the result of the same side domination in the orbito-frontal area by odor perception.

Sobel (1998), on the other hand, investigated olfaction using f-MRI, and reported that only right orbito-frontal fields were activated.

We also conducted the sniffing experiments for human olfaction and analysis of that the subject takes a sniff actively by MEG experiment of odor there (Tonoike, et al., 2001). Figure 9 shows the result of the sniffing experiment of odor and their analysis.

The upper figure in Figure 9 shows a typical MEG responding wave for sniffing experiment of odor and its analyzing process by SSP (Signal Space Projection) technique method.

The lowest wave in the upper-figure in Figure 9 is a typical sniffing original response of odor. The dashed line shows the starting time in sniffing. The second wave in the upper-figure shows the projection wave which was obtained at the sniffing non-odorant air only as a control data.

Figure 8. Olfactory cognitive response measured by "odd ball task" using MEG method

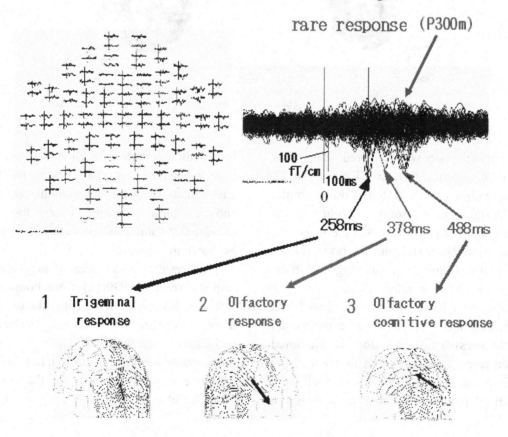

Figure 9. Olfactory MEG response in orbito-frontal area measured by "sniffing" method (with SSP technique)

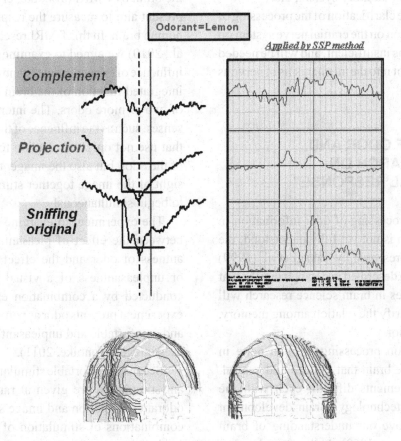

A SSP technique was applied to subtract the wave of sniffing non-odorant air from the original wave of sniffing odor. A most upper wave shows the result of the subtracted wave which means a real net-sniffing magnetic field response for odorant stimulation by the application of SSP method. From these analysis of SSP method, the clear response of about 350 ms latency (solid line) after sniffing odor was obtained and the signal source was estimated at the right orbito-frontal side only (see an ECD arrow in contour magnetic field map in the right frontal side) as the lower-figure in Figure 9.

From the result of MEG experiment by "sniffing" method a hypothesis of "right brain domination" on the brain activity of olfaction is suggested

because of the result of activation only in a right orbito-frontal field part (Tonoike, et al., 1998a, 1998b). The possibility that only the orbito-frontal field of the right hemisphere is activated was suggested in the "sniffing" stimulation method that takes a sniff actively but not in the passive odorant stimulation method that we executed.

What does the differential response in the orbito-frontal field on the same side by the dominant right side mean?

It is expected that the participation of a "top-down nervous process" is enough in active sensing of odor and passive sensing of odor though the meaning of this difference has still not been clarified. For example, "top-down process" in nervous networks is often found as the neural connection with a some kind of command from the center of nerve in visual or auditory system, etc.

However, the clarification of the processing of center information on the cranial nerve system on olfaction remains insufficient, and will be needed for further insight into the mechanisms of nervous system function.

MEMORY OF ODOR AND F-MRI RESEARCH ON "EMOTIONAL RESPONSE"

Although the processing of odor information in the human brain is not yet fully understood, the rhesus monkey research by Takagi et al. (1999) has already been described in detail. It may be that additional studies in brain science research will be needed to clarify the relation among memory, emotion, and odor.

Brain function processing is often done in a location in the brain that is deep and central, making measurements difficult even with the state-of-the-art technology. Brain development may help improve our understanding of brain evolution (Maclean, 1952). At the central part of the human brain is an area called the old subcortical brain, and this area is thought to correspond with the brains of ancient mammals and reptiles.

The surface part of the human brain, called the new substantia corticalis, has been extensively researched until now, because it is thought to be indispensable to human brain function.

Important processing in human brain is often done in new substantia corticalis in fields such as movement, vision, and audition, and it is thought that the research on the brain was comparatively done easily because of these parts on the surface brain.

On the other hand, as it remains uncertain whether the part of the brain that the processes such as memory and emotion (LeDoux, 1996) is deep within the brain, it is difficult to examine the function and processing of these parts.

We also are researching olfactory function in the brain by f-MRI (Tonoike, et al., 2008) and at present aim to measure the response deep in the human brain. In this f-MRI research (Tonoike, et al., 2010) we aimed to examine in particular the influence of odor on memory and emotion with the integrated function of the brain on the sensation of two or more odors. The interactions between senses, such as the influence of the visual stimulus that use not only the reaction to the stimulation of the odor, but also the image, the odor, and the sight of the image together stimulate the senses to begin simultaneously.

The experiment to examine the interrelation between the effect of pleasantness or unpleasantness of odor and the effect of pleasantness or unpleasantness of a visual image must be conducted by a combination experiment. This experiment presents odor as part of such research, and comfortable and unpleasant stimulation that uses images (Tonoike, 2011).

Because comfortable stimulation and unpleasant stimulation are given at random as for the odorant stimulation and image stimulation, four combinations of stimulation of pleasantness or unpleasantness of the unpleasantness and pleasantness/image of the odor will be presented to the subject, though it is presented to the subject to stimulate olfactory receptors and to stimulate the visual (image) receptors at the same time using the event-related design method by fMRI in this experiment.

The influence of odor on memory and emotion are expected to be strengthened by the synergistic effect of the combination of the odor and image stimulation; an analytical method that extracts the effect of "pleasantness/unpleasantness" and "matching/mismatching" is currently being examined. The amygdaloid body and the hippocampus exist near deep locations within the human brain as shown in Figure 10.

Figure 10. Results of activated areas by olfactory f-MRI imaging experiments (smell: iso-valeric acid)

These areas and the gyrus parahippocampalis were observed as the common specific regions activated by the stimulation of odor in our fMRI experimental results (Tonoike, et al., 2010). Such an experimental result illustrates the amygdaloid body, the hippocampus and the olfactory inputs in the brain, passing older parts of the brain.

Though the meaning of our experimental results mentioned above is still unkown, it suggests the important possibility of odorant information processing in these parts.

UNDERSTANDING OF OLFACTION GUIDED FROM THE INTEGRATED FUNCTION OF FIVE SENSES

We do not live using olfaction only but also five senses in daily life. Rolls (1996) proposed that our all five senses might be integrated at orbitofrontal areas through the control using the gated function of hypothalamus in the brain as shown in Figure 11.

His hypothesis may not be proven now, but it is estimated that every sensual information is brought together and terminated into orbitofrontal areas at last.

From the above viewpoint, we will need look at the study of perception and cognition on the human olfaction, again now.

RECOGNITION AND EXPECTATION FOR NEW ROLE OF OLFACTION

Information processing is done quite unconsciously by the deep parts in the brain under the substantia corticalis. We cannot consciously control processing such as memory and emotion, done deep within the brain.

However, in deep parts of the brains may exist unconscious information processing for olfaction and if the odor accesses these parts, the control of the part of the brain under unconsciousness might become possible by using information on the odor. The idea that information on odor might control memory and emotion was suggested. However, this has not yet been clarified using modern brain science.

The function (turnover) for abnormal sense of odor and the sense of odor decline to be defined in a cognitive syndrome of the Alzheimer's type and an initial symptom of Parkinson's disease (Imayoshi, et al., 2008). Classes of brain cells

Figure 11. The hypothesis of integrated function of five senses (Rolls, 1996)

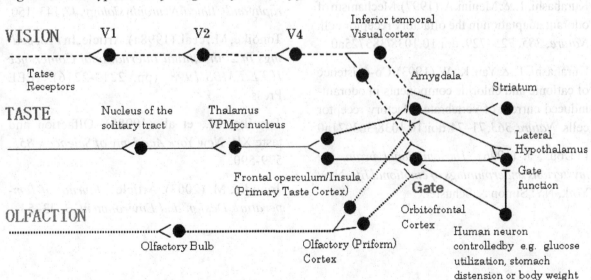

with the ability to rapidly turnover are limited to cells of the olfactory epithelium and olfactory bulb, and cells of the hippocampus.

The decline in olfactory function in illnesses with cognitive deficits adds more evidence for more detailed future study of the function of the olfactory system.

Though it had been thought up to now that human olfaction was sure to have only a secondary role compared with other sensory systems, the role of the nervous system in processing of olfactory information will be expected to be reassessed in near future.

REFERENCES

Buck, L., & Axel, R. (1991). A novel multigene family may encode odorant receptors: A molecular basis for odor recognition. *Cell, 65*, 175–187. doi:10.1016/0092-8674(91)90418-X

Imayoshi, I., & Sakamoto, M. (2008). Regenerating your senses: multiple roles for neurogenesis in the adult brain. *Nature Neuroscience, 11*, 1124–1126. doi:10.1038/nn1008-1124

Kobayakawa, K. (2007). Innate versus learned odour processing in the mouse olfactory bulb. *Nature, 450*, 503–508. doi:10.1038/nature06281

Kurahashi, T., & Menini, A. (1997). Mechanism of odorant adaptation in the olfactory receptor cell. *Nature, 385*, 725–729. doi:10.1038/385725a0

Kurahashi, T., & Yau, K.-W. (1993). Co-existence of cationic and chloride components in odorant-induced current of vertebrate olfactory receptor cells. *Nature, 363*, 71–74. doi:10.1038/363071a0

LeDoux, J. (1996). *The emotional brain, the mysterious underpinnings of emotional life*. New York, NY: Simon & Schuster.

Maclean, P. D. (1952). Some psychiatric implications of physiological studies on frontotemporal portion of limbic system (visceral brain). *Electroencephalography and Clinical Neurophysiology, 4*, 407–418. doi:10.1016/0013-4694(52)90073-4

Mori, K., Imamamura, K., & Mataga, N. (1992). Differential specificities of single mitral cells in rabbit olfactory bulb for a homologous series of fatty acid odor molecules. *Journal of Neurophysiology, 67*, 786–789.

Rolls, E. T. (1996). The orbitofrontal cortex. *Philosophical Transactions of the Royal Society of London. Series B, Biological Sciences, 351*, 1433–1444. doi:10.1098/rstb.1996.0128

Sobel, N. (1998). Sniffing and smelling: Separate subsystems in the human olfactory cortex. *Nature, 392*, 282–286. doi:10.1038/32654

Takagi, F. S. (1999). *Human olfaction*. Tokyo, Japan: University Tokyo Press.

Tanabe, T., Yarita, H., & Iino, M. (1975). An olfactory projection area in orbitofrontal cortex of the monkey. *Journal of Neurophysiology, 38*, 1269–1283.

Tonoike, M. (2011). The relation of human brain and olfaction. *Aroma Research, 46*, 121–128.

Tonoike, M. (1996). Article. *Electroencephalography and Clinical Neurophysiology, 47*, 143–150.

Tonoike, M., et al. (1998a). Article. In *Proceedings of 20th Annual International Conference IEEE/EMBS/1998*, (pp. 2213-2216). IEEE Press.

Tonoike, M., et al. (1998b). Olfaction and taste XII. *New York Academy of Sciences, 855*, 579-590.

Tonoike, M. (2003). Article. *Journal of Temperature Design and Environment, 3*, 43–53.

Tonoike, M., et al. (2004). Article. In *Proceedings of the 12th International Conference on Biomag2000*, (pp. 238-291). Biomag2000.

Tonoike, M., Miyamoto, K., Yokoo, Y., Toyofuku, T., Miwakeichi, F., & Uno, T. … Shintani, M. (2008). *Biomagnetsim–Transdiciplinary research and exploration.* Sapporo, Japan: Hokkaido University Press.

Tonoike, M., Uno, T., Yoshida, T., & Wang, L. Q. (2010). Article. *Electroencephalography and Clinical Neurophysiology, 121,* 217–218.

Tonoike, M., Yamaguchi, M., & Hamada, T. (2001). Article. In *Proceedings of Biomag2000,* (pp. 288-291). Biomag2000.

Yamanaka, T., Matsumoto, R., & Nakamoto, T. (2003). Article. *Sensors and Actuators. B, Chemical, 89,* 120–135. doi:10.1016/S0925-4005(02)00452-5

Yarita, H., Iino, M., & Tanabe, T. (1980). A transthalamic olfactory pathway to orbitofrontal cortex in the monkey. *Journal of Neurophysiology, 43,* 69–85.

Zatorre, R. (1992). Functional localization and lateralization of human olfactory cortex. *Nature, 360,* 339–340. doi:10.1038/360339a0

Chapter 3
Basics for Olfactory Display

Yasuyuki Yanagida
Meijo University, Japan

Akira Tomono
Tokai University, Japan

ABSTRACT

An olfactory display, which is the olfactory counterpart to a visual display, is controlled by a computer or information equipment and provides smells to a human user. Because we sense smells through the air, the role of an olfactory display is to make scented air from odor materials in a stocked form with the desired components and concentration and to deliver the scented air to the human olfactory organ. This chapter provides a survey of various technologies, categorized by scent generation methods and scent delivery methods, used to construct an olfactory display. For scent generation methods, vaporization/atomization techniques, scent switching techniques, and formulation techniques are discussed. For scent delivery methods, several approaches to convey odor material from the scent generator to the nose are discussed. In addition, a brief description of evaluation methods of olfactory displays is provided.

INTRODUCTION

An olfactory display is a computer-controlled device that generates scented air with the intended component and concentration of odor material and provides it to the human olfactory organ. In general, the term "display" has implicitly referred to a visual display, which provides information through visual stimuli including texts and images. As its counterpart, an olfactory display provides olfactory stimuli instead of visual stimuli.

Although the technical field of olfactory display might seem to be relatively new, it has a long history comparable to that of audio and visual displays. The first example of using scent in conjunction with cinema can be found in 1906 (Gilbert, 2008). Surprisingly, this example precedes the use of sound. A famous example of a system incorporating smells with other kinds of sensory displays is Heilig's "Sensorama," developed in the early 1960s (Heilig, 1962). Users could enjoy multimodal movies incorporating breezes and smells. However, compared with the use of sounds or stereoscopic images, the use of smells in media technology has not become widespread. Only recently have smells been presented interactively in cooperation with computers.

DOI: 10.4018/978-1-4666-2521-1.ch003

Copyright © 2013, IGI Global. Copying or distributing in print or electronic forms without written permission of IGI Global is prohibited.

Besides traditional ways of enjoying scents, such as aroma therapy and incense, several attempts have been made to apply computer-controlled olfactory displays in our life. Some entertainment attractions use scent; for example, McCarthy (1986) developed a scent emitting system that could emit a selected scent and produce a sequence of various smells. Toyota Motor Corporation, in the theater in their Amlux showroom, provided an aroma system that enhanced the experience of the audience. In 2005, the scent generator "Aromatrix" was used at a premium screening of the movie *Charlie and the Chocolate Factory*. The audiences were presented the aroma of chocolate, synchronous to the scene of being in the chocolate factory. NTT Communications conducted a social experiment to examine the effect of providing scents in an advertisement (Sakaino, 2008). On the academic side, an aroma blender was used as a part of a system that provided an interactive multimedia content showing a cooking procedure with the smell of foods (Nakamoto, et al., 2008). In 2011, Seems Inc. won the Ig Nobel Chemical prize (Improbable Research, 2011) with their alarm system to awaken sleeping people in case of a fire or other emergency by using the smell of wasabi (pungent horseradish) (Goto, Sakai, Mizoguchi, Tajima, & Imai, 2011).

In this way, computer-controlled scent presentation has been gradually spreading in our life. In this chapter, the technical basics for recent olfactory displays are described.

TECHNOLOGICAL ASPECTS OF OLFACTORY DISPLAYS

Unlike sensory channels for which display technologies are already highly developed, such as visual and auditory senses, olfaction is a chemical sense. This fact makes it difficult to introduce olfactory displays in a similar manner to sensory channels based on physical stimuli. One of the characteristics specific to a chemical sense is

its nonlinearity. The change of intensity of the stimuli (i.e., concentration of the odor material) can result in a qualitative change in subjective sensation. For example, a chemical compound that is recognized as having a good smell when its concentration is low can turn into a bad smell if the concentration is increased.

From the perspective of human-computer interaction, it would be interesting to examine how many kinds of smells are required to synthesize arbitrary smells. In addition, it would be helpful to compose a completely general olfactory display, if it was found that humans have a mechanism in olfaction comparable to the "three primary colors" in human vision. However, such a mechanism has not been found, or may not even exist. Previously, Amoore (1970), in his theory of stereochemistry, sophisticatedly categorized various odors into seven major groups of smells. Some researchers considered that these seven groups corresponded to the three primary colors, but recent progress in olfaction research shows that this does not sufficiently explain human olfaction. A breakthrough in olfactory research occurred in 1991. Using an approach from the field of genetics, Buck and Axel (1991) estimated the number of receptor proteins in mice to be approximately 1,000. Since then, physiological study on odorant receptors has made remarkable progress (Touhara, et al., 1999), and according to recent human genome analysis, 388 olfactory receptor genes have been found in humans (Niimura & Nei, 2003). Each receptor protein responds to multiple molecules, and a single chemical compound activates multiple receptors, resulting in very complex functions of human olfaction. The number of olfactory receptors can be an index that shows the order of required odor components for obtaining arbitrary smells, but researchers are still trying to find the minimum number of odor components required for achieving an acceptable quality of expressing arbitrary smells.

Nevertheless, from a practical point of view, we can proceed to develop olfactory displays without

Figure 1. Roles of an olfactory display: scent generation and scent delivery

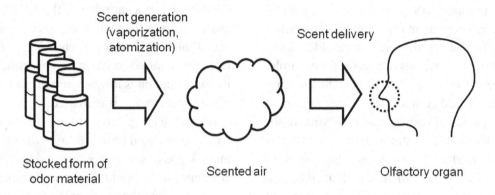

waiting for complete elucidation of the required number of odor components. We can significantly reduce the number of odor components if we restrict ourselves to a specific application. Blending from a relatively small set of component odors or switching among a set of pre-blended smells is considered to satisfy the required variety of presented smells.

Several technologies are applicable to the development of olfactory interfaces. Since people smell by using their nose, odorants should be vaporized and delivered to the nose (Figure 1). Thus, the major technical fields involved in creating olfactory interfaces include the generation and delivery of smells, defined as follows.

- **Generating Scents:** To produce scented air from the stocked form of odor materials, with the desired components and concentrations.
- **Delivering Scents:** To convey scented air from the scent generator to the human olfactory organ, by enabling spatial and temporal control of the olfactory stimuli.

These two functions might not be clearly separated, as many olfactory display systems include both. In this chapter, however, the authors discuss technologies applied to olfactory displays according to these categories, because enumerat-

ing all combinations of these technical areas is complicated and categorizing the technical areas might provide a somewhat better perspective of the emerging technologies.

In the following sections, most of the technologies listed in Table 1 are described, although, unfortunately, space does not allow all to be described in detail.

Many historical methods, such as using aroma pots and manual atomizers, are known to generate scents. Recent progress has led to the ability to control scent generation by a computer (Kaye, 2004). Details on scent generation technologies are described in the following section, "Scent Generation Methods."

Delivering scents is a relatively new technical area and is related to the concept of Virtual Reality (VR), by which a user interacts in three-dimensional space in real time. Early VR started with display technologies on audio and visual channels, and then VR was expanded to use haptic sensation. A natural progression has incorporated olfactory interfaces into VR systems (Barfield & Danas, 1996), which is an effective way to achieve a high level of presence. As real-time spatial interaction is essential in VR, spatio-temporal control of olfactory stimuli has become an important topic of study. In an analogy with visual displays, generating scents corresponds to graphics rendering and light emission on the

Table 1. Technologies applicable to an olfactory display. In principle, any combination of each technical category is possible for configuring a complete olfactory display.

Scent generation			Scent delivery
Vaporization	Switching	Formulation (blending)	

• Natural vaporization
• Airflow-based vaporization
• Heating
• Airflow-based atomization
• Direct atomization (ink jet)
• Ultrasonic atomization
	• Source switching
	  - Mechanical selection
	• Air switching
	  - Valve control
		• Liquid blending
		  - Drop-based blending
		• Gas blending (valve control)
		  - Mass flow control (analog)
		  - Digital control
		  - Pulse width modulation
		  - Δ-Σ modulation
		• Direct atomization control
		  - Number of droplets per unit time produced from each ink-jet head
			• Natural diffusion
			• Air convection
			  - Including heat
			• Wind
			  - Fans
			• Vortex ring
			  - Air cannon
			• Tube
			  - w/ air compressor or tank
			• Direct
			  - w/ tiny scent generator

surface of display devices; moreover, delivering scents corresponds to the spatial arrangement of display devices, such as Head-Mounted Displays (HMDs) and large-scale projection displays. Details on scent delivery technologies are described in the section "Scent Delivery Methods."

SCENT GENERATION METHODS

In general, two kinds of essences are known: natural essences extracted from animals and plants, and synthetic essences. The four kinds of animal extracts are musk, ambergris, civet, and castoreum, whereas approximately 1,500 kinds of plant extracts are known. The plant extracts are mainly the essential oils extracted from flowers, leaves, peels, seeds, roots, and stalks, of which approximately 150 kinds are currently on the market. As natural essences are rare, expensive, and easily spoiled, synthetic essences are often used. No variation exists in the quality of synthetic essences, and they provide a large, inexpensive, and stable supply. Of the approximately 5,000 kinds of synthetic essences, 320 kinds are produced

in compliance with industrial standards (Japan Perfumery and Flavoring Association, 2001).

It is possible to make a wide variety of scents by mixing these essences, but the technology of producing the target scents depends on their purposes. For example, when applying scents to a movie by choosing the proper scent for each scene, it is possible to switch scents prepared in advance. It is also possible to transmit a scent to a remote place by using a digital communication system, although this requires additional technologies to reproduce the scent identical (or similar) to the original one, based on the characteristic information extracted from the original scent by using a sensing system. Also, when applying the scent reproduction technique to aromatherapy, the best action to take is to mix perfumes at one place while listening to the patients' opinions in order to fit individual tastes, although it is a common practice to use only several preselected scents previously mixed for particular purposes.

Most of the essences are in a liquid form rather than a solid form, such as fragrant wood chips. Although it is easier to mix liquids rather than solid materials, liquids pose problems in handling, such as spilling the liquids and staining something. Therefore, ways to manage this problem are soaking an essence in porous materials, encapsulating them into microcapsules, or gelling them.

Scents are perceived when olfactory receptors (olfactory cells) inside the nose are stimulated. However, odorant molecules are not passed effectively when the essences are in the liquid or solid form, and so only relatively few molecules reach the receptors. Therefore, it is necessary to vaporize essences to deliver the molecules to one's nose. In the following subsections, methods to vaporize essences are discussed.

Vaporization Techniques

Various methods have been developed to emit molecules of scents from perfumes in accordance with the forms of essences. Many methods use well-known physical phenomena, although they depend on the state of the essence.

Natural Vaporization

In this method, essences are soaked in porous materials and naturally vaporized into the air. An aroma diffuser (or simply diffuser) refers to a device that diffuses aromas into the air. For example, when a decorative aroma diffuser, such as a perfume bottle with a cloth wick, is placed in a room, people can enjoy its subtle fragrance for a long time (e.g., on a monthly basis). In addition, sometimes a molded item, to which metal powder is sintered porously, has the ability to absorb perfume and maintain the scent. One factor to note when adapting this method is that a special container structure must be devised to keep the essence oil inside but effectively volatile when used. An aroma diffuser with a liquid perfume absorbing material inserted between porous covers is a typical example.

Figure 2 shows an aroma diffuser with a plate-like structure that which can be used for switching scents (Tomono & Uehara, 2006a). Its characteristic is that it has a mesh-structured breathable liquid absorbing board at its center. The board is put between cover plates with many specially shaped holes. Its evaporation performance is good, because air can pass in directions both parallel and perpendicular to the board, and because some spaces exist inside the holes, such that the structure is breathable. It is also possible to use this aroma diffuser for projected images by combining it with an airflow-based system or a heating-based system, as described later.

A natural vaporization method is simply structured, inexpensive, and easy to handle, but it has no function to control the emission rate of scents.

Figure 2. Evaporation-type aroma diffuser

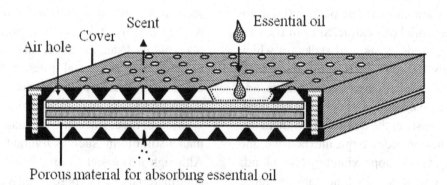

Airflow-Based Vaporization

As shown in Figure 3, this method works by letting air pass through the surface of a scent generating substance, thereby mixing the volatile component with the airflow. Many scent generators are based on this principle, as this method is simple and no special mechanism is required, except for devices to produce the airflow, such as fans, pumps, or air compressors.

As an example, Osmooze developed multi-channel scent diffusers that consist of vessels containing aromatic gels and a fan controlled via a USB communication line in 2002 (Osmooze, 2012). The system configuration is simple and straightforward, and was used in the project "Exhalia" handled by France Telecom S. A. (Messager & Takagi, 2002). The system was incorporated with practical audio-visual programs and demonstrated at various sites. In a typical program, called "Kaori-Web" ("kaori" is a Japanese word meaning aroma), the cooking process was dis-

played by images, sounds, and smells of the food being cooked. These multimodal stimuli are synchronously controlled by a PC (Tsuji, Takagi, Hirano, & Yoshihara, 2004).

This method is often used in wearable type and stationary type olfactory displays, where essences in solid or gel form are used. For the purpose of easily presenting scents in experiments involving the presentation of scents, one method is to put a perfume absorber, such as cotton wool, inside a tube. As we discuss later in the section "Scent delivery methods," the scent can be carried to the nose of subjects by sending air through the tube (Tomono, Kanda, & Otake, 2008). By placing a magnetic valve inside the tube and controlling it by a computer, it is possible to switch scents, as described in the subsection "Scent switching technology." In addition, various methods can deliver scents to a person's nose through the flow of air (Nakamoto, 2008), which is described in detail in the section "Scent delivery methods." The air flow method can control the emission of a scent

Figure 3. Ventilation-type aroma diffuser.

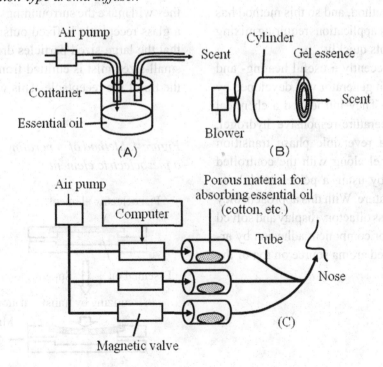

by switching it on or off. Therefore, if this system is used in a small room, it is relatively easy to control the direction and the amount of the scents.

Heating

Another method to promote vaporization is heating. In many countries, including Japan, traditional incense burners have been used to experience aromas (Pybus, 2001). By putting charcoal in ash and a fragrant wood chip on the ash, people in Japan have enjoyed the scents from the fragrant wood. Recently, aroma lamps have become popular. These are used by placing liquid perfume into a heat-resistant box and warming it by the heat from a lamp or the flame of a candle. The heating spreads a subtle scent over an entire room and is often used for aroma therapy. The aroma diffuser that uses the scent absorbing mechanism shown in Figure 2 has been developed, in which a desired scent can be generated at an appropriate time by the multiple scent absorbing parts mounted separately and a linked system to locally heat and control the diffuser. However, generally speaking, it is difficult to control the volatilization volume with the heating method, and so this method has not been suitable for applications requiring mixing and switching scents quickly.

Nevertheless, recently a useful heating- and cooling-based scent generator was developed by Kim et al. (2009). They introduced a chemical container of temperature-responsive hydrogel, which can have a reversible phase transition between sol and gel along with the controlled release of aroma by using a peltier module to control the temperature. With this approach, they achieved a soundless olfactory display and solved the problem of odor component adhesion by arranging a card-based aroma source on top of the olfactory display.

Airflow-Based Atomization

By arranging a nozzle (nozzle A) connected to the reservoir filled by essential oil and blowing the tip of the nozzle with a high-speed airflow generated by another air nozzle (nozzle B), the atmospheric pressure within nozzle A decreases by Bernoulli's law and the liquid is soaked up. Hence, at the tip of nozzle A, mist is generated as the liquid is blown with the air stream. This type of diffuser is well known among those people involved in the aroma business. The various designs of diffusers range from functional to decorative. What is characteristic about this method of scent generation is that a clear scent spreads evenly into a spacious room in a short time by the airflow of an air-conditioner, because the essential oil is directly turned into a mist and emitted.

Usually, glass is used for the nozzle placed in the reservoir and the air nozzle. The tip of the nozzle is precisely processed so that it can generate a fine mist. However, it is difficult to align the size of the mist droplets so that large droplets are not also generated, together with small ones. If large droplets of essential oil fly out of the device, they will make the surroundings dirty. Therefore, a glass receptacle is fixed outside the nozzle so that the large-sized particles drop in it and only small-sized mist is emitted from a small tube at the tip of the receptacle. This way of producing

Figure 4. Method of generating droplets by using a piezoelectric element

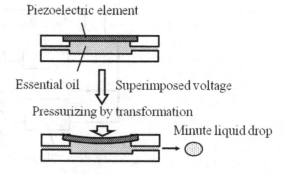

mist, however, suffers from several problems, among these, that the structure of the device is complicated and difficult to manufacture. In addition, the tip of the nozzle needs to be cleaned on a regular basis to prevent it from becoming clogged.

Direct Atomization

An on-demand ink-jet head for an ink-jet printer can be used as a scent generating device. "On-demand" means that it generates droplets when necessary. If a liquid flows through a tube or a material such as metal, on which minute holes are made and to which a strong pressure is applied from the side or back in pulses, fine droplets are emitted from the tip of each hole (Figure 4). It is possible to emit particles 70 microns in diameter and 200 pl per drop at an initial velocity of 2.0 m/s. The advantages of this approach include high performance in both temporal and quantitative control. This method was applied to the direct injection-type olfactory display (Yamada, Yokoyama, Tanikawa, Hirota, & Hirose, 2006), which is also discussed in the section "Scent Delivery Methods."

Because the on-demand type ink-jet head is simply structured, it is easy to miniaturize it and even make it multi-headed. Two methods are used to form droplets. One is to add instantaneous pressure on the liquid by using a deformed piezoelectric element (piezoelectric method) (Nakazawa, 1998), and the other is to generate bubbles within the liquid in a small tube by heating and utilizing the resulting pressure (thermal method). The piezoelectric method has the advantages that it can easily control the quantity of the liquid and it can use a liquid with high viscosity. Its disadvantage, however, is that the head structure is more complicated than that for the thermal method. The thermal method uses thermal resistance or induction heating, and its structure is simple and can be made into a small size. However, it may not work well with certain kinds of essences, because their chemical composition is denatured by high temperature. Kadowaki, Sato, Bannai, and Okada (2007) developed a thermal-type ink-jet-based scent generator. According to their comments, the degradation of essence was not noticeable, perhaps because the volume ratio of the essence that is heated to become a bubble is quite small and the remainder of the essence is just pushed out of the nozzle without a significant temperature increase.

Ultrasonic Atomization

This is a method to make fine particles from an essence in liquid form by ultrasonic energy and then to emit the particles. Lead Zirconate Titanate (PZT) ceramic or lithium niobate ceramic is used in ultrasonic transducers to atomize the liquid (Honda, 1994). As shown in Figure 5(a), if high-frequency voltage is applied to a disc-type piezoelectric element, it resonates toward its plate thickness direction, and the plate surface emits ultrasonic sound waves toward the vertical direction. A thin piezoelectric element can be driven by high-frequency waves of at least 2 MHz. When this transducer is immersed in water, ultrasonic waves are propagated through the water so that the water bulges by pushing up the water surface, and then the waves reach the boundary surface between the water and air. Due to the radical difference in the acoustic characteristic impedance of water and air, most of the ultrasonic waves are reflected on the boundary surface. The ultrasonic waves reflect successively in the upper part of the water bulge, and thus the collision and separation of liquid are repeated within the bulge. During this time, the portion of the bulge close to air is atomized by overcoming surface tension and flying out in the air. In this manner, a great amount of mist can be generated.

When the drive frequency of the ultrasonic transducer is adjusted to 2.5 MHz, the particles constituting the mist become very fine with a diameter of less than 3 microns. A mist of particles of this size feels less humid and has the charac-

Figure 5. Atomizer using an ultrasonic transducer

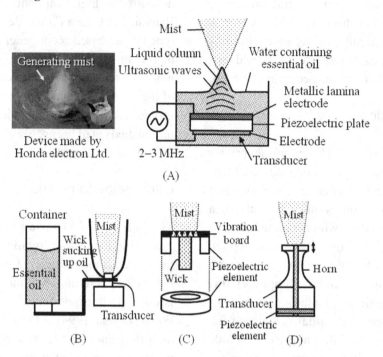

teristic of hovering in the air. An ultrasonic atomization method is often used in humidifiers. Therefore, if a perfume is put in it, the humidifier works as an aroma generator and makes a comfortable environment surrounded with soft, moisture-laden fragrance. Furthermore, because its responsiveness to atomization is good, the humidifier can instantaneously generate a scent. However, the problem is that, if a perfume is put in the water container, it will adhere to the water container and atomizer so that maintenance becomes necessary. In addition, if the volume of water becomes small, it causes a boil-dry state, and the ultrasonic transducer deteriorates or breaks. The adherence problem can be circumvented by using the method in which the essential oil is atomized in a small liquid container with an ultrasonic transmission membrane. The oil scatters only within this small liquid container, so that it can be removed and cleaned. As for the water volume problem, it is improved by developing a heat-resistant transducer element and a prevention circuit against the boil-dry state by using temperature detection of the element.

Another method to emit fine particles is breaking the surface tension by using the movement of the tip of an ultrasonic transducer (shape change). Figure 5(b) shows an atomizer in which a belt-shaped wick made of porous material is fixed on the mouth of the essential oil container. Through capillary action, the essential oil is sent to the tip of transducer, the transducer is vibrated at approximately 200 KHz, and the essential oil is atomized and emitted. Figure 5(c) shows an atomizer in which a vibration board with fine holes fixed on a piezoelectric element emits a fine mist (Toda, 1994). Figure 5(d) shows an atomizer using a Langevin-type transducer. Here, the piezoelectric element is fixed on the bottom of a metal part and the tip of the metal part is made into a horn shape. The essence goes through the horn and is atomized at the tip. The atomization method using the movement of the transducer has the advantages that it is simply structured and can be small in size. However, it still remains as an issue how to make the drive frequency higher and the diameter of the particles smaller.

These atomization methods are easy ways to control the quantity of the essence to be atomized and to be superior in responsiveness. These methods are also preferable for presenting the scent in a spacious space and for switching the scent, in comparison with the natural volatilization method, the blowing method, and the heating method. In order to take advantage of the merits of these multiple methods, a method combining the atomization, blowing, and heating methods is used as well.

Scent Switching Technology

When putting a scent suitable for the scene of a film and switching it to one suitable for the mood at that moment, a scent switching function is necessary. Various methods have been proposed. Some methods are based on mechanical switching so that one of the provided odors is selected by moving the containers. Others are based on airflow control so that one of the valves connected to the target scent source is opened. Here, as an example of a mechanical switching method, the authors' approach is introduced (Tomono & Uehara, 2006b).

Figure 6 shows an aroma diffuser in which several scents are absorbed on scent absorption plates of the structure shown in Figure 2, one of which is heated by a heater. In Figure 6, a mist is made to go through the absorption plate, then mixed with the scent and finally emitted. An ultrasonic transducer like the one shown in Figure 5(a) is used. The ultrasonic waves emitted from the ultrasonic transducer are reflected from a concave mirror and focused on the neighborhood of the water. Small water bulges are made on the surface, and effective atomization occurs in a narrow area. An ultrasonic reflection tube is fixed above the water so that it surrounds the space where the water splashes. When the water splashes, the ultrasonic waves that did not contribute to atomization are emitted into the tube, and they become traveling waves going toward the upper part of the tube. The mist is pushed up due

to the pressure of these waves and goes through the scent absorption plate. The stimulation of the scent moving into the mist is soft and pleasant. From several to 10 scents can be absorbed in the board of absorption plates. If several boards of absorption plates are used, the diffuser can switch dozens of scents. When no scent is required, it can be used as a humidifier. If Integrated Circuit (IC) memory is fixed on each scent absorption plate, it is possible for the plate to memorize the information of the Identification (ID) of scents. It is possible to read this information of identification of scent by an ID sensor to control the performance of scents by controlling the amount of mist that passes through it and interlocking the scent with other multimedia.

Formulation Technology

Formulation (blending) technology refers to the reproduction of a scent as closely as possible to the target scent, based on the information acquired by sensor outputs, human sensory evaluation, analysis (machine recognition), and so on. This technology is important for odor communication and olfactory virtual reality. Later, in Chapter 6, the latest system for odor recording and reproduction is described in detail. In this section, examples of the structure of a device generating a desired scent by mixing several essences, based on the conventional formulation method, are explained.

Extraction of Formulation Information and Replication

Figure 7 shows the extraction method of the formulation information of the targeted scent and the replication method using flow control (Yamanaka, Matsumoto, & Nakamoto, 2002). In Figure 7(a), the essence for the targeted scent is in scent bottle A. Essences of an ingredient of scent A or essences that can sensually replicate scent A are in scent bottles 1, 2, and 3. The process is given as follows. To begin, open valve A and close valve C.

Figure 6. Mist-type aroma diffuser that can switch scents

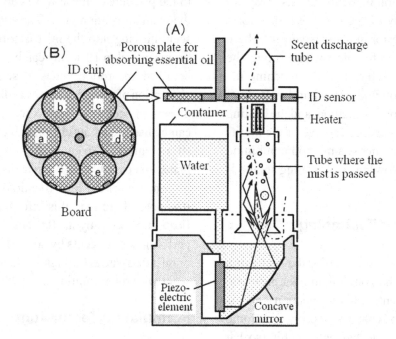

Then, let the targeted scent flow into the sensor array. Input the data of the sensor output into the computer for pattern recognition. Then, control the opening and closing of the flow regulators of scent bottles 1, 2, and 3 and mix the gases, close valve A and open valve C, send the gases to the sensor array, send the output to the computer, and compare it with the pattern of scent A. The system calculates the difference, feeds back the result into the mix-adjustment part, controls the flow regulators, makes the gas of the new mixing ratio, and compares the patterns again. The concentration determination of each essence component can be performed by repeating this procedure until the difference becomes less than the acceptable level.

Figure 7(b) shows the replication system. With this system, a scent like the scent of bottle A can be generated by adjusting the flow of the gas of each essence so that the mixing ratio takes the value obtained by the method illustrated in Figure 7(a).

As shown in this example, it is desired that the structures of the extraction system and the replication system of the formulation information of the scent are the same, because the extracted formulation information can be used for replication, and a high precision of replication can be attained. However, it should be pointed out that problems exist with this method, such as that the mass flow controller is expensive and large.

Formulation Method for Volatile Perfume

Figure 8 shows the example of the device (Aromageur, MIRAPRO Co., Ltd.) to formulate several scents using a relatively simple method of controlling the mixing ratio of each volatile essence by an electromagnetic valve when the mixing ratios of the essences are previously known, or when a recipe of the scent is given (Ando, Akiyama, Shouge, & Shimizu, 2007). As shown in the photo, an air pump and a driving circuit are fixed on the lower hemisphere of the spherical system, above which is an air supply room in which air is kept, and in the surrounding of which six scent bottles are mounted. The air flows are shown by arrows and numbers. The scents emitted from the six

Figure 7. Example of scent replication method (Tokyo Institute of Technology)

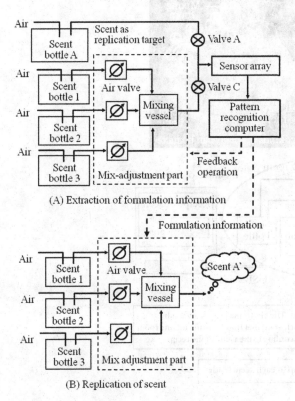

(A) Extraction of formulation information

Formulation information

(B) Replication of scent

bottles are mixed in a mixing room and emitted. The electromagnetic valves have one inlet and two outlets and are driven and controlled so that the outlets are switched by dividing one second into several equal segments. For example, if one movement supposedly takes 50 ms, the valves can be pulse-driven by dividing one second into 20 segments. In this case, if the electromagnetic valves are operated 20 times per second, the entire air flows to the scent bottle by the route from (1) to (3). If the electromagnetic valves are operated 10 times per second, half of the air flows to the scent bottle by route (3), and the other half returns to the air supply room by route (2). If the valves are operated one time per second, 5% of the air flows to the scent bottle. The volume of air to be sent to the scent bottle can be controlled in this manner.

The mixing ratio of the volatilization volume of each essence can be determined based on the frequency of vibration of each electromagnetic valve. For example, if the mixing ratios of six essences are 50%, 20%, 15%, 10%, 5%, and 0%, the frequency should be 10 Hz, 4 Hz, 3 Hz, 2 Hz, 1 Hz, and 0 Hz, respectively. By operating the six electromagnetic valves at 20 times per second, the mixing ratio can be manipulated while the total volatilization volume coming from the air supply room is fixed, and the air pressure in the air supply room is kept constant.

By increasing the speed of the electromagnetic valves, the system can blend the aromas at desired mixing ratio with resolution of 1%. The control of the formulation of scents is conducted by a computer. When the recipe of a scent is inputted, the air volume that flows to each scent bottle is controlled by the electromagnetic valves and the concentration of each essence can be adjusted to the value of the recipe in 10–20 seconds.

The maximum discharging amount of gas emitted from the mixing room is determined by the output power of the air pump. It is 1.5 L/min in this device. Enjoining the scent in the neighborhood of the device is not a problem, but, in order for the scent to be presented in a distant place, the device needs to send the scent to be used.

Formulation by Droplet Control

When the mixing ratio of essences is known, a method to mix droplets by the ratio and to emit the scent can be considered. It has been proposed to make a scent generating device that uses the method to measure the essences from essence receptacles and put them in a small liquid mixing container, vaporize or atomize the resulting essence, and send it by air (Tomono & Uehara, 2005). The technique to control droplets that uses the abovementioned piezoelectric element and static electricity, etc., is effective for the quantification of essences. Another method sets a small essence atomization device in front of an air cylinder, controls the mixing ratio by the atomization volume, and flows off the scent by the air that comes from the cylinder (Tomono, 2008).

Figure 8. Aroma formulation device using a solenoid-controlled valve (Mirapro Ltd.)

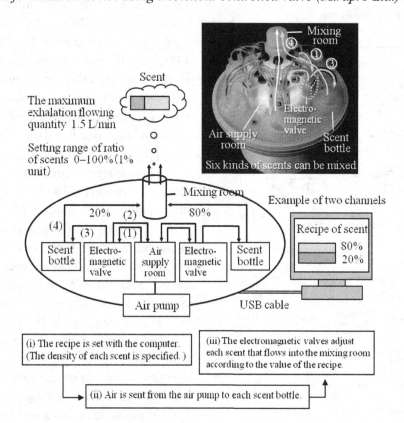

SCENT DELIVERY METHODS

Once an odor source is vaporized, it should be delivered to the nose. The method of delivery depends on the application style: to how many users should the system simultaneously send the smells, whether the users move or walk around, and how quickly different smells should be delivered to the users, and so on. When scents should be delivered to many people simultaneously (such as in theaters), a promising way is to diffuse scents into the entire space. In this case, a significant amount of odor material is diffused. Conversely, the area in which the scents are noticeable should be limited when the scents are provided for personal use. It would also be effective to use an enclosure or a booth to prevent the scent from unexpectedly spreading.

The duration that scents are noticeable has a close relationship with the range of scent diffusion. If the scents are diffused over a large volume, the scents are noticeable over a long duration. Otherwise, this duration is shorter if the scent diffusion is limited in a small area, because the diffused amount of odor material is so small that the concentration of odor compounds decreases rapidly. Such a scent presentation would be effective when scents are presented synchronously with audio-visual programs that have an instantaneous scene change.

If one wants the scents to be noticed only over a short duration, simple diffusion would not be sufficient. Once scents are diffused over a wide area, it is difficult to switch to a new scent within a short time, as the previously emitted scents remain in the space and the newly presented scent is mixed with the previous one. To address this problem, the following approaches can be considered.

- Incorporate scent-elimination equipment into the system.
- Provide a minimum amount of odor material to the user's nose.

In the scent-elimination approach, the concentration of the previously emitted scent is explicitly reduced by various equipment. If the amount of the smell is moderate, suction pumps and filters (such as a charcoal filter) can be used. For systems that emit a massive amount of scents, ventilating functions should be incorporated into the system. The use of ventilation equipment would be effective for dedicated facilities such as a theater or an amusement park, but it is difficult to be applied to ordinary homes and offices.

In the minimum material approach, the scents delivered to the nose dissipate over a short duration, if the amount of emitted odor material is quite limited. The user cannot notice the scent after a short time because the concentration of the scent becomes below the noticeable threshold. To achieve this, it is necessary to deliver a small amount of odor material to the nose effectively. This is the reason why scent delivery technology is also important for the spatio-temporal control of scents.

In the following subsections, we introduce various methods of delivering scents and categorize them by the means of scent delivery and the location of the scent generator. As the means of scent delivery, the following are considered: natural diffusion/convection, wind, vortex rings, tubes, and direct injection (Figure 9). We categorize the location of the scent generator as a fixed place in the environment, body-mounted, and nose-mounted. Examples of existing systems categorized by the combination of these two factors are shown in Table 2.

Natural Diffusion/Convection

Scents are naturally diffused from a high-concentration area to a low-concentration area. They are also conveyed by slow airflow, based on natural convection. Thus, the scents emitted from a scent generator in a room are gradually diffused into the entire room. The traditional way of enjoying smells involves diffusing aromas throughout a room, where they are continuously experienced by users for a sufficient period of time. Widespread, long-term aromas are sufficient for communicating environmental or ambient information. Such smells do not disturb users explicitly, but can nevertheless subtly communicate what is happening in the surrounding world.

Systems with Scent Generators Placed in the Environment

Most standalone aroma generators are categorized into this type, because they by themselves do not have an explicit function for controlling the spatio-temporal distribution of smells. Kaye (2001, 2004) developed various systems to emit scents in the context of ambient media. Air brushes are used in the system named "inStink" to emit 12 kinds of smells. Sprays driven by solenoids are used in the "Dollars & Scents," "Scent Reminder," and "Honey, I'm Home" systems that emit two smells, five smells, and a single smell, respectively.

To achieve the intended odor distribution, it is important to know how the odor material is diffused into the air. In an analogy with light emission, the odor concentration could be considered to decrease according to the distance from the odor source. However, the velocity of natural diffusion in a completely stationary atmosphere is rather slow. Instead, air convection plays an important role in spreading the scent from the source. To estimate how the scents are diffused or distributed in a room, it is useful to introduce computational fluid dynamics (Matsukura, Ohno, & Ishida, 2010). The temperature difference inside

Figure 9. Scent delivery methods: (a) natural diffusion/convection, (b) airflow/wind, (c) vortex ring, (d) tubes from a stationary scent generator, (e) tubes from a body-mounted scent generator, (f) direct injection

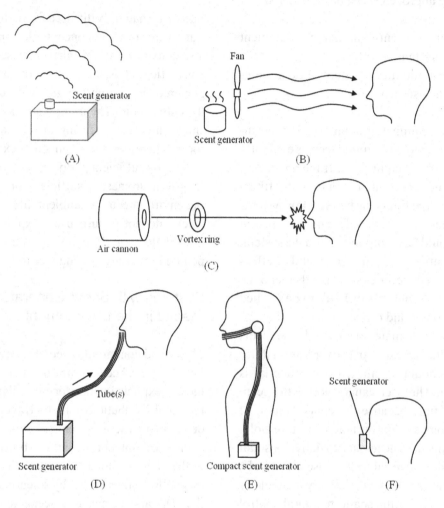

and outside the room, as well as the existence of a human (as an object with a heat source), can be important factors to determine the air convection. Details of this aspect are described in Chapter 21.

The heating-/cooling-based soundless olfactory display (Kim, et al., 2009), introduced in the "Heating Method" in the section "Scent Generation Methods" can also be categorized into this type. If the system is placed on a desk just in front of a user's chest, the odorants released from the sol/gel patches are naturally carried by the ascending air current to reach the nose.

Systems with Body-Mounted Scent Generators

Compact scent generators can be mounted on the body. Mounting scent generators to positions near the face, such as shoulders and chests, improves the spatio-temporal controllability of scents, while reducing the inconvenience of wearing devices. Such a configuration can result in natural human-computer interactions. At the University of Southern California, Morie et al. (2003) designed and implemented a necklace-shaped unit equipped with four wireless-controlled small

Table 2. Examples of systems categorized by the location of the scent generator and the means of scent delivery

	Diffusion/convection	Air flow (Wind)	Vortex ring	Tube	Direct
Environment (Stationary)	Diffusers, Atomizers, Single use of scent generators	"Scents of Space," MSFD	Scent projector	Olfactometers, Combination with scent generators	—
Body	"Scent Collar"			Wearable display, Arm-mounted display	—
Proximity to nose	—	—	—	—	Direct injection

scent emitters. This system is called the "Scent Collar." By emitting scents close to the nose, the collar enables location-specific olfactory stimuli without forcing users to wear encumbering tubes or devices near the face. To mount compact scent generators to the body under the nose seems to be effective, as scents generated at such positions would reach the nose, carried by the ascending air current caused by the body heat.

Using Wind (Stationary Airflow)

By using the wind (airflow), one can actively deliver a scent to the nose (Figure 9[b]). With this approach, the system designer can place the scent generator away from the user. As the user can notice the scent only when the air including the odor material reaches the nose, it is possible to present scents over a shorter duration, as compared with the natural diffusion/convection method.

"Scents of Space" developed by Haque (2004) is a large-scale example that uses airflow to deliver scents to the user. "Scents of Space" is a room-sized media art installation that presents lights and scents in coordination. In the enclosure, an array of fans generates slow airflow (0.2 m/s) so that visitors do not feel the movement of air. As this airflow starts from the entire wall at one side of the enclosure and goes out at the other side, a stable

laminar airflow is formed. Scents, generated in response to the visitor's movement, travel slowly to the visitor and constitute a three-dimensional placement of fragrances without dispersion. Visitors can move within the enclosure and enjoy the three-dimensional distribution of smells that changes in accordance with the visitors' motion.

Kadowaki et al. (2007) developed an olfactory display system that combines an ink-jet-based scent generator and a blower fan. The major advantage of this system, as described in the section "Scent generation methods," is its high performance of controlling scent generation, both in quantitative concentration and in time. After tiny droplets including odor material are pushed out of inkjet nozzles, they are completely vaporized to make scented air. Because the rate of generating droplets and the timings can be precisely controlled, their aroma generator achieved significant performance in controlling the concentration each time. By making use of this performance, they proposed a method to avoid the users' olfactory adaptation by providing short-term, pulse-like olfactory stimuli. Consequently, the user can feel the smell longer than when he/she is exposed to continuous olfactory stimuli. This system has a wide range of temporal control, from a short-term presentation to a long-term presentation. The outlet opening of the device is located approximately 10 cm in front of the user's face, providing precisely controlled scented air. Details of this system are described in Chapter 20.

Matsukura, Nihei, and Ishida (2011) developed a system named the multi-sensorial field display (MSFD). They placed a pair of fans facing each other with a computer display between them. The airflow generated by each fan collides in front of the computer display, and this collision position can be controlled by adjusting the balance of the fan speed. A part of the airflow is then directed to the user, resulting in a feeling that the wind blew out of the computer display. By incorporating a scent generator with the fan, a user can feel the scent in the wind in cooperation with the image on the computer display.

Using Vortex Rings

Although we can convey the scents using wind, the wind should be dispersed in accordance with the distance from the wind source (fans), except for specific configurations such as "Scents of Space" described above. If we use vortex rings to convey the scent, the emitted scent is encapsulated in the vortex ring and can reach a relatively long distance as long as the flying vortex ring keeps its shape (Figure 9[c]). To launch a vortex ring, a device called an "air cannon," which is a vessel with a circular aperture is used. By instantaneously reducing the inner volume of the air cannon, the air is pushed out of the aperture and forms a vortex ring (Figure 10[a, b]). As this vortex ring is composed of air located at the aperture before the shot, a scent can be conveyed in it to travel in free space. In contrast to a wind that is a continuous airflow, the use of a vortex ring is a "discrete" way of delivering scents. Because a vortex ring can contain a very small amount of scent and can keep its shape until it collapses, scents can be delivered locally both in time and space.

Watkins (2002) developed a scent emitting device that uses the principle of a vortex ring. Their device includes multiple scent generators

in a chamber, and the scented air that fills the chamber is pushed out of the aperture to compose a vortex ring by driving an actuator (loudspeaker) at the back of the chamber.

Yanagida and colleagues developed systems to deliver scents locally to moving users. They incorporated an image-based nose tracker so that the air cannon is automatically directed to a user's nose (Yanagida, Noma, Tetsutani, & Tomono, 2003). They also developed a prototype system in which the emitted scent can be switched to another one for each shot of the vortex ring by introducing a small cylinder-shaped chamber in front of the aperture of an air cannon (Yanagida, Kawato, Noma, Tomono, & Tetsutani, 2004) (Figure 10[c, d]: the camera for image-based nose tracking is not included in this photo). With this configuration, they avoided the main body of the air cannon to be filled with scents and achieved the scent switching function. They named their system "Scent Projector" after the characteristics of the vortex-ring-based scent delivering technique.

During the development of scent projectors, several issues emerged. For example, the feeling of suddenly being wind-blasted impairs the natural olfactory experience of the user. To solve this problem, a method was proposed to use two air cannons and let vortex rings collide with each other so that the vortex rings collapse in front of the user and the high-speed airflow composing the vortex rings is reduced (Nakaizumi, Yanagida, Noma, & Hosaka, 2006). Based on this configuration, a system was developed to provide scents locally, both in space and time, to people walking down an aisle (Murai, Serizawa, & Yanagida, 2011).

The limitations of vortex rings include the following: the conveyed volume of scents is decided by the size of the vortex ring, and the way of delivering scents is temporally discrete. Although this approach is suitable for short-term scent presentation in a limited space, it is not suitable for providing scents over a long duration, or continuously. Another limitation is that the trajectory of a vortex ring is affected by the

Figure 10. Vortex-ring-based scent delivery technique: (a) principle, (b) flying vortex ring, (c) overview of "scent projector" prototype with scent switching mechanism and a platform for nose tracking, and (d) its scent switching mechanism

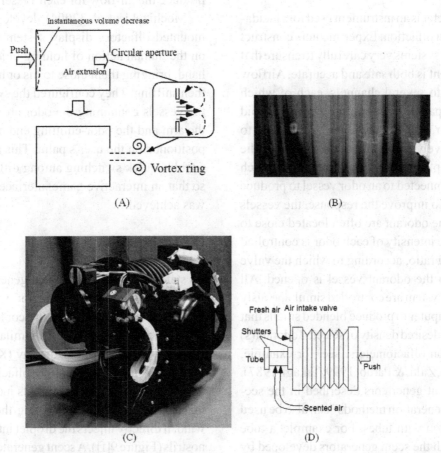

wind. A vortex ring can reach the target if the wind velocity is much smaller than the velocity of the vortex ring, but when the wind velocity is larger, the trajectory of the ring can be deflected from the intended one, or the ring can be collapsed by a strong wind.

Using Tubes

The use of tubes is an effective way to convey scented air from the scent generator to the nose (Figure 9[d, e]). Scents reliably reach the nose without being dispersed or mixing with the surrounding atmosphere. If we select an appropriate scent generator and control it adequately, this method can accommodate both continuous and short-term scent presentation. By releasing the scented air just under the nostril, the scent emission can be minimized to reduce the influence of previously presented smells. Special care should be taken so that the previously conveyed scents do not adhere to the inner wall of the tube, thus preventing previous scents from being mixed in the current scent. To avoid scent mixture in the tube, a bundle of tubes is often used so that each tube is exclusively used for a unique scent. A possible drawback of this approach as a human-computer interface is that attaching tubes is somewhat cumbersome.

Systems with Scent Generators Placed in the Environment

An olfactometer is an instrument used for elucidation of human olfaction. Experimenters construct olfactometer systems very carefully to ensure that the experiment is both safe and accurate. Airflow is divided into several channels, each of which consists of a pair of tubes equipped with solenoid valves. A pair of solenoid valves is controlled to open exclusively so that the total airflow of the channel is kept constant. One of the tubes in each channel is connected to an odor vessel to produce scented air. To improve the response, the vessels containing the odorant are often located close to the nose. The intensity of each odor is controlled by the timing ratio, according to which the valve connected to the odorant vessel is opened. All valves in the system are controlled simultaneously by a host computer to produce blended smells that consist of the desired density of selected odorant(s) (for details on olfactometers, see, for example, Lorig, Elmes, Zald, & Pardo, 1999; Takagi, 1987).

Many scent generators described in the section "Scent generation methods" can also be used in combination with tubes. For example, a tube was used with the scent generators developed by Nakamoto and colleagues (Nakamoto & Minh, 2007; Yamanaka, et al., 2002) to provide scents to a user. In this system, odor components are blended in real time to generate the intended scents synchronized with scenes in a video clip.

Systems with Body-Mounted Scent Generators

A wearable olfactory display system was developed at the University of Tokyo (Yamada, et al., 2004). By focusing on the spatial distribution of the virtual olfactory space and by making the entire system (including scent generators) compact and wearable, their system allows users to move around the environment and actively explore the virtual olfactory space (Figure 9[e]). This olfac-

tory display system has four odor vessels, and a micropump (driven by a DC motor) is used to produce the air flow for each vessel.

Mochizuki et al. (2004) developed an arm-mounted olfactory display system that focuses on the human action of holding objects in one's hand, bringing them close to his or her nose, and then sniffing. They configured the system so that the vessels containing the odor are mounted on the arm and the odor-emitting end of the tube is positioned on the user's palm. This arrangement enabled quick switching among different smells so that an interactive game interface using smell was achieved.

Direct Injection

As stated in the section "Scent generation methods," the direct injection method was proposed by Yamada et al. (2004) in the context of wearable olfactory displays. In a similar manner to an inkjet-based olfactory display (Kadowaki, et al., 2007), a direct-injection olfactory display generates fine droplets of liquids including odor material, but instead of carrying the scent by a wind, it directly injects the droplet into the human nostrils (Figure 9[f]). A scent generator is attached at the nose, and so it does not require any kind of scent delivery technique. An ideal response can be achieved, as the distance from the scent generator to the olfactory organ is minimized. A possible drawback of this approach, similar to that of the wearable olfactory display using a tube, is that it is somewhat cumbersome to wear a device. Likewise, for many other wearable devices, however, convenience will dominate the cumbersome feeling, if smaller and lighter devices become available in the future.

As an intermediate style between direct injection and other methods, Kim and Ando (2010) developed a directional olfactory display, which achieved both long-term preservation of the odor materials and miniaturization of the device. By arranging a set of micro air flow sources close to the nose (approximately 10–30 cm from the nose) and emitting a minimal amount of odor, scents can be delivered within a limited space. They also addressed the problem of the preservation of odor material after being set in the display device by introducing aroma-source containers, in which essential oil is perfused in porous material (a calcium silicate ball).

EVALUATION METHODS

Generally, two approaches are used to evaluate display devices and systems that stimulate human sensation: one is to evaluate the performance of devices or systems themselves, and the other is to evaluate the resulting effect on the human user. The evaluation regarding the human user is further categorized into the evaluation of objective measures and subjective measures.

Performance Evaluation of Devices/Systems

Factors to determine the performance of olfactory displays are listed in Table 3. Some of these factors can be determined by the specification of the device/system, and others are evaluated by measuring the scent output using sensors.

Performance Measure of Scent Generation

As a scent generator, the maximum ability of atomization/vaporization is an important factor for evaluation. If the scent emitting device/system is used to deliver a scent into an entire room, a significant amount of odor material should be vaporized. Users would not be able to feel the scent clearly if the vaporization capability is not sufficient. In contrast, if the scent generator is used in combination with a local scent delivery system, it is sufficient to vaporize only a small amount of odor material.

If we want to provide a variety of scents in an application, the number of odor components that can be blended or switched becomes an important factor. As mentioned in the section "Introduction" in this chapter, it would be ideal if the system could generate a sufficient variety of scents to cover arbitrary scents, but the required number of odor components has not been determined. Some scent generators developed so far can blend dozens of odor components (Nakamoto & Minh, 2007), which seem to be sufficient to generate a wide variety of scents, at least for a specified application.

The dynamic range refers to the maximum rate of scent generation divided by the minimum rate of scent generation. A scent generator with a large dynamic range can control the amount or

Table 3. Performance measures of olfactory displays

Scent generation	Scent delivery
Maximum ability of atomization/vaporization	Size of scent delivery area
Number of odor components	Duration of stimuli
Dynamic range	Response (temporal aspects)
Accuracy (stability, repeatability)	Efficiency
Crosstalk	
Dependence of volatility	
Response (temporal aspects)	

concentration of each odor component precisely. For example, the ink-jet-based scent generator developed by the research group of Keio University and Canon Inc. can vary the amount of emitted scent at 256 levels (Kadowaki, et al., 2007). The aroma blender developed by Nakamoto and Minh (2007) can also control the concentration level. This level depends on the fast valve response (1 ms) and the required repetition cycle time (1 s).

Accuracy, which means how exactly the specified emission amount or concentration level can be achieved, is another important factor. This can be also called stability or repeatability. In some scent generation methods, special care should be taken to keep the concentration constant. For example, in scent generators using airflow-based vaporization (Figure 3), the concentration of odor material in the vessel can change depending on the velocity of the volume that passes through the vessel. The concentration of vaporized odor material in the vessel is saturated if no airflow is present, whereas the concentration decreases when continuous airflow goes through the vessel. In many airflow-based scent generators, the system is designed such that this airflow is kept constant and the concentration of scent output from each channel is not affected regardless of whether the specific odor component is being presented.

For scent generators that can provide multiple scents, crosstalk can degrade the quality of the generated scent. Crosstalk refers to the phenomenon that unintended odor component(s) are mixed in the desired combination of odor components. In some scent generators and scent delivery systems, the crosstalk can occur in the tube(s) in which the scented air flows. The heating-/cooling-based scent generator developed by Kim et al. (2009) can be a good solution to this problem, as their system has an open structure and the odorants released from sol/gel patches, carried by the mild ascending air flow without adhering to any surface of the equipment (such as a tube), reach the nose.

In addition to the controllability of scent concentration, temporal response is also an important factor when using scents as a part of media technology. Major temporal aspects include delay, rising time, sustained period, and decay time. Figure 11 shows the general temporal aspects used to evaluate a pulse wave, where it is assumed that the target concentration level is set to C_t at $t = 0$ and reset to zero after a while. Since the concentration of scent output cannot be evaluated by the scent generator itself, odor sensors (described in Chapter 5) are used. Note that this aspect shows the overall response, including the response of both the scent generator and the sensor. The responses of the scent generator and the sensor often have an asymmetric feature, i.e., the decay time is longer than the rise time. Therefore, from the perspective of system engineering, these are regarded as nonlinear system elements.

The concentration and the temporal response can be affected by the volatility of the vaporized odor material. Especially with natural vaporization and airflow-based vaporization, vaporization for low-volatile material is slow, resulting in a lower concentration than that of a higher-volatile material. To achieve the concentration balance among odorants with higher and lower volatilities, micro-scale atomization is expected to be effective. Ariyakul and Nakamoto (2011) developed an ultrasonic-based atomizer by using electroosmotic pumps and a Surface Acoustic Wave (SAW) device, and confirmed the acceleration in the vaporization for a low-volatile compound. Ink-jet-based scent generators are also expected to effectively vaporize various odor materials regardless of their volatility.

Performance Measure of Scent Delivery

As described in the section "Scent delivery methods," the size of a scent delivery area is an important factor in scent delivery systems. The evaluation result for a scent delivery area depends on the application: to how many people should the scent be provided simultaneously, whether another person should be provided with different scents

Figure 11. Temporal aspects related to the response of an olfactory display

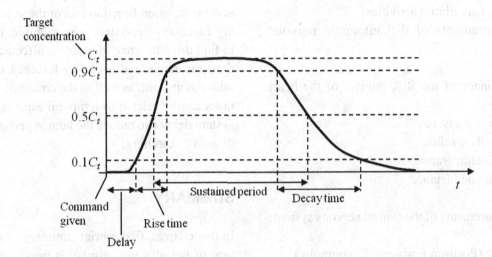

or whether the scent should not be provided, how quickly the presented scent should be switched, and so on.

The size of the scent delivery area is closely related to the sustained period and the decay time. Generally, the larger the size is, the longer the sustained period and the decay time are. The initial delay is related to the distance from the scent generator to the nose. It takes a longer time to convey scented air over a longer distance, regardless of which scent delivery method (wind, vortex ring, or tube) is applied. From this point of view, wearable olfactory displays have good potential to achieve a quick response.

Efficiency is the ratio of the amount of odor material required for scent presentation divided by the total amount of odor consumption. Better efficiency means that less odor material is uselessly scattered around the space. From this point of view, wearable olfactory displays again have good efficiency, followed by vortex-ring-based systems.

From the above discussions, the wearable approach has both good response and efficiency and therefore is a promising configuration for controlling scents in space and time. However, one can also notice the tradeoff between these desired

performances and the cumbersome impression of wearing a device. Therefore, it is important to select an appropriate method, depending on the application and the purpose of presenting scents.

Evaluation of the Effect on Users

Olfactory displays can also be evaluated by how the olfactory stimuli affect users. Evaluation methods in this category are common among other technical fields related to human-computer interactions. As the details of these methods are beyond the scope of this chapter, here we present a short summary on this topic. Evaluations performed by the subjective perception, cognition, and impression of the users are called sensory tests, which are described in the section "Sensory evaluation" in Chapter 5.

Physiological Measurement

Olfactory stimuli affect the activity of the human nerves and brain, and parts of these activities result in physiological responses. We can estimate the effect of olfactory stimuli by monitoring the physiological responses. Although the instrumentation of physiological responses is commonly used in a wide variety of fields to assess the effects on humans, here we just enumerate the measures related to nerve/brain activities.

Measurements of the automatic nervous system:

- Variance of the R-R interval of the heart rate
- Blood pressure
- Pupillary reflex
- Skin temperature
- Skin conductance

Measurements of the central nervous system:

- PET (Positron Emission Tomography)
- f-MRI (functional Magnetic Resonance Imaging)
- NIRS (Near Infra-Red Spectrometer)
- EEG (Electroencephalography)
- MEG (Magnetoencephalography)

Each method has advantages and limitations. For example, EEG has good temporal resolution, but its spatial resolution is limited when estimating the activity of specific parts of the brain. Non-invasive measurements of olfactory responses in the brain using EEG, MEG, and f-MRI are described in Chapter 2.

Task Performance

In some cases, a user can perform a task with an olfactory cue provided by a system. Examples of such tasks are listed below.

- A subject is asked to answer whether the scents presented in sequence are identical.
- A subject is asked to answer which scent is stronger.
- A subject is asked to reach the smell source by exploring in a field.
- A subject is asked to indicate the direction of the smell source.

Each task is related to the performance of the scent generation function and/or the scent delivery function of a system. For example, the task to find the difference of scents is affected by the dynamic range and accuracy for each blended odor component, as well as the crosstalk. Spatial tasks can be related to temporal aspects, as the system delay can reduce the human performance of active searching.

SUMMARY

In this chapter, first a brief summary of the history of the olfactory display is provided. Next, we categorize the roles of an olfactory display into two major functions: making scented air by vaporizing odor materials from their stocked form at the desired concentration and mixture ratio (scent generation), and bringing it to the human olfactory organ (scent delivery). A survey of scent generation methods and scent delivery methods is provided in each section. Finally, a brief summary of evaluating olfactory displays is provided. Computer-controlled olfactory displays are still a developing technology, and we expect a variety of novel and useful devices/systems to be developed in the future.

REFERENCES

Amoore, J. E. (1970). *Molecular basis of odor*. Springfield, IL: Charles C. Thomas.

Ando, T., Akiyama, S., Shouge, N., & Shimizu, T. (2007). *Japanese unexamined patent application. Publication 2007-236400*. Tokyo, Japan: Patent Office.

Ariyakul, Y., & Nakamoto, T. (2011). Improvement of olfactory display using electroosmotic pumps and a SAW device for VR application. In *Proceedings of International Conference on Artificial Reality and Telexistence (ICAT) 2011*, (pp. 15-21). Osaka, Japan: ICAT.

Barfield, W., & Danas, E. (1996). Comments on the use of olfactory displays for virtual environments. *Presence (Cambridge, Mass.)*, *5*(1), 109–121.

Buck, L., & Axel, R. (1991). A novel multigene family may encode odorant receptors: A molecular basis for odor recognition. *Cell*, *65*, 175–187. doi:10.1016/0092-8674(91)90418-X

Gilbert, A. (2008). *What the nose knows: The science of scent in everyday life*. New York, NY: Crown Publishing.

Goto, H., Sakai, T., Mizoguchi, K., Tajima, Y., & Imai, M. (2010). *Odor generation alarm and method for informing unusual situation*. U. S. Patent Application 2010/0308995. Washington, DC: US Patent Office.

Haque, U. (2004). *Scents of space: An interactive smell system. ACM SIGGRAPH 2004 Sketches*. New York, NY: ACM Press.

Heilig, M. L. (1962). *Sensorama simulator*. U. S. Patent 3,050,870. Washington, DC: US Patent Office.

Honda, K. (1994). *The world of ultrasound*. Tokyo, Japan: NHK Publishing Co., Ltd.

Improbable Research. (2011). *Winners of the Ig Nobel prize*. Retrieved February 10, 2012 from http://www.improbable.com/ig/winners/

Japan Perfumery and Flavoring Association. (2001). *Encyclopedia of scent*. Tokyo, Japan: Asakura Publishing Co., Ltd.

Kadowaki, A., Sato, J., Bannai, Y., & Okada, K. (2007). Presentation technique of scent to avoid olfactory adaptation. In *Proceedings of 17th International Conference on Artificial Reality and Telexistence*, (pp. 97–104). IEEE.

Kaye, J. N. (2001). *Symbolic olfactory display*. (Master's Thesis). Massachusetts Institute of Technology. Cambridge, MA.

Kaye, J. N. (2004). Making scents. *Interactions (New York, N.Y.)*, *11*(1), 48–61. doi:10.1145/962342.964333

Kim, D. H., & Ando, H. (2010). Development of directional olfactory display. In *Proceedings of the 9th ACM SIGGRAPH Conference on Virtual-Reality Continuum and its Applications in Industry (VRCAI 2010)*, (pp. 143–144). ACM Press.

Kim, D. H., Cho, Y. H., Nishimoto, K., Kawakami, Y., Kunifuji, S., & Ando, H. (2009). Development of aroma-card based soundless olfactory display. In *Proceedings of 16th IEEE International Conference on Electronics, Circuits, and Systems (ICECS) 2009*, (pp. 703–706). IEEE Press.

Lorig, T. S., Elmes, D. G., Zald, D. H., & Pardo, J. V. (1999). A computer-controlled olfactometer for fMRI and electrophysiological studies of olfaction. *Behavior Research Methods*, *31*(2), 370–375.

Matsukura, H., Nihei, T., & Ishida, H. (2011). Multi-sensorial field display: Presenting spatial distribution of airflow and odor. [IEEE Press.]. *Proceedings of IEEE Virtual Reality*, *2011*, 119–122.

Matsukura, H., Ohno, A., & Ishida, H. (2010). Fluid dynamic considerations for realistic odor presentation using olfactory display. *Presence (Cambridge, Mass.)*, *19*(6), 513–526. doi:10.1162/pres_a_00019

McCarthy, R. E. (1986). *Scent-emitting systems*. U. S. Patent 4,603,030. Washington, DC: US Patent Office.

Messager, J., & Takagi, S. (2003). The diffusion of fragrances in a multimedia environment. *Aroma Research*, *14*, 69–73.

Mochizuki, A., Amada, T., Sawa, S., Takeda, T., Motoyashiki, S., & Kohyama, K. … Chihara, K. (2004). Fragra: A visual-olfactory VR game. In *ACM SIGGRAPH 2004 Sketches*. New York, NY: ACM Press.

Morie, J. F., Iyer, K., Valanejad, K., Sadek, R., Miraglia, D., & Milam, D. … Leshin, J. (2003). Sensory design for virtual environments. In *ACM SIGGRAPH 2003 Sketches*. New York, NY: ACM Press.

Murai, K., Serizawa, T., & Yanagida, Y. (2011). Localized scent presentation to a walking person by using scent projectors. In *Proceedings of the First International Symposium on Virtual Reality Innovation (ISVRI) 2011*, (pp. 67–70). Singapore, Singapore: ISVRI.

Nakaizumi, F., Yanagida, Y., Noma, H., & Hosaka, K. (2006). SpotScents: A novel method of natural scent delivery using multiple scent projectors. [Alexandria, VA: IEEE Press.]. *Proceedings of IEEE Virtual Reality, 2006*, 213–218.

Nakamoto, T. (Ed.). (2008). *Olfactory display (multimedia tool for presenting scents)*. Tokyo, Japan: Fragrance Journal Ltd.

Nakamoto, T., & Minh, H. P. D. (2007). Improvement of olfactory display using solenoid valves. [Charlotte, NC: IEEE Press.]. *Proceedings of IEEE Virtual Reality, 2007*, 179–186.

Nakamoto, T., Otaguro, S., Kinoshita, M., Nagahama, M., Ohinishi, K., & Ishida, T. (2008). Cooking up an interactive olfactory game display. *IEEE Computer Graphics and Applications, 28*(1), 75–78. doi:10.1109/MCG.2008.3

Nakazawa, C. (1998). *Japanese unexamined patent application publication H10-182398*. Tokyo, Japan: Patent Office.

Niimura, Y., & Nei, M. (2003). Evolution of olfactory receptor genes in the human genome. *Proceedings of the National Academy of Sciences of the United States of America, 100*(21), 12235–12240. doi:10.1073/pnas.1635157100

Osmooze, S. A. (2012). *P@D diffusers*. Retrieved March 23, 2012, from http://www.osmooze.com/

Pybus, D. (2001). *Kodo: The way of incense*. Tokyo, Japan: Tuttle Publishing.

Sakaino, A. (2008). The concept of sensitivity communication using aroma and a plan of demonstration experiment: The digital signage with fragrance communication. *Technical Report of the Institute of Electronics. Information and Communication Engineers, 108*(291), 53–57.

Takagi, S. F. (1987). A standardized olfactometer in Japan. *Annals of the New York Academy of Sciences, 510*, 113–118. doi:10.1111/j.1749-6632.1987.tb43476.x

Toda, K. (1994). *Japanese unexamined patent application publication H6-7721*. Tokyo, Japan: Patent Office.

Tomono, A. (2008). *Gas discharger*. PCT Application, WO/2008/072744. Retrieved from http://patentscope.wipo.int/search/en/WO2008072744

Tomono, A., Kanda, K., & Otake, S. (2008). Effect that smell presentation has on an individual in regards to eye catching and memory. *IEEJ Transactions on Sensors and Micromachines, 128*(12), 478–486. doi:10.1541/ieejsmas.128.478

Tomono, A., & Uehara, A. (2005). *Japanese unexamined patent application publication 2005-296540*. Tokyo, Japan: Patent Office.

Tomono, A., & Uehara, A. (2006a). *Scent generator and scent generation device*. Japanese Patent Number 3874715. Tokyo, Japan: Patent Office.

Tomono, A., & Uehara, A. (2006b). *Mist generator and mist emission rendering apparatus*. PCT Application, WO/2006/095816. Retrieved from http://patentscope.wipo.int/search/en/WO2006095816

Touhara, K., Sengoku, S., Inaki, K., Tsuboi, A., Hirono, J., & Sato, T. ... Haga, T. (1999). Functional identification and reconstitution of an odorant receptor in single olfactory neurons. *Proceeding of the National Academy of Sciences, 96*(7), 4040–4045.

Tsuji, M., Takagi, S., Hirano, K., & Yoshihara, M. (2004). A new experiment in practical use of scent web. *Aroma Research, 20,* 34–39.

Watkins, C. J. (2002). *Methods and apparatus for localized delivery of scented aerosols.* U. S. Patent 6,357,726. Washington, DC: US Patent Office.

Yamada, T., Yokoyama, S., Tanikawa, T., Hirota, K., & Hirose, M. (2006). Wearable olfactory display: Using odor in outdoor environment. [Alexandria, VA: IEEE Press.]. *Proceedings of IEEE Virtual Reality, 2006,* 205–212.

Yamanaka, T., Matsumoto, R., & Nakamoto, T. (2002). Study of odor blender using solenoid valves controlled by delta-sigma modulation method for odor recorder. *Sensors and Actuators. B, Chemical, 87,* 457–463. doi:10.1016/S0925-4005(02)00300-3

Yanagida, Y., Kawato, S., Noma, H., Tomono, A., & Tetsutani, N. (2004). Projection-based olfactory display with nose tracking. [Chicago, IL: IEEE Press.]. *Proceedings of IEEE Virtual Reality, 2004,* 43–50.

Yanagida, Y., Noma, H., Tetsutani, N., & Tomono, A. (2003). An unencumbering, localized olfactory display. In *ACM CHI 2003 Extended Abstracts* (pp. 988–989). New York, NY: ACM Press.

KEY TERMS AND DEFINITIONS

Atomizer: Device that makes essential oil the minute particles and diffuses.

Piezoelectric Element: Ferroelectric element that does expansion and contraction transformation when voltage is added.

Ultrasonic: Cyclic sound pressure with a frequency greater than the upper limit (approximately 20,000 hertz) of human hearing.

Solenoid-Controlled Valve: Valve that opens and shuts with electromagnet.

Chapter 4
Interaction of Olfaction with Vision or Other Senses using Olfactory Display

Tomohiro Tanikawa
University of Tokyo, Japan

Michitaka Hirose
University of Tokyo, Japan

ABSTRACT

In this chapter, the authors introduce interaction of olfaction with other senses by showing two different types of case studies based on this interaction. Olfactory sensation is based on chemical signals whereas the visual sensation and auditory sensation are based on physical signals. By using this cross-modal effect between olfaction and vision, olfactory display can present various "pseudo olfactory experiences." One can produce an olfactory sensation different from the presented smell. In addition, by using cross-modal effect among olfaction, gustation, and vision, one can present various "pseudo gustatory experiences" with the same food via visual-olfactory displays. By utilizing the interaction of olfaction with other senses, it is possible to augment the capability of olfactory displays and achieve a high quality olfaction and gustation experience.

INTRODUCTION

Olfactory sensation is based on chemical signal, such as smell molecules, whereas the visual sensation and auditory sensation are based on physical signal, such as light, air vibration. Basic principle of information processing on olfactory sense has not yet been clarified. Therefore, most olfac-

tory displays which exist now have very limited functions. For example, most of the displays can only present the set of scents which was prepared beforehand because a set of "primary odors" has not been found. In order to implement olfactory displays for practical use, we have to improve them to present much more smells. For this purpose, we may need to find out a novel technology to synthesize wide range of smells from few element odors.

DOI: 10.4018/978-1-4666-2521-1.ch004

Copyright © 2013, IGI Global. Copying or distributing in print or electronic forms without written permission of IGI Global is prohibited.

By using instability and variability of olfaction, there would be a possibility that we can make such a technology. If we are able to present user smell other than the actual, we may be able to define several "element" odors or "primary odors," and we can generate various olfactory experiences by them.

Also, we may think about inter-sensory instability. For example, gustatory sensation has similar instability and variability with olfaction. Thus, we can change user's perceived taste of a food substance by changing appearance and scent with augmented reality technology.

In this chapter, the authors want to introduce display technology based on this kind of principle, that is, cross-sensory effect. This technology consists of very important part of "next generation VR technology."

OLFACTORY AND GUSTATORY DISPLAYS

Both olfactory and gustatory senses have instability different from the other senses. The new concept mentioned above can be applicable when implementing olfactory and gustatory displays.

Among five senses, it is said that olfaction activates our emotion most vividly. Therefore, it would be effective to use olfactory system as communication media. Olfaction is more unstable and variable than vision and audition. It is known that we can identify scents of daily materials only fifty percent of the time. For example, only half can answer "apple" when they sniff apples (Cain, 1979; Sugiyama, Kanamura, & Kikuchi, 2006).

Although olfactory displays are uncommon, many researchers are working to develop ways to display scents (e.g., Nakamoto & Minh, 2007; Yamada, Yokoyama, Tanikawa, Hirota, & Hirose, 2006; Nakaizumi, Yanagida, Noma, & Hosaka, 2006; Sato, Ohtsu, Bannai, & Okada, 2008). Moreover, some olfactory displays using vaporizers have already been commercialized (e.g.,

ScentAir; AromaJet; Trisenx; Scentcommunication; Osmooze; air aroma; Air/Q Whole Room Air Freshener). These display systems are used for appreciations with combination of other sensory displays (Heilig, 1992; Zybura & Eskeland, 1999; Mochizuki, Amada, Sawa, Takeda, Motoyashiki, Kohyama, ... Chihara, 2004). For example, "Let's cook curry" developed by Nakamoto, Otaguro, Kinoshita, Nagahama, Ohinishi, and Ishida (2008) is an olfactory display with interactive aroma contents, "a cooking game with smells." It presents smells of curry, meat, onion and so on by player's control. "Wearable olfactory display" developed by Yamada, Yokoyama, Tanikawa, Hirota, and Hirose (2006) generates a olfactory field by changing concentration of some kinds of aroma chemicals using position information.

However, both of them produced only combination of prepared element odors, they are, selected aroma chemicals, in each preceding studies. It is still difficult to generate infinite numbers of smells for current olfactory displays.

A gustatory display would be one of the last frontiers in the area of computer human interaction. Even comparing with the olfactory displays, very few studies are conducted regarding as this area.

Beidler (1971) provided a compendium of knowledge of the basis for the sense of taste as a pioneering work. More recently, Maynes-Aminzade offered a suggestion for "edible user interfaces" (Maynes-Aminzade, 2005) and developed some low-resolution gustatory displays. Iwata et al. have developed the "Food Simulator" (Iwata, Yano, Uemura, & Moriya, 2004) by integrating an interface that displays the biting force, auditory information, and the chemical sensation of taste. In the "Food Simulator," chemical sensation of taste was displayed by releasing prepared taste components using a micro injector. However, these studies have not focused on presenting various synthesized tastes.

There are several reasons why gustatory displays which can synthesize various tastes are so few. One of the most serious factor is that its basic mechanisms have not yet been fully understood. Another is that taste is largely affected by other factors such as vision, olfaction, thermal sensation, and memory. Thus, the complexity of the cognitive mechanisms underlying gustatory sensation makes it very difficult to develop a gustatory display.

However, our hypothesis is that the complexity of the gustatory system can be rather helpful for the realization of a pseudo-gustatory display, because we may use this cross-modal effect as a basic principle.

In this chapter, the authors want to stress that the cross-modal effect is very important principle to develop both olfactory and gustatory displays.

Conventionally, "perception" has been considered as a modular function. It has long been thought that different sensory modalities operate independently of each other. However, recent behavioral and brain imaging studies are changing this view by suggesting that cross-modal interactions have an important role in our perception (Shimojo, & Shams, 2001). In cross-modal effects, the perception of a sensation through one sense is changed by other stimuli that are simultaneously received through other senses. Indeed, many psychophysical studies have shown that the perception of taste is influenced by visual cues, auditory cues, smell, the trigeminal system, and touch. By using such effects, we may induce people to experience different flavors when they taste the same chemical substance.

VISUAL-OLFACTORY INTERACTIONS

The authors want to start the discussion with the instability and variability of olfaction. As mentioned before, in comparison with vision and audition, olfaction has more ambiguity. For example, it is very difficult for us to distinguish the name of flowers or foods only by scents, unlike by visual images. (Sugiyama, Kanamura, & Kikuchi, 2006) Thus, it is often said that olfaction is easily af-

Figure 1. Olfactory display is largely affected by visual display

fected by knowledge of smell and other sensation (Herz & Clef, 2001; Gottfried & Dolan, 2003). It means that it is very difficult to discuss olfactory display by itself, or independent to other senses. On the contrary, as shown in Figure 1, effective use of the cue of other sensation will give us better results (e.g., Zellner & Kautz, 1990; Grigor, Toller, Behan, & Richardson, 1999; Sakai, Imada, Saito, Kobayakawa, & Deguchi, 2005).

First, we want to introduce the methodology to generate various "pseudo olfactory experience" by using the cross modal effect between vision and olfaction. When the visual stimulus which contradicts the presented olfactory stimulus is presented, the visual stimulus influences olfaction (see Figure 1). We define this cross modal effect between vision and olfaction as "drawing effect" on olfaction by vision.

Cross-Modal Interactions between Vision and Olfaction

To demonstrate this drawing effect, Nambu, Narumi, Nishimura, Tanikawa, and Hirose (2008) implemented experimental installation called "nioi cafe" that enables to present pictures and scent sources at the same time (see Figure 2[a]).

Figure 2. experimental installation using cross-modal interactions between vision and olfaction (a) "Nioi-Café": Installation that uses visual-olfaction cross modal effect (b) "Flavor of Color": conflicts between scent and color of fruit syrups(c) Results of "Flavor of Color": the olfactory distance of the four scents: lemon, melon, strawberry, and vanilla. In case of "color:yellow/scent:lemon," "color:green/scent:melon," "color:red/scent:berry," there is no conflict between presented color and scent. Otherwise, there is conflict.

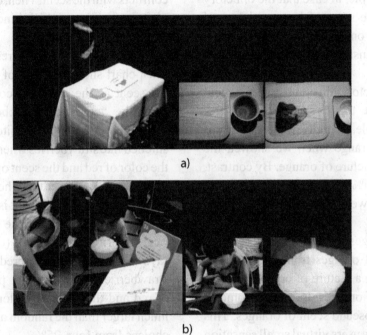

a)

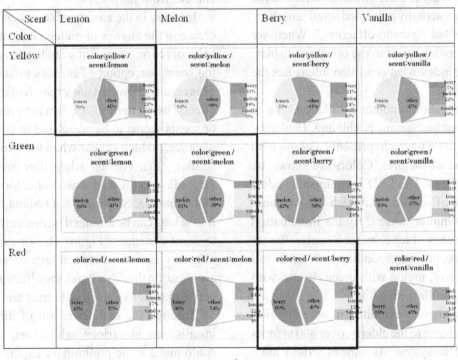

b)

Scent / Color	Lemon	Melon	Berry	Vanilla
Yellow	color:yellow / scent:lemon	color:yellow / scent:melon	color:yellow / scent:berry	color:yellow / scent:vanilla
Green	color:green / scent:lemon	color:green / scent:melon	color:green / scent:berry	color:green / scent:vanilla
Red	color:red / scent:lemon	color:red / scent:melon	color:red / scent:berry	color:red / scent:vanilla

c)

"Nioi" is a Japanese word meaning "scent." The system consists of an olfactory display, a projector and an empty dish. This system presents scents with pictures. In some case, scents and pictures have no conflicts, but the other case they do have conflicts. For example, in case that the olfactory display presents the scent of lemon, picture of apples is projected onto the dish, there are conflicts. Point of this installation is how people feel in such a situation.

As a result, olfactory illusion between a scent and a picture close to the scent occurred frequently. For example, as many as 50% of examinees smelled as orange when we showed the scent of tea and a picture of orange. By contrast, as few as about 15% of examinees smelled as apple when we showed the scent of coffee and a picture of an apple.

This result suggests the possibility of producing the scent of oranges from the aroma of apples, by showing a picture of oranges. In this case, the picture of oranges draws the aroma of apples toward the pseudo scent of oranges. This drawing effect gives users virtual smell sensation different from actually presented smell sensation, which is called "pseudo-olfaction." When we apply the drawing effect to the olfactory display, we need the index what condition intensifies the drawing effect.

Figure 2(b) shows another installation, "flavor of color" (Nambu, Narumi, Nishimura, Tanikawa, & Hirose, 2008) which presents colors with scent instead of pictures. Colors are shown by a full-color LED. The LED is equipped inside a food sample of shaved ice, which is a Japanese traditional summer dessert. By the illumination of LED, the shaved ice changes its color. We selected four scents corresponding with color: red with strawberry, melon with green, lemon with yellow and vanilla with white.

This system was exhibited in an exhibition and from children to the elderly, over 800 visitors experienced the system. As same as "Nioi-Café," some combinations have conflict between color and scent. This system presented a scent from the four scents—strawberry, melon, lemon, and vanilla—with a color from the four colors—red, green, yellow, and white. The color selected sometimes corresponds to the scent selected, otherwise conflicts with the scent. Then, demonstrator asked visitors to answer which kind of scent they felt among the four scents.

Figure 2(c) shows the result by pie charts. Each chart shows the rate of visitors answering the scent as the flavor of color presented. For example, "color:red/scent:berry (non-conflict case)" chart says 60% of visitors answered that it smelled like strawberries when they are presented the color of red and the scent of strawberries. This value was 10% larger than the identification rate of daily smells, 50%, thus it is suggested that the color of red emphasizes the scent of strawberries. "color:red/scent:melon (conflict case)" chart says 46% of visitors answered that it smelled like strawberries when they are presented the color of red and the scent of melons. This value was much larger than the random answering rate from choices from four, 25%.

Increase in the answer of strawberries and decrease in the answer of melons indicates that the color of red, metaphor of strawberries can change the scent perception of melons to strawberries. This results show that the strength of the drawing effect. The strength of the effect between two kinds of scents seems to be correlated to an "olfactory distance," which is near when the two scents are similar, otherwise far when they are different. According to the term-based olfactory map (Ito, Doi, Kameda, Shimoda, & Osajima, 1991), the four scents can be arranged on one axis according to scent distances (Figure 4). For example, the olfactory distance between lemons and melons are close, on the other hand, the olfactory distance between lemons and strawberries are far.

Through the demonstration of these artistic installations in various exhibitions, the authors could make some preliminary experiments concerning to olfactory-visual cross-sensory effect.

However, this is only a qualitative result. In order to make use of this effect in a realistic engineering system, more qualitative result will be required.

Visual-Olfactory Display using Cross-Modal Interactions

To realize visual-olfactory displays using the drawing effect, it is important to evaluate relationship between the strength of the drawing effect and the kind of the presented scent. Based on the preliminary implementations, it is expected that the drawing effect is generated easily between smells with high degree of similarity of the scent, while the drawing effect is not generated easily between scents with low degree of similarity of the scent. Then, we propose to use the degree of similarity of the smell, or the distance between scents, as an index in the drawing effect to the smell.

The distance between two scents is determined as an "olfactory distance" which is near when the two scents are similar, and far when they are different. The method of evaluating the degree of similarity of the scent includes a method using similarity according to the language and similarity of the chemical characteristics (Bensafi & Rouby, 2007), and Ito, Doi, Kameda, Shimoda, and Osajima (1991) proposed the olfactory map which is determined based on characterization of odor-descriptive terms.

Currently there is no fundamental research on the degree of similarity of the scent based on human's olfactory sensation. Then, we tried to construct a new olfactory map based on smell evaluation, which is more approximate to olfactory sensation than past olfactory maps.

The distance between scents can be evaluated more accurately and easily than before by making the olfactory map based on olfaction. Then, it becomes possible to operate the drawing effect to olfaction by vision more efficiently if we can prove that the closer the content of the olfactory source and the content of the picture aimed at, the stronger the drawing effect occurs.

It is difficult to take out a common part of multiple people's smell senses and to make it into the common map because olfaction has more individual variations than other senses (Lawless, 1989). Two kinds of approaches are thought for making an olfactory map. The first approach is making a personal olfactory map. It is required to measure distance, to make the map, and to prepare appropriate aromas for each user but the olfactory display completely suitable for each user can be achieved. The second approach is evaluating the distance between scents by many people, extracting a common part of olfaction not influenced to the individual variation, and making the map. The advantage of second approach is to be able to obtain the data of the distance between smells in which one map has generality. Therefore, when the individual variation of the result is not extremely large, it can be said that it is more advantageous for the development of an olfactory display suitable for practical use to use the approach of this common olfactory map.

Nambu, Narumi, Nishimura, Tanikawa, and Hirose (2010) constructed the olfactory map based on second approach. The procedure of constructing an olfactory map is as follows. First, they prepared 18-kinds of fruit flavored aroma chemicals. They confined the kinds of aroma chemicals among fruit flavors because we can compare the similarity between two aromas in the same category (fruits, flowers, dishes, etc.) easily than between two aromas in different categories. Then, they soaked test papers into each aroma chemicals and used them as smell samples. Seven subjects evaluated the degree of similarity of two smell samples by five stages from among them. For example, if a subject feels that the scent of oranges and the scent of melons are very similar, the similarity is "4." Then, they calculated smell distance between two smell samples as "5 minus similarity." Correspondence table between the similarity and the distance is illustrated in Table 1. This trial was done to the combination of all of the 18-kinds smell samples.

Table 1. Similarity and olfactory distance

Similarity		Distance
1	Different	4
2	less similar	3
3	fairly similar	2
4	very similar	1
5	hard to tell apart	0

The olfactory map can be constructed as an average subjects' result by mapping each aroma chemicals with keeping correlation by Isometric Multidimensional Scaling (isoMDS) (Kruskal, 1964). The relation of the distance of the 18-kinds of smell samples is shown as 18 dimensions square matrix. They analyzed the distance matrix by isoMDS and mapped the result into a two dimension olfactory map. Because it is important to evaluate the distance between scents by many people and extracting a common part of olfaction not influenced to the individual variation and making the map. The generated olfactory map makes it possible to categorize aroma chemicals based on each rough character of the smell like citrus fruits and the apples, etc. There is a possibility to implement the olfactory display with which small number of representative aroma chemicals can present various smells by selecting representative aromas from each category. Figure 3 shows the generated olfactory map based on this procedure.

If we prove that "the more similar the content of picture and the content of aroma chemicals are, the more the drawing effect is likely to happen," we can implement a brand-new olfactory display which can render more kinds and range of smells than the number and range of a few of prepared aroma chemicals.

Hardware of visual-olfactory display consists of the scent generator, the controller, the showing interface and PC monitor. The scent generator has four air pumps. Each pump is connected to a scent filter filled with aroma chemicals. The controller drives the air pumps in the scent generator accord-

ing to the command from PC. The scent filters add scents to air from the pumps and then the showing interface ejects air nearby user's nose.

The visual-olfactory display showed them a picture from 18-kind of pictures of fruits and an aroma from 4-kind of element aromas. The pictures of fruits correspond to 18 aroma flavors used in construction of the olfactory map one by one. Then, experimenters asked subjects, "What kind of smell you feel by sniffing the olfactory display?" As shown in Figure 4, the experiment was conducted in a well-ventilated large room to avoid mixing different aromas and olfactory adaptation.

The four kinds of element aromas were selected from 18-kinds of fruit used in construction of the olfactory map. First, according to limitation of the olfactory display, the 18-kinds of aromas should be categorized into four groups by features of scents as shown in Figure 3. Then one scent was selected from each group (apple, peach, lemon, lychee) so as to minimize the distance between a key aroma and each another aroma in the same category as the key aroma. Each picture was shown with the nearest key aroma.

If subjects answer that they feel the smell correspondent to the shown picture when the content of the picture and the content of the aroma are different, the drawing effect is considered to occur. Thus, we used the rate of answering the smell of the shown picture as an index of the drawing effect.

In order to prove "the more similar the content of picture and the content of aroma chemicals are, the more the drawing effect is likely to happen," we also conducted another experiment to evaluate the drawing effect between the picture and another aroma, which is not closest to the content of picture. We asked subjects to answer what smell they felt when we showed them a picture and the aroma second closest to the picture. The trials were done for 9-kinds of picture. We compared the drawing effect between trials using the closest aroma and trials using the second closest aroma.

Figure 3. Generated olfactory map by mapping and categorizing aroma camicals on two dimensional map

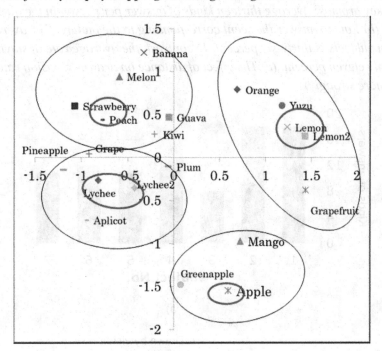

Each subject answered the scent of the picture in an average of 13 of 27 trials (36%) per person showing a picture and an aroma. This is statistically higher than the rate to answer the scent of the aroma, 11%. (p < 0.01) The number of description of answer for 27 trials per person was as many as an average of 13 kinds although we used only four kinds of aromas (Figure 5[a, b]). Moreover, we compared the rate to answer that the smell is like the content of the picture by olfactory distance on the map. The rate was 44%

when the picture and the aroma were close, while 27% when the picture and the aroma were distant. It means the close pair helped subjects to answer the smell influenced by the picture statistically significantly (p < 0.01) (Figure 5[c]).

There were much more answers that it smelled corresponding to the destined image than the answer that it smelled corresponding to the aroma chemical actually presented. Besides, the kind of a free answer included many kinds of smells. These results confirmed that we can generate

Figure 4. Prototype system of visual-olfactory display

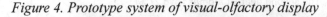

Figure 5. The experimental results of visual-olfactory display using cross-modal interactions (a) Kinds of answers from 4 key aromas: Average thirteen kinds of answer per person in the question "What kind of smell you felt?" (b) Rate to answer the scent corresponding to the picture: The average of drawn-by-vision rate of seven subjects is thirty-six percent. In contrast, the average rate of staying in the scent of the key aroma is only eleven percent. (c) The effect of distance on drawn-by-vision rate: Nearer aromas drawn by picture more strongly)

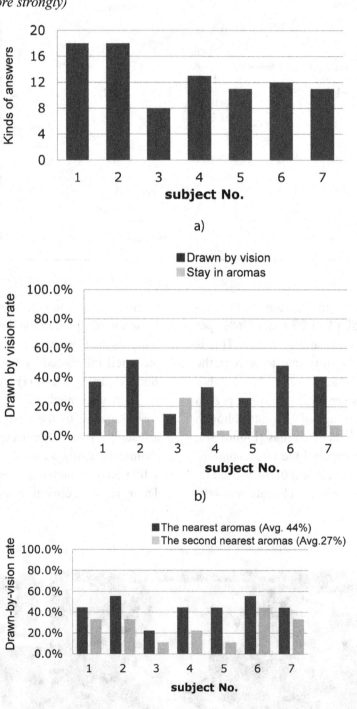

several times more kinds of pseudo smells than the number of prepared aroma chemicals.

In addition, the fact that a similar set of a picture and an aroma increases the rate of the drawing effect of the picture to the aroma proved the hypothesis that the closer the picture and the aroma on the olfactory map were, the stronger the drawing effect was. As well as the smell distance, positional relationship of smells in the map is available for a criterion of selecting element odors.

It proved to be possible to construct the olfactory map based on olfactory sensation according to the sensory evaluation of the smell similarity of two or more people. The common olfactory map suitable for people with various olfactory sensation patterns can be used as well as the language based olfactory map. Using the common olfactory map, we achieved an olfactory display presenting various smells virtually from a few aroma chemicals. It becomes possible to achieve olfactory virtual reality with a simpler system by reducing the number of aroma sources. Moreover, it is thought to be possible to make olfactory maps among other kinds of smells like flowers or dishes as far as the smells have visual cues in order for the olfactory cue.

OLFACTORY-GUSTATORY INTERACTIONS

Cross-Modal Interactions Underlying the Perception of Flavor

Taste is one of the traditional five senses. It refers to the ability to detect the flavor of substances such as food, certain minerals, and poisons. Humans receive gustatory input through sensory organs called taste buds concentrated on the upper surface of the tongue. According to physiological definitions, taste has the status of a minor sense modality, as a channel comprising only a limited number of sensations: sweetness, sourness, bitterness, saltiness, and umami (Delwiche, 2004).

Taste, as perceived by the tongue, can be measured using a biological membrane sensor that investigates the content of each basic taste (Toko, et al., 1994). However, it is difficult to synthesize a specific taste on demand by combining basic tastes. This is because the sense of taste is a multimodal sensation and is not determined solely by a combination of basic tastes.

The term "taste" signifies a perceptual experience that involves the integration of various sensations. When we use the common word "flavor" in place of taste, we again refer to what is a quite multi-faceted sensation. In fact, the International Standards Organization has defined flavor as a complex combination of olfactory, gustatory, and trigeminal sensations perceived during tasting (Chandrashekar, Hoon, Ryba, & Zuker, 2006). Auvray et al. reviewed the literature on multisensory interactions underlying the perception of flavor; they summarized their review by stating that flavor is not defined as a separate sensory modality but as a perceptual modality that is unified by the act of eating, and should be used as a term to describe the combination of taste, smell, touch, visual cues, auditory cues, and the trigeminal system (Auvray & Spence, 2008). These definitions suggest that it is possible to change the flavor that people experience from foods by changing the feedback they receive through modalities other than the sense of taste. Although it is difficult to present various tastes through a change in chemical ingredients, it is possible to vary other sensory information that people experience when eating without changing the chemical ingredients. In this way, people might be induced to experience various flavors.

Among the other senses, the sense of smell is most closely related to our perception of taste. This relationship between gustatory and olfactory sensations is commonly known, as is illustrated by the fact that we pinch our nostrils when eating food that we find displeasing (Ross, 2001). Indeed, it has been reported that most of what people commonly think of as the taste of food actually originates from the nose (Rozin, 1982).

Conversely, another set of studies on taste enhancement has provided strong support for the ability of odors to modify taste qualities (Stevenson, Prescott, & Boakes, 1999). These studies indicate the possibility of changing the flavor that people experience from foods by changing the scent.

Conversely, under many conditions, it is well known that humans have a robust tendency to rely upon vision more than other senses. Several studies have explored the effect of visual stimuli on our perception of flavor. For instance, the intensities of taste and flavor have been shown to increase as the color level in a solution increases (Zampini, Wantling, Phillips, & Spence, 2008). However, according to Spence et al., the empirical evidence regarding the role that food coloring plays in the perception of the intensity of a particular flavor or taste to which it is attributed (as reported by many researchers over the last 50 years) is rather ambiguous, although food coloring most certainly influences peoples' flavor identification responses (Spence, Levitan, Shankar, & Zampini, 2010). Nonetheless, their survey suggests the possibility of changing flavor identification by changing the appearance of food.

Gustatory Display Based on Edible Marker and Cross-Modal Interaction

Therefore, one gustatory display research focuses on the technological application of the appearance and scent of food and its effects on flavor perception. Narumi, Nishizaka, Kajinami, Tanikawa, and Hirose (2011) propose a method to change the perceived taste of a food by changing its appearance and scent (Figure 6). In this study, they use cookies as an example. They chose cookies because cookies have a wide variety of appearances, scents, and tastes, while being similar in texture and shape. Thus, they have developed a system to overlay the appearance and scent of a flavored cookie on a plain cookie to enable users to experience eating a flavored cookie while just eating a plain cookie.

The system configuration of "MetaCookie+" is shown in Figure 6. The Cookie Detection unit based on the Edible Marker system can obtain the 6 Degrees Of Freedom (6DOF) coordinate of the cookie and the distance between the cookie and the camera. In the Cookie Detection phase, two cameras are used in parallel. We used two cameras (angle of view: 76°) in this implementation. The layout of the cameras, a Head-Mounted Display (HMD). The range of the cameras is also illustrated in this figure. The two cameras are positioned to eliminate blind spots between the user's hands and mouth, in order to track the cookie from the time at which a user holds it to the time at which s/he puts it in her/his mouth.

They use an air-pump-type head-mounted olfactory display (Figure 6) to produce the scent of the selected cookie. The olfactory display comprises eight air pumps, a controller, and scented filters. One is to send fresh air and seven pumps are to send scented air. Each pump for scented air is connected to a scent filter filled with aromatic chemicals. It can eject fresh air and seven types of scented air. The scent filters add scents to air from the pumps, and the scented air is ejected near the user's nose. The strength of these scents can be adjusted to 127 different levels. By mixing fresh air and scented air, the olfactory display generates an odor in arbitrary level with same air volume. Users are unable to feel any change in air volume when the strength of the generated odor changes.

According to the position of the pattern-printed plain cookie, the controller drives the air pumps. Nearer the marked cookie from the user's nose, stronger scent ejects from the olfactory display. Response time for generating arbitrary odor is less than 50 ms. It is quick enough to let users experience the change of smell in synchronization with the change of visual information.

In order to evaluate the effectiveness of the proposed method for inducing people to experience various flavors, Narumi et al. conducted an explor-

Figure 6. "MetaCookie+" system (a) Layout of "MetaCookie+" system: two cameras and air-pump type head-mounted olfactory display (b) Participants eating cookies using "MetaCookie+" system

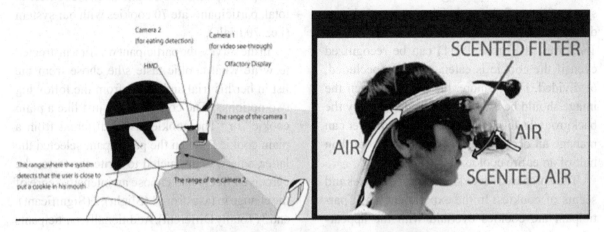

a)

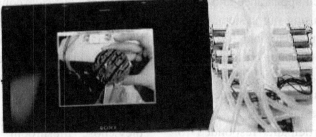

b)

atory study to investigate how people experience flavor in a cookie by using the "MetaCookie+" system. Figure 7 shows that the proposed object-detection system (Narumi, Kajinami, Nishizaka, Tanikawa, & Hirose, 2011) can be recognized even if the cookie is eaten, partially occluded, or divided. Furthermore, the area on which the image should be overlaid can be detected by the background subtraction method. The marker can manage an occlusion/division that is more than half of an entire cookie.

They prepared seven kinds of appearances and scents of cookies. In the experiment, each participant ate cookies overlaid with the appearances and scents of cookies prepared by "Meta-Cookie+" system and evaluated their tastes. (Figure 7) The combinations of scent and appearance, which were used in the exploratory study for representing flavored cookies, are illustrated in Figure 7. Six images of a chocolate cookie, an almond cookie, a tea cookie, a strawberry cookie, a maple cookie, and a lemon cookie, were captured and overlaid onto real cookies.

The study was conducted with 44 participants who had never received training in the anatomy of tastes. When they tested our system, we did not inform the participants beforehand that our system aimed to change perceived taste before they finished the experience.

First, the participant chose one taste from "chocolate," "almond," "tea," "strawberry," "lemon," "maple," and "mushroom" from a text-only list. After a taste was chosen by a participant, we overlaid the prepared appearance and scent of the selected cookie using our system. Next, the participant was instructed to hold the cookie, observe the overlaid appearance on the cookie, move it to her/his mouth, and eat it. After the trial, the participant was instructed to eat another plain cookie without our system.

After all trials, participants responded to surveys on the flavor they experienced for each cookie. To prevent subjects from knowing too much about the purpose of the experiment, they were given their survey form after all of their trials. Each participant selected one or two cookies. In total, participants ate 70 cookies with our system (i.e., 70 trials).

In the survey, the participant was first instructed to write what cookie taste s/he chose from the list in her/his trial and select from the following two options: "The cookie tasted just like a plain cookie" or "The cookie tasted different from a plain cookie." When the participant selected the latter, s/he was instructed to write the taste s/he perceived freely and choose an intensity score of the change in taste from 1 (Slight), 2 (Significant), and 3 (Totally Different). Additionally, participants were freely allowed to write some comments. Figure 6(a) illustrates participants eating cookies using "Meta Cookie+" system.

As shown in Figure 8(a), on 79.3% of the trials, the participants experienced a change in taste when they ate the simulated commercially available cookies with augmented appearance and scent. Moreover, on 72.6% of the trials, the participants identified the taste of the augmented cookie as the taste of the selected cookie, i.e., a participant tasted a chocolate cookie when s/he chose "chocolate" from the text-only list. This result suggests that our system can change a perceived taste and enable users to experience various tastes from a plain cookie by simulating other types of commercially available cookies.

Many participants commented that they were surprised to experience the significant change in the cookie's taste. Some participants expressed regret that our system could not change the texture of a plain cookie. On the other hand, on 85.7% of the trials, the participants experienced a change in the cookie's taste in case of representing an unfamiliar cookie. However, in only 42.9% of the trials did the participants identify the taste of the augmented cookie as the taste of mushroom when they chose "mushroom" from the text-only list. Many participants commented that they could not identify the taste of the cookie overlaid with the appearance and scent of a mushroom.

Figure 7. The appearances and scents of cookies presented by "MetaCookie+" system (a) Combination of food flavors and appearances (b) Edible Marker printed cookie: The Edible Marker can recognize the bitten/divided marker shown in the middle/bottom panels of the figure. Moreover, the remaining area can be detected to allow realistic superimposition.

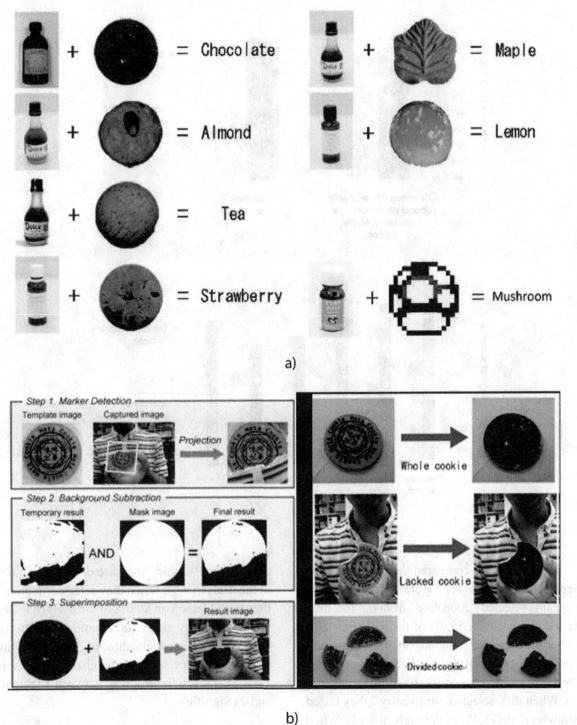

a)

b)

Figure 8. Results of exploratory study to investigate how people experience flavor in a cookie by using the "MetaCookie+" system (a) Comparison of the ratio of subjects who experienced the other/selected taste from plain cookie between emulation of commercial cookie and unfamiliar cookie (b) Percentage of subjects who experienced a change in taste from a plain cookie for each flavor

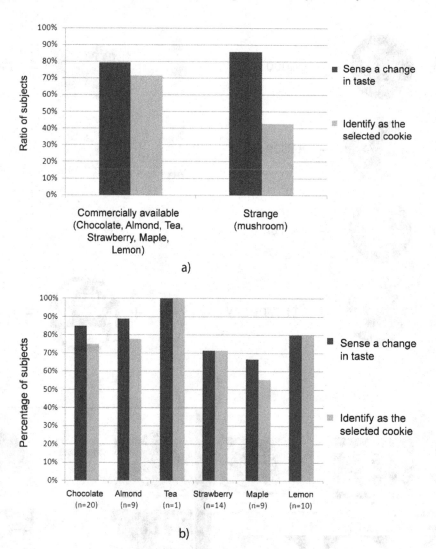

a)

b)

In addition, we compared the results of each represented flavor. (see Figure 8[b]) When participants selected "chocolate" from the list, they tasted chocolate on 75.0% of the trials (n = 20). When they selected "almond," they tasted almond on 77.8% of the trials (n = 9). When they selected "tea," they tasted tea on 100.0% of the trials (n = 1). When they selected "strawberry," they tasted strawberry on 71.4% of the trials (n = 14). When they selected "maple," they tasted maple on 55.6% of the trials (n = 9). When they selected "lemon," they tasted lemon on 80.0% of the trials (n = 10). The exploratory study gave similar results for every flavor except mushroom. Moreover, the average intensity score of the change in taste is 1.41. This score lies midway between 1 (Slight) and 2 (Significant).

The exploratory study shows that the participants experienced a change in the cookie's taste using the system on about 80% of the trials, although the intensity of the change in taste is modest. From the results, we cannot distinguish the different roles that visual cues with augmented reality and olfactory cues play in the perception of flavor. However, the results do suggest that our system can change the perception of taste, and allows users to experience various flavors by varying only the visual and olfactory information without changing the chemical composition.

Moreover, the exploratory study shows that the ratio of subjects who experienced a changed taste with an unfamiliar appearance and scent is similar to that of subjects who experienced a changed taste with a familiar appearance and scent, even though the ratio of subjects who identified the augmented cookie with an unfamiliar appearance and scent as the selected taste is lower than that of subjects who identified the augmented cookie with the familiar appearance and scent. The results suggest that our system changes both the perception of taste and the identification of flavor, and that knowledge has an important role in the identification of flavor. This indicates that it is difficult for our system to enable the user to experience and identify the taste of a cookie as intended when representing cookies with an unfamiliar appearance and scent, although the user perceives a change in the taste. In order to overcome this limitation, another method such as a method for synthesizing tastes from fundamental taste substances is required.

CONCLUSION

In this chapter, we introduce interaction of olfaction with other sense and show two different types of case studies based on this interaction. We proposed possibility to have audience feel various pseudo-olfaction and pseudo-gustation to overcome limitation of multi-modal display

systems; haptic, olfactory, gustatory display. Researchers are going to do experiments on more kinds of visual feedback and implement the new system representing realistic multi-modal sensation combining these feedback phenomena.

Olfactory sensation is based on chemical signals whereas the visual sensation and auditory sensation are based on physical signals. Using instability and variability of olfaction caused by its mechanism, there is a possibility that we can make people feel a smell different from the presented smell by using some techniques when a certain smell material is presented. It proved to be possible to construct the olfactory map based on olfactory sensation according to the sensory evaluation of the smell similarity of two or more people. The common olfactory map suitable for people with various olfactory sensation patterns can be used as well as the language based olfactory map.

Using the common olfactory map, we achieved an olfactory display presenting various smells virtually from a few aroma chemicals. It becomes possible to achieve olfactory virtual reality with a simpler system by reducing the number of aroma sources. Moreover, it is thought to be possible to make olfactory maps among other kinds of smells like flowers or dishes as far as the smells have visual cues in order for the olfactory cue.

The "pseudo-gustation" method to change the perceived taste of food when eaten by changing its appearance and scent. The "MetaCookie+" system was implemented based on the effect of cross-modal integration of vision, olfaction, and gustation. "MetaCookie+" is a system to change the perceived taste of a cookie by overlaying visual and olfactory information onto a real cookie with a special AR marker pattern. The system can recognize a cookie even if it is eaten or partially occluded, and detect the position and bitten/occluded area of the cookie using Edible Marker system.

Using this system, we performed an exploratory study that investigates how people experience the flavor of a plain cookie. The results of the experiment suggested that our system can change the perceived taste, and that this enables the user to experience various tastes simply by changing visual and olfactory information without changing the chemical ingredients in the cookie.

In future work, we will seek to quantify and assess the cross-modal integration effect. For example, we will attempt to reveal the role of visual feedback and olfactory feedback separately, and the relationship between the crossmodal effect and the strength of the odor produced using odor sensors. Through these assessments, we aim to realize a more effective pseudo-gustatory display system.

Furthermore, we believe we can build an expressive olfactory and gustatory display system by combining this pseudo-olfaction and pseudo-gustation method based on cross-modal integration and methods for synthesizing a rough taste from fundamental taste substances. By doing so, we can realize a gustatory display that can represent a wide variety of smells and tastes.

REFERENCES

Air Aroma. (2012). *Website.* Retrieved from http://www.air-aroma.com/ Air/Q Whole Room Air Freshener. (2012). *Website.* Retrieved from http://www.airq.com/store/whole-room-air-freshener

AromaJet. (2012). *Website.* Retrieved from http://www.aromajet.com/

Auvray, M., & Spence, C. (2008). The multisensory perception of flavor. *Consciousness and Cognition, 17,* 1016–1031. doi:10.1016/j.concog.2007.06.005

(1971). In Beidler, L. M. (Ed.). Handbook of sensory physiology: *Vol. 4. Chemical senses: Part 1: Olfaction.* Berlin, Germany: Springer-Verlag.

Bensafi, M., & Rouby, C. (2007). Individual differences in odor imaging ability reflect differences in olfactory and emotional perception. *Chemical Senses, 32,* 237–244. doi:10.1093/chemse/bjl051

Cain, W. S. (1979). To know with the nose: Keys to odor identification. *Science, 203,* 467–470. doi:10.1126/science.760202

Chandrashekar, J., Hoon, M. A., Ryba, N. J., & Zuker, C. S. (2006). The receptors and cells for mammalian taste. *Nature, 444,* 288–294. doi:10.1038/nature05401

Delwiche, J. (2004). The impact of perceptual interactions on perceived flavor. *Food Quality and Preference, 15,* 137–146. doi:10.1016/S0950-3293(03)00041-7

Gottfried, J., & Dolan, R. (2003). The nose smells what the eye sees: Crossmodal visual facilitation of human olfactory perception. *Neuron, 39*(2), 375–386. doi:10.1016/S0896-6273(03)00392-1

Grigor, J., Toller, S. V., Behan, J., & Richardson, A. (1999). The effect of odour priming on long latency visual evoked potentials of matching and mismatching objects. *Chemical Senses, 24,* 137–144. doi:10.1093/chemse/24.2.137

Heilig, M. L. (1992). El cine del futuro: The cinema of the future. *Presence (Cambridge, Mass.), 1*(3), 193–219.

Herz, R. S., & von Clef, J. (2001). The influence of verbal labeling on the perception of odors: Evidence for olfactory illusion? *Perception, 30,* 381–391. doi:10.1068/p3179

Ito, H., Doi, Y., Kameda, W., Shimoda, M., & Osajima, Y. (1991). Studies on characterization of odor-descriptive terms for food products, 6: Contribution of abstract terms to the characterization of concrete terms for odor-description. *Journal of the Japanese Society for Food Science and Technology, 38*(7), 588–594. doi:10.3136/nskkk1962.38.588

Iwata, H., Yano, H., Uemura, T., & Moriya, T. (2004). Food simulator: A haptic interface for biting. [IEEE Press.]. *Proceedings of IEEE Virtual Reality, 2004*, 51–57.

Kruskal, J. B. (1964). Multidimensional scaling by optimizing goodness of fit to a nonmetric hypothesis. *Psychometrika, 29*, 1–27. doi:10.1007/BF02289565

Lawless, H. T. (1989). Exploration of fragrance categories and ambiguous odors using multidimensional scaling and cluster analysis. *Chemical Senses, 14*(3), 349–360. doi:10.1093/chemse/14.3.349

Maynes-Aminzade, D. (2005). Edible bits: Seamless interfaces between people, data and food. In *ACM CHI 2005 Extended Abstracts*, (pp. 2207-2210). ACM Press.

Mochizuki, A., Amada, T., Sawa, S., Takeda, T., Motoyashiki, S., & Kohyama, K. … Chihara, K. (2004). Fragra: A visual-olfactory VR game. In *Proceeding of SIGGRAPH 2004 ACM SIGGRAPH 2004 Sketches*. ACM Press.

Nakaizumi, F., Yanagida, Y., Noma, H., & Hosaka, K. (2006). SpotScents: A novel method of natural scent delivery using multiple scent projectors. [IEEE Press.]. *Proceedings of IEEE Virtual Reality, 2006*, 207–212.

Nakamoto, T., Otaguro, S., Kinoshita, M., Nagahama, M., Ohinishi, K., & Ishida, T. (2008). Cooking up an interactive olfactory game display. *IEEE Computer Graphics and Applications, 28*(1), 75–78. doi:10.1109/MCG.2008.3

Nakomoto, T., & Minh, H. P. D. (2007). Improvement of olfactory display using solenoid valves. [IEEE Press.]. *Proceedings of IEEE Virtual Reality, 2007*, 179–186.

Nambu, A., Narumi, T., Nishimura, K., Tanikawa, T., & Hirose, M. (2008). Nioi cafe: Olfactory display system with visual feedback. In *SIGGRAPH Posters 2008* (p. 92). New York, NY: ACM Press.

Nambu, A., Narumi, T., Nishimura, K., Tanikawa, T., & Hirose, M. (2008). A study of providing colors to change olfactory perception - Using "flavor of color". In Proceedings of ASIAGRAPH in Tokyo 2008, (vol 2, pp. 265-268). ASIAGRAPH.

Nambu, A., Narumi, T., Nishimura, K., Tanikawa, T., & Hirose, M. (2010). Visual-olfactory display using olfactory sensory map. [IEEE Press.]. *Proceedings of IEEE Virtual Reality, 2010*, 39–42.

Narumi, T., Kajinami, T., Nishizaka, S., Tanikawa, T., & Hirose, M. (2011). Pseudo-gustatory display system based on cross-modal integration of vision, olfaction and gestation. [IEEE Press.]. *Proceedings of IEEE Virtual Reality, 2011*, 127–130.

Narumi, T., Nishizaka, S., Kajinami, T., Tanikawa, T., & Hirose, M. (2011). Augmented reality flavors: Gustatory display based on edible marker and cross-modal interaction. In *Proceedings of CHI 2011*, (pp. 93-102). ACM Press.

Osmooze. (2012). *Website.* Retrieved from http://www.osmooze.com/

Ross, P. W. (2001). Qualia and the senses. *The Philosophical Quarterly, 51*, 495–511. doi:10.1111/1467-9213.00243

Rozin, P. (1982). Taste-smell confusion and the duality of the olfactory sense. *Perception & Psychophysics, 31*, 397–401. doi:10.3758/BF03202667

Sakai, N., Imada, S., Saito, S., Kobayakawa, T., & Deguchi, Y. (2005). The effect of visual images on perception of odors. *Chemical Senses, 30*(1). doi:10.1093/chemse/bjh205

Sato, J., Ohtsu, K., Bannai, Y., & Okada, K. (2008). Pulse ejection technique of scent to create dynamic perspective. In *Proceedings of the 18th International Conference on Artificial Reality and Telexistence*, (pp. 167-174). IEEE.

ScentAir. (2012). *Website.* Retrieved from http://www.scentair.com/

Scentcommunication. (2012). *Website.* Retrieved from http://www.scentcommunication.com/

Shimojo, S., & Shams, L. (2001). Sensory modalities are not separate modalities: Plasticity and interactions. *Current Opinion in Neurobiology, 11*(4), 505–509. doi:10.1016/S0959-4388(00)00241-5

Spence, C., Levitan, C., Shankar, M., & Zampini, M. (2010). Does food color influence taste and flavor perception in humans? *Chemosensory Perception, 3*(1), 68–84. doi:10.1007/s12078-010-9067-z

Stevenson, R. J., Prescott, J., & Boakes, R. A. (1999). Confusing tastes and smells: How odours can influence the perception of sweet and sour tastes. *Chemical Senses, 24*(6), 627–635. doi:10.1093/chemse/24.6.627

Sugiyama, H., Kanamura, A., & Kikuchi, T. (2006). Are olfactory images sensory in nature? *Perception, 35*, 1699–1708. doi:10.1068/p5453

Toko, K., Matsuno, T., Yamafuji, K., Hayashi, K., Ikezaki, H., & Sato, K. (1994). Taste sensor using electric potential changes in lipid membranes. *Biosensors & Bioelectronics, 9*, 359–364. doi:10.1016/0956-5663(94)80036-7

Trisenx. (2012). *Website.* Retrieved from http://www.trisenx.com/intro.html

Yamada, T., Yokoyama, S., Tanikawa, T., Hirota, K., & Hirose, M. (2006). Wearable olfactory display: Using odor in outdoor environment. [IEEE Press.]. *Proceedings of IEEE Virtual Reality, 2006*, 199–206.

Zampini, M., Wantling, E., Phillips, N., & Spence, C. (2008). Multisensory flavor perception: Assessing the influence of fruit acids and color cues on the perception of fruit flavored beverages. *Food Quality and Preference, 18*, 335–343. doi:10.1016/j.foodqual.2007.11.001

Zellner, D. A., & Kautz, M. A. (1990). Color affects perceived odor intensity. *Journal of Experimental Psychology. Human Perception and Performance, 16*, 391–397. doi:10.1037/0096-1523.16.2.391

Zybura, M., & Eskeland, G. A. (1999). *Olfaction for virtual reality. Quarter Project, Industrial Engineering 543.* Seattle, WA: University of Washington.

Chapter 5
Odor Analysis Method

Kenshi Hayashi
Kyushu University, Japan

Jean-Jacques Delaunay
The University of Tokyo, Japan

Junichi Ide
T. Hasegawa Co., Ltd., Japan

Sigeru Omatu
Osaka Institute of Technology, Japan

ABSTRACT

Quantitative and qualitative measurements of odor are indispensable for the development of odor display systems that can reproduce odor at any place in any time. This chapter covers odor evaluation techniques based on human senses, instrumental analyses, odor sensors, and data analysis methods dedicated to odor measuring techniques. The chapter consists of the four following sections: sensory evaluation, gas analysis instruments, odor sensing system, and pattern analysis for odor sensing system. The first section describes odor evaluation methods with human senses. The second section gives an overview of instrumental laboratory techniques for olfaction research. The third section surveys sensor devices for odor detection. Finally, the last section gives the basic statistical methods and advanced pattern analysis for odor sensing systems.

SENSORY EVALUATION

This section covers sensory evaluation to examine sensory characteristics using human senses. First, methods generally used in sensory evaluation are briefly summarized. Second, important points to acquire reliable data in the sensory evaluation are given. Finally, a case study of sensory evaluation for the study on yuzu aroma is presented. Yuzu is widely used in Japanese cuisines for its pleasant flavor. To clarify the odor-active volatile compounds, which differentiate yuzu from other citrus

fruits, sensory evaluation methods were applied to yuzu peel oils. In order to extract information from the results of the evaluation, statistical analyses were performed using the comparison by cobweb chart, the analysis of variance, Tukey's multiple-comparison test and multivariate analysis.

According to the Institute of Food Technologists (IFT), sensory evaluation has been defined as "a scientific discipline used to evoke, measure, analyze, and interpret reactions to those characteristics of foods and materials as they are perceived by the senses of sight, smell, taste, touch, and hearing" (IFT, 1975).

DOI: 10.4018/978-1-4666-2521-1.ch005

Copyright © 2013, IGI Global. Copying or distributing in print or electronic forms without written permission of IGI Global is prohibited.

Table 1. Classification of sensory evaluation methods

Classification of methods	Appropriate methods
Analytical tests	
1. Discriminative tests	
	Paired-comparison test
	Duo-trio test
	Triangle test
	Two-out-of-five test
	Ranking test
2. Descriptive tests	
	Flavor profile analysis
	Texture profile analysis
	Quanititative descriptive analysis
Affective tests	Paired-comparison preference test
	Hedonic scaling test
	Ranking test

Sensory evaluation using the human senses is a method to measure the strength, texture, and preference of objects. The evaluation is subjective, sometimes ambiguous about reproducibility. Since such sensory evaluation is based on the human senses, it can be said that the evaluation includes subjective factors such as mistakes, overlooking, and sensory fatigue that do not arise with objective equipment. To solve these problems, proper designs of experiments that minimize the subjective influences caused by the assessor's mental and physical conditions is introduced.

Methods for Sensory Evaluation

Several methods have been developed for sensory evaluation. The experimenter should be thoroughly familiar with the advantages and disadvantages of each method. The most practical and efficient method should be selected for each situation as there is no method which can be used universally. The experimenter must precisely define the purpose of the test and the information he wants to acquire.

According to IFT, there are two classifications of sensory evaluations: analytical tests and affective tests. The general methods are briefly summarized in Table 1. Analytical tests are used for laboratory evaluation of products in terms of differences or similarities and for identification and quantification of sensory characteristics. There are two major types of analytical tests—discriminative tests and descriptive tests. General sensory evaluation techniques of analytical tests are given as follows (IFT, 1981).

Discriminative Tests: Difference tests measure whether samples can be differentiated at some predetermined levels of statistical confidence, e.g., $p < 0.05$. The difference tests are classified as follows.

1. **Paired-Comparison Test:** Two coded samples are evaluated simultaneously or sequentially in a balanced order of presentation. Fewer samples are required but the statistical efficiency is not as great, as the probability of a panelist selecting a sample by chance is 50%. For example, fifteen correct

judgments out of 20 were recorded. That is statistically significant at $p < 0.05$.

2. **Duo-Trio Test:** This test employs three samples, two identical and one different. One sample is identified as the standard and presented first, followed by two coded samples, one of which is identical to the standard. The judge is required to identify the sample which matches the standard. For example, fifteen correct judgments out of 20 were recorded. That is statistically significant at $p < 0.05$.

3. **Triangle Test:** This test employs three coded samples, two identical and one different, presented simultaneously. The judge is required to determine which of the three samples presented differs from the other two. For example, eleven correct judgments out of 20 were recorded. That is statistically significant at $p < 0.05$.

4. **Two-Out-of-Five Test:** This test employs five coded samples, two identical and three different, presented simultaneously. The judge is required to determine which of the five samples presented differs from the other three. Compared to the triangle test, in which the chance of choosing the correct sample is 1/3, the two-out-of-five test is more statistically efficient, as the probability of a panelist selecting a sample by chance is 1/10. For example, five correct judgments out of 20 were recorded. That is statistically significant at $p < 0.05$.

5. **Ranking Tests:** This test is used to make simultaneous comparisons of several samples on the basis of a single characteristic. It is rapid and allows the testing of several samples at once, as no identification of the size of the differences between samples is obtained.

Descriptive tests: There are also several types of descriptive analysis tests.

1. **Flavor Profile Analysis:** This technique provides a written record of a product's perceptible aroma and flavor components, feeling factors, and aftertastes.

2. **Texture Profile Analysis:** This is a descriptive technique based on the principles of the flavor profile method. It provides a systematic approach to measuring the textural dimensions of a food in terms of its mechanical, geometrical, fat, and moisture characteristic.

3. **Quantitative Descriptive Analysis:** This technique utilizes an unstructured category scale and a panel of not less than six trained panelists, and obtains repeated judgments from each panelist for test products. Sensory attributes of products are characterized in the order of their appearance, and relative intensities are assigned.

Affective Tests: There are three types of affective tests, namely, paired preference test, hedonic scaling test, and ranking test.

1. **Paired Comparison Preference Test:** The paired comparison preference test in preference testing is similar to that used for difference tests. When testing preferences, the panelist is presented with two coded samples and is asked which he prefers (Which of these samples do you prefer?)

2. **Hedonic Scaling Test:** The most commonly used scale for preference testing is the nine-point hedonic scale. The term "hedonic" is defined "having to do with pleasure." It should only be used in connection with scales in which the panelist expresses his degree of liking or disliking (e.g., please drink these samples and check how much you like or dislike each one)

3. **Ranking Test:** When ranking for preference, the panelist is presented with coded samples to rank in order of preference.

According to IFT, sensory evaluation panels can be grouped into two types. In the analytical tests, panelists are experienced and/or trained in advance. The panel size depends on product variability and judgment reproducibility. A usual number of panelists is more than ten and a recommended minimum number is five. In the affective tests, panelists are not trained, but are randomly selected from large to represent target or potential target populations or consumers of test products. A minimum number of the panelists is generally 24, which is sometimes considered rough product screening and 50-100 panelists are usually considered adequate (IFT, 1981).

Factors Influencing Sensory Evaluation

In the performance of sensory evaluation, factors which shall be taken to obtain reliable data are given below.

The purpose and the significance of the sensory evaluation should be clarified. Since different techniques have been developed for sensory evaluation, the experimenter should select the appropriate method and design the experiment.

All experiments should minimize the effect of psychological errors and physical conditions of the panelists or environment that influence human judgments (expectation error, stimulus error, logical error, halo effect, suggestion effect, order effect, and so on) (Larmond, 1977).

The experimenter should apply statistical analyses to extract information from results of the evaluation. For example, in addition to comparison by cobweb chart, analysis of variance (ANOVA), multiple-comparison test, and multivariate analyses are used in the analysis of assay results.

Without thorough consideration of the above factors in the experimental design, it is impossible to obtain reliable data from the sensory evaluation.

Application of Sensory Evaluation

Development of Yuzu Flavor

In order to reveal the yuzu aroma, sensory evaluation methods are applied. The yuzu (*Citrus junos* Sieb. ex Tanaka), a kind of sour orange belonging to the *Rutaeae* family, has a pleasant and fresh odor, and has been widely used in Japanese cuisines.

To clarify the odor-active volatile compounds that differentiate yuzu from other citrus fruits (orange, grapefruit, and lime), sensory evaluation were performed by seven males and four females, all of whom were employees of the Technical Research Center of T. Hasegawa Co., Ltd., Kawasaki, Japan (Miyazawa, et al., 2009).

The attributes used to describe the nature of citrus in their study were discussed by all panelists. As a result of several consultations, they reached a consensus on seven attributes to be used for their descriptive evaluations of the citrus aroma: fruity, sweet, floral, green, metallic, sour, and balsamic.

Each sample was put into a closed sensory vial and coded by a random three-digit number, and the panelists rated the intensity in seven attributes using a five-point linear scale from 1 (none) to 5 (very strong). The results of sensory evaluation of four kinds of citrus oil are shown in Table 2 and Figure 1. The cobweb chart reveals that the balsamic note is the dominant characteristic factor for yuzu aroma.

Statistical Analyses

To extract more information from the results of the evaluation, statistical analyses were performed.

The differences among the average scores of the evaluated samples were compared using the analysis of variance (ANOVA) and the Tukey's multiple-comparison test. For the ANOVA analysis, the Correction Factor (CF), Sum of Square

Table 2. Sensory evaluation of citrus oils

Attribute	Average Score			
	Yuzu	**Orange**	**Grapefruit**	**Lime**
Fruity	3.8	3.8	3.4	2.4
Sweet	3.5	3.5	3.3	1.7
Floral	3.8	3.1	3.3	2.6
Green	3.0	3.0	3.5	3.1
Metallic	2.8	2.5	3.0	4.5
Sour	2.9	3.6	3.5	3.5
Balsamic	4.4	2.8	2.3	1.7

Figure 1. Aroma profiles of citrus oils: (●) yuzu peel oil; (□) orange oil; (▲) grapefruit oil; (■) lime oil

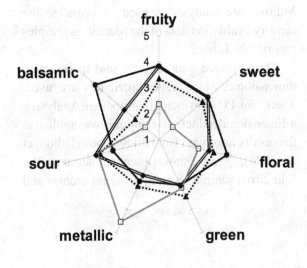

(SS), Degree of Freedom (df), Mean Square (ms), and F value for each attribute were calculated.

The result of the ANOVA for balsamic note is shown in Table 3. The value of $F = 18.601$ is highly significant, so that the null hypothesis can be rejected (i.e., there is no difference in the mean balsamic scores within the four citrus oils.) According to the distribution of $F(3,40)$, there is a significant difference at the 5% level, if the F value exceeds 2.84. Moreover, if it exceeds 4.31, there is a significant difference even at the 1% level.

Table 4 shows the results of the homogeneity of the variances. The parameters df1 and df2 are degrees of freedom obtained in the ANOVA analysis. Levene's test is designed to test the null hypothesis when the variances of the groups are equal. In this case, the significance value is > 0.05, therefore the variances of the four groups are not significantly different. Then means were compared with the Tukey's HSD (Honestly Significant Difference) test.

Tukey's Honestly Significant Difference (HSD) is simultaneous multiple comparison procedure (Meilgaard, 2006). Tukey's HSD can be applied regardless of the outcome of the overall test for differences among the samples. The general form of Tukey's HSD for the equal sample-size case for rating is

$$HSD = q \sqrt{MSE / n} \qquad (1)$$

where q are tabulated values of the studentized range statistics, n is the number of values we are dealing with in each group, and MES is the mean square within groups from the ANOVA, respectively.

According to the studentized range distribution, the value of $q(0.05,4,40)$ is 3.79 and HSD is 0.999.

Each mean is compared with the others to see if the difference is 0.999 or more.

For example, "Yuzu oil" – "Orange oil" = $1.55 > 0.999$

Table 3. Analysis of variance table (ANOVA: balsamic)

	Sum of squares	Degree of freedom	Mean square	F	P-value
Between groups	42.614	3	14.205	18.601	0.000
Within groups	30.545	40	0.764		
Total	73.159	43			

Table 4. Homogeneity of variances: balsamic

Levene statistic	df1	df2	P-value
0.407	3	40	0.748

The Tukey's HSD multiple-comparison test suggests that yuzu oil is significantly more balsamic than all the other oils.

On the basis of these sensory evaluation and analysis of volatile compounds (aroma extract dilution analysis, AEDA), multidimensional gas chromatography-mass spectrometry-olfactometry), Miyazawa and others, noted with interest that the balsamic note was the most characteristic factor in yuzu aroma. They finally revealed that YUZU-NONE ((6Z,8E)-undeca-6,8,10-trien-3-one) and YUZUOL((6Z,8E)-undeca-6,8,10-trien-4-ol), which were identified for the first time in natural products, contribute greatly to the yuzu aroma.

Multivariate Analyses

PCA

Multivariate analysis is used to visualize the sensory evaluation data of the four citrus samples reported in Table 2.

The obtained data may be said to be seven dimensional, since seven attributes are used. Therefore, PCA (Principal Component Analysis), a dimensional reduction technique, was applied to the results into two visual dimensions (Dillon, et al., 1984). Figure 2 shows a scatter diagram of the four citrus samples having different aromas and

Table 5. Multiple comparison

Dependent Variable: Balsamic

	(I)Citrus oil	(J)Citrus oil	Mean Difference (I-J)	Std.Error	P-value	95%Confidence Interval	
						Lower Bound	Upper Bound
Tukey HSD	1	2	1.55 *	0.373	0.001	0.55	2.54
		3	2.09 *	0.373	0.000	1.09	3.09
		4	2.64 *	0.373	0.000	1.64	3.64
	2	1	-1.55 *	0.373	0.001	-2.54	-0.55
		3	0.55	0.373	0.468	-0.45	1.54
		4	1.09 *	0.373	0.028	0.09	2.09
	3	1	-2.09 *	0.373	0.000	-3.09	-1.09
		2	-0.55	0.373	0.468	-1.54	0.45
		4	0.55	0.373	0.468	-0.45	-1.54
	4	1	-2.64 *	0.373	0.000	-3.64	-1.64
		2	-1.09 *	0.373	0.028	-2.09	-0.09
		3	-0.55	0.373	0.468	-1.54	0.45

* The mean difference is significant at the 0.05 level.
Citrus oils : 1 Yuzu oil , 2 Orange oil, 3 Grapefruit oil, 4 Lime oil

Figure 2. Principal component analysis of citrus oils for the first and second principal components

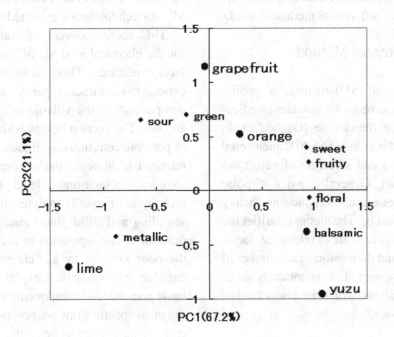

seven factor loadings. The total variance in the data obtained by this two-dimensional model is 88.3%. "Lime" is furthest removed from the other three samples. "Yuzu" is also separated from the two samples of "grapefruit" and "orange."

The two dimensions can be interpreted by examining the factor loading of the attributes on each dimension (Meilgaard, 2006). Factor loadings are similar to correlation coefficients. The value range of the factor loading is from -1 to +1. Large absolute values (> 0.6) indicate a strong association between the attribute and the principal. On the other hand, small absolute values (< 0.6) indicate a weak association. Focusing on the larger factor loadings helps in the interpretation of each of the principal components.

The relationships among the attributes and the citrus oils can now be illustrated on the scatter diagram. Figure 2 shows the relationships of the attributes and the citrus oils on the first two principal components. It can be seen, for example, that balsamic note is the most characteristic factor in the yuzu oil, whereas metallic note is the most characteristic factor in the lime oil. Moreover, it

is suggested that six attributes except green note contributed to the first principal component.

Magnitude Estimation

In order to estimate magnitude of sensation, relationship between the magnitude of a physical stimulus and its perceived intensity or strength is used. Weber-Fechner law and Stevens' power law are the most commonly used relationships: $S=a\log I/I0$ (Weber-Fechner law) and $S=kIa$ (Stevens' power law), where S is the perceived intensity caused by I the strength of the physical stimulus, and a and k are constants. In the case of Stevens' power law estimation, the estimated magnitude is called magnitude estimation, where a magnitude of a certain stimulus is expressed numerically by human panels comparing to a certain standard stimulus, then fitting to power law is conducted. The analysis is based on psychometrics or psychophysics, which quantitatively investigates the relationship between physical stimuli and the sensations and perceptions. In other words, sensory evaluation belongs to those psychological studies.

In the case of adjective or meaning scale, the following semantic differential method is used.

Semantic Differential Method

Semantic Differential (SD) method, or profile method, evaluates samples using scales on adjectives which relate to the samples (Osgood, et al., 1957). The method is a kind of Multi Dimensional Scaling. Extraction and selection of adjectives are very important. Generally, pairs of polar opposite adjectives are chosen such as "heavy smell" and "light smell." The method clarifies the semantic structure, i.e., scale of relevance, factorial composition and dimensions, and number of scales. The method uses PCA, factor analysis, or discrimination analysis, which are also a kind of multivariate analyses.

GAS ANALYSIS INSTRUMENTS

The purpose of gas analysis performed in laboratory is to accurately describe the physicochemical variables such as chemical structure, polarity, presence of double bonds of odorant molecules. These physicochemical variables provide the basis for the classification and synthesis of odorants. However, a general relation between the physicochemical variables and the olfactory properties of the odorants is still to be developed for the chemical analysis data to find its potential in the advancement of odor applications. Among olfactory properties, the olfactory threshold indicates the concentration threshold above which odor perception by the human olfactory system is made possible. The olfactory thresholds are very low and usually fall below the ppb range or even ppt range. These low thresholds put extreme challenge on the measurement techniques as sample contamination in the analysis chain and detection at these extremely low concentrations present difficult technological challenges. This is one of the reasons why on field analysis using portable devices is still an area of active research in which MEMS technologies is expected to play a key role.

This section covers laboratory techniques for the chemical analysis of gas samples in olfaction research. These techniques are used to concentrate, extract, separate, and identify the components of the volatile mixture making up an odor. The section begins with the description of pre-concentration techniques, which are often required to increase the concentration of odor samples to a measurable level. Then, extraction techniques of volatile analytes such as headspace sampling and solid phase micro-extraction are described. The separation of the components of the odor samples by gas chromatography in a capillary column is then explained. Finally, the basic principles of components identification using mass spectroscopy are reviewed. The section ends by describing systems that simultaneously enable both chemical analysis and sensory panel analysis of odor samples.

Pre-Concentration Techniques

Collect volatile organic vapor prior to separation and identification is an important step in the analysis of odor compounds because of their very low concentrations usually below the part per billion level. At this low level of concentration, most gas detectors do not have sufficient sensitivity and therefore the concentration of the odorants should be increased before odorants can be detected (Pillonel, 2002).

Trapping the odorants on adsorbent materials followed by thermal desorption is a standard technique for odor sample pre-concentration. The adsorbent materials are chosen to have very high specific surface areas (as large as 1000 m2/g). Among absorbent materials, the most effective are inorganic carbon based materials (carbon blacks, carbon molecular sieves, activated carbon and carbon nanotubes), polymer adsorbents (Tenax) and silicate based materials. Each material has advantages and drawbacks so that an optimum adsorbent material has to be selected for each specific application. Selection of the absorbent materials is done as a function of the range of boiling points and polarity of the sample molecules. Among drawbacks of adsorbent materials are false positive results generated by polymers based adsorbents caused by depolymerisation during thermal desorption. When the sampling of odorants has to be done under the condition of high moisture content, it is recommended to use hydrophobic adsorbent materials, so as to decrease the effect of water molecules. Adsorbent materials with low affinity with water (e.g. Tenax TA, carbosieve) are available. Odorants sampling often requires covering a wide range of molecules and, therefore, adsorbent materials are often used in combination. For example, carbotrap multibed adsorption is a combination of carbotraps and carbosieve that allows for trapping of low to high molecular weight components. Preconcentrator devices are available in the form of stainless tubes that can be filled with adsorbent materials and equipped with a needle for injection. The injection in the separation column is usually realized in two steps. First, rapid desorption with a ballistic heater and subsequent adsorption by a liquid nitrogen trap, which can use a small portion of the separation column as the trap. Second, the liquid nitrogen trap is heated to obtain a sharp peak of molecules that will carry through the separation column.

In addition, adsorbent materials have been incorporated in injection needles for GC (Shinwa/Shimadzu, 2011) to allow for direct injection of analytes into the separation column with a needle syringe. The needle absorbent material is first purged in the injection port by thermal desorption. Then the needle is used to trap odorants by active adsorption using a pump. Finally, the needle with its absorbent is directly inserted in the injection port and thermally desorbed odorant molecules are injected into the column with an inert gas stream. In this technique, no additional equipment such as a thermal desorption system is required. However, the technique is limited by the small amount of

adsorbent incorporated in the needle and by the types of adsorbent materials available from the maker. It is therefore not possible to optimize the adsorbent to a specific application.

A second technique of choice for trapping odorant molecules is the use of sorptive materials. In this technique, the odorant molecules are retained and concentrated in a polymer matrix by dissolution (Pawliszyn, 1997). For this purpose, a polymer is used with a glass transition temperature below the sampling temperature. The polymer is usually coated to a fiber that is directly inserted in the injection port of the GC system. Inertness and stability are the main advantages of the sorbent technique. The main drawback being a lack of sensitivity due to the limited amount of polymer that can be coated on the fiber. One widely used sorbent technique for odorants is the solid phase microextraction for which a wide variety of coating has been developed (Pawliszyn, 1997).

Recently, microfabrication techniques have been used to micro-fabricate preconcentrators in silicon. Deep etching is used to form structures such as channels, slats and posts, which can hold materials of the adsorbent in the form of beads, grains or layers (Tian, et al., 2003; Hussain, 2008; Takada, et al., 2010). Integrated heaters are used to desorb and inject the volatile compounds into the separation column and/or detector. These preconcentrators have limited sampling flow rates and capacity due to their small sizes. Therefore, development of new adsorbent materials with high capacity is needed. Single wall carbon nanotubes have been proposed as a potential candidate for high performance adsorbent materials in microfabricated preconcentrators (Hussain, 2008; Takada, et al., 2010).

Separation and Identification

Gas Chromatography (GC) in combination with a flame ionization detector is the most widely used instrument in the analysis of odorants (Dorman, et al., 2008; Grob & Barry, 2004). The separation of odorants is achieved on high performance capillary columns providing high resolution that permits the separation of hundreds of compounds. The detection is achieved using sensitive detector such as flame ionization detector, which has the ability to detect and quantitate compounds in the ppb range. Further, compounds identification and detailed description of the odorant physico-chemistry is possible using mass spectrometry (Hubschmann, 2009). Finally, the advance of automated gas chromatographic systems has made possible the analysis of large number of samples in laboratory at low cost.

Chromatography separates odorant components by partitioning the components between the stationary phase (coating of the capillary column) and the mobile phase (inert carrier gas). The odorant components are dissolved in the coating of the capillary column, thus forming equilibrium between the stationary phase and the mobile phase. Usually absorption of odorant molecules in the coating of the separation column is used for separation, but adsorption may be present. Thus, the major process at play for separation is a differential sorption process between the stationary phase and mobile phase. The carrier gas transports the mobile phase as it is passing through the stationary phase, thus resulting in a series of equilibrium operations. As a result of the series of equilibria, the odorant components emerge of the separation column at different times (retention times) rendering their detections possible in the form of a chromatogram.

Flame-Ionization Detectors (FID) are the most widely used GC detectors owning to their high sensitivity, good linearity, and versatility of detected molecules. In FIDs, the effluents are burned in an oxygen-hydrogen atmosphere. This process produces ions that are collected on the detector electrode. The collected ions generate a current that is used as a signal. The FID signal is proportional to the amount of carbon in the effluents enabling quantitation of effluents. One further advantage of FIDs lies in the lack of sensitivity to water vapor, a common interference gas in odorant analysis. The FID main drawback is that FIDs require calibration of retention times for molecule identification and, therefore, do not permit direct molecule identification. For direct molecule identification, Mass Spectrometry (MS) is used. In MS, the separated molecules are first ionized to generate ions that are separated by mass analyzers (e.g. quadrupole mass analyzer) and detected according to their mass to charge ratio (electron multiplier). The generated mass spectrum exhibiting intensity of the detected ions versus mass to charge ratio is finally compared with standard spectra of known molecules recorded in well-established databases. The GC-MS technique performs best with volatile and thermally stable odorants.

Injection in the separation column is realized in the injection port by vaporizing the odorant samples. The effect of any thermal process on the odorant molecules should be carefully investigated because many odorant molecules are thermally unstable. For example, sulfur-containing molecules in garlic oils (Block, et al., 1992; Cai, et al., 1995) require special attention as thermal degradation of molecules during the analysis is a known cause for erroneous identification in analysis. The possibility of decomposition of the odorant molecules on heating at the injection port, column and transfer line of GC-MS systems should be investigated.

Combination of Analytical and Sensory Data for Odor Analysis

The chemical analysis of odorants provides analytical data that does not relate to any odor perception. It is therefore necessary to combine analytical data with sensory data in order to perform odor analysis. Both analytical and sensory data can be combined in Gas Chromatography-Olfactometry (GC-O) method, as depicted in Figure 3 (Friedrich & Acree, 2000; Curioni & Bosset, 2002; Lee & Noble, 2003). In GC-O, odorant molecules are first separated by chromatography and, then,

Figure 3. GC-O system and its output information; chromatogram and aromagram by AEDA

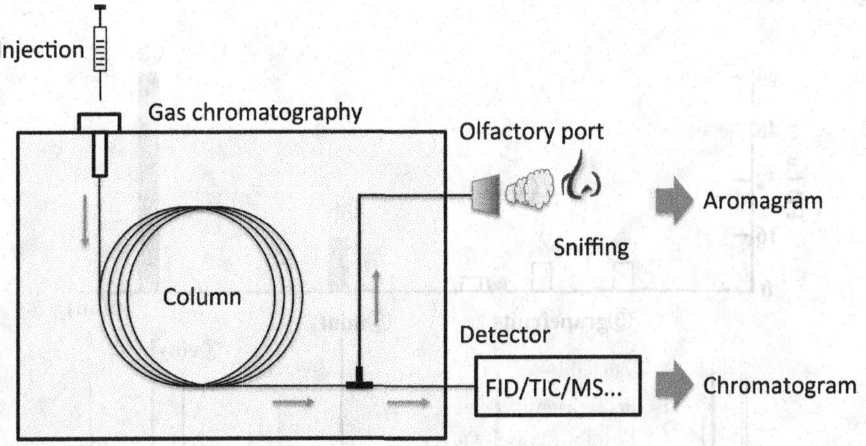

concurrently detected by human olfactometry (aromagram of sniffer) and analytical detection (mass spectra of GC-MS). Thus, the odor activity of the odorant molecules can be related to their chemical structures through the comparison of the aromagrams and the mass spectra. This method allows for the discrimination of odor-active molecules from odor-less molecules. Control of humidity and flow at the sniffing port of the GC-O system are provided to improve the reproducibility of sensory data. The drawbacks associated with human olfactometry caused by natural variations in sensory ability within and between sniffers can be addressed by using standardized procedures. Successful strategies to collect and quantify odorant information by olfactometry are based on successive dilutions of the original sample. The charm analysis procedure records the duration and quality of the odor during successive dilutions. This data is used to calculate a charm value that is graphed as a function of retention time. In the Aroma Extract Dilution Analysis (AEDA) procedure, a dilution factor is computed as the ratio between the original concentration of the odorant and the concentration at the highest dilution at which an odor is still detected (Figure 4). AEDA has been applied to the screening of the potent odorants of various foods and flavors (Grosch, 1994). Bias caused by the sampling

techniques (pre-concentration) is often an issue in the GC-O method. Odorant perception is realized through headspace sampling by the nose so that the odorant sampling should respect the property of headspace sampling. Aromagrams obtained from extracts may differ from real aromagrams obtained by head space sniffing. Active headspace with subsequent pre-concentration of odorants is the usual technique for sampling, although the balance of odorant molecules may be changed upon the pre-concentration step (relative loss of the low versus high boiling volatiles). It is therefore recommended to try several sampling techniques and compare their results.

Finally, it should be noted that the prediction of odor perception from the information gained by chemical analysis is still difficult.

ODOR-SENSING SYSTEM

This section covers odor-sensing system based on combinations of various sensors and signal processing units. The sensors corresponding to the five senses of human, sight, hearing, touch, smell and taste are being developed, however, many difficulties exist for sensing odor because odor sensors must detect a large variety of chemicals and exhibit specific detecting performance similar to

Figure 4. Aromagram by AEDA and gas chromatogram from a GC detector by courtesy of Prof. T. Matsui (Kobayashi, et al., 2006)

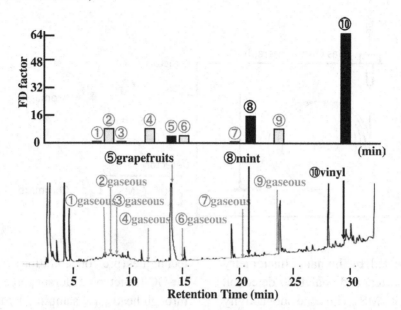

biological olfaction. The section describes the detection principles of gas sensors, recent progresses, and applications of the odor sensors using metal oxide semiconductor gas sensor (MOX), Quartz Crystal Microbalance sensor (QCM), cantilever sensor, surface acoustic wave sensor, conducting polymer sensor, electrochemical sensor, optical sensor, biosensor, and their combinations. Various odor sensor applications, for example food analyses, environmental monitoring, security sensing, and medical diagnoses are also surveyed. The limitations of the described odor sensing systems are also discussed.

Requirement for Odor-Sensor

Needless to say, odor is an olfactory sensation brought about by volatile chemicals. A very large number of volatile chemicals have the ability to cause olfactory sensation. In biological olfactory system, a great number of olfactory cells receives odor substances transported into olfactory mucus layer through the nasal cavity. Olfactory cilia sprouted into the mucus layer from olfactory cell

catches the odor molecules on its surface. Thus, the large number of chemicals is translated into multivariate signals of activated olfactory cells, and the signals are processed in the central nervous system. Even the processing detail is very complex and still a subject of research, central brain recognizes odor chemicals and thus we feel odor sensation. Consequently, artificial biomimetic odor sensors can be realized by constructing an artificial sensor array that generates multivariate signals and process signals in the same way as the central nervous system (Figure 5).

Olfactory Receptors (ORs) recognize a specific feature of odor molecules, therefore, a molecule is received by several receptors and a receptor detects several kinds of odor molecules. Consequently, selectivity of odor receptors generally has wide tuning properties and sensitivity to odorants depends on intermolecular forces that interact between a recognized substructure of odorants, i.e., odotopes and a recognizing site of ORs.

It is important that biological sensation is not a quantitative analysis and relationship between

Figure 5. Biological olfactory system and artificial odor sensing system

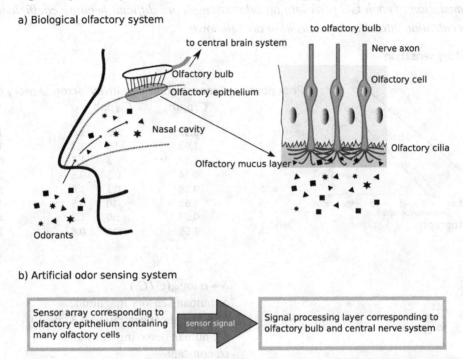

a) Biological olfactory system

to central brain system

Olfactory bulb

Olfactory epithelium

Nasal cavity

Olfactory mucus layer

Odorants

to olfactory bulb

Nerve axon

Olfactory cell

Olfactory cilia

b) Artificial odor sensing system

| Sensor array corresponding to olfactory epithelium containing many olfactory cells | sensor signal | Signal processing layer corresponding to olfactory bulb and central nerve system |

magnitude of physical stimulus and perceived intensity is well quantified as in the Weber-Fechner law. Hence, in human olfaction, magnitude of subjective sensation increases in proportionally to the logarithmic concentration of odor chemical. The relationship comes from a logarithmic term of chemical potential and adsorption amount of chemicals in certain concentration ranges. As shown in Figure 6, relationship between odorant concentrations and sensory magnitudes can be simply summarized by two parameters, a detection limit (threshold concentration) Ct and a constant factor α. Even if each chemical component can be quantified by gas chromatography as described in the previous section, we must translate each concentration using the formula in Figure 6. It is tremendous work to determine the parameters for all odor chemicals, and to quantify chemicals that have very different threshold values. Therefore, the AEDA method is indispensable, in which chemicals are diluted by a geometric series, and human olfactory sense is utilized as a sensory detector.

Thus, odor sensors should have the ability to reproduce the logarithmic concentration dependencies of odor sensation, where concentration can vary by a factor 104. In actual odor vapor, chemicals with various Ct values are mixed and measured at the same time. Therefore, the required precision for a total measurement should be five to six digits. It means that quantitative analytical methods such as GC are not very suitable for the odor detection. Consequently, sensors which respond to chemicals logarithmically are useful, even these sensors cannot be used as quantitative analytical methods.

As the sensor response time is concerned, biological olfactory sense is fast and, therefore, sensors should have comparable response times with biological olfactory of ~1 s. For example, in the case of a robot using circumstance recognition to behave according to surrounding space, odor sensors must respond very fast. Current instrumental analyses as well as gas sensors reported below are far from such high-performance fast

Figure 6. Concentration dependency of human olfactory sensation, gas chromatograph of odor chemicals, and translation of each GC peak into an odor strength are difficult because coefficients used to convert concentration into olfactory sensation are unknown

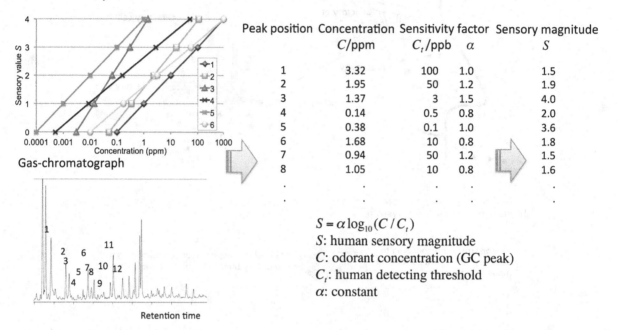

Human olfactory sensation

Gas-chromatograph

Retention time

Peak position	Concentration C/ppm	Sensitivity factor C_t/ppb	α	Sensory magnitude S
1	3.32	100	1.0	1.5
2	1.95	50	1.2	1.9
3	1.37	3	1.5	4.0
4	0.14	0.5	0.8	2.0
5	0.38	0.1	1.0	3.6
6	1.68	10	0.8	1.8
7	0.94	50	1.2	1.5
8	1.05	10	0.8	1.6

$$S = \alpha \log_{10}(C / C_t)$$

S: human sensory magnitude
C: odorant concentration (GC peak)
C_t: human detecting threshold
α: constant

response time. However, further improvements in sensor response time characteristics are expected to solve this drawback and thus improve monitoring ability of sensors.

Gas Sensing Devices

MOX Sensors

Metal Oxide (MOX) gas sensors are well-developed sensor devices which are widely used in various home appliance products as well as in gas leak detection systems (Seiyama, et al., 1962; Taguchi, 1962). The sensors can be easily obtained commercially and have long lifetime, high stability and high sensitivity.

The structure of a MOX gas sensor together with a photograph of a commercialized sensor are shown in Figure 7. Metal oxide semiconductors are sensitive layers fabricated on insulator substrates that are heated at a few hundred degrees Celsius

(e.g. 400°C) to promote chemical reactions on their surfaces. Response mechanisms are also shown in Figure 8, where grain boundary conductivity of a small crystal made of metal oxide semiconductor changes under reductive gas atmosphere. It is noted that humidity and O2 concentration also affect the sensor response.

As shown in Figure 7(c), concentration dependencies of a typical MOX sensor to some gases are logarithmic and thus MOX sensors can mimic biological olfactory sensation. Therefore, these MOX sensors could be applied in odor sensor systems. However, MOX sensors are sensitive to a limited range of gas vapors because MOX sensors mainly respond to reductive gases.

Even if the MOX sensors can be fabricated with good performance for practical applications, biological olfactory sense has much higher sensitivities for some odor chemicals such as hydrogen sulfides, geosmine (musty smell) and 2-methylisoborneol (2-MIB, smell of ditch) which

Figure 7. (a) Structure of metal oxide gas senor, (b) commercialized sensor, and (c) typical responses of a metal oxide gas sensor (courtesy of Figaro Engineering Inc., Japan)

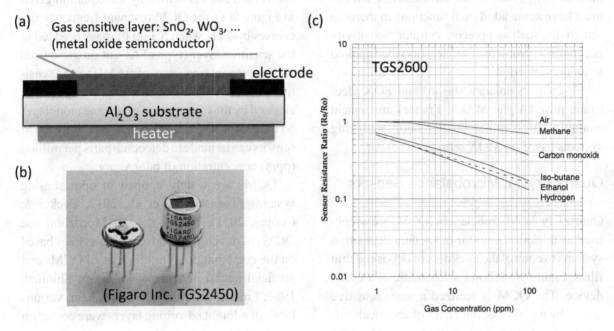

Figure 8. Response mechanism and energy diagram of a MOX gas sensor device

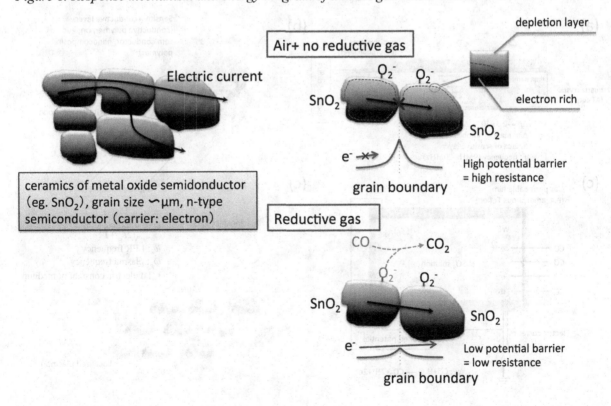

can be detected at the ppt level. Therefore, the odor sensing systems that utilize MOX sensors must have some additional functions to increase sensitivity, such as a preconcentrator. Sensitivity is a common problem of gas sensors when applied to indoor detection.

FF-2020 (Shimadzu, Japan) and FOX electronic nose (Alpha M.O.S, France) are typical examples of commercialized odor analyzing systems based on MOX sensors.

Quartz Crystal Microbalance Sensors

Quartz Crystal Microbalances (QCM) are widely used as thickness monitor in vacuum deposition systems to control the thickness of deposited thin films. Figure 9(a) shows a schematic of a QCM device. The QCM is realized a mass-sensitive sensor by a mass loading effect of chemicals ad-

sorbed on very thin sensing layers deposited on QCM surfaces. As shown by the equation given in Figure 9(a), the QCM resonant frequency decreases by 1 Hz when 5.3 ng of mass is added in the sensitive layer (typical AT-cut quartz crystal with a resonant frequency of f=9MHz and a sensitive surface S=1cm2). Such a mass change can be attained by the formation of a benzene monolayer on the sensor surface. Thus high sensitivity QCM sensors can be made to detect sub parts per million (ppm) concentration of odor vapor.

QCMs are widely applied in odor sensing systems (Tuantranont, et al., 2011; Becker & Cooper, 2011). Nakamoto and Moriizumi use QCMs to develop an odor sensing system based on the combination of multi-channel QCMs and artificial neural network (Okahata & Shimizu, 1987; Ema, et al., 1989). In this system, various kinds of odorant adsorbing layers were coated on

Figure 9. Gas sensitive devices: (a) QCM odor sensor, (b) nanocomposite polymer, organic semiconductor, (c) LPR gas sensing mechanism, and (d) controlled potential electrochemical sensor cell

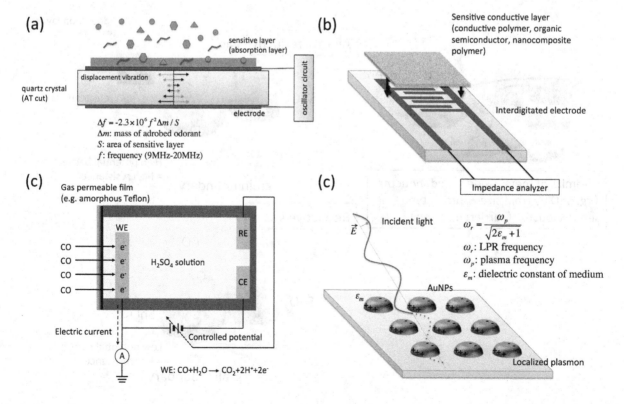

the QCM surfaces. The sensing layers are decisive to control QCM sensitivity and selectivity to odor chemicals (Wyszynski, et al., 2009). Typically adsorbing properties depends on the Langmuir equilibrium equation and, therefore, the QCM response is quasi-logarithmic with odor concentration in a defined concentration range. Generally, QCM sensors are suitable for odor sensing but their performances are limited by the availability of coating materials and techniques.

Organic Semiconductors

Organic semiconductors have high compatibility to organic materials and can be synthesized in a wide variety of materials. Therefore, it is expected that sensitivity and selectivity to various odorants can be tuned using different organic semiconductors. Conductivity of organic semiconductors is low in general so that interdigitated electrodes are used to decrease the resistance of the sensitive organic semiconductor layer. Figure 9(b) shows a basic structure of an electrode for sensitive conductive organic semiconductor layers (Bernards, et al., 2010; Eurochem, 2011; Liu, et al., 2010).

Conductive Polymer Composites

Odor sensors made of conductive polymer composites have been developed by N. Lewis (Lewis, 2000) and commercialized by Cyrano Sciences (Smith detection) as Cyranose. Cyranose is equipped with 32 channels consisting of conductive polymer nanocomposites. Carbon black is a common material used to obtain composite electrical conductivity. Similar carbon-polymer composites were already used as humidity sensors. The odor sensors based on conductive polymer composites have the same response mechanism to odor chemicals, where conductance of the material changes by swelling of the polymer through absorption of odor chemicals. This mechanism has high sensitivity near the percolation threshold. Carbon Nanotubes (CNT) have also been

applied to this type of sensors with the purpose of sensitivity enhancement. The basic structure of sensors made of conductive polymer composites is similar to that used for organic semiconductor materials shown in Figure 9(b).

Electrochemical Sensors

Amperometric Gas Sensors (AGS) are widely used to detect gases, such as oxygen, carbon monoxide, hydrogen sulfide, and nitrogen oxide (Hollowell & McLaughlin, 1973; Stetter, 2008). Particularly, AGS have been successfully commercialized for the detection of hazardous gases. The sensor has its own lifetime, and sensitivity is relatively high. The sensor measures electric current (Faradaic current) under a certain electrode potential, where a certain chemical species reacts at a certain redox potential. The potential is specific to the chemical; therefore, selectivity can be achieved by controlling the potential. Output current depends on the amount of chemical reaction occurred on the electrode surface, therefore the response increases with the analyte concentrations (Figure 9[c]). Consequently, the sensor is not very suitable for odor analyses.

Electrochemical impedance, surface impedance of electrode, is also a candidate of sensor signals where changes of impedance and its spectroscopy give information about odor chemicals (Izumi, et al., 2008). Chemical reaction required in AGS is not indispensable for impedance measurements, because surface impedance will be changed by adsorption of chemicals onto the electrode surface. In this method, concentration dependency of adsorption generally follows an adsorption isotherm that increases logarithmically in a defined concentration range.

Plasmonic Sensors

Nanoparticles (NPs) of noble metals have unique optical properties. Light of a certain wavelength excites a plasmon resonance in the particle that results in light extinction (ohmic and scattering losses) at this particular wavelength. This effect is called Localized Plasmon Resonance (LPR) and is being actively researched. The characteristic wavelength for the light extinction depends on the size of NPs and the refractive index of the NP surrounding. As shown in Figure 9(d), the extinction wavelength increases when the NP surrounding is filled with chemical substances that change the refractive index of the NP surrounding. This change in refractive index modifies the plasmon resonance conditions, thus shifting the extinction wavelength. Consequently, NPs respond to odor chemicals when the odorants adsorb on the NPs.

Modification of the surface of NPs by functional materials allows for a better control of sensitivity and selectivity to odor chemicals. LPR in NPs present the advantage of high sensitivity and fast response time. Interaction of light with metallic nanoparticles through LPR may provide a means to develop molecular recognition schemes for odor sensors (Mayer, 2011).

Other Sensor Devices

Surface Acoustic Wave (SAW) based devices are similar to QCM devices, in which an oscillator is fabricated on a piezoelectric substrate and connected to a pair of electrodes and delay line. The sensor responds to gases by means of mass-loading effect on sensitive layer coated on the delay line. Higher operating frequencies of SAW oscillators lead to high sensitivity in gas detection.

Photo Ionization Detector (PID) detects an electric current that is caused by the photo-ionization of chemicals. Some PID sensors (RAE Systems, USA/Ion Sciences, UK) are commercialized for monitoring VOCs. This detector has fast response time (~s) and high sensitivity (ppb order). However, PID detector response is linear with chemical concentration (electric current increases linearly with ionized chemical concentration) and therefore the PID detector output signal does not represent olfactory sensation well.

Optical methods such as infrared absorbance, dye color change, and dye fluorescence are also used to detect gases (Lubbers & Opitz, 1975; Walt, 2010). Optical methods present the advantage of remote sensing ability. Combination of optical detection methods with optical fibers is very powerful to realize sensing systems (Rakow & Suslick, 2000).

Biosensors that utilize biological materials such as enzyme and antibody exhibit very high performance in terms of sensitivity and selectivity (Hun & Park, 2010). In addition, olfactory receptors have been used in odor sensor systems (Misawa, et al., 2010; Ling, et al., 2010).

Electronic-Nose System

Odor sensing systems are usually referred to as electronic noses (e-nose) and consist of array of gas sensors (Persaud & Dodd, 1982; Rock, et al., 2008; Arshak, et al., 2004, Wilson & Baietto, 2009). Even if each sensor has low selectivity to odor chemicals, the e-nose architecture of sensor array makes it possible to evaluate odor sensation using sensor signal processing (Figure 10). However, the very large number of odor chemicals restricts the applications of e-nose systems, because unknown or unexpected odor chemicals may disturb the responses of the sensor systems by generating sensor errors. Examples of e-nose systems are the metal oxide sensors based FS-2020 (Shimadzu, Japan), the FOX system (Alpha M.O.S, France), the Cyranose 320 system (Cyranose Sciences, USA). All these systems use the sensor array design described in Figure 10.

To convert the data collected with e-nose systems into olfactory sensory values, data processing plays a crucial role as explained in the section on pattern analysis which follows.

Figure 10. Electronic nose system

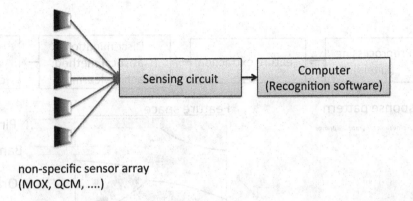

non-specific sensor array
(MOX, QCM, ...)

Applications of Odor Sensing Systems

Odor recognition is used in a broad range of fields and therefore a very large number of odor sensing system applications have been reported to date (Mahdi, et al., 2010; Thaler, et al., 2001; Wilson & Baietto, 2011; Laothawornkitkul, et al., 2008; Sankaran, et al., 2010; Sekhar, et al., 2010; Smith, et al., 2008). The major fields are:

- **Environment:** Water quality, air pollution, offensive odor
- **Medical Diagnosis and Health Monitoring:** Breathe analysis, cancer detection, and body odor
- **Food Quality and Production:** Meat, fruit, vegetable, oil, wine, beer, beverages, dairy foods, coffee, and agriculture
- **Safety:** Landmine detection, explosive detection, gas leakage, fire detection, illegal drug, biometrics and human investigation
- **Cosmetics:** Perfume, aromatics
- **Robotics:** Odor source localization, self-propelled robot

Finally, it should be noted that the prediction of odor perception from the information gained by chemical analysis is still difficult.

PATTERN ANALYSIS FOR ODOR SENSING SYSTEM

This section covers odor classification techniques based on standard statistical classification methods and more advanced pattern classification approaches based on statistical theory, neural networks, and optimization theory. The classification methods are first surveyed, and then, the typical classification algorithms are presented which seems to be useful for classification of odor data. Emphasis is given on widely available data collected with metal oxide gas sensors and quartz crystal microbalance sensors for various kinds of odors.

Pattern Recognition Systems

The purpose of pattern recognition is to capture information in the raw data so as to take a decision based on categories (Young & Fu, 1986; Duda, et al., 2001). The pattern recognition enables us to recognize an object, understand spoken words, read handwritten characters, classify fresh fruits by the smells, etc. To achieve the recognition, sensing, segmentation and grouping, feature extraction, classification, and evaluation processes are used. In this section, we will explain these processes in more detail from the viewpoint of odor recognition.

Figure 11. Pattern analyses for a multivariate signal from an odor sensing system

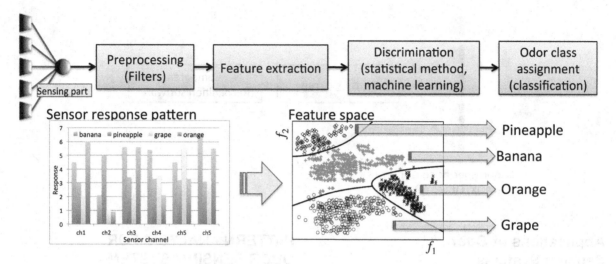

Preprocessing

Odor data is obtained in the form of time variations in the output of a sensor as voltage series or a resonant frequency series. These series include noise of several types. For example, the data acquired with metal-oxide semi-conductor gas sensor data show irregular changes and the quartz crystal microbalance sensors include spikes. It is important to remove such irregular changes and spikes in order to correctly extract features for classification (Figure 11). It is well known that a low pass filter is useful to smooth irregularities and a median filter is applicable to reduce spikes. This step is called data preprocessing and is used to reduce noise in the data before extracting features.

Low-Pass Filter

$H(j\omega)$ A low-pass filter attenuates the high frequencies of the transfer function . Since edge and other sharp intensity transitions such as noise are characterized by high frequencies, the effect of a low-pass filter is to blur the data. One of the most popular low-pass filters is the Butterworth filter whose frequency response function is given by:

$$|H(j\omega)|^2 = \frac{1}{1 + \varepsilon^2 (\omega / \omega_c)^{2n}} \qquad (2)$$

where n is the order of the filter, ω is the angular frequency, ω_c is the cutoff frequency, and ε is the gain parameter which determines the tolerance level. The phase property of the filter is a linear phase shift which means that in the time domain the input signal is simply shifted without distortion.

Obviously, low-pass filters result in the blurring of sharp details in the data series. The sharpness may include important information. This blurring can often be reduced significantly by the use of median filters.

Median Filter

A median filter replaces the measurement value at each time by the median of the values in a predefined neighborhood of that value instead of taking the average. The median m of a set of values is such that half of the values in the set are less than m and half of the values are greater than m . In order to perform median filtering in the neighborhood of a value at a specific time, we first sort the values in its neighbors, determine the median, and assign this value to the original value at a specific time. For example, in a three neighborhood configuration, the median is the second largest value, in a five neighborhood configuration, it is the third largest value. The principal function of median filtering is to force points with very distinct values from their neighbor values to be close to their neighbor values. Spikes that appear isolated in the area of the filter mask can therefore be eliminated by the application of median filtering.

Feature Selection and Extraction

In the feature selection and extraction step, features of the pattern will be chosen so that similar patterns having closed feature values and can be classified in the same category, and different patterns having different values that represent different categories (Young & Fu, 1986; Duda, et al., 2001). In other words, in this step the data dimensionality will be reduced so that patterns can be represented with few parameters named pattern descriptors. Pattern descriptors constituting a low-dimensional representation of the pattern are called features since they play an important role in characterizing the distinguishing properties of pattern classes.

FORMULATION OF FEATURE SELECTION AND EXTRACTION

The feature selection and extraction step corresponds to dimensionality reduction of the dataset and can be achieved in two different ways (Young & Fu, 1986; Duda, et al., 2001). One way is to identify the features which contribute to separability of categories. The problem is to select a small subset of d features $x_j, j = 1, 2, \cdots, d$ out of the available D measurements (sensor outputs) $y_k, k = 1, 2, \cdots, D$. This dimensionality reduction process is called feature selection. In this case the

redundant and irrelevant sensor outputs are ignored.

Another approach is to use the sensor outputs and map the useful information into a lower-dimensional d feature space given by:

$$x_j = f_j(y_1, y_2, \cdots, y_D), j = 1, 2, \cdots, d.$$

This approach is called feature extraction. We denote a set of mapping $f_j, j = 1, 2, \cdots, d$ by F and the sensor outputs (available measurements) $y_k, k = 1, 2, \cdots, D$ by y. We assume that each representation pattern y belongs to one of M possible pattern classes $\omega_i, i = 1, 2, \cdots, M$ and representation pattern y can be characterized by conditional probability density function $p(y / \omega_i)$ and a priori class probabilities $P(\omega_i), i = 1, 2, \cdots, M$.

A set of candidate features $\eta_j, j = 1, 2, \cdots, d$ is denoted by κ and

$$x = \{x_j \mid j = 1, 2, \cdots, d\}$$

is the set of optimal features in the sense of some cost function J. In the case of feature selection, optimization is performed over all possible candidate feature sets such that

$$J(\kappa^0) = \max_\kappa J(\kappa) \qquad (3)$$

where κ^o is an optimal selection among y.

In feature extraction, the optimization is carried out over all admissible mappings such that:

$$J(F^o) = \max_F J(F) \qquad (4)$$

where F^o is an optimal feature extractor.

Then we have:

$$x = F^o(y). \qquad (5)$$

We will show the criterion functions in terms of the model characteristics $P(\omega_i)$ and $p(y / \omega_i)$ or the conditional probability density functions:

$$p(\kappa / \omega_i). \tag{6}$$

FEATURE SELECTION CRITERIA

Below, we introduce four criterion functions used to measure performance in feature selection and extraction. The four measure functions are error probability measure, probabilistic distance measure, probabilistic dependence measure, and interclass distance measure (Young & Fu, 1986; Duda, et al., 2001).

Error Probability Measure

In the d-dimensional feature space defined by a candidate set of features $\eta_i, i = 1, \cdots, d$, the error probability e is given by:

$$e = \int \left(1 - \max_i P(\omega_i / \eta)\right) p(\eta) d\eta,$$
$$d\eta = d\eta_1 d\eta_2 \cdots d\eta_d \tag{7}$$

where the integration is taken over all regions of the variables, $\eta = (\eta_1, \eta_2, \cdots \eta_d)$ which is the feature vector composed of candidate features. $P(\omega_i / \eta)$ is the a posteriori probability of the ith class and $p(\eta)$ denotes the mixture density function satisfying:

$$p(\eta) = \sum_{i=1}^{M} p(\eta / \omega_i) P(\omega_i). \tag{8}$$

Note that the a posteriori probability function $P(\omega_i / \eta)$ is related to the ith class conditional probability density function by:

$$P(\omega_i / \eta) = \frac{p(\eta / \omega_i) P(\omega_i)}{p(\eta)}. \tag{9}$$

Probabilistic Distance Measure

The concept of probabilistic distance can be introduced by considering the error probability e in the two-class case. Noting that

$$P(\omega_1) + P(\omega_2) = 1$$

and

$$P(\omega_i / \eta) p(\eta) = p(\eta / \omega_i) P(\omega_i),$$

we have:

$$e = \frac{1}{2}\left[1 - \int | p(\eta / \omega_1) P(\omega_1) - p(\eta / \omega_2) P(\omega_2) | d\eta\right]. \tag{10}$$

The above equation means that the error becomes maximal when the integrand is zero, that is, the probability density functions are completely overlapped, and it becomes zero when the probability density functions $p(\eta / \omega_i), i = 1, 2$ do not overlap. The integral in the above equation can be considered to quantify the probabilistic distance between the two probability density functions $p(\eta / \omega_i), i = 1, 2$, that is, the greater the distance, the smaller the error and vice versa.

The following measures have been used widely.

$$J_C = -\ln \int p^s(\eta / \omega_1) p^{1-s}(\eta / \omega_2) d\eta, s \in [0, 1]$$
(Chernoff) $\tag{11}$

$$J_D = \left\{\int p(\eta / \omega_1) - p(\eta / \omega_2)\right\} \ln\left[\frac{p(\eta / \omega_1)}{p(\eta / \omega_2)}\right] d\eta$$
(Divergence) $\tag{12}$

Probabilistic Dependence Measure

The pattern recognition process can be considered to involve two random variables. One is the pattern vector η and the other is the class ω. The observation of an outcome of the pattern enables us to make a decision about the class. The dependence of the two variables is embodied in the conditional probability density functions $p(\mu / \omega_i), i = 1, 2, \cdots, M$. If η and ω_i are independent, then $p(\mu / \omega_i) = p(\eta)$, that is, the ith class-conditional probability density function is identical to the mixture probability density function. In that case, we do not learn anything about its class membership by observing the pattern vector η.

It is clear that the degree of dependence between the variable η and a particular realization ω_i can be measured by the distance between the conditional probability density function $p(\mu / \omega_i)$ and the probability density function $p(\eta)$. The overall dependence can be assessed by computing the weighted average of these class-conditional distances which yields a multiclass criterion of feature effectiveness.

Interclass Distance Measure

Many feature selection criteria are based on the heuristic notion of interclass distance. Given a set of patterns which is representative of the mixture distribution (training set), it is reasonable to assume that pattern vectors of each class occupy a distance region in the observation space. The average pair-wise distance between the patterns in the set is a measure of class separability in the space.

Let us denote a metric for measuring the distance between the kth pattern of the ith class and the lth pattern of the jth class by $\delta(\eta_{ik}, \eta_{jl})$, the average distance J_δ can be defined as:

$$J_\delta = \frac{1}{2} \sum_{i,j=1}^{M} P(\omega_i)$$

$$P(\omega_i) \frac{1}{N_i N_j} \sum_{i=1}^{N_i} \sum_{j=1}^{N_j} P(\omega_i) P(\omega_i) \delta(\eta_{ik}, \eta_{jl})$$

(13)

where N_i is the number of pattern vectors belonging to class ω_i.

The following metrics have been used in association with the criterion J_δ.

$$\delta_C(\eta_k, \eta_l) = \left| \eta_{kj} - \eta_{lj} \right| \quad \text{(city metric)} \tag{14}$$

$$\delta_E(\eta_k, \eta_l) = \sqrt{\sum_{j=1}^{d} (\eta_{kj} - \eta_{lj})^2} \quad \text{(Euclid metric)}$$

(15)

FEATURE EXTRACTION CRITERIA

Feature Extraction Measures

In the feature extraction step, a lower-dimensional feature space is to be found (Young & Fu, 1986; Duda, et al., 2001). Although the mapping required to achieve high-discriminatory information compression $x = F^o(y)$ may be nonlinear, a linear mapping may have the advantage of having some degree of analytical tractability and of being computationally feasible. Thus, we consider linear mapping only, that is, we will look for a feature extractor A where A is a $D \times d$ matrix, to transform the pattern vector y into a feature vector x according to:

$$x = A^T y. \tag{16}$$

The feature extractor should be optimal in the sense of a suitable criterion function $J(A)$. In contrast to the problem of feature selection where optimization procedures and criterion functions are independent, the feature extraction is closely linked with the criterion used.

Parametric Measures

The parametric measures can be used for feature extraction by expressing the mean vectors and covariance matrices of the class-conditional probability density functions in terms of the distributed parameters in the observation space $\tilde{\mu}_i$ and $\tilde{\Sigma}_i$ for any class i. Note that the relevant relationships are:

$$\mu_i = A^T \tilde{\mu}_i \tag{17}$$

and

$$\Sigma_i = A^T \tilde{\Sigma}_i A. \tag{18}$$

FEATURE SEARCH ALGORITHMS

Feature Selection on the Individual Measurements

Given a set of measurements, $y_j, j = 1, 2, \cdots, D$, the problem of selecting the optimal subset of $d < D$ of these measurements as features involves the evaluation of effectiveness of all the possible candidate feature sets κ of cardinality d that can be constructed from measurements $y_j, j = 1, 2, \cdots, d$. The search for the optimum is a combinatorial problem, that is, the number of sets for searching equals $D! / (D - d)! d!$. Furthermore, the assessment of each set κ may involve the estimation of probability density functions in multivariate space, the computation of the func-

tion defining the separability measure used, and numerical integration. Thus, the feature selection problem fails to be computationally feasible.

In a special case of two Gaussian distribution classes with equal diagonal covariance matrices, that is, the measurements are conditionally independent, the Mahalanobis distance becomes:

$$J_M(\kappa) = \sum_{j=1}^{d} \frac{(\mu_{1j} - \mu_{2j})^2}{\sigma_{jj}} \tag{19}$$

where μ_{ij} is the jth component of the ith class mean vector and σ_{jj} is the jth diagonal element of the covariance matrix. In this case, the contribution of class separability of one measurement is independent of all the other measurements. Thus, the optimal set of d features is determined by selecting d individually best measurements. Therefore, after computing $J_M(y_j), j = 1, 2, \cdots, D$, we rank the measurements such that the magnitudes of the criterion function become decreasing order. Then we select the best feature set $x = \{y_j \mid j = 1, 2, \cdots, d\}$.

Branch and Bound Algorithm

Feature set selection by brute-force search becomes computationally prohibitive. But it is possible to determine the optimal feature set without explicit evaluation of all the possible combinations of d measurements by using the branch and bound method. We assume that the goal is to find the minimum value of a function $J(x)$ where x ranges over some set S of admissible solutions over the search space. We can find the maximum value of $J(x)$ by finding the minimum of $J(x)$.

A branch and bound procedure requires two tools. The first one is a splitting procedure that, given a set S of candidates, returns two or more smaller sets $S_1, S_2, \cdots$ whose union covers S. Note that the minimum of $J(x)$ over S is $\min\{v_1, v_2, \cdots\}$ where each v_i is the minimum of $J(x)$ within S_i. This step is called branching, since its recursive application defines a tree structure (the search tree) whose nodes are the subsets of S.

Another tool is a procedure that computes upper and lower bounds for the minimum value of $J(x)$ within a given subset of S. This step is called bounding. The key idea of the branch and bound algorithm is that if the lower bound for some tree node (set of candidates) A is greater than the upper bound for some other node B, then A is discarded from the search. This step is called pruning, and is usually implemented by maintaining a global variable m (shared among all nodes of the tree) that records the minimum upper bound seen among all sub-regions examined so far. Any node whose lower bound is greater than m can be discarded.

The recursion stops when the current candidate set S is reduced to a single element, or when the upper bound for set S matches the lower bound. Either way, any element of S will be a minimum of the function within S. The algorithm is applicable under the assumption that a feature selection criterion satisfies the monotone property. Denoting a candidate feature set containing j features by κ_j, the monotone property means that for nested feature sets feature sets κ_j such that:

$$\kappa_1 \subset \kappa_2 \subset \cdots \subset \kappa_j \subset \cdots \subset \kappa_D \qquad (20)$$

The criterion function $J(\kappa_j)$ satisfies:

$$J(\kappa_1) \leq J(\kappa_2) \leq \cdots \leq J(\kappa_j) \leq \cdots \leq J(\kappa_D). \qquad (21)$$

Feature Extraction Algorithms

In order to find the maximal values for $J_C(A)$ and $J_E(A)$, we will take the derivatives for the measures with respect to A. Generally, the optimal solutions can be obtained by using the gradient method. But analytical solution is obtained for $J_C(A)$ when the covariance matrix are identical, that is, $\tilde{\Sigma}_1 = \tilde{\Sigma}_2 = \tilde{\Sigma}$.

The optimal feature extractor becomes a $D \times 1$ matrix given by:

$$A = \tilde{\Sigma}^{-1}(\tilde{\mu}_2 - \tilde{\mu}_1). \qquad (22)$$

When the mean vectors are identical, that is, $\tilde{\mu}_2 = \tilde{\mu}_1$, the optimal solution A becomes the matrix of eigenvectors $u_1, u_2, \cdots, u_D$ of the matrix $\tilde{\Sigma}_2^{-1}\tilde{\Sigma}_1$. Therefore, components of the eigenvalues ranked in descending order can be chosen until d to extract the features.

Classification Algorithms

In the classification step, the object is assigned to a category by using the feature vectors obtained with the algorithms described in the previous section. As perfect classification performance is difficult, a more general task is to determine the probability for each of the possible categories. The abstraction provided by the feature vector representation of the input data enables the development of a largely domain-independent theory of classification (Omatsu, et al., 1996; Dayhoff, 1990; Kohonen, 1997).

The degree of difficulty of the classification problem depends on the variability in the feature values for objects in the same category relative to the difference between feature values for objects in different categories. In what follows, we consider typical types of classification and new methods. Bayesian estimation and maximum likelihood estimation for the former case, and neural network approach for the latter case.

CONVENTIONAL CLASSIFICATION

Bayesian Classification

Let $\omega_i, i = 1, 2, \cdots, M$ be category with the probability $P(\omega_i)$ and let $x \in R^D$ be a feature vector where R^D is a D-dimensional Euclidian space. Let $\alpha_j, j = 1, 2, \cdots, N$ be actions and let $l(\alpha_j / \omega_i)$ be a loss function when the category is ω_i and the action α_j has been taken. If we define a conditional density function for x conditioned on ω_i by $p(x / \omega_i)$ which has been called a likelihood function. Then the posterior probability density function $P(\omega_i / x)$ can be computed from $p(x / \omega_i)$ by Bayesian formula:

$$P(\omega_i / x) = \frac{p(x / \omega_i)P(\omega_i)}{p(x)} \tag{23}$$

where the evidence $p(x)$ is given by:

$$p(x) = \sum_{j=1}^{M} p(x / \omega_j)P(\omega_j). \tag{24}$$

The Bayesian formula is described by:

$$posterior = \frac{likelihood \times prior}{evidence}. \tag{25}$$

Here, the Bayesian formula means that by observing x we can convert the prior probability $P(\omega_i)$ to the a posterior probability $P(\omega_i / x)$, that is, the probability of ω_i given that the feature vector x has been observed. $p(x / \omega_i)$ is called the likelihood of ω_i with respect to x, the term indicates that, other things being equal, the category ω_i for which $p(x / \omega_i)$ is large is more likely to the true category.

Assume that we observe a particular x and that we contemplate taking action α_i. If the true category is ω_j, by definition there occurs the loss

function $l(\alpha_i / \omega_j)$ and the expected loss function $L(\alpha_i / x)$ associated with taking action α_i is given by:

$$L(\alpha_i / x) = \sum_{j=1}^{M} l(\alpha_i / \omega_j)P(\omega_j / x). \tag{26}$$

Then the overall loss function L is given by:

$$L = \sum_{i=1}^{N} \int L(\alpha_i / x)p(x)dx \tag{27}$$

where the integral extends over the entire feature space.

Let us consider the special case of two-category classification problems. The action α_1 corresponds to deciding that the category is ω_1 and the action α_2 corresponds to deciding that the category is ω_2. Let $l_{ij} = \sum_{j=1}^{M} l(\alpha_i / \omega_j)$ be the loss incurred for deciding ω_i when the true category is ω_j. Then $L(\alpha_i / x)$ becomes:

$$\begin{aligned} L(\alpha_1 / x) &= l_{11}P(\omega_1 / x) + l_{12}P(\omega_2 / x) \\ L(\alpha_2 / x) &= l_{21}P(\omega_1 / x) + l_{22}P(\omega_2 / x). \end{aligned} \tag{28}$$

There are various ways to express the minimum-risk decision rule. The fundamental rule is to decide ω_1 if $L(\alpha_1 / x) < L(\alpha_2 / x)$, that is,

$$(l_{21} - l_{11})P(\omega_1 / x) > (l_{12} - l_{22})P(\omega_2 / x). \tag{29}$$

Since the loss incurred for making an error is greater than the loss incurred for being correct, both $(l_{21} - l_{11})$ and $(l_{12} - l_{22})$ are positive.

The above rule results in the equivalent rule, to decide ω_1 if:

$$(l_{21} - l_{11})P(x / \omega_1)P(\omega_1) > (l_{12} - l_{22})P(x / \omega_2)P(\omega_2) \tag{30}$$

and otherwise decide ω_2.

Assuming $l_{21} > l_{11}$, from the above inequality we have the rule to decide ω_1 if:

$$\frac{P(x \, / \, \omega_1)}{P(x \, / \, \omega_2)} > \frac{l_{21} - l_{11}}{l_{12} - l_{22}} \frac{P(\omega_2)}{P(\omega_1)} \equiv \theta_1. \qquad (31)$$

Here, θ_1 is called threshold and the right hand side of the above inequality is called the likelihood ratio. Thus, the Bayesian decision rule can be interpreted as the rule to decide ω_1 if the likelihood ratio exceeds a threshold θ_1.

Maximum-Likelihood Classification

The concept and meaning of maximum-likelihood function $p(x \, / \, \omega_j)$ has been explained in Bayesian classification part. We will define the maximum-likelihood function in more detail since it has many attractive attributes. One of them is good convergence properties as the number of training samples increases. The other one is that maximum-likelihood classification can be simpler than alternative methods, such as Bayesian methods or other methods.

Assume that we will separate a collection of samples according to class so that we have N data sets, $\Omega_1, \Omega_2, \cdots, \Omega_N$ and the samples in Ω_j have been drawn independently with the probability density function $p(x \, / \, \omega_j)$. Such samples are called independent and identically distribution and denoted as *i.i.d.* Furthermore, we assume that $p(x \, / \, \omega_j)$ has a known parametric form such as Gaussian distribution, which means that it is determined uniquely by the value of a parameter vector θ_j. For example, if we assume the Gaussian distribution $N(\mu_j, \Sigma_j)$ where μ_j and Σ_j are mean vector and covariance matrix, then θ_j means (μ_j, Σ_j). The problem is to estimate the unknown parameter vectors $\theta_1, \theta_2, \cdots$ and θ_N associated with the categories $\Omega_1, \Omega_2, \cdots$ and Ω_N, respectively based on the information provided by the training samples.

For the sake of simplicity, we assume that the samples in Ω_i gives no information about θ_j for $i \neq j$, which means that the parameter vectors for the different classes are independent. Thus, we treat the work distinctions separately and simplify the notation by deleting indications of class and the problem has been described as follows: Let Ω be a set of training samples drawn independently from the probability density function $p(x \, / \, \theta)$ to estimate the unknown parameter vector θ.

Assume that Ω contains n samples, $x_1, x_2, \cdots, x_n$ with the probability density functions $p(x_i \, / \, \theta), i = 1, 2, \cdots, n$. Since the samples were drawn independently, we have:

$$p(\Omega \, / \, \theta) = \prod_{i=1}^{n} p(x_i \, / \, \theta). \qquad (32)$$

Here, $p(\Omega \, / \, \theta)$ which has been considered as a function of θ, is called the likelihood of θ with respect to the set of samples, Ω. The maximum-likelihood estimate of θ is defined by the maximum value of $p(\Omega \, / \, \theta)$ with respect to θ and denoted by $\hat{\theta}$, that is,

$$\hat{\theta} = \arg \ \max_{\theta} p(\Omega \, / \, \theta). \qquad (33)$$

Intuitively, this estimate corresponds to the value of θ that agrees with the actual observed training samples. Furthermore, the log-scale representation may be useful, especially in the case of Gaussian distribution. It is called as log-likelihood function, that is,

$$\hat{\theta} = \arg \ \max_{\theta} \ln p(\Omega \, / \, \theta). \qquad (34)$$

In the case of Gaussian distribution with unknown mean vector μ, we consider a sample point x_i. Then logarithm of the probability density function $p(x_i \, / \, \mu)$ becomes:

$$\ln p(x_i \,/\, \mu) = -\frac{1}{2}\left(\begin{array}{l} \ln\left((2\pi)^D \det(\Sigma)\right) \\ +(x_i - \mu)^T \Sigma^{-1}(x_i - \mu) \end{array} \right)$$

$$(35)$$

and taking the derivative with respect to μ and letting it be 0, we have:

$$\Sigma^{-1}(x_i - \hat{\mu}) = 0 \qquad (36)$$

where $\hat{\mu}$ denotes the optimal value which satisfies the maximum-likelihood function.

As the above relation must hold for any $i, i = 1, 2, \cdots, N$, we have:

$$\hat{\mu} = \frac{1}{N}\sum_{i=1}^{N} x_i. \qquad (37)$$

In the case of Gaussian distribution with unknown mean vector μ and covariance matrix Σ, taking the derivative with respect to μ and Σ, and letting them equal to 0, we have:

$$\hat{\mu} = \frac{1}{N}\sum_{i=1}^{N} x_i \qquad (38)$$

and

$$\hat{\Sigma} = \frac{1}{N}\sum_{i=1}^{N} (x_i - \hat{\mu})(x_i - \hat{\mu})^T. \qquad (39)$$

Thus, the maximum-likelihood estimates of mean vector and covariance matrix are given by the above relation. However, it is easy to prove that the covariance matrix $\hat{\Sigma}$ does not satisfy the unbiased property and the unbiased estimate $\hat{\Sigma}_{ub}$ becomes:

$$\hat{\Sigma}_{ub} = \frac{1}{N-1}\sum_{i=1}^{N} (x_i - \hat{\mu})(x_i - \hat{\mu})^T. \qquad (40)$$

NEW TYPES OF CLASSIFICATION ALGORITHMS

Compared with the conventional classification, there have been new classification algorithms based on neural networks in pattern recognition. These methods do not require the specific models of the underlining probability distributions. New methods consist of procedures for estimating the probability density functions from sample patterns instead of assigning a model. If these estimates are satisfactory, they can be substituted for the true probability density functions when we design the classifier. Furthermore, they consist of directly estimating the a posteriori probabilities $P(\omega_i \,/\, x)$. We will explain four typical methods such as the layered neural networks, the self-organizing feature maps, the learning vector quantization, and the vector support machine.

Layered Neural Networks

Neural networks are networks mimicking our brain which consist of a large number of neurons to achieve intelligent information processing, especially, pattern recognition, learning ability, and associative memories.

The layered neural network consist of more than three layered networks among which there are three types of layers, input layer, hidden layer, and output layer. The input layer consists of neurons corresponding to a feature vector. The output layer consists of neurons corresponding to the number of classification. The hidden layer consists of suitable number of neurons that connect the neurons in the input layer to those of the output layer. Each neurons are connected to each other and connection weights are adjustable such that the input could be classified correctly. The adjustment can be achieved based on trial and error as the network will learn everything step by step.

Let $O_i, i = 1, 2. \cdots, I$ be the inputs (feature vector components) and let $O_k, k = 1, 2, \cdots, K$ be the outputs (number of classes). For the sake of notational simplicity, we consider the case of one hidden layer while any number of hidden layers could be treated in the same way. Thus, we denote the hidden neuron output by O_j, $j = 1, 2, \cdots, J$. A mathematical model of the layered neural network can be given by:

$$O_j = f(\text{net}_j), \quad \text{net}_j = \sum_{i=1}^{I} w_{ji} O_i - \theta_j,$$

$$f(x) = \frac{1}{1 + e^{-x}}$$

$$(41)$$

$$O_k = f(\text{net}_k), \quad \text{net}_k = \sum_{j=1}^{J} w_{kj} O_j - \theta_k \quad (42)$$

where $f(x) \in (0, 1)$ is the sigmoid function, w_{ji} and w_{kj} are connection weights from neuron i to neuron j and from neuron j to neuron k, respectively, and θ_j is the threshold of neuron j.

Here, $f(x)$ is called as the output function of the neuron and net_j is a net weighted sum of outputs of neurons connected to neuron j.

Let the desired outputs be d_k, $k = 1, 2, \cdots, k$ which corresponds to the output of neural network O_k, $k = 1, 2, \cdots, K$. Let us denote the error between the desired output d_k and the actual output of neural network O_k by e_k:

$$e_k = d_k - O_k, k = 1, 2, \cdots, K \quad (43)$$

and the total sum of errata by:

$$E = E(w_{kj}, w_{ji}) = \frac{1}{2} \sum_{k=1}^{K} e_k^2. \quad (44)$$

Using the gradient method, we have the following recursive algorithm which is called the error back-propagation.

$$\Delta w_{kj} = \eta \delta_k O_j$$

$$\delta_k \equiv e_k f'(\text{net}_k) = e_k O_k (1 - O_k)$$

$$w_{kj}^{\text{new}} = w_{kj}^{\text{old}} + \Delta w_{kj}$$

$$\Delta w_{ji} = \eta \delta_j O_j$$

$$\delta_j = \eta \sum_{k=1}^{K} \delta_k w_{kj} f'(\text{net}_j) = \eta \sum_{k=1}^{K} \delta_k w_{kj} O_j (1 - O_j)$$

$$w_{ji}^{\text{new}} = w_{ji}^{\text{old}} + \Delta w_{ji}.$$

$$(45)$$

where $\eta > 0$ and $f'(x)$ is the derivative of $f(x)$ with respect to x.

Note that if $f(x) = x$, that is, linear, $f'(x) = 1$ and $\delta_k = e_k$. Since δ_k shows the nonlinear effect, δ_k is called the generalized error. The generalized error δ_j is obtained from δ_k by changing the direction the connection arrow with connection weight w_{kj} and calculating the weighted sum of δ_k. Thus, this algorithm is called as the error back-propagation algorithm. The number of neurons in the hidden layer can be selected by trial and error. If we increase the number of neurons in the hidden layer or increase the number of hidden layers, we can obtain the more precise classification. But if we increase number of neurons too much, the neural network can learn the noise, that is, over-learning occurs.

Self-Organizing Feature Map

The self-organizing feature map is a two-layered network. The first layer is called as the input layer and the second layer is organized as a two-dimensional grid. All interconnections go from the first layer to the second layer and the two layers are fully interconnected. Each input unit is connected to all of the units in the competitive layer with connection weights. Each unit in the competitive layer has a connection weight vector. The initial values of the connection weight vectors are set in a random way or in such a way that small random numbers are added to the average of all connection weight vectors.

When an input vector (feature vector) is presented, the distances between the input vector and connection weight vectors for all units in the competitive layer are calculated and find the minimum distance unit in the competitive layer which is called as the winner unit. Connection weight vectors located near the winner neuron have been altered such that connection weight vectors will become similar to that of the winner neuron. In the beginning the distance to be affected is long and the distance will be shortened step by step. The connection weight vector is updated during the training of the network.

An input vector to the self-organizing feature map is denoted as:

$$u = (u_1, u_2, \cdots, u_D). \tag{46}$$

The connection weight vector from this input to a single neuron in the competitive layer is:

$$w_i = (w_{i1}, w_{i2}, \cdots, w_{iD}) \tag{47}$$

where i identifies the number of neuron in the competitive layer.

The first step in the operation is to compute a similarity index for each neuron in the competitive layer with the input vector. This similarity index measures the extent to which the weights of each neuron match the corresponding values of the input vector. The matching value for unit i is:

$$d_i \equiv \|u - w_i\| \text{ or } e_i \equiv \|u_i\| \ \|w_i\| \cos\theta \tag{48}$$

where $\|\ \|$ denotes Euclidean norm and θ denotes the angle between u and w_i.

The neuron with the lowest matching value of d_i (the highest matching value of e_i) is called the best match vector or the winner vector. Here, we denote the neuron with the best much as neuron c and chosen such that:

$$\|u - w_c\| = \min_i \ \|u - w_i\| \tag{49}$$

where the minimum is taken over all neurons i in the competitive layer.

After the winning neuron is identified, the next step is to identify the neighborhood around it. The neighborhood consists of those processing neurons that are close to the winner neuron in the competitive layer grid. The size of neighborhood changes every updating. The neighborhood is denoted by the set of neurons N_c. Connection weighting vector is updated for all neurons that are in the neighborhood of the winning neuron. The update relation is given by:

$$\Delta w_{ij} = \begin{cases} \alpha(u_i - w_{ij}), & i \in N_c \\ 0, & i \notin N_c \end{cases} \tag{50}$$

and

$$w_{ij}^{\text{new}} = w_{ij}^{\text{old}} + \Delta w_{ij}. \tag{51}$$

This adjustment results in the winning neuron and its neighbors having their connection weight vectors modified, becoming more like the input vector. The winner vector becomes more likely to win the competition if the same or a similar input vector will be presented subsequently.

There are two parameters that must be specified: The value of α, the learning rate parameter in the connection weight adjustment relation, and the size of the neighborhood N_c. An acceptable rate of decrease for α is given by:

$$\alpha_t = \alpha_0 \left(1 - \frac{t}{T}\right) \tag{52}$$

where t is the current training iteration and T is the total number of training iterations to be done. Thus, α begins at a value α_0 and is decreased until it reaches the value of 0.

The size of the neighborhood is the second parameter to be specified. Typically the initial neighborhood width is relatively large, and the width is decreased over many training iteration. Let d be distance from the winner neuron c. Since the width of the neighborhood decreases over the training iterations, the value d decreases. Initially d is set at a chosen value d_0 and then it will be decreased according to the equation:

$$d_t = d_0 \left(1 - \frac{t}{T}\right) \tag{53}$$

where t is the current training iteration and T is the total number of training iterations to be done. Thus, d begins at a value d_0 and is decreased until it reaches the value of 0.

Learning Vector Quantization Algorithm

This algorithm is a kind of self-organizing feature maps and it uses the teacher for classification. Let us consider the classification problem such that we wish to classify an input $x \in R^D$ into one of the classes $c_1, c_2, \cdots, c_K$ where each class has some sub-classes. The neural network is a two-layered network like the self-organizing feature map where the first layer is the input layer and the second layer is a competitive layer with the same number of neurons as sub-classes allocated in a class. For example, we specify L neurons for the class $c_i = \{c_{i1}, c_{i2}, \cdots, c_{iL}\}$ although they are regarded as the same class c_i. Note that all neurons in the competitive layer have been renumbered from $1, 2, \cdots, N$, where N is the total number of neurons including the subclasses. As in the self-organizing feature map, all neurons in the competitive layer are connected to the neurons in the input layer with connection weights. The connection weight vector m_i is updated during the training of the network.

An input vector to the self-organizing feature map is denoted as:

$$x = (x_1, x_2, \cdots, x_D). \tag{54}$$

The connection weight vector from this input to a single neuron in the competitive layer is:

$$m_i = (m_{i1}, m_{i2}, \cdots, m_{iD}) \tag{55}$$

where i identifies the ith neuron among all neurons N in the competitive layer.

Note that the connection weight vector to the winner neuron by m_i instead of w_i according to the original notation. The only difference compared with the self-organizing feature map is that the learning vector quantization algorithm can use the information of the class to which the input vector belongs. In other words, in the case of the learning vector quantization algorithm we have been informed the class of the input vector in advance and we will train the neural network such that all the training samples could be classified correctly by adjusting the connection weight vectors. In this sense, the learning vector quantization is a classifier with teacher.

The first step in the operation is to compute a similarity index for each neuron in the competitive layer with the input vector. This similarity index measures the extent to which the weights of each neuron match the corresponding values of the input vector. The matching value for unit i is:

$$d_i \equiv \|x - m_i\| \text{ or } e_i \equiv \|x\| \, \|m_i\| \cos \theta. \tag{56}$$

The neuron with the lowest matching value of d_i (the highest matching value of e_i) is called the best match vector or the winner vector. Here, we denote the neuron with the best much as neuron c and chosen such that:

$$\|x - m_c\| = \min_i \ \|x - m_i\| \tag{57}$$

where the minimum is taken over all neurons i in the competitive layer.

After the winning neuron is identified, the next step is to judge whether the winning neuron in the competitive layer belongs to the same class of the feature of the input vector or not. Connection weighting vector is updated only for the winning neuron. The update relation is done according the following rule:

If the class of m_i is the same class of x

$$m_j(t+1) = \begin{cases} m_j(t) + \alpha(t)(x - m_j(t)), & j = i \\ m_j(t), & j \neq i. \end{cases} \tag{58}$$

If the class of m_i is not the same class of x

$$m_j(t+1) = \begin{cases} m_j(t) - \alpha(t)(x - m_j(t)), & j = i \\ m_j(t), & j \neq i. \end{cases} \tag{59}$$

This adjustment results in the winning neuron belonging to the same class to the input vector having its connection weight vector modified, becoming more like the input vector, but the winning neuron belonging to the different class to the input vector having its connection weight vector modified, becoming more unlike the input vector.

An acceptable rate of decrease for is given by:

$$\alpha_t = \alpha_0 \left(1 - \frac{t}{T}\right) \tag{60}$$

where t is the current training iteration and T is the total number of training iterations to be done. Thus, α begins at a value α_0 and is decreased until it reaches the value of 0.

Support Vector Machine

In training a classifier, the aim is to maximize the classification accuracy for the training data. If we try to achieve the learning to much for the training data, classification ability (generalization ability) for unknown data may decrease. This is called over-fitting. The vector support machine is useful to increase the generalization ability. In what follows, we will discuss the concept of the support vector machine in the case of two-class problems.

Let M training inputs $x_i \in R^m, i = 1, 2, \cdots, M$ belong to Class 1 or Class 2 and associated labels be $y_i = 1$ for Class 1 and $y_i = -1$ for Class 2. If these data are linearly separable, we can determine the decision function:

$$D(x) = w^T x + \theta \tag{61}$$

where w in an m-dimensional vector, θ is a bias term and for $i = 1, 2, \cdots, M$ we have:

$$w^T x_i + \theta = \begin{cases} > 0, & \text{for} \quad y_1 = 1 \\ < 0, & \text{for} \quad y_1 = -1. \end{cases} \tag{62}$$

Since the training data are assumed to be linearly separable, there is no training data on the discrimination line $w^T x_i + \theta = 0$. Thus, to adjust separability, we consider the following inequalities.

$$w^T x_i + \theta = \begin{cases} \geq 1, & \text{for} \quad y_1 = 1 \\ \leq -1, & \text{for} \quad y_1 = -1. \end{cases} \tag{63}$$

This relation is equivalent to:

$$y_i(w^T x_i + \theta) \geq 1 \quad \text{for} \quad i = 1, 2, \cdots, M. \tag{64}$$

The distance between the separating hyperplane and the training data nearest to the hyperplane is called the margin. Assuming that the hyper-planes $D(x) = 1$ and $D(x) = -1$ include at least one training data, the hyper-plane $D(x) = 0$ becomes the maximum margin. The separating hyper-plane with maximum margin is called the optimal separating hyper-plane. Assume that no outlier is included in the training data and that unknown test data will obey the same probability law as that of the training data. Then it is intuitively clear that the generalization ability is maximized if the optimal separating hyper-plane is selected. Since $w^T x_i = 0$ means that w and x_i are orthogonal, this hyper-plane passes origin and is perpendicular to the vector w. Thus, the hyper-plane $w^T x_i + \theta = 0$ is obtained by shifting the plane $w^T x_i = 0$ by θ. In order to find the suitable separating hyper-plane, it is essential to adjust vector w such that two classes could be separated. The following relation is most important to find the optimal separating hyper-plane analytically.

The Euclidean distance d_i between a training data x_i and the separating hyper-plane becomes:

$$d_i = \frac{|D(x_i)|}{\|w\|}. \tag{65}$$

Therefore, to make the optimum margin we can minimize $\|w\|$ or equivalently $\frac{1}{2}\|w\|^2$ under the constraints:

$$y_i(w^T x_i + \theta) \geq 1 \quad \text{for} \quad i = 1, 2, \cdots, M.$$

This problem could be solved by using quadratic programming technique.

Conclusion for Pattern Analyses

We have reviewed several methods for pattern classification. First, noise filtering methods were introduced. Then feature selection and extraction methods were discussed. Then Bayesian method and maximum-likelihood method have been discussed. Finally, some new techniques using neural networks were reviewed.

Detail algorithms were not described due to the limitation of the pages. However, the basic concepts of these algorithms have been stated. The details of them would be referred the original references.

REFERENCES

Arshak, K., Moore, E., Lyons, G. M., Harris, J., & Clifford, S. (2004). A review of gas sensors employed in electronic nose applications. *Sensor Review*, 24(2), 181–198. doi:10.1108/02602280410525977

Becker, B., & Cooper, M. A. (2011). A survey of the 2006–2009 quartz crystal microbalance biosensor literature. *Journal of Molecular Recognition*, 24, 754–787. doi:10.1002/jmr.1117

Block, E., Putman, D., & Zhao, S. H. (1992). Allium chemistry: GC-MS analysis of thiosulfinates and related compounds from onion, leek, scallion, shallot, chive, and Chinese chive. *Journal of Agricultural and Food Chemistry*, 40, 2431–2438. doi:10.1021/jf00024a018

Cai, X.-J., Block, E., Uden, P. C., Quimby, B. D., & Sullivan, J. J. (1995). Allium chemistry: Identification of natural abundance organoselenium compounds in human breath. *Journal of Agricultural and Food Chemistry*, 43, 1751–1753. doi:10.1021/jf00055a001

Curioni, P. M. G., & Bosset, J. O. (2002). Key odorants in various cheese types as determined by gas chromatography. *International Dairy Journal*, 12, 959–984. doi:10.1016/S0958-6946(02)00124-3

Dayhoff, J. (1990). *Neural network architecture*. London, UK: International Thomson Computer Press.

Dillon, W. R., & Goldstein, M. (1984). *Multivariate analysis methods analysis methods and applications*. New York, NY: John Wiley and Sons.

Dorman, F. L., Overton, E. B., Whiting, J. J., Cochran, J. W., & Gaedea-Torresdey, J. (2008). Gas chromatography. *Analytical Chemistry, 80*, 4487–4497. doi:10.1021/ac800714x

Duda, D. O., Hart, P. E., & Stork, D. G. (2001). *Pattern classification*. New York, NY: John Wiley & Sons.

Ema, K., Yokoyama, M., Nakamoto, T., & Moriizumi, T. (1989). Odour-sensing system using a quartz-resonator sensor array and neural-network pattern recognition. *Sensors and Actuators, 18*(3-4), 291–296. doi:10.1016/0250-6874(89)87036-2

Friedrich, J. E., & Acree, T. E. (2000). Issues in gas chromatography-olfactometry methodologies. In Rish & Ho (Eds.), *Flavor Chemistry*, (pp. 124-132). New York, NY: ACS Publications.

Ghasemi-Varnamkhasti, M., Mohtasebi, S. S., & Siadat, M. (2010). Biomimetic-based odor and taste sensing systems to food quality and safety characterization: An overview on basic principles and recent achievements. *Journal of Food Engineering, 100*, 377–387. doi:10.1016/j.jfoodeng.2010.04.032

Grob, R. L., & Barry, E. F. (2004). *Modern practice of gas chromatography*. New York, NY: Wiley-Interscience. doi:10.1002/0471651141

Grosch, W. (1994). Determination of potent odorants in foods by aroma extract dilution analysis and calculation of odour activity values. *Flavour and Fragrance Journal, 9*, 147–158. doi:10.1002/ffj.2730090403

Hollowell, C. D., & McLaughlin, R. D. (1973). Instrumentation for air pollution monitoring. *Environmental Science & Technology, 7*(11), 1011–1017. doi:10.1021/es60083a012

Hubschmann, H. J. (2009). *Handbook of GC/MS: Fundamentals and applications*. New York, NY: Wiley-VCH.

Hussain, C. M. (2008). Carbon nanotubes as sorbents for the gas phase preconcentration of semi-volatile organics in a microtrap. *Analyst (London), 133*, 1076–1082. doi:10.1039/b801415a

IFT. (1975, June 10). *Minutes of sensory evaluation*. Chicago, IL: IFT.

IFT. (1981). *Sensory evaluation guide for testing food & beverage products*. Chicago, IL: Sensory Evaluation Division of IFT.

Kobayashi, A., Kagawa, S., Ishikawa, Y., Matsubara, H., Matsui, T., & Matsumoto, K. (2008). Identification of plastic off-odors from linear-low density polyethylene. *Journal of Packaging Science & Technology Japan, 17*(6), 427–432.

Kohonen, T. (1997). *Self-organizing maps*. Heidelberg, Germany: Springer. doi:10.1007/978-3-642-97966-8

Laothawornkitkul, J., Moore, J. P., Taylor, J. E., Possell, M., Gibson, T. D., Hewitt, C. N., & Paul, N. D. (2008). Discrimination of plant volatile signatures by an electronic nose: A potential technology for plant pest and disease monitoring. *Environmental Science & Technology, 42*(22), 8433–8439. doi:10.1021/es801738s

Larmond, E. (1977). *Laboratory methods for sensory evaluation of food*. Ottawa, Canada: Agriculture Canada.

Lee, S. H., & Park, T. H. (2010). Recent advances in the development of bioelectronic nose. *Biotechnology and Bioprocess Engineering, 15*, 22–29. doi:10.1007/s12257-009-3077-1

Lee, S.-J., & Noble, A. (2003). Characterization of odor-active compounds in Californian chardonnay wines using GC-olfactometry and GC-mass spectrometry. *Journal of Agricultural and Food Chemistry, 51,* 8036–8044. doi:10.1021/jf034747v

Ling, S., Gao, T., Liu, J., Li, Y., Zhou, J., & Li, J. (2010). The fabrication of an olfactory receptor neuron chip based on planar multi-electrode array and its odor-response analysis. *Biosensors & Bioelectronics, 26,* 1124–1128. doi:10.1016/j.bios.2010.08.071

Lubbers, D. W., & Opitz, N. (1975). *Die pCO2-/p02-Optode: Eine Neue pCO2-bzw. p02-Messsonde zur. Meilgaard, M., Civille, G. V., & Thomas, B. (2006). Sensory evaluation techniques* (4th ed.). Boca Raton, FL: CRC Press.

Mayer, K. M., & Hafner, J. H. (2011). Localized surface plasmon resonance sensors. *Chemical Reviews, 111*(6), 3828–3857. doi:10.1021/cr100313v

Miyazawa, N., Tomita, N., Kurobayasi, Y., Nakanishi, A., Ohkubo, Y., Maeda, T., & Fujita, A. (2009). Novel character impact compounds in yuzu. *Journal of Agricultural and Food Chemistry, 57,* 1990–1996. doi:10.1021/jf803257x

Okahata, Y., & Shimizu, O. (1987). Olfactory reception on a multibilayer-coated piezoelectric crystal in a gas phase. *Langmuir, 3,* 1171–1172. doi:10.1021/la00078a054

Omatu, S., Marzuki, K., & Rubiyah, Y. (1996). *Neuro-control and its applications.* London, UK: Springer. doi:10.1007/978-1-4471-3058-1

Osgood, C. E., Suci, G. J., & Tannenbaum, P. H. (1957). *The measurement of meaning.* Urbana, IL: University of Illinois Press.

Pawliszyn, J. (1997). *Solid phase microextraction, theory and practice.* New York, NY: Wiley-VCH.

Persaud, K., & Dodd, G. (1982). Analysis of discrimination mechanisms in the mammalian olfactory system using a model nose. *Nature, 299,* 352–355. doi:10.1038/299352a0

Pillonel, L. (2002). Rapid preconcentration and enrichment techniques for the analysis of food volatiles: A review. *Lebensmittel-Wissenschaft + [i.e. Und] Technologie. Food Science + Technology. Science + Technologie Alimentaire, 35,* 1–14. doi:10.1006/fstl.2001.0804

Rock, F., Barsan, N., & Weimar, U. (2008). Electronic nose: Current status and future trends. *Chemical Reviews, 108,* 705–725. doi:10.1021/cr068121q

Sankaran, S., Mishra, A., Ehsani, R., & Davis, C. (2010). A review of advanced techniques for detecting plant diseases. *Computers and Electronics in Agriculture, 72*(1), 1–13. doi:10.1016/j.compag.2010.02.007

Seiyama, T., Kato, A., Fujiishi, K., & Nagatani, M. (1962). A new detector for gaseous components using semiconductive thin films. *Analytical Chemistry, 34,* 1502–1503. doi:10.1021/ac60191a001

Sekhar, P. K., Brosha, E. L., Mukundan, R., & Garzon, F. H. (2010). Chemical sensors for environmental monitoring and homeland security. *Electrochemical Society Interface.* Retrieved from http://shinwa-cpc.co.jp/gc/product/needl.html and http://www2.shimadzu.com/applications/GC/G261.pdf

Smith, R. G., D'Souza, N., & Nicklin, S. (2008). A review of biosensors and biologically-inspired systems for explosives detection. *Analyst (London), 133,* 571–584. doi:10.1039/b717933m

Stetter, J. R. (2008). Amperometric gas sensors - A review. *Chemical Reviews, 108*(2), 352–366. doi:10.1021/cr0681039

Stevens, S. S. (1957). On the psychophysical law. *Psychological Review, 64*(3), 153–181. doi:10.1037/h0046162

Taguchi, N. (1962). Gas alarm device. *Japanese Pat., 45*(38200).

Takada, S., Nakai, K., Thurakitseree, T., Shiomi, J., Maruyama, S., & Takagi, H. (2010). Micro gas preconcentrator made of a film of single-walled carbon nanotubes. *IEEJ Transactions on Sensors and Micromachines, 130*(6), 207–211. doi:10.1541/ieejsmas.130.207

Thaler, E. R., Kennedy, D. W., & Hanson, C. W. (2001). Medical applications of electronic nose technology: Review of current status. *American Journal of Rhinology, 15*(5), 291–295.

Tian, W.-C., Pang, S. W., Lu, C.-J., & Zellers, E. T. (2003). Microfabricated preconcentrator-focuser for a microscale gas chromatograph. *Journal of Microelectromechanical Systems, 12*, 264–272. doi:10.1109/JMEMS.2003.811748

Tuantranont, A., Wisitsora-at, A., Sritongkham, P., & Jaruwongrungsee, K. (2011). A review of monolithic multichannel quartz crystal microbalance. *Analytica Chimica Acta, 687*, 114–128. doi:10.1016/j.aca.2010.12.022

Walt, D. R. (2010). Bead-based optical fiber arrays for artificial olfaction. *Current Opinion in Chemical Biology, 14*, 767–770. doi:10.1016/j.cbpa.2010.06.181

Wilson, A. D., & Baietto, M. (2009). Applications and advances in electronic-nose technologies. *Sensors (Basel, Switzerland), 9*, 5099–5148. doi:10.3390/s90705099

Wilson, A. D., & Baietto, M. (2011). Advances in electronic-nose technologies developed for biomedical applications. *Sensors (Basel, Switzerland), 11*, 1105–1176. doi:10.3390/s110101105

Wyszynski, B., Somboon, P., & Nakamoto, T. (2009). Self-assembled lipopolymers with physisorbed amphiphilic GC materials for QCM odor sensors. *IEEJ Transactions on Sensors and Micromachines, 129*(9), 273–277. doi:10.1541/ieejsmas.129.273

Young, T. Y., & Fu, K. S. (1986). *Handbook of pattern recognition and image processing.* San Diego, CA: Academic Press.

Chapter 6
Odor Recorder

Takamichi Nakamoto
Tokyo Institute of Technology, Japan

ABSTRACT

An odor recorder is a gadget to record smells as well as reproduce them. The odor recorder to record the recipe of multiple-component odor, the dynamical change of the odor recipe even under the environmental change, such as humidity and temperature, has been so far studied. The methods to solve the mixture quantification problem, such as multiple linear regression, partial least squares, neural network, etc., are described. Furthermore, the active odor sensing system, which explores the recipe of the blended odor with its output pattern's similarity to that of the target odor, is described. Then, an example of the actual implementation of the odor recorder based upon a QCM sensor array is shown. Based upon that odor recorder, the experimental result of the fruit flavors made up of 4-8 odor components is described. Then a mass spectrometer without GC for determining the recipe of a few dozen odor components is explained. The mass spectrometry is useful to overcome the collinearity problem. However, the accuracy of the recipe estimation is insufficient when the number of odor-component candidates is more than a few hundred. The selection methods of odor components among the huge number of candidates and its application to the fruit flavors are explained. Finally, the method to find an appropriate set of odor components and the simulation result using mass spectrum database are described.

INTRODUCTION

Vision and audition among five senses can be nowadays easily recorded and reproduced under multi-media environment. Since the fields of vision and audition have been so far mature, it is indispensable to open the new field in addition to those senses. The study of recording olfactory information is very challenging.

DOI: 10.4018/978-1-4666-2521-1.ch006

Although odors have been analyzed using GC/MS (Gas Chromatography/Mass Spectrometry) for long time, odor-sensing systems often called electronic noses have been studied for last two decades (Pearce, Schiffman, Nagle, & Gardner, 2003). The odor sensing system offers simple, rapid, and objective evaluation method in place of GC/MS. Its principle is based upon the pattern recognition of the outputs of the multiple sensors with partially overlapping specificities in

Copyright © 2013, IGI Global. Copying or distributing in print or electronic forms without written permission of IGI Global is prohibited.

the same manner as that of a biological olfactory system. The group of UK proposed that principle first (Persaud & Godd, 1982), the concept of the similarity was introduced by Japanese group (Kaneyasu, Ikegami, Arima, & Iwanaga, 1987), and then a combination of a sensor array with neural network was proposed (Nakamoto & Moriizumi, 1988). Thereafter, many researchers came into this field and the research on the odor sensing system became popular (Nagle, Schiffman, & Gutierrez-Osuna, 1998; Gardner & Bartlett, 1994). Nowadays the international symposium on olfaction and electronic noses is held every two years.

On the other hand, an olfactory display, a device for smell presentation, was recently studied in virtual reality (Kaye, 2004). A computer-controlled scent diffuser connected to Internet (Messager, 2002), an odor-source localization in virtual space (Hirose, 2002) and the olfactory display for delivering smell to a single user's nose were studied (Yanagida, Kawato, Noma, Tomono, & Tetsutani, 2004).

An odor recorder with the capability of reproducing smells as well as recording them in the same manner as that realized in VCR (Video Cassette Recorder) was proposed (Nakamoto, Nakahira, Hiramatsu, & Moriizumi, 2001). This is the new field since the odor sensing system and the olfactory display have been independently studied. There are many consumer products related to smell such as food, beverage, cosmetics, toothpaste, air fresheners for breath, room, and bathroom, etc. It is possible to apply the odor recorder to a variety of fields such as e-commerce, game, virtual reality, cinema, etc.

Moreover, the odor recorder can be used for the research on cultural anthropology of the senses. The olfactory information about historically and ethnologically important objects can be preserved and be reproduced. Objects with scents around the world such as Asian, African, Caribbean, and European areas can be recorded. Especially, cooking is strongly related to scents. A variety of foods

and beverages around the world accompanied with scents can be reproduced using the odor recorder.

In the odor recorder, the odor quality is represented as the recipe of the multiple odor components. It is feasible to express a variety of odors by blending multiple ingredients. The recipe can be determined so that the similarity of the blended odor to the original one can be maximized. Thus, the mixture quantification technique is indispensable although the classification is focused on in most of odor sensing system. The mixture quantification technique is described in the next section.

There are two types of odor recorder. One determines the odor recipe kept constant during recording. The other is the odor recorder for obtaining the recipe of dynamically changing the odor. These two types of the odor recorder are reviewed here.

When we quantify odors composed of many components, mass spectrometry is useful. However, the selection of odor components among huge number of candidates is necessary to perform the quantification. This technique is also described.

One of the fundamental issues is to determine a appropriate set of odor components. You can think about the aspect from the physiology of olfaction. Buck and Axel reported the multigene family of G-protein coupled ORs (Olfactory Receptors) in 1991, and then molecular biology of olfaction rapidly progressed (Buck & Axel, 1991). They won the Nobel Prize in Physiology or Medicine in 2004. However, primary smells have not been so far discovered unlike primary colors in vision although the stereochemical theory was proposed by Amoore (1970).

Unlike the primary colors in the vision, however, the combination of several odor components does not cover whole range of the smell. Thus, the technique to select odor components so that the range of the smell can be maximized is described in the latter part of this chapter.

METHOD TO QUANTIFY MIXTURE COMPOSITION

The fundamental technique for an odor recorder is to obtain the composition of the gas mixture. In this section, the author describes the analysis method of sensor-array data, high-speed gas chromatography and mass spectrometry.

Analysis Method of Sensor-Array Data

Although many researchers study the odor classification using an odor sensing system, the mixture quantification is another research field. The simplest method is MLR (Multiple Linear Regression) (Dillon & Goldstein, 1983). The linear regression model involving the dependent variable Y_i and independent variables such as X_2, X_3,...,X_p can be written as:

$$Y_i = \beta_1 + \beta_2 X_2 + \beta_3 X_3 + \cdots \beta_p X_p + \varepsilon_i,$$

(1)

where β_1 denotes the intercept, and $\beta_2 \ldots \beta_p$ are the coefficients and ε_i is the residual of the ith measurement. In case of the sensor array, X_2, X_3,...., X_p correspond to sensor responses and Y_i is the concentration of the ith vapor in the mixture, assuming that the linear superposition is valid for each gas sensor response. In MLR, $\beta_2 \ldots \beta_p$ are obtained using the observed data so that the sum of the residual can be minimized. However, the linear superposition cannot be applied to most of actual gas sensors.

The important problem to be solved in the mixture quantification is the collinearlity problem. Let us assume that the two sensors are used to obtain the composition of the binary mixture as is illustrated in Figure 1. Each line shows the sensor characteristics and the solution is the intersection point of the two lines. However, these two lines become almost parallel if two sensor characteristics are very close. Then, the solution becomes instable even if the measurement data deviate just a little. In Figure 1, the location of the

Figure 1. Explanation of collinearity problem. Case of two sensors for binary mixture.

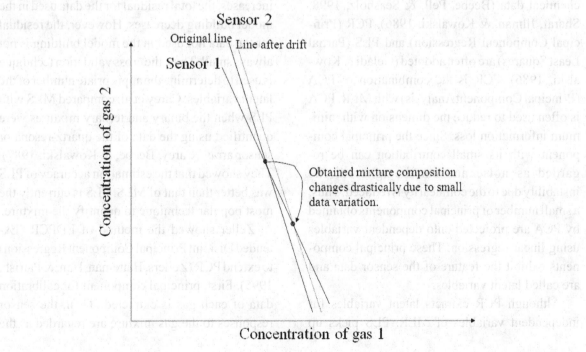

Figure 2. Principle of PLS method

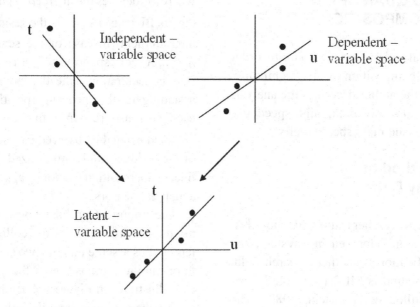

intersection point drastically changes with small noise. This problem is called collinearity and is the same as the calculation of the inverse matrix with the determinant approaching zero.

There are several methods to reduce the collinearity in chemometrics where statistical and mathematical techniques are used to analyze chemical data (Beebe, Pell, & Seasholz, 1998; Sharaf, Illman, & Kowalski, 1986). PCR (Principal Component Regression) and PLS (Partial Least Squares) are often adopted (Geladi & Kowalski, 1986). PCR is the combination of PCA (Principal Component Analysis) with MLR. PCA is often used to reduce the dimension with minimum information loss. Since the principal component with its small contribution can be regarded as noise and can be ignored, the instability due to the collinearity is reduced. Thus, a small number of principal components obtained by PCA are projected onto dependent variables using linear regression. These principal components exhibit the feature of the sensor data and are called latent variables.

Although PCR extracts latent variables for independent variables of MLR, PLS picks up

latent variables both for independent and dependent variables as is illustrated in Figure 2. Latent variables in space of independent variables are projected onto space of dependent variables using regression equation. Number of latent variables is an important parameter for raising estimation accuracy. When the number of latent variables increases, the total residual for the data used in the model building decreases. However, the residual for the data not used in the model building is not always small. Thus, the cross validation technique is used to determine the appropriate number of the latent variables. Carey et al. compared MLS with PLS when the binary and ternary mixtures were quantified using the data of the quartz-resonator sensor array (Carey, Beebe, & Kowalski, 1987). They showed that the estimation accuracy of PLS was better than that of MLS. PLS is currently the most popular technique to quantify the mixture.

Zeller showed the method of EDPCR (Extended Disjoint Principal Component Regression) to extend PCR (Zellers, Batteman, Han, & Patrish, 1995). First, principal component for calibration data of each gas is extracted. Then, the sensor responses to the gas mixture are regarded as the sum of the principal-component vector for each gas. The coefficient for each principal-component vector, the ratio of the corresponding component, is determined so that the residual can be minimized. Although this method is straightforward and is easy to understand, the accuracy deteriorates if each sensor has nonlinearity.

Another method is LWR (Locally Weighted Regression) (Wang, Isaksson, & Kowalski, 1994) where linear analysis method is partially applied in spite of the nonlinearity for the whole concentration range. The sensor response around the measurement point is approximated using linear function and calibration data. The accuracy of the quantification depends upon the number of calibration data. This method is useful when large amount of the data are available.

Those methods mentioned above are linear ones. However, it is expected to raise the accuracy of the mixture quantification when nonlinear method is used. Sensors such as metal oxide gas sensors have highly nonlinear properties. Although QCM (Quartz Crystal Microbalance) gas sensors or SAW (Surface Acoustic Wave) gas sensors have relatively linear characteristics, the accuracy of the mixture quantification is still influenced by the nonlinear portion. Thus, a neural network is useful to overcome the nonlinear characteristics (Duda, Hart, & Stork, 2001). One of the typical methods of neural networks is MLP (Multi-Layer Perceptron) composed of input layer, intermediate layer and output layer. Since Funahashi et al. showed that it was possible to realize arbitrary mapping with arbitrary accuracy using MLP (Funahashi, 1989), MLP is useful for nonlinear mapping. The typical algorithm for training MLP is an error back propagation often called BP method (Rumelhart, McClelland, & PDP Research Group, 1986). In the quantification phase, each sensor signal is fed into each neuron in the input layer and then the concentration of each gas component is output at each neuron in the output layer. In the training phase, the neural network is repeatedly trained when the concentration of each gas component

is presented as target input of each neuron in the output layer, followed by the weight modification using BP method.

Sundgren et al. trained MLP neural network using BP method so that the gas mixture composition could be obtained from the MOS FET gas sensor array (Sundgren, Winquist, & Lundstrom, 1991). Linear superposition is not valid for MOS FET gas sensor. They reported that they obtained good quantification accuracy in comparison with PLS method.

Wang et al. proposed a neural network called Chemnets especially designed for metal oxide gas sensors (Wang, Hwang, & Kowalski, 1995). The model of Taguchi gas sensor is combined with MLP. A priori knowledge of gas sensor enhanced the network capability. The rough model of Taguchi gas sensor reduces the number of parameters in the neural network, resulting in the reduction of training epochs and the improvement of generalization capability.

Although several methods work well to quantify the mixture, it is indispensable to build a model for mapping sensor space onto concentration space. It is necessary to have many data points to obtain the accurate model. Moreover, the model should be reconstructed when we encounter the sensor drift or aging problem. The active sensing method described below is suitable for solving the problems.

MEMS Gas Chromatograph

Although the data from a sensor array are analyzed to obtain the mixture composition in the previous section, the complicated analysis is not required if the single peak of each component in the mixture is temporally separated. This is achieved by gas chromatography. However, the conventional gas chromatography consumes much time and the size of the equipment is large. Although micro GC was proposed by Stanford University in 1979 (Terry, Jerman, & Angell, 1979), recent progress of micro fabrication technique made that research field activated. A small and high speed gas chromatography has been studied using MEMS (Micro Electro Mechanical System) technology. The small column fabricated using MEMS technology performed the gas separation to some extent, followed by pattern recognition of a gas sensor array (Zellers, et al., 2007). Although the typical problem of GC system is to consume much time to obtain the result, MEMS GC system is relatively fast. In case of the apparatus made by University of Michigan, it took four minutes to analyze the sample gas made up of 19 compounds. They integrated a micropreoconcentrator, dual separation columns, and an array of nanoparticle-coated chemiresistors using MEMS technology. It is expected to use MEMS GC system in the way similar to that of a sensor if the separation performance will be increased in the future.

Mass Spectrometry

Mass spectrometry, abbreviated as MS, without GC can be used to quantify the mixture as well as to classify samples. Although GC/MS is a typical

tool for gas analysis, it takes much time to analyze the gas when we use GC. Since it does not take much time to measure the sample only using MS, MS without GC is also useful when the accurate identification of the gas component included in a sample is not necessary. That system is called MS-based e-nose (Dittman, Nitz, & Horner, 1998; Miura, Nakamoto, & Moriizumi, 2003). In an odor recorder, it is possible to reproduce the odor even if we do not know the gas components. Since it is possible to reproduce the odor based upon the output pattern of the sensor array, the gas-component identification is not required.

An example of mass spectrum is shown in Figure 3. MS provides a variety of mass spectra of many compounds using more than 100 m/z, which correspond to elements in a sensor array. Many peaks appear due to the ion fragmentation since the ionization method is EI (Electron Ionization). Different mass spectra are obtained even if molecular weights of two different compounds are the same. Thus, collinearity problem is drastically reduced since a variety of mass spectra dependent upon samples are observed. The advantage of

Figure 3. Example of mass spectrum (sample: trans-2-hexenyl acetate)

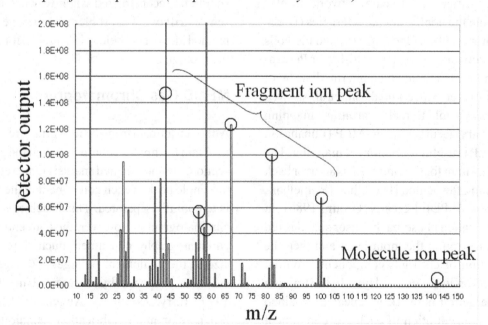

MS over other type odor sensing system is the capability of recording smell composed of many components. Moreover, stable responses can be obtained compared with other chemical sensors since the temperature or humidity in the ambient air do not influence the measurement result, whereas many chemical sensors suffer from aging or drift problem. Thus, we used MS and PLS methods mentioned before to quantify the recipe of an orange flavor composed of 14 components (Miura, Nakamoto, & Moriizumi, 2003). Later we describe the method to pick up actual odor components among huge number of candidates.

Most of mass spectrometers require the liquid injection for the measurement. However, a real-time mass spectrometer to suck the ambient air has been developed and was used for recording odor (Somboon, Wyszynski, & Nakamoto, 2009). The disadvantage of MS is the difficulty in miniaturization.

ODOR RECORDER

Research Trend

In the development of food product, food prototype is repeatedly modified followed by the sensory-test evaluation so that the prototype can approach the final product. It takes much time to develop food product because of the sensory-test evaluation. The similar process is required in an odor recorder although the process is accelerated due to the replacement of the sensory test with sensor measurement. Thus, the development of food product is described first.

In the process of food development, the subjects evaluate foods by sniffing them. The typical method of evaluation is SD (Sematic Differential) method where subjects determine scores for several evaluation items. Score takes a few discrete values, e.g., from 0 to 5. Evaluation items should express the feature of the product. For example, let us think about an ice cream development.

Sweetness, milk sense, vanilla sense, richness, oiliness, flouriness, clearness, total balance are evaluation items for the ice cream. The result of SD method is analyzed using principal component analysis and can be plotted on a scattering diagram as is shown in Figure 4. Positive direction of first principal axis shows the impression of sweetness while that negative direction expresses clearness. After modifying the prototype several times from A to E, the acceptable product is finally completed. Although it is possible to make a target product in this way, it consumes much time and labor during the development of the food product. In an odor recorder, this laborious task is automated and the time required for exploring the target becomes as short as possible.

Next, the researches related to the odor recorder are described. Although there have been many reports of odor sensing systems, the reports aimed for odor reproduction are just a few ones. It was proposed that the odor classified at one site was reproduced at remote site (Keller, Kouzes, Kangas, & Hashem, 1995). The output pattern of a sensor array composed of nine semiconductor gas sensors, humidity and temperature sensors was recognized using MLP (MultiLayer Perceptron). The classification result was transmitted to the remote site via Internet and the same smell was generated there. Although they did the experiment on odor classification, the actual experiment on the smell generation was not performed. Moreover, they did not blend odors but aimed to generate the same odor identified at the sensing site.

When we blend several odor components, the range of the smell to be covered becomes much larger. In the previous example of food-product development, the recipe of the ingredients is modified so that the prototype odor can approach the target one in sensory space. Since the sensory test consumes much time and labor, it can be replaced with an array of sensors. Although odor components are typically prepared in advance, F.Davide proposed the framework of the olfactory display,

Figure 4. Process of food development using sensory test

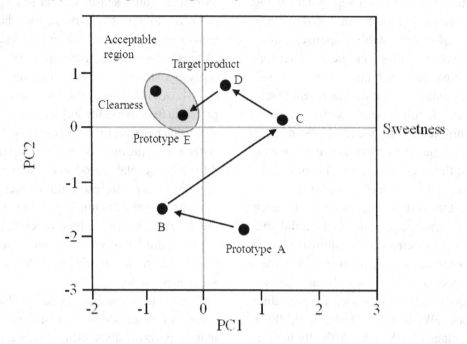

which not only blend odors but generate the new odor using a precursor (Davide, Holmberg, & Lundstrom, 2001). Since this is just the concept and has not been so far realized, the following portion of this chapter deals with blending odor components.

Matsushita et al. developed the equipment composed of conducting polymer sensor array and an odor generator using syringes (Matsushita, 2002). They just used linear regression method to obtain the recipe of the mixture. Based on that recipe, flavors were injected using the syringes driven by stepping motors and the flavor mixture was vaporized using a heater. Although the principle is close to an odor recorder, the feedback in active sensing, which enhances the flexibility and the accuracy of the system, is not included.

Carmel reported the algorithm to determine the mixture composition so that the sensor-array output pattern of the blended odor could match that of the target odor. They used 8 QCM gas sensors and obtained the mixture composition of the odor made up of five components. Although

they would like to synthesize the target odor, they only did the mixture quantification (Carmell & Harel, 2007).

Hayashi et al. tried to express odor focusing on partial structure of odorant. They expressed the single compound by blending several odor components. Odor components were selected using charge distribution and molecular structure, and the mixture composition was calculated using QSAR (Quantitative Structure-Affinity Relationship) method, followed by the sensory test. They claimed that the blended odor approached the target odorant in comparison with any single odor component (Iwasa, Izumi, Hayahsi, & Toko, 2004).

The trend of the research toward odor recorder is summarized as follows. The matching between target and reproduced odors should be ideally achieved in sensory space. Although this matching is investigated in food-product development, it consumes much time and labor. Thus, the sensory test should be replaced with a sensing system. The concept of the reproduction of the identified odor at remote site or the reproduction by automatically blending odor components have been reported. However, the report of the odor reproduction using a sensing system is only a few one whereas many researchers study odor-sensing systems. The odor recorder might be a next target in the field of electronic nose. In the next section, the principle of odor recorder using the active sensing is introduced.

Odor Recorder Using Active Sensing

An active sensing is a concept to raise sensing capability, efficiency, and flexibility. A conventional sensor works passively to convert physical or chemical quantities into electrical signals. The information flows in the order of detection, recognition, judgement, and action, and the information direction is only one way. However, the exploration behavior prior to recognition is important and the information circulation of exploratory behavior, detection, and recognition enables the remarkable enhancement of sensing system capability.

Its principle is illustrated in Figure 5. First, a target odor is introduced into a sensor array and its output pattern is memorized. Then, the array is exposed to the mixture of multiple odor components from an odor blender to obtain the pattern of the blended odor. The pattern matching, i.e., the distance between the target and the blended odors in sensor feature space, is calculated and the recipe of the blended odor is modified so that the pattern-matching index can be improved. The recipe modification, the measurement of the sensor responses to the blended odor and the pattern matching calculation are repeatedly performed until the sufficient pattern matching is achieved. After convergence, the recipe of the target odor is

Figure 5. Principle of odor recorder

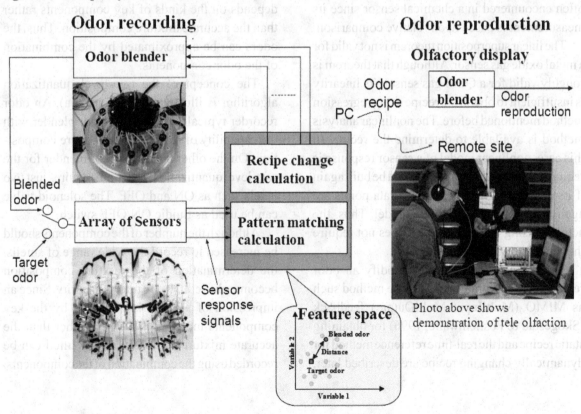

indirectly obtained from that of the blended one. Once the recipe is obtained, it can be transferred to the remote site via Internet. It is possible to reproduce the same smell even at the remote site (Nakamoto, 2005).

In a sensor array, a variety of sensors such as metal oxide semiconductors, QCM gas sensors, SAW (Surface Acoustic Wave) gas sensors, conducting polymer sensors and even mass spectrometry are used. Another important component in the odor recorder is the odor blender, which can be used as an olfactory display (Yamanaka, Matsumoto, & Nakamoto, 2002) in the odor reproduction phase.

The odor recorder is based upon an active odor sensing system since it explores the space of odor recipe in addition to the pattern-matching index. It deals with the mixture quantification problem, which many researchers tried to solve using PLS, PCR, neural net etc as is described in the previous section. The odor recorder is flexible and is robust against nonlinearlity, drift, and aging often encountered in a chemical sensor since its measurement is based upon relative comparison.

The linear superposition theorem is not valid for a metal oxide gas sensor. Although that theorem is roughly valid for a QCM gas sensor, its linearity is insufficient to obtain the recipe using regression method mentioned before. The nonlinear analysis method is available to determine the recipe. In this case, nonlinear model of a sensor response is required. However, its model should be built again if its characteristic varies. Many data points are again necessary to rebuild the model. Thus, the active sensing is useful since it does not require the model but does the feedback.

There are several ways to modify an odor recipe in the exploratory phase. The method such as MIMO (MultiInput MultiOutput) feedback (Skogestad & Postlethwaite, 1996) for obtaining static recipe and the real-time reference method for dynamically changing recipe are described later.

VARIOUS TYPES OF ODOR RECORDER

It is possible to record odor using the component odors less than the number of the components included in the target odor. This technique is called an odor approximation (Munoz, Yoshino, Nakamoto, & Moriizumi, 2007). Since there are variety of odors, the smaller numbers of odor components without the deterioration of the odor quality is preferable. Thus, we studied the odor approximation technique to reduce the number of the odor components. When the number of odor components is reduced, the collinearity problem is also reduced.

2-Level Quantization Method

One of the methods to reduce the collinearity our group proposed is two-level quantization method (Yamanaka, Matsumoto, & Nakamoto, 2003). In general, the human impression on the odors mostly depends on the kinds of key components rather than the accurate mixture composition. Thus, the odors can be approximated by the combination of the odor components.

The concept of the two-level quantization algorithm is illustrated in Figure 6(a). An odor recorder typically requires an odor blender with the capability of realizing any mixture composition. On the other hand, the odor blender for the two-level quantization algorithm requires just two levels such as ON and OFF. The solenoid valve can be used as fluidic ON/OFF switch.

Although the number of the components should be increased to record the wide range of smells, the determination of the mixture composition becomes difficult due to the collinearity. Since an impression of a smell is governed by the key components included in a smell rather than the accurate mixture composition, the smell can be recorded using the combination of the components.

Figure 6. Two-level quantization method: (a) principle and (b) recording result of five fruit flavors (copyright Elsevier, 2006). Odor-component number in parenthesis appears in the reference (Somboon, et al., 2007).

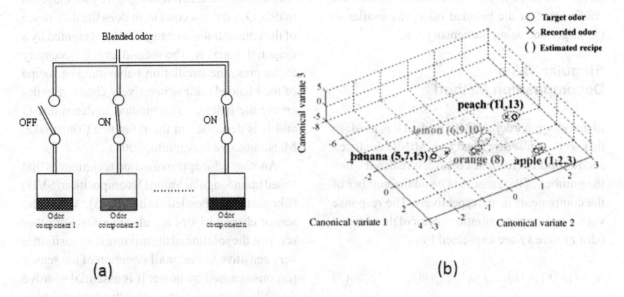

(a)   (b)

Since two-level quantization method reduces the recipe space to be explored, it is useful to record odors composed of many components avoiding the collinearity problem.

When we use N odor components to approximate odors, there are 2^N-1 recipe combinations. Although we can take three or more levels to quantify the mixture, two-level method was adopted here for simplicity. Since it is difficult to test all the combinations when the number of the odor components is increased, the sophisticated algorithm for the recipe exploration is required.

First, each odor component is measured and the combination of the odor components with its response pattern the closest to the target odor is estimated assuming that the linear superposition is valid. The deviation from the linear superposition is calculated after measuring the point among several ones around the ideal point. Then, the point to be explored is updated taking the deviation into account. This procedure is repeatedly performed until the convergence.

One of the examples of the experiment on two-level quantization is shown in Figure 6(b) (Som-

boon, Wyszynki, & Nakamoto, 2007). Five fruit flavors such as apple, orange, lemon, banana and peach were recorded using 13 odor components. The concentration of each odor component was adjusted so that the magnitude of each sensor-response vector could be the same. Each odor was automatically blended in the liquid phase using the autosampler (Somboon, Wyszynski, & Nakamoto, 2007). The autosampler is useful to blend large number of odor components whereas it takes much time to blend odor components. 13 QCM sensors (20MHz, AT-CUT) with different coatings were used here. Moreover, not only steady-state responses but also time constants both of response and recovery phases were used as variables. After selecting appropriate variables among 39 ones using canonical discrimination technique, the recipe was explored in 3 dimensional space of canonical discrimination analysis.

The circle in Figure 6(b) indicates the response pattern of the target odor and x does the response pattern of the recorded odor. The numbers in the parentheses mean the odor-component number required for each fruit (Somboon, Wyszynki, &

Nakamoto, 2007). Gray plots are predicted ones. As is shown in the figure, the blended odor each flavor was close to the target one. Moreover, we confirmed that the blended odor was similar to the target one using the sensory test.

Singular Value Decomposition Method

In an odor recorder, MIMO feedback is used. In this section, it is described how MIMO feedback such as optimal feedback control is realized when the number of the sensors is n and the number of the components is m, respectively. The response vector and the concentration vector of the blended odor at time kT are expressed by:

$$\mathbf{s_k} = [s_1(k), s_2(k), .., s_i(k), .., s_n(k)]^T \qquad (2)$$

and

$$\begin{aligned}\mathbf{u_k} &= [u_1(k), u_2(k), .., u_j(k), .., u_m(k)]^T \\ &= [c_1(k) - c_1(k-1), c_2(k) - c_2(k-1), .., c_j(k) \\ &\quad -c_j(k-1), .., c_m(k) - c_m(k-1)]^T\end{aligned}$$
$$(3)$$

where $s_i(k)$, $u_j(k)$, $c_j(k)$ are the ith sensor response, the jth component concentration change and the jth component concentration, respectively. The state-space equation is expressed by:

$$\mathbf{s_{k+1}} = F\mathbf{s_k} + G\mathbf{u_k}. \qquad (4)$$

In the optimal feedback control, the index value:

$$J = \sum_{k=0}^{p-1} \{(\mathbf{s_{k+1}} - \mathbf{s_{target}})^T Q(\mathbf{s_{k+1}} - \mathbf{s_{target}}) + \mathbf{u_k}^T R\mathbf{u_k}\}$$
$$(5)$$

is minimized by modifying the recipe of the blended odor where p is the number of the concentration change during the odor-recipe exploration. The first term in Equation(5) expresses the difference of the sensor response vector between the target odor and the blended one weighted by the diagonal matrix Q and the second term does the difference of the concentration-change vector weighted by a diagonal matrix R. The second term is necessary to suppress the oscillation behavior. The recipe of the blended odor is iteratively changed to decrease the index J. The method to determine Q and R is described in the reference (Yamanaka, Matsumoto, & Nakamoto, 2003).

Another odor approximation technique is that based upon Singular Value Decomposition (SVD) (Skogestad & Postlethwaite, 1996). When the sensor characteristics are close to those of other sensors, the solution of the mixture composition is very sensitive to the small variation of the sensor response caused by noise. It is essential to solve the collinearity problem so that the stable solution can be obtained.

The sensor responses s (s=Ac, A can be expressed as UWV^T) is:

$$\mathbf{s} = UWV^T\mathbf{c} \qquad (6)$$

where U is a column orthogonal matrix and V is a square orthogonal matrix. W is a diagonal matrix:

$$W = \begin{bmatrix} w_1 & & 0 \\ & \ddots & \\ 0 & & w_m \end{bmatrix}, w_1 \geq \cdots \geq w_m, \qquad (7)$$

where the diagonal elements are the singular values. When the vectors:

$$\mathbf{x} = V^T\mathbf{c} \qquad (8)$$

and

$$\mathbf{y} = U^T\mathbf{s} \qquad (9)$$

are used, the relationship between y and x is:

$$\mathbf{y} = W\mathbf{x} \tag{10}$$

according to eqs. (6, 8, 9. Since the elements of x corresponding to the small singular values in Equation (7) seldom contributes to y, those elements are set to 0s to suppress the influence of noise and to reduce the dimension of the space to be explored. The elimination of the small singular values contributes to the increase in the solution stability because the collinearity problem is suppressed. The recipe of the blended odor is modified so that the following index value at time k can be minimized instead of Equation (5).

$$J_k = (\mathbf{y_{k+1}} - \mathbf{y_{target}})^T Q(\mathbf{y_{k+1}} - \mathbf{y_{target}}) \\ + (\mathbf{x_k} - \mathbf{x_{k-1}})^T R(\mathbf{x_k} - \mathbf{x_{k-1}}) \tag{11}$$

y_{target} is the transformed sensor response vector of the target odor by SVD method (Yamanaka, Matsumoto, & Nakamoto, 2003).

Then, the experiment on the exploration of the recipe composed of 8 component odors was performed. The target odor was the apple flavor composed of 9 odor components such as trans-2 hexenyl acetate, trans-2-hexenal, isobutyric acid, ethyl valerate, propionic acid, 1-hexanol, 1-butanol, butyl isobutyrate and butyl propionate. The first 8 compounds were used as odor components in the blended odor. The 8 sensors used here were the QCMs coated with Apiezon L, Thermol-1, polyphenylether (6ring), tricresyl phosphate, Versamid 900, PEG 1000, cerebroside, and ethyl cellulose. The experimental result of the apple flavor recording using 8 components is

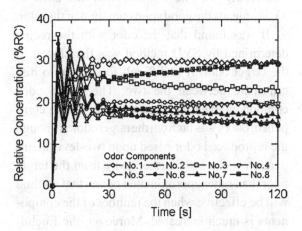

Figure 7. Recipe exploration process of 8 odor components using SVD method

depicted in Figure 7. The unit % RC in the figure means the concentration relative to the full scale in an odor blender. 4 singular values were used in this experiment. It was found that the stable convergence was obtained even when the 8 odor components were used, whereas the report by other researchers includes the quantification of the gas mixtures with at most four (Amrani, Dowdeswell, Payne, & Persaud, 1997).

Then, the evaluation by sensory test was performed. The triangle test, where the panelists pick up the sample different from the two same ones among the three samples, was performed. The result of the triangle test to evaluate the approximated odor using various methods is summarized in Table 1. The odors generated by the odor blender were filled with the sampling bag made of fluorine-contained resin. The 5-component approximation in total indicates that the target odor was approximated using 5 odor components

Table 1. Result of triangle tests for reproduced odors with their recipes determined by two-level quantization method (8 components), basic method (5 components), and SVD method (8 components)

Method	Selection rate (%)	Euclidean distance
Two-level quantization	58.3	0.0402
5-component approximation	47.2	0.0398
SVD	33.3	0.0144

without SVD method. The number of the panelists was totally 36. The low selection rate close to 33.3% means the good approximation of the odor.

It was found that the odor with the recipe determined by SVD method was the closest to the target odor. It is difficult for people to discriminate between the two. The single odor component even the closest among all the component odors was far from the target odor. Although the reproduced odor based upon two-level quantization was a little farther away from the target odor than other approximated odors, that method will be effective when the number of the components is much increased. Moreover, the Euclidean distance in the sensor space agreed with that in sensory space. Thus, QCM sensor response pattern is a good indicator of the odor approximation since there is correlation between its sensitivities to odorants and the human thresholds.

Real-Time Reference Method

The apple flavor made up of 8 odor components was successfully determined using the odor recorder as is described in the previous section. Although the constant recipe was obtained in most of previous studies, the actual odor in the atmosphere is continuously and dynamically changed. The dynamical recording and regeneration are useful to have much presence in the odor reproduction. Hence, the technique of recoding dynamically changing odor has been developed.

First approach to record the dynamical change of odor is based upon the neural network using the feedback error learning (Miyamoto, Kawato, Setoyama, & Suzuki, 1988). Since the odor recorder using a feedback-error-learning was a little complicated and consumed much time for the neural-network training (Nakamoto & Hiramatsu, 2002), the real-time reference method for recording dynamical change of odor was developed (Yamanaka & Nakamoto, 2003). This method is useful for recording dynamical change of odor as

well as for compensating for change of environment such as temperature and humidity (Yamanaka & Nakamoto, 2002). Although the odor recorder in the previous section has robustness against temperature and humidity, the real-time reference method is more robust especially against abrupt change of the environment.

The comparison of real-time reference method with conventional one is illustrated in Figure 8(a, b). In the previous method in Figure 8(a), the steady-state response to the target odor with constant concentration is measured for the first time. Then, the recipe of the blended odor is adjusted so that the response to the blended odor can match that to the target odor. Since it takes a few minutes to determine the concentration, the change during the process of the recipe determination cannot be detected.

On the other hand, the target and blended odors are alternately introduced into the sensor array every sampling interval (several seconds) in the real-time reference method in Figure 8(b). Although the sensor response to the blended odor disagrees with that to the target odor at first due to the concentration difference, it soon approaches the response to the target odor. Once the convergence occurs, the blended odor concentration tracks that of the target odor. The real-time reference method achieves the time resolution of a few seconds to record dynamical change of odor. This method is also effective to compensate for the rapid environmental change encountered during the process of the recipe determination.

Then, the experiment on recording the dynamically changing odor using the real-time reference method is described. The concentrations of four odor components of the apple flavor were independently changed in the experiment. The odor components used here were trans-2-hexenyl acetate (green note, Comp1), trans-2-hexenal (smell of grass, Comp2), isobutyric acid (sour sweet, Comp3), ethyl valerate (fruity, Comp4). The sensors used here were four quartz resonators

Figure 8. Real-time reference method for recoding dynamical change of odor: (a) previous method, (b) real-time reference method, (c) recorded dynamic concentration change of each odor component, and (d) temperature and humidity change during experiment (copyright Elsevier, 2003)

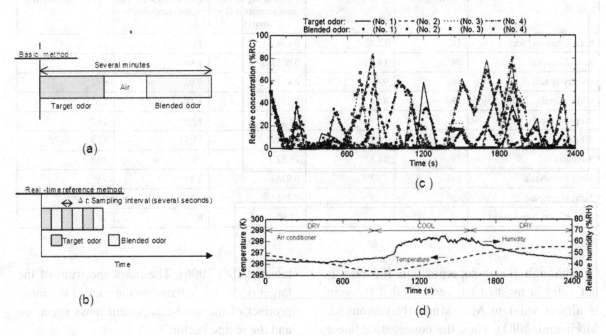

(20MHz, AT-CUT) coated with polphenyl ether, polyethylene glycol 1000, tricresyl phosphate, Apiezon L, respectively. The sampling interval was 4s.

The temperature and the humidity were intentionally changed during the experiment since the robustness against the temperature and humidity changes was also studied. The change of the air conditioner mode (DRY/COOL) caused 2.5°C of the temperature change and 20% of the humidity change during the experiment.

The experimental result is shown in Figure 8(c). The solid and dashed lines are the concentrations of the component odors in the target odor and plots are the recorded concentrations of the component odors. Since the recorded concentration of each component odor almost agreed with that of the target odor, it was found that the real-time reference method achieves the record of dynamical change of odor even under the environment of the temperature and the humidity changes as is shown in Figure 8(d). The real-time reference

method can be speeded up when the blended odor is measured simultaneously with the target odor using the two same sensor arrays (Yamanaka, Yoshikawa, & Nakamoto, 2004).

Mixture Quantification Using a Huge Number of Odor-Component Candidates

Although the number of odor components was extended, it is still insufficient to realize an odor recorder for general purpose. Then, MS (Mass Spectrometer) without GC (Gas Chromatograph) was used as is described in the previous section. It was reported that MS without GC was useful to classify smells for short time (Vinaixa, et al., 2005). MS provides a variety of mass spectra of many compounds using more than 200 m/z. Each m/z corresponds to a sensor element in a sensor array. The advantage of MS over other type odor sensing system is the capability of recording smell composed of many components.

Table 2. Result of recipe estimation using large-scale mass spectrum data (target odor: apple flavor)

Odor component	Molecular weight	apple recipe (%)	Estimated recipe (%) using 1040 components (after step1)	Estimated recipe (%) using selected odor components	Estimated recipe (%) (Experiment)
trans-2-hexenyl acetate	142	12.72	0.1343	12.72	13
trans-2-hexenal	98	1.69	0.002735	1.69	0
isobutyric acid	88	9.05	0.435	9.05	6.1
ethyl valerate	130	8.14	6.434	8.14	5.4
propionic acid	74	12.9	12.22	12.9	13.2
1-hexanol	102	15.74	4.698	15.74	12.4
1-butanol	74	28.32	25.87	28.32	20.8
butyl isobutyrate	144	1.67	0.9743	1.67	1.9
butyl propionate	130	9.77	7.274	9.77	9.2
sum of other components			61.97	0	18

Although linear superposition theorem is not valid in most of gas sensors, that theorem is almost valid in MS (Miura, Nakamoto, & Moriizumi, 2003). Thus, the nonnegative linear least squares method was used considering that the concentration of any odor component should not be negative. We solve a kind of optimization problem with nonnegativity constraint to obtain the recipe when we use a nonnegative least squares method. However, the iterative procedure is still required to select odor components among huge number of candidates (Nakamoto, 2008).

If many odor components are prepared but not included in a target odor, the contributions of those odor components should be zero. However, small percentages of those components remain after the calculation of the nonnegative least squares. Because of too many actual zero odor components, the cumulative error of those odor components is not negligible. Thus, the recipe should be calculated after eliminating the odor components with zero contributions.

The number of odor component candidates extracted from NIST database (NIST 2005), which is commercially available, was about 10,000. The intensity of the mass spectrum at each m/z is included in that database. Moreover, the recipe of the essential oil can be obtained from the da-

tabase (ESO 2006). The mass spectrum of the target odor is calculated as the sum of the inner product of the odor-component mass spectrum and the recipe vector.

The typical apple flavor consists of only 9 odor components in Table 2. That table shows the recipe calculation result using 1040 odor candidates among 10,000 ones. Other candidates can be excluded since its intensity is not zero at m/z where the intensity of the target odor is zero. The recipe calculation result of the apple flavor was quite different from the actual recipe as is shown in Table 2. The error becomes larger when too many odor components are used because of numerical-calculation problem. Thus, it is indispensable to select appropriate odor components. We proposed the method of selecting odor components among 10,000 candidates using the following procedure.

Step 1: Eliminate the candidates with nonzero m/z which the target odor does not include.

Step 2: The nonnegative least squares method is applied to remaining odor components. The odor components with their ratios less than 10% in the odor-component recipe are removed. This step is repeatedly performed until the number of remaining odor components is less than 40.

Step 3: At step 2, there is possibility that the odor components actually included are removed. Thus, an odor candidate removed at step 2 is temporally added to the set of remaining odor components again and the nonnegative least squares method is applied to that set. After this procedure is performed for all the odor components removed at step 2, the odor candidate with the minimum residual error among them is determined to join the set of the remaining odor components.

Step 3 is repeatedly performed until the minimum residual error increases.

The number of remaining odor components at step 2 was determined to be 40 because most of the samples in ESO database have less than 40 components.

1040 odor components remained after step 1. At step 2, the number of odor components gradually decreased together with residual error. The number of remaining odor components was 40 at the end of step 2. At step 3, the residual error became zero since the odor components incorrectly eliminated were added at this step. The nonnegative least squares method was about 3000 times performed at step 3. The recipe of the apple flavor was correctly obtained after step 3 as is shown in Table 2.

In addition to apple flavor, the recipes of basil, bitter orange flower, citrus, ginger, jasmine, melon, peach, ylangylang, grapefruit leaf were correctly estimated when the recipe data in ESO2006 database were used. Especially, the recipe was correctly obtained even when 38 odor components were actually included in grapefruit leaf.

Next, the actual data of 82 candidates obtained from the mass spectrometer (QP5050A, Shimadzu) were used to estimate the odor recipes. The ionization method was EI (Electron Ionization) with its energy of 70eV. We performed the recipe estimation using the actual measurement data. The range of m/z was from 10 to 250 except 43 and 58, the main peaks of the solvent (acetone). The injection volume was 1μL and the measurement was automatically performed using an autosampler (AO-5000, Shimadzu). The target odor used in this study was apple composed of 9 odor components. The 82 odor candidates used in this experiment is tabulated in Table 3. All the target odors and odor components were 10 times measured and the averaged data were used to estimate the recipe. Since the number of odor candidates was small compared with the simulation, step 1 was skipped. The estimated recipe is shown in Table 2. Although trans-2-hexenal included in the target odor was not selected as an odor component, the recipe of the odor components was estimated within the error of 6%.

Thereafter, sensory test was performed. The target sample and the sample with recorded recipe were prepared in the liquid phase. First, a subject sniffs the smell of the target sample. Then, a subject is required to pick up one of the two prepared samples closer to the sample presented first. 9 subjects joined the sensory test and 5 subjects picked up the sample with recorded recipe. Since two smells were very similar, a half of them picked up the target one while other half of them picked up the sample with the recorded recipe. Thus, we found that the recorded smell was close to the target one.

The same experiment was performed for peach, banana, strawberry, melon, lemon, orange and grape. The sensory test revealed that the recorded smell was similar to the target one (Mamun & Nakamoto, 2008).

ODOR APPROXIMATION BASED UPON EXTRACTED ODOR COMPONENTS

Although MS-based sensor is effective to quantify the mixture composed of many odor components, it is not practical to prepare for a few hundred

Table 3. Odor-component candidates for experiment in Table 2

1	1,7-octadiene	42	DL-2-methylbutyric acid methyl ester
2	1-decene	43	n-butyric acid methyl ester
3	1-nonene	44	n-caproic acid ethyl ester
4	2-octene	45	n-caprylic acid isopropyl ester
5	n-nonane	46	nerol
6	trans-e-hexen-1-yl-aldehyde	47	1-octanol
7	(r)-(+)-limonene	48	1-pentanol
8	1,8-cineole	49	2-octanol
9	beta-caryphyllene	50	2-propanol
10	geraniol	51	acetic acid isobutyl ester
11	perilaldehyde	52	acetic acid isopropyl ester
12	n-butyric acid isoamyl ester	53	acetic acid n-amyl ester
13	n-caproic acid	54	cis-5-octen-1-ol
14	n-octanal	55	lactic acid ethyl ester
15	n-valeraldehyde	56	n-butyric acid ethyl ester
16	2-phenyl ethyl alcohol	57	n-butyric acid isopropyl ester
17	acetic acid isoamyl ester	58	n-pentane
18	cis-3-octen-1-ol	59	n-valeric acid methyl ester
19	isovaleric acid isoamyl ester	60	propionic acid ethyl ester
20	n-caprylic acid ethyl ester	61	1-butanol
21	butyl acetate	62	1-hexanol
22	citronellyl acetate	63	butyl isobutyrate
23	DL-2-methylbutyric acid ethyl ester	64	butyl propionate
24	neryl acetate	65	ethyl valerate
25	n-nonyl alcohol	66	isobutyric acid
26	1-nonanol	67	propionic acid
27	3-buten-1-ol	68	trans-2-hexen-1-al
28	4-penten-1-ol	69	trans-2-hexenyl acetate
29	acetic acid cis-3-hexen-1-yl ester	70	benzaldehyde
30	acetic acid npropyl ester	71	delta-decanolactone
31	n-caproic acid isopropyl ester	72	ethyl acetate
32	(+-)-citronellol	73	formic acid ethyl ester
33	2-methyl-1-propanol	74	gamma-decanolactone
34	3-methyl-1-butanol	75	gamma-hexanolactone
35	5-hexen-1-ol	76	gamma-octanolactone
36	acetic acid 2-phenylethyl ester	77	geranyl acetate
37	acetic acid benzyl ester	78	isobutanol
38	acetic acid n-heptyl ester	79	trans-2-hexen-1-ol
39	acetic acid n-octyl ester	80	acetic acid n-hexyl ester
40	beta-ionone	81	butyric acid
41	cis-3-hexen-1-ol	82	n-amyl n-butyrate

or more odor components. Thus, it is important to find a set of odor components to cover wide range of smells.

There are three primary colors such as red, green, and blue in vision. Thus, color can be quantitatively expressed in color space. Although Amoore proposed seven primary smells (Buck & Axel, 1991), it seems difficult to express sufficient number of odors using only seven components. The approach from the aspect of olfactory receptors was also tried. Although the molecular biology of olfaction rapidly progressed (Buck & Axel, 1991), it is too complicated to find primary smells since 3-400 receptor types are used in a living body (Schiffman & Pearce, 2003). However, it might be possible to express a smell using smaller number of odor components since 350 odor receptors have partially overlapping specificities.

Even if primary smells have so far not been found, it is still important to blend smells because the blending process is currently essential in creating new smells, particularly in the flavor and fragrance industry. In addition to novel scent creation in the flavor and fragrance industry, a variety of applications related to odor reproduction are feasible using an olfactory display. Those applications are an odor recorder, a movie with scents, games, exhibitions, on-line shopping, restaurants, educational tools, medical-diagnostic tools, museums, art etc. if smell can be expressed using at most a few tens odor components. It is not practical to realize the olfactory display for general purpose if the number of odor components is more than 100.

The olfactory display can be applied to a cooking game with scents, where smells are essential to enhance reality (Nakamoto, Otaguro, Kinoshita, Nagahama, Ohnishi, & Shida, 2008). In the cooking game, each odor component was assigned to the corresponding ingredient such as meat, onion, curry, rue, etc. However, it is important to select more general odor components to extend the range of smells.

It has not been so far clear how many odor components are necessary and how we can organize odor components. When we study this topic, the best way is to use the data of the sensory test. However, it consumes huge labor and time to make the reliable large-scale database of the sensory test. Although the large-scale database of the sensory test was previously made in the United States (Andrew, 1985), it is still insufficient.

Several researchers in virtual reality aimed to cover wider range of smells with aid of cross-modal interaction of olfaction with vision (Nambu, Narumi, Nishimura, Tanigawa, & Hirose, 2010; Kawai & Noro, 1996). The smell which exactly matches the corresponding object is not always necessary if the smell is presented together with vision. The cross-modal sensory interaction certainly helps the reduction of the number of odors prepared for the olfactory display. However, it is more essential to search for a set of odor components to cover wide range of odors although many people tend to avoid this problem.

Then, we focus on the database of mass spectrometry. The huge amount of mass spectrum data is available to investigate the odor components. Moreover, its selectivity and stability are sufficient compared with other electronic noses so that collinearity problem can be avoided.

When the large database of odor is available, the mathematical method to extract the basis vectors corresponding to odor components is required. Moreover, the basis vector should be synthesized using the vectors of existing compounds. Then, NMF (Nonnegative Matrix Factorization) method was applied to extract basis vectors (Lee & Seung, 1999) and the nonnegative least squares method was used to determine the mixture composition of the odor corresponding to the basis vector. The selection method of odor components followed by the simulation result is shown in this section.

NMF can be used with the constraints that all the elements of data vectors are not negative and that the ratio of each odor component in the mixture is not negative (Pauca, Piper, & Plemmon,

2006; Cichocki, Zdunek, Phan, & Amari, 2009). NMF was applied to the extractions of features of face images and semantic features in the text.

Those constraints are important when the data of the mass spectra are analyzed. The detector output at each m/z should not be less than zero in the mass spectrometry. Furthermore, the ratio of each odor component in the target odor should not be less than zero.

There is a well-known feature extraction method such as principal component analysis (Dillon & Goldstein, 1983). However, it cannot be used because of the constraints of this problem mentioned above. There is no negative value in the mass spectrum. Moreover, it is not possible to use negative coefficient when we synthesize the mass spectrum of the target odor. Then, NMF was adopted to search for a set of odor components. The non-negativity constraints lead to parts-based representation since they allow only additive, not subtractive combinations. In case of face images, several versions of mouths, noses etc were extracted as basis images.

The outline of NMF is briefly described here. Let V a data matrix, WH an approximated matrix, W a basis matrix and H a coefficient matrix. V is factorized as:

$$V \cong WH = W \times H , \qquad (12)$$

where n is the number of m/z, m the number of the mass spectrum data, r is the number of basis vectors. The r columns of W are the basis vectors of odor components. The encoding is composed of the coefficients by which the mass spectrum vector of the target odor is represented with a linear combination of basis vectors corresponding to the odor components. The elements of W and H are initially set at random. When r is given, the matrices W and H are obtained according to the iterative procedure (Lee & Seung, 1999). W is determined regardless of actual mass spectra

of existing compounds. Thus, the basis vector should be approximated using mass spectra of existing compounds.

The mass spectrum database used here was NIST05 including data of 163,000 compounds. All the data were measured at the ionization energy of 70 eV. In the database, the range of m/z is between 0 and 700. Each mass spectrum is normalized by its maximum intensity, which is scaled to 999.

The molecular weight of compound with odor is generally at most 300. Any intensity at m/z higher than molecular weight is zero. The compound with molecular weight greater than 300 does not have volatility enough for people to sniff. Then, the total dimension of the data vector was 300. The data of 9,987 compounds were picked up from the database for the simulation. The matrix size of V was 300 x 9,987.

NMF method was applied to the data matrix V. Its result is shown in Figure 9(a, b). The lateral axis means ID number of compounds and the vertical axis is m/z. Almost 10,000 mass spectra are shown in both figures. The color of each plot expresses the intensity. Figure 9(a) shows the original data of V, whereas Figure 9(b) shows the approximated matrix of WH in the case of r=100. The number of iterations for updating W and H was 5,000. It was found that the peak at m/z below 150 appeared clearly. The approximation was almost successful since both figures are almost the same.

Next, the residual error as a function of number of basis vectors was evaluated. The residual error is the sum of the squares of the difference between the element of V and that of WH. The approximation becomes better as the residual error decreases. NMF calculation was performed when r=10, 25, 32, 50, 64, 100, 150, and 200, respectively.

Although basis vectors could be extracted from mass spectra of single compounds, actual smell is composed of multiple compounds. Then, the mass spectrum of the target odor composed of multiple

Figure 9. Intensity image composed of 10,000 mass spectra (a) matrix data V and (b) approximated matrix WH (copyright IEEE, 2009)

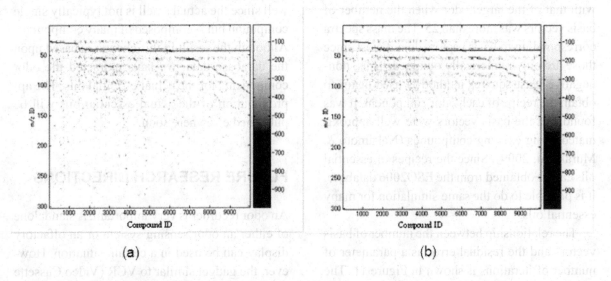

(a)   (b)

compounds was synthesized using basis vectors extracted by NMF method. The target odor is typical apple flavor with the recipe tabulated in Table 2. The mass spectra of compounds shown in Table 2 were obtained from NIST05 database and the mass spectrum of the target odor was synthesized according to equation:

$$\mathbf{m}_t = \sum_{i=1}^{p} \alpha_i \mathbf{m}_i \tag{13}$$

where $\mathbf{m}_t$ is the mass spectrum of the target odor, $\mathbf{m}_i$ the mass spectrum of odor component i, the ratio of the odor component i and p the number of odor components.

Next, the non-negative least squares method was used to approximate the mass spectrum of the target odor. The non-negative least squares method is a kind of optimization method to solve the linear equations with the constraint that all the elements in the solution vector are not negative. In this method, the solution vector x is obtained so that the minimized index I:

$$I = \min_{\mathbf{x}} |C\mathbf{x} - \mathbf{d}| \tag{14}$$

can be obtained. C is the basis matrix W extracted by NMF, $\mathbf{d}$ the mass spectrum of the target odor, x the mixture composition. x to minimize the residual error is obtained under the constraint that all the elements in x are not negative. $\mathbf{d}$ can be replaced with $\mathbf{m}_t$ here.

The comparison of the mass spectrum of the blended odor with that of the target odor is shown in Figure 10. The number of NMF iterations was 1,000 and 25 basis vectors were used. The mass spectrum of the blended odor almost agreed

Figure 10. Comparison of mass spectrum of target odor with that of blended odor using NMF method (copyright IEEE, 2009)

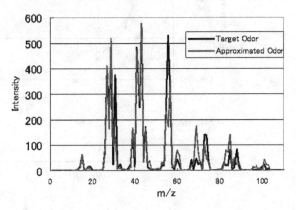

with that of the target odor. Moreover, the mass spectrum of the blended odor agreed completely with that of the target odor when the number of basis vectors was more than 25. The mass spectra corresponding to basis vectors do not exist since those are only numerically obtained. Thus, non-negative least squares method is used again to obtain the recipe of each odor component. It was found that the basis vectors were well approximated using existing compounds (Nakamoto & Murakami, 2009). Since the recipes of essential oils can be obtained from the ESO2006 database, it is possible to do the same simulation for many essential oils.

The relationship between the number of basis vectors and the residual error as a parameter of number of iterations is shown in Figure 11. The accuracy became better as the number of iteration increased. It was found from the figure that 1,000 iterations were sufficient for NMF calculation. Moreover, it was found that the approximation accuracy became better as the number of basis vectors increased. When we did the simulation for 10,000 compounds, at least 64 odor compo-

nents seems to be required. However, less number of odor components might still approximate odors well since the actual smell is not typically single compound but is composed of many compounds. Although the result in this chapter is based upon the database data, we have extracted the odor components for the actual essential oils. The approximation of the actual essential oils will be published elsewhere soon.

FUTURE RESEARCH DIRECTIONS

An odor recorder is very important. A standalone of either an odor sensing system or an olfactory display can be used in a certain situation. However, the gadget similar to VCR (Video Cassette Recorder) in vision is indispensable in the olfaction. Currently the researchers of odor recorder are not so many. The reason is that the primary smells have not been so far revealed. It is impossible to make a general-purpose odor recorder without primary smells.

Figure 11. Relationship between number of basis vectors and residual error when 10,000 mass spectra were analyzed using NMF method (copyright IEEE, 2009)

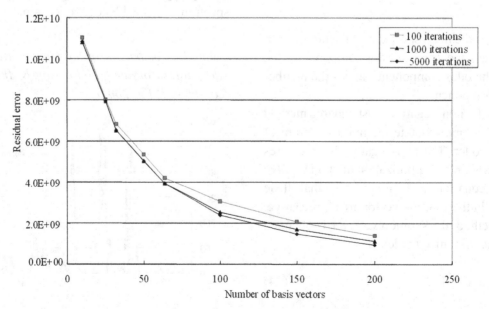

However, the selection method of odor components was recently proposed. Although we do not find a few primary smells, any odor might be approximated using a few tens odor components when we analyzed the 10,000 mass spectra. There is tradeoff between the accuracy of the odor approximation and the number of odor components. However, a few tens odor components are not far from the realistic number. Since it is possible to realize the olfactory display with more than 30 odor components (Nakamoto & Dinh Minh, 2007), we can reproduce any odor to certain degree of the approximation.

Since this method is based upon mass spectrometry, several researchers are worried about the correlation between the mass spectrum and the sensory test. Although the data from the mass spectrometer does not completely match the characteristic of the olfactory perception, it can explain the similarity between odors to some extent. Especially the data at high m/z region exhibits the strong correlation (Ohno, Nihei, & Nakamoto, 2011). It is possible to use mass spectrometry at the current stage although it might be replaced with more biologically-plausible sensor (Goldsmith, et al., 2011) in the future when it has enough capability and can accumulate huge amount of the data.

Many people want to have an odor recorder. When you search for an odor recorder at the Internet, you will find many articles. Because of the possibility of realizing the odor recorder for general purpose, its development should be accelerated.

CONCLUSION

In this chapter, the fundamentals of an odor recorder such as the quantification method of the mixture composition was described. Then, the research trend of the odor recorder, the ac-

tual implementation and the experiments were explained. Moreover, the application of mass spectrometry to the odor recorder, and the exploration of odor components were shown. Although the odor recorder can be used in a limited situation at the current stage, the range of odor is gradually extended. More than two decades have passed since an odor sensing system often called an e-nose appeared. The reproduction technique using both odor sensing and olfactory display will open the new direction of machine for the artificial olfaction.

REFERENCES

Amoore, J. E. (1970). *Molecular basis of odor*. Springfield, IL: Charles C Thomas Publisher.

Amrani, M. E. H., Dowdeswell, R. M., Payne, P. A., & Persaud, K. C. (1997). An intelligent gas sensing system. *Sensors and Actuators. B, Chemical, 44*, 512–516. doi:10.1016/S0925-4005(97)00240-2

Andrew, D. (1985). *Atlas of odor character profiles*. Philadelphia, PA: ASTM.

Beebe, K. R., Pell, R. J., & Seasholz, M. B. (1998). *Chemomrtrics –Practical guide*. New York, NY: Wiley.

Buck, L., & Axel, R. (1991). A novel multigene family may encode odorant receptors: Molecular basis for odor recognition. *Cell, 65*, 175–187. doi:10.1016/0092-8674(91)90418-X

Carey, W. P., Beebe, K. R., & Kowalski, B. R. (1987). Multicomponent analysis using an array of piezoelectric crystal sensors. *Analytical Chemistry, 59*, 1529–1534. doi:10.1021/ac00138a010

Carmell, L., & Harel, D. (2007). Mix-to-mimic odor synthesis for electronic noses. *Sensors and Actuators B, 125*, 635-643.

Cichocki, A., Zdunek, R., Phan, A. H., & Amari, S. (2009). *Nonnegative matrix and tensor factorizations*. New York, NY: Wiley. doi:10.1002/9780470747278

Davide, F., Holmberg, M., & Lundstrom, I. (2001). Virtual olfactory interfaces: electronic noses and olfactory displays. In Riva, G., & Davide, F. (Eds.), *Communications through Virtual Technologies* (pp. 193–220). Amsterdam, The Netherlands: IOS Press.

Dillon, W. R., & Goldstein, M. (1983). *Multivariate analysis*. New York, NY: Wiley.

Dittman, B., Nitz, S., & Horner, G. (1998). A new chemical sensor on a mass spectrometric basis. *Advances in Food Science, 30,* 115.

Duda, R. O., Hart, P. E., & Stork, D. G. (2001). *Pattern classification*. New York, NY: Wiley-Interscience.

Funahashi, K. (1989). On the approximate realization of continuous mappings by neural networks. *Neural Networks, 2,* 183–192. doi:10.1016/0893-6080(89)90003-8

Gardner, J. W., & Bartlett, P. N. (1994). A brief history of electronic noses. *Sensors and Actuators. B, Chemical, 18,* 210. doi:10.1016/0925-4005(94)87085-3

Geladi, P., & Kowalski, B. R. (1986). Partial least-squares regression: A tutorial. *Analytica Chimica Acta, 185,* 1–17. doi:10.1016/0003-2670(86)80028-9

Goldsmith, B. R., Mitala, J. J., Josue, J., Castro, A., Lerner, M. B., & Bayburt, T. H. … Johnson, C.J. (2011). Biomimetic chemical sensors using nanoelectronic read out of olfactory receptor proteins. In *Proceeding of 14th International Symposium on Olfaction and Electronic Nose*. New York, NY: IEEE.

Hirose, H. (2002). Sensory info-communication technology and olfactory media. *Aroma Research, 10,* 60.

Iwasa, Y., Izumi, R., Hayahsi, K., & Toko, K. (2004). *Synthesis of odor based on substructures and physicochemical properties of odorants*. Retrieved from http://sciencelinks.jp/j-east/article/200507/000020050705A0243286.php

Kaneyasu, M., Ikegami, A., Arima, H., & Iwanaga, S. (1987). Smell identification using a thick-film hybrid gas sensor. *IEEE Transactions on Components. Hybrids and Manufacturing Technology, 10,* 267. doi:10.1109/TCHMT.1987.1134730

Kawai, T., & Noro, K. (1996). Psychological effect of stereoscopic 3-D images with fragrances. *Ergonomics, 39,* 1364–1369. doi:10.1080/00140139608964556

Kaye, J. J. (2004). Making scents. In *ACM Interaction* (p. 49). New York, NY: ACM Press.

Keller, P. E., Kouzes, R. T., Kangas, L. J., & Hashem, S. (1995). Transmission of olfactory information for telemedicine. In Morgan, K., Satava, R. M., Sieburg, H. B., Matteus, R., & Christensen, J. P. (Eds.), *Interactive Technology and the New Paradigm for Healthcare* (pp. 168–172). Amsterdam, The Netherlands: IOS Press and Ohmsha.

Lee, D. D., & Seung, H. S. (1999). Learning the parts of objects by non-negative matrix factorization. *Letters to Nature, 401*(21), 788–791.

Mamun, A. L., & Nakamoto, T. (2008). Recipe estimation using mass spectrometer and large-scale data. *Transactions of the Institute of Electrical Engineering of Japan, 128,* 467–471.

Matsushita, Y. (2002). A virtual space with aroma and wind. *Aroma Research, 3,* 42–49.

Messager, J. (2002). *The diffusion of fragrances in a multimedia environment*. Paper presented at the 3rd Aroma Science Forum. Tokyo, Japan.

Miura, T., Nakamoto, T., & Moriizumi, T. (2003). Study of odor recorder using mass spectrometry. *Transactions of IEEJ, 456*, 513-518.

Miyamoto, H., Kawato, M., Setoyama, T., & Suzuki, R. (1988). Feedback-error-learning neural network for trajectory control of a robotic manipulator. *Neural Networks, 1*, 251. doi:10.1016/0893-6080(88)90030-5

Munoz, S., Yoshino, A., Nakamoto, T., & Moriizumi, T. (2007). Odor approximation of fruit flavors using a QCM odor sensing system. *Sensors and Actuators. B, Chemical, 123*, 1101–1106. doi:10.1016/j.snb.2006.11.025

Nagle, H. T., & Schiffman, S., & Gutierrez-Osuna. (1998). The how and why of electronic noses. *IEEE Spectrum, 35*, 22. doi:10.1109/6.715180

Nakamoto, T. (2005). Odor recorder. *Sensor Letters, 3*, 136–150. doi:10.1166/sl.2005.018

Nakamoto, T. (2008). Odor recorder using mass spectrometry. *Sensor Letters, 6*, 1–5. doi:10.1166/sl.2008.548

Nakamoto, T., & Dinh Minh, H. P. (2007). Improvement of olfactory display using solenoid valves. In *Proceeding of IEEE Virtual Reality*, (pp. 171-178). Charlotte, NC: IEEE Press.

Nakamoto, T., & Hiramatsu, H. (2002). Study of odor recorder for dynamical change of odor using QCM sensors and neural network. *Sensors and Actuators. B, Chemical, 85*, 263–269. doi:10.1016/S0925-4005(02)00130-2

Nakamoto, T., & Moriizumi, T. (1988). Odor sensor using quartz-resonator array and neural-network pattern recognition. In *Proceedings of the IEEE Ultrasonics Symposium*, (p. 613). Chicago, IL: IEEE Press.

Nakamoto, T., & Murakami, K. (2009). Selection method of odor components for olfactory display using mass spectrum database. In *Proceedings of IEEE Virtual Reality*, (pp. 159-162). Lafayette, LA: IEEE Press.

Nakamoto, T., Nakahira, Y., Hiramatsu, H., & Moriizumi, T. (2001). Odor recorder using active odor sensing system. *Sensors and Actuators. B, Chemical, 76*, 465. doi:10.1016/S0925-4005(01)00587-1

Nakamoto, T., Otaguro, S., Kinoshita, M., Nagahama, M., Ohnishi, K., & Ishida, T. (2008). Cooking up an interactive olfactory game display. *IEEE Computer Graphics and Applications, 28*, 75–78. doi:10.1109/MCG.2008.3

Nambu, A., Narumi, T., Nishimura, K., Tanigawa, T., & Hirose, M. (2010). Visual-olfactory display using olfactory sensory map. [Waltham, MA: IEEE Press.]. *Proceedings of IEEE Virtual Reality, 2010*, 39–42.

Ohno, M., Nihei, Y., & Nakamoto, T. (2011). Study of odor approximation by using mass spectrometer. In *Proceeding of 14th International Symposium on Olfaction and Electronic Nose*. New York, NY: IEEE.

Pauca, V. P., Piper, J., & Plemmon, R. J. (2006). Nonnegative matrix factorization for spectral data analysis. *Linear Algebra and Its Applications, 416*, 29–47. doi:10.1016/j.laa.2005.06.025

Pearce, T. C., Schiffman, S. S., Nagle, H. T., & Gardner, J. W. (Eds.). (2003). *Handbook of machine olfaction*. Weinheim, Germany: Wiley-VCH.

Persaud, K. C., & Godd, G. (1982). Analysis of discrimination mechanisms in the mammalian olfactory system using a model nose. *Nature, 299*, 352. doi:10.1038/299352a0

Rumelhart, D. E., & McClelland, J. L. PDP Research Group. (1986). *Parallel distributed processing*. Cambridge, MA: MIT Press.

Schiffman, S., & Pearce, T. C. (2003). Introduction to olfaction: Perception, anatomy, physiology and molecular biology. In Nagle, H. T., Gardner, J. W., Schiffman, S. S., & Pearce, T. C. (Eds.), *Handbook of Machine Olfaction* (pp. 1–32). Weinheim, Germany: Wiley-VCH. doi:10.1002/3527601597.ch1

Sharaf, M. A., Illman, D. L., & Kowalski, B. R. (1986). *Chemometrics*. New York, MY: Wiley.

Skogestad, S., & Postlethwaite, I. (1996). *Multivariable feedback control*. Chichester, UK: Wiley.

Somboon, P., Wyszynki, B., & Nakamoto, T. (2007). Realization of recording wide range of odor by utilizing both of transient and steady-state sensor responses in recording process. *Sensors and Actuators. B, Chemical, 124*, 557–563. doi:10.1016/j.snb.2007.01.030

Somboon, P., Wyszynski, B., & Nakamoto, T. (2007). Novel odor recorder for extending range of recordable odor. *Sensors and Actuators. B, Chemical, 121*, 583–589. doi:10.1016/j.snb.2006.04.105

Somboon, P., Wyszynski, B., & Nakamoto, T. (2009). Development of odor recorder with enhanced recording capabilities based on real-time mass spectrometry. *Sensors and Actuators. B, Chemical, 141*, 141–146. doi:10.1016/j.snb.2009.06.005

Sundgren, H., Winquist, F., & Lundstrom, I. (1991). Artifical neural networks and statistical pattern recognition improve MOSFET gas sensor array calibration. [IEEE.]. *Proceedings of the Technological Digest of Transducers, 1991*, 574–577.

Terry, S. C., Jerman, J. H., & Angell, J. B. (1979). A gas chromatographic air analyzer fabricated on a silicon wafer. *IEEE Transactions on Electron Devices, 26*, 1880–1886. doi:10.1109/T-ED.1979.19791

Vinaixa, M., Vergara, A., Duran, C., Llobet, E., Badia, C., & Brezmes, J. (2005). Fast detection of rancidity in potato crisps using e-noses based on mass spectrometry or gas sensors. *Sensors and Actuators. B, Chemical, 106*, 67–75. doi:10.1016/j.snb.2004.05.038

Wang, Z., Hwang, J., & Kowalski, B. R. (1995). ChemNets: Theory and application. *Analytical Chemistry, 67*, 1497–1504. doi:10.1021/ac00105a003

Wang, Z., Isaksson, T., & Kowalski, B. R. (1994). New approach for distance measurement in locally weighted regression. *Analytical Chemistry, 66*, 249–260. doi:10.1021/ac00074a012

Yamanaka, T., Matsumoto, R., & Nakamoto, T. (2002). Study of odor blender using solenoid valves controlled by delta-sigma modulation method. *Sensors and Actuators. B, Chemical, 87*, 457–463. doi:10.1016/S0925-4005(02)00300-3

Yamanaka, T., Matsumoto, R., & Nakamoto, T. (2003). Odor recorder for multi-component odor using two-level quantization method. *Sensors and Actuators. B, Chemical, 89*, 120–125. doi:10.1016/S0925-4005(02)00452-5

Yamanaka, T., Matsumoto, R., & Nakamoto, T. (2003). Study of recording apple flavor using odor recorder with five components. *Sensors and Actuators. B, Chemical, 89*, 112–119. doi:10.1016/S0925-4005(02)00451-3

Yamanaka, T., Matsumoto, R., & Nakamoto, T. (2003). Fundamental study of odor recorder for multi-component odor using recipe exploration based on singular value decomposition. *IEEE Sensors Journal, 3*, 468–474. doi:10.1109/JSEN.2003.815778

Yamanaka, T., & Nakamoto, T. (2002). Improvement of odor-recorder robustness against environmental change using real-time reference method. *IEEJ Transactions on Sensors and Micromachines, 122*, 317.

Yamanaka, T., & Nakamoto, T. (2003). Real-time reference method in odor blender under environmental change. *Sensors and Actuators. B, Chemical, 93*, 51–56. doi:10.1016/S0925-4005(03)00202-8

Yamanaka, T., Yoshikawa, K., & Nakamoto, T. (2004). Improvement of odor-recoder capability for dynamical change of odor. *Sensors and Actuators. B, Chemical, 99*, 367. doi:10.1016/j.snb.2003.12.004

Yanagida, Y., Kawato, S., Noma, H., Tomono, A., & Tetsutani, N. (2004). Projection-based olfactory display with nose tracking. In *Proceedings of the IEEE Virtual Reality 2004*, (p. 43). Chicago, IL: IEEE Press.

Zellers, E. T., Batteman, S. A., Han, M., & Patrish, S. J. (1995). Optimal coating selection for the analysis of organic vapor mixtures with polymer-coated surface acoustic wave sensor arrays. *Analytical Chemistry, 67*, 1092. doi:10.1021/ac00102a012

Zellers, E. T., Reidy, S., Veeneman, R. A., Gordenker, R., Steinecker, W. H., & Lambertus, G. R. … Wise, K. D. (2007). An integrated micro-analytical system for complex vapor mixtures. In *Proceedings of the Technological Digest of Transducers 2007*, (pp. 1491-1494). IEEE.

ADDITIONAL READING

Barfield, W., & Danas, E. (1996). Comments on the use of olfactory display for virtual environments. *Presence (Cambridge, Mass.), 5*, 109–121.

Carey, W. P., & Yee, S. S. (1992). Calibration of nonlinear solid-state sensor arrays using multivariate regression technique. *Sensors and Actuators. B, Chemical, 9*, 113–122. doi:10.1016/0925-4005(92)80203-A

Hines, E. L., Llobet, E., & Gardner, J. W. (1999). Electronic noses: a review of signal processing. *IEE Proceedings on Circuit Devices Systems, 146*, 297-310.

Nakamoto, T. (2005). Record of dynamical change of odor using odor recorder. *Sensors and Materials, 17*(7), 365–384.

Nakamoto, T., Hirota, Y., & Ide, J. (2005). Record of mint flavor using mass spectrometry. In *Proceedings of the IEEE Sensors Conference*, (pp. 393-396). Irvine, CA: IEEE Press.

Nakamoto, T., & Ishida, H. (2008). Chemical sensing in spatial/temporal domains. *Chemical Reviews, 108*, 680–704. doi:10.1021/cr068117e

Nakamoto, T., Ishida, H., & Matsukura, H. (2011). Olfactory display using solenoid valves and fluid dynamics simulation. In Ghinea, G., Andres, F., & Gulliver, S. (Eds.), *Multiple Sensorial Media Advances and Applications: New Developments in MulSeMedi*. Hershey, PA: IGI Global. doi:10.4018/978-1-60960-821-7.ch007

Nakamoto, T., Nimsuk, N., Wyszynski, B., Takushima, H., Kinoshita, M., & Cho, N. (2008). Experiment on teleolfaction using odor sensing system and olfactory display synchronous with visual information. In *Proceedings of ICAT*, (pp. 85-92). Yokohama, Japan: ICAT.

Nakamoto, T., Okazaki, N., & Moriizumi, T. (1997). High speed active gas/odor sensing system using adaptive control theory. *Sensors and Actuators. B, Chemical, 41*, 183–188. doi:10.1016/S0925-4005(97)80293-6

Nakamoto, T., & Yamanaka, T. (2011). Odor reproduction with movie and its application to teleolfaction. In Hines, E., & Leeson, M. (Eds.), *Intelligent Systems for Machine Olfaction: Tools and Methodologies.* Hershey, PA: IGI Global. doi:10.4018/978-1-61520-915-6.ch005

Narumi, T., Kajinami, T., Nishizaka, S., Tanikawa, T., & Hirose, M. (2011). Pseudo-gustatory display system based on cross-modal integration of vision, olfaction and gustation. In *Proceedings of the IEEE Virtual Reality,* (pp. 127-130). Singapore, Singapore: IEEE Press.

Nayak, M. S., Dwivedi, R., & Srivastava, S. K. (1994). Application of iteration technique in association with multiple regression method for identification of mixtures of gases using an integrated gas sensor array. *Sensors and Actuators. B, Chemical, 2,* 11–16. doi:10.1016/0925-4005(93)01203-G

Somboon, P., Wyszynski, B., & Nakamoto, T. (2009). Odor recorder capable of wide dynamic recordable range based on higher-order sensing and signal extraction technique for small signal. *IEEE Sensors Journal, 9,* 93–102. doi:10.1109/JSEN.2008.2011072

Yamanaka, T., Nimsuk, N., & Nakamoto, T. (2007). Concurrent recording and regeneration of visual and olfactory information using odor sensor. *Presence (Cambridge, Mass.), 16,* 307–317. doi:10.1162/pres.16.3.307

Zellner, D. E., & Whitten, L. A. (1999). The effect of color intensity and appropriateness on color-induced odor enhancement. *The American Journal of Psychology, 112,* 585–604. doi:10.2307/1423652

Section 2
Latest Studies

Chapter 7
Olfactory Sensing Using Quartz Crystal Microbalances with Radio-Frequency Sputtered Organic Films Based on Phenomenological Gas-Sorption Dynamics

Iwao Sugimoto
Tokyo University of Technology, Japan

Michiko Seyama
NTT Microsystem Integration Laboratories, Japan

ABSTRACT

Olfactory information is made up of a wide range of volatile chemical compounds that can be detected by gas sensors with sensing layers, which play a crucial role in gas detection. The sorption-desorption dynamics in the vicinity of the top surface of the sensing layer are largely responsible for the sensor response. Carbonaceous films produced by the radio frequency sputtering of organic materials have granular structures with unsaturated chemical bonds that make them promising olfactory sensing layers. The pre-adsorbates of carbonaceous films, such as water in realistic circumstances, are regarded as dynamic active sites that affect the gas sorption characteristics. The authors have focused on surface water as the most common pre-adsorbate and ionic liquid as an artificial ionic pre-adsorbate. These pre-adsorbates modulate the structures of the sensing layers and act as an absorbent that generates dynamic changes in the sensory responses.

DOI: 10.4018/978-1-4666-2521-1.ch007

Copyright © 2013, IGI Global. Copying or distributing in print or electronic forms without written permission of IGI Global is prohibited.

INTRODUCTION TO GAS-SORPTION SUBJECTS AT A SENSING LAYER

Human olfactory interfaces for virtual reality devices can be developed by organizing a coder and decoder of olfactory information via information networks. The coder is generally referred to as an odor sensing system, and the decoder is termed an olfactory display, and is designed to be wearable and suitable for use as a human interface. Recent studies have revealed that the perception of olfactory information is profoundly affected when combined with visual information (Matsukura, 2009; Nishiguchi, 2010; Narumi, 2011).

An odor sensing system is symbolically called an electronic nose or an artificial olfaction (a machine olfaction) (Pearce, 2003). The representative odor sensing system is basically composed of a multiple gas sensor array that is generally made up of a sensing layer, a transducer/amplifier, and a signal processor. The sensor array consisting of various different types of sensors is considered to expand the chemospectrum of detectable species, and discrimination capability is also enhanced by a combination of specific sensor responses.

Environmental odor sensors must provide precise olfaction information reproducibly despite the continuous fluctuation of environmental conditions as characterized by temperature, humidity, and flow rate (Peter, 2009; Mumyakmaz, 2010). Gas sensors are required to extract electrical signals from physicochemical phenomena occurring

at the atmospheric interface of adsorption/absorption (sorption) layers on the transducer. Irrespective of application, the gas-sorption dynamics of the sensing layer will determine the functionality of the gas sensor.

The molecular structure and surface morphology of the sensing layers are basic determinants of the gas sorption characteristics. The material design and structure of the sensing layer provide unique opportunities for tailoring functionality by means of intermolecular interactions between sorbate gases and sorbent (solvent) films, as depicted in Figure 1. In an ideal situation, the gas-sorption dynamics at sensing layers without pre-adsorbates can be characterized by physicochemical molecular descriptors, such as polarity, polarizability, chirality, volume, flexibility, and proton acidity (basicity) (Abraham, 2004; Abraham, 1994; Grate, 1991). The adsorbed gas molecules at the top surface of the sensing layer are likely to diffuse successively into the film in the vicinity of the top surface. The predominant process will differ with different combinations of film and gas.

In the realistic circumstances in which an electronic nose will be used, the pre-adsorbates in the vicinity of the top surface of the sensing layer will play crucial roles as regards sensor response. The pre-adsorbates at the sensing layer are regarded as dynamic active sites that profoundly affect the gas sorption characteristics.

Figure 1. Sorption behaviors of sorbate vapors at the sensing layers of a sorbent with pre-adsorbates

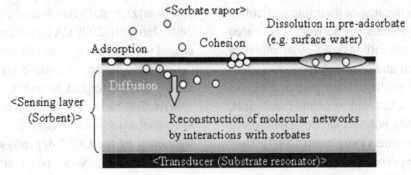

The main objective of this chapter is to show the role of pre-adsorbates in diversifying the sensor responses and thus making it possible to distinguish a single carbon difference in an aliphatic carbon chain of acetyl esters or normal alcohols, which are familiar odorants in our daily lives, as an indices for evaluating food quality/safety. We have focused on the omnipresent water vapor, which is a typical pre-adsorbate, owing to its high cohesive and adsorptive properties. The agglomeration of adsorbed water is considered to form localized islands in hydrophilic areas near the top surface (Figure 1). The surface water can be regarded as an additional sensing moiety, which should generate various response patterns by acting as an absorbent or an evaporant corresponding to the chemical impulse in an olfactory environment.

We have also used a non-volatile ionic liquid as an artificial pre-adsorbate, which is expected to act as an ionic absorbent and a surface potential modulator (Keskin, 2007; Armand, 2009; Feng, 2010). Ionic liquids that are miscible with water are likely to reduce the electrostatic characteristics by neutralizing the polar sites of the sensing layer. Therefore, an ionic liquid pre-adsorbate should enhance the capability of sensing layers to discriminate carbon chains of odorant molecules by restraining the polar characteristics, which in turn increase the non-polar characteristics.

The pre-adsorbate will have a pronounced effect on the sensing layers by acting as a surface potential modulator or sorption-desorption moieties responding to the chemical impulse. We have used plasma-derived carbonaceous films as the sensing layer because of their fine particulate structures with molecular networks activated by the unsaturated carbons and polar moieties including oxygen and/or nitrogen atoms. These carbonaceous films have been prepared by the radio frequency sputtering of organic materials, such as amino acids, polysaccharides, DNA bases, and synthetic polymers (Sugimoto, 2007). During the sputtering process, organic materials are carbonized to form granular or pillar aggregates, in combination with the oxygenation and nitridation of film constituents that are suitable for pre-adsorption by polar species (Sugimoto, 2010). The specific surface area of the carbonaceous sputtered film consisting of pillar aggregates is at least $109 \, m^2/g$. This value is comparable to that of mesoporous carbon adsorbents (Sugimoto, 2010).

This chapter has four parts. The first part describes the preparation and characterization of the carbonaceous sputtered films deposited on a quartz crystal resonator, which has been widely used as a mass-sensitive transducer. The second part reports the demonstration of a Quartz Crystal Microbalance (QCM) sensor array where it detects a tea leaf aroma generated in humid conditions. The third part describes the single carbon discrimination of a carbon chain in a series of aliphatic acetate esters by the QCM sensors. The inverse directional responses of the hydrophilic and hydrophobic films inspire the modeling of surface water behavior in the vicinity of sensing layers. The last part reports the discrimination of normal alcohols by using a non-volatile ionic liquid as a pre-adsorbate that can minutely modify the electrostatic force in carbonaceous films.

QUARTZ CRYSTAL MICROBALANCE COATED WITH PLASMA ORGANIC FILMS

A piezoelectric quartz crystal resonator is widely used as a sub-nanogram gravimetric transducer for a broad range of chemical species, and is known as a Quartz Crystal Microbalance (QCM) (Smith, 2007; Janshoff, 2000). A quartz crystal resonator coated with a sensing layer can provide mechanical information about sensing layers, which are mainly parameterized by mass, viscoelasticity, and friction force. If we disregard the changes in viscoelasticity and friction force, the resonant frequency of the QCM depends exclusively on the effect of mass. When polymer film is used as a sensing layer, this situation is realized as long as the polymer thickness is less than about 1 μm (Lucklum, 1997).

A QCM coated with a sensing layer is one of the most promising olfactory sensors since it has a relatively simple structure and can directly reflect the gas sorption-desorption dynamics in an electrical signal. The gas selectivity of the sensing layer generally depends on the molecular thermodynamics and kinetics of the sensing layer during gas sorption. In addition, each sensing layer has a range for detecting chemical species, or a chemical spectrum range. Therefore, a sensor array that is selective towards a wide range of chemical species can be prepared by combining sensing layers with different selectivities and chemical spectrum ranges.

The QCM was coated with a sensing layer prepared by the radio frequency sputtering of an organic material source consisting of either biomaterials or synthetic polymers. The organic material sources were D-phenylalanine (Phe), D-tyrosine (Tyr), DL-histidine (His), D-glucose

(Glu), adenine (Ade), polyethylene (PE), and polychlorotrifluoroethylene (PCTFE).

The sputtered species in plasma tend to be decomposed by carbonization on the substrate, to which the carbonized films are tightly bound in the plasma sputtering process. Both sides of the QCM substrate were kept at 293 K and coated with carbonaceous film approximately 0.5 μm thick by plasma sputtering.

The arrayed QCMs and the surface elemental ratios of their sensing layers evaluated by X-ray Photoelectron Spectroscopy (XPS) are shown in Figure 2. Carbonized films formed by sputtering tend to reflect the elemental ratios of their raw molecules, which would be carbonized by elimination and crosslinking reactions under sputtering conditions. Moreover, the residual air components in the sputtering chamber induce the oxidation and nitridation of the sputtered species, which are reconstructed into carbonized frameworks with polar groups in the resulting sputtered films.

The carbonaceous structures are characterized by unsaturated moieties, such as dangling bonds

Figure 2. Arrayed QCM sensors coated with radio-frequency sputtered organic films and their structural characteristics

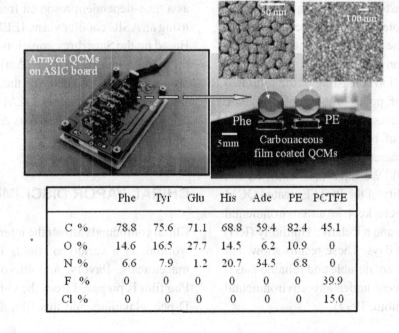

	Phe	Tyr	Glu	His	Ade	PE	PCTFE
C %	78.8	75.6	71.1	68.8	59.4	82.4	45.1
O %	14.6	16.5	27.7	14.5	6.2	10.9	0
N %	6.6	7.9	1.2	20.7	34.5	6.8	0
F %	0	0	0	0	0	0	39.9
Cl %	0	0	0	0	0	0	15.0

and multiple bonds, in addition to the electron withdrawing elements of nitrogen and oxygen. These characteristic moieties are likely to interact specifically with gaseous species.

The SEM image shows that the Phe film is composed of granular aggregates or a bundle of capped pillars, which are separated by grooves. This characteristic surface structure is commonly observed for other sputtered films made up of biomaterials. They are expected to be hydrophilic owing to their bundled pillars characterized by polar moieties in molecular networks. Therefore, the gas-sorption is considered to derive significantly from adsorption at an interface with a coarse structure (Sugimoto, 2010).

The PE film is made up of densely packed granules that have piled up to form a finely rugged surface. In addition to surface adsorption, the diffusion into inner sites should contribute to the gas-sorption behavior of the PE film. In phenomenological terms, the inward diffusion can be regarded as absorption into the film. In combination with the elemental composition, these morphological characteristics should reduce the hydrophilicity of the PE film, which accounts for its amphiphilic nature (Kasai, 1999).

On the other hand, the PCTFE film has a pinhole-free and extremely flat surface consisting of halogenated moieties. These structural characteristics provide the hydrophobic and absorption-driven gas-sorption properties.

Under a condition consisting of the saturated vapor pressure of polar or non-polar organic solvents, we have ascertained the gas-induced frequency shifts of our QCM sensors without changes in resistance by impedance analysis (Sugimoto, 1999). We have also clarified the long-term durability of the PCTFE-coated QCM sensors, which were kept in an environmental chamber at 333 K and a Relative Humidity (RH) of 85% for 1,100 days. These results show that our QCM sensors are durable and reliable mass-sensitive transducers under any environmental conditions (Sugimoto, 1999).

APPARATUS FOR TESTING OLFACTORY SENSORS IN HUMID FLOW

To assess the gas-sorption dynamics that occur at the sensing layers, it is important to understand the step response of the QCM sensors to the sample gas flow while suppressing the disturbance by changing the reference gas flow. Here we describe our test apparatus based on the differential flow measurement method. The gas line connected to the sensor cell can be changed instantaneously and reversibly by turning a four-way valve between the reference and sample lines, as shown in Figure 3. While changing the gas lines, the flow rate (100-200 mL/min) of the sensor cell is kept constant by adjusting each mass flow controller individually. The carrier N_2 is humidified by flowing it through the headspace of a temperature-controlled bottle containing deionized water.

A liquid sample can be vaporized from a sustained release bead placed in a U-shaped Teflon tube (4.35 mm inner diameter). Alternatively, a sealed bottle (100 mL volume) can be used to generate the sample gas from solid and volume samples, such as tea leaves (5 g).

The response of the QCM sensors was recorded as a time-dependent resonant frequency shift by using an ASIC counter via an IEEE 485 interface. Based on the Sauerbrey equation (Mecea, 1994), the loading/unloading mass (Δm) on the QCM is proportionally correlated with the shift in resonant frequency (Δf). Using our QCM resonating at 9 MHz, the relation is shown as Δm [ng] = -1.05 Δf [Hz].

CHIRAL VAPOR DISCRIMINATION

Chiral compounds attract the interest of scientists working in a variety of fields including pharmaceuticals, flavors, and life-origin research. Phe film is prepared from the chiral amino acid, D-phenylalanine, and this film deposited QCM

Figure 3. Olfactory test apparatus of QCM sensors under a constant aroma flow

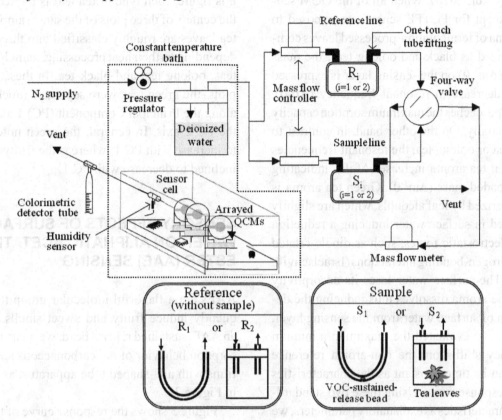

exhibits different vapor sorption characteristics to the chirality of mono-terpene group odorants, limonene, and α-pinene (Sugimoto, 2000). The Phe sensor exhibits a larger sorption capacity for lemon-scented (-)-limonene vapor than for oily-scented (+)-limonene vapor in the 1 to 15 ppm concentration range. Another chiral odorant (-)-α-pinene is also adsorbed more by Phe film than (+)-α-pinene when they are supplied at the same concentration level. This preferred sorption characteristic as regards one of the chiral forms appears to be due to the molecular structure of the Phe film. When mint-scented carvone, which has a polar structure (C=O), was applied to the Phe sensor, there was no significant difference in the sorption capability with the (-) and (+)-forms. Such a polar structure in the vapor molecule induces a stronger interaction with the Phe film than the favored chiral conformation that may exist in the Phe film.

AROMA SENSING OF TEA LEAVES

We demonstrate the utility of the test apparatus for sensing the aroma of a solid sample. The aroma of tea leaves generated in a sealed bottle using RH30% N_2 as a carrier was measured with the arrayed sensors, as shown in Figure 2. Tea leaves are generally classified in terms of the extent of their fermentation by polyphenol-oxidizing enzymes, which can be deactivated by heat processing. The fruity aroma of black teas mainly originates in terpene alcohols and aromatic alcohols, which are generated by the enzymatic oxidation of tea leaves. On the other hand, the green note aroma characterizing green tea is based on leaf alcohols and leaf aldehydes (Wilson, 1992).

The time-course of a frequency shift should theoretically obey the adsorption-diffusion model (Fischerauer, 2007) or the adsorption-desorption model (Okur, 2010). When all of the QCM sensors, except for PCTFE sensor, are exposed to the aroma of fermentation-processed leaves commercialized as black and oolong teas, the mass loaded ($\Delta m > 0$) on the sensing layer is expressed by the decrease in resonant frequency ($\Delta f < 0$), which approaches the maximum sorption capacity exponentially. On the other hand, in contrast to black tea or oolong tea, the resonant frequencies for green tea aroma increase ($\Delta f > 0$), indicating the unloaded mass ($\Delta m < 0$). Green tea aroma is characterized by leaf alcohols, which are slightly dissolved in surface water inducing a reduction in its electrostatic forces, such as dipole-related and hydrogen-bonding interactions (Israelachvili, 1985). The surface water loses its adsorptivity when the aroma dissolves thus inducing the desorption of surface water from the sensing layer.

We have evaluated the maximum/minimum frequency shift from the non-aroma reference level and its time constant as the characteristics of the response curve. Using these two standardized characteristics as explanatory parameters, we classified various tea leaves by Principal Component Analysis (PCA), as shown in Figure 4. In

this figure, each type of tea leaf is plotted using the centers of three plots of the same sample. The tea leaves are roughly classified into three types depending on their heat processing, namely, green teas, oolong tea, and black tea. In these scatter plots, the green teas were separated much more along the Principal Component (PC) 1 axis than the PC 2 axis. In general, the green note tends to increase with PC 1, whereas the fruity note is inclined to decrease with PC 1.

SENSORY EFFECTS OF SURFACE WATER ON ALIPHATIC ACETATE ESTER (AAE) SENSING

AAEs are a flavorful molecular group that frequently induce fruity and sweet smells. Using an AAE-sustained release bead, we measured the sorption behavior of the carbonaceous sputtered films with a U-shaped tube apparatus, as shown in Figure 3.

Figure 5 shows the response curve of the Phe film-coated QCM for a series of AAEs (Sugimoto, 2011). The relative humidity and temperature were

Figure 4. Score plots of principal component analysis to aroma of tea leaves

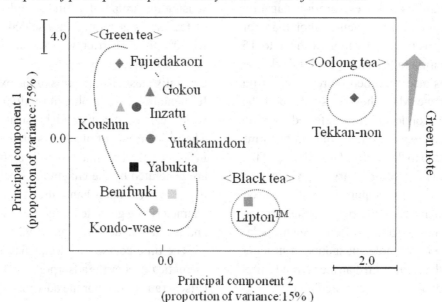

Figure 5. Responses of the Phe sensor to AAEs at RH 60% and 298 K

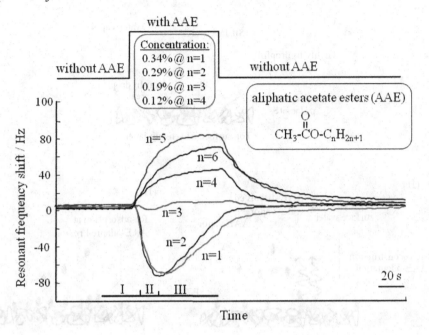

set at 60% and 298 K, respectively. The smaller acetates, such as methyl and ethyl esters, induce V-shaped curves during exposure to AAEs. The initial downward shifts, indicating unloading mass, are considered to originate in the desorption of pre-adsorbed water dissolving the AAEs.

Having reached the minimum value after 30 sec, the frequency shifts began to increase, indicating loading mass. And when humid N_2 without esters flowed again 1 min later, the slope of the upward shift became gentler. This behavior suggests that the upward shifts after the minimum point are mainly derived from the sorption of AAEs in a humid carrier.

We used the Phe sensor to measure the humidity dependence of unloading mass on the small acetates, such as methyl and ethyl acetates (Sugimoto, 2011). There is a tendency with both of the acetates for the unloading mass to decrease as the relative humidity decreases from 60% to 30%. The magnitude of the reduction is more pronounced for ethyl acetate than for methyl acetate. At lower humidity, the unloading mass is prominent for

methyl acetate, which has the highest solubility in water. The humidity dependence of the unloading mass suggests that the unloading mass at the initial stage can be attributed to the desorption of pre-adsorbed water induced by the dissolvation of acetate vapor.

We present a plausible explanation for the V-shaped response curves based on a patchwork model in the vicinity of the top surface of the Phe film exposed to the small amphiphilic AAEs, as shown in Figure 6. (1) Baseline in sensory curve; the water vapor is adsorbed in the vicinity of the surface of the hydrophilic region, forming pre-adsorbed water clusters. (2) Downward shift (unloading mass) in sensor curve; the AAEs are dissolved in the pre-adsorbed water clusters inducing a distortion of the structured molecular networks of water adapted to the film interface. This structural change reduces the adsorption force of the AAE-dissolved water clusters. In addition to the rearrangement of molecular networks for adaptation to AAEs, the AAE-dissolved surface water is desorbed by the weakened hydrophilic

Figure 6. Modeling of sorption of amphiphilic small AAEs in the vicinity of the top surface of the Phe film

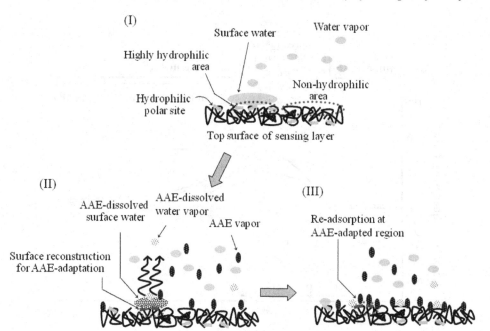

interactions. (3) Upward shift (loading mass) in sensor curve; the AAE and water are cooperatively adsorbed in the reconstructed surface.

The mass loading amounts of AAEs on a series of QCM sensors are shown in Figure 7. The sensors can generally be classified into two groups.

One is composed of the Phe, PE, and His sensors, which possess incremental tendencies that increase with the aliphatic carbon chains. The other group consists simply of the PCTFE sensor, which shows the opposite tendency to the former group. We can roughly characterize both groups by their

Figure 7. Amounts of mass loading on a series of QCM sensors induced by the AAEs at RH 60% and 298 K

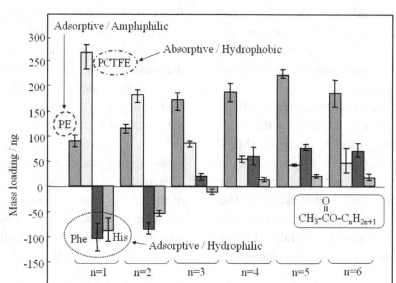

affinity to water. The former group is hydrophilic and can be divided into two classes; one consists of the His and Phe sensors, which are highly hydrophilic. They exhibit negative responses (unloading mass) to small AAEs. Other sensors, which originate in biomaterials, such as Ade, Glu, and Tyr sensors, have shown the same tendencies as the His and Phe sensors, even though their response intensities were smaller. The other class is the PE sensor, which provides positive responses (loading mass) for a range of AAEs. There are considered to be fewer pre-adsorbed water clusters in the amphiphilic PE film than in the former group. The extremely high sorption capacity of PE film is considered to suppress the desorption of pre-adsorbed water even when the small AEEs have been dissolved.

On the other hand, the PCTFE sensor exhibits a unique carbon length dependence; the sorption capacity tends to decrease as the carbon chain length of the AAEs increases. Unlike the carbonaceous films, the hydrophobic PCTFE film without pre-adsorbed water has absorption-driven gas-sorption

properties. As the carbon chain length increases, the diffusion into the inside film should decrease. This reduction in absorption is attributable to the reduction in the sensor response in addition to the reduction in the vapor concentration.

IONIC-LIQUID ADDED SPUTTERED ORGANIC FILMS

With the array of sputtered organic films prepared from different solid materials, we can discriminate groups of chemicals, such as alcohols, aromatic compounds, and saturated lipids. However, there is a problem as regards discriminating such vapor chemical groups generated with different concentrations, since the sensitivity of each sputtered organic film to each group was different.

We considered the addition of ionic liquids with different concentrations to one kind of sputtered film to construct a sensor array. Ionic liquid is a salt that keeps its liquid form at room temperature (Welton,

Figure 8. Score plots of principal component analysis to four alcohols. Each plot represents different concentrated alcohol vapor.

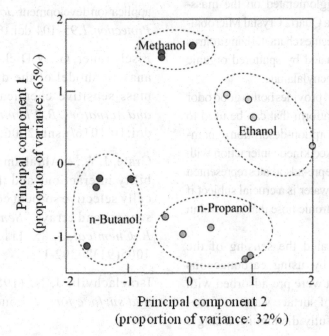

1999) and various compounds are synthesized for applications in many fields for example as solvents for synthesis, batteries, and waste recycling. We added different concentrations of one of the stable ionic liquids, 1-ethyl-3-methyl imidazolium tetrafluoroborate (EMI-BF4), to the Phe film and confirmed that EMI-BF4 dispersed in the film as investigated with XPS (Seyama, 2006). Four types of alcohol vapor (methanol, ethanol, n-propanol, and n-butanol) were applied to the sensor array at different concentrations between 15.6 to 81.4 ppm, and it was found that the relative sorption capability among the Phe films with different concentrated EMI-BF4 remained constant. Therefore, as shown in Figure 8, the plots for the same alcohol gather in the plane of PC 1 and PC 2. Each plot represents a different concentrated vapor. Considering the variety of ionic liquids, this modification method is a powerful tool with which to diversify the sorption characteristics of sputtered organic film for olfactory sensors.

CONCLUSION

We used the radio-frequency sputtering of biomaterials to prepare carbonaceous films composed of granular particulates agglomerated on the mass-sensitive transducers of a Quartz Crystal Microbalance (QCM). Chiral molecules characterizing a citrus aroma can be discriminated by sputtered organic film of the D-form of phenylalanine.

The film coated QCM provides both a good odor sensing device and a platform that can be used to understand various gas sorption-desorption dynamics. In particular, the mixed kinetic interaction with gas molecules and surface pre-adsorbates represented by omnipresent surface water is a crucial subject if we are to realize an electronic nose that is useful in the real world.

We have demonstrated the sensing of the aroma of tea leaves by using carbonaceous film coated QCMs that were pre-adsorbed with water. The utilization of surface water as a pre-adsorbate can successfully distinguish a single

carbon difference in a carbon chain in aliphatic acetate esters. The QCM sensors can differentiate normal alcohols using a non-volatile ionic liquid as a pre-adsorbate.

REFERENCES

Abraham, M. H. (1994). New solute descriptors for linear free energy relationships and quantitative structure-activity relationships. In Politzer, P., & Murray, J. S. (Eds.), *Quantitative Treatments of Solute/Solvent Interactions*. Amsterdam, The Netherlands: Elsevier.

Abraham, M. H., Ibrahim, A., & Zissimos, A. M. (2004). Determination of sets of solute descriptors from chromatographic measurements. *Journal of Chromatography. A, 1037*, 29–47. doi:10.1016/j.chroma.2003.12.004

Armand, M., Endres, F., MacFarlane, D. R., Ohno, H., & Scrosati, B. (2009). Ionic-liquid materials for the electrochemical challenges of the future. *Nature Materials, 8*, 621–629. doi:10.1038/nmat2448

Feng, R., Zhao, D., & Guo, Y. (2010). Revisiting characteristics of ionic liquids: A review for future application development. *Journal of Environmental Protection, 1*, 95–104. doi:10.4236/jep.2010.12012

Fischerauer, G., & Dickert, F. L. (2007). An analytic model of the dynamic response of mass-sensitive chemical sensors. *Sensors and Actuators. B, Chemical, 123*, 993–1001. doi:10.1016/j.snb.2006.11.002

Grate, J. W., & Abraham, M. H. (1991). Solubility interactions and the design of chemically selective sorbent coatings for chemical sensors and arrays. *Sensors and Actuators. B, Chemical, 3*, 85–111. doi:10.1016/0925-4005(91)80202-U

Israelachvili, J. N. (1985). *Intermolecular and surface forces*. London, UK: Academic Press.

Janshoff, A., Galla, H.-J., & Steinem, C. (2000). Piezoelectric mass-sensing devices as biosensors-an alternative to optical biosensors? *Angewandte Chemie International Edition*, *39*, 4004–4032. doi:10.1002/1521-3773(20001117)39:22<4004::AID-ANIE4004>3.0.CO;2-2

Kasai, N., & Sugimoto, I. (1999). Effects of aging on radio frequency-sputtered polyethylene film. *Journal of Applied Polymer Science*, *73*, 1869–1877. doi:10.1002/(SICI)1097-4628(19990906)73:10<1869::AID-APP6>3.0.CO;2-7

Keskin, S., Kayrak-Talay, D., Akman, U., & Hortaçsu, Ö. (2007). A review of ionic liquids towards supercritical fluid applications. *The Journal of Supercritical Fluids*, *43*, 150–180. doi:10.1016/j.supflu.2007.05.013

Lucklum, R. (1997). Determination of polymer shear modulus with quartz crystal resonators. *Faraday Discussions*, *107*, 123–140. doi:10.1039/a703127k

Matsukura, H., Yoshida, H., Saitoh, A., & Nakamoto, T. (2009). Odor presentation with a vivid sense of reality: Incorporating fluid dynamics simulation into olfactory display. [IEEE Press.]. *Proceedings of IEEE Virtual Reality*, *2009*, 295–296.

Mecea, V. M. (1994). Loaded vibrating quartz sensors. *Sensors and Actuators. A, Physical*, *40*, 1–27. doi:10.1016/0924-4247(94)85026-7

Mumyakmaz, B., Özman, A., Ebeoğlu, M. A., Taşaltin, C., & Gürol, İ. (2010). A study on the development of a compensation method for humidity effect in QCM sensor responses. *Sensors and Actuators. B, Chemical*, *147*, 277–282. doi:10.1016/j.snb.2010.03.019

Narumi, T., Kajinami, T., Nishizaka, S., Tanikawa, T., & Hirose, M. (2011). Pseudo-gustatory display system based on cross-modal integration of vision, olfaction and gestation. [IEEE Press.]. *Proceedings of the IEEE Virtual Reality*, *2011*, 127–130.

Nishiguchi, M., Sakamoto, K., Nomura, S., Hirotomi, T., Shiwaku, K., & Hirakawa, M. (2010). Tabletop life review therapy system using olfactory display for presenting flavor. In *Proceedings of the International MultiConference of Engineers and Computer Scientists 2010*, (vol. 1). IEEE.

Okur, S., Kuş, M., Özel, F., & Yilmaz, M. (2010). Humidity adsorption kinetics of water soluble calix[4]arene derivatives measured using QCM technique. *Sensors and Actuators. B, Chemical*, *145*, 93–97. doi:10.1016/j.snb.2009.11.040

Pearce, T. C., Schiffman, S. S., Nagle, H. T., & Gardner, J. W. (Eds.). (2004). *Handbook of machine olfaction*. Weinheim, Germany: Wiley-VCH.

Peter, A. L., & Dickert, F. L. (2009). Chemosensors in environmental monitoring: Challenges in ruggedness and selectivity. *Analytical and Bioanalytical Chemistry*, *393*, 467–472. doi:10.1007/s00216-008-2464-3

Seyama, M., Iwasaki, Y., Tate, A., & Sugimoto, I. (2006). Room-temperature ionic-liquid-incorporated plasma-deposited thin films for discriminative alcohol-vapor sensing. *Chemistry of Materials*, *18*, 2656–2662. doi:10.1021/cm052088r

Smith, A. (2007). The quartz crystal microbalance. In Brown, M., & Gallagher, P. (Eds.), *Handbook of Thermal Analysis and Calorimetry* (*Vol. 5*). Amsterdam, The Netherlands: Elsevier Science.

Sugimoto, I., Mitsui, K., Nakamura, M., & Seyama, M. (2011). Effects of surface water on gas sorption capacities of gravimetric sensing layers analyzed by molecular descriptors of organic adsorbates. *Analytical and Bioanalytical Chemistry*, *399*, 1891–1899. doi:10.1007/s00216-010-4556-0

Sugimoto, I., Nagaoka, T., Seyama, M., Nakamura, M., & Takahashi, K. (2007). Classification and characterization of atmospheric VOCs based on sorption/desorption behaviors of plasma polymer films. *Sensors and Actuators. B, Chemical, 124*, 53–61. doi:10.1016/j.snb.2006.11.045

Sugimoto, I., Nakamura, M., & Muzunuma, M. (1999). Structures and VOC-sensing performance of high-sensitivity plasma-polymer films coated on quartz crystal resonator. *Sensors and Materials, 11*, 59–70.

Sugimoto, I., Nakamura, M., Seyama, M., Ogawa, S., & Katoh, T. (2000). Chiral-discriminative amino acid films prepared by vacuum vaporization and/or plasma processing. *Analyst (London), 125*, 169–174. doi:10.1039/a907149k

Sugimoto, I., Okamoto, M., Sone, K., & Takahashi, K. (2010). Structures and gas-sorption properties of carbonaceous film prepared by radio-frequency sputtering of polysaccharides pectin. *Polymer Degradation & Stability, 95*, 929–934. doi:10.1016/j.polymdegradstab.2010.03.023

Sugimoto, I., & Sekiguchi, H. (2010). Structure and N_2-sorption properties of carbonaceous films prepared by high-powered sputtering of D-phenylalanine. *Thin Solid Films, 518*, 2876–2882. doi:10.1016/j.tsf.2009.10.002

Welton, T. (1999). Room-temperature ionic liquids: Solvents for synthesis and catalysis. *Chemical Reviews, 99*, 2071–2083. doi:10.1021/cr980032t

Willson, K. C., & Clifford, M. N. (1992). Aroma of green tea. In *Tea* (pp. 428–439). London, UK: Chapman & Hall. doi:10.1007/978-94-011-2326-6

Chapter 8
Materials Design of Sensing Layers for Detection of Volatile Analytes

Mutsumi Kimura
Shinshu University, Japan

Tsuyoshi Ikehara
National Institute of Advanced Industrial Science and Technology, Japan

Tadashi Fukawa
Shinshu University, Japan

Takashi Mihara
Olympus Corporation, Japan

ABSTRACT

The authors developed highly sensitive sensing layers for detection of Volatile Organic Compounds (VOCs) by using polymeric nanomaterials. In this chapter, they describe their recent progress on the design of polymeric sensing layers for the chemical sensors. The nanostructures of polymeric sensing layer strongly influenced the sensitivity and selectivity for VOCs sensings.

INTRODUCTION

We are constantly exposed to health and safety hazards as a result of dynamic and unpredictable conditions. On-site and real-time analyses of ambient information on factors such as sounds, colors, and odors provide us with situational awareness to manage these hazards. Among the ambient factors, odorants are detected and discriminated though olfaction and the physicochemical properties of odorants induce specific odor sensations by selective binding with odorant receptors in the nasal cavity. The chemical features of the odorants activate multiple receptors and all of the signals are sent to the brain as activation patterns to recognize a specific group or feature of the target odorant.

Artificial electronic nose systems have been developed for the detection of volatile odorants. These systems mimic the mammalian olfactory system by producing sensing patterns of cross-responsive sensor arrays. The systems comprise a chemical sensor array together with an interfacing electronic circuitry, as well as a pattern recognition unit that acts as a signal processing system. The chemical sensor arrays are capable of converting chemical information into an output signal and each sensor in the array can generate different signals in response to the concentration and the specific interaction with target odorants. Target odorants cannot be identified from the response of a single sensor element. A response pattern from multiple sensors in the arrays can provide a fingerprint that allows classification and

DOI: 10.4018/978-1-4666-2521-1.ch008

Copyright © 2013, IGI Global. Copying or distributing in print or electronic forms without written permission of IGI Global is prohibited.

identification of the odorant. To yield the sensing patterns requires a variety of sensing layers with different responses for odorants.

Mass sensors have been applied to chemical sensing in the electronic nose systems by the use of various sensing materials. When VOCs are captured within the sensing layers on the mass sensors, the sorption amounts can be monitored by resonant frequency shifts of the sensors. The determination of weight changes is directly related to the interactions between the sensing layers and target compounds. Quartz Crystal Microbalances (QCMs) have been widely used as the platform for mass sensing by the deposition with the sensing layers. The resonance frequency has been proven to decrease linearly upon the increase of weight on the QCM electrode in a nanogram level. Recently, silicon resonators such as microcantilevers and microdisks have come to be expected to provide an alternative platform for mass sensors. The microfabrication processes of silicon makes it possible to significantly downsize of sensor arrays and integrate various components onto one chip.

We have developed highly sensitive sensing layers for detection of VOCs by using nanomaterials such as the polymer thin films, the dense surface of polymer brushes, and sterically protected metal complexes. In this chapter, we describe our recent progress on the design of the sensing layers for the chemical sensors. The sensitivity, selectivity, and responsibility for VOCs sensing systems depend on the chemical structure of polymeric sensing layers and microenvironment around the receptor molecules.

POLYMER-BASED RECOGNITION LAYERS

Polymer-Coated QCM Sensor Arrays

Polymers have been used as sensing layers owing to their great design flexibility. The polymers offer an advantage as a sorbent coating for the detection of analytes by using QCM sensors because they provide specific interactions with analytes as well as form stable thin films (Matsuguchi & Ueno, 2006; Kikuchi, Tsuru, & Shiratori, 2006; Zeng, et al., 2007; Si, et al., 2007; Ichinohe, Tanaka, & Konno, 2007; Matsuguchi, et al., 2008; Ju, et al., 2008; Ayad & Torad, 2009; Du, et al., 2009; Baimpos, 2010; Wang, et al., 2010; Nomura, et al., 2010) . Polymers can offer enhanced sensitivity and a real-time response in the QCM sensor systems. The responses of polymer-coated QCM sensors to exposure to VOCs were studied under various operational conditions and were also applied to the detection of VOCs by the response analyses of QCM sensor arrays.

The chemical structures of four polymers are shown in Figure 1a. Four polymers, polystyrene (PS), polybutadiene (PBD), poly(acrylonitrile-*co*-butadiene) (PAB), and poly(styrene-*co*-butadiene) (PSB), were deposited onto the gold electrode of 9 Mz QCMs by the spin-coating method. The SEM image of the PBD-coated QCM shows a smooth and uniform surface. The thickness of the PBD layer was 400 nm as observed in the cross-sectional SEM image shown in Figure 1b. The deposition of polymer films on QCMs induced the frequency decrease at approximately 7000 Hz. Using the Sauerbrey equation (Sauerbrey, 1959), this frequency decrease is equivalent to a mass coating of 7400 ng. The thickness of the deposited polymer films is about 400 nm, estimated from the weight obtained from the frequency decrease, the density of polymers, and the area of the electrode. The estimated thicknesses agree with those observed from the SEM images.

The polymer-coated QCMs were set into the measurement chamber and the sensing properties of polymer-coated QCMs were investigated by measuring the frequency changes when the film was exposed to VOC vapors in the measurement chamber. Toluene, n-octane, acetone, and ethanol were chosen as common representatives of different classes of solvents. The measurements consist of an exposure phase and a regeneration

Figure 1. a) Chemical structures PS, PBD, PAB, PBD; b) cross-sectional SEM image of PBD film

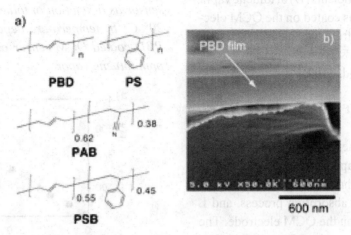

phase. During the exposure phase, the films on QCMs act as sensing layers for VOC molecules and the incorporation of VOC molecules within the polymer film causes the frequency to decrease. After reaching a constant frequency, the incorporated VOC molecules are released by the supply of pure carrier gas. During the regeneration process, the frequency of the sensors rises due to the mass decreasing in the polymer film.

Figure 2 shows time courses of sensor responses (ΔF) of the QCMs coated with PS and PBD responding to exposure to 1000 ppm toluene vapor at 20 °C. The sensor responses ΔF were ob-

Figure 2. Frequency changes in PBD- (solid line) and PS- (dotted line) coated QCMs (film thickness is 500 nm) on exposure to 1000 ppm toluene vapor measure at 20° C

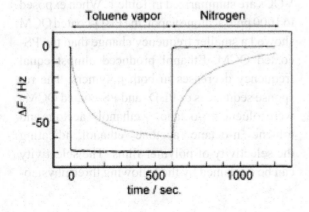

tained from the frequency differences between the corresponding QCM frequencies at the beginning and end of the exposure phase. When the PBD thin film was employed, the frequency of the QCM decreased rapidly in response to the exposure to toluene vapor and saturated at -ΔF= 69 Hz within 20 s. When the carrier gas was changed to pure nitrogen gas, the frequency returned to the original value within 20 s, which indicates fast adsorption and desorption processes of toluene in the PBD film. On the other hand, the PS-coated QCM exhibited a very slow frequency change in the adsorption and desorption of toluene vapor and −ΔF after 600 s reached 60 Hz. The response time of PS-coated QCM ($t_{90\%}$ = 275 s) was a significantly longer than that of the PBD-coated QCM ($t_{90\%}$ = 7 s). The difference in sensing response speed between PS- and PBD-coated QCMs may be based on the chemical structures of the polymers. Since the glass transition temperature (T_g) of PS is 95 °C, PS is solid state at room temperature. In contrast, PBD is a flexible elastic material at room temperature owing to its low T_g (T_g < -90 °C). The diffusion of toluene within the hard PS film is slow compared with that within the soft PBD film. Thus, the PS-coated QCM sensor needs a long period to reach a saturated state in response to the expose to toluene vapor.

The diffusion coefficients (D) of toluene vapor into PBD and PS films coated on the QCM electrode are determined from the analyses of sensor responses using Fick's second equation (Ayad, El-Hefnawey, & Torad, 2009):

$$\Delta F_t/\Delta F_\infty = 4(D/\pi)^{1/2}\,(t^{1/2}/L) \qquad (2)$$

where ΔF_t is the frequency change due to the absorption of toluene vapor into the polymer films at any time t, ΔF_∞ is the frequency change in the saturated state in the absorption process, and L is the film thickness on the QCM electrode. The D values of toluene vapor in PBD and PS films were obtained from plots of $\Delta F_t/\Delta F_\infty$ as a function of $t^{1/2}/L$. The D values of toluene vapor were estimated to be 5.4×10^{-11} and 2.7×10^{-13} cm²/s for PBD and PS films, respectively. The D value of the PBD film was 200 times higher than that of the PS film, indicating a rapid diffusion of toluene vapor in flexible PBD films.

Figure 3a shows the ΔF_∞ change of PBD-coated sensors in sensing toluene with various concentrations of 50-6000 ppm. A linear correlation was obtained with a correlation coefficient of 0.992 and a slope of 0.095 Hz/ppm. The linear correlation between ΔF and toluene concentrations makes it possible to determine the concentration of toluene vapor in unknown samples. The limit for the detection of toluene concentration was 20 ppm for the PBD-coated sensor. The sensor responses were recorded versus time until reaching the steady state and then the complete desorption of toluene vapor from PBD film was obtained using pure nitrogen. The experiment was repeated ten times to ensure complete reproducibility and reversibility of the sensor. The PBD-coated QCMs showed good reproducibility and reversibility in the toluene sensing. Figure 3b shows the dependence of ΔF_∞ on the temperature of the tested chamber. The sensor response of the PBD-coated QCM at 0 °C is about 4 times higher than that at 20 °C and ΔF_∞ decreased with increasing temperature. When the PBD film is exposed to toluene vapor,

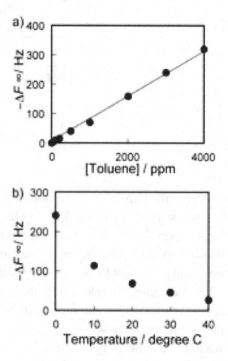

Figure 3. a) Responses to PBD-coated QCM sensor as a function of toluene concentration at 20° C; b) temperature dependence of ΔF_∞ for PBD-coated QCM sensor on exposure to 1000 ppm toluene vapor

gaseous toluene condenses within the PBD film. The ΔF_∞ decreasing with rising temperature can be explained by the increase in the equilibrium vapor pressure. The sensor responses strongly depend on the ambient temperature as well as the concentration of target VOCs.

The ΔF_∞ and $t_{90\%}$ values of PBD- and PS-coated QCMs under the exposures to 1000 ppm VOCs are summarized in Table 1. When exposed to 1000 ppm acetone vapor, the PBD-coated QCM showed a smaller frequency change than the PS-coated QCM. Ethanol produced almost equal frequency decreases in both polymers. The response sequences of PBD- and PS-coated QCMs were toluene = n-octane >> ethanol > acetone and toluene > n-octane > acetone > ethanol, indicating the selectivity of polymer films. The selectivity can be explained by the following three physico-

Table 1. -ΔF_∞ and $t_{90\%}$ values of PBD and PS-coated QCMs under the exposures with 1000 ppm VOCs

| | $-\Delta F_\infty$ (Hz) | $t_{90\%}$ (s) | PS | |
			$-\Delta F_\infty$ (Hz)	$t_{90\%}$ (s)
Toluene	69.0	7	60.0[1)]	275*
n-Octane	72.0	8	18.0[1)]	400*
Acetone	2.2	6	6.2	12
Ethanol	2.9	6	3.1	6

* The absorptions of toluene and n-octane in PS film did not saturate even after 6000 s. Values are determined at 6000 s.

chemical properties of VOCs and polymers: the molecular weight of VOCs, the equilibrium vapor pressure of VOCs, and the affinity of the polymer for VOC vapor. PBD and PS exhibited different patterns of selectivity in VOC sensing, suggesting a difference in the affinity of the polymers for VOC vapors.

The affinity of polymers for VOC vapors mainly coincides with the solubility parameter (δ) towards organic solvents (Vandemburg, et al., 1999). The solubility parameter provides a numerical estimate of the degree of intermolecular interaction between different two materials. The solubility parameter of PBD (δ = 7.3) is closer to that of n-octane (δ = 7.0), but is smaller than that of ethanol (δ = 12.7) (Gamsjäger, et al., 2008). The closer solubility parameters between PBD and n-octane will be able to interact with each other, resulting in higher response of the sensor coated with PBD to n-octane vapor. Toluene and n-octane, having closer parameters with PBD and PS, shows larger responses than ethanol and acetone. Since PS showed very slow responses in toluene and n-octane, the detection of VOCs at the saturated state needs long periods of over 6000 s. On the other hand, the response times of the PBD-coated QCM for all the VOC are less than 20 s. Flexible polymers having low T_g are suitable as sensing layers for the detection of VOCs.

The thickness of the polymer film on the QCM would affect the sensitivity of the sensors. The QCMs having different PBD film thicknesses were prepared by changing the rotation speed of

spin-coating processes and the PBD concentration of the solution. While the ΔF_∞ linearly increased with increasing film thickness upon exposure to 1000 ppm toluene vapor, the QCM coated with a 1-μm-thick PBD film showed an unstable oscillation under the same voltage. To evaluate the quality of oscillations, the electrical characteristics of the PBD-coated QCMs using a network impedance analyzer were studied. As shown in Figure 4, the peaks were significantly broadened by the deposition of a 1-μm-thick PBD film. The

Figure 4. Frequency-dependent impedance for PBD-coated QCMs having different film thicknesses at 20° C: a) only QCM; b) 500 nm thick QCM coated with PBD; and c) 1 μm thick QCM coated with PBD. The film thicknesses were estimated by the frequency changes.

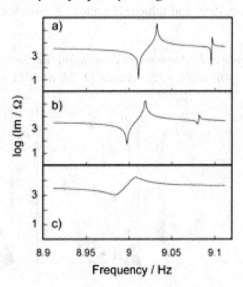

viscoelastic effects of the flexible PBD films contribute strongly to the resonance properties of QCMs. From these results, the film thickness of PBD should be less than 1 μm to obtain a stable oscillation. Although the deposition of flexible polymers on QCMs leads to high sensitivities of sensors, the enhancement of sensitivity by increasing the film thicknesses is limited.

To change the affinity of polymers for VOC vapors, PBD-based copolymers PAB and PSB were used as sensing layers of VOC sensors. PAB and PSB are random copolymers containing 38 wt% polar acrylonitrile and 45wt% aromatic polystyrene segments, respectively. The presence of different polarity segments in the polymer chains will influence the responsibility and selectivity of sensors. Figure 5 shows the changes of absorption amounts in PBD, PAB, and PSB films during exposure to VOCs as a function of the analyte's vapor pressure, P/P_0 (Severin & Lewis, 2000). Polymer films show linear dependences of absorption amount for the four VOCs on P/P_0. The differences in the slopes of P/P_0 dependence are due to the differences in chemical affinity between the polymer film and VOCs as well as the molecular properties of the VOCs such as their molecular volume. The slope sequences of PBD, PAB, and PSB-coated QCMs are toluene > acetone = n-octane > ethanol, acetone > toluene > ethanol > n-octane, and toluene > acetone > n-octane >

ethanol, respectively, indicating different selectivities for VOCs in PBD-, PAB-, and PSB-coated QCM sensors. The affinities of polar VOCs are enhanced by the introduction of a polar acrylonitrile segment, resulting in higher responses for these polar VOCs in the PAB film. The response times of PAB and PSB for all VOCs are almost the same as that of PBD, indicating the fast diffusion of VOCs within the PAB and PSB films. The above difference in sensitivity produces response patterns for the classification and identification of unknown VOC vapors. The responses for three QCMs coated with PBD, PAB, and PSB produce a recognition pattern that can be used to detect VOCs (Jin, et al., 2009).

Three flexible polymers, PBD, PAB, and PSB, exhibited different selectivities for four VOCs. The sensitivity of sensor can tune by the combination of polybutadiene segments and the other segment in the copolymers. The simultaneous measurement of the QCM array having different sensitive polymer films provides the recognition pattern for the detection of VOCs.

QCMs Modified with Polymer Nanobrushes

Polymer was coated by the several techniques including vapor-deposition, spin-coating, electrophoresis, and electropolymerization. However,

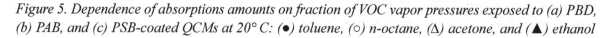

Figure 5. Dependence of absorptions amounts on fraction of VOC vapor pressures exposed to (a) PBD, (b) PAB, and (c) PSB-coated QCMs at 20° C: (●) toluene, (○) n-octane, (△) acetone, and (▲) ethanol

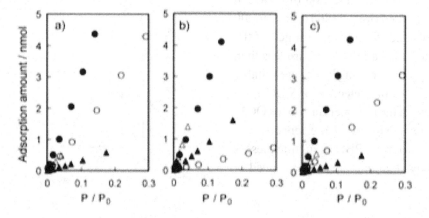

it is difficult to provide uniform nanostructures in molecular level because of their long flexible nature. Recently, the attractive approach to control nanostructures on the solid substrates has been developed by the combination of self-assembling monolayer formation (SA) and living radical polymerization (Jordan, et al., 1999; Tsujii, et al., 2006). At the first, the thiols were attached with the gold surface by the formation of covalently bond Au-S and the Self-Assembled Monolayers (SAMs) were formed on the surface of substrates. The other side of thiols possesses the attachment units for polymer chains and the corresponding monomers are polymerized from the attachment unit on the surface of SAMs. The spatial arrangement of polymer chains is observed due to the close distance of grafted points. Hence, the polymers deform and stretch in the direction perpendicular to the surface like brushes (Milner, 1991).

Atom Transfer Radical Polymerization (ATRP) have been developed by Matyjaszewski, Patten, and Xia (1997). ATRP allows the reaction to be carried out in a controlled way to generate a living growth end during the polymerization, and can be used to obtain polymers with high molecular weight and low polydispersity index. ATRP from the surface of substrates induces the condense polymer brush formation with controlled length of polymer brush. The combination of SA with ATRP can produces uniform nanostructures composed of densed polymer brushes on the solid surface. These methods have been applied to the polymer-brush patterns and nanostructured surface for the attachment of biomolecules (Bao, Bruening, & Baker, 2006; Shah, et al., 2000).

We demonstrated the fabrications of mass sensors by the polymer-brush coating on QCMs through SA and ATRP. Polymer naostructures can be provides uniform and high sensitive surface for absorption of gas molecules and the absorption on the polymer brushes may induce the rapid and precise detection of weights of atmospheric gas molecules. Polymer brushes were attached with the surfaces of QCMs, and the morphologies and chemical structures, and analyzed their sensing abilities for Volatile Organic Compounds (VOCs) were characterized.

The polymerizations of several vinyl monomers were carried out by the ATRP method from the initiator-modified substrates (Scheme 1). Au-coated Si substrates were cleaned in piranha solution (3:1 [v/v] conc. H_2SO_4 and 30% H_2O_2) for 30 min, then were rinsed completely with DI (18.2 MΩ/cm) water and dried under a stream of dry nitrogen. SAMs of thiol having a initiator segment for ATRP were formed onto the cleaned gold surface by immersion into 1 mM toluene solutions of 13,13'-dithio-bis-(2-bromo-3-tridecanone) at 60° for 1 day. Polymer brushes prepared from the initiator-modified gold surface at 60° for 3 h in the presence of $FeBr_2$, triphenylphosphine and ethyl-2-bromoisobutyrate. After the polymerization, the substrates were washed with methanol and toluene to remove no-attached polymer chains.

(Dimethylamino)ethyl acrylate (DMAEA) was used for the monomers for the polymer brushes on the substrates. Au-evaporated Si wafers and Quartz Crystal Microbalances (QCMs) were used as substrates. The morphologies and chemical structures of polymer brushes were analyzed by SEM, AFM, and IR-RAS using Au-evaporated Si substrates. Furthermore, the thickness of polymer brushes was estimated from the frequency increasing of QCMs after the polymerization and the polymer brush-modified QCMs were used for the absorption properties of VOCs.

The FT-IR spectra of polymer brushes exhibited similar spectra of each parent polymers suggesting the successful polymerization by ATRP form the initiator-modified substrate surface. The morphologies of these polymer-modified surfaces were monitored by AFM and SEM. AFM images of polymer brushed Au substrate revealed a smooth surface with a thickness of approximately 40-60 nm. SEM image also indicates that the formations of polymer brush membrane on QCM surface were accomplished by this method.

Scheme 1. Synthetic approaches of polymer brushes

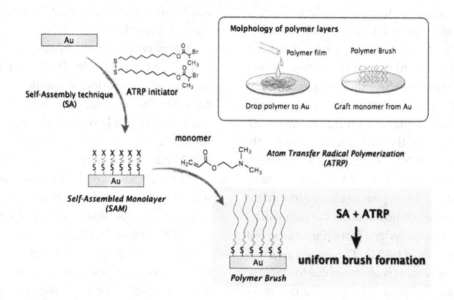

Acetone, ethanol, and toluene were chosen as tested VOC sources and the concentration of these VOCs in the chamber were fixed at 4000 ppm. QCMs were coated with three polymer brushes were 50 nm thickness on average. When the acetone and ethanol were injected into QCM coated with polymer brushes, the decreasing of frequency value was observed. It suggests the weight increase of the polymer brush layer. The vapor sensing properties of polymer brushes on QCMs were investigated by measuring the frequency changes when the film was exposed to three VOCs vapors (Figure 6). We found that poly((2-dimethylamino)ethyl methacrylate) (PDMEAMA) brush shows a strong affinity for every vapors than other polymer brushes and the response sequence of PDMEAMA was ethanol > acetone > toluene, indicating the selectivity of polymer brush.

QCMs Coated with Nanostructured Macromolecular Metal Complexes

The olfactory receptor superfamily in biological noses provides a basis for the remarkable abil-ity to recognize and discriminate among a large number of structurally diverse odorants (Buck & Axel, 1991; Katada, et al., 2005). The olfactory receptors are incorporated on the surface of many tiny hair-like cilia. The cilia provide an effective high surface area that reacts to odorants. If the molecular receptors recognize the chemical properties of VOCs based on their size and polarity, the incorporation of receptors within cilia-like polymer brushes on QCMs can enhance the selectivity and sensitivity for VOC sensing. We designed and synthesized a novel receptor including metallophthalocyanine (MPcs) and a three-dimensional phenylene structure. Müllen and coworkers reported selective detection with a high sensitivity to polar aromatic target molecules by using polyphenylene dendrimers (Schlupp, et al., 2001; Vossmeyer, et al., 2002; Krasteva, et al., 2002). The sensitivity and selectivity for VOCs depended on the chemical structure and size of dendrimers. Incorporating MPcs within the polyphenylenes can create a unique microenvironment for a sensing event. Planar phthalocyanine (Pc) ligand can coordinate with various metal ions, and the central metals can interact with small

Figure 6. Sensor responses of QCM sensors modified with only three polymer brushes to 4000 ppm acetone, ethanol, and toluene vapors at 20° C

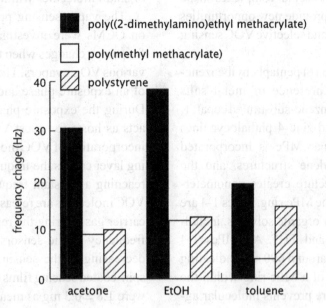

molecules through a coordination bond (Snow & Barger, 1989; Fietzek & Mack, 2007; Ceyhan, et al., 2007; Bohrer, et al., 2008). However, non-substituted Pcs do not dissolve in any solvents due to their strong aggregation tendency. The aggregation between MPcs hindered the access of small molecules into the central metal. To diminish the intermolecular aggregation of MPcs, bulky substituents have been introduced at the

peripheral positions of MPcs. When bulky oligo-phenylene units were introduced at the peripheral positions of the Pc ring, they served to prevent direct interaction between the MPcs (Walsh & Mandal, 2000). The selective control of ligation through steric recognition within the pocket of sterically protected MPcs was reported (Kimura, et al., 2003). Trapping sterically protected MPcs within a polymer brush structure can tune the

Scheme 2. Structures of sterically protected MPcs

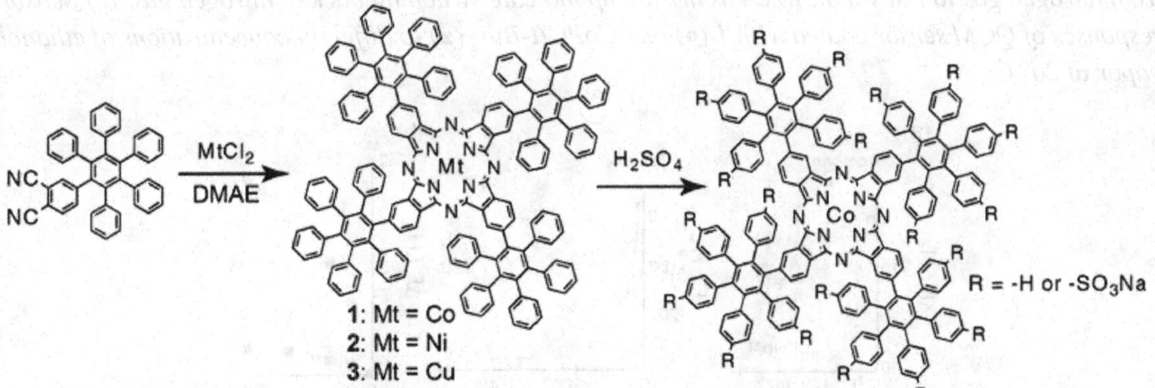

sensing of VOCs. We believe that fabricating nanostructured macromolecular complexes on the surface of QCMs will provide new opportunities for the highly sensitive and selective VOC sensing systems to be used.

Cyclotetramerization of pentaphenylbenzene-phthalonitrile in the presence of metal salts yielded pentaphenylbenzene-substituted cobalt 1, nickel 2, copper 3, and zinc 4 phthalocyanines (Scheme 2). The planar MPc is incorporated within the polyphenylene structures, and the polyphenylene architecture creates nanometer-sized cavities around the MPc ring. MPcs 1-4 are highly soluble in many organic solvents, including toluene, CH_2Cl_2, and THF. All MPcs 1-4 exhibit a sharp Q band around 690 nm, indicating that the incorporation of a MPc ring within the polyphenylene structure prevents molecular aggregation between MPc rings in solid thin films (Stillman & Nyokong, 1989). However, spin-coated films of tetrakis(*tert*-butyl)phthalocyanine metal complexes (MPc(*t*-Bu)$_4$) lacking bulky pentaphenylbenzene substituents exhibited a broad band around 620 nm, which can be attributed to the aggregation of MPcs. The prevention of intermolecular aggregation among MPc rings allows small molecules to penetrate central metals. Furthermore, cavities of the rigid polyphen-

ylene structures may provide penetration pathways of small molecules within the thin film.

The vapor sensing properties of MPc films on QCMs were investigated by measuring the frequency changes when the film was exposed to various VOCs vapors. The measurements consist of an exposure phase and a regeneration phase. During the exposure phase, the film on QCMs acts as hosts for guest VOC molecules and the incorporation of VOC molecules within the sensing layer causes the frequency to decrease. After reaching a constant frequency, the incorporated VOC molecules are released by the supply of pure carrier gas. During the regeneration process, the frequency of the sensors rises due to the mass decreasing in the sensing film. The masses of spin-coated sensing films deposited on the QCMs were 1.8 ± 0.3 mg as measured by the frequency changes. The QCMs coated with host molecules in a temperature-controlled measurement cell at 25 °C were exposed to the different VOCs at various concentrations. The sensor responses ΔF were obtained from the frequency differences between the corresponding QCM frequencies at the beginning and the end of the exposure phase.

Figure 7a shows the response signals of QCM sensors coated with 1 and CoPc(*t*-Bu)$_4$ exposed to acetone, ethanol, and toluene vapors at a con-

Figure 7. (a) Response signals of QCM sensors coated with 1 (solid line) CoPc(t-Bu)$_4$ (dotted line) to 4000 ppm acetone, ethanol, and toluene vapors at 20° C. Arrows pointing down indicated switching from nitrogen gas to test vapor, whereas arrows up indicate switching back to nitrogen gas. (b) Sensor responses of QCM sensor coated with 1 (●) and CoPC(t-Bu)$_4$ (■) to different concentrations of ethanol vapor at 20° C.

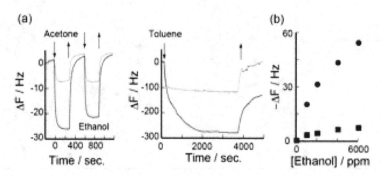

centration of 4000 ppm. Sterically protected CoPc 1 has much larger responses to all VOCs than CoPc(*t*-Bu)$_4$. Sterically protected CoPc 1 shows ca. 6-fold higher adsorption capability in acetone relative to CoPc(*t*-Bu)$_4$. The large responses of 1 to all VOCs are due to the rigid and poor packing of molecular components within the thin film. The sensor responses of 1 are reversible and reproducible to acetone and ethanol vapors, and the sensor is ready for the next measurement after 300 sec. However, the incorporation and releasing of toluene vapor in 1 required a very long time, and the time until 90% of the equilibrium sensor response was 1250 sec. The sensor response reached 275 Hz at 2000 sec after the start of the supply of 4000 ppm toluene vapor.

In addition to the mass of incorporated VOCs within the MPc film on QCMs, other factors such as sample viscoelasticity, surface roughness, and interfacial slippage will also affect the QCM's resonance frequency. Acoustical rigidity of the film in the presence and absence of VOCs was proven by analyzing the bandwidth of the admittance spectra of the MPcs-coated QCMs. When the film was exposed to VOCs vapors, the bandwidth increase was not observed suggesting that the change in viscoelastic properties is almost negligible.

Figure 7b shows the sensor response of 1 and CoPc(*t*-Bu)$_4$ sensors in sensing ethanol with different concentrations of 1000, 2000, 4000, and 6000 ppm. The sensor responses increased as the concentration of ethanol increased. The response sequence of 1 was toluene > acetone > ethanol, indicating the selectivity of host molecules. The selectivity can be explained by the following three physicochemical properties of VOCs and host molecules: the molecular weight of VOCs, boiling temperature of VOCs and the affinity of the host molecule for VOC vapor. When the molecular weight or boiling point of VOC is higher, the sensor response is greater. The sensor responses were converted to the molar concentrations of

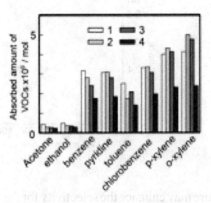

Figure 8. Sensor responses of QCM sensors coated with 1-4 various VOC vapors at the concentration of 4000 ppm. The inset shows a photograph of MPcs-coated QCM.

VOCs within thin films by using the Sauerbrey equation and the molecular weights of VOCs.

Figure 8 shows the molar concentrations of adsorbed VOC molecules in QCM sensors coated with 1-4 having different central metals. Despite the chemical structure of the ligand being the same in 1-4, the different central metals have different response patterns to various VOCs vapors. We found that CoPc 1 shows a strong affinity for acetone, ethanol, and pyridine vapors than other MPcs. These coordinative VOC vapors can form a weak coordination interaction with the central metal, and the formation of coordination bonds enhances the selectivity of sensors. Pentaphenylbenzene substituted MPcs react very selectively to aromatic VOCs, which can be attributed to their aromatic skeleton. Accordingly, MPcs incorporated into the polyphenyelene structures can adsorb VOC guest molecules very selectively into their cavities, whereby the selectivity of VOCs depends upon the central metal.

Polymer brushes of PDMAEMA tethered directly on the gold surface of QCMs were prepared through SA-ATRP from initiator-modified SAMs. The films coated with cationic PDMAEMA brushes can trap anionic molecules within the brush structure. The trapping of sterically protected CoPc within the cationic polymer brush

Figure 9. (a) Absorption spectrum of 5 ([5]=0 mg/ml) in water. (b) Sensor responses of QCM sensors modified only poly(DMAEA) brushes and PDMAEA brush with 5 to 4000 ppm acetone, ethanol, and toluene vapors at 20° C.

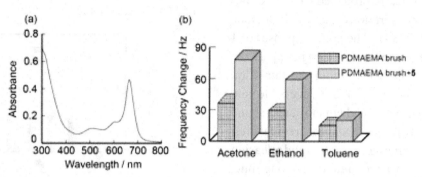

structure may enhance the selectivity for the VOC detection. We synthesized an anionic CoPc 5 by the sulfonation of 1 using a treatment with concentrated sulfonic acid. The ^{1}H NMR spectrum of 5 in D_2O showed that some aromatic proton peaks disappeared, indicating the pentaphenylbenzene substituents sulfonated in 1. The absorption spectra of 5 in water exhibited a sharp peak at 665 nm (Figure 9a). The position of the observed Q band agreed with the reported position of monomeric cobalt (II) tetrasulfonated phthalocyanine (CoTSPc) in water. Rollmann and Iwamoto reported a spectral change due to the association of CoTSPc above 1.0×10^{-5} M concentration in water (Rollmann & Iwamoto, 1968). The spectra of 5 having bulky pentaphenylbenzene units did not change until 2.0×10^{-4} M. The introduction of pentaphenylbenzene substituents prevents molecular aggregation between hydrophobic phthalocyanine moieties in water. The trapping of 5 within PDMAEMA brushes (5-PDMAEMA) was conducted by the immersing modified QCMs into a 1 mM aqueous solution of 5. Dimethylamino groups in a PDMAEMA brush protonate in the neutral pH region and the negatively charged 5 was trapped in a positively charged PDMAEMA brush structure through an electrostatic interaction. The apparent mass increase after the immersion into the aqueous solution of 5, washing with pure water, and drying under a steam of nitrogen is

561 ng/cm^2. Thus, 2.47×10^{-11} mol of 5 was trapped into the PDMAEMA brush structure. An increase in the peak for SO_3^- at 1300 cm^{-1} in the FT-IR-RAS showed the presence of sulfonated 5 at the surface of the gold substrate.

Figure 9b shows the results for sensor responses of QCMs modified with only PDMAEMA or 5-PDMAEMA due to the exposition to acetone, ethanol, and toluene vapors at the concentration of 4000 ppm. While the sensor response of 5-PDMAEMA for non-polar toluene vapor was almost the same as that of only PDMAEMA, the other responses for polar ethanol and acetone were enhanced by the trapping of 5 within the PDMAEMA brushes (He et al, 2007). On the other hand, CoTSPc trapped into the PDMAEMA brushes did not enhance any sensor responses of VOC vapors. The observed increase in sensor responses to ethanol and acetone in 5-PDMAEMA suggests that the trapped 5 works as a receptor within the PDMAEMA brushes. Furthermore, the times until 90% of the equilibrium sensor response were less than 60 sec for all VOCs vapors. The PDMAEMA brushes can accumulate polar VOC vapors such as acetone and ethanol. The trapped CoPc 5 reacts with these polar and coordinative VOC vapors within the brush structure though the formation of coordination bond with the central metal of 5. Thus, the incorporation of 5 within the PDMAEMA brushes allows polar VOC vapors to be selectively detected. The combination of polymer brushes with receptors enables fine-tuning of the sensor properties.

We demonstrated the VOC sensing by modifying weight-detectable QCMs with polymer brushes and sterically protected MPcs. PD-MAEMA brushes could be grown through SA-ATRP from the initiator-terminated surface of QCMs. The brushes were highly hydrophilic and functioned very well as anion exchangers. Metallophthalocaynines having bulky pentaphenlyenes were synthesized, and their sensing abilities for VOC vapors were investigated. The selectivity and sensitivity of MPcs strongly depended on the structure of peripheral substituents and the central metals. When the polymer brushes were loaded with sulfonated CoPcs, we showed that the sensor responses were enhanced for polar VOC vapors. The incorporation of sterically protected CoPc within the polymer brushes on QCMs works as molecular receptors to recognize the chemical properties of VOC vapors based on their size and polarity. The selectivity and sensitivity of the sensing layer on QCMs can be tuned by modifying receptors and polymer brushes.

CONCLUSION

We have demonstrated that chemical mass sensors coated with polymeric nanomaterials can detect VOCs through analyses of frequency change in their sensing layer. Nanostructures and viscoelestic properties of the films affected their sensitivity to VOC gases. The tunability is an important advantage of organic polymers that aids the preparation of a variety of sensing layers for the detection of target VOCs.

Electronic nose systems that include microcantilever sensor arrays can serve as the sensory part of an intelligent safety system by embedding them into various devices such as mobile phones and home electronics products. On-site and real-time analyses of odors surrounding us can assist our olfactories to manage health and safety hazards. Research in this area has the potential of eventually enabling the development of electronic nose systems that can continuous monitor odors from our body.

REFERENCES

Ayad, M. M., El-Hefnawey, G., & Torad, N. L. (2009). A sensor of alcohol vapours based on thin polyaniline base film and quartz crystal microbalance. *Journal of Hazardous Materials*, *168*, 85–88. doi:10.1016/j.jhazmat.2009.02.003

Ayad, M. M., & Torad, N. L. (2009). Alcohol vapours sensors based on thin polyaniline salt film and quartz microbalance. *Talanta*, *78*, 1280–1285. doi:10.1016/j.talanta.2009.01.053

Baimpos, T., Boutikos, P., Nikolakis, V., & Kouzoudis, D. (2010). A polymer-Metglas sensor used to detect volatile organic compounds. *Sensors and Actuators. A, Physical*, *158*, 249–253. doi:10.1016/j.sna.2010.01.020

Bao, Z., Bruening, M. L., & Baker, G. L. (2006). Rapid growth of polymer brushes from immobilized initiators. *Journal of the American Chemical Society*, *128*, 9056–9060. doi:10.1021/ja058743d

Bohrer, F. I., Colesniuc, C. N., Park, J., Ruidiaz, M. E., Schuller, I. K., Kummel, A. C., & Trogler, W. C. (2008). Comparative gas sensing in cobalt, nickel, copper, zinc, and metal-free phthalocyanine chemiresistors. *Journal of the American Chemical Society*, *131*, 478–485. doi:10.1021/ja803531r

Buck, L., & Axel, R. (1991). A novel multigene family may encode odorant receptors: A molecular basis for odor recognition. *Cell*, *65*, 175–187. doi:10.1016/0092-8674(91)90418-X

Ceyhan, T., Altmdal, A., Özkaya, A. R., Erbil, M. K., & Bekaroğlu, Ö. (2007). Synthesis, characterization, and electrochemical, electrical and gas sensing properties of a novel *tert*-butylcalix[4]arene bridged bis double-decker lutetium(III) phthalocyanine. *Polyhedron, 26*, 73–84. doi:10.1016/j.poly.2006.07.035

Du, X., Wang, Z., Huang, J., Tao, S., Tang, X., & Jiang, Y. (2009). A new polysiloxane coating on QCM sensor for DMMP vapor detection. *Journal of Materials Science, 44*, 5872–5876. doi:10.1007/s10853-009-3829-5

Fietzek, C., & Mack, H.-G. (2007). Influence of different transition metals in phthalocyanines on their interaction energies with volatile organic compounds: An experimental and computational study. *Journal of Molecular Modeling, 13*, 11–17. doi:10.1007/s00894-006-0118-y

Gamsjäger, H., Lorimer, J. W., Scharlin, P., & Shaw, D. G. (2008). Glossary of terms related to solubility. *Pure and Applied Chemistry, 80*, 233–276. doi:10.1351/pac200880020233

He, J., Wu, Y., Wu, J., Mao, X., Fu, L., & Qian, T. (2007). Study and application of a linear frequency-thickness relation for surface-initiated atom transfer radical polymerization in a quartz crystal microbalance. *Macromolecules, 40*, 3090–3096. doi:10.1021/ma062613n

Ichinohe, S., Tanaka, H., & Konno, Y. (2007). Gas sensing by AT-cut quartz crystal oscillator coated with mixed-lipid film. *Sensors and Actuators. B, Chemical, 123*, 306–312. doi:10.1016/j.snb.2006.08.024

Jin, X., Hung, Y., Mason, A., & Zeng, X. (2009). Multichannel monolithic quartz crystal microbalance gas sensor array. *Analytical Chemistry, 81*, 595–603. doi:10.1021/ac8018697

Jordan, R., Ulman, A., Kang, J. F., Rafailovich, M. H., & Sokolov, J. (1999). Surface-initiated anionic polymerization of styrene by means of self-assembled monolayers. *Journal of the American Chemical Society, 121*, 1016–1022. doi:10.1021/ja9813481

Ju, J. F., Syu, M.-J., Teng, H.-S., Chou, S.-K., & Chang, Y.-S. (2008). Preparation and identification of β-cyclodextrin polymer thin film for quartz crystal microbalance sensing of benzene, toluene, and *p*-xylene. *Sensors and Actuators. B, Chemical, 132*, 319–326. doi:10.1016/j.snb.2008.01.052

Katada, S., Hirokawa, T., Oka, Y., Suwa, M., & Touhara, K. (2005). Structural basis for a broad but selective ligand spectrum of a mouse olfactory receptor: Mapping the odorant-binding site. *The Journal of Neuroscience, 25*, 1806–1815. doi:10.1523/JNEUROSCI.4723-04.2005

Kikuchi, M., Tsuru, N., & Shiratori, S. (2006). Recognition of terpenes using molecular imprinted polymer coated quartz crystal microbalance in air phase. *Science and Technology of Advanced Materials, 7*, 156–161. doi:10.1016/j.stam.2005.12.004

Kimura, M., Sakaguchi, A., Ohta, K., Hanabusa, K., Shirai, H., & Kobayashi, N. (2003). Selective ligation to sterically isolated metallophthalocyanines. *Inorganic Chemistry, 42*, 2821–2823. doi:10.1021/ic026149o

Krasteva, N., Fogel, Y., Bauer, R. E., Müllen, K., Joseph, Y., & Matsuzawa, N. (2007). Vapor sorption and electrical response of Au-nanoparticle-dendrimer composites. *Advanced Functional Materials, 17*, 881–888. doi:10.1002/adfm.200600598

Matsuguchi, M., & Ueno, T. (2006). Molecular imprinting strategy for solvent molecules and its application for QCM-based VOC vapor sensing. *Sensors and Actuators. B, Chemical, 113*, 94–99. doi:10.1016/j.snb.2005.02.028

Matsuguchi, M., Ueno, T., Aoki, T., & Yoshida, M. (2008). Chemically modified copolymer coatings for mass-sensitive toluene vapor sensors. *Sensors and Actuators. B, Chemical, 131*, 652–659. doi:10.1016/j.snb.2007.12.052

Matyjaszewski, K., Patten, T. E., & Xia, J. (1997). Controlled/"living" radical polymerization: Kinetics of the homogeneous atom transfer radical polymerization of styrene. *Journal of the American Chemical Society, 119*, 674–680. doi:10.1021/ja963361g

Milner, S. T. (1991). Polymer brushes. *Science, 251*, 905–914. doi:10.1126/science.251.4996.905

Nomura, E., Hosoda, A., Takagaki, M., Mori, H., Miyake, Y., Shibakami, M., & Taniguchi, H. (2010). Self-organized honeycomb-patterned microporous polystyrene thin films fabricated by Calix[4]arene derivatives. *Langmuir, 26*, 10266–10270. doi:10.1021/la100434b

Rollmann, L. D., & Iwamoto, R. T. (1968). Electrochemistry, electron paramagnetic resonance, and visible spectra of cobalt, nickel, copper, and metal-free phthalocyanines in dimethyl sulfoxide. *Journal of the American Chemical Society, 90*, 1455–1463. doi:10.1021/ja01008a013

Sauerbrey, G. (1959). Verwendung von schwingquarzen zur wägung dünner schichten und zur mikrowägung. *Zeitschrift fur Physik, 155*, 206–208. doi:10.1007/BF01337937

Schlupp, M., Weil, T., Berresheim, A. J., Wiesler, U. M., Bargon, J., & Müllen, K. (2001). Polyphenylene dendrimers as sensitive and selective sensor layers. *Angewandt Chemie International Edition, 40*, 4011-4015.

Severin, E. J., & Lewis, N. S. (2000). Relationships among resonant frequency changes on a coated quartz crystal microbalance, thickness changes, and resistance responses of polymer-carbon black composite chemiresistors. *Analytical Chemistry, 72*, 2008–2015. doi:10.1021/ac991026f

Shah, R. R., Merreceyes, D., Husemann, M., Rees, I., Abbott, N. L., Hawker, C. J., & Hedrick, J. L. (2000). Using atom transfer radical polymerization to amplify monolayers of initiators patterned by microcontact printing into polymer brushes for pattern transfer. *Macromolecules, 33*, 597–605. doi:10.1021/ma991264c

Si, P., Mortensen, J., Komolov, A., Denborg, J., & Møller, P. J. (2007). Polymer coated quartz crystal microbalance sensors for detection of volatile organic compounds in gas mixture. *Analytica Chimica Acta, 597*, 223–230. doi:10.1016/j.aca.2007.06.050

Snow, A. W., & Barger, W. R. (1989). Phthalocyanine films in chemical sensors. In Lezonoff, C. C., & Lever, A. B. P. (Eds.), *Phthalocyanines: Properties and Applications* (pp. 341–392). New York, NY: John Wiley and Sons.

Stillman, M. J., & Nyokong, T. (1989). Absorption and magnetic circular dichroism spectral properties of phthalocyanines part 1: Complexes of the dianion Pc(-2). In Lezonoff, C. C., & Lever, A. B. P. (Eds.), *Phthalocyanines: Properties and Applications* (pp. 133–290). New York, NY: John Wiley and Sons.

Tsujii, T., Ohno, K., Yamamoto, S., Goto, A., & Fukuda, T. (2006). Structure and properties of high-density polymer brushes prepared by surface-initiated living radical polymerization. *Advances in Polymer Science, 197*, 1–46.

Vandenburg, H. J., Clifford, A. A., Bartle, K. D., Carlson, R. E., Carroll, J., & Newton, I. D. (1999). A simple solvent selection method for accelerated solvent extraction of additives from polymers. *Analyst (London), 124*, 1707–1710. doi:10.1039/a904631c

Vossmeyer, T., Guse, B., Besnard, I., Bauer, R. E., Müllen, K., & Yasuda, A. (2002). Gold nanoparticle/polyphenylene dendrimer compodite films: Preparation and vapor-sensing properties. *Advanced Materials, 14,* 238–242. doi:10.1002/1521-4095(20020205)14:3<238::AID-ADMA238>3.0.CO;2-#

Walsh, C. J., & Mandal, B. K. (2000). A novel method for the peripheral modification of phthalocyanines: Synthesis and third-order nonlinear optical absorption of β-teterakis(2,3,4,5,6-pentaphenylbenzene) phthalocyanine. *Chemistry of Materials, 12,* 287–289. doi:10.1021/cm9907662

Wang, X., Ding, B., Sun, M., Yu, J., & Sun, G. (2010). Nanofibrous polyethyleneimine membranes as sensitive coating for quartz crystal microbalance-based formaldehyde sensors. *Sensors and Actuators. B, Chemical, 144*, 11–17. doi:10.1016/j.snb.2009.08.023

Zeng, H., Jiang, Y., Xie, G., & Yu, J. (2007). Polymer coated QCM sensor with modified electrode for the detection of DDVP. *Sensors and Actuators. B, Chemical, 122*, 1–6. doi:10.1016/j.snb.2006.04.106

Chapter 9
Development of Highly Sensitive Compact Chemical Sensor System Employing a Microcantilever Array and a Thermal Preconcentrator

Takashi Mihara
Olympus Corporation, Japan

Sunao Murakami
National Institute of Advanced Industrial Science and Technology, Japan

Tsuyoshi Ikehara
National Institute of Advanced Industrial Science and Technology, Japan

Ryutaro Maeda
National Institute of Advanced Industrial Science and Technology, Japan

Mitsuo Konno
National Institute of Advanced Industrial Science and Technology, Japan

Tadashi Fukawa
Shinshu University, Japan

Mutsumi Kimura
Shinshu University, Japan

ABSTRACT

The authors developed a highly sensitive compact chemical sensor system employing a polymer-coated microcantilever sensor array and a thermal preconcentrator with an airpump. The theory, design, structure, fabrication, and experiment results are reported here. This sensor system had 1) sub-ppb detection limit enhanced by a carbon-fiber filled preconcentrator with an air pump and 2) analysis function by thermal desorption of the adsorbed VOCs in the preconcentrator and multiple cantilevers (acting as mass sensors) with different polymers. Eight silicon microcantilevers in one silicon chip fabricated by Micro Electro Mechanical Systems (MEMS) technology were driven by a PZT actuator plate mounted in the package, and four of them were wire bonded.

DOI: 10.4018/978-1-4666-2521-1.ch009

Copyright © 2013, IGI Global. Copying or distributing in print or electronic forms without written permission of IGI Global is prohibited.

Using the 4th vibration mode (resonant frequency: 764 kHz) of a polybutadiene (2.52 μm thick)-coated cantilever, the sensitivity was 514 Hz/ppm for toluene and 850 Hz/ppm for p-xylene with a 5 min preconcentration time. The estimated detection limit of the sensor system was 0.6ppb for toluene and 0.4ppb for p-xylene with a 5 min preconcentration time, which was good enough for application to environmental monitoring. Separate detection of the mixed toluene and p-xylene was achieved as different time peaks. The authors also estimate the concentration of mixed acetone and 1-propanol by the method of the fitting of two Gaussian curves model.

INTRODUCTION

The development of a chemical sensor system to detect Volatile Organic Compounds (VOCs) species has been receiving much attention for environmental monitoring and ultrafast medical diagnostics, which are strongly demanded to a safety and aged society. To date, the widely used sensor to detect VOCs has been Metal Oxide Semiconductor (MOS) sensor; however, it was difficult to analyze the VOC elements owing to the relatively poor selectivity of compounds. Quartz Crystal Microbalance (QCM) and Surface Acoustic Wave (SAW) devices with sensing films have also been widely investigated; however, it was also difficult to integrate with electronic devices as a smart sensor and mass-productive sensor chip. New highly sensitive micromass sensors using a microcantilever have been developed recently including first optical detection (Maute, et al., 1988; Battiston, et al., 2001; Kim, et al., 2001) an integration with electronic devices (Lang, et al., 1999; Lange, et al., 2002) and sensing analysis (Dufour & Fadel, 2003). However, previous investigations show a not so high sensitivity, such as 0.01 Hz/ppm for ethanol and 0.1 Hz/ppm for toluene.

We have been developing an integrated chemical analysis system with focus on the resonant micromass sensor made by MEMS technology for this purpose. We have reported the studies on the mass sensitivity of the silicon microcantilever with high resonant modes (Ikehara, et al., 2007; Lu, et al., 2006), sensing films using copolymer-based elastic polymers (Liu, et al., 2007), and the first

prototype sensor system including preconcentrator (Mihara, et al., 2008). We consider that silicon micromass sensors including cantilever are potential smart and flexible used sensors because they can be easily integrated with electronic devices to install intelligent functions in a chemical sensor system and many different kinds of sensing materials can be used on the MEMS resonators. To increase the sensitivity, we used a preconcentrator. To obtain the analysis function, we utilized the desorption characteristics of adsorbed VOCs from a preconcentrator and cantilever arrays with different sensing materials (Mihara, et al., 2009, 2008). We also reported the estimation of concentration factors and system efficiencies using basic formulas on the cantilever-type chemical sensor system (Mihara, et al., 2010, 2011). Several previous investigations to combine a preconcentrator with SAW devices and QCM-type sensors have been reported to date. By using the TENAX-TA (polymer beads based on 2.6 diphenyl-p-phenylene oxide by Teijin)-filled preconcentrator and 433 MHz SAW sensor, the detection limit for toluene was reported to be 0.08 ppm and that for ethanol was 33 ppm after 3-min concentration (Groves, et al., 1998; Bender, et al., 2003). Another report showed the separation of the components with the thermal preconcentrator combined with QCM devices (Nakamoto, et al., 2005).

In this study, we report the theory, design, fabrication and evaluation results of a newly developed sub-ppb-detectable sensor system possessing a preconcentration and analysis functions at the same time. This book chapter is an expanded version of a previous report submitted to Sensor and Materials (Mihara, et al., 2011), including a detailed description of theoretical consideration, system architecture, desorption characteristics from preconcentration, evaluation details and detailed experimental results.

THEORY, DESIGN, MATERIALS, AND METHODS

Design of Sensor System

The potential applications of our chemical sensor system are in environmental monitoring and medicine. The environmental monitoring requires toxic VOC (including toluene and xylene) sensing at extremely low concentration of sub-ppb order for a relatively large air volume (more than 10 liters). Medical application requires the detection of specific gases, for example, acetone in a few liters of sample to diagnose diabetes (Henderson, et al., 1952). We also require the compact size and low-cost operation in addition to on-site measurement in the sensing field. These requirements allow the sensor system to implement an analysis function and a preconcentrator. Thus, our sensor system comprised an air pump, a preconcentrator and a cantilever array as a sensing device, as shown in Figure 1(a). The sample gas was introduced into the preconcentrator by pumping at room temperature. Then, the temperature of the preconcentrator was gradually increased by the heater, and the desorbed gases at a specific temperature were delivered into a sensor chamber with pure nitrogen carrier gas. This desorbed gas was detected by a cantilever array coated with different polymers under the control of temperature. The shifts of frequency are appeared at different time as shown in Figure 1(a). The response curves of the sensors have distinguished peaks corresponding to the specific VOC. We can also apply a principal component analysis using peak values and peak times from different sensors.

We introduced the detailed description of important formulas including the frequency shift of the cantilever sensor, the condition of oscillation for multiple cantilevers, preconcentration and analysis of VOC, the definition of sensitivity, efficiencies, and concentration factor of our system, and the detection limit. We added a detailed description formulas of the VOC desorption from adsorption materials and precise estimation method from mixed VOC in addition to the previous report (Mihara, et al., 2010, 2011). On the basis of these formulas, the sensor system was designed and its performance was evaluated. This sensor system is not limited to the medical and environmental application, but broadly used to the other application including factories and inspections subject to the selecting the sensing materials.

Sensitivity of Cantilever Mass Sensor

We chose a microcantilever as a mass-sensing resonator because its characteristics are well known, the fabrication is well established, and the combination with electronic devices is easy. The resonant frequency of the nth flexural mode of resonant frequency $f_{n,0}$ of a cantilever with length L_{Si} and thickness t_{Si} is shown as:

$$f_{n,0} = k_n \frac{t_{Si}}{L_{Si}^2} \sqrt{\frac{E_{Si}}{\rho_{Si}}},\tag{1}$$

where E_{Si} is Young's modulus, ρ_{Si} density of silicon and k_n, coefficient dependent on mode n (Blevins, 1979). If the density of cantilever is change from ρ_{Si} to $\rho_{Si+\Delta}\rho_{Si}$, the shift of resonant frequency is derived by differential of Equation (1) as:

$$\Delta f_{n,0} = -\frac{1}{2} f_{n,0} \frac{\Delta \rho_{Si}}{\rho_{Si}}.\tag{2}$$

Figure 1. (a) Sensing concept and (b) principle of our sensor system

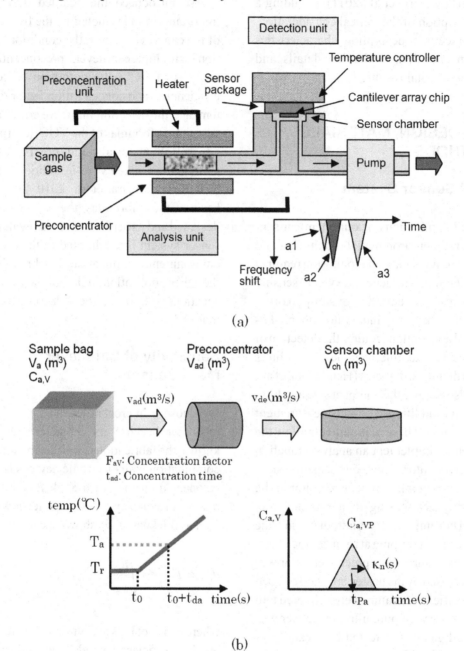

(a)

(b)

Then the shift of frequency is proportional to the change of cantilever's mass.

After the deposition of polymers that act as VOC sensing materials, the resonant frequency $f_{n,P}$ of the nth mode vibration is reduced by the change in the cantilever's mass as:

$$f_{n,P} = f_{n,0} - \frac{1}{2} f_{n,0} \frac{\sigma_{Poly}}{\sigma_{Si} + \sigma_{Pad}}, \qquad (3)$$

where σ_{Poly} is the surface densities of the polymer, σ_{Si} silicon and σ_{Pad} adhesive layer between them in kg/m^2.

The frequency shift $\Delta f_{n,a}$ of the polymer-coated cantilever after the exposure to diluted VOC of component "a" is described as:

$$\Delta f_{n,a} = -\frac{1}{2} f_{n,P} \frac{\Delta m_c}{m_c}, \qquad (4)$$

where m_c is the mass of the cantilever and Δm_c is the change of m_c by the VOC exposure (Blevins, 1979; Chen, et al., 1995). The Δm_c is estimated using a product of K_a, the concentration of gas phase and volume of polymer as:

$$\Delta m_c = \frac{K_a C_a M_a A_c t_{Poly}}{0.0224}, \qquad (5)$$

where K_a is the distribution factor (or K-factor) of VOC for related polymer, which is defined as the ratio of the volume concentrations of VOC in the polymer to that in the surround gas in equilibrium state. C_a and M_a are the concentration of VOC in mole ratio, mole weight of diluted VOC, respectively. A_c and t_{Poly} are the area of cantilever and thickness of polymer, respectively. The value 0.0224 (m^3) is a mole volume in ideal state of gas state and used to transform the mole ratio to the volume one. A discussion using K-factor is presented in the reference (Dufour & Fadel, 2003). Then $\Delta f_{n,a}$ is expressed using the surface densities of cantilever as:

$$\Delta f_{n,a} = -\frac{1}{2} f_{n,P} \frac{K_a C_a M_a t_{Poly}}{0.0224(\sigma_{Si} + \sigma_{Pad} + \sigma_{Poly})}. \qquad (6)$$

Hence, the sensitivity of the cantilever sensor s_a (Hz/ppm) defined as the ratio of the change in frequency to the concentration in ppm is shown as:

$$s_a = -\frac{1}{2} f_{n,P} \frac{K_a M_a t_{Poly}}{0.0224 \cdot 10^6 (\sigma_{Si} + \sigma_{Pad} + \sigma_{Poly})}. \qquad (7)$$

The sensitivity is proportional to the resonant frequency, K_a, t_{Poly} and the inverse of the surface density of the cantilever.

Circuit Design and Oscillation Condition of Cantilever Array

The design of an oscillation circuit of cantilever sensors is described. Figure 2(a) shows the schematic of the two-cantilever oscillation system. This circuit contains two cantilevers with stress gauges, two front-end amplifiers with gain g_i (i = 1, 2), a Multiplexer (MPX), a Phase Shifter (PS), a Bandpass Filter (BPF), and a PZT plate as an actuator. At first, we explain the design for one cantilever sensor. The driving signal $p_i(t)$ fed to PZT actuation plate is expressed using the amplitude P_{0i}, the driving frequency f_{PZT} and the phase χ_i of driving signal as:

$$p_i(t) = P_{0i} \sin(2\pi f_{PZT} t + \chi_i). \qquad (8)$$

When MPX selects ith cantilever, the signal $u_i(t)$ of the piezoresistive gauge with specific vibration mode of ith cantilever is expressed with the amplitude U_{0i}, the resonant frequency f_i and the phase shift φ_i as:

$$u_i(t) = U_{0i} \sin\{2\pi[f_i(1 + \beta_i \Delta T_c)]t + \varphi_i + \delta\varphi_i\}. \qquad (9)$$

Equation (9) also includes temperature coefficient β_i, the change in cantilever temperature ΔT_c and phase variation $\delta\varphi_i$. The temperature dependence of frequency produced by β_i is a major origin of the frequency drift and should be compensated by the measurement of chip temperature (Ikehara, et al., 2011). The $\delta\varphi_i$ produces the short-range variation of frequency that determines the detection limit of chemical sensors.

We designed the oscillation circuit of cantilever subject to the following three items.

Figure 2. Sensor and component: (a) schematic of two cantilevers oscillation system, and (b) schematic of an integrated on-chip temperature measurement

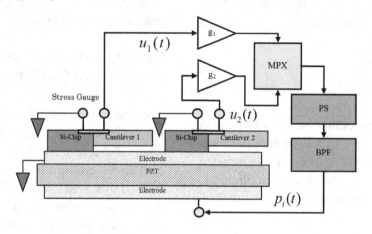

(a)

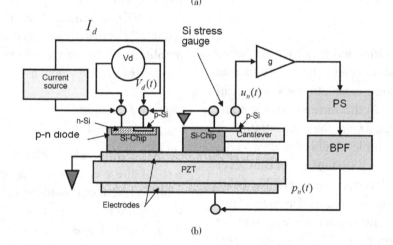

(b)

The f_{PZT} is adjusted by the central frequency of BPF to match the resonant frequency of cantilever as:

$$f_{PZT} = f_i(1 + \beta_i \Delta T_c). \qquad (10)$$

The total gain G_i of the circuit including g_i of front-end amplifier is set to be larger than the ratio of P_{0i} to U_{0i} as:

$$\frac{P_{0i}}{U_{0i}} \le G_i. \qquad (11)$$

The g_i is adjusted to the particular value for ith cantilever and G_i is automatically adjusted by AGC to the adequate value of $G_i = P_{0i}/U_{0i}$ when the stable oscillation occurs.

The phase π_i of PS is adjusted to that the sum of phases φ_i, χ_i, π_i and a phase θ_i of other circuits including the amplifier, BPF and MPX should be multiple of 2π as:

$$\varphi_i + \chi_i + \pi_i + \theta_i = 2\pi I, \qquad (12)$$

where I is an integer. In actual experiment, the central frequency of BPF is adjusted to obtain the maximum values of P_{0i}, after that π_i of PS is adjusted to obtain the maximum values of U_{0i}. Then the stable resonant vibration of the cantilever occurs. Note that the G_i is varied with so many mechanical parameters including efficiency/coupling factor of PZT, piezoresistive gauge and adhesive glue.

Then, we explain the case of the cantilever array. We applied electrical multiplexing to achieve the driving of multiple cantilevers, because the oscillation circuit became complicated for obtaining stable oscillation. After the switching of the sensor signal from i to $i+1$ using MPX, $u_i(t)$ is altered to $u_{i+1}(t)$ by the specific U_{0i+1}, f_{i+1}, and φ_{i+1} for each cantilever, as shown in Equation (9). The design and oscillation conditions should also be satisfied on $(i+1)$th cantilever as shown in Equations (10) to (12). We found that the U_{0i}, f_i and φ_i for each cantilever with polymer are not the same and these values should be adjusted after multiplexing. Then, we utilized a presetting circuit with memories as described in sect. *"Oscillation circuit"* in this chapter

Suppression of the Drift by Temperature Compensation

As described in the previous section, the time dependence of the actual resonant frequency $f_{id}(t)$ detected by the sensor has a drift component, which is derived from Equation (9) and expressed as:

$$f_{id}(t) = f_i\{1 + \beta_i \Delta T_c(t)\} + \Gamma_i(t), \quad (13)$$

where $\Gamma_i(t)$ is a short-time variation of the resonant frequency. $\Gamma_i(t)$ can be derived from the phase variation $\delta\varphi_i$. To suppress the drift in frequency, precise measurement of the cantilever temperature is essential (Ikehara, et al., 2011). Figure 2(b) also shows the p-n diode on a chip as the temperature sensor, in addition to one cantilever and the oscillation circuit. This p-n diode is fabricated by the same process as that for fabricating the p-type

diffusion layer (which serves as the cathode) of the Si piezoresistive gauge. To isolate the voltage at the n-type diffusion layer (as the anode) from the n-isolation layer of the Si-piezoresistive gauge, the n-type diffusion layer is thoroughly etched. The change in the cantilever temperature, ΔT_c, is measured using the change in the forward voltage ΔV_d (mV) of the p-n diode when the forward current is constant; ΔT_c can be expressed as:

$$\Delta T_c(t) = \beta_d \Delta V_d(t) \quad (14)$$

where β_d is the temperature coefficient of the diode, expressed in °C/mV. Hence, the p-n diode is driven by a current source with a constant current I_d. In addition, a short time deviation is very important to improve the detection limit, as described in sect. "Detection Limit of Sensor System with Preconcentration" in this chapter. However, we could not develop formulas based on actual device parameters such as the quality factor of the cantilever.

Preconcentration

We applied a preconcentrator to improve the detection limit of the system at the ppb level. Figure 1(b) shows the schematic diagram of the flow of gas sample from sample bag to sensor. The VOC gas with component "a" and mass m_a(kg) in the gas state is diluted in the volume V_a(m³) with concentration $C_{a,V}$ as shown in Figure 1(b). When the gas of V_a is introduced to the preconcentrator of V_{ad}(m³) with the flow of a volume velocity of v_{ad}(m³/s) and adsorption time t_{ad}(s), the part of component "a" will be adsorbed in the adsorption material. The mass of component "a" in the preconcentrator $m_{a,ad}$(kg) is reduced by the preconcentrator's efficiency η_a as:

$$m_{a,ad} = \eta_a m_a = \eta_a \frac{M_a V_a C_{a,V}}{0.0224} = \eta_a \frac{M_a v_{ad} t_{ad} C_{a,V}}{0.0224},$$

$$(15)$$

Then, $(1-\eta_a)$ stands for the part that escapes from preconcentrator when sample gas is adsorbed.

Peak Time and Desorption Temperature of Sensor System with Preconcentrator

The adsorbed VOC in the preconcentrator is desorbed by the heating of preconcentration and streamed to the sensor chamber by the high purity nitrogen carrier gas with a volume velocity of v_{de}(m³/s) as shown in Figure 1(b). The peak time t_{Pa}(s) of component "a" measured with the sensor is presented as:

$$t_{Pa} = t_0 + \frac{T_a - T_r}{r_t} + \frac{S_t L_t}{v_{de}} + \frac{V_{ch}}{v_{de}}, \qquad (16)$$

where t_0(s) is start time of heating, as shown in Figure 1(b). The second term stands for time to reach desorption t_{da}(s), in which T_r is room temperature, T_a(s) desorption temperature of VOC "a" and r_t(m²/s), heating rate of preconcentrator. The third term is the delivery time from the preconcentrator to the sensor chamber by the carrier gas, in which S_t(m²) is the cross-sectional area of the gas tube, L_t(m) the length of the tube, and v_{de}(m³/s) the volume velocity of the carrier gas. The fourth term is filling time of VOC in the sensor chamber with volume V_{ch}(m³). If the sample gas is a mixture of several VOCs, multiple peaks are observed because of the difference in T_a among VOCs.

Response Curve for Desorption of Preconcentrator

The desorption response of the adsorbed gas is explained on the basis of the theory of Temperature

Programmed Desorption (TPD) (Redhead, 1962). The time t dependence of desorption molecules, $N_d(t)$ (molecules/s), is expressed using the adsorbed amount of gases on a surface Ω_z (molecules/cm²), reaction order of desorption z, absorption rate γ_z (molecules/s), desorption energy E_a (eV), Boltzmann constant k_B, and temperature T (°C) of the adsorbed surface as:

$$N_d(t) = -\frac{d\Omega_z}{dt} = \gamma_z \Omega_z{}^z \exp\{\frac{E_a}{k_B(T + 273.15)}\}.$$

$$(17)$$

The Ω_z in Equation (17) is obtained by integration from T_1 to T_2 as:

$$-\int_{\Omega_{Z1}}^{\Omega_{Z2}} d\Omega_Z \frac{1}{\Omega_Z} = \ln(\frac{\Omega_{Z1}}{\Omega_{Z2}})$$
$$= \frac{\gamma_z}{r_t} \int_{T_1}^{T_2} dT \exp\{\frac{E_a}{k_B(T + 273.15)}\} \qquad (18)$$

when the desorption is of the first order, i.e., $z=1$. We assume that the temperature of the preconcentrator is $T = T_r + r_t t$, using the same parameters as Equation (16). Therefore, the following function $F(T_r, T_2)$ defined using the relation $T_1 = T_r$ and T_2 as:

$$F(T_r, T_2) = \frac{\gamma_z}{r_t} \int_{T_r}^{T_2} dT \exp\{\frac{E_a}{k_B(T + 273.15)}\}$$
$$= \frac{\gamma_z}{r_t} \sum_{T_r}^{T_2} \Delta T \exp\{\frac{E_a}{k_B(T + 273.15)}\} \qquad (19)$$

is calculated by numerical integration. Subsequently, Ω_z is derived as a function of T_2 as:

$$\Omega_Z(T_2) = \exp\{-F(T_r, T_2)\}. \qquad (20)$$

Finally, $N_d(t)$ is expressed using the differential of time for a short period Δt as:

$$N_d(t) = -\frac{d\Omega_Z(T_r + r_t t)}{dt}$$

$$= -\frac{\Omega_Z\{T_r + r_t t\} - \Omega_Z\{T_r + r_t(t - \Delta t)\}}{\Delta t}.$$

$$(21)$$

The actual response time is increased by t_0, and the transfer time of carrier gas is expressed as:

$$N_d(t') = N_d\{t - (t_0 + \frac{S_t L_t}{v_{de}} + \frac{V_{ch}}{v_{de}})\}, \quad (22)$$

where t' is the actual time required to measure the response, in the same manner as shown in Equation (16).

Response Curve by Multiple Gaussian Functions Approximation

Although the formula in previous section provides a response curve from physical process, Ω_z in Equation (17) is solved by the numerical integration with adsorption temperature, and $N_d(t)$ is solved by the numerical differential, which is too complicated to fit an actual sensing response curve to determined the concentration of each component in mixed VOC. Therefore, we use the linear combination of several Gaussian functions as:

$$\Delta f_{mix}(t) = \Delta f_{0mix} + \sum_{j=1}^{N} \Delta f_{Pa,j} Exp\{-\frac{(t - t_{Pa,j})^2}{\kappa_{a,j}^2}\}$$

$$(23)$$

to explain the actual sensor response. Hence, $\Delta f_{mix}(t)$ is response of frequency shift by mixed VOCs, Δf_{0mix} baseline of $\Delta f_{mix}(t)$, $\Delta f_{Pa,j}$ peak value of frequency shift for jth component, $t_{Pa,j}$ peak time for jth (or "a") component and $\kappa_{a,j}$, standard deviation of the peak width for jth (or "a") component. Note that t_{Pa} in Equation (16) is equal to $t_{Pa,j}$ when $j = 1$. When the fitting to the actual sensor response to Equation (23) has carried out, system sensitivity (defined in next section) in this

chapter), $t_{Pa,j}$ and $\kappa_{a,j}$ should be determined by the actual experimental data as the calibration step. We use second-order polynomials for the concentration $C_{a,V}$ dependence of $\Delta f_{Pa,j}$, $t_{Pa,j}$ and $\kappa_{a,j}$ are as:

$$\Delta f_{Pa,j}(C_{a,V}) = \Delta f_{Pa0,j} + \Delta f_{Pa1,j} C_{a,V} + \Delta f_{Pa2,j} C_{a,V}^2,$$

$$(24)$$

$$t_{Pa,j}(C_{a,V}) = t_{Pa0,j} + t_{Pa1,j} C_{a,V} + t_{Pa2,j} C_{a,V}^2,$$

$$(25)$$

and

$$\kappa_{a,j}(C_{a,V}) = \kappa_{a0,j} + \kappa_{a1,j} C_{a,V} + \kappa_{a2,j} C_{a,V}^2,$$

$$(26)$$

respectively. These coefficients of polynomial $\Delta f_{Pa0,j}$, $\Delta f_{Pa1,j}$ and $\Delta f_{Pa2,j}$ for $\Delta f_{Pa,j}$, $t_{Pa0,j}$, $t_{Pa1,j}$, and $t_{Pa2,j}$ for $t_{Pa,j}$, and $\kappa_{a0,j}$, $\kappa_{a1,j}$, and $\kappa_{a2,j}$ for $\kappa_{a,j}$ are determined by the $C_{a,V}$ dependence of $\Delta f_{Pa,j}$, $t_{Pa,j}$ and $\kappa_{a,j}$, which are carried out prior to the fitting of actual sensor measurements of mixed VOC.

Concentration Factor and Efficiency of Sensor System

The final sensing mass $m_{a,de}$(kg) of component "a" detected by the sensor is calculated with the desorption response as:

$$m_{a,de} = \frac{M_a}{0.0224} v_{de} \sum_{\Delta t_{de}} \Delta t_{de} C_{a,de}(t)$$

$$= \frac{M_a}{0.0224} v_{de} \sum_{\Delta t_{de}} \Delta t_{de} s_a \Delta f_{aV}(t)$$

$$(27)$$

where Δt_{de} is time interval of sensing, $C_{a,de}(t)$ is the observed concentration of VOC by the cantilever sensor at time t, and Δf_{aV} is a shift of frequency of the cantilever with preconcentrator. Note that Δf_{mix} in Equation (23) is a specific case of Δf_{aV} of a mixed VOC-sample. This $m_{a,de}$ is a part of the mass $m_{a,ad}$ of absorbed VOC in the preconcentrator; then, $m_{a,de}$ is presented by another efficiency ξ_a as:

$$m_{a,de} = \xi_a m_{a,ad} = \xi_a \eta_a m_a = \xi_a \eta_a \frac{M_a V_a C_{a,V}}{0.0224} . \tag{28}$$

We can evaluate the total efficiency $\xi_a \eta_a$ of the system by taking the ratio of $m_{a,de}$ to m_a. The concentration factor F_{aV} of a sensor system is defined using the ratio of $C_{a,deP}$ (peak value of $C_{a,de}(t)$ in Figure 1[b]) to $C_{a,V}$, and the peak value Δf_{aVP} of the time response $\Delta f_{aV}(t)$ as:

$$F_{aV} = \frac{C_{a,deP}}{C_{a,V}} = \frac{\Delta f_{aVP} s_a}{C_{a,V}}, \tag{29}$$

which is proportional to V_a. In practical use, the sample volume is determined from the volume of sample bag or the time of aspiration t_{ad}(s) into the preconcentrator by an air pump. Then, we defined the system sensitivity S_{a10L}(Hz/ppm when $V_a = 10$ L) as:

$$S_{a10L} = \frac{\Delta f_{a10LP}}{C_{a,10L}} = F_{a10L} s_a \tag{30}$$

where Δf_{a10LP} and $C_{a,10L}$ are the peak values of measured frequency shift and the concentration when $V_a = 10$L respectively, and F_{a10L} is the measured concentration factor when $V_a = 10$L. The coefficients of Equation(24) is also explained by the mth concentration factors of polynomial and s_a as:

$$\Delta f_{Pam,j} = F_{am,j} s_a . \tag{31}$$

Detection Limit of Sensor System with Preconcentration

Finally, the detection limit DL_{a10L} (ppb when $V_a = 10$ L) is derived from the standard deviation λ of $\Delta f_{n,a}$ (or $\Gamma_i(t)$ in Equation [13]) in short time and S_{a10L} as:

$$DL_{a10L} = \frac{3\lambda}{10^{-3} S_{a10L}} = \frac{3\lambda}{10^{-3} F_{a10L} s_a}, \tag{32}$$

where 10^{-3} is used to transform ppm to ppb. To obtain a low detection limit, the efforts to reduce λ, including to increase the high quality factor of the cantilever and to reduce an electric noise are essential, as well as the high sensitivity.

We expressed the important formulas of our sensor system described above for purposes of designing the sensor system. We used Equations (1) to (7) to analyze and design a cantilever sensor, Equations (8) to (14) to design an oscillation circuits and temperature compensation, and Equations (15) to (32) to design the operation parameters and analyze the performance.

SYSTEM COMPONENTS

Cantilever Sensors and Packaging

Silicon cantilevers were fabricated using microfabrication techniques from an SOI wafer (Ikehara, et al., 2007). The length, width and thickness of the cantilever were 200 to 500, 50 to 100, and 5 µm, respectively, as shown in Figure 3(a) in which photograph of 300 µm length and 100 µm width is shown. A set of bridged piezoresistive stress gauges was formed at the root of the cantilever by the p-type layer in the n-type active layer employing boron implantation and thermal diffusion. The substrate under the cantilever was removed by deep RIE from the backside to eliminate the squeezed air damping effect. A gold pattern was formed on the upper surface of the cantilever to obtain an adequate adhesion characteristic with polymers as shown in Figure 3(b).

Eight cantilevers in one silicon chip were packaged in a ceramic flat package and driven by a PZT actuator plate mounted in the package. The silicon chip was adhered to the PZT plate with epoxy, and the PZT plate was mounted on the flat

Figure 3. Cantilever sensor and the assembly: (a) before coating of polymer, (b) after PBD coating, (c) sensor chamber and flat package of cantilever chip with PZT plate, and (d) photograph of packaged sensor

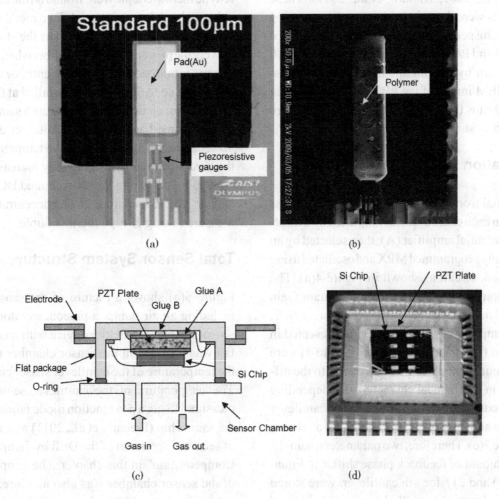

(a) (b)

(c) (d)

package with epoxy (glue A) at four corners and Ag paste (glue B) at the center to get the electric contact, as shown in Figure 3(c). Four of the eight cantilevers were wire bonded and used as sensors. Figure 3(c) also shows the attached sensor chamber and a temperature controller (not in the figure) to the package. This sensor package was mounted in a sensor chamber with miniature o-ring made of silicon lubber for sealing. The volume of sensor chamber (V_{ch}) was 0.03 cc. Figure 3(d) shows the magnified photograph of the sensor package with PZT actuator plate.

Polymer (Sensing Material)

In this sensor system, we require the short response time of the adsorption and desorption against VOCs because a concentrated pulse-like VOCs from heated preconcentrator is delivered to sensors. Two types of polymer as VOC sensing films among the elastomer-type materials were used in this requirement. One was poly-butadiene (PBD): sensitive to aromatic VOC gases including toluene and xylene. The other was poly(acrylonitrile-co-butadiene)(PAB): sensitive to alcohol and acetone. We found that the PBD and PAB films showed fast response to adsorption and desorption while these films were exposed to the various VOCs (Liu, et al., 2007; Kimura, et al., 2011). These thin films were deposited on the cantilever using the microdispensing technique. The thicknesses of the PBD and PAB films were controlled from 300 to 2500 nm by varying the duration of dispensing. A SEM image of the PBD-coated cantilever demonstrates that flat and smooth surfaces were obtained as shown in Figure 3(b).

Oscillation Circuit

The signal from the bridged piezoresistive stress gauge on each cantilever was amplified by a front-end differential amplifier (A), then selected by an electrically programmed MPX and oscillated using a feedback circuit as shown in Figure 4(a). The oscillation circuit consisted of an Automatic Gain Controller (AGC), a PS and a second-order BPF. The f_i, amplitude U_{0i} and phase φ_i as presented in Equation (9) for each cantilever ($i = 1$ to 4) were varied much among cantilevers owing to the difference in mechanical characteristics depending on the coated materials, the site of the cantilever in a chip and method of PZT mounting as shown in Figure 3(c). Therefore, two parameters, namely, 1) the amount of feedback phase shift π_i in Equation (12) and 2) f_i for i-th cantilever, were stored in memories on the oscillation circuit board and used when multiplexing to oscillate under the best condition. Hence, the amplitude U_{0i} was automatically adjusted with AGC. Figure 4(a) shows the additional AD and DA converters and Random Access Memories (RAMs) in conjunction with PS and BPF to preset and stores them. Thanks to these preset circuits, we could oscillate any cantilever of various sizes, modes and polymer materials.

Preconcentrator

A preconcentrator was made of a 6.35 mm-diameter stainless steel tube, in which 0.03 g of carbon fiber (Kuraray Chemical: maximum surface area is about 2500 m²/g) was filled as shown in Figure 4(b, c). A 1 mm-diameter sheathed heater and a K-type thermocouple were wound on the tube with a thermal insulation material. Two metal meshes at both sides of carbon fiber act as the stopper to prevent the movement of carbon fiber when the carrier gas introduces. This preconcentrator capable of heating up to 600 mm was installed at the inlet of the sensor chamber to concentrate a sample gas in the sample bag or environmental air directly. To separate the mixed VOCs, the temperature of the preconcentrator was gradually increased at r_t = 1.0 to 1.3 m/s using the programmed DC power supply. The temperature of preconcentrator was measured using K-type thermocouple.

Total Sensor System Structure

Figure 5(a) shows a picture of the sensor unit including an air pump, a preconcentrator, and a sensor chamber. A Peltier device with an electric fan was installed in the sensor chamber to keep the temperature of the cantilever sensor constant. The temperature of the cantilever sensor was measured using a p-n junction diode fabricated in the same chip (Ikehara, et al., 2011) as a manner of sect. "Suppression of the Drift by Temperature Compensation" in this chapter. The temperature of the sensor chamber was also measured using a thermistor attached to the sensor chamber. The size of the total system was 280 x 200 x 80 mm³.

Figure 5(b) also shows an electronic unit incorporating three electrical circuit boards for an oscillation, a monitor, and a power electronic circuit. Figure 5(c) shows the block diagram of the electrical circuits. The power unit includes five electrical power supplies, the voltages of which are controlled by control commands provided using an R8c micro computer (Renesas Electronics Corporation) combined with a power controller. The monitor unit includes the measurement circuits of the p-n diode, mass flow meter (MFM), and thermocouples (TC). The constant current is fed to the p-n diode using the current source, and the terminal voltage is monitored. In

Figure 4. Oscillation circuit and preconcentrator: (a) block diagram of oscillation circuit with phase and resonant frequency presetting at MPX switching, (b) cross sectional schematic, and (c) picture of covered preconcentrator

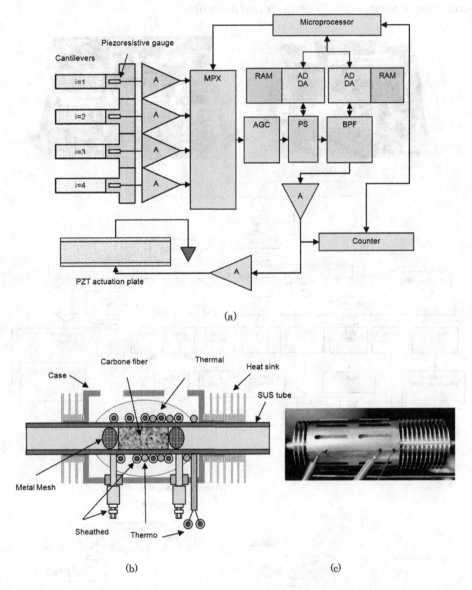

(a)

(b)   (c)

an oscillation unit, the frequency counter circuits are embedded in a Field Programmable Gate Array (FPGA). All control commands and measured data were transferred to a Personal Computer (PC) via Universal Serial Bus (USB) and Recommended Standard 232 (RS232c) interface. Visual Basic was used to program the measurement and analysis software, which incorporated several

design formulas in this chapter to evaluate the system parameters.

Figure 5(d) shows the sample-gas-flow diagram of our sensor system shown in Figure 5(a), in which three-port manual valves (V), MFM and needle valve are shown. Figure 5(e) shows two measurement steps of actual application: (1) preconcentration step: a pump pulls the sample

Figure 5. Total system and the configuration: (a) picture of the sensor system including air pump, pre-concentrator, and sensor chamber, (b) electrical cases with three circuit boards, (c) block diagram for control and measurement, (d) configuration of our sensor system, and (e) VOC flow at actual operation, 1) preconcentration of sample gas, 2) analysis and detection

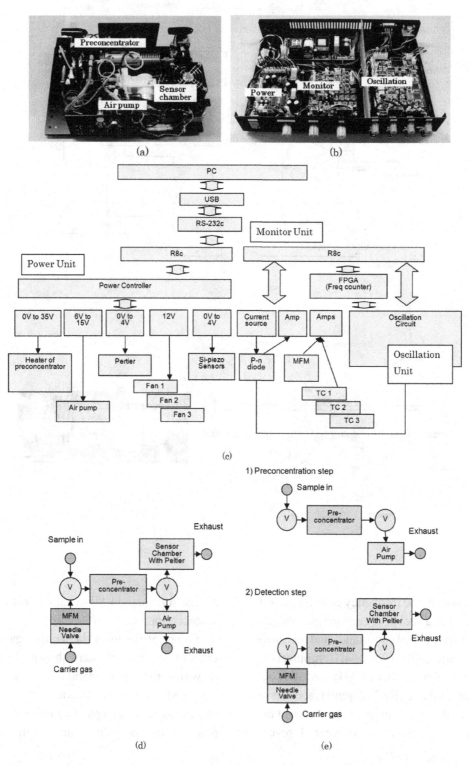

gas though a preconcentrator at room temperature, and (2) detection step: pure nitrogen carrier gas pushes the desorbed VOCs from the heating preconcentrator into the sensor chamber, where a needle valve is maintaining volume velocity v_{de} of carrier gas constant and a MFM monitors them.

RESULTS

Performance of Polymer-Coated Cantilever without Preconcentrator

Frequency Characteristics of Polymer Coated Cantilever

After the fabrication of flat package as shown in Figure 3(d), we evaluated the frequency characteristics of PBD coated cantilever. The length, width, and thickness of the cantilever were 500, 100, and 5 µm, respectively. Figure 6(a) shows the evaluation setup for this purpose. An output terminal of a network analyzer (Anritsu MS4630B) connected to the lower electrode of PZT plate. A magnified differential signal from the set of bridged piezoresistive gauges consists of reference and sensor gauges connected to input analysis terminal (TA) of MS4630B. Figure 6(b) shows the frequency dependence of the sensor signal in dBm unit when the frequency varied 10 to 1500 kHz. Four peaks corresponded to the second to fifth flexural vibration mode were observed. The operation of higher mode brings the higher sensitivity derived from Equation (7), however λ_i of higher mode becomes large one too. Then we used fourth flexural vibration mode in this chapter for the cantilever with L_{si} = 500 µm.

Estimations of Thickness of Polymers

At first, we estimated the thicknesses of polymers as a sensing material. The polymers were PAB and PBD. We evaluated the 4th mode of resonant frequency $f_{4,0}$ (before coating) and $f_{4,P}$ (after coat-

ing) to determine the thickness using Equations (1) to (3). The thickness t_{Si} was determined using $f_{4,0}$ in Equation (1), and t_{Poly} was calculated using Equation (3) from the difference between $f_{4,P}$ and $f_{4,0}$ as shown in Table 1. Thus, the thicknesses of PBD and PAB were evaluated to be 2520 and 640 nm, respectively. The thicknesses of polymers in this chapter were evaluated using the same method.

Temperature Measurement and Drift Compensation

To reduce the drift component as shown in Equation (10), we evaluated the temperature of the cantilever chip using the p-n diode in the setup shown in Figure 2(b). The junction area of the p-n diode was 6000 µm², and I_d = 10 µA. The precision of the temperature measurement was less than 0.01 °C (in other words, a typical standard deviation was less than 0.003 °C). Prior to the drift measurement, we evaluated the temperature coefficient β_d = 2.18 mV/degree and V_d = 573 mV using Equation (14) with temperature being maintained at 25 °C using a thermostatic oven. Figure 6(c) shows Δf_{id} in Equation (13) and the temperature measured by the p-n diode when a Peltier cooler attached to the back of the sensor package was operated. Note that f_{id} is the same as the change of $\Delta f_{4,a}$ in Equation (4); the width and length of the cantilever were 50 and 500 µm, respectively; and the polymer was not coated. Assuming a correlation between f_{id} and ΔT_C, β_i was estimated to be -34.1 ppm using Equation (13). Then we simply substituted Δf_{id} from Equation (13) and obtained a small drift with a variation within 1 Hz, as shown in Figure 6(d). The theory and detailed description of the temperature dependence are provided in Ikehara et al. (2011).

Frequency Shifts of Cantilever Sensors by VOC Exposure

We evaluated the frequency shift of the fourth mode, $\Delta f_{4,a}$, in the case where a cantilever sensor

Figure 6. Resonant oscillation and temperarature compensation: (a) measurement circuit of frequency characteristics of cantilever with actuator, (b) frequency dependence of signal of stress gauge on cantilever, (c) time dependence of frequency shift and temperature of on-chip p-n diode, and (d) time dependence of frequency shift after temperature compensation of resonant frequency

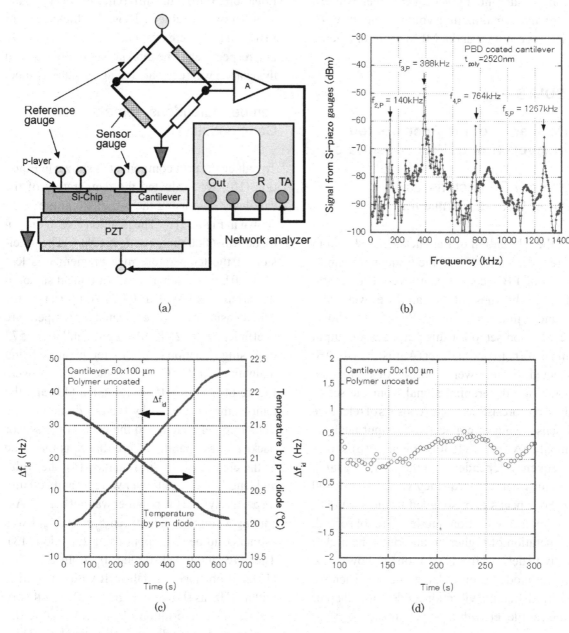

(a)   (b)

(c)   (d)

Table 1. Sensitivities and K-factors for VOCs for PAB and PBD coated cantilevers

Polymer	$f_{4,0}$(kHz)	$f_{4,P}$ (kHz)	t_{Si}(µm)	t_{Poly}(nm)	Acetone		1-Propanol		Toluene		p-Xylene	
					s_{ace}	K_{ace}	S_{1pl}	K_{1pl}	s_{tol}	K_{tol}	s_{pxy}	K_{pxy}
PAB	911.4	885.2	4.87	640	0.036	605	0.15	2380	0.25	2650	0.63	5800
PBD	862.5	764.3	4.69	2520	0.025	141	0.076	420	0.62	2200	1.85	5800

was exposed to a diluted VOC gas. To make a diluted VOC sample, a diluted gas generation system was employed, as shown in Figure 7(a). The gas generation system consisted of a pure nitrogen cylinder, Mass Flow Controllers (MFCs), bubblers with thermostat (not shown), diluted nitrogen line, and a 4-way valve. Vaporized VOC component "1" or "2" in pure nitrogen gas with the specific mass flow adjusted using MFC was diluted by the dilute nitrogen line. The 4-way valve acts as a switch to alter the proportion of the diluted and pure nitrogen gas. The outlet of "diluted VOC" is connected to the "Gas in" port of a sensor chamber, as shown in Figure 3(c). Thus, we can obtain the pulsed diluted VOC with a specific concentration.

Figure 7(b) and 7(c) shows $\Delta f_{4,a}$ for four VOCs without a preconcentrator as (a) 640-nm-thick PAB thin film and (b) 2520-nm-thick PBD thin film. The drift component of $\Delta f_{4,a}$ was compensated by β_i (183 ppm/°C for PAB, 78 ppm/°C for PBD), and ΔT_c was measured using the on-chip p-n diode (Ikehara et al, 2011), as given in Equation (13). The diluted 1800 ppm acetone, 500 ppm ethanol, 500 ppm 1-propanol, and 590 ppm toluene gases were injected sequentially into the sensor chamber separated by pure nitrogen gas. The two polymers PAB and PBD had different characteristics of sensitivity among the four VOCs: PBD had a high selectivity for toluene, and PAB had a relatively high sensitivity for acetone and alcohol.

Figure 8(a) shows the PBD-thickness dependence of $\Delta f_{4,a}$ for toluene and acetone. $\Delta f_{4,a}$ is linearly dependent on t_{poly} up to 2500 nm, as confirmed from Equation (6), and the sensitivity is proportional to t_{poly} as well. This implies that the VOC molecules are adsorbed by polymer films to a depth of at least 2500 nm.

Estimations of Sensitivity and K-Factor

Then, we evaluated the C_a dependence of $\Delta f_{4,a}$ for several VOCs to determine the K_a. Figures 8(b)

and 8(c) show the concentration dependence of $\Delta f_{4,a}$ among several VOCs. Then, we estimated the sensitivity s_a among VOCs as shown in Table 1. Using Equation (7) with s_a, we also calculated the K_a for several VOCs as shown in Table 1. For example, K_{ace} (for acetone) was 605 for PAB and 141 for PBD. K_{tol} (for toluene) was 2650 for PAB and 2200 for PBD. Note that K_{pxy} (for p-xylene) for PAB and PBD had an extremely large value of 5800. Since these K_a values are independent of t_{Poly}, $\Delta f_{n,P}$ and C_a, and K_a are adequate parameters of gas adsorption selectivity for polymers.

Performance of Sensor System

Sensor Signal from Preconcentrated Mixed VOCs Using One Cantilever

This section described the performance of sensor system with preconcentrator shown in Figure 5. The prepared samples were described in previous section, and the polymers were PAB. The typical conditions were as follows: $V_a = 10$ L (10^{-2}m³), $v_{ad} = 2.0$ L/min (3.3×10^{-5}m³/s), $v_{de} = 17.2$ sccm (2.86×10^{-7}m³/s), $T_r = 27$ °C and the maximum preconcentrator temperature was 520 °C. Prior to evaluation by sensor system, the temperature profile of our preconcentrator was established. Figure 9(a) shows the typical temperature profile with $t_0 = 182$ sec, $T_r = 27$ s and $r_t = 1.26$ m³/s in this experiment. Note that the temperature is lineally increased with temperature from 50 to 500°. This profile is controlled by a programmed applied voltage in a power unit as shown in Figure 9(b).

To explain the analysis function of our sensor system, we evaluated the response of Δf_{a10L} from preconcentrated mixed VOCs employing one cantilever sensor without multiplexing (MPX is fixed to the particular cantilever). The volume of mixed gas V_a was 10 L and the components of VOC were 1-propanol ($C_{1pl,10L} = 1.8$ppm), toluene ($C_{tol,10L} = 0.69$ppm) and p-xylene ($C_{pxy,10L} = 0.5$ppm). The selected cantilever was PAB coated with $t_{Poly} = 640$ nm. The response of Δf_{a10L} had

Figure 7. VOCs evaluations: (a) apparatus for diluted VOCs generation (two VOCs case), (b) and (c) frequency shift of polymer coated cantilever for four VOCs without preconcentrator in the case of (b) 640nm thickness PAB thin film, and (c) 2520nm thickness PBD thin film

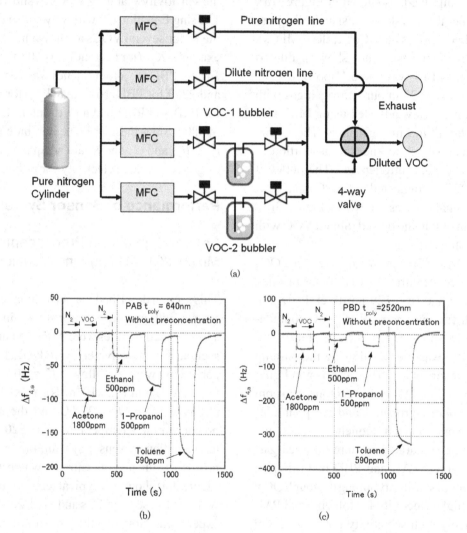

(a)

(b)

(c)

three distinct peaks corresponding to 1-propanol, toluene and p-xylene. These peaks are supposed to be corresponding different T_a of each VOC, which are discuss in sect. *"Estimation of desorption temperature in"* this chapter.

Sensor Signal from Preconcentrated Mixed VOCs using Cantilever Array

Now we use multiple cantilevers with different polymers. Two types of cantilever sensors namely,

1) PAB of different thicknesses for acetone-toluene mixed gas and 2) PBD of different thicknesses for toluene-xylene mixed gas, are prepared and attached to the package and sensor system as shown in Figures 3(c), 3(d) and 4(a). Figures 9(c) and 9(d) show the typical signal $u_i(t)$ from sensor and the typical applied voltage $p_i(t)$ to PZT actuator when $i = 1$ and 4 ($i = 1$: PAB-coated cantilever $t_{Poly} = 330$ nm; $i = 4$: not coated). While the phase between $u_1(t)$ and $p_1(t)$ was about zero, that between $u_4(t)$ and $p_4(t)$ was about 180 degree. Note

Figure 8. The sensitivities of cantilever sensors: (a) thickness dependence of frequency shift of PBD coated cantilever for toluene and acetone without preconcentrator, (b) frequency shift of polymer coated cantilever for four VOC without preconcentrator for 640nm thickness PAB thin film, and (c) 2520nm thickness PBD thin film

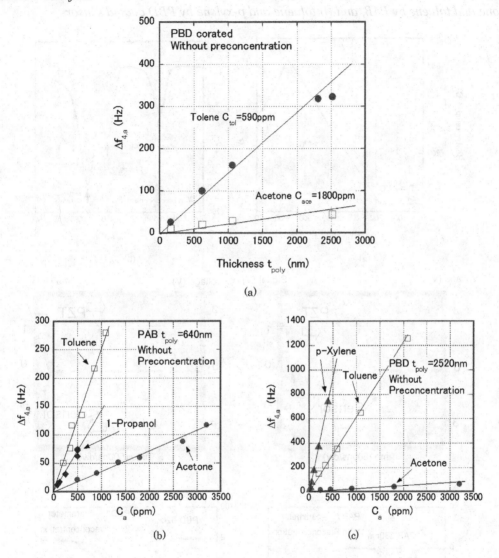

(a)

(b)

(c)

that the U_{0i} are adjusted by the gain of front-end amplifier. As shown in this example, the each phase between $u_i(t)$ and $p_i(t)$ when $i=1$ to 4 was varied. Then the circuit with preset of phase was essential to obtain the stable oscillation when multiple cantilevers are used.

Figure 9(e) shows the frequency shift Δf_{a10L} by a desorbed mixed gas of acetone ($C_{ace,10L}$ = 1.8 ppm) and toluene ($C_{tol,10L}$ = 0.69 ppm) using

two PAB-coated cantilever sensors with different thicknesses (t_{Poly} = 330 and 640 nm). The response curves had two distinct peaks corresponding to acetone and toluene. Figure 9(f) shows Δf_{a10L} by the desorbed mixed gas of toluene ($C_{tol,10L}$ = 0.69 ppm) and p-xylene ($C_{pxy,10L}$ = 0.5 ppm) using three PBD-coated cantilever sensors with different thicknesses (t_{Poly} = 620, 1060 and 2520 nm). Three response curves were also distinguished with two

Figure 9. Analysis and results from multi-sensors: (a) temperature profile of preconcentrator, (b) desorption response of PAB coated cantilever for 1-propanol, toluene and p-xylene with preconcentrator, (c) (d) signal of sensor (u$_i$(t)) and applied voltage to PZT (p$_i$(t)) observed by oscilloscope with (c) for i=1, (d) for i=4, (e) desorption response of polymer coated cantilever for VOCs with preconcentrator for acetone and toluene by PAB, and (f) toluene and p-xylene by PBD coated sensor

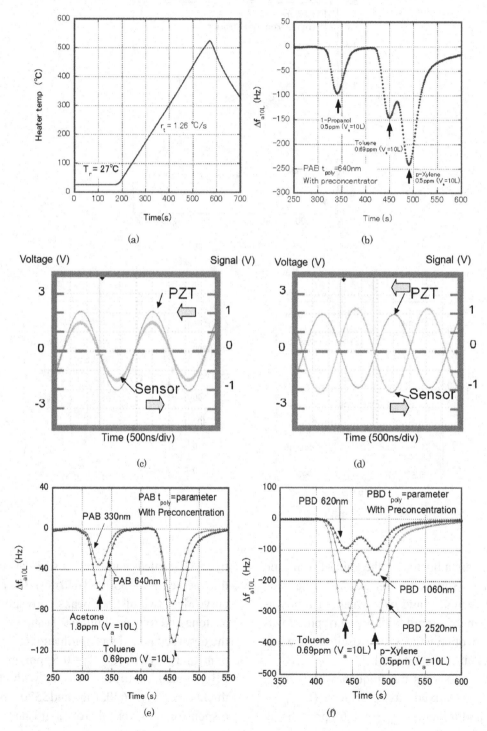

peaks, and the peak values of Δf_{a10L} among the different thicknesses were proportional to t_{Poly}. We could evaluate the response of the desorption gas at the same time using a multiple cantilever system in a preset method for phase and frequency as shown in Figure 4(a).

Estimation of Desorption Temperature

To estimate the desorption temperature T_a derived from Equation (16), v_{de} dependence of Δf_{a10LP} was performed. The polymers were PAB (t_{Poly} = 640 nm) and PBD (t_{Poly} = 2520 nm). Figure 10(a) shows four response curves of Δf_{a10L} according to different v_{de} values ranging from 17.2 to 133 sccm for 1-propanol when cantilever was coated with PAB with t_{poly} = 640 nm. The small v_{de} values yielded large values of t_{Pa} and a large maximum Δf_{a10LP}. The analysis of this response curve for small values of v_{de} is described in the next section. Figure 10(b) shows the v_{de} dependence of t_{Pa} using 1-propanol, toluene, and p-xylene. These values of t_{Pa} tend to be constant when v_{de} is large.

Considering the $1/v_{de}$ dependence of t_{Pa} and using Equation (16) subject to given t_0 and T_r, we can estimate the desorption temperature T_a at $1/v_{de} = 0$ for each VOC, as shown in Figure 10(c). This figure shows that t_{Pa} was 271, 379, and 417 s, and T_a was 138, 275, and 325 °C for 1-propanol, toluene, and p-xylene, respectively, taking into account the temperature profile of the preconcentrator, as shown in Figure 9(a). The slopes of these three lines had the same value, i.e., 26.2 mL, which was supposed to be the value of $(S_t L_t + V_{ch})$ in Equation (16). The actual value of $(S_t L_t + V_{ch})$ in our sensor system, as shown in Figure 5(a), was approximately 6 mL, which was much smaller than that estimated from Figure 10(c). Because the pipes between the preconcentrator and the sensor are complicated with many narrow places including values and connectors, the fluid resistance of the pipes may cause the increase in this value. Table 2 shows t_{Pa} and T_a estimated from

v_{de} dependence of Δf_{a10LP} for PAB and PBD sensing materials.

Estimations of Preconcentration Factor and Efficiency

To estimate other important parameters including preconcentration factor F_{a10L} and system efficiency $\xi_a \eta_a$ as shown in Equations (27) to (30), the v_{de} dependence of Δf_{a10L} was evaluated because v_{de} was largest variable parameter by which the concentration factor and sensitivity are affected. The polymers were PAB (t_{Poly} = 640 nm) and PBD (t_{Poly} = 2520 nm). Figures 11(a) and (b) show the v_{de} dependence of F_{a10L} and $\xi_a \eta_a$ of (a) acetone for PAB and (b) toluene for PBD. F_{a10L} was calculated using Equation (19), and $\xi_a \eta_a$ was calculated from the mass of detected VOCs $m_{a,de}$ using Equations (27) and (28). Although $\xi_a \eta_a$ was almost constant from 0.7 to 0.9 among v_{de} = 3 to 68 sccm, F_{a10L} decreased while v_{de} increased. We considered that the response time of Δf_{a10L} from the VOC sensing might be an important rule of this phenomenon because a small v_{de} made Δf_{a10L} high. The lower the v_{de} produced, the higher the F_{a10L}; however, it made the width of the peaks (or deviation of Gaussian curve κ_a, we neglected j when $j = 1$) long and gave poor separation capability among VOCs. Here, κ_a was estimated by a parameter fitting of the Gaussian curve using Equation (23) with $j = 1$. Thus, we decided that an adequate v_{de} was 17.2 sccm (2.8×10^{-5} m³/s). In this case, the typical κ_a was 12 to 13 s for four VOCs. Table 2 showed the important values estimated from v_{de} dependence of Δf_{a10L}, including $\xi_a \eta_a$, F_{a10L} and κ_a at the values of v_{de} = 17.2 sccm. Maximum F_{a10L} was 910 for acetone with 640nm PAB and 2520nm PBD, and minimum was 460 for p-xylene with 2520nm PBD.

Estimation of System Sensitivity

To estimate the system sensitivity S_{a10L} as shown in Equation (30), the $C_{a,10L}$ dependence of Δf_{a10LP}

Figure 10. Effect of V_{de} in preconcentration, (a) desorption response of PAB coated cantilever for 1-pnopanol with preconcentrator, 4 lines show these for different V_{de}, (b) V_{de} dependence of peak time for VOCs, and (c) $1/V_{de}$ dependence of peak time for VOCs.

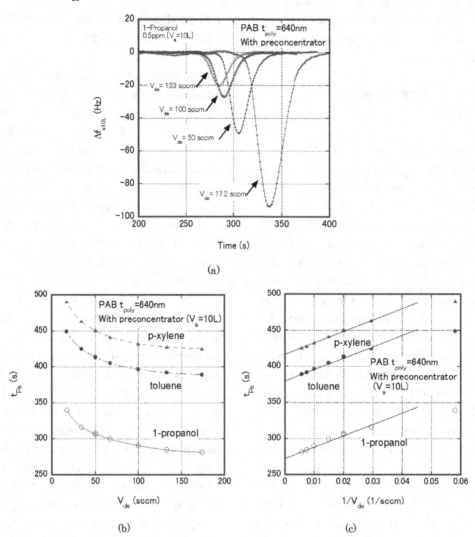

(a)

(b)

(c)

was measured for the same samples in the previous section. Figure 11(c) shows the $C_{a,10L}$ dependence of Δf_{a10LP} of the PAB-coated cantilever for acetone, 1-propanol and toluene; Figure 11(d) shows that of the PBD-coated cantilever for toluene and p-xylene. The tangent of the straight line for each VOC was S_{a10L}, and listed in Table 2. The maximum S_{a10L} was 850 Hz/ppm when $V_a = 10$ L for p-xylene with 2520 nm PBD and the minimum was 22.7 for acetone with 2520 nm PBD.

Fitting of Response Curve to Theoretical Model

In the previous few sections, we reported the estimation of the essential parameters required for actual applications of this system, including environmental monitoring. In this section, we have tried to fit the actual sensor response of Δf_{aV} to the curves derived from a theoretical consideration. We introduced the simple desorption model from

Table 2. System sensitivities, efficiency, and detection limit for VOCs for PAB and PBD coated cantilevers

Items	Unit	PAB 640nm			PBD 2520nm		
		Acetone	1-Propanol	Toluene	Acetone	Toluene	p-Xylene
T_a	°C	132	138	275	131	276	325
Sensitivity s_a	Hz/ppm	0.036	0.15	0.25	0.025	0.62	1.85
System sensitivity S_{a10L}	Hz/ppm (V_a=10L)	32.7	88.5	148	22.7	514	850
F_{a10L} (v_{de}=17.2sccm)	(V_a=10L)	910	590	590	910	830	460
$\xi_a \eta_a$ (v_{de}=17.2sccm)	s	0.88	0.53	0.6	0.8	0.78	0.45
κ_a (v_{de}=17.2sccm)	s	12.2	11.5	12.9	11.9	12.6	13
t_{Pa} (t_0=182s,v_{de}=17.2sccm)	s	327.5	345.7	456	320.6	446.6	493.1
Standard dev. λ	Hz	0.13	0.13	0.13	0.11	0.11	0.11
DL_{a10L}	ppb (V_a=10L)	12	4.4	2.6	14.5	0.6	0.4

the adsorbed carbon fiber with a large surface area as shown in sect. *"Response curve for desorption of preconcentrator"* in this chapter, and the formulae of desorption rate (molecules/s) were applied in Equations (17) to (21). We also applied this formula to our sensor system in Equation (22). The coated polymers were PAB (t_{poly} = 640 nm) and PBD (t_{poly} = 2520 nm). The typical conditions were as follows: V_a = 10L, v_{ad} = 2.0 L/min, v_{de} = 17.2 sccm, T_r = 27 °C, and t_0 = 179 s. The value of $(S_t L_t + V_{ch})$ in Equation (22) is 26.2 mL, which was estimated from Figure 10(c). Figure 12(a) shows the fitting results of the desorption curve of Δf_{a10L} as two peaks with $C_{ace,10L}$ = 1.8 ppm and $C_{tol,10L}$ = 0.69 ppm.

The estimated values of fitting parameters are E_a = 0.28 eV (27.0 KJ/mole) for acetone and E_a = 0.56 eV (54.0 KJ/mole) for toluene, respectively. These E_a values were fixed so as to correspond to times at which each peak occurs because E_a is a unique parameter from which T_a is determined. Hence, the peak value of $N_d(t)$ in Equation (22) is taken to be Δf_{a10LP} for comparison with the actual response. The values ranging from 15.2 to 42 KJ/mole were reported is previous papers as the enthalpy of adsorption (equal to $96.5E_a$) for acetone adsorption on carbon fiber (Barton, et al.,

1998; Delage, et al., 2000; Hsieh & Chen, 2002; Popescu, et al., 2003) and from 30.4 to 46.4 KJ/mole for toluene (Delage, et al., 2000; Yu, et al., 2002). These papers stated that the values varied according to the kind of adsorption materials, evaluation conditions, and analysis methods. Therefore, the estimated values mentioned earlier were considered to be the rough values for describing this phenomenon. The response curves of Δf_{a10L} were much sharper than the theoretical curves; however, the reason behind this was not clear.

Separation of Acetone and 1-Propanol using Two-Gaussian Model

As described in previous section, the measured response curve Δf_{a10L} was not explained using the response from the theoretical adsorption model in Equations (17) to (21) and the formula were too complicated to fit them by several parameters. Then, we tried to use simpler formula by Gaussian curves as explained in Equation (23). As the example, we estimated the concentrations of acetone and 1-propanol from a mixed gas sample by fitting of two Gaussian curves using a PAB

Figure 11. Concentration factor, total system efficiency, and system sensitivity for our system, (a) acetone by PAB coated sensor, (b) toluene PBD coated sensor, (c) frequency shift of polymer coated cantilever for four VOCs with preconcentrator with 640nm thickness PAB thin film, and (d) 2520nm thickness PBD thin film

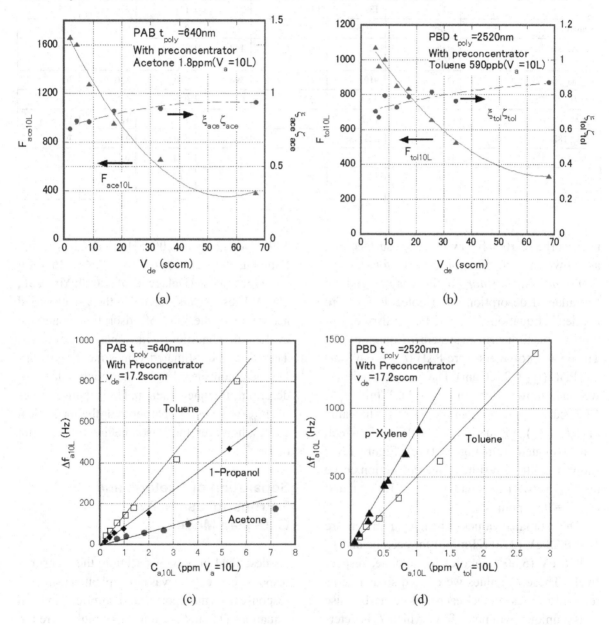

(a)　　　　　　　　　　　　　(b)

(c)　　　　　　　　　　　　　(d)

(t_{Poly} = 640nm)-coated cantilever sensor. Since T_{ace} (for acetone) = 132 °C and T_{1pl} (for 1-propanol) = 138 °C were similar, it was very difficult to distinguish the peaks on the response curve. Therefore, we used Equation (23) to explain the actual response curve taking account of adequate

fitting parameters. Although Equation (23) has three fitting parameters ($\Delta f_{Pa,j}$, $t_{Pa,j}$ and $\kappa_{a,j}$) for each Gaussian function, $t_{Pa,j}$ and $\kappa_{a,j}$ was constant values which were explained by a second ordered polynomial according to the concentration in Equations (25) and (26). The coefficients of each

Figure 12. Desorption characteristics, (a) comparisons between the calculated response curves with estimated E_a and measured Δf_{a10L} with preconcentrator, (b) decomposition results from two Gaussian curve fitting using parameters shown in Table 2, and (c) t_{ad} dependence of frequency shift on PBD 2520nm coated cantilever for toluene with preconcentrator

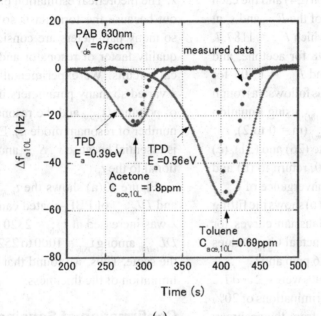

(a)

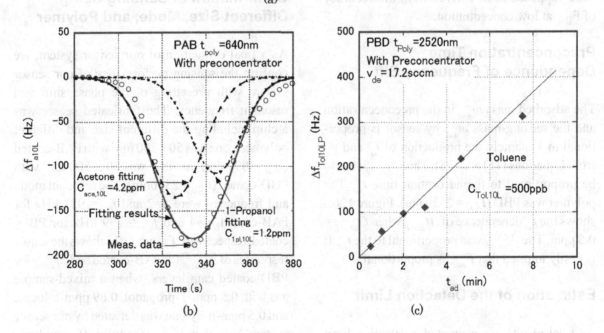

(b)   (c)

polynomial were; $t_{Pa0,j} = 333.93$, $t_{Pa1,j} = -2.0058$, $t_{Pa2,j} = 0.05911$, $\kappa_{a0,j} = 11.627$, $\kappa_{a1,j} = 0.1901$, $\kappa_{a2,j} = -0.00336$ for acetone; $t_{Pa0,j} = 351.02$, $t_{Pa1,j} = -5.8$, $t_{Pa2,j} = 0.58689$, $\kappa_{a0,j} = 11.162$, $\kappa_{a1,j} = 0.30637$, $\kappa_{a2,j} =$

0 for 1-propanol. These coefficients were obtained by obtaining the $C_{a,10L}$ dependence of Δf_{a10LP}, $t_{Pa,j}$ and $\kappa_{a,j}$ for acetone and 1-propanol.

The purpose of this fitting is to estimate the each concentration of acetone and 1-propanol of mixed gas. Therefore fitting parameters of Δf_{a10LP} are the coefficients of Equation (24) and the each coefficients are the products of the $F_{am,j}$ and s_a at each m as Equation (31), in which $F_{a0,j}$ = 1187.7, $F_{a1,j}$ = -106.7, and $F_{a2,j}$ = 3.98 for acetone, and $F_{a0,j}$ = 656.6, $F_{a1,j}$ = -95.5, and $F_{a2,j}$ = 17.05 for 1-propanol. Fitting process is as follows: (a) rough estimation of $C_{a,10L}$ by the Δf_{a10LP} using Equation (29), (b) determination of $F_{am,j}$ (m = 0 to 2), $t_{Pa,j}$ and $\kappa_{a,j}$ using Equations (24) to (26) and (31), (c) fitting to the shape of $\Delta f_{a10L}(t)$, return to (b) and repeat (b) and (c) until the convergence of $C_{a,10L}$ of each component. Figure 12(b) shows the fitting result to decomposed two Gaussian curves for acetone and 1-propanol. The actual $C_{a,10L}$ values of mixed gas were $C_{ace,10L}$ = 3.6 ppm and $C_{pnl,10L}$ = 1.0 ppm, but the evaluated values were 4.2 and 1.2 ppm, respectively. These discriminations of 20% were supposed to be derived from the accuracy of F_{a10L} at low concentration.

Preconcentration Time Dependence of Frequency Sift

The adsorbed mass $m_{a,ad}$ in the preconcentration and the sensing-mass $m_{a,de}$ by sensor is proportional to V_a namely the production of t_{ad} and v_{ad} from Equations (15) and (28). Thus Δf_{a10LP} should be proportional to the adsorption time t_{ad}. The polymer was PBD (t_{Poly} = 2520 nm). Figure 12(c) shows the t_{ad} dependence of Δf_{a10LP} when $C_{tol,10L}$ = 0.5 ppm. The Δf_{a10LP} was proportional to the t_{ad}. It is easily implied that F_{a10L} is proportional to t_{ad}.

Estimation of the Detection Limit

As final results, we estimated a detection limit DL_{a10L} using Equation (32). A standard deviation λ was calculated with 11 points (for 33 s) of Δf_{a10L} at the same time of measurement. The estimated values were 12 ppb for acetone, 0.6 ppb for toluene and 0.4 ppb for p-xylene, as shown in Table 2. Note that the detection limit is proportional to λ. The theoretical estimation of λ has not carried out because the formula is so complicated and so many parameters are considered such as the quality factor of resonator and noise of electrical circuits. We experimentally found that the λ varied so many parameters including the type of polymer, t_{Poly}, and the resonant frequency (or number of resonant mode n). Especially, the t_{Poly} is essential because s_a, S_{a10L} and F_{a10L} are proportional to the t_{Poly}.

Figure 13(a) shows the t_{Poly} dependence of λ and DL_{tol10L} of PBD-coated cantilever. Since the λ was increased at t_{Poly} = 2320 and 2520nm, the DL_{tol10L} among t_{Poly} = 1000 to 2520nm were almost the same. Thus, we found that t_{Poly} had practical limitation of the thickness.

Confirmation of Sensing Using Different Size, Mode, and Polymer

As a final evaluation of our sensor system, we confirm the sensing performance of our sensor system with presetting of the phase shift and resonant frequency. The fabricated sensor was a chip including the different size and different polymers, one was 50 x 200 μm² with PAB-coated (t_{Poly} = 890 nm), another was 50 x 500 μm² with PBD-coated (t_{Poly} = 2320nm). The resonant mode and frequency were n=2 and $f_{2,P}$ = 938 kHz for PAB-coated, n=4 and $f_{4,P}$ = 799 kHz for PBD-coated, respectively. Figure 13(b) shows the sensor responses of $\Delta f_{2,a10L}$ for PAB-coated and $\Delta f_{4,a10L}$ for PBD-coated cantilevers, when a mixed-sample gas with 0.5 ppm-1-propanol, 0.69 ppm-toluene, and 0.5 ppm-p-xylene was detected by our sensor system. Note that $\Delta f_{n,a10L}$ stands for Δf_{a10L} with nth vibration mode. These two curves had three peaks corresponding to the three VOCs and each peak had different peak values in terms of the difference

Figure 13. (a) Thickness dependence of λ and DL$_{Tol10L}$ on PBD coated cantilever for toluene with preconcentrator, and (b) sensor responses of Δf$_{2,a10L}$ for PAB-coated and Δf$_{4,a10L}$ for PBD-coated cantilevers

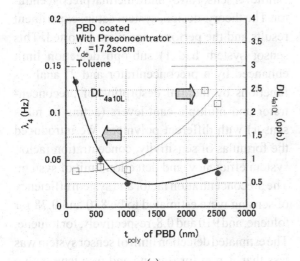

(a)

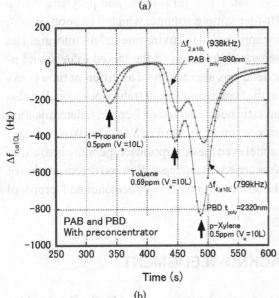

(b)

of sensitivity. Since two cantilevers had different size, type of polymer, t_{Poly}, mode and the resonant frequency, $f_{n,P}$ and these phases between $u_i(t)$ and $p_i(t)$ were much different. However, thanks to the presetting of the $f_{n,P}$ and the phase shown in this chapter, we could obtain stable sensor responses.

DISCUSSION

The theory, design, structure and experimental results of a compact chemical sensor system employing polymer-coated multiple-cantilever-type mass sensors were presented. This sensor system had two merits for actual applications: (1) high sensitivity and (2) analysis function, as follows.

High Sensitivity

High sensitivity was achieved using a preconcentrator of 6.35 mm diameter, an air pump with a large flow rate of 2.0 L/min and a small sensor chamber of 0.3 cc. A 10-liter of VOC sample was concentrated for 5min and a 60-liter volume for 30 min for practical application. We confirmed the frequency shift and the sensitivity were proportional to the pumping time as shown in Figure 12(c). This large sample volume made the concentration factor high. A textile structure of carbon fiber as the preconcentration material was also distributed for taking a large sample volume. The sensitivity, concentration factor and detection limit for the 10-liter toluene sample in 5 min of pumping were 514 Hz/ppm, 830 and 0.6 ppb, also 3084 Hz/ppm, 4980 and 0.1 ppb for the 60-liter sample in 30 min pumping, respectively. It is considered that the detection limit for actual application is 3 to 5 times larger than estimated one. Since the indoor concentration guideline values of chemicals are 70 ppb for toluene and 200 ppb for xylene in Japan (Guideline in Japan, 2000), these detection limits of our chemical sensor system are good enough for monitoring these environmental solvents in a room.

Analysis Function

This system had analysis functions by two methods: (a) distinguished by peak delay time of sensor response caused by desorption temperature difference of heated preconcentrator and (b) by use of multiple cantilever sensors with different polymers. Our system was capable of distinguishing toluene and p-xylene from the difference in peak time. Even though the peak time (or the desorption temperature) between the two VOCs was similar, the concentrations of the two were estimated in terms of parameter fitting of multiple Gaussian functions from an actual response curve. We confirmed the decomposition of the acetone and 1-propanol mixed sample by these methods. A key of operation for multiple cantilevers was to install the circuits of preset for resonance frequency and feedback phase at the cantilever switching by MPX. Since the resonant frequency varied with the thickness of polymers, the feedback phase and the site of the cantilever in a chip, it was very difficult to achieve an adequate oscillation with multiple cantilevers with different thicknesses and different polymers. We confirmed that two cantilevers with different length of 200 and 500 μm, different polymers of PAB and PBD, and different mode of 2 and 4, detected three mixed gas including 1-propanol, toluene and p-xylene as shown in Figure 13(b).

In this chapter, we integrated eight microcantilevers including stress gauges and a p-n diode as a temperature sensor on a chip, and four cantilevers among them were operated by multiplexing. Other electronic circuits consisted of discrete parts, operational amplifiers, ICs and microcomputers. In the future, all electronic circuits can be integrated in the same silicon chip, as well as cantilevers, and act as a smart sensor with various intelligent functions. We also consider that this system is the first compact chemical sensor system using a MEMS mass sensitive resonator for the purpose of environmental monitoring.

CONCLUSION

We developed a highly sensitive compact chemical sensor system employing a polymer-coated microcantilever sensor array and a thermal preconcentrator. The theory, design, system setup, experiment results and the performance were reported. This sensor system had 1) sub-ppb detection limit enhanced by a preconcentrator and 2) analysis functions by thermal desorption of preconcentrator and multiple cantilevers (acting as mass sensor) with different polymers. We introduced the formulas of sensitivity, concentration factor, system efficiency, and detection limit of system. The preconcentration factor and system efficiency of sensing were estimated to be 830 and 0.78 for toluene, and 910 and 0.8, respectively, for toluene. The estimated detection limit of sensor system was less than 1 ppb for toluene and p-xylene with a 10-liter sample volume, which was good enough for application to environmental monitoring. The separated detection of the mixed toluene and p-xylene was also achieved as different time peaks on the heating preconcentrator operation. We also investigate the method of the precise determination of concentration of mixed VOCs by two Gaussians model even the desorption temperature is so close. We carried out the separation and determination of the concentration of mixed acetone and 1-propanol with 20% precision.

ACKNOWLEDGMENT

This research was supported by the Regional Innovation Cluster Program of Nagano, granted by Ministry of Education, Culture, Sports, Science, and Technology (MEXT), Japan.

REFERENCES

Barton, S. S., Evans, M. J. B., & Macdonald, J. A. F. (1998). Adsorption and immersion enthalpies on BPL carbon. *Carbon, 36*(7-8), 969–972. doi:10.1016/S0008-6223(97)00224-8

Battiston, F. M., Ramseyer, J. P., Lang, H. P., Baller, M. K., Gerber, C., & Gimzewski, J. K. (2001). A chemical sensor based on a microfabricated cantilever array with simultaneous resonance-frequency and bending readout. *Sensors and Actuators. B, Chemical, 77*, 122–131. doi:10.1016/S0925-4005(01)00683-9

Bender, F., Barie, N., Romoudis, G., Voigt, A., & Rapp, M. (2003). Development of a preconcentration unit for a SAW sensor micro array and its use for indoor air quality monitoring. *Sensors and Actuators. B, Chemical, 93*, 135–141. doi:10.1016/S0925-4005(03)00239-9

Blevins, R. D. (1979). *Formulas for natural frequency and mode shape.* Malabar, India: Krieger Publishing. doi:10.1115/1.3153712

Chen, G. Y., Thundat, T., Wachter, E. A., & Warmack, R. J. (1995). Dsorption-induced surface stress and its effects on resonance frequency of microcantilevers. *Journal of Applied Physics, 77*, 3618–3622. doi:10.1063/1.359562

Delage, F., Pre, P., & Cloirec, P. L. (2000). Mass transfer and warming during adsorption of high concentrations of VOCs on an activated carbon bed: Experimental and theoretical analysis. *Environmental Science & Technology, 34*, 4816–4821. doi:10.1021/es001187x

Dufour, I., & Fadel, L. (2003). Resonant microcantilever type chemical sensors: Analytical modeling in view of optimization. *Sensors and Actuators. B, Chemical, 91*, 353–361. doi:10.1016/S0925-4005(03)00110-2

Groves, W. A., Zellersa, E. T., & Fryec, G. C. (1998). Analyzing organic vapors in exhaled breath using a surface acoustic wave sensor array with preconcentration: Selection and characterization of the preconcentrator adsorbent. *Analytica Chimica Acta, 371*, 131–143. doi:10.1016/S0003-2670(98)00294-3

Henderson, M. J., Karger, B. A., & Wrenshall, G. A. (1952). Acetone in the breath: A study of acetone exhalation in diabetic and nondiabetic human subjects. *Diabetes, 1*, 188–193.

Hsieh, C. T., & Chen, J. M. (2002). Adsorption energy distribution model for VOCs onto activated carbons. *Journal of Colloid and Interface Science, 255*, 248–253. doi:10.1006/jcis.2002.8668

Ikehara, T., Konno, M., Murakami, S., Fukawa, T., Kimura, M., & Mihara, T. (2011). Integration of p-n junction diode to cantilever mass sensor for frequency drift compensation due to temperature fluctuation. *Sensors and Materials, 23*, 381–396.

Ikehara, T., Lu, J., Konno, M., Maeda, R., & Mihara, T. (2007). High quality-factor silicon cantilever for high sensitive resonant mass sensor operated in air. *Journal of Micromechanics and Microengineering, 17*, 2491–2494. doi:10.1088/0960-1317/17/12/015

Japanese Ministry of Health, Labor, and Welfare. (2000). *Guideline and standard evaluation method of the VOC indoor concentration in room.* Tokyo, Japan: Japanese Ministry of Health, Labor and Welfare.

Kim, B. H., Prins, F. E., Kern, D. P., Raible, S., & Weimar, U. (2001). Multicomponent analysis and prediction with a cantilever array based on gas sensor. *Sensors and Actuators. B, Chemical, 78*, 12–18. doi:10.1016/S0925-4005(01)00785-7

Kimura, M., Liu, Y., Sakai, R., Sato, S., Hirai, T., Fukawa, T., & Mihara, T. (2011). Detection of volatile organic compounds by analyses of polymer-coated quartz crystal microbalance sensor arrays. *Sensors and Materials, 23*, 359–368.

Lang, H. P., Baller, M. K., Berger, R., Gerber, C., Gimzewski, J. K., & Battiston, F. M. (1999). An artificial nose based on a micromechanical cantilever array. *Analytica Chimica Acta, 393*, 59–65. doi:10.1016/S0003-2670(99)00283-4

Lange, D., Hagleitner, C., Hierlemann, A., Brand, O., & Baltes, H. (2002). Complementary metal oxide semiconductor cantilever arrays on a single chip: Mass-sensitive detection of volatile organic compounds. *Analytical Chemistry, 74*, 3084–3095. doi:10.1021/ac011269j

Liu, Y., Mihara, T., Kimura, M., Takasaki, M., & Hirai, T. (2007). Polymer film-coated quartz crystal microbalances sensor for volatile organic compounds sensing. In *Proceedings of the 24th Sensor Symposium Funabori*, (pp. 309-312). Tokyo, Japan: IEEJ.

Lu, J., Ikehara, T., Zhang, Y., Maeda, R., & Mihara, T. (2006). Energy dissipation mechanisms in lead zirconate titanate thin film transduced micro cantilevers. *Japanese Journal of Applied Physics, 45*, 8795–8800. doi:10.1143/JJAP.45.8795

Maute, M., Raible, S., Prins, F. E., Kern, D. P., Ulmer, H., Weimar, U., & Goepel, W. (1998). Detection of volatile organic compounds (VOCs) with polymer-coated cantilevers. *Sensors and Actuators. B, Chemical, 58*, 505. doi:10.1016/S0925-4005(99)00110-0

Mihara, T., Ikehara, T., Konno, M., Maeda, R., Kimura, M., & Fukawa, T. (2010). Design and fabrication of high-sensitive chemical sensor system with preconcentration and analysis functions employing a micro cantilever sensor. *IEEJ Transactions on SM, 130*, 275–282. doi:10.1541/ieejsmas.130.275

Mihara, T., Ikehara, T., Konno, M., Murakami, S., Maeda, R., Kimura, M., & Fukawa, T. (2011). Design, fabrication and evaluation of highly-sensitive compact chemical sensor system employing a microcantilever array and a preconcentrator. *Sensors and Materials, 23*, 397–417.

Mihara, T., Ikehara, T., Lu, J., Maeda, R., Fukawa, T., & Kimura, M. … Hirai, T. (2008). Integrated chemical sensor system employing micro cantilever and adsorption tube. In *Proceedings of the 12th International Meeting on Chemical Sensors*, (pp. 533-534). Columbus, OH: IEEE.

Mihara, T., Ikehara, T., Lu, J., Maeda, R., Fukawa, T., & Kimura, M. … Hirai, T. (2008). Sensitivity improvement of a chemical sensor system employing a micro cantilever sensor and an adsorption tube. In *Proceedings of the 25th Sensor Symposium*, (pp. 591-594). Okinawa, Japan: IEEJ.

Mihara, T., Ikehara, T., Lu, J., Maeda, R., Fukawa, T., & Kimura, M. (2009). High-sensitive chemical sensor system employing a higher-mode operative micro cantilever sensor and an adsorption tube. In *Proceedings of the 13th International Symposium on Olfaction and Electronic Nose*, (pp. 79-82). Brescia, Italy: American Institute of Physics.

Nakamoto, T., Sukegawa, K., & Sumitomo, E. (2005). Higher order sensing using QCM sensor array and preconcentrator with variable temperature. *IEEE Sensors Journal, 5*, 68. doi:10.1109/JSEN.2004.839894

Popescu, M., Joly, J. P., Carre, J., & Danatoiu, C. (2003). Dynamical adsorption and temperature-programmed desorption of VOCs (toluene, butyl acetate and butanol) on activated carbons. *Carbon, 41*, 739–748. doi:10.1016/S0008-6223(02)00391-3

Redhead, P. A. (1962). Thermal desorption of gases. *Vacuum, 12*, 203–211. doi:10.1016/0042-207X(62)90978-8

Yu, F. D., Luo, L. A., & Grevillot, G. (2002). Adsorption isotherms of VOCs onto an activated carbon monolith: Experimental measurement and correlation with different models. *Journal of Chemical & Engineering Data, 47*, 467–473. doi:10.1021/je010183k

Chapter 10
Odor Sensing Using Spherical Surface Acoustic Wave Sensors (Ball SAW Sensors) with Organic Sensing–Films

Bartosz Wyszynski
Tokyo Institute of Technology, Japan & Westpomeranian University of Technology, Poland

Takamichi Nakamoto
Tokyo Institute of Technology, Japan

Noritaka Nakaso
Toppan Printing Corporation, Japan

ABSTRACT

As the olfactory modality gains a well-deserved importance and understanding among the human senses, there are numerous attempts to mimic performance of the sense of smell using man-made machine olfaction. One of the important problems in the machine olfaction field is the availability of miniature, bio-inspired gas/odor sensors capable of working in conditions similar to those for olfactory receptors. One of the emerging technologies with enormous potential for odor sensing is the spherical surface acoustic wave—ball-SAW—sensors. The chapter introduces the ball-SAW technology and presents the developments made in the field by describing methods of fabricating the chemically interactive membranes onto the ball-SAW devices, properties of the obtained sensors, and their practical implementation. A subsection is devoted to the perspectives of the gas/odor sensing using the ball-SAW sensors.

DOI: 10.4018/978-1-4666-2521-1.ch010

Copyright © 2013, IGI Global. Copying or distributing in print or electronic forms without written permission of IGI Global is prohibited.

INTRODUCTION

Biological olfaction is a powerful "instrument" enabling reception and processing of chemical stimuli. Thought to be one of the earliest senses developed in course of evolution, the sense of smell is common among virtually all eukaryotes—from insects to humans (Firestein, 2001). The human sense of smell has for long time seemed less important than the senses of vision and audition. Advances in studying and understanding biological/human olfaction make for a gradual increase of the sense's significance (Buck & Axel, 1991). From the technological standpoint, the growing importance of the sense of smell can be measured in a number of initiatives to incorporate olfactory modality into everyday technology such as odor reproduction and/or presentation techniques.

An indispensable prerequisite for development of the above-mentioned techniques for odor reproduction and/or presentation is presence of a technique to measure odors. To date, detection and quantification of odors has been commonly made using techniques of odorimetry and ol-

factometry (Steinhart, et al., 2000). However, serious limitations of the techniques called for studies and development of the machine capable of detecting and quantifying odors—an "electronic nose" or "artificial olfaction" systems (Persaud & Dodd, 1982; Nakamoto, et al., 1994). The parallel between the biological and artificial olfaction systems is shown schematically in Figure 1. In simplistic brevity, when we smell an aroma or odor, the air containing mixture of volatile compounds passes through nasal cavity and comes in contact with olfactory receptors. Signals of those receptors are then processed in the specialized part of the brain called olfactory cortex. As the odor sensing systems are intended to mimic performance of the biological olfaction, the artificial olfaction needs to be composed of the two described, general stages—(1) reception and (2) processing of the received signals.

In this chapter our main interest will be in the reception stage—the odor sensors. In humans, the olfactory epithelium—an odor reception field in the nose—hosts $10^7 - 10^8$ receptors on an area as small as 5 cm^2 (Pearce, 1997). Mimicking the

Figure 1. Analogy between biological and artificial olfaction systems

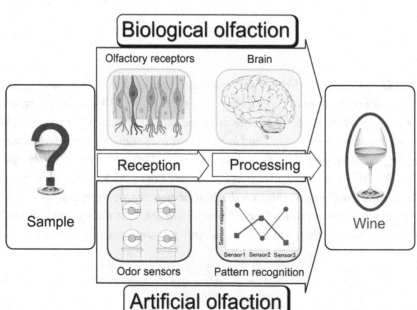

biological olfaction must therefore mean miniaturization of the sensors. For this reason we will pay special attention to the novel odor-sensing technology of the spherical Surface Acoustic Wave (SAW) devices—so called ball-SAW devices. Firstly, we will shortly review various technologies applied in the field of odor sensors. Then, we will focus more on the SAW sensors, explaining basics of the planar devices and differences between the planar and spherical SAW devices. In the main part of the chapter, we will introduce techniques used so far for fabrication of the ball-SAW odor sensors, results of the experimental evaluation of the fabricated ball-SAW sensors, and example application of the ball-SAW odor sensors. Finally we will discuss perspectives of the research on ball-SAW odor sensors.

ODOR SENSORS: VARIOUS TECHNOLOGIES, ONE GOAL

The first stage of the odor reception in the biological system occurs at the olfactory epithelium, where the odorant molecules interact with the Olfactory Receptors (ORs). In the artificial olfaction systems, the interaction takes place at the

odor sensors. Importantly, the gas sensors used in the artificial olfaction need to be non-specific, i.e. they respond rather to group of odorants than to a single analyte. This is based on the concept of electronic noses inspired by the biological olfactory system that uses large number of non-specific olfactory receptors. Although the receptors themselves posses remarkably high sensitivity toward odorants, their responses are not analyte-specific. Signals of those receptors are run through several processing stages leading to an output that not only makes sense of odors/odorants but does so on a remarkable level of sensitivity. For this reason, mimicking performance of the biological olfaction sets a very strict requirement for the sensing elements to be used in its artificial counterpart (i.e. detection limits, conditions of operation, flexibility in engineering the chemically interactive materials, size, etc.).

Just as the ORs are chemical receptors, the odor sensors belong to a large group of chemical sensors. Chemical sensors are devices capable of capturing and converting a chemical quantity into a measurable electric signal (Nagle, et al., 1998). Figure 2a shows a simple schematic of the chemical (odor) sensors' principle of operation. Each type of the chemical sensors is equipped

Figure 2. Chemosensor technology: (a) schematic depiction of the chemosensors' principle of operation, (b) planar surface acoustic wave (SAW) sensor (Figure 2b: © 1984, Elsevier[1], used with permission)

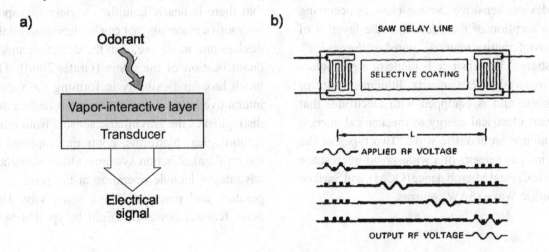

with a material capable of interacting with the airborne molecules (*vapor-interactive material*). The interaction causes a change in properties of the material, which results in a measurable electrical signal being generated. The chemical sensors most often used in the artificial olfaction applications can be generally classified into four main groups: chemoresistors, chemocapacitors, chemotransistors, and gravimetric sensors (Nanto & Stetter, 2003).

In chemoresistors, the vapor-interactive layer is composed of an electrically resistive material (e.g. the metal oxide or conductive polymer). The airborne molecules (i.e. odorants) interact chemically with the interactive material's surface, which results in changes of the material's resistance/conductance.

The chemocapacitors are usually composed of a substrate with a polymeric layer coated between electrodes. When the odorants are present in the environment, they are absorbed in the polymeric, which results in measurable changes of the capacitance.

The chemotransistor sensors use conductive materials (e.g. conducting polymers) as vapor-interactive layers. Upon presence of the analyte, a measurable shift in gate voltage occurs. The chemoresistors, chemocapacitors and chemotransistors are described in greater detail in other chapters of this book.

The gravimetric sensors, as the name implies, are devices sensitive to mass-changes occurring upon sorption of the odorant in the layer(s) of vapor-interactive material coated on the device's substrate. The substrate is made of a piezoelectric material such as quartz, lithium niobate or langasite and is equipped with electrodes that convert electrical energy to mechanical energy, i.e. induce an acoustic wave. Two types of the gravimetric sensors of a widespread interest are Quartz Crystal Microbalance (QCM), and Surface Acoustic Wave (SAW) sensors.

In the QCMs, the substrate plate is equipped with metallic electrodes attached to both sides of the plate. The suitable voltage applied to the electrodes induces bulk transverse waves that travel perpendicular to the substrate's surface—so called thickness shear mode (Nakamoto & Moriizumi, 1990). In given conditions, the QCM resonates with a given resonant frequency (usually 5, 10, or 20 MHz). Application of the mass to the device's surface results in a negative shift of the resonant frequency—a measurable change of the device's properties (Sauerbrey, 1959).

A more complex gravimetric sensor is the surface acoustic wave device. The classic, planar SAW sensors are made of piezoelectric substrate plate with Interdigital Transducer electrodes (IDT) fabricated on its surface—a transmitter and receiver IDTs on opposite sides of the substrate (see Figure 2b, top). Radio Frequency (RF) voltage applied to the transmitter IDT generates a Rayleigh surface wave in the substrate. The Rayleigh wave is composed of the longitudinal and vertical shear components and travels parallel to the substrate surface until it reaches the receiver IDT. On its way, the Rayleigh wave interacts with the coating in contact with the SAW delay line (Wohltjen, 1984).

Both QCM and SAW sensors seem to be the best suited for the application in the odor sensing systems due to their arguably best mimicking of the olfactory receptors. This comes from a fact that there is nearly countless variety of vapor-interactive materials that can be deposited on the devices and made use of in the detection and/or quantification of the odors (Grate, 2000). The much broader flexibility in forming the vapor-interactive layers is an advantageous feature that distinguishes the gravimetric sensors from other technological platforms, commonly applied in the artificial olfaction systems. Other important advantages include operation at the room temperature and potentially high sensitivity. This latter feature, however, might be spoiled by a negative impact of humidity, seen quite well when the devices are coated with materials highly suitable for odor sensing (e.g. gas-chromatography stationary phases with high affinity to organic vapors). Another disadvantageous feature of the gravimetric odor-sensors might be the necessity to equip them with interface electronics. This requirement combined with the fact that the typical QCM or SAW sensors seem rather bulky might mean that the whole sensing system would be of an undesirably large size—a feature hard to accept in modern odor-sensing systems, striving for portability. The call for size-reduction of the whole system is being answered in a research on ways to miniaturize its components including research and development of novel, miniaturized odor-sensing platforms.

SPHERICAL SAW DEVICES AS ODOR SENSORS

Ball-SAW Devices vs. Planar SAW Devices

In the field of acoustic wave-based sensors, miniaturization of the sensing devices follows usually the way of size-reduction and fine-tuning of the already existing platforms. The development process can be observed in the usually used, planar SAW devices. A little more than a decade ago, size of a typical planar SAW sensor was in a range of several centimeters. Size of the recent "miniaturized" planar SAW sensors could be reduced below one centimeter (Barie, et al., 2006). As impressive as it might seem, the quest for miniaturization of the planar SAW sensors might be seriously limited by the geometrical constraints (length of the SAW delay line). As indicated in the Figure 2b, the planar SAW sensors operate on the principle of the acoustic wave travelling between a pair of Interdigital Transducer electrodes (IDT). The area between the IDTs is coated with the chemically-interactive material capable of selective, revers-

ible sorption of the airborne molecules. In most such cases, the SAW velocity can be considered to be a linear function of the mass sorbed by the interactive coating per unit area—a mass loading effect (Wohltjen, 1984). Actual distance between the IDTs—length of the SAW propagation path – is an important factor affecting S/N ratio of the designed SAW vapor/gas-sensor (Kobari, et al., 2009). In an ideal situation, extending the length of the SAW propagation path should therefore translate into higher sensitivity of the SAW sensor. The miniaturization requirement might mean a rather non-desired compromise between the size and sensitivity of the planar SAW sensor.

Given the size-sensitivity constraint, further improvement of the SAW sensor technology requires a completely novel approach to design of the sensing device. One of such novel approaches assumes that the SAW would propagate along a circular path realized on a piezoelectric sphere and called a ball-SAW device (Yamanaka, et al., 2000, 2006; Nakaso, et al., 2002).

Schematic depiction of the ball-SAW sensor is given in Figures 3 (a)-(c). As shown in Figure 3 (a), the ball-SAW device is composed of a single piezoelectric substrate molded into a sphere, and equipped with a single IDT serving as both SAW-generating and detecting transducer. The IDT is carefully designed and deposited in such a spot that the generated SAW is collimated and can travel in multiple trips (roundtrips) around the device's equator (Yamanaka, et al., 2006). Similar to other acoustic wave-based odor sensors, the odor-sensing function of the ball-SAW device is activated by coating a sensitive film on the SAW propagation path – depicted schematically in Figure 3 (b). Amplitude of the SAW travelling around the ball-SAW sensor's surface decreases due to attenuation. Maximum number of round trips for obtaining measurable signal of the ball-SAW device (3.3 mm diameter, 150MHz) is typically 100, which corresponds to the SAW propagation path of 1m. Figure 3 (c) shows a photographic image of the actual ball-SAW devices.

Figure 3. Schematic depiction of the spherical SAW (ball-SAW) sensor: (a) general view and depiction of the waveform at the nth roundtrip of SAW,(b) principle of operation, and (c) photograph of the ball-SAW devices

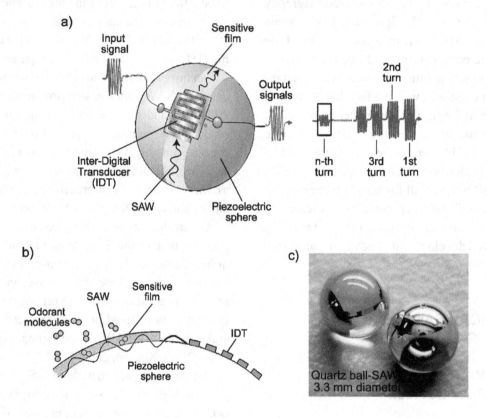

Assuming the ball-SAW device is coated with the isotropic sensitive film, the sensor's response mechanism is similar to that of the planar devices, i.e. delayed propagation of the SAW due to sorption of the vapor/gas molecules (mass loading). Since the ball-SAW sensor is equipped with an appropriately designed and deposited IDT, the SAW roundtrip time can be precisely measured (Yamanaka, et al., 2000). The typical measurable output of the ball-SAW sensor is the change of delay-time, expressed often as phase shift. In addition, when coated with the materials prone to a viscoelastic effects, one might also observe changes in the SAW amplitude.

Fabrication of the ball-SAW sensor begins with a spherical substrate. The piezoelectric materials used typically for the ball-SAW devices are mostly quartz and langasite. The spherical shape is obtained by molding in the grinder. To date, typical diameters of the resulting substrates were 10, 3.3, and 1 mm. The IDT is then deposited by photolithography. It has to be stressed once again that design and placement of the IDT is of capital importance for the proper operation of the ball-SAW sensor—the diffraction—and reflection-lossless propagation of the SAW (collimated SAW). The final stage of the ball-SAW sensor fabrication process is deposition of a vapor/gas sensitive coating. Depending on the purpose and target analyte, there is a variety of methods used for coating the vapor/gas-interactive films. The advantage of the ball-SAW over the planar SAW sensor can be mostly appreciated when the device is coated with a very thin sensitive film. In such a situation, the attenuation loss is relatively small and the ultramultiple roundtrips of SAW effectively amplify sensitivity of the ball-SAW sensor. Additionally, the thin coating might allow for a fast response of ball-SAW sensor. For this reasons, appropriate coating of the sensing film is of a paramount importance to the quality of the resulting ball-SAW sensors. The methods used for coating the sensitive films over the ball-SAW sensors' surface are summarized in the subsequent section.

Deposition of Gas/Vapor Sensing Films onto Ball-SAW Sensors

Deposition of a chemically interactive film is a final step in fabrication of the ball-SAW sensor. The methods used to date for formation of the sensitive films can be divided into methods for deposition of all-inorganic, metallic films and methods for deposition of organic and organic-inorganic films.

From the chronological standpoint, the first method used for fabrication of gas-sensitive film was thermal evaporation of the metallic Pd or PdNi films. The method resulted in a uniformly deposited film with a thickness of 20 nm or 40 nm (Yamanaka, et al., 2009). Compared to the other methods to be introduced in course of this paragraph, the thermal evaporation method is the

only one dealing with deposition of all-inorganic, metallic films. The sensors coated with the Pd-containing films were used for detection of hydrogen (Yamanaka, et al., 2006, 2009). The method was also used for preparation of the ball-SAW substrate for self-assembling techniques described later. In that case, the Au/Cr films were deposited on the ball-SAW surface.

Among the methods used for deposition of the organic and organic-inorganic films, one can distinguish direct deposition of organic films using an ultrasonic atomizer, direct deposition of organic films using an electrospray, formation of the hybrid organic films using self-assembling techniques, and formation of the hybrid organic-inorganic films using self-assembling techniques. Schematic representation of the methods is depicted in Figures 4(a)-(c).

Ultrasonic atomizer is the first of the direct methods for coating the all-organic films onto acoustic wave-based sensors (Wyszynski, et al., 2007). The method requires an apparatus—ultrasonic atomizer—composed of properly set-up deposition chamber, flow-channels and atomization stage. The ball-SAW substrate is put in the deposition chamber. The sensing material is dissolved in organic solvent (i.e. chloroform) and put in the atomization stage. When irradiated with

Figure 4. Schematic comparison of the main methods for fabrication of the sensing films, green color signifies outer, the most active layer of the sensing films: (a) direct deposition, (b) basic self-assembling of the all-organic films, and (c) refined self-assembling of the organic-inorganic films containing nano-composites (with inorganicAu nanoparticles as a core)

a)
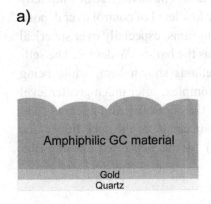

b)
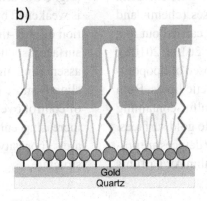

c)
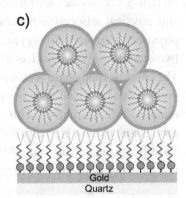

the ultrasonic wave, the solution is atomized into fine particles that are carried through the flow-channels into the deposition chamber.

The ultrasonic atomizer is a highly-efficient but quite basic method, resulting in rather thick films. For that reason it is used generally for larger sensors (e.g. QCMs). More effective for the ball-SAW sensor fabrication is another direct deposition method—the electrospray (Sekine, et al., 2008; Wyszynski, et al., 2010). The method is a refinement of the most basic airbrush spray method with the essential modification consisting in charging the sprayed droplets/particles by using the high voltage AC/DC. Charging allows for creation of a very well defined and precise "beam" of very fine droplets. Deposition using electrospray allows for much better control of the deposited material in terms of placement and thickness. Both direct-deposition methods are schematically depicted in Figure 4(a). Depending on the method, the film thickness, its uniformity, and specific surface area might vary.

Despite the greater scope of control, the electrospray method might still be ineffective when used for coating of very small substrates such as the ball-SAW devices. One of the main requirements for the ball-SAW device's coating method is that it results in a uniformly thin sensing film, deposited in a specifically designed spot of the device, i.e. on a SAW propagation path. Such level of control can be offered by a group of methods commonly called the self-assembling. The self-assembling methods used for formation of the sensing films on ball-SAW devices are based on the chemical and physical adsorption processes (chemi- and physisorption, respectively) and carried out in a two-step flow (Wyszynski, et al., 2010a, 2010b). The chemisorbed phase is composed of lipopolymers, alone or mixed with synthetic lipids. Both materials are terminated with sulfur-containing groups that exhibit high affinity to gold surfaces. To utilize the effect, the ball-SAW devices are pre-fabricated by deposition of very thin Au/Cr films

on the SAW propagation path (formed by thermal evaporation). Formation of the chemisorbed film is carried out by immersion of the pre-fabricated ball-SAW devices in the ethanolic solution of appropriate material. The ball-SAW devices with the chemisorbed material(s) are then immersed in ethanolic solution of the physisorbing phase composed either of lipopolymers or amphiphilic GC materials. General view of the basic self-assembling method is shown in Figure 4(b).

A refinement of the general self-assembling method has been devised to allow for formation of the hybrid, organic-inorganic films containing lipopolymer-Au nanocomposites (Wyszynski, et al., 2010). The method consists of 4 steps. Firstly, the lipopolymeric Self-Assembled Monolayers (SAM) are formed on the inorganic part—the Au nanoparticles (lipopolymer-Au nanoparticles, step 1). The lipopolymeric SAM is formed onto the ball-SAW devices (step 2) and the nanocomposites are precipitated onto the ball-SAW device with SAM (step 3). Finally, the amphiphilic GC materials are physisorbed onto the SAM-nanocomposite complex (step 4). Schematic depiction of the refined self-assembling method is shown in Figure 4(c).

Compared to the direct coating methods shown in Figure 4(a), the self-assembling methods in Figures 4(b) and (c) differ rather significantly in both application and the resulting sensing-film. The two direct methods presented in this chapter—ultrasonic atomizer and electrospray—are simple and convenient methods used commonly for coating of sensors with relatively large surfaces (e.g. QCM sensors). The advantage of simplicity is weakened by low level of control over deposition of very-thin films, especially over spherical surfaces, such as the ball-SAW device. The self-assembling methods shown here, while being slightly more complex, offer much greater level of control over the deposited film thickness and increasing enhancement of the specific surface area (porosity) of the deposited sensing-film structure.

Ball-SAW Odor Sensors Fabricated Using Various Techniques

The ball-SAW sensors fabricated using the techniques described above have been validated in numerous experiments of gas/vapor sensing. Our main focus in this chapter is on ball-SAW odor sensors intended to be used in the artificial olfaction applications. Such sensors need to have broad specificities, i.e. respond to group of gas/vapors rather than a one target. The first actual realization of the ball-SAW sensors were the devices with metallic Pd or NiPd alloy films, devised for specific detection of hydrogen gas (Yamanaka, et al., 2004). Specificity of that sensor was an important feature intended for the hydrogen sensing but would be a hindrance when used in the artificial olfaction. Sensing materials offering the postulated broad specificity are in most cases organic materials—polymers, lipids, lipopolymers, etc. In fact, virtually all of the ball-SAW odor sensors have been coated with one or a combination of the organic materials.

The ball-SAW odor sensors described in this chapter were based on 3.3mm quartz balls (operating frequency: 150 MHz). Each device was equipped with a single Au/Cr IDT fabricated on the ball's z-axis by photolithographic process. The IDT had ten pairs of electrodes, with a period of 21.38μm and an aperture of 265.59μm. Time required for a roundtrip was 3.20μs. The devices used for self-assembling fabrication methods were equipped with thin Au/Cr film deposited on the SAW propagation path. The gold film was required for covalent coupling of the self-assembled lipopolymer/lipid materials.

The first actual ball-SAW odor sensors were coated using ultrasonic atomizer method, with four Gas Chromatography (GC) stationary phase materials: Siponate DS-10, Polyethylene glycol, Apiezon-L and Tricresyl phosphate (Nakamoto, et al., 2008). Use of the GC materials as coatings for odor sensors is highly recommended due to their good sorption properties and reversibility

of responses. The sensitive films deposited using the ultrasonic atomizer were rather thick and caused a significant attenuation of the SAW. For that reason, the sensor responses could be measured at rather low 4th and 5th roundtrips of SAW. Still, the fabricated ball-SAW sensor-array was successfully used for discrimination of various artificial flavors. The study proved viability of applying the organic films as sensitive coatings in ball-SAW odor sensors.

Further investigation of ball-SAW odor sensors with organic coating was made upon application of another coating method—the electrospray. The method was first used for coating a potentially highly-sensitive GC material—Siponate DS-10 (Sekine, et al., 2008). Comparing to the ultrasonic atomizer, the electrospray method offers much more control over the deposited film's thickness—a feature paramount to the ball-SAW sensor's quality and sensitivity. The Siponate DS-10 ball-SAW sensors coated using the method exhibited dramatically larger number of the available SAW roundtrips allowing for the measurements to be performed at 40-50 rounds of SAW. This quality improvement translated directly into the enhancement of sensitivity as the electrospray-coated ball-SAW sensors could detect n-butanol vapors at concentrations levels of parts per billion (ppb) in dry-air.

Successful application of the electrospray method paved the way to the subsequent study in which the ball-SAW sensors were coated with lipopolymers (Wyszynski, et al., 2010). The lipopolymers are relatively novel group of materials in which the polymeric and lipidic moieties are covalently linked in one macromolecule (Marsh, et al., 2003). The resulting structure has hybrid lipidic-polymeric properties that can be utilized for formation of thin membranes—the feature extremely interesting for the odor sensing applications.

Electrospray-coated lipopolymer films were rather thin and of a relatively good quality—indicated by a small attenuation of SAW and a large number of the available SAW roundtrips. Unfortunately, the responses of electrospray-coated lipopolymeric ball-SAW sensors were not impressive. The lower-than-expected responses prompted application of another fabrication method—the basic self-assembling method (Wyszynski, et al., 2010a).

As indicated previously, in the self-assembling methods, the ball-SAW devices need to be equipped with thin metallic Au/Cr films to facilitate chemisorption of the lipopolymers. The chemisorbed phase was composed of 1,2-distearoyl-sn-glycero-3-phosphoethanolamine-N-[PDP (polyethylene glycol) 2000] (PDP-LD2K). Once the chemisorbed layer was deposited, a physisorption stage was performed. The physisorbed phase was composed of 4 ether-terminated lipopolymers—1,2-distearoyl-sn-glycero-3-phosphoethanolamine-N-[methoxy (polyethylene glycol)] with four different lengths of the polyethylene glycol tether—1000, 2000, 3000, and 5000 Da (LD1K, LD2K, LD3K and LD5K, respectively).

Figure 5(a) shows comparison of the SAW attenuation curves obtained for the ball-SAW sensors coated with lipopolymers using ultrasonic atomizer and self-assembling techniques. As can be seen, the number of available roundtrips of SAW was very low in case of atomizer-coated sensor (11 rounds) while there were more than 60 available SAW roundtrips in the ball-SAW sensor fabricated by self-assembling. Since the number of available SAW roundtrips can be considered a good indication of the ball-SAW sensor quality, it can be concluded that the ball-SAW sensor fabricated using the self-assembling technique was way superior to that coated using the atomizer. Despite only slightly better propagation of the SAW as compared to the electrospray-coated ball-SAW sensors, the sensors with self-assembled lipopolymers were much more sensitive to vapors of various odorants. Quality of the ball-SAW sensors with lipopolymers coated using the electrospray method was comparable to that of the sensors fabricated by self-assembling methods.

Despite that fact, the sensors with self-assembled lipopolymeric films were much more sensitive to odorant-vapors than their electrospray-coated counterparts. The difference in recorded sensitivity occurred despite very similar amounts of the coated sensing material and was attributed to higher porosity obtained as a result of self-assembling.

The significant enhancement of sensitivity was an encouragement for further studies of the self-assembling method, this time employing the amphiphilic GC material—Siponate DS-10 (Wyszynski, et al., 2009, 2010b). The material was physisorbed over a specially prepared, chemisorbed phase composed of the mixed film of lipid with lipopolymer at a molar ratio of 1:1000 (Sup#3). The carefully executed deposition of the materials resulted in the ball-SAW sensors of extremely high quality. Figure 5(b), consecutive stages of fabrication—chemisorption of the Sup#3 and physisorption of the Siponate DS-10. Clearly, the consecutive steps of fabrication did not cause significant attenuation of the SAW. The resulting ball-SAW sensor had around 60 available roundtrips of SAW and allowed for the optimum measurement performed at as high as 50th roundtrip.

In order to compare the sensing properties of the ball-SAW sensors fabricated using the atomizer, electrospray and self-assembling techniques (Siponate DS-10 coating), sensors with relatively the same amounts of coating were experimentally exposed to vapors of n-butanol at various concentrations in the humidified air. The measurements were performed at the optimum roundtrip of SAW, i.e. the one producing the highest response at the given conditions (Sekine, et al., 2008). The obtained results are summarized in form of the sensitivity curves in Figure 6. Apparently, the ball-SAW sensor with self-assembled film was much more sensitive than the sensors fabricated using the direct coating techniques.

An important problem facing researchers working on the sensors coated with organic films is influence of the humidity. In most of sensors,

Figure 5. Comparison of the ball-SAW's attenuation curves obtained from impulse responses of: (a) ball-SAW sensors coated with lipopolymers using two different techniques, and (b) the ball-SAW odor sensors at each stage of fabrication with lipid-derivatives (Sup#3) and amphiphilic GC material (DS-10)

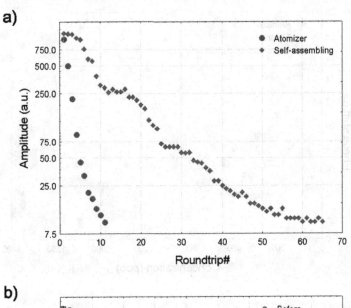

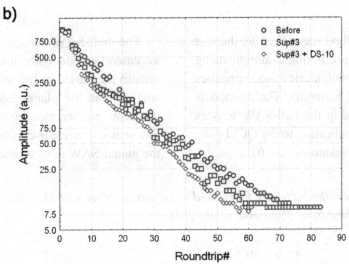

especially ones coated with polar materials such as Siponate DS-10, the sensitivity is suppressed by the increasing level of humidity. The effect was seen profoundly in case of the sensors coated using the direct techniques (atomizer, electrospray). The dramatically enhanced sensitivity of the sensors fabricated using the self-assembling method implied potential for overcoming the negative effect of the humidity. Figure 7 shows sensitivity curves of n-butanol obtained upon

results of experiments performed with the self-assembled Siponate DS-10 ball-SAW sensor at various humidity levels. Although the humidity influence was apparent, the fabricated ball-SAW sensors seemed to cope with it rather graciously, allowing them to respond to a very low concentration of the analyte at an elevated humidity. The result clearly confirms validity of the self-assembling fabrication method applied for the ball-SAW odor sensors.

Figure 6. Sensitivity to n-butanol for three Siponate DS-10 ball-SAW sensors fabricated using atomizer, electrospray, and chemi-/physisorption technique (measurements at 10th, 50th, and 50th roundtrip, respectively, RH ~ 35%)

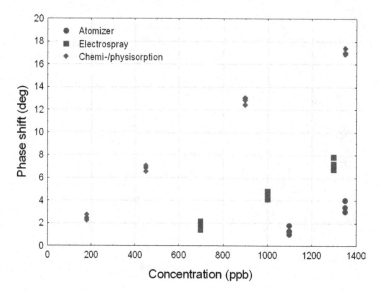

A fabrication method mentioned as the last was the refined self-assembling technique using the lipopolymers, lipopolymeric nanocomposites and amphiphilic GC materials. The method is currently investigated in the ball-SAW sensors after its successful application to the QCM platform (Wyszynski & Nakamoto, 2010).

The ball-SAW sensors technology is still an emerging one with intended goals of high sensitivity provided by sensing devices much smaller than the planar SAW sensors. Despite numerous publications regarding the planar SAW gas-sensors, a clear-cut comparison between the planar SAW devices and the ball-SAW odor

Figure 7. Sensitivities of the ball-SAW fabricated by self-assembling with DS-10 to n-butanol at various humidity levels (adapted from Wyszynski, et al., 2010b)

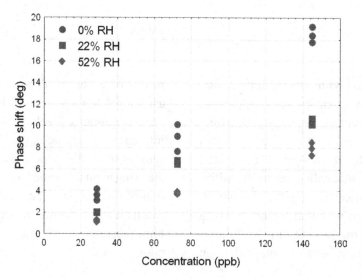

sensors presented herein is quite difficult at the current stage. On one hand, the vast majority of the planar SAWs with organic sensing-films are intended to be specific vapor/gas-sensors. A good example would be the sensors for explosives and chemical warfare agents (Nimal, et al., 2009). On the other hand, the planar sensors with reported sensitivity to similar analytes (e.g. alcohols) are characterized in greatly different circumstances, such as analyte concentrations or measurement conditions (Ippolito, et al., 2006; Chevallier, et al., 2011). Further progress in development of the ball-SAW vapor/gas-sensors should provide more opportunities for comparison between these two closely related technologies.

Application of the Ball-SAW Odor Sensors

The ball-SAW odor sensors are being developed for intended use in a variety of odor/aroma sensing tasks. One of the potential applications of the sensors could be detection and discrimination between various aromas. The section herein describes a pilot study performed using the ball-SAW odor sensors aimed at detecting and discriminating between vapors from beverages.

The ball-SAW sensor array used in the study was composed of 3 ball-SAW odor sensors fabricated by means of physisorption of the amphiphilic GC materials—Siponate DS-10, Triton X-305, and TWEEN 80—over chemisorbed lipid-lipopolymer layer (Sup#3), while 1 ball-SAW sensor was made by self-assembling the lipopolymers, lipopolymeric nanocomposites (nano-Au) and Siponate DS-10. The ball-SAWs were placed in a cylindrical flow-cell with matching circuits. The sensors were put in the cell on a specially designed electrical contacts and immobilized using screws. The flow was induced by an air pump and was kept at the level of 0.6 L/min. A generator was used to supply 150 MHz RF burst signal (duration – 2.5µs) to the Ball-SAWs to induce acoustic wave travelling a fixed number of roundtrips on the device's surface. The output signal was then digitized and analyzed in terms of phase shift and amplitude change (number of averaging – 250) (Wyszynski, et al., 2010b).

The samples were 2 commercially available beverages and a mineral water. The sensors were exposed to dynamic headspace of the samples at two concentrations. The "low" concentration was adjusted to be equivalent of the vapor concentration resulting from evaporating 0.1mL of a beverage in a 40 L box. The "high" concentration was chosen to be 10 times higher than the "low" one. In layman terms, the human nose could not detect the "low" concentration while the "high" one was close to the detection threshold level. The sensor array was exposed to each concentration of the samples 3 times.

The obtained sensor responses formed a 4 x 18 matrix. The matrix was preprocessed by auto-scaling and fed to a Principal Component Analysis (PCA) implemented in the MATLAB software. Figure 8 shows a PCA scattering diagram generated upon the experimental results. As can be seen, the data were clustered into 6 separate groups, each referring to a certain concentration of the sample. The samples were neatly separated even at the "low" concentration and distance between the respective clusters was significant.

As argued in the previous sections, advantage of using the ball-SAW odor sensors lies in their expected high sensitivity toward odorants. As the ball-SAW sensors are developed to be used in the highly sensitive odor-sensing systems, the presented result is a very good illustration of the potential practical application of the ball-SAW-based odor sensing system.

PERSPECTIVES OF THE RESEARCH ON BALL-SAW ODOR SENSORS

Results of the experimental evaluation of the ball-SAW odor sensors described in this chapter show an enormous potential for the growth of this

Figure 8. PCA scattering diagram for vapors of two beverages and water

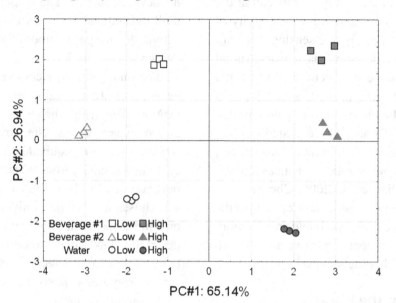

sensing platform. The perspectives of the research on ball-SAW odor sensors can be generally divided into two parts—related to the sensing film fabrication and related to the development of the ball-SAW sensor-based sensing system.

In an already realized project, it was possible to overcome an ever-present negative influence of humidity and to detect vapors of alcohol at the concentration as low as ca. 30 ppb. To put this into perspective, the human detection threshold for the same chemical is reported to be in the range of 20 – 200 ppb. This exciting result was obtained for the sensors coated using the self-assembling technique with lipopolymer/lipid and amphiphilic GC material. Additional enhancement of the sensitivity is expected in the ongoing project where the ball-SAW odor sensors are fabricated using the refined self-assembling, using the lipopolymers, lipopolymeric nanocomposites and amphiphilic GC materials. Such complex sensing structure has been shown to be extremely sensitive and very robust against influence of humidity. The ball-SAW sensors coated with this technique are

expected to be highly sensitive, robust, and reliable in a broad range of the operating conditions.

Exploration of other novel sensing materials and coating techniques constitutes the foremost direction in the research on the ball-SAW odor sensors. Another is the research on the overall sensing system employing the ball-SAW odor sensors as the detecting/sensing stage. The system being currently developed envisions a compact, small-size (portable) sensing unit equipped with an array of ball-SAW odor sensors. Depending on the application, the sensor module would be easily replaced to fulfill requirements posed by the actual sensing problem. Such versatile system would be welcomed as a universal tool to be used in various industries.

The presented two areas of development discussed above are not the only ones in which the ball-SAW sensor technology is capable of growth. In fact, since the ball-SAWs are the novel and emerging technology, there seem to be enormous potential and very broad perspectives limited barely by the researchers' imagination.

CONCLUSION

The ball-SAW sensors are a relatively novel and fresh branch of the acoustic wave-based sensing technology. Since the first reports of the hydrogen-gas ball-SAW sensors, one could see a rapid development directed mostly into a field of odor sensing. This direction determined development of the fabrication methods—techniques for depositing thin organic films aimed at realization of the non-specific ball-SAW sensors.

The fabrication methods to be used in the ball-SAW sensors have to be constrained by the strict requirements of the film's thickness and integrity. Following the principles, a number of techniques have been studied, each offering gradual improvements of the resulting ball-SAW sensors' quality and sensitivity toward odorants. To date, the best results have been obtained when the ball-SAW devices were coated using the self-assembling technique, employing chemisorptions of mixed synthetic-lipids with lipopolymers, and physisoprtion of amphipihilic GC materials. The ball-SAW odor sensors fabricated this way were characterized by limit of detection challenging the values of the human detection threshold.

Current developments—application of the novel hybrid materials coated by means of self-assembling using the lipopolymers, lipopolymeric nanocomposites, and amphiphilic GC materials—are expected to offer further enhancement of the ball-SAW sensors' performance. Results indicate high usefulness of the novel ball-SAW sensors for the practical tasks—such as detection of the extremely small amounts of beverages, in packaging process.

Given the rapid emergence of the ball-SAW sensor technology and the clear perspectives of its development, one might assert that the ball-SAW sensors might be one of the most significant sensing technologies of the future.

REFERENCES

Barié, N., Bücking, M., & Rapp, M. (2006). A novel electronic nose based on miniaturized SAW sensor arrays coupled with SPME enhanced headspace-analysis and its use for rapid determination of volatile organic compounds in food quality monitoring. *Sensors and Actuators. B, Chemical, 114*(1), 482–488. doi:10.1016/j.snb.2005.06.051

Buck, L., & Axel, R. (1991). A novel multigene family may encode odorant receptors: a molecular basis for odor recognition. *Cell, 65*(1), 175–187. doi:10.1016/0092-8674(91)90418-X

Chevallier, E., Scorsone, E., & Bergonzo, P. (2011). New sensitive coating based on modified diamond nanoparticles for chemical SAW sensors. *Sensors and Actuators. B, Chemical, 154*(2), 238–244. doi:10.1016/j.snb.2010.01.042

Firestein, S. (2001). How the olfactory system makes sense of scents. *Nature, 413*, 211–218. doi:10.1038/35093026

Grate, J. W. (2000). Acoustic wave microsensor arrays for vapor sensing. *Chemical Reviews, 100*(7), 2627–2648. doi:10.1021/cr980094j

Grate, J. W., Martin, S. J., & White, R. M. (1993). Acoustic wave microsensors. *Analytical Chemistry, 65*(22), 940A–948A.

Ippolito, S. J., Ponzoni, A., Kalantar-Zadeh, K., Wlodarski, W., Comini, E., Faglia, G., & Sberveglieri, G. (2006). Layered WO3/ZnO/36° LiTaO3 SAW gas sensor sensitive towards ethanol vapour and humidity. *Sensors and Actuators. B, Chemical, 117*(2), 442–450. doi:10.1016/j.snb.2005.12.050

Kobari, K., Yamamoto, Y., Sakuma, M., Akao, S., & Yamanaka, K. (2009). Fabrication of thin sensitive film of ball surface acoustic wave sensor by off-axis spin-coating method. *Japanese Journal of Applied Physics, 48*(7), 07GG13-1 – 07GG13-6.

Marsh, D., Bartucci, R., & Sportelli, L. (2003). Lipid membranes with grafted polymers: physicochemical aspects. *Biochimica et Biophysica Acta, 1615*(1-2), 33–59. doi:10.1016/S0005-2736(03)00197-4

Munro, J. C., & Frank, C. W. (2004). Adsorption of lipid-functionalized poly(ethylene glycol) to gold surfaces as a cushion for polymer-supported lipid bilayers. *Langmuir, 20*(8), 3339–3349. doi:10.1021/la036062v

Nagle, H. T., Gutierrez-Osuna, R., & Schiffman, S. S. (1998). The how and why of electronic noses. *IEEE Spectrum, 35*(9), 22–31. doi:10.1109/6.715180

Nakamoto, T., Aoki, K., Ogi, T., Akao, S., & Nakaso, N. (2008). Odor sensing system using ball SAW devices. *Sensors and Actuators. B, Chemical, 130*(1), 386–390. doi:10.1016/j.snb.2007.09.022

Nakamoto, T., & Moriizumi, T. (1990). A theory of a quartz crystal microbalance based upon a mason equivalent circuit. *Japanese Journal of Applied Physics, 29*(5), 963–969. doi:10.1143/JJAP.29.963

Nakamoto, T., Ustumi, S., Yamashita, N., Moriizumi, T., & Sonoda, Y. (1994). Active gas/odor sensing system using automatically controlled gas blender and numerical optimization technique. *Sensors and Actuators. B, Chemical, 20*(2-3), 131–137. doi:10.1016/0925-4005(93)01193-8

Nakaso, N., Tsukahara, Y., Ishikawa, S., & Yamanaka, K. (2002). Diffraction-free propagation of collimated SAW around a quartz ball. In *Proceedings of the 2002 IEEE Ultrasonic Symposium,* (pp. 47–52). IEEE Press.

Nanto, H., & Stetter, J. R. (2003). Introduction to chemosensors. In Pearce, T. C. (Eds.), *Handbook of Machine Olfaction* (pp. 79–104). New York, NY: Wiley-VCH.

Nimal, A. T., Mittal, U., Singh, M., Khaneja, M., Kannan, G. K., & Kapoor, J. C. (2009). Development of handheld SAW vapor sensors for explosives and CW agents. *Sensors and Actuators. B, Chemical, 135*(2), 399–410. doi:10.1016/j.snb.2008.08.040

Pearce, T. C. (1997). Computational parallels between the biological olfactory pathway and its analogue 'the electronic nose': Part I – Biological olfaction. *BioSystems, 41*(2), 43–67. doi:10.1016/S0303-2647(96)01661-9

Persaud, K., & Dodd, G. (1982). Analysis of discrimination mechanisms in the mammalian olfactory system using a model nose. *Nature, 299*, 352–355. doi:10.1038/299352a0

Sauerbrey, G. (1959). Verwendung von schwingquarzen zur wägung dünner schichten und zur mikrowägung. *Zeitschrift fur Physik, 155*(2), 206–222. doi:10.1007/BF01337937

Sekine, M., Wyszynski, B., Nakamoto, T., Nakaso, N., & Noguchi, K. (2008). Sensitivity improvement of the odor sensors using Ball SAW device. *IEEJ Transactions on Sensors and Micromachines, 128-E*(12), 487–492. doi:10.1541/ieejsmas.128.487

Steinhart, H., Stephan, A., & Bücking, M. (2000). Advances in flavor research. *Journal of High Resolution Chromatography, 23*(7-8), 489–496. doi:10.1002/1521-4168(20000801)23:7/8<489::AID-JHRC489>3.0.CO;2-O

Wohltjen, H. (1984). Mechanism of operation and design considerations for surface acoustic wave device vapor sensors. *Sensors and Actuators. B, Chemical, 5*(4), 307–325. doi:10.1016/0250-6874(84)85014-3

Wyszynski, B., Gutierrez-Galvez, A., & Nakamoto, T. (2007). Improvement of ultrasonic atomizer method for deposition of gas-sensing film on QCM. *Sensors and Actuators. B, Chemical, 127*(1), 253–259. doi:10.1016/j.snb.2007.07.052

Wyszynski, B., & Nakamoto, T. (2010). Humidity-robust and highly-sensitive QCM odor sensors with amphiphilic GC-materials physisorbed over-lipopolymer-protected nano-Au. In *Proceedings of the 27th Sensor Symposium*, (pp. 375-378). IEEE.

Wyszynski, B., Nakamoto, T., Akao, S., & Nakaso, N. (2010b). Odor sensing system using ball SAW devices functionalized with self-assembled lipid-derivatives and GC materials. In *Proceedings of the 9th IEEE Conference on Sensors*, (pp. 342-345). IEEE Press.

Wyszynski, B., Sekine, M., Nakamoto, T., Nakaso, N., & Noguchi, K. (2010a). Spherical ball-SAW devices functionalized with self-assembled lipo-polymers for odor-sensing. *Sensors and Actuators. B, Chemical*, *144*(1), 247–254. doi:10.1016/j.snb.2009.10.059

Wyszynski, B., Somboon, P., & Nakamoto, T. (2009). Self-assembled lipopolymers with physisorbed amphiphilic GC materials for QCM odor sensors. *IEEJ Transactions on Sensors and Micromachines*, *129*(9), 273–277. doi:10.1541/ieejsmas.129.273

Yamanaka, K., Cho, H., & Tsukuhara, Y. (2000). Precise velocity measurement of surface acoustic waves on bearing ball. *Applied Physics Letters*, *76*(19), 2797–2799. doi:10.1063/1.126481

Yamanaka, K., Ishikawa, S., Nakaso, N., Takeda, N., Mihara, T., & Tsukuhara, Y. (2004). Ball SAW device for hydrogen gas sensor. In *Proceedings of the 2003 IEEE Ultrasonic Symposium*, (pp. 299-302). IEEE Press.

Yamanaka, K., Ishikawa, S., Nakaso, N., Takeda, N., Sim, D. Y., & Mihara, T. (2006). Ultramultiple roundtrips of surface acoustic wave on sphere realizing innovation of gas sensors. *IEEE Transactions on UFFC*, *53*(4), 793–801.

ADDITIONAL READING

Auld, B. A. (1990). *Acoustic fields and waves in solids*. Malabar, FL: Robert E. Krieger Publishing Company.

Ballantine, D. S., White, R. M., Martin, S. J., Ricco, A. J., Zellers, E. T., Frye, G. C., & Wohltjen, H. (1996). *Acoustic wave sensors: Theory, design, and physico-chemical applications*. London, UK: Academic Press.

Devos, M., Patte, K. F., Roualt, J., Laffort, P., & Van Gemert, L. S. (1990). *Standardized human olfactory thresholds*. London, UK: Oxford University Press.

Ullman, A. (1996). Formation and structure of self-assembled monolayers. *Chemical Reviews*, *96*(4), 1533–1554. doi:10.1021/cr9502357

ENDNOTES

[1] Reprinted from Wohltjen, H. (1984). Mechanism of operation and design considerations for surface acoustic wave device vapor sensors. *Sensors and actuators b*, *5*(4), 307-325. With permission from Elsevier.

Chapter 11

Real Time Monitoring Mass Spectrometry:
Walkthrough Portal to Detect Improvised Explosive Devices

Yasuaki Takada
Hitachi, Ltd., Japan

Masuyuki Sugiyama
Hitachi, Ltd., Japan

Yuichiro Hashimoto
Hitachi, Ltd., Japan

Masuyoshi Yamada
Hitachi, Ltd., Japan

Hisashi Nagano
Hitachi, Ltd., Japan

Minoru Sakairi
Hitachi, Ltd., Japan

ABSTRACT

Monitoring or detection of illicit chemicals has become one of the most important issues worldwide due to the spreading global use of explosives and illicit drugs. To improve security, the authors have started developing a real time monitoring technology based on mass spectrometry. In this technology, a sample gas is directly introduced into an ion source without any pre-treatments of the sample gas, and ions produced by the ion source are analyzed by a mass spectrometer. Various organic compounds can be detected by analyzing the mass number of the observed ions. The real time monitoring technology has been applied to monitor environmental pollutants such as Polychlorinated Biphenyls (PCBs) and to detect explosives, chemical warfare agents, and illicit drugs. High-throughput detection of an improvised explosive has also been successfully demonstrated by the real time monitoring technology.

INTRODUCTION

Mass spectrometry is a well-known technique in an analytical chemistry field, which has high sensitivity and high selectivity. However, it is difficult to analyze mixtures and crude samples

for mass spectrometry due to several reasons; for example, mixtures cause complicated mass spectra, which are difficult to make interpretation of the mass spectra, and an existence of impurities in the crude sample decreases ionization efficiencies of sample molecules at an ion source of a mass

DOI: 10.4018/978-1-4666-2521-1.ch011

Copyright © 2013, IGI Global. Copying or distributing in print or electronic forms without written permission of IGI Global is prohibited.

spectrometer. To avoid these problems, several pre-treatment processes such as extraction, concentration and separation are adopted before the mass analysis. Figure 1(a) shows a typical mass analysis procedure in a chemical laboratory. Especially, a combination of a separation technique, such as gas chromatography and liquid chromatography, and mass spectrometry is so popular to obtain simple mass spectra and high sensitivity. The pre-treatment procedure in laboratory is time-consuming processes and needs several minutes or several hours in a typical analysis situation.

In the last two decades, the use of mass spectrometry has been strongly demanded for the screening or detection of hazardous materials such as environmental pollutants (Wise & Guerin, 1997, p. 26A), explosives, and illicit drugs at a contaminated site or a security checkpoint to reduce false alarms by using its high sensitivity and selectivity. To respond the social needs for mass spectrometry, we have started to develop a real time detection system by using mass spectrometry.

In our system, almost all the pre-treatment processes are omitted. In the monitoring or detection of a vaporized sample, the sample gas is directly introduced into an ion source of a mass spectrometer as shown in Figure 1(b). The mass analysis process that includes ionization of the gaseous sample molecules and mass analysis of the ionized molecules is fast, and the typical analyzing interval is 0.1 s/scan. Therefore, the change in concentration of chemicals included in the sample gas is continuously monitored by the mass spectrometer. The vapor detection procedure is useful to monitor or detect volatile compounds such as environmental pollutants, chemical warfare agents, improvised explosives, and inflammable liquids.

In the detection of fine particles attached onto an object to be checked, on the other hand, a vaporization step (heating process) is needed to obtain gaseous molecules as shown Figure 1(c). The vaporization step needs 10 s. The particle detection procedure is useful to detect non-volatile compounds such as military explosives and illicit drugs.

We name these methods shown in Figures 1(b) and (c) as a real time monitoring mass spectrometry. To develop the real time monitoring mass spectrometry, improvements in sensitivity, selectivity, and robustness are important technological issues.

Figure 1. Analysis procedures in mass spectrometry for (a) typical analysis at chemical laboratory, (b) real time monitoring mass spectrometry for vapor detection, and (c) real time monitoring mass spectrometry for particle detection

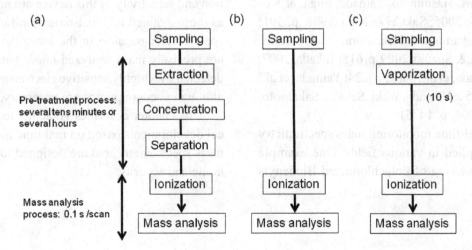

In our real time monitoring mass spectrometry, a sample gas is continuously introduced into an Atmospheric Pressure Chemical Ionization (APCI) ion source. The ions produced at atmospheric pressure are transferred to a mass analyzing region through a differential pumping region to obtain a mass spectrum. In a mass spectrum, the horizontal axis represents the *m/z* value (mass to charge ratio) of ions, while the vertical axis represents ion intensity. This information is very useful for identifying samples because specific ions of sample molecules can be observed. Our original APCI ion source can achieve long-term stable measurements by drastically reducing the contamination of the discharge electrode for ionization with organic compounds. In addition, a wire-type liner ion trap mass spectrometer (wire-LIT) was developed to improve sensitivity. A tandem mass spectrometry (mass spectrometry/mass spectrometry; MS/MS) technique can be used by colliding sample ions with helium buffer gas in an ion trap region, followed by dissociation of the sample ions. This Collision-Induced Dissociation (CID) method is very useful for obtaining abundant structural information of sample molecules and for reducing chemical noise. We can detect various kinds of organic compounds with high sensitivity by analyzing the mass number of observed ions or combinations of ions with different mass numbers (Hashimoto, et al., 2000, p. 49; Kojima, Sakairi, Takada, & Nakamura, 2000, p. 360; Sakairi, Hashimoto, Yamada, Suga, & Kojima, 2004, 2005; Sakairi & Kato, 1998, p. 391; Sakairi, Nakamura, & Nakamura, 1998; Sakairi, Nishimura, & Suzuki, 2009, p. 618; Takada, 2007, p. 91; Takada, et al., 2002, p. 224; Yamada, et al., 2001, p. i559; Yamada, Waki, Sakairi, Sakamoto, & Imai, 2004, p. 1475).

Our real-time monitoring mass spectrometry can be applied in various fields. One example is the monitoring of Polychlorinated Biphenyls (PCBs) at PCB treatment facilities (Hashimoto, et al., 2000, p. 49; Sakairi, et al., 2004; Takada, et al., 2002, p. 224; Yamada, et al., 2001, p. i559; Yamada, et al., 2004, p. 1475). Continuous monitoring is necessary for these facilities in Japan because citizens living nearby fear the possible threat of a leakage of untreated PCBs. PCB monitoring systems are therefore used at all PCB treatment facilities.

Another application field is the detection of explosives and illicit drugs at security checkpoints (Kojima, et al., 2000, p. 360; Sakairi, et al., 1998; Sakairi, et al., 2004, 2005; Takada, et al., 2002, p. 224; Takada, 2007, p. 91). The Transportation Security Administration (TSA), part of the US Department of Homeland Security, says, "Explosive trace detection technology is a critical tool in our ability to stay ahead of evolving threats to aviation technology" (http://www.tsa.gov). This is one of the reasons we have focused on developing a trace detection system based on real-time monitoring mass spectrometry. In the US, a trace detection method based on ion mobility has been used in public spaces. In this method, sample ions produced by a beta ray are drifted under atmospheric pressure by electric fields and detected with an electrometer. The principle of this method is that the drift time of ions depends on the mass number of the ions. No vacuum pump is needed, which makes it possible to miniaturize the device. However, the resolution and sensitivity of this device are not as high as those attained in a real-time monitoring mass spectrometer because in the latter device, ions are precisely mass analyzed under vacuum and detected by a highly sensitive electron multiplier, although vacuum pumps are necessary.

This chapter describes Hitachi's technological developments based on real time monitoring mass spectrometry that are designed to improve homeland security.

BACKGROUND: EXPLOSIVES TRACE DETECTION SYSTEM

Due to various changes in world circumstances, the threat of terrorism has become a serious problem for all countries. For example, military explosives are traded on the black market, and the general public can find information on making explosives on the Internet. Therefore, to maintain a safe society, detection technologies for hidden explosives are in great demand.

Two types of detection methods are primarily used: bulk detection (which uses x-rays to determine the existence of suspicious objects such as knives and firearms based on their shapes), and trace detection (which detects the presence of explosives by chemically analyzing the vapor emitted from nitro-compounds). Bulk detection has been in wide use for many years, but trace detection technologies have become increasingly necessary as security concerns have grown. Combined use of bulk detection and trace detection has become much more common to improve security at important facilities.

An image of an explosives trace detection system by mass spectrometry is illustrated in Figure 2. Typical operating procedures for baggage screening at an airport or other important facility are as follows. The most common sampling method for detecting explosives involves wiping the object being tested, a piece of luggage for example, with a wiping sheet. Chemical substances adhering to the surface of a passenger's baggage are wiped with the wiping sheet. The wiping sheet is then inserted into a heating unit of the explosives detector, and vapors from the sheet are introduced into an ionization source. Ions produced by the ionization source are introduced into a vacuum region and analyzed by a mass spectrometer. A data processor analyzes the obtained signals using predetermined detection logic and determines whether the molecules on the wiping sheet are explosives. The total detection time is about 10 seconds for all explosives.

KEY TECHNOLOGIES

Counter Flow Atmospheric Pressure Chemical Ionization

Cross-sectional views of (a) a conventional APCI ion source and (b) our developed APCI ion source are shown in Figure 3. In the conventional

Figure 2. Image of explosive trace detection system based on mass spectrometry, and a resulting mass spectrum

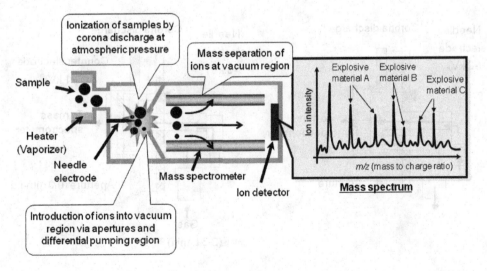

ion source, a sample gas flows directly into the region where the corona discharge is generated using a needle electrode. High negative voltage (about -2 kV) is applied to the needle electrode to produce a negative corona discharge at the tip of the electrode. Ion molecular reactions occur between sample molecules and reactant ions produced by the negative corona discharge. These ions are transferred to the sampling aperture of a differential pumping region by the gas flow and an electric field produced between the needle electrode and the aperture electrode. Then, the sample ions are introduced into a mass-analyzing region under vacuum. In the new APCI ion source shown in Figure 3(b), sample gas flows into a second chamber region and then into the first corona discharge region. The negative ions are extracted in the direction opposite the gas flow by the electric field in the first corona discharge region. Then, ions are introduced into the mass-analyzing region through the second chamber region and the sampling aperture. An electric field is also applied to the second chamber region for focusing ions. We call this method the atmospheric pressure chemical ionization method

with counter-flow introduction (APCI-CFI). This is because the directions of the sample gas flow and extracted ions are opposite each other in the first corona discharge region.

The negative ionization process of sample molecules *(M)* is expressed as follows in the conventional APCI ion source.

$$O_2 + e^- \rightarrow O_2^-$$

$$O_2 + N_2 \rightarrow 2NO$$

$$O_2^- + NO \rightarrow NO_3^-$$

$$O_2^- + M \rightarrow (M\text{-}H)^- + HO_2$$

Here, *(M-H)*$^-$ represents a negative ion with a removed proton from *M*. In this process, nitrogen monoxide *(NO)* is produced by the negative corona discharge, and *NO* easily reacts with O_2^- to produce NO_3^-. This reaction reduces the concentration of O_2^- and affects the ionization efficiency of the sample molecules *M*. However, in the new ion source, neutral *NO* molecules are eliminated from the ion-molecule reaction region by the gas flow.

Figure 3. Cross-sectional view of (a) conventional atmospheric pressure chemical ionization (APCI) ion source, and (b) our APCI ion source with counter-flow introduction (APCI-CFI)

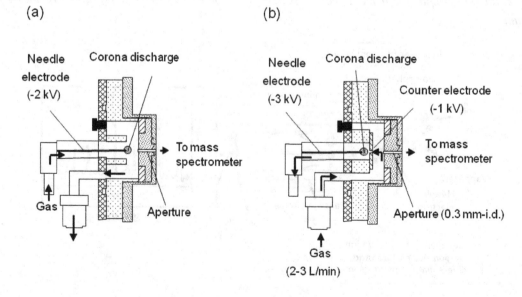

This is very effective for driving the ion-molecule reaction $(O_2^- + M \rightarrow (M\text{-}H)^- + HO_2)$ instead of the ion-molecule reaction $(O_2^- + NO \rightarrow NO_3^-)$.

We used 2,4-dichlorophenol (DCP) as a model compound to evaluate the new ion source because it is easily ionized using the negative APCI-CFI ion source. Typical mass spectra of DCP obtained with the conventional APCI ion source and the APCI-CFI ion source are shown in Figures 4(a) and 4(b), respectively. The observed ion intensity of $(DCP\text{-}H)^-$ was greatly improved by using the APCI-CFI ion source. The relationships between the gas flow rates and observed ion intensities of various ions $(O_2^-, NO_3^-,$ and $(DCP\text{-}H)^-)$ are shown in Figure 4(c). The intensities of the O_2^- and DCP ions increased with the gas flow rate, but that of NO_3^- decreased. These data support the explanation that higher gas flow is useful for eliminating NO from the ion-molecule reaction region and

also show the effectiveness of the APCI-CFI ion source. In addition to the improved efficiency in ionizing sample molecules, a stable corona discharge can be maintained for a long period of time in the APCI-CFI ion source. This is a very important feature for a monitoring system that requires stable operation over a long period; a system without this feature cannot really be called a "monitoring system." One reason a stable corona discharge cannot be maintained for a long period when there is no counter gas flow against the tip of the needle electrode used for corona discharge is that various kinds of compounds are deposited on the tip, which increases its curvature and thus causes instability in the corona discharge. This results in fluctuation in the discharge current, which makes the ionization unstable and also leads to fluctuation of the ion intensity measured by the mass spectrometer.

Figure 4. Characteristics of our novel APCI ion source. Comparison of negative APCI mass spectra of 2, 4-dichlorophenol (DCP) obtained by (a) conventional ion source and (b) our developed ion source, and (c) relationship between gas flow rate and observed ion intensity with our counter flow introduction mode (Takada, et al., 2002, p. 224).

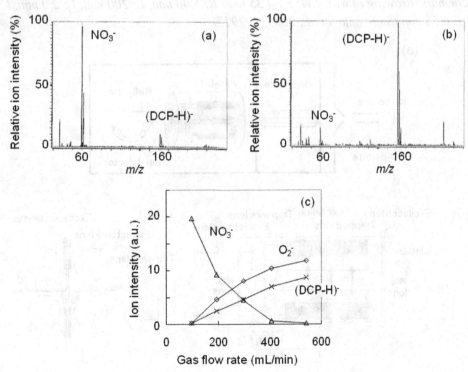

Wire-Type Linear Ion Trap Mass Spectrometer

To improve sensitivity, we developed a novel mass spectrometer called a wire-type linear ion trap (wire-LIT). This section briefly describes the wire-LIT used for mass analysis. Recently, linear ion traps (LITs) have been used as mass selective ejection devices due to their higher transmission compared to the conventional Three-Dimensional Quadrupole Ion Trap (3D-QIT). For sensitive detection of ions that are produced in the ion source, we developed a new method using a device called a wire-LIT that extracts ions axially with a DC extraction field (Sugiyama, Hasegawa, & Hashimoto, 2009, p. 2917). The wire-LIT, depicted in Figure 5, consists of an inlet lens, exit lens, quadrupole rods, trap wire lens, extraction wire lens, and excitation lenses. The rod length of the wire-LIT (L) is 50 mm, the rod radius (R) is 5.00 mm, and the distance between the rod and center

axis (r_0) is 4.35 mm. Two phases of trapping RF voltage (~1 MHz) are applied to each rod pair. Then, 1 mTorr of helium buffer gas is introduced into the wire-LIT to trap and cool the ions inside.

The trapping efficiency from the ion guide to the wire-LIT is high at almost 100%; in contrast, the trapping efficiency of the 3D-QIT is less than 10%. Controlled voltages are applied to these lenses to confine, dissociate, and mass-selectively eject ions during each sequence. In this LIT, trapped ions are mass-selectively excited by applying supplemental AC voltage to the excitation lenses. Excited ions pass over the trap wire lens while non-excited ions are confined by the trap wire lens. Ions that have passed over the trap wire lens are extracted from the LIT by the extraction wire lens with a high ejection efficiency of about 40%. The total transmission of the wire-LIT is about 40%, whereas it is less than 5% for the 3D-QIT, which indicates a nearly 10 times higher signal enhancement. This enhanced S/N

Figure 5. Schematic drawing of wire-LIT: r_0: 4.35 mm, R: 5.00 mm, L: 200 mm, l_1: 2.0 mm, l_2: 2.0 mm, l_3: 2.0 mm, d: 6.53 mm (Sugiyama, et al., 2009, p. 2917)

(a)

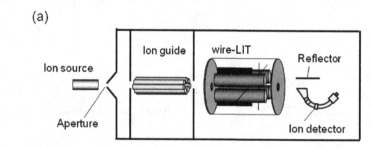

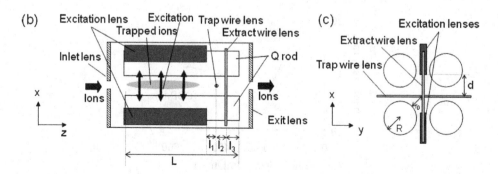

Figure 6. Detection of TATP vapor emitted from trace contamination of TATP attached onto cotton swab by using (a) conventional 3D-QIT, and (b) our wire-LIT (Takada, et al., 2011, p. 2448). The arrows show the TATP signals. Monitored m/z was 77.

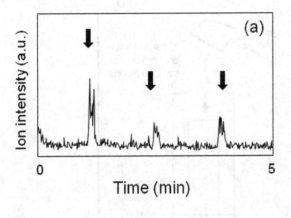
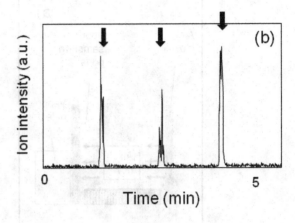

comes from higher transmission of the wire-LIT compared to the 3D-QIT. Figure 6 shows detection results of Triacetone Triperoxide (TATP) which is a popular improvised explosive used for terrorism (Takada, et al., 2011, p. 2448). Trace amounts of TATP, approximately 100 µg, attached onto a cotton swab was moved close to our mass spectrometer for ten seconds, and vapors emitted from the TATP were detected. In the case of a conventional 3D-QIT, observed S/σ was 17 as shown in Figure 6(a), where S shows the ion intensity and σ shows the standard deviation of background signal. On the other hand, the observed S/σ with the wire-LIT was 170, which was one order of magnitude higher than that of conventional 3D-QIT.

High-Throughput Detection of Explosives Using Real-Time Monitoring Mass Spectrometry

For further improvement of public security, the next-generation trace detector, namely, a high-throughput walkthrough detection systems, is currently under development (Takada, 2008, p. 149; Takada, et al., 2011, p. 2448). This system is being designed to prevent future terrorist attacks in public transportation areas, sports stadiums, shopping malls, and other high-density areas. The system 'sniffs' vapors emitted from the body and luggage and checks whether the 'smell' of explosives is present. Figures 7(a) and 8(b) schematically illustrate two versions of the explosive detection system. When a terrorist prepares an explosive device, their hands, clothes, luggage, and other everyday belongings are contaminated with trace amounts of the explosive they handled. In the portal version (targeting use at airports, for example) shown in Figure 7(a), when the terrorist passes through the portal, vapors from the explosive contaminants on their body, clothes, and luggage are detected. The target throughput of this system is 1,200 people per hour. In contrast, the "automatic ticket gate" version shown in Figure 7(b) is designed to detect explosive contaminants on hands, tickets, and IC cards. The target throughput of this system is 3,600 people per hour.

A prototype of the portal version is shown in Figure 8(a). In preliminary trials, vapors emitted from a small amount of a common improvised explosive, Triacetone Triperoxide (TATP), were clearly detected within only two seconds of a test

Figure 7. Schematic images of two versions of the explosive detection system, (a) portal version and (b) automatic ticket gate version. The arrows show flow of air and sample gas.

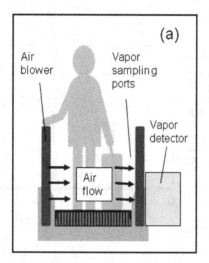
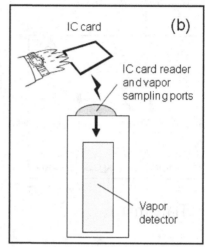

subject bearing traces of TATP passing through the portal, as shown in Figure 8(b). The arrows in the figure highlight the characteristic signals of TATP. This system will therefore be useful in preventing suicide attacks by terrorists. We tested a prototype of the portal version at Tokyo International Airport (Haneda) and at Akihabara train station in Tokyo to estimate the false positive rate. Passengers of local trains arriving at the airport and at the station passed through the prototype portal. The field tests will be described in detail in another paper. Briefly, though, no false positive alarms for TATP were obtained from 5,000 passengers. The estimated false positive rate calculated from the background signals of the airport and the train station for the TATP detection was therefore about 0.001%.

Figure 8. (a) Prototype for use in train stations, and (b) detection example: one of the authors passed through the prototype three times with a cotton swab on which a small amount of TATP, approximately 100 μg, had been placed. Three signals show positive detection of TATP by overall body suction system. Monitored m/z was 77.

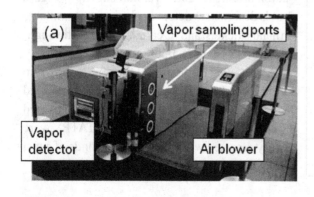
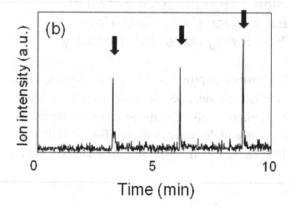

The high-throughput walkthrough detection project was supported by the Ministry of Education, Culture, Sports, Science, and Technology ("Science and Technology Project for a Safe and Secure Society").

FUTURE RESEARCH DIRECTIONS

To improve social security, we believe that the trace detection technologies described above must be connected to Information Technologies (IT). For example, if the high-throughput explosives detectors are installed in many places throughout the terminal and are connected to video monitoring systems, a passenger detected with traces of explosive contaminants is identified by an alarm on the explosives detector and automatically tracked by the video monitoring systems. Therefore, we will start to collaborate with IT researchers for a security system integration.

CONCLUSION

Homeland security technologies based on mass spectrometry were described. Systems using these technologies have significant advantages in sensitivity and selectivity and have a very low false-positive rate compared to other methods such as ion mobility although they tend to be larger in size due to the use of evacuation pumps. A new APCI technique was also described. It was found to be very effective for continuous monitoring due to its stable operation.

REFERENCES

Hashimoto, Y., Yamada, M., Suga, M., Kimura, K., Sakairi, M., & Tanaka, S. (2000). Online measurement of organic chlorides using an atmospheric-pressure chemical ionization ion-trap mass spectrometer. *Bunseki Kagaku, 49*, 49–54. doi:10.2116/bunsekikagaku.49.49

Kojima, K., Sakairi, M., Takada, Y., & Nakamura, J. (2000). Vapor detection of TNT and RDX using atmospheric pressure chemical ionization mass spectrometry with counter-flow introduction (CFI). *Journal of Mass Spectrometry Society of Japan, 48*, 360–362. doi:10.5702/massspec.48.360

Sakairi, M., Hashimoto, Y., Yamada, M., Suga, M., & Kojima, K. (2004). *Mass spectrometer, mass spectrometry, and monitoring system*. Patent US 6,686,592 B1. Washington, DC: US Patent Office.

Sakairi, M., Hashimoto, Y., Yamada, M., Suga, M., & Kojima, K. (2005). *Mass spectrometer, mass spectrometry, and monitoring system*. Patent US 6,838,664 B2. Washington, DC: US Patent Office.

Sakairi, M., & Kato, Y. (1998). Multi-atmospheric pressure ionization interface for liquid chromatography-mass spectrometry. *Journal of Chromatography. A, 794*, 391–406. doi:10.1016/S0021-9673(97)01220-X

Sakairi, M., Nakamura, H., & Nakamura, J. (1998). Highly sensitive vapor detection of nitro-compounds by atmospheric pressure chemical ionization mass spectrometry. In *Proceedings of 6th International Symposium on Analysis and Detection of Explosives*. IEEE.

Sakairi, M., Nishimura, A., & Suzuki, D. (2009). Olfaction presentation system using odor scanner and odor-emitting apparatus coupled with chemical capsules of alginic acid polymer. *IEICE Transactions on Fundamentals, E92*(A), 618-629.

Sugiyama, M., Hasegawa, H., & Hashimoto, Y. (2009). Mass-selective axial ejection from a linear ion trap with a direct current extraction field. *Rapid Communications in Mass Spectrometry, 23*, 2917–2922. doi:10.1002/rcm.4204

Takada, Y. (2007). Explosives trace detection by mass spectrometry. *Journal of the Mass Spectrometry Society of Japan, 55*, 91–94. doi:10.5702/massspec.55.91

Takada, Y. (2008). High-throughput walkthrough portal to detect improvised explosive devices. *Safety Engineering, 4*(8), 149.

Takada, Y., Nagano, H., Suga, M., Hashimoto, Y., Yamada, M., & Sakairi, M. (2002). Detection of military explosives by atmospheric pressure chemical ionization mass spectrometry with counter-flow introduction. *Propellants, Explosives. Pyrotechnics, 27*, 224–228. doi:10.1002/1521-4087(200209)27:4<224::AID-PREP224>3.0.CO;2-V

Takada, Y., Nagano, H., Suzuki, Y., Sugiyama, M., Nakajima, E., Hashimoto, Y., & Sakairi, M. (2011). Detection of military high-throughput detection of triacetone triperoxide (TATP) by atmospheric pressure chemical ionization ion trap mass spectrometry (APCI-ITMS). *Rapid Communications in Mass Spectrometry, 25*, 2448–2452. doi:10.1002/rcm.5147

Transportation Security Administration. (2012). *Homepage*. Retrieved from http://www.tsa.gov/

Wise, M. B., & Guerin, M. R. (1997). Direct sampling MS for environmental screening. *Analytical Chemistry, 69*, 26A–32A. doi:10.1021/ac971504r

Yamada, M., Sakairi, M., Hashimoto, Y., Suga, M., Takada, Y., & Waki, I. (2001). On-line monitoring of dioxin precursors in flue gas. *Analytical Sciences, 17*, i559–i562.

Yamada, M., Waki, I., Sakairi, M., Sakamoto, M., & Imai, T. (2004). Real-time-monitored decrease of trichlorophenol as a dioxin surrogate in flue gas using iron oxide catalyst. *Chemosphere, 54*, 1475–1480. doi:10.1016/j.chemosphere.2003.10.031

ADDITIONAL READING

Japan Explosives Society (Ed.). (2002). *Explosives analysis handbook*. Tokyo, Japan: Maruzen.

Japan Explosives Society (Ed.). (2010). *Explosives detection handbook*. Tokyo, Japan: Maruzen.

March, R. E., & Todd, J. F. J. (Eds.). (1995). *Practical aspects of ion trap mass spectrometry*. Boca Raton, FL: CRC Press, Inc.

Schubert, H., & Kuznetsov, A. (Eds.). (2006). *Detection and disposal of improvised explosives*. Berlin, Germany: Springer. doi:10.1007/978-1-4020-4887-6

Schubert, H., & Kuznetsov, A. (Eds.). (2008). *Detection of liquid explosives and flammable agents in connection with terrorism*. Berlin, Germany: Springer. doi:10.1007/978-1-4020-8466-9

Yinon, J. (Ed.). (1995). *Forensic applications of mass spectrometry*. Boca Raton, FL: CRC Press, Inc.

Yinon, J., & Zitrin, S. (1993). *Modern methods and applications in analysis of explosives*. New York, NY: John Wiley & Sons Ltd.

KEY TERMS AND DEFINITIONS

Atmospheric Pressure Chemical Ionization: An ionization method for mass spectrometry based on ion-molecule reactions under atmospheric pressure.

Ion Trap: A method of concentrating ions by trapping them in a limited space.

Chapter 12

Electronic Mucosa:
A Natural Successor to the Electronic Nose System?

Julian W. Gardner
University of Warwick, UK

James A. Covington
University of Warwick, UK

Fauzan Khairi Che Harun
Universiti Teknologi Malaysia, Malaysia

ABSTRACT

The field of electronic noses (e-noses) has advanced tremendously over the past ten years. This progress has mainly been achieved through addressing two key components; namely, the nature of the sensor array by employing more chemically-selective layers, and the method of pattern recognition by employing better algorithms for odour classification. Firstly, the field of chemical sensors has seen considerable advances: focused mainly on the development of more sensitive, more selective, faster responding materials, new sensing structures, and larger arrays to improve the overall ability of e-noses to solve problems. Such improvements have been coupled with a better understanding of how a sample is taken, a steady increase in the number of sensors, and the use of sample pre-concentration to improve the limit of detection. Secondly, improved and novel algorithms for feature extraction/selection, signal processing, and methods to classify/identify simple and complex odours. For example, there has been considerable effort in the field of machine olfaction to make use of transient (i.e. time-varying) signals rather than extracted pre-processed features (e.g. maximum change in sensor resistance) in order to improve classification rates. Yet, in spite of all these advances, the e-nose today still struggles to solve complex olfactory problems and cannot compete with the performance of the biological olfactory system.

In this chapter, the authors discuss a new concept that involves the development of a new type of sensor array and a new type of time-dependent signal processing method that they call an artificial (or electronic) olfactory mucosa. This so-called e-mucosa employs large sets of spatially distributed odour

DOI: 10.4018/978-1-4666-2521-1.ch012

Copyright © 2013, IGI Global. Copying or distributing in print or electronic forms without written permission of IGI Global is prohibited.

sensors and gas chromatographic-like retentive micro-columns. It has been inspired by the architecture of the human nose with the olfactory epithelium region located in the upper turbinate. The authors describe the fabrication of an e-mucosa and the use of a convolution method to analyse the time-varying signals generated by it and thus classify different odours. They believe that as this concept evolves it could result in a superior instrument to the sensor-based e-noses currently available today.

INTRODUCTION

Many common electronic devices have been inspired by our understanding of nature, or more specifically biology. The associated area of research is often referred to as *biomimetics* and focuses upon mimicking the concepts, mechanisms, functions, and design features that are often observed in nature. One of the earliest attempts of bio-inspired design was probably the airplane, when Leonardo de Vinci sketched diagrams showing the way that birds fly using their wings. Even with significant advancements in engineering materials and techniques, we are still learning from the way that biology solves challenging engineering problems. The field of artificial (or machine) olfaction is no different, as we attempt to compare and replicate the human biological system in terms of sensitivity, selectivity, ability to deal with extremes in environment and repeatability. Yet in spite of many years of effort our electronic noses (e-noses) still have some way to go if they are to perform as well as mammals and insects (see Pearce, et al., 2003 for review of machine olfaction).

In this chapter, we introduce the concept of an electronic olfactory mucosa (or *e-mucosa*) instrument. We believe that the e-mucosa is the next generation electronic nose, which has been inspired by our understanding of the olfactory epithelium or mucosa and so attempts to mimic more closely the human nose than conventional e-nose instrumentation.

Here we are interested in implementing *in silica*, a built-in advantage of the human olfactory system that is derived from the existence of *nasal*

chromatography. In essence an e-mucosa adds another dimension to an electronic nose instrument by utilizing the temporal information from sensors - as well as the spatial information in an advanced pattern recognition process. Here our embodiment of an e-mucosa is essentially an e-nose instrument with the addition of two retentive columns (mimicking two nasal paths), placed in between two sensor arrays. The retentive column acts like the olfactory mucosa by delaying some odour molecules while letting other molecules pass through with minimal delay. This provides differential temporal data, which are complementary to the conventional e-nose response. Future opportunities of this concept are also mentioned at the end of the chapter.

BACKGROUND

The sense of smell has always been seen as the least significant amongst the five major human senses (i.e. sight, touch, taste, hearing, and smell). Evolution created the sense of smell for several uses, such as a warning mechanism for avoiding predators, finding a suitable food source, and locating/choosing a mate for reproduction. However, as humans have evolved, the human olfactory system has degraded in function, probably due to its reduced importance for our survival and our reproductive process.

An electronic nose (or *e-nose*) is essentially an instrument that comprises an array of chemical sensors with partial specificity coupled with an appropriate pattern recognition system, and used to classify different simple and complex odours. There is no standard definition of what exactly we mean by an e-nose and it is often a topic of discussion amongst researchers. But the definition above is that defined by Gardner and Bartlett over ten years ago (Gardner & Bartlett, 1999) and covers the essential elements of a *sensor-based* electronic nose as opposed to one based upon, say, Field Asymmetric Ion Mobility Spectroscopy (FAIMS).

In the mammalian olfactory system, lungs are used to draw gases and Volatile Organic Compounds (VOCs) through our nostrils and transport them into the upper chamber or turbinate inside our nasal cavity and so across the olfactory epithelium. This epithelium consists of millions of olfactory neurons containing odour-sensitive receptor cells. In addition, the human epithelium has a mucous coating with cilia (see Figure 1) that acts as both a chemical headspace filter and pre-concentrator as the molecules move along its surface. The olfactory receptor neurons then convert the chemical responses to electronic nerve impulses, i.e. a spike train. The unique patterns of nerve impulses are propagated by neurons through a complex network of glomeruli nodes and mitral cells before going through the higher brain (hypothalamus) for interpretation. For further details see Pearce *et al.* (2003).

In our artificial system, an electronic nose utilizes a mechanical pump to draw in the odorant headspace and passes it into a chamber containing an array of chemical sensors. An electronic nose instrument also has an inlet sampling system that provides sample filtration, possible pre-concentration and conditioning to protect the sensor array and to enhance selectivity. In an effort to mimic the biological system, an electronic nose has a number of sensors that have different selectivity and sensitivity to a particular odour molecule or note. Similarly, to the human nose, when the chemical sensors react with the odorant molecules, a set of time-dependent electrical signals are

Figure 1. Mammalian olfactory system showing the olfactory mucosa in the upper turbinate. Olfactory receptors are located in cilia that extend into a thick aqueous mucous layer through which odour molecules pass, signals are generated and passed to the glomeruli and mitral cells located within the olfactory bulb.

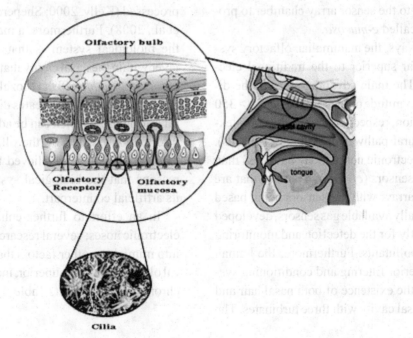

Figure 2. Schematic representation of the component parts of a conventional sensor-based electronic nose and (below) its extension to create an electronic olfactory mucosa or e-mucosa

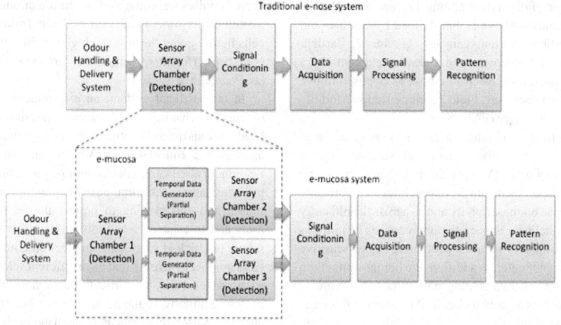

produced. This pattern of signals is then processed and interpreted using some form of intelligent pattern classification algorithm that mimics the olfactory cortex. Figure 2 shows a basic functional block of an electronic nose showing modification to the sensor array chamber to produce our so-called *e-mucosa*.

In many ways, the mammalian olfactory system is still far superior to the traditional electronic nose. The main advantages are in the diversity and magnitude of sensors/receptors (> 350 and > 50 million, respectively), and the complexity of the neural pathways (>100,000 neurons). Almost all electronic noses today have less than 50 chemical sensors (*cf* >350 in nature) that are placed in an array; with the sensors being based on commercially available gas sensors, developed pre-dominantly for the detection and monitoring of airborne pollutants. Furthermore, the human nose has superior filtering and conditioning system through the existence of both nasal hair and a complex nasal cavity with three turbinates. The

nasal cavity or *nasal fossa* is the air filled area located behind the nose and in front of the face. Its function is to precondition the sniffed air by warming and humidifying the air in such a way that it prepares the odour before being sensed and processed (Kelly, 2000; Sheperd, 2004; Gardner, et al., 2008). Furthermore, a major advantage of the biological system is that it has a mucous layer within the nasal cavity that produces a *nasal chromatographic* effect (Mozell, 1974). The addition of this structure creates differential temporal information, which can be added to the spatial information created by the olfactory receptors. This combination is believed to be one of the reasons that the biological system outperforms its artificial counterpart.

In an effort to further enhance the current electronic noses; several researchers have looked into mimicking other factors that makes biological olfactory system superior, including this nasal chromatograph effect. Table 1 shows the rela-

Table 1. Similarity between an electronic mucosa and human nose

Human Olfactory System	Electronic Mucosa	Comments
Lung	Pump	Sample delivery system
Nasal Cavity	Pre-Concentrator	Pre-concentration and temperature conditioning
Nose Hair	Air Filter and Conditioner	To filter dust and big particles from entering the system
Nasal Mucous	Retentive Column	Generate spatio-temporal response from the 'nasal chromatograph' effect.
Olfactory Epithelium and Receptor	Large Sensor Array	Large number of sensors with different tunings
Stereo Olfaction	Multi-dimensional retentive column	Different flow rates on the two nostrils provide additional information.
Olfactory Bulb	Signal Processing	Pattern recognition
Olfactory Cortex/Brain	Pattern Analyzer	Central Processing Unit

tionship between the human nose and the e-nose instrument indicating the similarities.

Here our e-mucosa is designed to mimic the way the mammalian nose functions by using a large sensor array combined with two retentive micro-columns focused on mimicking specifically the olfactory mucosa (Gardner, et al., 2007). Furthermore, it has an embedded pre-concentrator that tries to improve the system by concentrating the odour/sample being tested; similar to the function of the nasal cavity. In the next section we discuss the design and specification of our e-mucosa and its fabrication by researchers at Warwick University. The choice of microcontroller, data acquisition, and storage method will also be explained that create the entire instrument.

ELECTRONIC MUCOSA: CONCEPT

The nasal chromatograph component of the e-mucosa can be viewed in some way as a conventional Gas Chromatography (GC) column. Traditionally, GC is used to separate out different chemical components based upon the interaction between the molecules (mobile phase) and a retentive coating (stationary phase) inside a long column. The output from a GC is a series of chemical pulses that emanate from the end of the column at different points in time. This output is then detected by either a flame ionization detector, for example, or a mass spectrometer, which aids in identifying each chemical component within an odour through its elution time.

Here, the concept is slightly different, but in execution, it has many similarities. First, we are not attempting to separate the chemical constituents out into a series of peaks, but simply to gain information about the concentrations of the chemical compounds within a complex headspace. Thus, the sensor array in our e-mucosa does not try to detect the gas individually but as a whole pattern. Furthermore, like the biological system, we use normal air as the carrier gas, instead of helium or hydrogen. The difference between the two systems is that the column only partially separates the odour (broadly) instead of complete separation, as shown in Figure 3. In our case the long column or micro-channels are formed from micro-fabrication techniques (described later) instead of being a glass capillary like structure. Such an approach does reduce the length of the column, but allows simpler integration into the electronic nose instrument. Then odour sensors need to be located before and after the micro-columns to enable us to measure the retentive

Figure 3. e-Mucosa concept diagram based on one retentive micro-channel and two large sensor arrays

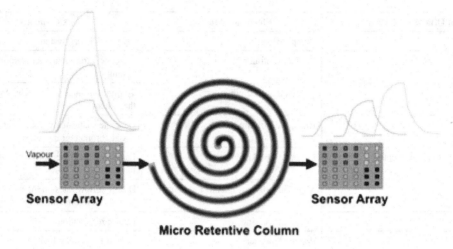

Figure 4. Normalised response of two sensor array before and after the column

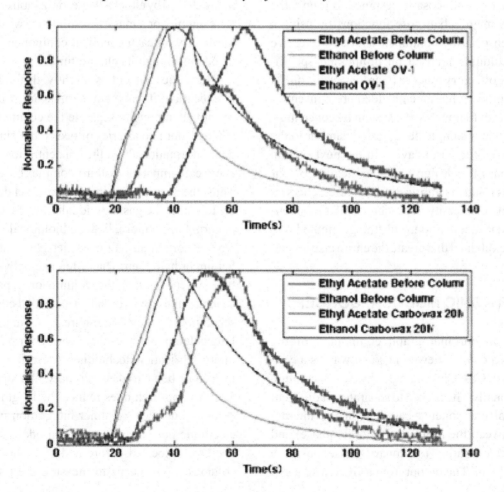

effect of the coatings made from polymers or rubber like materials.

There are several ways to use the retentive micro-channel to generate this spatio-temporal signal. Figure 3 shows a one dimensional setup; one retentive channel is used to delay the odour going from the first sensor array, producing a delayed response on the output. The pattern recognition technique used in e-mucosa will have to include the temporal information gathered by the system.

Figure 4 shows the separation produced by a column of two chemical compounds of ethanol and ethyl acetate in air. Here, two micro-columns were tested, namely one column coated with the stationary phase compound of Carbowax 20M and the other OV-1. We can see that the same odour is delayed differently when different coatings are used, e.g. polar, non-polar. Here ethyl acetate was delayed the most in OV-1 column while ethanol with Carbowax 20M.

The purpose of this experiment was to demonstrate the difference between the separation power of polar (Carbowax 20M) and non-polar (OV-1) stationary phase coatings employing a micro-retentive column. In general, it is expected

that ethanol vapour, being more polar than ethyl acetate, will be delayed more through a polar column (Carbowax 20M) and vice versa. As expected here, we see that ethanol is delayed further than ethyl acetate on the Carbowax20M, while ethyl acetate is delayed more after the OV-1 column—as expected.

We can roughly estimate the retention caused by the stationary phase by calculating the partition coefficients between the mobile and stationary phase compounds. This can be done using the Linear Solvation Energy Relationship (LSER) equation. The partition coefficient for ethyl acetate, acetone and ethanol towards SE-30 and Carbowax 20M can be calculated and plotted, shown in Figure 5. Here, SE-30 was used because the constant values are available and it is the same material as OV-1 (100% PDMS). For further details and the equations for LSER, see Gardner and Bartlett 1999.

Figure 5 clearly shows that ethyl acetate and ethanol vapours have contradictory reactions towards SE-30 and Carbowax 20M. This supports the results we gained from our earlier experiment, shown in Figure 4, where we saw that ethanol vapour is delayed more with a Carbowax 20M

Figure 5. Partition coefficients for three different chemicals of ethyl acetate, ethanol and acetone with two stationary phases of SE-30 and Carbowax 20M. These are used to calculate the overall partition coefficient K_p for the solute (odour) / solvent (polymer) interaction.

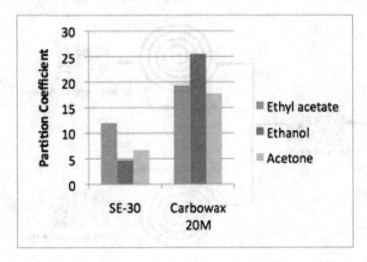

coated retentive column and ethyl acetate vapour is delayed more with an OV-1 column.

Carbowax 20M and OV-1 are exemplar materials that can be used to separate odours within the e-mucosa. Figure 6 illustrates the more advanced block diagram of an e-mucosa system now employing a second retentive column and an additional large sensor array. In our configuration, each array is formed from 300 discrete sensors and becomes in effect three conventional electronic noses (when combined with pattern recognition) by themselves. In this setup, three sets of sensor arrays were used with two differently coated micro retentive columns to produce the nasal chromatograph effect in stereo. Thus, we can make a differential e-mucosa system based upon say polar and non-polar coatings.

The flow of odours through the instrument starts by passing over the initial sensor array, where the response of chemoresistive sensors is similar to that of a traditional e-nose (i.e. spatial information). The sample flow is then divided (controlled via two valves) and passed through two retentive micro channels coated with Carbowax 20M and OV-1 (polar and non-polar compounds) with channel dimensions of 0.25 mm × 0.38 mm × 1.0 m. As the odours are emitted from the micro channels they pass over additional sensor arrays, producing spatio-temporal data.

The e-mucosa, offers a number of extra parameters (or features) that can be either selected or extracted to reduce the dimensionality of the problem and thus improve classification performance over a conventional e-nose. Spatial data are produced by all three, similarly fabricated, large sensor arrays with similar coatings or "tunings." However, the response of all three sensor arrays will be different in terms of spatial data. The initial sensor array will produce a high *magnitude* response towards the odour, similar to a traditional e-nose. The second and third sensor arrays will produce significantly smaller sensor responses, in terms of magnitude when compared to the first sensor, but produce additional *temporal* data. There are several reasons for this. Firstly, the volumetric flow rate of odour going through the output sensor arrays is halved by the two micro retentive columns, thus producing lower magnitude of responses. Furthermore, the odour being tested is now partially separated through time, which means some molecules will reach the sensors earlier than the others; hence, the smaller response in magnitude. Another factor is the absorption of molecules by the first large

Figure 6. More advanced e-mucosa with two retentive micro columns and three large odour sensor arrays

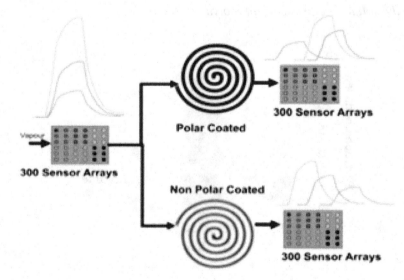

sensor array, which might contribute to the small sensor response at the end array. In term of spatial data, we can say that it is possible to extract three different spatial data sets from this system.

The temporal data are calculated by looking at the delayed sensor responses between the first sensor array and the two arrays after the retention column. There are several parameters that can be extracted from the e-mucosa system. The first is

the delay between sensor array 1 and sensor array 2, also between sensor array 1 and sensor array 3. This gives an additional two features regarding the delays produced by the e-mucosa compared with the e-nose. Another temporal feature that can be extracted is the delay between sensor array 2 and sensor array 3, where the difference in temporal information between the same odours through a different column can be used, as shown in Figure 7.

Figure 7. Sensor response towards ethanol and ethyl acetate vapour in ambient air before and after the retentive micro-columns: thus showing partial separation of the signals (unlike a proper but slower GC unit)

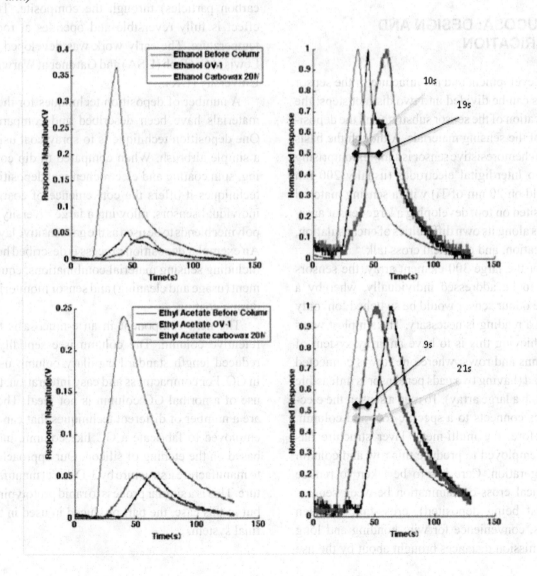

The right hand side figure shows that ethyl acetate is delayed more that ethanol on the OV-1 channel. The distinction for ethanol between both channels is not so clear cut, however the ethyl acetate delay shows that OV-1 is reacting more towards this molecule compared to ethanol. This shows the non-linearity in the temporal data formation. This last feature not only shows the difference between a polar and non-polar column, but that the signals have a reduced signal to noise ratio. In the next section we describe the design and fabrication of the e-mucosa with further details found elsewhere (Che Harun, 2010).

E-MUCOSA: DESIGN AND FABRICATION

The development and manufacture of the sensor arrays can be divided into two distinct steps; the fabrication of the sensor substrate and the deposition of the sensing materials. Although the basis of the chemoresistive sensor is simple, comprising of two interdigital electrodes (usually 200 nm of gold on 20 nm of Ti) with a sensing material deposited on top, developing a large sensor array brings along its own difficulties of encapsulation, fabrication, and electrical cross talk.

For the large 300 element array, the sensors have to be addressed individually, whereby a single odour sensor would be switched 'on' only when a reading is necessary. The simplest ways of achieving this is to have an array system of columns and rows; where one row is connected to a pad (having two pads per sensor is unfeasible for such a large array). To read a sensor, the electronics connects to a specific row and column. Therefore, the multi-metal layer structure has been employed to produce this row and column configuration. Care has to be taken to reduce chemical cross-contamination between sensors (whilst being deposited), cross-talk between tracks, convenience for wire bonding and long transmission distances brought about by the use of shared pads. A resistive-based gold temperature sensor was designed on-chip to aid temperature monitoring during testing. The temperature sensor was designed with a baseline resistance of 200 Ω at room temperature.

For this array, carbon black composite materials were used as the gas sensitive layer. These materials combine an insulating polymer with carbon nano-spheres (*ca.* 30 nm) that endow conductive properties to the resultant mix. Gas detection is based on a swelling effect, whereby absorption of the odorant molecules causes the polymer to expand and thus increase the length of conductive paths (created by interconnected carbon particles) through the composite. This effect is fully reversible and operates at room temperature. The early work was developed by Lewis at CalTech (USA) and Gardner at Warwick University (UK).

A number of deposition techniques for these materials have been described and compared. One deposition technique is to spray coat using a simple airbrush. When compared to dip coating, spin coating and electrochemical deposition techniques it offers the convenience of coating individual sensors, allowing a large diversity of polymer blends to be used as the gas sensitive layer. An exemplar deposition process is described here including sensing material combinations, equipment (usage and cleaning) and sensor monitoring during coating.

The next component in an e-mucosa is the retentive column. The column is essentially a reduced length standard capillary column used in GC. For compactness and easy integration, the use of a normal GC column is not ideal. There are a number of different techniques that can be employed to fabricate a GC like column, most based on the etching of silicon. Our approach is to manufacture a structure by 3-D direct manufacture. This is a similar process to rapid prototyping, but in this case, the part produced in used in the final system.

The creation of a 3-D object starts with a 3-D CAD design, using CAD software, in our case Solidworks. We used a commercial stereolithographic rapid prototyping machine (EnvisionTec Perfactory Mini system) that accepts object data files in the form of "STL" (stereolithography) file. This file format is widely used in most rapid prototyping systems and 3-D direct manufacture applications, especially among stereolithographic systems. The CAD design is saved as "STL" file in Solidworks before the next step. This 3-D object is then sliced to 2-D layers using the Envisiontec Perfactory Direct application. If part of the object has irregular 'non-flat' surfaces, it is necessary to build a support to hold the part during the build process. In cases where support is needed, Magics 11 from Materialise Software is used to generate 3-D support before the object is sliced. The slice data are then sent to the machine to start the building process. Each 2-D slice is projected into the resin surface, layer by layer, to produce the 3-D object, thus it is an additive layer process. An advantage of this process is that it allows fittings and connectors to be integrated into the part to simplify connectivity.

Upon completion, the object is washed to remove any uncured resin on its surfaces and within the microchannels. The object is cleaned by placing it in a beaker filled with isopropanol before being immersed in an ultrasonic bath. After ultrasonic cleaning, the object is blown with compressed air to dry and cured using a UV light box (Metalight QX1, Primotec, Germany) for 5 minutes. The steps for MSL fabrication process is summarised in Figure 8.

In gas chromatography, the stationary phase compound is one of the most important elements of the technique. The greater the partitioning of a chemical compound, the more it will be retained, thus the slower the compound will advance through the column. There are many types of stationary phases, which are mainly classified based on their interaction with a sample (polar, non-polar, and ionic). The most common method used to evaluate a stationary phase is the McReynolds system (McReynolds, 1966). McReynolds constant can be used to determine the selection of a stationary

Figure 8. Retentive column fabrication process: from CAD design to 3D structure

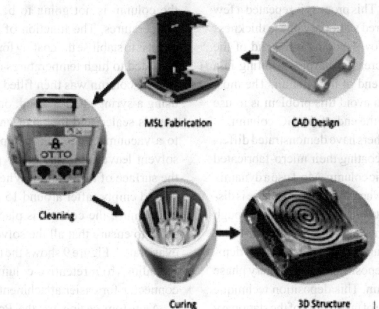

phase for a specific compound. McReynolds has analyzed more than 200 stationary phases (Eugene, 2007) from which Delley suggested, four phases: OV-101, OV-17, OV-225, and Carbowax 20M, can provide satisfactory GC analysis for over 80% of all applications (Delley & Friedrich, 1977). The general rule, when choosing a stationary phase, is to use a polar phase for polar compounds and a non-polar phase for non-polar compounds, with further fine-tuning according to the McReynolds system. Non-polar phases are more resistant to oxidation and hydrolysis than polar phases. Polysiloxane based phases are the most common stationary phases used in GC because of their high thermal stability and the wide range of polarities. Here, we have chosen OV-1(100% Polydimethylsiloxane) as our non-polar stationary phase because of its wide range of polarities and Carbowax 20M (polyethylglycol) as our polar stationary phase.

Conventional gas chromatography column stationary phase coating techniques are mainly divided into two groups, namely dynamic and static coating (Lee, 1984). Generally, dynamic coating is performed by driving a plug of stationary phase solution through the column. This causes a thin layer of stationary phase to adhere to the wall of the column. This process is repeated a few times until the desired stationary phase thickness is achieved. The flow velocity at the end of the column usually increases sharply, resulting in a thicker film at the end of the column. The most common method to avoid this problem is to use a buffer column at the end of the GC column.

Various researchers have demonstrated different techniques for coating their micro-fabricated gas chromatographic column. Most use a dynamic coating technique, whereby stationary phase is dissolved in a volatile solvent and then pushed through the column at a constant velocity (Reston, 1994; Reidy, 2006). Noh and Kolesar (2002) have demonstrated vapour deposition of a stationary phase onto a micro-column. This deposition technique offers the advantage of uniformity of the stationary phase layer on a micro sized column. Noh (2002)

coated their micro-column with parylene using a vapour deposition machine from Specialty Coating System. Kolesar used sublimation technique to evaporate the stationary phase onto an unsealed silicon micro-GC column (Reston, 1994). Then, the wafer was polished prior to anodically bonding it to a Pyrex lid to seal the column creating a coated micro-GC column.

We have tested several methods of coating our micro retentive columns including spray coating, static coating and vapour deposition. We found that static coating gave to most repeatable and reliable results. The static coating technique was conducted in a similar way as demonstrated by Reidy (where they successfully coated 0.1 to 0.2 μm of stationary phase (OV-1) onto a silicon fabricated micro-GC channel (Reidy, 2006).

The stationary phase solution was prepared by dissolving 0.05g of OV-1(non-polar) or Carbowax 20M (polar) (both acquired from Sigma Aldrich UK), in 10 ml dichloromethane. The mixture was then agitated for 30 min by shaking it in a flash shaker (George and Griffin, UK) to ensure complete dissolution. Although Reidy suggested adding dicumyl peroxide, a cross-linking agent, to the stationary phase before coating, we have decided not to use the agent due to the fact that the column is not going to be exposed to high temperatures. The function of the cross-linking agent is to stabilise the coating for when the column is heated to high temperatures during operation.

The column was then filled with the solution using a syringe. Once filled, one end of the column is sealed and the other end was connected to a vacuum pump. The pump removed all the solvent leaving the stationary phase coating on the surface of the column. When the column appeared empty (after around 15 minutes for a 0.5 m column), the column is placed in an oven at 50°C to ensure that all the solvent is completely evaporated. Figure 9 shows the (a) sealed column including (b) a retentive column complete with connector for easier attachment to the system.

A custom casing for the Portable e-Mucosa (PeM) was designed and fabricated at the Uni-

Figure 9. (a) Sealed retentive micro column; (b) retentive column with flow connector

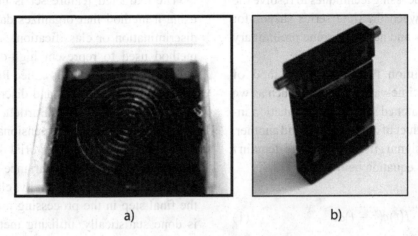

a)   b)

versity of Warwick. This was design in Solidworks 2009 and the casing itself was fabricated using a Fused Deposition Modeller (FDM) technique, using Dimension from Stratasys ©.

Figure 10(a) shows the PeM PCB boards connected together, forming an instrument with dimensions of 96 mm × 180 mm × 86 mm. The casing itself was designed to be slightly bigger at 110 mm × 200 mm × 100 mm so that the board can fit in properly. The casing was designed in 3 pieces; main body, top cover and bottom cover.

The three boards are screwed onto the main body with all the pipefittings. The odour inlet, air inlet and exhaust are placed on different sides of

the instrument to avoid contamination between the inlet and the exhaust. A Luer lock connector is fitted on the inlet to allow different sample collection methods to be deployed. The LCD, keypad and buttons are fitted onto the top cover. Figure 10 (c) shows the perspective view of the PeM instrument.

Solutions and Recommendations

Signal processing techniques that fully utilize the additional information held in the e-mucosa data are still under investigation. For example we have been exploring the application of *convolution-*

Figure 10. (a) Stacked PCB of the e-mucosa system, (b) bottom of system showing three sensors with chambers, and (c) complete portable e-mucosa system

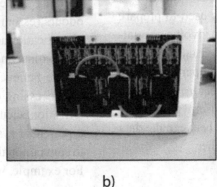

a)   b)   c)

based signal processing techniques to resolve the differences between the time series shapes for different odours and have had some preliminary success.

The convolution function is a method of combining two time-varying signals (such as we get from two matched sensors). The function integrates the product of one signal *f(t)* and another, time-reversed, signal *g(t)*, over the time domain *t* as shown in the equation below.

$$f(t) * g(t) = \int_{-\infty}^{\infty} f(t)g(\tau - t)dt \qquad (1)$$

The combined signal f*g peaks where both signals are best matched, producing the highest integration area when multiplied. Convolution is usually used in system analysis to operate a transfer function on an input signal to define an output signal. However, here we are using it to seek out the similarities between two odour sensor signals in a novel way. The peaks and troughs of the convolution signal highlight periods of the two signals that are most and least similar. It is thus a simple way of extracting information from two time series signals in an elegant and efficient manner to have a simple feature such as the peak height H or area A of the convolution integral. Further details of the use of a convolution algorithm have been reported previously (Gardner & Taylor, 2009).

Briefly, the convolution method is based upon several stages in processing the sensors data. First, a signal pre-processing stage is used to prepare the data for processing. This can involve normalizing and/or filtering the data. Normalization will make each set of data directly comparable. Then, feature extraction using single feature processing method is performed to extract useful parameters that can be used to differentiate between the data from one input source and another.

The extracted feature set is then processed using a method that organizes data for pattern discrimination or classification. Most common method used to represent high-dimensionality but correlated data-sets is called Principal Components Analysis (PCA) and discriminant function analysis (Gardner & Bartlett, 1999). These functions present high-dimensional data sets in a manner by in essence vectorial decomposition so that there is maximum variance in a minimum number of dimensions. Finally, classification is the final step in the processing procedure. This is done statistically, utilizing methods such as linear metrics and nearest neighbour linkage or non-linear metrics and linkage. More advanced methods employ non-linear classifiers such as genetic algorithms and probabilistic neural networks.

The methods presented hence focus on the feature extraction stage. These methods will be combined with different standard normalization techniques in the preprocessing stage. The extracted feature set will then be processed using PCA (or DFA), and benchmarked based on the quality of the separation in the principle component (PC) plots. Classification is not carried out explicitly, because we are seeking excellent linear separability of the samples. For further details on pattern analysis methods see Gardner and Bartlett (1999), Hines *et al.* (1999), and Pearce *et al.* (2003).

Previously reported experimental results on simple odours (e.g. ethanol and toluene) indicate that using convolution-based methods can offer an improved image for classification, and work utilizing larger data sets with more complex odours (essential oil) shows an improvement in classification accuracy. For details of these studies see Gardner and Taylor (2009) and Taylor (2010).

We believe that convolution-based methods of processing can be used to improve the classification accuracy of not only novel e-mucosa type sensor systems but may even be applicable to conventional sensor-based e-nose technologies. For example, we can analyse convolution within a sensor array and thus find the time differences between different sensor technologies like metal oxide chemoresistors and quartz crystal microbalances. Figure 11 shows a PCA plot of the convolution area *A* for the time series responses of a set of 4 metal oxide sensors with themselves (MOX*MOX), a set of 4 QMB sensors with themselves (QMB*QMB) and between MOX and QMB sensors (MOX*QMB). In this case it is possible to separate out very easily the simple compounds of anisole, cyclohexanol, propanol and toluene using the convolution method. Interesting, the convolution of MOX sensors with QMB has no physical meaning but did prove to add additional discriminatory information. Again, for details see Gardner and Taylor (2009). In practice it is simpler to discriminate using conventional

electronic noses and just the maximum change in resistance or frequency shift but in some cases this approach could provide additional information to a more complex problem.

This study into metal oxide and quartz microbalance sensors does show that other types of chemical could be used within our e-mucosa and analysed using the time series convolution method. The sensitivity of metal oxide and QMB sensors are known to be in the ppb to ppm level and so could be used to enhance the capability of our system. In fact, we have some recently that QCMs are capable of discriminating between different complex odour blends with a neuromorphic model of an insect macroglomerular complex (Karout, et al., 2011).

Figure 11. Convolution-based approach has been used to classify successfully different odours based upon a mixture of gas sensing technologies. The feature extracted is the area under the convolution integral for all pairs of sensors in the set of sensors. The results are presented using a principal components plot of the first two scores (from Gardner & Taylor, 2009).

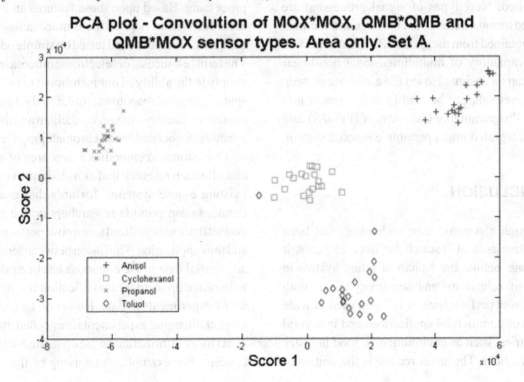

However, here our ultimate aim is to develop an e-mucosa that successfully compares with the human olfactory system and comprises a large set of receptors (sensing elements), internal temperature and humidity controller, filter and multi-dimensional nasal chromatograph and advanced time series signal processing methods like convolution integrals combined with a probabilistic neural classifier.

FUTURE RESEARCH DIRECTIONS

Research into the field of e-mucosa is still relatively new and expanding. In terms of further advances in signal processing not that much effort is being directed towards the temporal information. Therefor the fusion of transient, spatial, and temporal data fusion might help us to improve the way our e-mucosa performs and start to approach more the capabilities of the human nose.

In terms of application, the e-mucosa promises a new area of research with more information available than conventional e-noses that can be exploited. New types of signal processing are needed to make better use of the large and complex data obtained from the system. Pattern recognition with capability of multidimensional non-linear data can be designed to aid the e-mucosa system. Such methods can be readily implemented into Field-Programmable Gate Arrays (FPGAs) and thus integrated into a portable e-mucosa system.

CONCLUSION

Although electronic nose technology has been an active area of research for over 25 years, it still lags behind the human olfactory system in term of selectivity and sensitivity. Even with this lower performance, it is being used in wide range of commercial applications and in several industries, such as environmental, food industry and medical. The main reason is the ability of an electronic nose to solve specific problems at a lower cost and within a short period of time.

An e-nose system provides an alternative to the use of organoleptic panels and is better in several areas. Using humans to evaluate the smell of products, such as perfumes, foods and beverages, is a costly process, because trained panels of experts are required and they can only work for relatively short periods of time. Furthermore, in areas such as explosive detection and several medical applications, it is impossible or undesirable to use human organoleptic panels to classify toxic and dangerous odorants.

Motivated to improve the performance, size, and cost of existing e-nose instruments, this chapter described our effort towards developing an artificial olfactory mucosa or epithelium in order to improve upon the current limited performance of e-nose technology. In an attempt to extract the features that contribute to the superiority of the biological olfactory system, this study has focused on several key features such as a large sensor count, the nasal chromatograph effect, stereo micro channel "olfaction," and differential signals processing. Based upon these features an instrument referred to here as the e-mucosa has been designed, fabricated, and tested on simple odours. The term 'e-mucosa' or 'electronic mucosa' refers simply to the ability of our instrument to generate spatio-temporal responses similar to the function of human olfactory mucosa/epithelium and thus recreate the associated 'nasal chromatograph' effect.

Our e-mucosa embodies a new area of artificial olfaction research that aims to improve upon existing e-nose systems. Towards that goal, an e-mucosa can provide researchers with a richer dataset that can be utilized to improve performance and thus application. The fusion between temporal and spatial data in the e-mucosa has been shown to improve upon odour classification in a modest set of experiments to date. However, further and more challenging experiments are needed that extracts more information based upon the e-mucosa concept. For example, the solving of the odour segmentation problem, i.e. the detection of low levels of one odour molecule within high levels of other background molecules. Only then will be now if this concept realises its full potential.

REFERENCES

Che Harun, F. K., Taylor, J. E., Covington, J., & Gardner, J. W. (2009). An electronic nose employing dual-channel odour separation columns with large chemosensor arrays for advanced odour discrimination. *Sensors and Actuators. B, Chemical, 141*(1), 134–140. doi:10.1016/j.snb.2009.05.036

Delley, R., & Friedrich, R. A. (1977). System CG 72 von bevorzugten trennflüssigkeiten für die gas-chromatographie. *Chromatographia, 10*(10), 593–600. doi:10.1007/BF02265037

Eugene, F. (2007). *Columns for gas chromatography: Performance and selection*. New York, NY: Wiley-Interscience.

Gardner, J. W., & Bartlett, P. N. (1999). *Electronic noses: Principles and application*. Oxford, UK: Oxford University Press.

Gardner, J. W., Covington, J., Tan, S. L., & Pearce, T. C. (2007). Towards an artificial olfactory mucosa for improved odour classification. *Proceedings of the Royal Society of London. Series A, 463*, 1713–1728. doi:10.1098/rspa.2007.1844

Gardner, J. W., Nadarajan, S., & Kimber, P. (2008). Modelling and measurement of odour transportation within the human naval cavity. In *Proceedings of the 6th IASTED International Conference on Biomedical Engineering*, (pp. 145-150). IASTED.

Gardner, J. W., & Taylor, J. E. (2009). Novel convolution-based signal processing techniques for an artificial olfactory mucosa. *IEEE Sensors Journal, 9*, 929–935. doi:10.1109/JSEN.2009.2024856

Hines, E. L., Llobet, E., & Gardner, J. W. (1999). Electronic noses: A review of signal processing techniques. *Proceedings of the IEE: Circuits, Systems and Devices, 146*, 297-310.

Karout, S., Racz, Z., Capurro, A., Cole, M., Gardner, J. W., & Pearce, T. C. (2011). Ratiometric chemical blend processing with a neuromorphic model of the insect macroglomerular complex. In *Proceedings of the AIP Conference*, (vol 1362, pp. 77-78). AIP.

Kelly, J. T., Prasad, A. K., & Wexler, A. S. (2000). Detailed flow patterns in the nasal cavity. *Journal of Applied Physiology, 89*(1), 323–337.

Lee, F., Lee, M., Yang, F., & Bartle, K. (1984). *Open tubular column gas chromatography: Theory and practice*. Chichester, UK: John Wiley & Sons.

Li, J. R. (2003). Carbon black/polystyrene composites as candidates for gas sensing materials. *Carbon, 41*(12), 2353–2360. doi:10.1016/S0008-6223(03)00273-2

Lonergan, M. C. (1996). Array-based vapor sensing using chemically sensitive, carbon black polymer resistors. *Chemistry of Materials, 8*(9), 2298–2312. doi:10.1021/cm960036j

McReynolds, W. O. (1966). *Gas chromatographic retention data*. Niles, IL: Preston Publications Inc.

Mozell, M. M. (1974). Mechanisms underlying the analysis of odorant quality at the level of the olfactory mucosa I: Spatiotemporal sorption patterns. *Annals of the New York Academy of Sciences, 237*, 76–90. doi:10.1111/j.1749-6632.1974.tb49845.x

Noh, H., Hesketh, P., & Frye-Mason, G. (2002). Parylene gas chromatographic column for rapid thermal cycling. *Journal of Microelectromechanical Systems, 11*(6), 718–725. doi:10.1109/JMEMS.2002.805052

Pearce, T. C., Schiffman, S., Nagle, H. T., & Gardner, J. W. (2003). *Handbook of machine olfaction.* Dordrecht, The Netherlands: Wiley-VCH.

Reidy, S. (2006). High-performance, static-coated silicon microfabricated columns for gas chromatography. *Analytical Chemistry, 78*(8), 2623–2630. doi:10.1021/ac051846u

Reston, R., & Kolesar, E. (1994). Silicon-micromachined gas chromatography system used to separate and detect ammonia and nitrogen dioxide: Design, fabrication, and integration of the gas chromatography system. *Journal of Microelectromechanical Systems, 3*(4), 134–146. doi:10.1109/84.338634

Röck, F., Barsan, N., & Weimar, U. (2008). Electronic nose: Current status and future trends. *Chemical Reviews, 108*(2), 705–725. doi:10.1021/cr068121q

Shepherd, G. M. (2004). The human sense of smell: are we better than we think? *PLoS Biology, 2*(5), 146. doi:10.1371/journal.pbio.0020146

Taylor, J. E. (2010). *Novel convolution-based processing techniques for applicationn in chemical sensing.* (PhD Thesis). University of Warwick. Coventry, UK.

Terry, S., Jerman, J., & Angell, J. (1979). A gas chromatographic air analyzer fabricated on a silicon wafer. *IEEE Transactions on Electron Devices, 26*(12), 1880–1886. doi:10.1109/T-ED.1979.19791

Xu, Z., Gu, A., & Fang, Z. (2007). Electric conductivity of PS/PA6/carbon black composites. *Journal of Applied Polymer Science, 103*(2), 1042–1047. doi:10.1002/app.25300

Yates, J., Chappell, M. J., & Gardner, J. W. (2007). Novel phenomena based dynamic model of carbon-black/composite vapour sensors. *Proceedings of the Royal Society of London. Series A, 463,* 551–568. doi:10.1098/rspa.2006.1776

Chapter 13
The Technology Demonstration of the Third Generation JPL Electronic Nose on the International Space Station

Abhijit V. Shevade
Jet Propulsion Laboratory (JPL),
California Institute of Technology, USA

Liana M. Lara
Jet Propulsion Laboratory (JPL),
California Institute of Technology, USA

Margie L. Homer
Jet Propulsion Laboratory (JPL),
California Institute of Technology, USA

Hanying Zhou
Jet Propulsion Laboratory (JPL),
California Institute of Technology, USA

Adam K. Kisor
Jet Propulsion Laboratory (JPL),
California Institute of Technology, USA

Kenneth S. Manatt
Jet Propulsion Laboratory (JPL),
California Institute of Technology, USA

Shiao-Ping S. Yen
Jet Propulsion Laboratory (JPL),
California Institute of Technology, USA

Scott Gluck
Jet Propulsion Laboratory (JPL),
California Institute of Technology, USA

Margaret A. Ryan
Jet Propulsion Laboratory (JPL),
California Institute of Technology, USA

ABSTRACT

This chapter describes the development, operation, and experimental results of the Third Generation JPL Electronic Nose (ENose), which operated on board the International Space Station (ISS) as a technology demonstration for seven months from 2008-2009. The JPL ENose is an array of chemiresistive sensors designed to monitor the environment for the sudden release of targeted chemical species, such as leaks or spills. The Third Generation JPL ENose was designed to detect, identify, and quantify eleven chemical species, three inorganic, ammonia, mercury, and sulfur dioxide, and eight organic compounds, which represent common classes of organic compounds such as alcohols, aromatics, and halocarbons. Chemical species were quantified at or below their 24 hour Spacecraft Maximum Allowable Concentrations

DOI: 10.4018/978-1-4666-2521-1.ch013

Copyright © 2013, IGI Global. Copying or distributing in print or electronic forms without written permission of IGI Global is prohibited.

(SMAC), generally in the parts-per-million range; some targeted species were detected in the parts-per-billion range. Analysis of third generation JPL ENose monitoring data on ISS show the short term presence of low concentrations of alcohols, octafluoropropane, and formaldehyde as well as frequent short term unknown events. Repeated unknown events were identified post-flight as sulfur hexafluoride.

INTRODUCTION

The JPL Electronic Nose (Ryan, 1997, 1998, 2000, 2001, 2004a, 2004b) is an event monitor designed and built for near real time air quality monitoring in crew habitat aboard the space shuttle/space station. This is an array–based sensing system which is designed to run continuously and to monitor for the presence of selected chemical species in the air at parts-per-million (ppm) to parts-per-billion (ppb) concentration ranges. The Jet Propulsion Laboratory (JPL) is a federally funded research and development facility managed by the California Institute of Technology for the National Aeronautics and Space Administration (NASA) (http://www.jpl.nasa.gov/). Its mission is to enable space exploration for the benefit of humankind by developing robotic spacecraft and instruments.

There have been three phases of development of the JPL Electronic Nose. In the first phase, arrays of sensors were investigated and a device capable of detecting, analyzing, and quantifying ten analytes at the 1-hour Spacecraft Maximum Allowable Concentration (SMAC) (Toxicology Group, 1999) was developed. This device was tested successfully for six days on Space Shuttle flight STS-95 in 1998 (Ryan, 2004a). In the second phase, the ENose was miniaturized and the capabilities were significantly expanded to include 21 analytes and detection at varying humidity and temperature. This device, the Second Generation ENose, was tested extensively on the ground, and was demonstrated to be able to detect, identify, and quantify the 21 analytes at or below their 24-hour SMACs. The third phase of development was designed to monitor spacecraft cabin air quality in near real-time. A technology demonstration of the Third Generation JPL ENose

aboard the International Space Station (ISS) was performed in 2008-09. Analytes included ammonia, mercury and sulfur dioxide, and eight organic compounds, which represent common classes of organic compounds. Analytes and targeted detection concentrations are shown in Table 1.

Development of the Third Generation JPL ENose required two major areas of development. One area is the design and fabrication of an interface unit which allowed the ENose to be operated through the EXPRESS Rack (EXpedite The PRocessing Of Experiments To Space Station) on the ISS; installation on this rack allows experimental devices to be tested in a realistic space environment. In the other area, the capabilities of the sensing platform, the Second Generation ENose, including sensing materials, sensor substrate, and data analysis routines were expanded

Table 1. Target analytes for the third generation JPL ENose technology demonstration aboard the international space station. SMAC refers to the Spacecraft Maximum Allowable Concentration.

ANALYTE	QUANTITATIVE TARGET (ppm)	24-Hour SMAC (ppm)
1. Ammonia	5.0	20
2. Mercury	0.010	.0020
3. Sulfur Dioxide	1.0	NA
4. Acetone	200	200
5. Dichloromethane	10	35
6. Ethanol	500	2000
7. Freon 218	20	11,000
8. Methanol	10	10
9. 2-Propanol	100	100
10. Toluene	16	16
11. Formaldehyde	0.10	0.10

to include the ability to detect the inorganic species mercury and sulfur dioxide and to provide quasi-real time data analysis with read-out.

Previous experimental investigations reported for spacecraft air quality monitoring applications include event monitors, designed to detect anomalous events such as leaks or spills, and trace gas monitors, designed to monitor the concentrations of potential contaminants known to be present in the air. Devices for monitoring have been tested on the MIR space station and on the International Space Station (ISS). An experimental event monitor using two sensing arrays, one of conducting polymer chemiresistive sensors and one of coated Quartz Crystal Microbalance (QCM) sensors operated on the MIR space station for 40 days within a six month period and again for several days more than a year later (Persaud, 1999). In that experiment, data were downloaded and analyzed after the monitoring period; the device was able to detect changes in the composition of the air and changes were correlated to recorded events. The European Space Agency (ESA) sponsored an ISS test of a sensor array event monitor composed of metalloporphyrin coated crystals in a QCM array device (Martinelli, 2007). That device was operated in several experiments over a period of 9 days and data analyzed afterward. The purpose of that test was demonstration of microgravity operation. NASA's Volatile Organics Analyzer (VOA) is a trace gas monitor composed of a gas chromatograph-ion mobility spectrometer (Limero, 2006). VOA was operated intermittently on ISS for several years. It was designed to detect several tens of constituents in the air with samples taken once a day and included on-board data processing. Finally, the Analysing Interferometer for Ambient Air (ANITA), sponsored by ESA, is a trace-gas monitor based on a Fourier transform infra-red spectrometer (Stuffler, 2008). ANITA operated on-board ISS for one year, taking a sample one time every 40 minutes, with on-board, near real time data analysis. This device was able to detect and identify changes in the atmosphere on ISS.

In the following sections, we will focus on the Third Generation JPL ENose device development, the selection and performance of organic and inorganic sensing materials for the new target analytes elemental mercury and sulfur dioxide, ground testing of the ENose device prior ISS deployment, results of ISS technology demonstration and analysis, and post-flight testing.

DEVELOPMENT OF THE THIRD GENERATION JPL ENOSE FOR ISS TECHNOLOGY DEMONSTRATION

The Third Generation ENose was a modified Second Generation ENose Sensor Unit coupled with an Interface Unit, as shown in Figures 1 and 2. The Interface Unit was designed and built by Oceaneering Space Systems (OSS). The ENose Interface Unit fully encloses ENose Sensor Unit and provides power conditioning and distribution, thermal management and a display. It also includes computers for device control, data acquisition, and data analysis, and interfaces directly with the EXPRESS Rack for power and for data transfer.

The ENose Sensor Unit consists of an anodized aluminum chassis, which houses the sensor array and pneumatic system. The ENose Sensor Unit also contains the electronics to route power, relay data, and commands between the sensor array and the ENose Interface Unit. The Sensor Unit for the Third Generation ENose was designed and built by JPL; it is based on the platform developed as the Second Generation JPL ENose, which has previously been discussed in detail (Shevade, 2007).

The sensor unit monitors the environment by pumping air from the surroundings into the sensor chamber, where sensors in an array respond to the vapors in the environment. Before entering the sensing chamber, the air is directed either through an activated charcoal filter which is put in line to provide cleaned air for baseline data or through a glass bead filter which serves as a particle filter and

Figure 1. The Third Generation JPL ENose sensor unit for the ISS technology demonstration

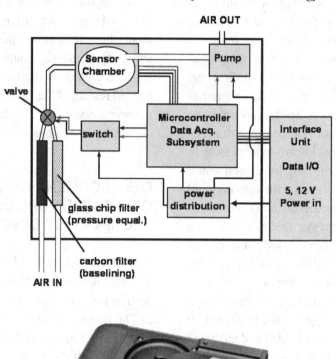

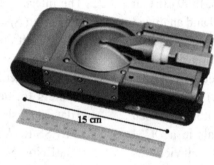

Figure 2. The Third Generation JPL ENose for the technology demonstration on-board ISS. Sensor unit is enclosed in the interface unit which was connected to the ISS EXPRESS Rack.

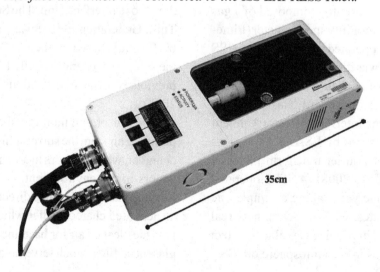

which is in line to provide a pressure drop equal to that in the charcoal filter. A solenoid valve is programmed to open the path to the charcoal filter and provide clean airflow for a programmable period of time at programmable time intervals; otherwise, the air is directed through the glass beads. When air enters the sensing chamber, the resistance of each individual sensing element in the 32-sensor array is measured. A baseline of background air is established at the beginning of a sensing period, and deviations from that baseline are recorded as changes in resistance of the sensors. The pattern of distributed response of the sensors is deconvoluted, and chemical species to which the device has been trained are identified and quantified by using a set of software analysis routines developed for this purpose.

The ENose Interface Unit was designed to draw power at 28 VDC from the EXPRESS Rack (Shevade, 2007); it converts this power from the ISS into voltages compatible with interface unit computer systems and functions and to the electronic and pneumatic systems of the ENose Sensor Unit. The computers in the Interface Unit manage data collection, data storage and data analysis for the ENose. The Interface Unit also controls the thermal environment of the ENose Sensor Unit.

In previous versions of the JPL ENose, sensors in the 32 element sensing array were made from polymer-carbon composite sensing films (Ryan, 1997, 1998, 2000, 2001, 2004a, 2004b) and deposited on 2 mm x 1 mm Pd-Au electrode sets, where electrode spacing is approximately 250 μm. Polymer deposition and the electrode sets have previously been discussed in detail (Ryan, 2001, 2004a, 2004b). In order to detect elemental mercury vapor and sulfur dioxide, it was necessary to develop alternative sensing materials as well as alternative sensor substrates. The substrates developed were designed to fit into the Sensor Unit platform with no changes to the Sensor Unit enclosure and minimal changes to the electronics. Materials were developed specifically to respond to these two analytes. The sensor

material selection for the new analytes mercury and sulfur dioxide is discussed below. The sensor substrates developed for use with materials to detect these analytes are microhotplates, which allow sensing and regeneration of the sensor to take place at temperatures ranging from environmental temperature (20-25° C) up to 200° C. Microhotplate substrates were selected in order to minimize the power requirements of heating the sensor. The sensing chamber as well as the 32 sensor array for the Third Generation JPL ENose is shown in Figure 3.

SELECTION OF SENSING MATERIALS

The Third Generation JPL ENose ISS Technology Demonstration was designed to detect, identify and quantify eleven chemical species, including eight organic compounds as well as ammonia, mercury and sulfur dioxide, at concentrations shown in Table 1. These target concentrations are based on Spacecraft Maximum Allowable Concentrations in human-occupied spacecraft and do not reflect limits of detection of the ENose. The chemical species elemental mercury and sulfur dioxide were not tested in the earlier JPL ENose devices and were added to the list in the Third Generation. The challenge in this project was to develop and select new sensing materials that could be integrated into to the current platform. We will discuss the sensing materials selection for both these new target analytes in the following sections using combined modeling and experimental approaches.

Sensing Materials for Sulfur Dioxide (SO_2)

One approach to development of sensing materials has been to develop molecular models of the interaction energies of the analyte with functional groups present on polymers (Shevade, 2006, 2009;

Figure 3. Sensing chamber of the third generation JPL ENose sensor unit. Seen are sensor array on 4 chips (8 sensors per chip) optimized for target analytes. The sensing array consists of polymer-carbon, gold and palladium chloride films operating at 25-200° C on Si/alumina substrates. Sensors for temperature, pressure, and relative humidity are also included in the sensing chamber.

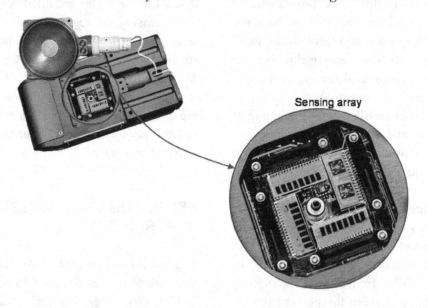

Belmares, 2004; Blanco, 2009). These interaction energies are used to predict which types of polymers are likely to bind to the analyte, and thus may respond to the presence of analyte with a change in resistance in a polymer-carbon composite sensing film. Following the prediction of candidate polymers, sensors are made and tested for response to the analyte, in this case SO_2.

A first principles quantum mechanical model was used to predict the strength of interactions between SO_2 and organic molecules. This methodology involves calculating interaction energies for organic-SO_2 binary systems. Common classes of organic structures are considered as functionalities, which may be found on polymer chains. The calculations undertaken include interaction energies of alkanes, alkenes, aromatics, amines (primary, secondary or tertiary), aldehydes, and carboxylic acids with sulfur dioxide. Interaction energies were calculated using Becke-three-parameter-Lee-Yang-Parr (B3LYP) flavor of Density Functional Theory (DFT) (Becke, 1993; Lee, 1998). DFT is a quantum mechanical model-

ing method that is used to investigate electronic structures and energetics of atoms / molecules / condensed phases. To calculate energetics in DFT, the challenge is in evaluating the exchange correlation part of an effective potential, which has been achieved using hybrid functional forms. Of the many exchange-correlation functions investigated, B3LYP is a popular choice for organic systems as it has been shown to predict the electronic structure and energy well (Tirado-Rives, 2008). These quantum mechanical results were used to develop a first principles force field for use in the calculation of interaction energies (E_{bind}) of SO_2 molecules with various polymers. Only interaction energies less than zero will result in binding between analyte and functional group such that there it may result in a change in resistance in a polymer-carbon composite film. Results of modeled interaction energies of organic-SO_2 systems indicate that a polymer candidate for SO_2 detection would be one containing amine functional groups, preferably primary or secondary. An example of interaction energy calculations

Figure 4. Modeled binding energy of SO$_2$ with amines using quantum mechanics (QM) tools

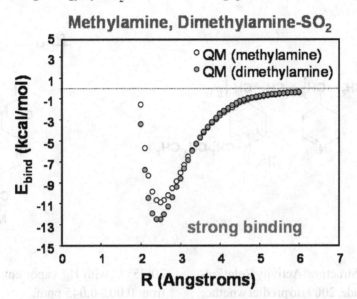

is shown in Figure 4, where E_{bind} is strong, ~ -11 kcal/mole. Other chemical functionalities that have moderate to strong binding with SO$_2$ are amides, aldehydes, and carboxylic acids. Ethane and benzene showed either no binding ($E_{bind} > 0$) or weak binding ($0 > E_{bind} > -4$ kcal/mol).

Two polymers were selected and made into polymer carbon black composite sensors (Ryan, 2006). These two polymers are both poly-4-vinyl pyridine derivatives with a quaternary and a primary amine as shown in Figure 5. The polymers were synthesized from poly-4-vinyl pyridine and made into polymer-carbon composite sensing films using protocols which have been previously described (Ryan, 2001, 2004a, 2004b). These films were loaded with 8-10% carbon by weight and solution deposited onto microhotplate sensor substrates with a sensor area of 200 μm by 200 μm ($4 \times 10_{-8}$ m$_2$). The baseline resistance of each sensor was ~ 10 kΩ. These sensors were exposed to SO$_2$ in 22-25° C air with water content of 10,000 ppm (~40% relative humidity). SO$_2$ concentrations ranged from 0.2 to 20 ppm at atmospheric pressure. Sensors made from both polymers showed strong repeatable response to SO$_2$ in air, as predicted by the modeled interaction

energy between SO$_2$ and primary amines. These two sensing materials were selected in the final sensor set for use in the ISS Technology Demonstration; when integrated into the sensing array, the responses of these polymers to SO$_2$ made distinct patterns which allowed identification and quantification of SO$_2$ vapor.

Sensing Materials for Elemental Mercury (Hg)

As a first step in selection of materials to detect elemental Hg vapor, a literature search was made to determine what had previously been used (Shevade, 2007). It was clear from that search that while there were some developmental materials, metallic gold films are the most reliable method of detecting mercury vapor.

We used several modeling approaches to screen materials for use in the JPL ENose, prior to experiments. We modeled the interaction energies of analytes with polymers using molecular modeling tools (Shevade, 2006, 2009; Belmares, 2004; Blanco, 2009). These interaction energies are used in semi-empirical models developed using multivariate statistical analysis technique

Figure 5. Polymers selected as sensor material to detect SO$_2$. These polymers also showed weak response to elemental mercury (Hg).

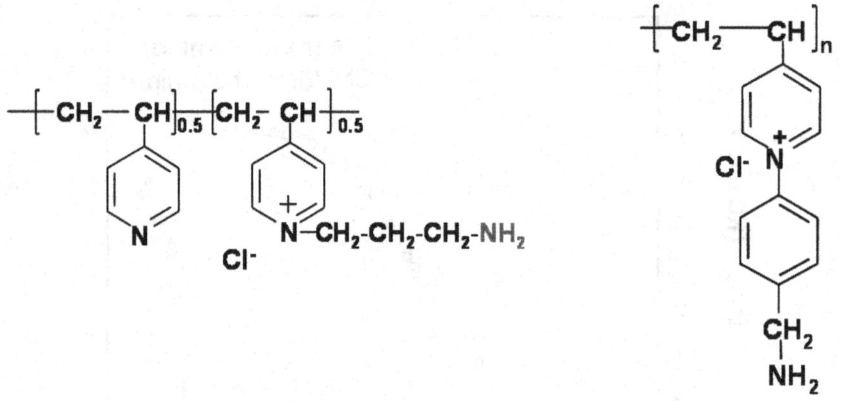

such as Quantitative Structural Activity Relationships (QSAR) (Shevade, 2009) to predict whether particular polymers will respond to the presence of particular analytes with a change in resistance in a polymer-carbon composite sensing film. QSAR studies did not predict any response to Hg from polymers which had previously been used as sensing materials in the JPL ENose.

A second modeling approach as discussed in the previous section is based on Quantum Mechanical techniques, was developed to model the interaction energies of analytes and functional groups present on polymers (Belmares, 2004; Blanco, 2009). Both inorganic and organic materials were investigated as sensing materials for Hg. This modeling technique predicted that polymers containing amines would respond to Hg vapor. The interaction of the amine functionality with elemental mercury, shown in Figure 6, is weak as compared to the interaction with SO$_2$, as discussed in the previous section.

We tested several sensing materials for Hg detection, including gold films, treated gold films, sintered Palladium Chloride (PdCl$_2$) thick films, polymer-carbon composite thick films, and thin gold films on polymer-carbon composites. All materials were tested in flowing cleaned, humidified air (relative humidity ~30%) at

20-25° C with Hg vapor concentrations ranging from 0.002-0.045 ppm.

The two materials selected for the Technology Demonstration were thin gold films, the standard material for vapor phase Hg detection, and sintered PdCl$_2$ thick films. With these two materials, the Third Generation ENose includes dissimilar redundancy for Hg detection. Neither of these materials shows significant response to other analytes selected for this Technology Demonstration and so worked well within the sensing array to distinguish Hg from other analytes.

Materials which showed good response to mercury vapor but which were not used in the Third Generation ENose include abraded gold films and gold-on-polymer films (Shevade, 2007). Abraded gold films require further work to make the response reproducible. Gold-on-polymer films have excellent response to mercury vapor, but it was found that it would be necessary to develop deposition methods to impart batch-to-batch reproducibility in these films; thus, they were not included in the ENose sensing array for this application. In addition, amine containing polymers selected for SO$_2$ detection (discussed above) showed minor response to Hg, and may be used to follow clean up processes if there is high concentration of mercury released into the air by a containment failure.

Figure 6. Modeled binding energy of elemental Hg with amines using quantum mechanics (QM) tools. Circles (open and filled) are calculated binding energy of elemental mercury with methylamine and dimethylamine. Lines are Morse potentials calculated separately.

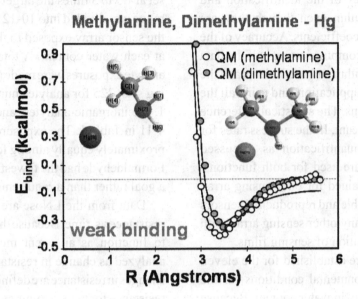

GROUND VALIDATION PRIOR TO ISS DEPLOYMENT

Prior to deployment on International Space Station (ISS) the Third Generation JPL ENose was ground tested for the performance of the device (Ryan, 2008).

Environmental Conditions

The environmental conditions under which testing was done were defined according to conditions which can be expected in the US Lab on the ISS. Background air composition was based on allowed ISS atmospheric concentrations of water, carbon dioxide, and methane. Relative Humidity (%RH) may vary from 25-75% at temperatures of 18-30° C, CO_2 concentration may be as much as ~15 mm Hg partial pressure and CH_4 may be several hundred ppm. Atmospheric pressure in the ISS may vary from 538-760 torr (10.4 to 14.7 psi) and may rise for brief periods (minutes) as high as 830 torr (16 psi).

Temperature may vary over the range 18-30° C. Nominal conditions are 760 torr, temperature 21-23° C and relative humidity 30-40%. Testing was done under all conditions, but not all concentrations of all analytes were tested under all conditions. For repeatability in testing, water content was controlled as ppm water rather than as relative humidity. Nominal conditions on orbit in ISS correspond approximately to 21-22° C, 10,000 ppm water, and atmospheric pressure.

Training Sets

As the ENose is an array-based chemical sensor device, before it can be used as an air quality monitor, training sets must be acquired. Based on the training sets, the patterns of array response to targeted analytes under specified conditions are included in the data analysis algorithm. Training sets give insight into the conditions under which ENose operates best, which conditions cause difficulties in identification and quantification, and allow calculation of performance as accuracy of identification and quantification, number of false negatives and number of false positives using a large number of trials. Training sets can be used to judge the accuracy of the identification and quantification algorithm even though they are used to establish the coefficients. Accuracy of the algorithm has been computed using half the data to establish the algorithm and coefficients and the other half to test the application, and using all the data for both functions. The statistical difference in results is insignificant. In the success rates for identification and quantification as discussed below, all the data are used for both functions. The training set obtained for one sensing array consisting of repeatable and reproducible sensors could be applied to any other sensing array with same set and distribution of sensing films.

Training sets were established for the eleven analytes. The environmental conditions for the training sets vary only in water content. Because there is temperature control in the sensing chamber in the ENose, the environmental temperature does not influence the temperature at which analytes are detected, identified and quantified. Detection temperature is held at 25-27° C for all training sets. Detection temperature rises above 27° C only when environmental temperature approaches 30° C, the maximum temperature for ENose operation, in which case detection temperature will be 27-28° C. The relative humidity of the environment will be altered if the temperature of the sensing chamber is different from the temperature of the environment, so for training sets, the humidity is regulated as ppm water. Training sets were made in a background of filtered house air with water concentrations of 5000, 10,000, 15,000, and 20,000 ppm. These concentrations correspond roughly to 20%, 40%, 60%, and 80% relative humidity at 21° C, and cover the specified range of humidities for the specified range of temperatures. The response of the sensors in the JPL ENose have been shown to be pressure-insensitive in response (Ryan, 2004a), and so varied pressure training sets were not made, although performance validation tests were done at diminished pressures.

In designing training sets, the range of analyte concentration to which sensors are exposed was set at 1/3 to 3 times the target concentration. This range was divided into 10-12 concentrations, and the sensor array exposed to those concentrations at each water content. A total of 1599 different analyte exposures were made to establish the training sets; 325 for analytes numbered 1-3 in Table 1, the inorganic analytes, and 1274 for analytes 4-11 in Table 1. The exposures were divided approximately equally among four humidity levels. Formaldehyde had the fewest exposures, as it was a goal rather than a requirement in this program.

Data from the ENose are recorded as sensor resistance vs. time. Because the ENose is designed to function as an event monitor, the data are analyzed as change in resistance vs. time, where changes in resistance are defined against the sensor resistance for the 3-5 minutes immediately before resistance started changing. Individual sensor resistances are recorded simultaneously, with a point being taken every twenty seconds. While it would be possible to take data more or less frequently than three times a minute, this data rate has been established as an optimum rate to show fairly rapid changes in the environment without overwhelming computer memory with data. Our data analysis approach defines an "event" as a change in the composition of the environment which lasts longer than ten minutes, or thirty points at the standard data rate, in part because events of duration shorter than ten minutes cannot practically be addressed or mitigated using either breathing apparatus or clean-up techniques. The data analysis algorithm needs about ten points (~ three minutes) to establish that resistance has changed significantly. Based on the data rate and needs of the data analysis algorithm, training sets were established using vapor deliveries, or events, of 30-45 minutes duration.

The data analysis uses a Levenberg-Marquart non-linear least squares fitting approach to deconvolute changes in resistance across the sensing array into identification and quantification of the analyte causing response in the sensors. It has been discussed in detail previously (Zhou, 2006). As important as the analysis approach itself is, the challenge is to extract accurate ENose resistance change (sensor response peak height relative to its base response) from the time-series data due to the baseline drift problem. The causes for baseline drift can be multiple (variations in temperature, humidity, pressure, aging of the sensors, and sensor saturation), while the underlying mechanism of each one of the causes is not fully understood at the present time. Direct compensation (e.g. baseline subtraction from humidity or temperature readings) was found to be unreliable. In our work we use the fact that the baseline drift is generally slowly-varying in nature compared to the response time of a detectable gas event. This difference in time scale enables us to use a long-length digital filter to determine the approximate baseline drift over an extended time (say, 2 hours or longer). Specifically, for baseline estimation purpose, we first retain non-event regions as baseline points (A). Any gas event regions over the time period are carefully blanked out (with detected events information) and filled in with piece-wise linear fit (B). Newest data are held at the level either of last checked point (when it is not an event at the last check) or of the last event beginning level (if an event is detected at the last check) (C). Baseline drift can then be estimated by filtering points made of (A+B+C) and removed from the raw responses. This approach provides a practical and effective method to accommodate the baseline drift effect. Humidity caused change is not currently treated as baseline change; instead it is treated as an analyte (as it often exhibits itself as an event). During sensor array training, libraries for analyte training sets at different relative humidity conditions are recorded. During the ENose operation, data recorded from the humidity sensor in the JPL ENose sensor chamber is used to select the appropriate training library for analyte identification and quantification. Data analysis is

returned 10-30 minutes from the start of an event, depending on the analyte and the concentration.

Success Rates

Success in detection signifies that the analyte was detected, identified correctly, and quantified within +/- 50% of the measured delivered concentration of analyte. A false positive is detection of an "event," defined as a change in environment caused by the presence of a targeted species, where there was none, or mis-identification of an event (*e.g.* identification of toluene as methanol), or quantification outside the required range even if identified correctly. A false negative is failure to identify that an event has happened, without respect to identification or quantification.

In a total of 1599 exposures, the overall success rate for the inorganic analytes, numbered 1-3 in Table 1 was 89%, and was 80% for analytes 4-10, over all humidity and pressure conditions. Weighting these success rates for the number of chemical species in each category, inorganic or organic, the success rate for identification and quantification of delivered species in training sets was 83% over all conditions.

At nominal conditions, environmental temperature of 21-22° C and 10,000 ppm water (about 40% RH), the success rate for inorganic analytes 1-3 was 93%, and was 85% for organic analytes. The overall success rate for all species under nominal conditions was 87%.

OPERATION ON THE INTERNATIONAL SPACE STATION

The JPL ENose was launched on STS-126 on November 14, 2008. It was unstowed, installed on EXPRESS Rack 2 in the US Lab and activated at 08:46 GMT, December 9, 2008 and ran continuously while powered until it was disconnected for return to earth on July 15, 2009. ENose operated for a total of 4855 hours and took data continuously.

Figure 7. Third generation JPL ENose GUI, showing instrument operating parameters (voltage, current, and power; environmental information such as temperature and pressure; interior temperature; sensor raw resistances)

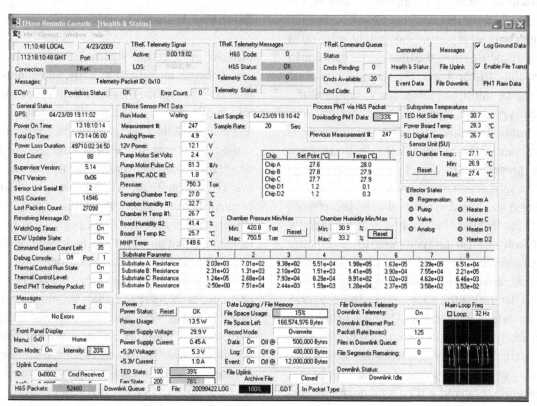

Within minutes of activation, data from ENose were received at JPL. Data were streamed through a Graphical User Interface (GUI) designed for the process. Streamed data included instrument status data for EXPRESS Rack monitoring, device health information and sensor data. Some key device health information includes (as shown in Figure 7): input power data information from the EXPRESS Rack, the temperature data on the interface unit / sensor unit, sensor unit pump performance data, as well as resistances and temperature data from individual sensing substrates. The data stream could be read whenever there was signal from space to ground. Figure 7 shows a snapshot of the GUI as it was running on a JPL local computer.

A photo of the ENose installed on EXPRESS Rack 2 is shown in Figure 8. Instrument health and status data are transmitted from the EXPRESS Rack to ground one time per second; ENose data acquisition and storage was designed to fold raw sensor data into the health and status data, and so we are able to capture real time ENose sensor as well as instrument health data on the ground.

INITIAL DATA FROM ISS

Humidity Cycles

Initial data sets acquired by the ENose on ISS showed a periodic rise and fall of about 3 percent relative humidity with a period of 144 minutes. Figure 9a shows an example of a 24-hour data file; the upper trace is percent relative humidity, as measured by a humidity sensor installed in the same chamber as the ENose sensors (y-axis

Figure 8. The ENose deployed on ISS; it is located on EXPRESS Rack 2, on the "ceiling" above a hatch (circled in red), shown on the left and zoom-in picture of the JPL ENose shown on the right.

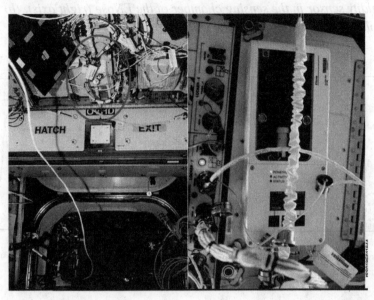

on right), and the lower traces are normalized change in resistance of eight polymer-carbon black sensors (y-axis on left; dR/R_0 where R_0 is set arbitrarily to the first point in the file.) This plot shows that sensor resistance change follows humidity change with little or no time offset. If the species detected had been at low concentration, there might have been somewhat more of a time offset as sufficient analyte sorbed into sensors to cause a resistance change.

Figure 9b shows the results of the automated analysis of sensor data. The analysis program detected a rise and fall of about 1000 ppm water on a 144 minute period, with little or no time delay. This plot shows percent relative humidity on the left y-axis and ppm change in water content on the right y-axis. The two axes are set to span the same range; *i.e.* a change of 4.5 percent relative humidity is equivalent to a change of 1700 ppm water.

Earlier laboratory work on the ability of ENose to detect changes in the environment showed that changes of 5–10 percent relative humidity over a period of a minute would interfere with the ability

of the ENose analysis program to deconvolute the data and recognize target species; however, the humidity changes detected on ISS occur over 20–30 minutes and do not interfere with the data analysis process.

The periodic rise and fall of humidity was present for the first several days of operation on ISS, then stopped, and humidity and temperature were steady. Comparison of ENose data with the schedule of operation of another instrument under test at the time ENose was activated, the Carbon Dioxide Removal Assembly (CDRA) showed a correlation in time between when the CDRA was operating and the presence of regular rise and fall of humidity detected by the ENose. Over the entire period of operation of the ENose on ISS, the CDRA was turned on and off several times, and each time the operation of CDRA correlated with the presence of periodic humidity change. The CDRA has a 144 minute half cycle and can expel humidity during the desiccant bed regeneration; thus, we assigned the periodic humidity rise and fall to the CDRA.

Figure 9. Third generation JPL ENose sensor data taken on ISS. Shown (a) eight sensors plotted with change in resistance against the initial point in the trace. The trace on the top is relative humidity as measured by a humidity sensor in the sensing chamber of the ENose (right axis). (b) Relative humidity in the sensing chamber varied by about 3% RH with a period of 144 minutes.

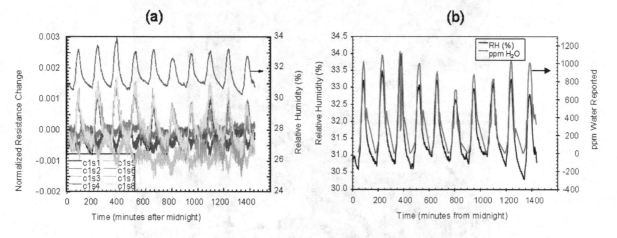

Confirmational Event

To confirm that the JPL ENose was working nominally, the ISS crew members were asked to perform a "confirmational event" periodically. In a confirmational event, a crew member held a disinfectant wipe in front of the air-inlet of the device. Sensors would respond to this event and we could analyze the data to confirm nominal operation. The first confirmational event for ENose was done about two weeks after activation. A crew member held a disinfectant wipe in front of the ENose air inlet for one minute, to provide a stimulus to the sensors at a recorded time. The first confirmational event was easily seen in the sensor resistance data and was detected by the automated analysis program. The analysis program reported the stimulus as "unknown." The sensor response signature of the disinfectant wipe was not included in the ENose data library, as this event gave us the opportunity to confirm that ENose was able to report unknowns. Subsequent to this first confirmational event, a crewmember performed one once every two weeks. No confirmational event was mis-identified as a targeted species.

Events Reported

In normal operation on ISS, and in the absence of real-time monitoring, very few changes in environment which might be considered to be events are reported. The source of these reports is generally crew observation. Samples of air are taken in the US Lab Destiny of ISS about once a month. Analysis of those samples lags considerably in time from when they are taken because they must be transported to the ground and analyzed at Johnson Space Center.

ENose detected several events during the seven-month period of operation. Most events detected by ENose on ISS lasted 30-60 minutes; the longest lasting event was less than two hours. That events did not last longer than two hours indicates that events detected by ENose were truly chemical release events, where a chemical species was released and concentration rose, then concentration fell as the air in the US Lab was taken up by the Environmental Control and Life Support System (ECLSS), cleaned and returned to the environment. The airflow rate within the US Lab is 663 m³/hour; with a volume of 122 m³, US Lab air will be replaced one time in about 11 minutes. With this replenishment rate, a single release should be cleaned from the US lab in 30-60 minutes. The airflow rate into and out of the US Lab from other modules in ISS is about 1/3 the flow rate within the lab (230 m³/hour), so chemical species entering the lab from other modules would have to be at a rather high concentration in order to travel to a single point monitor to be detected.

Previous work in testing air quality instruments on ISS has included the NASA's Volatile Organics Analyzer (VOA), a gas chromatograph-ion mobility spectrometer (Limero, 2006), and the European Space Agency's Analysing Interferometer for Ambient Air (ANITA), a Fourier transform infrared spectrometer (Stuffler, 2008). VOA measurements were taken up to a few times a day, and so provide a snapshot of the presence (or absence) of some forty chemical species, but does not give insight into air constituent changes lasting less than several hours. ANITA measurements were taken more frequently, and the instrument was designed to run continuously. However, measurements were reported about forty minutes apart, and so would not give insight into changes lasting less than one or two hours. Results from ANITA experiments showed that there was much greater fluctuation in the composition of air in the US Lab

than had previously been thought (Honne, 2009). In particular, the ANITA experiment showed a persistent presence of low-concentration Freon 218 (octafluoropropane) with occasional spikes in concentration.

With this knowledge, we expected that we might see changes in Freon 218 concentration in the environment, along with other small organic molecules previously measured in the ISS atmosphere, such as alcohols and formaldehyde. A summary of events detected by ENose is shown in Table 2. There were several events related to changes in Freon 218 concentration in the environment, along with other small organic molecules previously measured in the ISS atmosphere, such as alcohols and formaldehyde. There are several reports of "unknown" species causing a stimulus to the ENose sensors. The identity of these unknowns is discussed below.

CHARACTERIZATION OF UNKNOWN EVENTS

During its operation on ISS, as discussed above, the JPL ENose detected several short lived, low concentration events of ethanol, methanol, Freon 218 and formaldehyde. In addition, there were sev-

Table 2. Summary of the analytes detected by the third generation JPL ENose during continuous operation aboard the international space station during December, 2008 and July, 2009. SMAC refers to Spacecraft Maximum Allowable Concentration. "Unknown" refers to the chemical species outside the set of target analytes (Table 1).

Species	Number of Events	Minimum Concentration detected (ppm)	Maximum Concentration detected (ppm)	One Hour SMAC (ppm)
Ethanol	1	450	800	5000
Methanol	24	3	40	200
Formaldehyde	57	0.18	0.22	0.8
Freon 218	19	6	91	11,000
Confirmational Event	13	na	na	na
Unknown	22	-	-	-

eral events classified as "unknown," events caused by chemical species outside the set of targeted analytes. After the full experimental period, the array response fingerprint patterns of the unknown events were analyzed statistically to determine whether they were similar enough to be considered to be caused by a single stimulus. A 90% overlap in fingerprint patterns is considered to be a result of the same stimulus. Of the 22 unknown events, 11 were clearly caused by the same stimulus, with 90% or greater overlap. Five events were clearly similar to each other and possibly similar to the first 11, with 80-90% overlap between these 5 and the first 11 events. Six events were unrelated to each other or other events.

We have developed and applied modeling approaches to identify the chemical nature of the analyte(s) producing unknown events (Shevade, 2010). Identification was achieved by using sensor response models based on molecular principles developed using Quantitative Structure-Activity Relationships (QSAR) and First Principles Molecular Dynamics approaches.

Quantitative Structure-Activity Relationships (QSAR) Model

The QSAR approach used in modeling polymer-carbon black sensor response (Shevade, 2006, 2009) uses a novel molecular descriptor set that was developed at JPL for this purpose; this set combines descriptors of sensing film-analyte interactions, representing sensor response, with a basic analyte descriptor set (e.g., molar refractivity, molecular volume, number of hydrogen bond donor/acceptor sites, dipole, etc.). Statistically validated QSAR models have been developed using Genetic Function Approximations (GFA) for a sensor array for a given training data set. Using this modeling approach, molecular descriptors for the unknown species were calculated from eight polymer-carbon composite sensor responses. These molecular descriptors were then compared with descriptors for a selection of chemical species,

as shown in Table 3. The chemical species which has molecular descriptors closest to the calculated ones is sulfur hexafluoride (SF_6).

First Principles Molecular Dynamics Hansen Solubility Model

A second sensor response model used to determine the identity of the unknown is based on Hansen solubility parameters for the analytes and amorphous polymers (Belmares, 2004; Blanco, 2009). This model was developed by the Materials and Process Simulation Center at Caltech. Hansen solubility parameters are fitted to measured polymer-carbon sensor responses with physically rooted analytical models. Sensor responses for eight polymer-carbon composite sensors were used to calculate a solubility parameter and molecular volume, and compared with known values for a selection of chemical species. As with the Hansen solubility model, the chemical species with a solubility parameter and molecular volume closest to the values calculated from sensor responses is SF_6. The match between calculated descriptors and those of SF_6 is not exact, but rather represents the best fit among candidate chemical species.

A ground experiment with SF_6 on the flight unit after it was returned to JPL showed that the sensing array responds to SF_6 at concentrations above 1000 ppm and that the array fingerprint matches the unknown fingerprint with an 85% overlap. This degree of overlap is borderline in indicating that the two fingerprints come from the same species. Thus, while calculations show that it is possible that the unknown species is likely to be SF_6, experiment offers only moderate support to this conclusion. It is possible that the unknown species is another species altogether, or a mixture of SF_6 with another species. The similarities of calculated values to literature values in Table 3 also give moderate support to the conclusion that the unknown is SF_6, but the differences also support the idea that the unknown is a mixture of species.

There are several chemical species that might have parameters similar to those calculated, and so this identification of the unknown as SF_6 is not certain. Calculated parameters do not match those of SF_6 exactly, although they match SF_6 better than any other species considered. As can be seen from Table 3, there is a possibility that the unknown species is Halon 1301, and the unknown species may be some other compound or chemical species not considered. In an earlier experiment, the European Space Agency's ANITA technology demonstration, found a signal corresponding to about 1 ppm SF_6 in ISS air (Honne, 2009). In the same experiment, Halon 1301 was found, but only during a shuttle docking. Thus, SF_6 is a good candidate for the chemical species, which caused the unknown signal seen during ENose's seven months of operation.

POST-FLIGHT VERIFICATION

The ENose flight unit was returned to JPL in October, 2009, after returning to earth on shuttle flight 17A (STS-128). On receipt, the ENose was inspected. It had no nicks or scratches, no bent pins, and all caps and covers were in place. It looked as it did when delivered.

The ENose was installed on the laboratory bench at the main gas handling system, where training sets were developed. ENose was exposed to two concentrations each of three of the four species detected on orbit. The exposures were ethanol 450 and 800 ppm, methanol 3 and 10 ppm, and formaldehyde 0.21 and 0.25 ppm. These exposures were selected based on the quantities of each of these three analytes detected on orbit, the target detection range, and the quantities, which could be delivered without modifying the vapor delivery system. The quantities detected on orbit were ethanol 800 ppm, methanol 3–40 ppm (detection range 1–10 ppm), and formaldehyde 0.17 to 0.23 ppm (detection range 0.1–0.3 ppm).

Each of the analytes delivered by the vapor delivery system was detected, identified, and quantified correctly by ENose. Ethanol was quantified as 350 and 630 ppm for 400 and 800 ppm delivered. Methanol was quantified as 3 and 8 ppm. Formaldehyde was quantified as 0.19 and 0.23 ppm. In each case, the quantification is accurate to better than +/- 50%, as required. Freon 218 was not tested in post-flight verification

Table 3. Molecular descriptors of chemical species and calculated descriptors for unknown events. The columns dipole, molecular weight, molar volume, etc. are some of the molecular descriptors used in the JPL ENose sensor response model.

Possible chemical species	Dipole	Mol. weight	Mol. volume (A^3)	H-bond acceptor sites	H-bond donor sites	Molar refractivity	Solubility Parameter (cal/ cm^3)$^{1/2}$
Sulfur hexafluoride	0.001	146.05	73.41	6	0	9.01	1.5
2-ethoxyethanol	3.836	90.12	96.65	2	1	24.05	11.47
Bromotrifluoromethane (Halon 1301)	3.105	148.91	61.93	4	0	15.54	4.83
Ethylene glycol	3.579	62.07	61.89	2	2	14.55	16.11
Hexamethyl cyclotrisiloxane	0.021	222.46	209.37	3	0	39.70	
Model predictions							
Unknown (QSAR)	0.01				0	5	
Unknown (Hansen solubility)			50				2.16

because to do so would have required modifying the vapor delivery system. We concluded that if three of the four analytes were identified and quantified correctly, that post-flight operation verified the accuracy of the events detected during the operational period on ISS.

CONCLUSION

The JPL ENose Technology Demonstration on-board ISS showed that the Third Generation ENose operated autonomously, continuously and reliably in the ISS environment, and that it can be used as an event monitor. The overall vision for development of air quality monitoring using a sensing array such as ENose goes further than developing the instrument. For a technology such as ENose to be useful, it would be necessary to distribute several around the crew habitat. In this way, the differences among various locations could be monitored, and the development of an event could also be monitored and pinpointed in space as well as time. Finally, a truly autonomous system would integrate environmental control functions with the monitoring functions provided by a distributed network of sensing arrays. In this way, crew habitat would include a system in which deviations from healthy air detected by the monitor would initiate environmental control measures such as closing off areas and triggering additional clean-up functions.

During the operational period, JPL ENose detected one instance of ethanol and several events of Freon 218, formaldehyde and methanol. In no case did the concentration approach hazardous levels. In addition to detecting the four targeted species, ENose detected 22 events which were classified as "unknown." A subset of 11 of these unknown events are tentatively identified as SF_6 or a mixture of another species plus SF_6. It has not been possible to correlate the events detected with activities within the US Lab, although many of the daily changes in humidity content of the environment can be correlated with crew exercise or meal periods. Without detailed logs of activities, their duration and their location, it will not be possible to determine a cause for any of the events detected, and even then, it may not be possible to pinpoint sources for events detected.

Sensor response models based on molecular understanding of polymer-carbon sensing film response to an analyte were used to identify the chemical nature of the analyte(s) causing the unknown events. The predicted molecular descriptors using unknown events show a close but not exact match to the molecular descriptors of sulfur hexafluoride (SF_6). The match represents the best fit among candidate chemical species. There are several chemical species and possibilities of mixtures that might have parameters similar to those calculated, and so this identification of the unknown as SF_6 is not certain. In order to refine the understanding of the sensor response, further work will be necessary.

As NASA moves towards deep space and long duration exploration, including human missions, monitoring space and/or surface habitats will become more important. Long-term build up of contaminants as well as events involving potential chemical hazards can compromise the safety of the life support system and crew health. The return of air and water samples for ground analysis will become cost and time prohibitive and the need for *in situ* monitoring and analysis capabilities will become crucial with long duration human missions. Possible directions of future ENose work will include increasing the number of analytes, improving the identification of unknowns, extending the lifetime of the sensors, and development of adaptive software for self-calibration.

ACKNOWLEDGMENT

The research reported in this chapter was carried out at the Jet Propulsion Laboratory, California Institute of Technology, under a contract with the

National Aeronautics and Space Administration and supported by the Advanced Environmental Monitoring and Control Program, ESMD, NASA.

REFERENCES

Becke, A. D. (1993). Density-functional thermochemistry 3: The role of exact exchange. *The Journal of Chemical Physics*, *98*, 5648–5652. doi:10.1063/1.464913

Belmares, M., Blanco, M., & Goddard, W. A. (2004). Hildebrand and Hansen solubility parameters from molecular dynamics with applications to electronic nose polymer sensors. *Journal of Computational Chemistry*, *25*(15), 1814–1826. doi:10.1002/jcc.20098

Blanco, M., Shevade, A. V., & Ryan, M. A. (2009). Quantum mechanics and first-principles molecular dynamics selection of polymer sensing materials. In Ryan, M. A., Shevade, A. V., Taylor, C. J., Homer, M. L., Blanco, M., & Stetter, J. R. (Eds.), *Computational Methods for Sensor Material Selection*. New York, NY: Springer. doi:10.1007/978-0-387-73715-7_3

Honne, A., Schumann-Olsen, H., Kaspersen, K., Limero, T., Macatangay, A., et al. (2009). Evaluation of ANITA air monitoring on the international space station. In *Proceedings 39th International Conference on Environmental Systems*. Society of Automotive Engineers (SAE).

Lee, C. T., Yang, W. T., & Parr, R. G. (1998). Development of the Colle-Salvetti correlation-energy formula into a functional of the electron-density. *Physical Review B: Condensed Matter and Materials Physics*, *37*, 785–789. doi:10.1103/PhysRevB.37.785

Limero, T., Cheng, P., & Boyd, J. (2006). Evaluation of gas chromatography-differential mobility spectrometry for measurement of air contaminants in spacecraft. In *Proceedings 36th International Conference on Environmental Systems*. Society of Automotive Engineers (SAE).

Martinelli, E., Zampetti, E., Pantalei, S., Lo Castro, F., Santonico, M., & Pennazza, G. (2007). Design and test of an electronic nose for monitoring the air quality in the international space station. *Microgravity Science and Technology*, *19*(2), 46–49.

Persaud, K. C., Pisanelli, A. M., Szyszko, S., Reichl, M., Horner, G., & Rakow, W. (1999). A smart gas sensor for monitoring environmental changes in closed systems: Results from the MIR space station. *Sensors and Actuators. B, Chemical*, *55*, 118–126. doi:10.1016/S0925-4005(99)00168-9

Ryan, M. A., Homer, M. L., Buehler, M. G., Manatt, K. S., Lau, B., Karmon, D., & Jackson, S. (1998). Monitoring space shuttle air for selected contaminants using an electronic nose. In *Proceedings 28th International Conference on Environmental Systems*. Society of Automotive Engineers (SAE).

Ryan, M. A., Homer, M. L., Buehler, M. G., Manatt, K. S., Zee, F., & Graf, J. (1997). Monitoring the air quality in a closed chamber using an electronic nose. In *Proceedings 27th International Conference on Environmental Systems*. Society of Automotive Engineers (SAE).

Ryan, M. A., Homer, M. L., Zhou, H., Manatt, K., & Manfreda, A. (2001). Toward a second generation electronic nose at JPL: Sensing film optimization studies. In *Proceedings 31st International Conference on Environmental Systems*. Society of Automotive Engineers (SAE).

Ryan, M. A., Homer, M. L., Zhou, H., Manatt, K., Manfreda, A., & Kisor, A., Shevade, A., & Yen, S. P. S. (2006). Expanding the capabilities of the JPL electronic nose for an international space station technology demonstration. In *Proceedings 36th International Conference on Environmental Systems*. Society of Automotive Engineers (SAE).

Ryan, M. A., Homer, M. L., Zhou, H., Manatt, K. S., Ryan, V. S., & Jackson, S. (2000). Operation of an electronic nose aboard the space shuttle and directions for research for a second generation device. In *Proceedings 30th International Conference on Environmental Systems*. Society of Automotive Engineers (SAE).

Ryan, M. A., Shevade, A. V., Kisor, A. K., Manatt, K. S., Homer, M. L., Lara, L. M., & Zhou, H. (2008). Ground validation of the third generation JPL electronic Nose. In *Proceedings 38th International Conference on Environmental Systems*. Society of Automotive Engineers (SAE).

Ryan, M. A., Shevade, A. V., Zhou, H., & Homer, M. L. (2004b). Polymer-carbon-composite sensors for an electronic nose air quality monitor. *MRS Bulletin, 29*, 714. doi:10.1557/mrs2004.208

Ryan, M. A., Zhou, H., Buehler, M. G., Manatt, K. S., Mowrey, V. S., & Jackson, S. P. (2004a). Monitoring space shuttle air quality using the JPL electronic nose. *IEEE Sensors Journal, 4*, 337. doi:10.1109/JSEN.2004.827275

Shevade, A. V., Homer, M. L., Taylor, C. J., Zhou, H., Jewell, A. D., & Manatt, K. S. (2006). Correlating polymer-carbon composite sensor response with molecular descriptors. *Journal of the Electrochemical Society, 153*, H209–H216. doi:10.1149/1.2337771

Shevade, A. V., Homer, M. L., Zhou, H., Jewell, A. D., Kisor, A. K., Manatt, K.S., Torres, J., Soler, J., Yen, S.-P. S., Blanco, M., Goddard III, W. A., & Ryan, M. A. (2007). Development of the third generation JPL electronic nose for international space station technology demonstration. *Journal of Aerospace SAE Transactions, 2007-01-3149*. Retrieved from http://enose.jpl.nasa.gov/publications/ICES-Amy-2007.pdf

Shevade, A. V., Ryan, M. A., Homer, M. L., Kisor, A. K., Lara, L. M., & Zhou, H., Manatt, K. S., & Gluck, S. (2010). Characterization of unknown events observed by the 3rd generation JPL electronic nose using sensor tesponse models. In *Proceedings 40th International Conference on Environmental Systems*. American Institute of Aeronautics and Astronautics (AIAA).

Shevade, A. V., Ryan, M. A., Homer, M. L., & Zhou, H. (2009). Chemical sensor array response modeling using quantitative structure-activity relationships. In Ryan, M. A., Shevade, A. V., Taylor, C. J., Homer, M. L., Blanco, M., & Stetter, J. R. (Eds.), *Computational Methods for Sensor Material Selection*. New York, NY: Springer. doi:10.1007/978-0-387-73715-7_8

Stuffler, T., Mosebach, H., Kampf, D., Honne, A., Schumann-Olsen, H., & Kaspersen, K., Supper, W., & Tan, G. (2008). ANITA air monitoring on the international space station part 1: The mission. In *Proceedings 38th International Conference on Environmental Systems*. Society of Automotive Engineers (SAE).

Tirado-Rives, L., & Jorgensen, W. L. (2008). Performance of B3LYP density functional methods for a large set of organic molecules. *Journal of Chemical Theory and Computation, 4*, 297–306. doi:10.1021/ct700248k

Toxicology Group. (1999). *Spacecraft Maximum Allowable Concentrations for airborne contaminants*. Houston, TX: National Aeronautics and Space Administration (NASA).

Zhou, H., Homer, M. L., Shevade, A. V., & Ryan, M. A. (2006). Nonlinear least-squares based method for identifying and quantifying single and mixed contaminants in air with an electronic nose. *Sensors (Basel, Switzerland)*, 6, 1–18. doi:10.3390/s6010001

Chapter 14
Improving the Robustness of Odor Sensing Systems by Multivariate Signal Processing

Marta Padilla
University of Barcelona, Spain

Jordi Fonollosa
University of Barcelona, Spain

Santiago Marco
University of Barcelona, Spain

ABSTRACT

Electronic noses or artificial olfaction systems based on chemical gas sensors present lack of robustness, a problem that is mainly technological and requires more research to improve fabrication processes and develop new technologies. However, statistical signal processing can help to mathematically reduce those unwanted effects on the sensors responses before the prediction step. In this chapter, the authors explore the concept of robustness in electronic nose instruments and the use of several multivariate signal processing techniques to deal with two specific problems related to such lack of robustness: time instability (drift) and the detection of a possible faulty sensor in the array. In particular, three different techniques that deal with drift problems are reviewed. These techniques address drift by correction of unwanted variance, by taking advantage of the characteristics of a three-way data arrangement, or by using a blind strategy to extract information with chemical meaning. Finally, a method based on principal component analysis is presented for fault detection, faulty sensor identification, and correction of a fault in a sensor array.

DOI: 10.4018/978-1-4666-2521-1.ch014

Copyright © 2013, IGI Global. Copying or distributing in print or electronic forms without written permission of IGI Global is prohibited.

INTRODUCTION

Persaud and Dodd proposed the first electronic nose (e-nose) in 1982. Electronic noses (e-noses) or Artificial Olfaction (AO) systems were very promising for many qualitative and quantitative applications in the nineties. Researchers expected to develop a device capable of recognizing odors and characterize them with attribute descriptors such fruity, grassy, earthy, malty, etc., just like human sense of smell does. Electronic noses were also designed to be an alternative to the use of other instruments for gas analysis or detection. At that time, e-noses were expected to present a set of very interesting characteristics such as being of small size, low cost, low power consumption, fast, easy to use and to provide a prediction of the human odor impression. Consequently, especially interesting applications for these instruments were on-field fast detection and/or quantification of target gases or volatiles and global evaluations of aroma, even replacing human sensory panels, which would considerably reduce the related costs. However, despite these many potential advantages, nowadays, almost 30 years after the first device, e-noses have not reached the initially expected success. The main reason lies in the sensing area of the instrument, which exhibits poor selectivity and bad stability. Moreover, these instruments cannot mimic olfaction, and thus, give a human odor impression with the actual technology.

Nowadays, several sensing technologies are available for AO systems, but typically, these instruments are based on chemical gas sensors. In particular, these types of sensors suffer from cross sensitivities, time instability, dependence on previous gas exposures, different responses among identical sensors, etc. Such shortcomings affect negatively the reproducibility and reliability of the final instrument, and thus, its robustness. Therefore, instruments based on these sensors suffer from lack of robustness and do not give enough reproducible results. Consequently, e-noses are not (yet) suitable for industry. The nature of the

problems and the lack of robustness that chemical gas sensors show are mainly technological and affect sensors of all state of the art technologies, though to different degrees. In the future, those deficiencies will be mostly overcome by improving the fabrication process and by developing new technologies. However, while more research is made on these areas, statistical signal processing can help to mathematically compensate or reduce the effect of the mentioned issues before pattern recognition.

The aim of this chapter is to explore the concept of robustness in AO systems and the use of several statistical signal-processing techniques, along with sensor operation methods, that may improve the robustness of such AO systems. In particular, these techniques aim to correct or compensate the responses of the sensors affected by two specific problems related to the lack of robustness: sensor drift and failure of one or more sensors of an array. In order to improve time stability, three different signal-processing approaches recently proposed are reviewed. Such strategies make use of sensors time information either due to sampling transient or temperature modulation from different points of view. The first one uses the method Orthogonal Signal Correction to correct unwanted variance related to drift. The second approach proposes the use of an unsupervised Multiway technique (PARAFAC) on sensors transient signals to take advantage of the characteristics of a three way data arrangement. The last approach consists of the use of Multivariate Curve Resolution Alternating Least Squares (MCR-ALS) on temperature modulated metal oxide (MOX) sensors. MCR-ALS is a blind deconvolution strategy that extracts information with special meaning without any calibration step, by introducing prior knowledge into the data matrix decomposition through constraints. Finally, a method based on Principal Component Analysis (PCA) is presented for fault detection, faulty sensor identification, and correction in an array of chemical gas sensors. For this, a subtle fault based on the change on sensitivity produced by sensor poisoning is considered. Indeed, the detection of change in sensor sensitivity is a relevant problem that has received poor attention by the AO community.

This document is organized in four sections. In the first one, the concept of robustness is briefly discussed, the nature of the specific problems is treated, and their effects on the sensor responses are exposed. In the following section, some evidence of lack of robustness due to drift and sensor faults are shown, together with a brief state of the art on the advances to compensate them by signal processing techniques. In the third section, a short revision is made on the above-mentioned three methods for drift counteraction and for fault detection. Finally, conclusions are given in section four.

ROBUSTNESS OF AO SYSTEMS

As exposed in the introduction, electronic noses or Artificial Olfaction (AO) systems are instruments with very interesting capabilities for fast analysis of volatiles. However, they present some shortcomings that have to be solved in order to become a reliable instrument for industry. Different problems come from incorrect measurement procedures, sampling methods or system design. Others come from the area of sensor technology, such as sensor drift, which degrades the sensors performance along the time. Furthermore, since the core of an electronic nose is an array of gas sensors, an additional problem to be considered is the possible failure of one or more sensors in the array. In general, most of these problems are also present in other analytical instruments, which are highly used in industry. Indeed, industry is increasingly requiring for instruments able to give fast measurement with suitable precision, accuracy, and long-term stability under variable (industrial) conditions. Moreover, industry is subjected to strict regulatory requirements and costs. In consequence, technical users demand analytical

instruments to fulfill certain requirements, within which robustness is one of the most important ones. The measurement of system robustness and model transferability has become two key points in the development of new measurement technologies.

Although robustness has always been considered an important property of a measurement method, there is not an official definition for the term itself valid for all type of measurements. Many similar definitions can be found in literature, most of them related to specific problems in specific applications, thus, sometimes different definitions can be found within one domain. Nevertheless, some international organizations, such as International Organization for Standardization (ISO), the International Conference on Harmonization of Technical Requirements for Registration of Pharmaceuticals for Human Use (ICH) and US Pharmacopoeia (USP), give some guidelines to characterize the quality of a measurement method. For instance, USP and ICH definition of robustness concur: the robustness of an analytical procedure is a measure of its capacity to remain unaffected by small, but deliberate variations in method parameters and provides an indication of its reliability during normal usage (Dejaegher & Heyden, 2007).

In a robustness test, problematic variables, specific of the given instrument, are first identified. Then, the behavior of the instrument to variations in such variables is deeply studied, taking into account all aspects of the measurement and methodology: sampling, instrumental (mechanical and sensors), environmental characteristics, and calibration models. In particular, the robustness of the (multivariate) calibration models is an important task for signal processing and includes the evaluation of the calibration method and algorithms involved in the prediction step. On the other hand, in multivariate calibration, robustness is often evaluated by the use of indices based on minimizing the objective function of prediction error (Zeaiter, et al., 2004). Indeed, a calibration model is often selected to be the one that shows

Figure 1. Example of the performance of two calibration models: (a) the model showing better prediction rates may degrade faster, or (b) the model better prediction rates may need more calibration samples

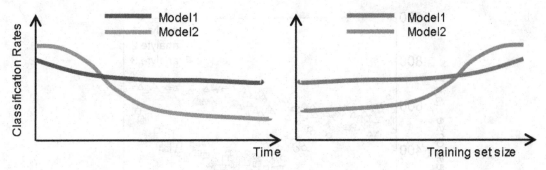

less error of prediction on computation using the cross validation technique, and less attention is paid to their robustness. Later, models are commonly tested by the Root Mean Square Error of Prediction (RMSEP) index. Other indices are also sometimes presented as a measurement of robustness, such as the calibration model dependence on training samples, on the training set size or results from permutation tests. Nevertheless, in a study on the sensitivity of multivariate calibration models (Swierenga, et al., 1999), the authors consider that the robustness of models cannot be judged only in terms of their prediction error; indeed, models may possess a small prediction error and at the same time be very sensitive to small perturbations in experimental conditions (Figure 1). Besides, the robustness of calibration models can be improved by using several statistical techniques that enhance prediction model performance. Zeaiter et al. (2005) presented an interesting overview of these techniques in the field of Near Infrared (NIR) spectroscopy.

On the other hand, calibration model transferability is also an important issue for industry, since the systems need maintenance and parts of them have to be repaired or replaced, This means that calibration has to be repeated very often, which is very time consuming and expensive. The aim of the field named *calibration transfer* is to minimize the cost and time expense of repeated calibration tasks by transferring the information in the calibration model of a first instrument to

the calibration model for a second instrument using as few measurements as possible. Both instruments should be comparable, so that it can be assumed that measurements in similar environments change in a similar way in both instruments (Holmberg, 2003).

AO systems are relatively young, and general standards and concepts for the study of their robustness have not been established yet. However, some of the concepts derived in other instrumentation areas, such as the variety of methods in chromatography, spectroscopy, etc. could be adapted and transferred to the field of artificial olfaction. In relation with a method based on an AO system, there are a number of factors that may be varied to evaluate its robustness. Typical parameters that may need to be studied are the sampling method (sample preparation, sampling time), influence of temperature, flow rates and humidity as these parameters influences the sensors responses. In particular, time stability is an important factor to be included in a robustness test. Therefore, factors influencing sensor drift should also be studied.

DRIFT AND SENSOR FAULTS IN A GAS SENSORS ARRAY

Among the factors that influence AO systems degrading their robustness, two are specially treated in this document: sensor drift and failure of one or more sensors in an array.

Figure 2. Example of the evolution of the response of a sensor affected by (simulated) drift to three types of analytes along 100 days

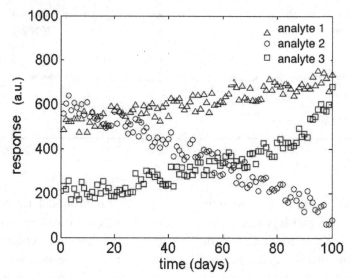

Sensor *drift* is considered to be one of the most serious limitations to the extensive use of the e-noses. It is a common problem for all chemical sensors, although different causes for drift dominate depending on the sensor types. Drift consists of random temporal variation of the individual sensor response when the sensor array is exposed to the same analyte under identical conditions. In the field of chemical gas sensors, it is considered to be strictly due to the degradation of the sensor's sensing material (aging and poisoning) although other authors include environmental agents such as changes in humidity, temperatures, and flow rates, into the causes of drift (Figure 2). In fact, also other sources that influence the sensor measurements over time and that are not due to drift can be considered and treated as drift from the point of view of signal processing. Examples of such sources are hysteresis or systematic errors due to fixed sampling sequences, short-term effects such as system warm-up or thermal trends, noise or even the degradation of the samples themselves (Hierlemann, 2008; Holmberg, 2003), which are mostly due to a bad design of the measurement system or an unsuitable measurement procedure.

Besides, *poisoning* is a change in the response of a sensor to the same analyte measured under the same conditions, due to irreversible interactions between the sensing material and the poisonous analyte. As a result of these effects, the sensor responds with changed sensitivities, baseline, selectivity and magnitude along the time, even the speed of the response can be also altered (Holmberg, 2003). In general, both effects are considered to degrade the sensors in a gradual way but this degradation may be speeded up depending on the conditions of the sensor operation, such as the temperature (Holmberg, 2003) or the poisonous substance and its concentration. Moreover, since drift influences different sensors in different ways, the relative relationship between these different sensors changes, and thus the characteristic pattern of a given target gas may not be preserved over time. All these changes in the sensors response lead to the performance degradation of the overall instrument. Indeed, in a multi-sensor system, a visual inspection on data affected by drift by means of an exploratory tool as PCA, shows (Artursson, et al., 2000) that drift may tend to move data mainly in one direction, which is similar for all similar gas mixtures, but which may differ for different gas mixtures. Figure 3 shows this fact on two subsets of samples collected with an array of 17 conductive polymer sensors in an experiment lasting 10 months. The first subset corresponds to measurements from firsts 15 days and the second one shows samples collected 4 months later. All three gas species are represented in both subsets. In general, in both subsets, the main drift component has similar direction for all classes except one (ammonia). Further, we can see that the second subset is shifted from the first one due to an additional long-term drift, and the direction of the main drift component of ammonia has also changed slightly.

A common situation in a multisensory system is the possibility of failure of individual sensors in the array, which can be of different nature: instrumental or derived from the sensor technol-

ogy. As a result, errors are introduced in the measurements, which may give place to misclassifications. Therefore, in order to minimize such errors, the faulty sensor must be replaced as soon as possible. For this, automatic algorithms are needed, which can fast detect a fault, identify the faulty sensor, and correct its response if the sensor cannot be immediately removed. In the case that the sensor fault is subtle, such as when the sensitivity of one sensor in the array is slightly changed (poisoning), the detection and identification of the faulty sensor is a challenge. Furthermore, after a faulty sensor is replaced, the instrument performance may be substantially changed. This is a common case in gas sensor arrays, since the new and the replaced sensor signals can differ significantly although they are supposed to be identical. Therefore, in this case, techniques of calibration transfer can be used to reduce the costs of the re-calibration of the system.

Figure 3. Example of a PCA scores plot of two subsets of samples measured in an experiment lasting 10 months. The first subset corresponds to measurements from firsts 15 days and the second one shows samples collected 4 months later.

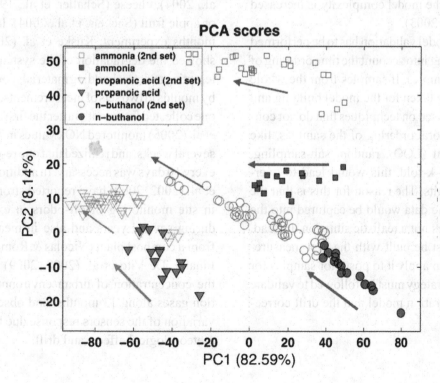

As a result of lack of robustness, calibration models may become obsolete over a relatively short time (on the order of few weeks). Therefore, to keep the performance of an AO system along the time, periodical full re-calibrations may be required, which are laborious, expensive and time-consuming tasks. Even in the case of sensor failure, a full recalibration must be performed, since the new sensor and its predecessor response are different although are supposed to be identical.

On the other hand, an important issue in signal processing is the evaluation methodology of the applied drift or fault correction techniques. For this, several strategies can be followed, such as the comparison of the prediction capabilities of the classification/quantification model with and without drift counteraction. For classification applications, a measure of the effectiveness of the method is the relative change of the evaluation of the Fisher ratio. In quantification applications, the relative change in the Root Mean Squared Error in Prediction (RMSEP) value can be used. The improvement of the prediction ability must be significant, otherwise the method should not be used since the model complexity is increased (Pearce, et al., 2003).

Besides, model validation has to be performed with care, taking into account the time ordering of the training samples. If samples from the whole time period are taken for the model building and validation is based on techniques that do not consider the temporal ordering of the samples, like Leave-One-Out (LOO), random sub-sampling, bootstrap, and k-fold, this would lead to over-optimistic results. The reason for this is that the evolution of the data would be captured into the model, which is not a realistic situation. Instead, the model must be built with the first measurements, and then apply it to posterior samples for testing. This strategy must be followed to validate both, the calibration model and the drift correction method.

Much effort is being made on research in new and better sensing materials for gas sensors, but is a difficult task. However, signal processing methods and the use of different operation modes can be used to help to improve the system robustness and, in consequence, the gas identification capability can be maintained for a longer time period.

EVIDENCE AND STATE OF THE ART IN DRIFT CORRECTION AND FAULT DETECTION

From the beginning of the development of e-noses instruments, the effect of drift in array of gas sensors have been observed in a broad variety of applications, such as food applications, environment monitoring, etc. with time duration of only few days to months.

For instance, drift was observed in experiments lasting few days on food samples such as fish (Haugen, et al., 2000) milk (Haugen, et al., 2000; Labreche, et al., 2005), tea (Dutta, et al., 2003), tomatoes (Concina, et al., 2009; Berna, et al., 2004), cheese (Schaller, et al., 1999, 2000), or apple fruit (Saevels, et al., 2004). In a several months experiment, Kuske et al. (2005, 2006) showed the degradation of the system when attempting to detect building materials contaminated by moulds in two sets of measurements, the second one collected five months after the first one. Tsujita et al. (2005) monitored NOx values in Tokyo over several weeks, and realized that one re-calibration every 10 days was necessary. In addition, Romain et al. (2002, 2009) have reported strong drift for in site monitoring of off-odors in experiments during several years and also in measurements from a compost plant (Nicolas & Romain, 2004). Finally, De Vito et al. (2008, 2009) monitored the concentration of urban environment pollution gases along 13 months, and observed large variation of the sensors response due to seasonal meteorological effects and drift.

Moreover, some authors have also reported the occurrence of faults during long measurement series. Besides the presence of drift, Romain and Nicolas (2009) also mentioned the need to replace some sensors in their long experiment in monitoring odors on a landfill site. In other experiments, the sensors had to be exposed to certain substances, such as sulphur compounds, hexamethyldixyloxane (Pratt & Williams, 1997) or some acids (e.g. acetic) in the samples, cheeses (Schaller, et al., 1999, 2000), wines, vinegars, cruciferous vegetables or lampant virgin olive oils (García-González & Aparicio, 2002). There, sensor poisoning became a serious problem. It may happen that one or few sensors are more affected by sensor poisoning than the others. Therefore, in those situations, the failing sensors must be detected and identified in the array, in order to be immediately replaced.

BRIEF STATE-OF-THE-ART FOR DRIFT COUNTERACTION AND FAULT DETECTION BY SIGNAL PROCESSING TECHNIQUES

In general, given the amount of literature about AO systems, most of it is related to the sensitivity of the instruments and poor attention has been paid to its robustness (Figure 4). However, important and interesting contributions can be found in literature, although here only some of them are mentioned due to space restrictions. In relation with drift correction, different approaches can be found in the AO literature, which address the problem from several different points of view, depending on the situation. Some of these ones are reviewed next.

For instance, Wilson et al. (1995) and Bednarczyk et al. (1995) attempted to build robust features by transforming the values of the sensors response into a new pattern. Wilson and DeWeerth (1995) converted the sensors signals into binary outputs by calculating a threshold with the median values

Figure 4. Pentagon diagram which nodes represent the main features in a general measurement instrument. The red line shows the abundance of literature in the e-nose field related to each node (adapted from Graf, 2009).

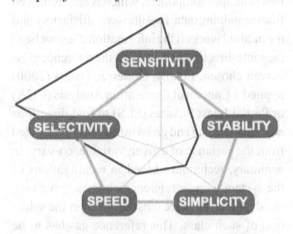

for every sensor. Besides, Bednarczyk et al. (1995) modified the sensors signals pattern by pattern. However, both techniques remove much information to discriminate sufficiently, especially among chemicals within a large range of concentration.

Other approaches are based on the estimation of the drift effect on the system to be later removed. Drift effect estimation can be made, for instance, by measuring the change in the sensor responses to one (or more) reference gas, which is measured with some intervals along the experiment. This strategy can be applied in a univariate way (sensor-by-sensor) or in a multivariate way by removing the directions of dispersion of the reference data in the feature space. In literature, we can find works by Fryder et al. (1995) and Haugen et al. (2000), who performed re-calibrations with a reference gas sensor by sensor. In particular, Haugen et al. (2000) re-calibrated their system in two steps: within a single measurement sequence and between measurement sequences. This strategy provided very good results, however, many calibration measurements have to be made and this is not possible in many situations. Examples of drift correction by multivariate methods include

Arthursson et al. (2000), who proposed a method named Component Correction (CC) based on PCA and PLS. In this technique, a reference gas is used to estimate its main direction of drift, given by the first principal component, which is later removed from remaining data. Results were satisfactory and the method works if the information does not lie in the same direction as drift and if the reference class is well chosen. Finally, Gutierrez-Osuna (2000) applied a Canonical Correlation Analysis (CCA) or Partial Least Squares (PLS) to find directions along which data and given information, extracted from the variance of a given variable, co-vary. In summary, techniques based in recalibrations of the system using a reference class can give very good results, but care must be taken in the selection of such class. This reference gas has to be representative of all the classes being measured, since they are supposed to drift in similar ways. It should also be stable along the time, available and easy to measure (Salit & Turk, 1998).

In order to avoid frequent re-calibrations, the drift effect on the sensors measured within the calibration subset, can be assumed to be constant along the time and thus be compensated for in future samples. The CC proposal by Arthursson et al. (2000) is an example of this strategy. Other example was proposed by Ziyatdinov et al. (2010), who exposed a new technique based on Common Principal Component Analysis (CPCA), to find the direction of variance common to all classes present in the dataset, which is then removed from data. This method is very interesting because it takes into account the variability of all clusters to calculate the component to be removed, thus avoiding the (sometimes) difficult selection of a reference class. However, Ziyatdinov needed too many train samples for a model, about 1000 samples, which is not usually feasible. In other works (Di Natale, et al., 2002; Kermit, et al., 2003), Independent Component Analysis (ICA) has been used to find statistically independent components of the sensor array response, which could be associated to drift and discriminatory information.

Obtained results were good but Kermit et al. (2003) applied ICA in an off-line way, and did not tested the method with new incoming samples, and Di Natale et al. (2002) used the validation method of leave one out, which is not suitable for validation in drift conditions.

Adaptive strategies, by which calibration models are updated with oncoming samples, have also been used. These techniques are very interesting in applications such as process monitoring, provided events and faults can be distinguished from normal data evolution and data evolves gradually. If abrupt and unpredictable changes are present in data, adaptive methods may not be suitable. Adaptive methods with Self-Organizing Maps (SOM) have been applied with resulting small errors in Davide et al. (1994), Marco et al. (1998), and Zuppa et al. (2004). A drawback of adaptive methods appears when several classes are present in the experiment. These classes have to be alternatively measured; otherwise, the adaptive models may lose the tracking of some of them. Perera et al. (2006) also proposed an adaptive technique for event detection, based on recursive dynamic PCA (Ku, et al., 1995) that can operate under drift conditions, however, the tested drifting data was synthetic.

Finally, Wavelets decomposition method has also been used as a drift correction method, since Discrete Wavelet Transform (DWT) may give information of the frequency content and time localization of drift components on a time signal (Hui, et al., 2003; Zuppa, et al., 2007). Both papers show good results, but signals were collected during few days (Hui, et al., 2003) or drift was simulated (Zuppa, et al., 2007). Both approaches are interesting and should be tested on real drift conditions.

Some authors have also contributed with comparisons among different drift correction methods, Zuppa et al. (2004), Sisk and Lewis (2005), and Romain and Nicolas (2009). Sisk and Lewis (2005) and Romain and Nicolas (2009) compared multivariate and univariate approaches for drift correction in different applications, and concluded that the univariate approach was the most adequate for their respective problems. However, in such experiments the e-nose instrument contained few sensors (max. 15 sensors [Sisk & Lewis, 2005])

On the other hand, the case of sensor failure has not been as extensively considered as the problem of drift, and only few works can be found in the AO literature in which the aim is to detect and correct a fault in an array of gas sensors (Pardo, et al., 2000; Tomic, et al., 2002). For instance, in order to detect a possible fault, Pardo et al. (2000) estimated the outputs of an array of five sensors from the actual signals and then compared them to the real values. Finally, Tomic et al. (2002) studied calibration transfer techniques for their application in sensor replacement problems.

SIGNAL PROCESSING METHODS FOR IMPROVING ROBUSTNESS

Although there are a variety of different proposals to deal with drift problems: univariate (Haugen, et al., 2000; Sisk & Lewis, 2005), multivariate (Arthursson, et al., 2000; Marco, et al., 1998), linear (Arthursson, et al., 2000), and non-linear (Davide, et al., 1994; Marco, et al., 1998), no technique is valid for all situations, and thus more research is needed to find strategies that could be adjusted to specific scenarios.

In this section, we revise three recently proposed useful strategies for drift counteraction and subtle fault detection, identification and correction. Such methods address the problem of drift from different point of view, as it is shown next.

Orthogonal Signal Correction (OSC)

OSC was presented by Wold et al. in 1998, and after that date, many other similar methods inspired by OSC have appeared. So nowadays, all these techniques are grouped in the family of Orthogonal Projection (OP) methods. The main action of OP methods is a reduction of the data

dimensionality, searching for dimensions of the subspace that describe the maximum variance of the data X unrelated to certain information of interest Y in the multivariate space, usually target species or concentration levels. For this, different approaches have been developed. For instance, in order to extract the X data structure to be related to Y, these approaches can be based on Partial Least Squares (PLS), which relates X with a subspace orthogonal to Y. Therefore, these methods remove the influence of non-desired variations in the data, what simplifies data, improve model interpretation, and thus increase the robustness of the system. Further, they may also show an improvement of the model predictive performance, even outside the calibration range, and in the presence of different factors that may influence the signals. Several works comparing some of these techniques can be found in literature (Goicoechea & Olivieri, 2001; Svensson, et al., 2002; Zeaiter, et al., 2005; Gabrielsson & Trygg, 2006).

The AO community does not normally use these techniques, only few applications can be found in literature with the aim of removing local data dispersion (Tomic, et al., 2002; DiNatale, et al., 2002). However, a recently presented contribution (Padilla, et al., 2010) explored the ability of one of the OP techniques, Orthogonal Signal Correction (OSC) algorithm, to diminish the influence of drift on an experiment lasting 10 months. This experiment consisted of measurements of three types of analytes at several concentration levels by using an array of 17 conducting polymer gas sensors, including the whole sensors transient signals. In addition, Component Correction (CC) method (Arthursson, et al., 2000) was applied on the same dataset in order to be compared with OSC and with prediction when no preprocessing stage to counteract drift was employed. In addition, the calculated components of non-desired variance (to be removed from data) were analyzed and the robustness of both methods was tested, in relation with the sufficient size of the calibration set to provide stable results.

Results showed that both methods extended the lifetime of the system by improving its classification ability along about four months. However, OSC outperformed CC during that period of time, probably due to the fact that all the classes were taken into account into the OSC algorithm whereas CC only uses one reference class. Thus, the application of OSC resulted in compact clusters (Figure 5, to be compared with Figure 3), which therefore implied an easier classification task. Finally, after those months, both methods performed similarly bad, which indicated that a new recalibration was needed, since a long-term drift component could not be removed. On the other hand, the study of the removed components by both methods, revealed that the part of the sensors transient signal which most contributed to sample dispersion are the rise and fall regions.

Multivariate Curve Resolution (MCR)

The objective of MCR is similar to the so-called blind source separation (BSS) problem, well known in signal processing. BSS deals with situations that involve the recovery of the original speech signals of different speakers from the mixed sound. In analytical chemistry, the set of Multivariate Curve Resolution (MCR) methods tries to solve a similar problem. Such problem consists of blindly extracting information about the pure components from a mixture, which may contain many components to be simultaneously analyzed or may include a few interesting analytes in the presence of many other chemical interferences, as in environmental samples. This self-modeling method is therefore very interesting for e-nose systems because it extracts information from data without the need of a calibration model and thus it is not affected by drift.

To extract the pure components, MCR methods use simple Least Squares (LS) technique. The most common MCR algorithm performs LS in an iterative way, thus it is named MCR Alternating Least Squares (MCR-ALS) (de Juan & Tauler, 2006). Specifically, MCR methods de-mix a data matrix X, containing the raw measurements of mixtures, into the contributions related to each of the pure components in the system. De-mixing is

Figure 5. PCA scores plot after correction by OSC

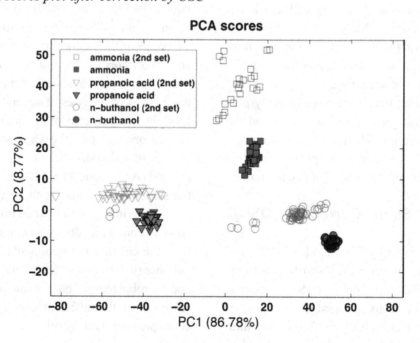

done by the decomposition of the initial mixture data matrix X into the product of two chemically meaningful data matrices C and S^T. Each of these matrices contains the pure response profiles of the n mixture components associated with the row and the column directions of the initial data matrix, respectively. In matrix notation, the expression has the form:

$$X = C \ S^T + E \qquad (1)$$

where $X \ (r \times c)$ is the original data matrix, $C \ (r \times n)$ and $S^T \ (n \times c)$ are the matrices that contain n pure-component profiles related to the data variation in the row direction and in the column direction, respectively, and $E(r \times c)$ is the residual variation of the data set not related to any chemical contribution. Matrices C and S^T, often refer to concentration or component profiles and spectra, but they can refer to other factors in other problems (de Juan & Tauler, 2006). However, additional information about the problem is needed to avoid the ambiguities related with this decomposition, and also, a prior step is necessary to find an initial estimates for matrix C or S^T. Those ambiguities make that several solutions of the equation, pairs of matrices C and S^T, can be found that reproduce the original data set with the same fit quality. There is a rotational and scale freedom, since the obtained component profiles may differ in shape (rotational ambiguity) or in magnitude (intensity ambiguity) from the true ones. Nevertheless, the needed information to restrict such ambiguities can be derived from the physical nature of the system and from prior knowledge of the problem under study. For instance, non negativity in C (when referred to concentration profiles) or peak uni-modality for S^T (for spectra chromatographic problems) are often used (de Juan & Tauler, 2006; Rutan & de Juan, 2009). Besides, initial estimates can be obtained by techniques such as Evolving Factor Analysis (EFA) (Gampp, et al., 1987) or Self-Modelling Mixture Analysis (SIMPLISMA) (Windig & Guilment, 1991).

Although MCR is widely used in analytical instrumentation, where its capabilities for qualitative analysis have been proven, it had never been applied in AO systems until now. In this unique contribution to our field, Montoliu et al. (2010) presented an application of MCR-ALS where the evolution of two species of gases in a mixture was measured with an array of four metal oxide sensors thermally modulated. It is known that thermal modulation provides higher selectivity and sensitivity than isothermal heating. Temperature modulation screens the thermal sensitivity of every sensor to the analytes in the mixture, which thus gives more information about the analytes themselves. In this experiment, MCR-ALS determined the resolution of the gas mixture resulting in concentration C and also temperature sensitivity profiles S^T to both analytes in the mixture. Further, the analysis was made on measures from a single

Figure 6. Resolution of the concentration profiles in the mixture of two gas species, in Montoliu's experiment, for two different concentrations of both gases (adapted from Montoliu, et al., 2010)

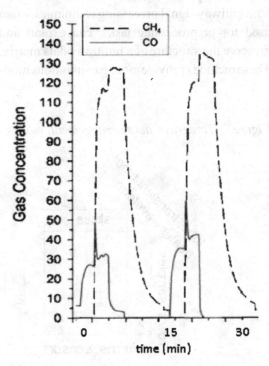

sensor, and later on data containing responses from all sensors, which could improve the resolution of the analytes in the mixture. However, non-linear effects were observed, which distorted the final resolution profile, particularly in the overlapping region (Figure 6).

Multiway (N-Way) Methods

The different operation modes of the AO instrument allow obtaining every single sensor response to temperature modulation or transient to a sudden exposition to the target analyte. By including any of this extra information in a data set, the dimension of the feature space is increased, which therefore implies richer information that increases the prediction ability of the system. Such data set can be organized in the form of a cube or a three way matrix, e.g. a tensor where every edge or mode; row, column and tube, refers to either the samples, the sensors and every sensor transient signal or response to temperature modulation (Figure 7). Even a four way matrix with dimensions *samples × sensors × temperature modulation response × transient response* could be considered.

Multiway signal processing techniques, often used for preprocessing tasks, can exploit and preserve the structure of a multiway data matrix. These methods provide more parsimonious mod-

els than classical methods. Moreover, extracted features are meaningful and easier to interpret and can also be used to build posterior models for prediction. The most common multiway techniques are parallel factor analysis (PARAFAC) and Tucker, and extensions and modifications proposed for both (PARAFAC2, Tucker3, etc.). If the dataset is trilinear, PARAFAC, can decompose the cube into three two-way matrix, each one referring to a mode and having all the same number of factors. On the contrary, Tucker3 method does not require trilinearity but the model building and final interpretation become much more complex. Tucker3 decomposes the multiway dataset into three matrices and another multiway matrix, named *core matrix G*, which contains the non-trilinear part of the original multiway data and which allows different interactions among the modes. The decomposition of the three-way matrix X, according to two multiway methods, is given by:

$$PARAFAC: \quad x_{ijk} = \sum_{f=1}^{F} a_{if} b_{jf} c_{kf} + e_{ijk} \quad (2)$$

$$Tucker3: \quad x_{ijk} = \sum_{d=1}^{D} \sum_{f=1}^{F} \sum_{h=1}^{H} a_{id} b_{jf} c_{kh} g_{dfh} + e_{ijk} \quad (3)$$

Figure 7. Three-way data arrangement, modes, and row-wise unfolding

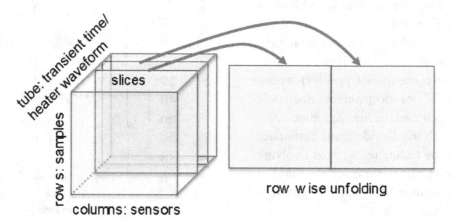

where x_{ijk} represents the ijkth element in the three-way data set, a_{if}, b_{jf}, c_{kf} are the elements in the decomposition matrices A, B, and C, e_{ijk} is the residual term and g_{dfh} is the dfhth element of a core array (in Tucker model) of size $D \times F \times H$. D, F and G are the selected number of factors in each decomposition matrix. A deep study on multiway methods can be found in Smilde and Bro (2004). In addition, in 2001, de Juan and Tauler make a comparison of three-way resolution methods for non-trilinear chemical data sets.

The usual approach in AO is to use classical methods on the three-way matrix, which is unfolded often in a row-wise way (Figure 7). Therefore, the relationship among the three modes is destroyed and interesting information lost. However, recent contributions to the use of N-way methods to AO systems can be found in literature (Skov & Bro, 2005; Padilla, et al., 2006). For instance, Skov and Bro (2005) applied PCA, PARAFAC and PARAFAC2 on a dataset consisting of measurements of commercial licorice product of several qualities with an array of 12 MOX sensors, including the sensors transient response. PARAFAC2 was preferred to classical PARAFAC because of its ability to handle shifted sensors transient profiles. The authors compared this technique with PCA and conclude that, although PARAFAC2 offers some advantages compared to PCA, the structure of the model required a more careful interpretation of the model parameters. Besides, Padilla et al. (2006) used PARAFAC in an application for quality control of a processed food product, consisting of fried potato chips with different concentration of a flavoring agent. The measurements were performed with an array of 13 metal oxide sensors, the sensors transient response were included in the three-way dataset. One of the obtained features from PARAFAC was related to the concentration of aroma and could be used to build an Inverse Least Squares (ILS) model to predict the concentration of aroma of new incoming samples. Remaining loadings from

PARAFAC gave information about the influence of every individual sensor on the multiway model and identified the time window when the sensors are exposed to the volatiles.

Fault Detection and Isolation (FDI) Methods

As mentioned above, the detection, identification, and correction of a fault in an array of sensors, avoids incorrect results that could lead to erroneous decisions. In industry, fault detection and isolation is a key point, given the increasing degree of automation and the growing demand for higher performance, efficiency, reliability, and safety in their systems. For these reasons, the control research community has put a great effort in developing methods to automatically detect and identify a possible faulty sensor by using the available remaining sensor signals.

FDI methods can follow two different approaches: model-driven and data-driven. Data-driven methods are especially useful, since they do not need models describing the physical/chemical principles underlying the process. At the same time, data-driven methods groups different strategies such as signal based, multi-variable statistics based, and knowledge based. Multi-variable statistics based FDI methods are very interesting to implement in AO systems; in particular, PCA is a simple and robust technique that can reduce the high dimensionality in a few features containing most of the information of the original data. PCA has been applied in other fields with great success (Ding, et al., 2009), and recently also in our AO field (Padilla, et al., 2007). In that work (Padilla, et al., 2007), the authors used a technique based on Principal Component Analysis (PCA) to fast detect a fault, identify one or two failing sensors and correct its responses on an array of 17 conductive polymer gas sensors measuring several gases. Additionally, PCA (Dunia, et al., 1996) was compared with other techniques, such as Partial Least Squares (PLS) and another method based on structured residuals of PCA (Qin & Li, 1999) for faulty sensor identification.

Since PCA divides the sensor space X into model space $\hat{X}$ and its residual space $\tilde{X}$, orthogonal to the former one, the PCA technique measures the norm of a new incoming sample in the residual space to detect the presence of a fault in such sample (Figure 8). That sample is faulty if $\|\tilde{x}\|$ exceeds a given threshold. The failing sensor is identified by projecting the residual vector $\tilde{x}$ on the axes of the original space, which correspond to every sensor. Finally, the sample is corrected by subtracting the calculated value of the fault to the identified faulty sensor. Besides, the technique based on the PCA structured residuals attempt to find a matrix W by means of which the primer PCA residuals can be structured into new ones which show maximum sensitivity to given faults and minimum sensitivity to others. This method may add accuracy to the identification of the faulty sensor and moreover, W can be designed so that given combinations of sensors failing at the same time can be fast identified (Li & Shah, 2002; Xu & Kwan, 2003).

Finally, the method based on PLS consist on building a model for every sensor, so that for one sample, the response of every sensor can be estimated from the PLS model and the signals from remaining sensors. Then, the estimated and the real value are compared and, if this difference is higher than a certain threshold, a fault is detected on the sensor being evaluated. This strategy is similar to the one used by Pardo et al. (2000), though their models were built with artificial neural networks, they also compared estimated and actual sensors responses to detect a fault.

It is worthy to note that the considered failure was a subtle type of fault typically affecting chemical gas sensors. Such fault was simulated with the main effect that sensor poisoning has on the sensors signals, e.g. a change on the sensitivity profile of the faulty sensor. Poisoning is difficult to detect compared with other type of faults, because the sensor keeps working under apparently normal conditions. All three techniques were compared in every task, detection, identification and correction, and provided very good results with slight differences, which are significant only in the case of two sensors failing at the same time, where some methods degrades more than others.

Figure 8. A faulty sample out of the PCA model space

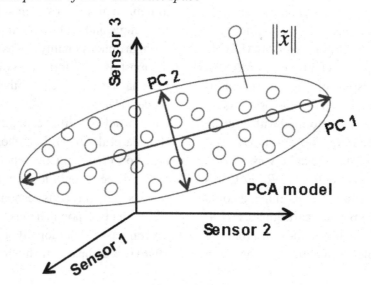

CONCLUSION AND FUTURE RESEARCH DIRECTIONS

AO systems based on an array of gas sensors and multivariate signal processing show lack of robustness. For instance, AO systems exhibit poor time stability, chemical sensors are in general influenced by environmental variables and the operation conditions can make the system to be dependent on variables such as flow rate, heating time and heating cycle for MOX sensors. Moreover, in an array of sensors one or more sensors may fail due to a variety of reasons such as instrumental or poisoning in the case of chemical sensors. Consequently, the metrologic characteristics of the instrument are degraded and therefore need frequent re-calibrations, which is time consuming and expensive. However, multivariate signal processing techniques can improve the robustness of e-nose instruments and therefore extend the lifetime of the system between re-calibrations.

In this chapter, we have made a discussion about the concept of robustness for e-nose instruments, in particular, for calibration models. Since lack of robustness in AO systems comprises many related problems, we have focused in two specific ones, which are the mainly contributing: time instability or sensor drift, and (subtle) fault detection, isolation and correction. A brief revision of literature, regarding evidences of such problems and main signal processing techniques to compensate them was presented. Finally, we included four methods that have recently been applied in AO systems and that can improve the e-nose robustness, in relation with drift and fault detection.

Orthogonal Signal Correction (OSC) has proven to provide very good results during a reasonable long period of time in an experiment where the sensors were affected by a very irregular drift. The analysis of OSC and CC calculated components to be removed from data, also provide information of the region of the sensors transient signal that contributes most to sample dispersion. Besides, two examples in literature show that Mul-tiway methods are able to provide parsimonious models for e-nose data structure containing sensor transient responses. In particular, PARAFAC decomposition leads to direct interpretation of the role of the different modes. In addition, MCR-ALS applied on temperature modulated MOX sensors signals is able to provide approximated concentration and sensitivity profiles without any previous recalibration step, although non-linearities in the sensors responses may introduce some distortion in the final profiles. Finally, simple multivariate techniques such as PLS, PCA, and structured residuals, have proven to be very useful for the detection of a subtle fault, caused by sensor poisoning, and identification of the faulty sensor. Further, these methods permit the reconstruction of the faulty sensor signal, keeping the system working with minor performance degradation.

It is important to note that the presented works that use Multiway and MCR methods are examples that show some of the characteristics of such techniques in specific situations but not under general drift conditions. However, we believe that these methods may be able to isolate a significant part of drift component. This characteristic will be tested in future contributions. In relation with fault detection and isolation, new methods and modifications to the shown simple techniques can much improve all the three tasks involved in it. For instance, sensors signal can be previously decomposed by wavelet transform (Padilla, et al., 2010), which improves results even under drift conditions.

REFERENCES

Artursson, T., Eklöv, T., Lundström, I., Mårtensson, P., Sjöström, M., & Holmberg, M. (2000). Drift correction for gas sensors using multivariate methods. *Journal of Chemometrics*, *14*(5-6), 711–723. doi:10.1002/1099-128X(200009/12)14:5/6<711::AID-CEM607>3.0.CO;2-4

Bednarczyk, D., & DeWeerth, S. (1995). Smart chemical sensing arrays using tin oxide sensors and analog winner-take-all signal processing. *Sensors and Actuators. B, Chemical, 27*(1-3), 271–274. doi:10.1016/0925-4005(94)01600-M

Berna, A., Lammertyn, J., Saevels, S., Natale, C., & Nicolaï, B. M. (2004). Electronic nose systems to study shelf life and cultivar effect on tomato aroma pro□le. *Sensors and Actuators. B, Chemical, 97,* 324–333. doi:10.1016/j.snb.2003.09.020

Concina, I., Falasconi, M., Gobbi, E., Bianchi, F., Musci, M., & Mattarozzi, M. (2009). Early detection of microbial contamination in processed tomatoes by electronic nose. *Food Control, 20,* 873–880. doi:10.1016/j.foodcont.2008.11.006

Davide, F., DiNatale, C., & D'Amico, A. (1994). Self-organizing multisensor systems for odour classi□cation: Internal categorization, adaptation and drift rejection. *Sensors and Actuators. B, Chemical, 18,* 244–258. doi:10.1016/0925-4005(94)87090-X

De Juan, A., & Tauler, R. (2001). Comparison of three-way resolution methods for non-trilinear chemical data sets. *Journal of Chemometrics, 15*(10), 749–771. doi:10.1002/cem.662

De Juan, A., & Tauler, R. (2006). Multivariate curve resolution. In Gemperline, P. (Ed.), *Practical Guide to Chemometrics* (pp. 417–467). New York, NY: Taylor and Francis Group.

De Vito, S., Massera, E., Piga, M., Martinotto, L., & De Francia, G. (2008). On □eld calibration of an electronic nose for benzene estimation in an urban pollution monitoring scenario. *Sensors and Actuators. B, Chemical, 129,* 750–757. doi:10.1016/j.snb.2007.09.060

De Vito, S., Piga, M., Martinotto, L., & De Francia, G. (2009). CO, NO_2 and NOx urban pollution monitoring with on-□eld calibrated electronic nose by automatic bayesian regularization. *Sensors and Actuators. B, Chemical, 143,* 182–191. doi:10.1016/j.snb.2009.08.041

Dejaegher, B., & Heyden, Y. (2007). Ruggedness and robustness testing. *Journal of Chromatography. A, 1158*(1-2), 138–157. doi:10.1016/j.chroma.2007.02.086

DiNatale, C., Martinelli, E., & D'Amico, A. (2002). Counteraction of environmental disturbances of electronic nose data by independent component analysis. *Sensors and Actuators. B, Chemical, 82*(2-3), 158–165. doi:10.1016/S0925-4005(01)01001-2

Ding, S. X., Zhang, P., Naik, A., Ding, E. L., & Huang, B. (2009). Subspace method aided data-driven design of fault detection and isolation systems. *Journal of Process Control, 19,* 1496–1510. doi:10.1016/j.jprocont.2009.07.005

Dunia, R., Qin, S., Joe, E. T. F., & McAvoy, T. J. (1996). Use of principal component analysis for sensor fault identification. *Comprehensive Chemical Engineering, 20,* 713–718. doi:10.1016/0098-1354(96)00128-7

Dutta, R., Hines, E., Gardner, J., & Kashwan, K. (2003). Tea quality prediction using a tin oxide-based electronic nose: An arti□cial intelligence approach. *Sensors and Actuators. B, Chemical, 94,* 228–237. doi:10.1016/S0925-4005(03)00367-8

Fryder, M., Holmberg, M., Winquist, F., & Lundstrom, I. (1995). Calibration technique for an electronic nose. In *Proceedings of the 1995 8th International Conference on Solid-State Sensors and Actuators and Eurosensors,* (pp. 683-686). Stockholm, Sweden: IEEE.

Gabrielsson, J., & Trygg, J. (2006). Recent developments in multivariate calibration. *Critical Reviews in Analytical Chemistry, 36*(3), 243–255. doi:10.1080/10408340600969924

Gampp, H., Maeder, M., Meyer, C., & Zuberbuehler, A. (1987). Evolving factor analysis. *Comments on Inorganic Chemistry: A Journal of Critical Discussion of the Current Literature, 6*(1), 41–60.

García-González, D., & Aparicio, R. (2002). Sensors: From biosensors to the electronic nose. *Grasas y Aceites-Sevilla, 53*(1), 96–114.

Goicoechea, H., & Olivieri, A. (2001). A comparison of orthogonal signal correction and net analyte preprocessing methods: Theoretical and experimental study. *Chemometrics and Intelligent Laboratory Systems, 56*, 73–81. doi:10.1016/S0169-7439(01)00110-1

Gutierrez-Osuna, R. (2000). Drift reduction for metal-oxide sensor arrays using canonical correlation regression and partial least squares. In *Proceedings of the 7th International Symposium on Olfaction and Electronic Nose*. Brighton, UK: IEEE.

Haugen, J., Tomic, O., & Kvaal, K. (2000). A calibration method for handling the temporal drift of solid state gas-sensors. *Analytica Chimica Acta, 407*(1-2), 23–39. doi:10.1016/S0003-2670(99)00784-9

Hierlemann, A., & Gutierrez-Osuna, R. (2008). Higher-order chemical sensing. *Chemical Reviews, 108*, 563–613. doi:10.1021/cr068116m

Holmberg, T. A. M. (2003). Drift compensation, standards, and calibration methods. In Pearce, T. C., Schiffman, S. S., Nagle, H. T., & Gardner, J. W. (Eds.), *Handbook of Machine Olfaction - Electronic Nose Technology* (pp. 325–346). Weinheim, Germany: WILEY-VCH.

Hui, D., Jun-Hua, L., & Zhong-Ru, S. (2003). Drift reduction of gas sensor by wavelet and principal component analysis. *Sensors and Actuators. B, Chemical, 96*, 354–363. doi:10.1016/S0925-4005(03)00569-0

ISO. (2012). *International organization for standardization (ISO)*. Retrieved from http://www.iso.org

Kermit, M., & Tomic, O. (2003). Independent component analysis applied on gas sensor array measurement data. *IEEE Sensors Journal, 3*(2), 218–228. doi:10.1109/JSEN.2002.807488

Ku, W., Storer, R., & Georgakis, C. (1995). Disturbance detection and isolation by dynamic principal component analysis. *Chemometrics and Intelligent Laboratory Systems, 30*, 179–196. doi:10.1016/0169-7439(95)00076-3

Kuske, M., Padilla, M., Romain, A., Nicolas, J., Rubio, R., & Marco, S. (2006). Detection of diverse mould species growing on building materials by gas sensor arrays and pattern recognition. *Sensors and Actuators. B, Chemical, 119*(1), 33–40. doi:10.1016/j.snb.2005.02.059

Kuske, M., Rubio, R., Romain, A., Nicolas, J., & Marco, S. (2005). Fuzzy k-nn applied to moulds detection. *Sensors and Actuators. B, Chemical, 106*, 52–60. doi:10.1016/j.snb.2004.05.066

Labreche, S., Bazzo, S., Cade, S., & Chanie, E. (2005). Shelf life determination by electronic nose: Application to milk. *Sensors and Actuators. B, Chemical, 106*, 199–206. doi:10.1016/j.snb.2004.06.027

Li, W., & Shah, S. (2002). Structured residual vector-based approach to sensor fault detection and isolation. *Journal of Process Control, 12*, 429–443. doi:10.1016/S0959-1524(01)00046-4

Marco, S., Ortega, A., Pardo, A., & Samitier, J. (1998). Gas identiᐤcation with tin oxide sensor array and self-organizing maps: Adaptive correction of sensor drifts. *IEEE Transactions on Instrumentation and Measurement, 47*(1), 316–321. doi:10.1109/19.728841

Montoliu, I., Tauler, R., Padilla, M., Pardo, A., & Marco, S. (2010). Multivariate curve resolution applied to temperature-modulated metal oxide gas sensors. *Sensors and Actuators. B, Chemical, 145*(1), 464–473. doi:10.1016/j.snb.2009.12.051

Nicolas, J., & Romain, A. (2004). Establishing the limit of detection and the resolution limits of odorous sources in the environment for an array of metal oxide gas sensors. *Sensors and Actuators. B, Chemical, 99*, 384–392. doi:10.1016/j.snb.2003.11.036

Padilla, M., Montoliu, I., Pardo, A., Perera, A., & Marco, S. (2006). Feature extraction on three way enose signals. *Sensors and Actuators. B, Chemical, 116*(1-2), 145–150. doi:10.1016/j.snb.2006.03.011

Padilla, M., Perera, A., Montoliu, I., Chaudry, A., Persaud, K., & Marco, S. (2007). Poisoning fault diagnosis in chemical gas sensor arrays using multivariate statistical signal processing and structured residuals generation. In *Proceedings of the IEEE International Symposium on Intelligent Signal Processing, WISP 2007*. IEEE Press.

Padilla, M., Perera, A., Montoliu, I., Chaudry, A., Persaud, K., & Marco, S. (2010). Fault detection, identification, and reconstruction of faulty chemical gas sensors under drift conditions, using principal component analysis and multiscale-PCA. In *Proceedings of the IEEE World Congress on Computational Intelligence, WCCI 2010*. IEEE Press.

Padilla, M., Perera, A., Montoliu, I., Chaudry, A., Persaud, K., & Marco, S. (2010). Drift compensation of gas sensor array data by orthogonal signal correction. *Chemometrics and Intelligent Laboratory Systems, 100*(1), 28–35. doi:10.1016/j.chemolab.2009.10.002

Pardo, M., Faglia, G., Sberveglieri, G., & Corte, M. (2000). Monitoring reliability of sensors in an array by neural networks. *Sensors and Actuators. B, Chemical, 67*, 128–133. doi:10.1016/S0925-4005(00)00402-0

Pearce, T. C., Schiffman, S. S., Nagle, H. T., & Gardner, J. W. (Eds.). (2003a). *Handbook of Machine Olfaction - Electronic Nose Technology*. Berlin, Germany: WILEY-VCH.

Pearce, T. C., Schiffman, S. S., Nagle, H. T., & Gardner, J. W. (2003b). Applications and case studies. In Pearce, T. C., Schiffman, S. S., Nagle, H. T., & Gardner, J. W. (Eds.), *Handbook of Machine Olfaction - Electronic Nose Technology* (pp. 419–578). Weinheim, Germany: WILEY-VCH.

Perera, A., Papamichail, N., Barsan, N., Weimar, U., & Marco, S. (2006). On-line novelty detection by recursive dynamic principal component analysis and gas sensor arrays under drift conditions. *IEEE Sensors Journal, 6*(3), 770–783. doi:10.1109/JSEN.2006.874015

Persaud, K., & Dodd, G. (1982). Analysis of discrimination mechanisms in the mammalian olfactory system using a model nose. *Nature, 299*, 352–355. doi:10.1038/299352a0

Pratt, K., & Williams, D. (1997). Self diagnostic gas sensitive resistors in sour gas applications. *Sensors and Actuators. B, Chemical, 45*(2), 147–153. doi:10.1016/S0925-4005(97)00288-8

Qin, S. J., & Li, W. (1999). Detection, identification and reconstruction of faulty sensors with maximized sensitivity. *AIChE Journal. American Institute of Chemical Engineers, 45*(9), 1963–1976. doi:10.1002/aic.690450913

Romain, A., Andre, P., & Nicolas, J. (2002). Three years experiment with the same tin oxide sensor arrays for the identification of malodorous sources in the environment. *Sensors and Actuators. B, Chemical, 84*, 271–277. doi:10.1016/S0925-4005(02)00036-9

Romain, A., & Nicolas, J. (2009). Long term stability of metal oxide-based gas sensors for e-nose environmental applications: An overview. *AIP Conference Proceedings, 146*(2), 502–506.

Rutan, R. S. C., & de Juan, A. (2009). Introduction to multivariate curve resolution. In Brown, S. D., Tauler, R., & Walczak, B. (Eds.), *Comprehensive Chemometrics* (*Vol. 2*, pp. 249–258). London, UK: Elsevier. doi:10.1016/B978-044452701-1.00046-6

Saevels, S., Lammertyn, J., Berna, A., Veraverbeke, E., Natale, C., & Nicolaï, B. (2004). An electronic nose and a mass spectrometry-based electronic nose for assessing apple quality during shelf life. *Postharvest Biology and Technology, 31*, 9–19. doi:10.1016/S0925-5214(03)00129-7

Salit, M., & Turk, G. (1998). A drift correction procedure. *Analytical Chemistry, 70*, 3184–3190. doi:10.1021/ac980095b

Schaller, E., Bosset, J., & Escher, F. (1999). Practical experience with 'electronic nose' systems for monitoring the quality of dairy products. *CHIMIA International Journal for Chemistry, 53*, 98–102.

Schaller, E., Bosset, J., & Escher, F. (2000). Instability of conducting polymer sensors in an electronic nose system. *Analusis, 28*, 217–227. doi:10.1051/analusis:2000113

Sisk, B., & Lewis, N. (2005). Comparison of analytical methods and calibration methods for correction of detector response drift in arrays of carbon black-polymer composite vapor detectors. *Sensors and Actuators. B, Chemical, 104*, 249–268. doi:10.1016/j.snb.2004.05.010

Skov, T., & Bro, R. (2005). A new approach for modelling sensor based data. *Sensors and Actuators. B, Chemical, 106*, 719–729. doi:10.1016/j.snb.2004.09.023

Smilde, A., & Rasmus, B. (Eds.). (2004). *Multiway analysis with applications in the chemical sciences*. New York, NY: John Wiley & Sons. doi:10.1002/0470012110

Svensson, O., Kourti, T., & MacGregor, J. F. (2002). An investigation of orthogonal signal correction algorithms and their characteristics. *Journal of Chemometrics, 16*, 176–188. doi:10.1002/cem.700

Swierenga, H., Weijer, A. D., & Wijk, R. V. (1999). Strategy for constructing robust multivariate calibration models. *Chemometrics and Intelligent Laboratory Systems, 49*, 1–17. doi:10.1016/S0169-7439(99)00028-3

Tomic, O., Ulmer, H., & Haugen, J. (2002). Standardization methods for handling instrument related signal shift in gas-sensor array measurement data. *Analytica Chimica Acta, 472*(1-2), 99–111. doi:10.1016/S0003-2670(02)00936-4

Tsujita, W., Yoshino, A., Ishida, H., & Moriizumi, T. (2005). Gas sensor network for air-pollution monitoring. *Sensors and Actuators. B, Chemical, 110*, 304–311. doi:10.1016/j.snb.2005.02.008

USP. (2012). *United States pharmacopeial convention (USP)*. Retrieved from http://www.usp.org

Wilson, D., & DeWeerth, S. (1995). Odor discrimination using steady-state and transient characteristics of tin-oxide sensors. *Sensors and Actuators. B, Chemical, 28*(2), 123–128. doi:10.1016/0925-4005(95)80036-0

Windig, W., & Guilment, J. (1991). Interactive self-modeling mixture analysis. *Analytical Chemistry, 63*, 1425–1432. doi:10.1021/ac00014a016

Wold, S., Antti, H., Lindgren, F., & Öhman, J. (1998). Orthogonal signal correction of near-infrared spectra. *Chemometrics and Intelligent Laboratory Systems, 44*, 175–185. doi:10.1016/S0169-7439(98)00109-9

Xu, R., & Kwan, C. (2003). Robust isolation of sensor failures. *Asian Journal of Control, 5*, 12–23. doi:10.1111/j.1934-6093.2003.tb00093.x

Zeaiter, M., Roger, J., & Bellon-Maurel, V. (2005). Robustness of models developed by multivariate calibration: The infuence of pre-processing methods. *Trends in Analytical Chemistry, 24*(5), 437–445. doi:10.1016/j.trac.2004.11.023

Zeaiter, M., Roger, J., Bellon-Maurel, V., & Rutledge, D. (2004). Robustness of models developed by multivariate calibration: The assessment of robustness. *Trends in Analytical Chemistry, 23*(2), 157–170. doi:10.1016/S0165-9936(04)00307-3

Ziyatdinov, A., Marco, S., Chaudry, A., Persaud, K., Caminal, P., & Perera, A. (2010). Drift compensation of gas sensor array data by common principal component analysis. *Sensors and Actuators. B, Chemical, 146*, 460–465. doi:10.1016/j.snb.2009.11.034

Zuppa, M., Distante, C., Persaud, K., & Siciliano, P. (2007). Recovery of drifting sensor responses by means of DWT analysis. *Sensors and Actuators. B, Chemical, 120*(2), 411–416. doi:10.1016/j.snb.2006.02.049

Zuppa, M., Distante, C., Siciliano, P., & Persaud, K. (2004). Drift counteraction with multiple self-organising maps for an electronic nose. *Sensors and Actuators. B, Chemical, 98*, 305–317. doi:10.1016/j.snb.2003.10.029

Chapter 15
Methods and Graphical Tools for Exploratory Data Analysis of Artificial Olfaction Experiments

Matteo Falasconi
University of Brescia, Italy

Matteo Pardo
Institute of Applied Mathematics and Information Technology, Italy

Giorgio Sberveglieri
University of Brescia, Italy

ABSTRACT

Visualization and initial examination of the Electronic Nose data is one of the most important parts of the data analysis cycle. This aspect of data investigation should ideally be performed iteratively together with data collection in order to optimize experimental protocols and final results. Once exploration has been completed, a complete supervised data analysis on a full dataset can be run, leading to prediction and thereby to e-nose performance evaluation. Exploratory Data Analysis (EDA) comprises three tasks: checking the quality of the data, calculating summary statistics, and producing plots of the data to get a feel of their structure. Graphical visualization of data allows checking for instrumental malfunctioning, discovering human errors, removing outliers, understanding the influence of experimental parameters, verifying the ability of the machine in discriminating the examined samples, and eventually formulating new hypotheses. A number of different techniques have been developed for data visualization, including multivariate statistical analysis, non-linear mapping, and clustering techniques. This chapter will present an overview of methods, tools, and software for EDA of artificial olfaction experiments. These will cover visualization and data mining tools for both raw and preprocessed data, such as: histograms, scatter plots, feature and box plots, Principal Component Analysis (PCA), Cluster Analysis (CA), and Cluster Validity (CV). Some case studies that demonstrate the application of the methods to specific chemical sensing problems will be illustrated.

DOI: 10.4018/978-1-4666-2521-1.ch015

Copyright © 2013, IGI Global. Copying or distributing in print or electronic forms without written permission of IGI Global is prohibited.

INTRODUCTION

Since almost three decades of experience with chemical sensing devices (Persaud, 1982) it is known that the applicative success of this technology strongly depends on proper selection and subsequent optimization of crucial experimental parameters. The experimental outcomes depend on a tremendously high number of variables, such as: sensor type (Röck, 2008; Pardo, 2004) and variables selection (Pardo, 2007; Roussels, 1998), odour sampling approach (Šetkus, 2010; Roussels, 1999), humidity level and/or presence of interfering species (Vezzoli, 2008), time progression and sensor stability (Padilla, 2010; Sharma, 2001; Ionescu, 2000). Therefore, the successful design of an Electronic Nose (EN) requires a careful consideration of the various issues involved in the experimental procedure (Gutierrez-Osuna, 2002).

The visualization and initial examination of the data—also called Exploratory Data Analysis (EDA) (Tukey, 1977)—is one of the most important parts of the data analysis cycle (Webb, 2002). Indeed, EDA is a necessary step in which the user can interact with the machine to check the quality of experimental results before embarking in successive, more automated steps, thus saving lot of unnecessary efforts.

The aims of EDA are manifold: maximize insight into a data set, uncover underlying structure, extract important features, and detect outliers. A most valuable outcome of EDA is to check for prior assumptions, understand how they affect the EN response, and determine the optimal experimental settings.

EDA includes three relevant aspects:

1. **Checking the quality of the data.** A first look at the sensor responses serves to control the correct functioning of the equipment. For example, in the case of the responses of chemical sensors to controlled as mixtures in ENs, the expected form of the response is known. Malfunctioning of the equipment (sampling system, sensors, electronics) can be spotted by plotting the sensor dynamic response vs the acquisition time.

2. **Calculating summary statistics.** Summary statistics can be used to characterize the data: few numbers can convey the fundamental properties of the data set, e.g., by calculating (sample) mean and variance for each feature and for each class it is possible to detect the (more obvious) outliers and to get clues about the variables important for discriminating particular classes.

3. **Producing plots of the data in order to get a feel of their structure.** This aspect of data investigation should ideally be performed iteratively together with data collection in order to adjust the experimental conditions for maximizing the system performance (e.g. samples classification by the EN).

Graphical views of the data (Chernoff faces, radar plots, histograms, scatter plots, multivariate data projections (linear or nonlinear), and cluster analysis) are the most useful tools for providing an insight into the nature of multivariate data. Visual data mining is especially useful at the initial stage of the process when little is known about the data and the exploration goals are vague. Since the user is directly involved in the process, shifting and adjusting the experimental design and the data acquisition can be easily implemented.

This Chapter will provide an overview of single and multiple variable displays techniques and of cluster analysis and cluster validity approaches. A set of Matlab functions (a toolbox) including several graphical tools has been developed in the SENSOR Lab to interactively implement such functionalities for EN data examination. The presentation of the techniques is accompanied by some case studies that demonstrate the practical application of these tools.

METHODS AND TECHNIQUES

Exploratory Analysis with Single and Multiple Variable Displays

In this section, we present the possibilities given by three standard exploratory data analysis methods: feature plot, box plot and Principal Component Analysis (PCA). To this aim, we report a substantial shortened and emended version of a previous paper of ours (Vezzoli, 2008). In that study, we tested the detection properties of four metal oxide sensors toward different ozone mixtures to identify sets of sensing layers and interfering compounds concentrations most suitable for reliable ozone detection.

Ozone detection is not only an environmental priority but also an industrial requirement to keep workplaces healthy. The Occupational Safety and Health Association (OSHA) has defined strict exposure limits (Threshold Limit Value [TLV] is 100 ppb while normal background level of O_3 in workplaces is 30 ppb). Gas sensors arrays (or electronic nose) offer a cheaper but reliable alternative approach to ozone analyzers, which are, up to now, the only available solution for ozone monitoring.

During the last years different metal oxide sensors such as gold catalyzed tin oxide (SnAu), tungsten oxide (WO_3), mixed indium and iron oxide (InFe), and cobalt oxide (CoO) revealed suitable for ozone sensing (see references in Vezzoli, 2008).

The focus of the present book chapter is methodological, so that the actual results, e.g. relative to the best sensing layers or in general the discussion of the evidence coming from the explorative analysis, are not detailed.

We initially tested four interfering gases: ammonia, ethylene, ethanol, and carbon monoxide. For three compounds (ammonia, ethanol, and carbon monoxide) we observed a very low interfering behaviour with respect to ozone so, after some preliminary measurements, we discarded ammonia and ethanol. Carbon monoxide was chosen as representatives of this class of low-interfering gases. Ethylene showed a stronger interfering effect. Thus, we prepared samples mixing dry air and ozone or dry air, ozone and an interfering compound (ethylene or carbon monoxide). We tested 581 samples divided in 30 different binary mixtures during an eleven months campaign.

The concentrations of the analytes employed are: ozone (0, 70, 140, 280, 560 ppb), carbon monoxide (0, 5, 10 ppm), ethylene (0, 5, 10, 30, 60 ppm). The measurements are performed at different humidity concentrations: 3 and 20% at 20°C. Different humidity levels are considered to increase the system complexity and match more realistic industrial environments. The detailed experimental setup is to be found in (Vezzoli, et al., 2008).

Two different features were extracted from each sensor response: R_{ss} (steady state resistance) and $\Delta R = R_{ss} - R_0$. R_{ss} is the average sensor response between 10 and 20 minutes after injection. Averaging is done to filter electric noise and spurious signals that can invalidate a punctual sensor response sampling. R_0 (baseline) value was evaluated for all the sensors only once at the beginning of each measurement session and then applied to the calculation of ΔR for all the measurements in that session.

The preprocessing step, including feature extraction, can affect the EDA results, for instance if the sensors are non-linear. However, this task is not further discussed here; instead, the reader might refer to previous topical publications (Hines, 1999; Pardo, 2000; Gutierrez-Osuna, 2002; Pardo & Sberveglieri, 2007).

The measurements' variability depends on a high number of variables: sensor type, ozone concentration, interfering species and their concentrations, humidity level and time progression. In order to visually understand how the variables affect the sensor response, we applied EDA techniques, implemented in the "EDA software," a

Matlab® toolbox developed over the years at the Sensor Lab, starting with (Pardo, 2000).

The EDA software consists of several customized descriptive statistics functions and tools that enable for: the definition of a data structure (both the measurement matrix and the data covariates), easy data manipulation (e.g. data sub-sampling, data set fusion) and plots customization. EDA software has some useful plotting feature as the possibility to describe data points with a double labeling. This means that the legend is characterized by two labels: the first label refers to a data category, e.g. ozone concentration, so that data points are colored with different colours relating to different ozone concentrations. The second label refers to a diverse category, e.g. humidity level, and points are marked with diverse markers relating to diverse humidity levels. This simple customization is useful to retrieve more information out from the same figure reducing the number of needed plots. In particular, the advantage of this graphical mode is that the user is able to observe how data points are spatially located referring simultaneously to two categories and to recognize particular data structures more easily.

Sensor Selection

Initially, with feature plots and box plots, we visually selected the best sensors. Feature plots depict the value of a characteristic extracted from a sensor versus time or another data category. For example in Figure 1 the feature is plotted with respect to the category ozone concentration and category classes are 35, 70, 140, 280, and 560 ppb. The subset of measurements depicted are (1) the measurement session of December 2005 (the other sessions give similar results) (2) all the sensors composing the array (3) at fixed humidity (RH = 20%) (4) without interfering gases. Each subplot refers to a sensor while points are grouped with respect to different ozone concentrations on the x axis. WHT and SnAu are the two best sensors. For the WHT sensor, measurements at different ozone concentrations do not overlap (except for

a few measurements at 35 and 70 ppb). For the other three sensors an overlapping is present. Yet, for SnAu the within class spread is noticeably minor that for the other two.

A further indicator of sensor performance is stability over different sessions. In Figure 2 we expand the values of Figure 1 with the second, third and fourth session. We also change the label, which now reflects the session name. This plot confirms that sensor WHT is performing best and the sensor SnAu is the second best.

Such deduction is also supported by the box plot of the sensor WHT and CoO (Figure 3). The box plot summarize different properties of a data distribution: (1) the box has lines at the lower or first quartile (bottom blue line), median or second quartile (red line in the middle) and upper or third quartile (top blue line) values; (2) whiskers are lines extending from each end of the box showing the extent of the tails of the sample distribution. Whiskers extend from the box out to the most extreme data value within 1.5*IQR, where IQR is the inter-quartile range (i.e. difference between 3rd and 1st quartile values) of the sample; (3) outliers are data with values beyond the ends of the whiskers and they are marked with a red cross. If there is no data outside the whisker, a dot is placed at the bottom whisker.

Box plots convey more synthetically the different performance of WHT and CoO. You should compare these figures with the relative plots in Figure 2. For the WHT, the boxes are well separated and a neat increasing relation with respect to ozone concentration is observed. The contrary is true for CoO. As you note in Figure 3 (bottom), there is only a slight negative correlation between the ozone concentration and the sensor response. Note that the CoO sensor (p-type) is expected to behave in an opposite way with respect to the WHT sensor (n-type). The actual problem is clear from Figure 2: the dependence on ozone is smaller than the dependence on the session number (you could attempt to counterbalance drift, we did not).

Figure 1. Feature plot of the characteristic Rss. Ozone concentration is on the x axis (from 35 to 560 ppb). The sensors that better discriminate different ozone concentration are WHT and SnAu. All the measurements reported were collected only in December 2005. The measurements collected at 35 and 560 ppb of ozone were collected only in the first session. From (Vezzoli, 2008).

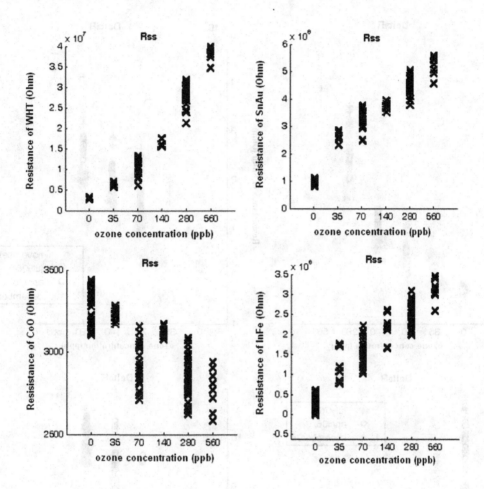

Explaining the Variance

The three interfering compounds play an important role in the determination of the ozone concentration. In fact, as we will see in this section, in a mixture of ozone, ethylene, carbon monoxide and water steam at the concentrations of interest in this study, the data variability depends, sorting with descending importance, on:

1. Humidity Level
2. Sensor Drift
3. Ozone Concentration (with a resolution of circa 50 ppb)
4. Ethylene Concentration (if less than 10 ppm)
5. CO Concentration (any)

The interfering effect of humidity is well known for all metal oxide sensors and represents the major drawback of this type of sensors. Humidity level estimation is almost necessary when sensors are placed in a workplace in which humidity variations are not negligible. In the following, we perform successive principal component analysis plots on

Figure 2. Top) Feature plots of the ΔR feature extracted from WHT and SnAu sensors over four measurement sessions: November 06, July 06, April 06, December 05. Bottom) The same feature extracted from CoO and InFe sensors presents a visible drift. Measurements with 35 and 560 ppb ozone have been performed only in the first measurement session. From (Vezzoli, 2008).

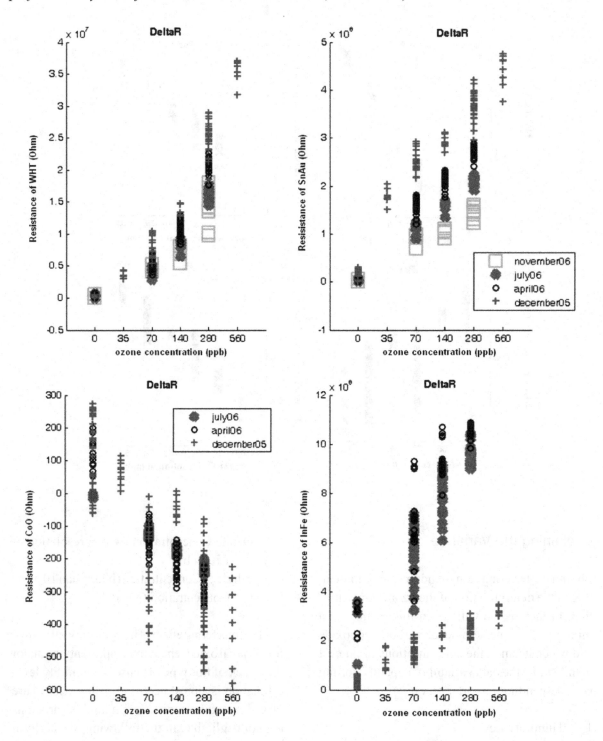

Figure 3. Box plots of R_{SS} characteristic extracted from the sensors WHT (top) and CoO (bottom), one for each ozone concentration (from 0 to 560 ppb). The points marked with a red cross are outliers. From (Vezzoli, 2008).

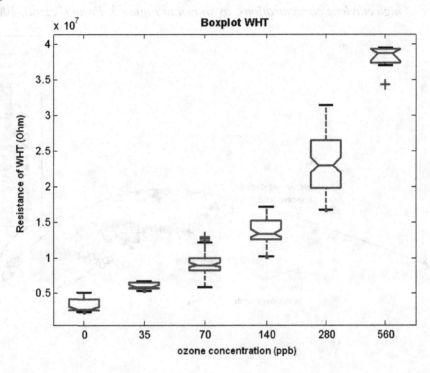

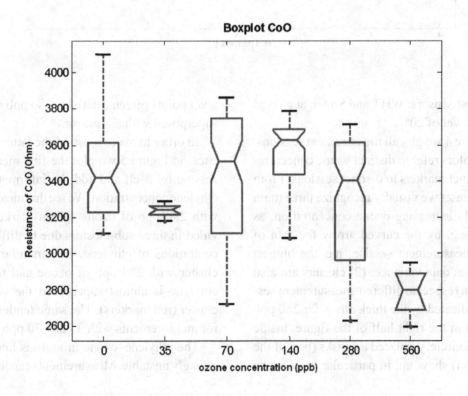

Figure 4. Different ozone concentrations (from 0 to 560 ppb) are reported with different colours. The clusters are ordered and quite separated with respect to both ozone concentration and session (arrows), apart from those located close to 0 ppb of ozone (dashed circle). The anomalous measurements are due to the presence of high ethylene concentrations, as shown in Figure 5. From (Vezzoli, 2008).

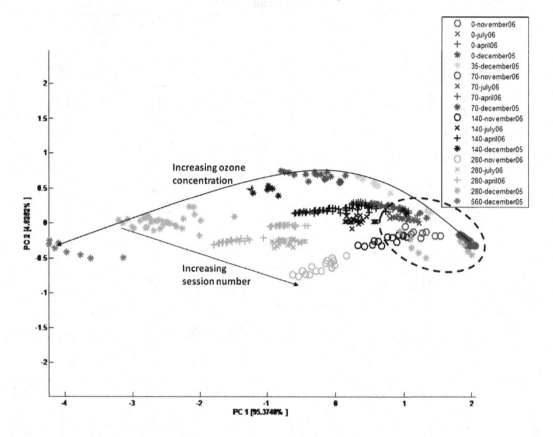

the two best sensors: WHT and SnAu, at a fixed humidity level of 20%.

In Figure 4 we plot all measurement sessions. Distinct colors refer to distinct ozone concentrations, distinct markers to distinct sessions. From this big dataset we visually recognize three main aspects: (1) increasing ozone concentration, as indicated e.g. by the curved arrow for data of the first measurement session, has the biggest influence on data variance; (2) clusters are also spread with respect to different measurement session, as indicated by the thick arrow for 280 ppb ozone; (3) in the right half of the figure, inside the dashed circle, displaced asterisks (part of the first session) show up; in particular high ozone

level points (green asterisks, 280 ppb ozone) are superposed with simple air.

In order to make sense of the latter incongruence, in Figure 5 we plot the first measurement session by itself and add the information about ethylene concentration. We see that measurements with 280 ppb of ozone (green marker) are divided in three sub-clusters due to different concentrations of ethylene. In particular, the sub-cluster with 280 ppb of ozone and 60 ppm of ethylene is almost superposed the zero ozone cluster (red markers). The same tendency is true for measurements with 35 and 70 ppb of ozone.

The ethylene–ozone mixture is known to be strongly unstable. Measurements carried out with

Figure 5. A subset of the data displayed, covering the first measurement session only (ozone- ethylene mixtures). The first column of each entry in the legend refers to the ozone concentration (in ppb) whilst the second one to the ethylene concentration (in ppm). The arrows show the effect of increasing ethylene concentrations (0 to 30 to 60 ppm). From (Vezzoli, 2008).

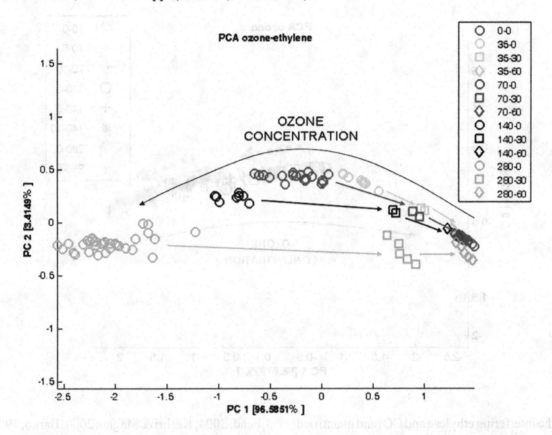

an ozone analyzer revealed that the ozone concentration decreases of about 2-5% once ethylene is added. However sensor response is decreased more than 2-5% when ethylene is added to ozone. It is reasonable to ascribe this to the catalytic effect of the metal oxide surface, which enhances ozone-ethylene interaction. It is apparent that the sensor system is not able to detect ozone in presence of more than 30ppm of interfering ethylene. For this reason, we performed measurements with high concentration of ethylene (30 and 60 ppm) just in the first session and we subsequently tested only mixtures with low ethylene concentrations (≤ 10 ppm) in later sessions. Extreme concentrations of ozone (35 and 560 ppb) were also not measured in the last sessions.

Figure 6 shows the second measurement session with several ozone-ethylene mixtures. If the ethylene is present at low concentrations (up to 5 ppm) ozone concentration differences are still bigger than ethylene differences. Ten ppm of ethylene, at least for higher ozone concentrations, still represents a big interference.

As for CO interference, in Figure 7 we see that it is not noticeable up to the CO level tested (10 ppm): different CO concentrations fall within the same ozone-dependent cluster (same color).

Finally, if we consider all sessions without the interfering effect of high ethylene concentrations (10, 30, and 60 ppm) and without the 35 and 560 ppb of ozone, we obtain Figure 8. The different ozone levels can be distinguished independently

Figure 6. A subset of the data displayed, covering the second measurement session (ozone- ethylene mixtures). The first column of each entry in the legend refers to the ozone concentration (ppb) whilst the second one to the ethylene concentration (ppm). The spreading of clusters at different ozone concentrations are still bigger than those of ethylene (up to 5 ppm). From (Vezzoli, 2008).

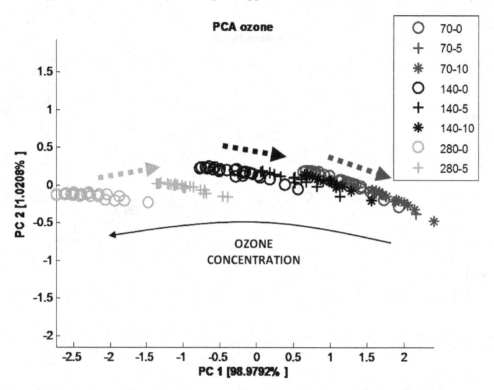

Cluster Analysis and Validity

Cluster Analysis (CA) is an unsupervised learning method frequently used in EDA to make a preliminary assessment of the data structure, to discover hidden structures in the data sets, and to extract (or compress) the information by drawing data prototypes (Jain, 1999; Gordon, 1999).

CA has been introduced in the chemical sensor field almost two decades ago (Gardner, 1991; Jurs, 2000) and then has been often adopted in combination with PCA for data mining and visualization (Shagal & Magan, 2008; Zhang, 2006;

of the interfering ethylene and CO (and quantified with a very small error, see [Vezzoli, et al., 2008]). In particular, the right half of the plot is not confused anymore as it was in Figure 4.

Fend, 2004; Keshri & Magan, 2000; Barkó, 1999; Holberg, 1995).

CA enables the user to summarize information, e.g. by representing classes through prototypes, and can help detecting important relationships within the data sets, make predictions or formulate hypotheses about the data structure. Furthermore, a more rational organization of information facilitates the subsequent step of supervised learning.

The present book chapter will first illustrate CA strategies and some common graphical tools for visualization of clustering outcomes; then it provides a brief overview of Cluster Validity (CV) techniques (Halkidi, 2001; Milligan & Cooper, 1985; Dubes & Jain, 1979), a set of statistical procedures for judging the merits of the clustering outcome in a quantitative manner and they can be used to objectively assess the resulting clustering structure.

Figure 7. A subset of the data displayed, relative to ozone-CO mixtures. Different colours refer to different ozone concentrations, whilst different markers refer to 0, 5 and 10 ppm of CO. From (Vezzoli, 2008).

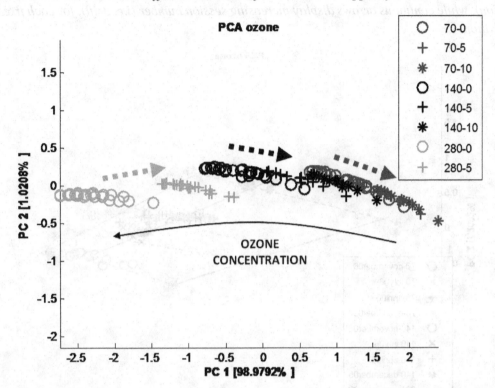

Here we disregard most of mathematical and computational concepts, which are widely reported in the literature (the reader might refer to the additional readings section).

Clustering Strategies and Related Visualization Tools

CA essentially refers to the assignment of patterns into groups (clusters) so that the objects belonging to the same group are *more similar* to each other than those within different groups.

Similarity is usually measured by a distance function defined on pairs of patterns. The most popular metric for continuous features is the Euclidean distance (Zhang, 2006; Magan, 2000; Holmberg, 1995).

The similarity measure directly affects the formation of the resulting clusters, hence the distance measure must be chosen carefully by the user. For instance, Euclidean distance works well with Gaussian distributed clusters while linear correlation among features, which is often the case of sensor array data, can distort the distance measures; this distortion can be alleviated by using the squared Mahalanobis distance (Mao and Jain, 1996).

Given the proximity measure, the construction of a data partition represents an NP-hard optimization problem, which is solved by approximate, often empirical, solutions. A wealth of algorithms has been developed in different frameworks. To date there is no clustering algorithm that can be universally used to solve all problems; therefore the user must carefully investigate the characteristics of the problem at hand, in order to select the appropriate approach (Xu and Wunsch, 2005).

A widely agreed taxonomy classifies the clustering techniques as hierarchical and partitional clustering, based on the properties of generated clusters (see Jain, 1999 Section 5).

Figure 8. A subset of the data displayed, where extreme ozone values and high ethylene concentrations are omitted. From (Vezzoli, 2008). Dashed arrows display increasing ozone concentrations (one arrow per session), while continous arrows display increasing session number (i.e. drift), for each fixed ozone concentration.

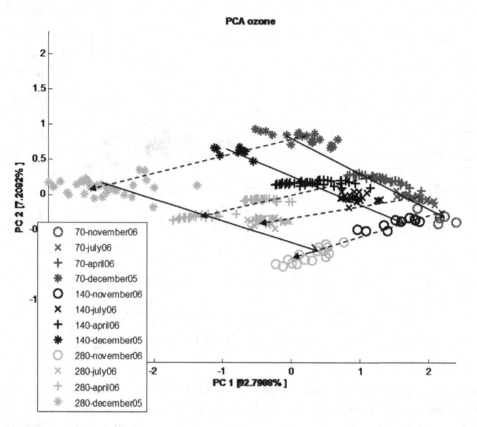

Hierarchical Clustering

Hierarchical Clustering (HC) organizes the data into a hierarchical structure, i.e. a nested set of subsequent non-overlapping partitions.

Algorithms for HC are mainly classified as divisive and agglomerative methods. Divisive HC begins with all objects in one cluster and then splits it in subsequent nested sub-clusters until all object belong to individual clusters; this is not very used in practice due to exponentially diverging computational cost with the number of objects to be clustered. Agglomerative HC starts with clusters that include exactly one object, then a series of merge operations are followed out to bring all objects into the same group. The most popular methods are: single link (SL), average

link (AL), complete link (CL) and Ward strategy (Ward).

The results of HC are graphically depicted by a *binary tree* or *dendrogram* (see an example in Figure 9). The root node of the dendrogram represents the whole data set and each leaf node is regarded as a data object. The intermediate nodes, thus, describe the extent that the objects are proximal to each other; and the height of the dendrogram usually expresses the distance between each pair of objects or clusters, or an object and a cluster. A data partition can be obtained by cutting the tree at different distance levels.

To judge the quality of HC results the user can check the value of the so called Cophenetic Correlation Coefficient (CPCC) (Jain & Dubes, 1988, section 4.3). This represents the linear correlation

Figure 9. Graphical visualization of hierarchical CA results. In these experiments the EOS835 EN was used to analyze the headspace of maize grain samples contaminated by Fusarium fungi. Grains were contaminated by Fusarium verticillioides, able to produce the mycotoxin Fumonisin B, and by other four species (F. oxisporum, F. semitectum, F. solani, and F. subglutinans), which are not expected to produce Fumonisin. Thus the label FB+ denotes the ability to produce Fumonisin, whilst FB− the inability. Some maize samples were left uncontaminated as reference ("maize" label). Data source: Falasconi (2007).

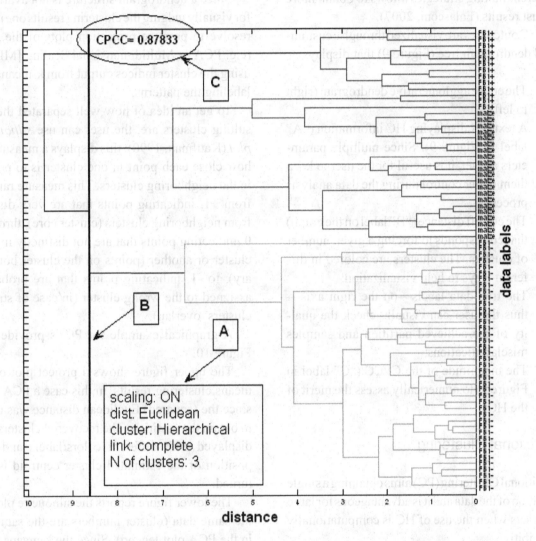

coefficient between the cophenetic distance (the level of the dendrogram at which two objects are placed in the same cluster) obtained from the tree, and the original distance used to construct the tree. Thus, it measures how faithfully the tree represents the dissimilarity matrix. The CPCC value is between -1 and 1, and should be very close to 1 for a high-quality clustering solutions,

although it is not an absolute reference of HC goodness but is more likely a relative quality index (Rohlf & Fisher, 1968).

HC has been often used for checking the classification ability of artificial noses in a number of different applicative scenarios (Naraghia, 2010; Sahgal, 2008; Zhang, 2006; Fend, 2004; Magan, 2000) or to investigate the similarity among the sensors included in an array (Chaudry, 2000; Penza, 2001).

The SENSOR clustering package implements all the above cited agglomerative HC strategies; in fact using more than one clustering method and different linking strategies allows to obtain more robust results (Falasconi, 2007).

HC outcomes are visualized through a customized dendrogram tree (Figure 9) that displays:

1. The entire agglomerative dendrogram (right to left);
2. A text box displaying HC information ("A" label in Figure 9). Since multiple parameters are set, it is useful for the user to keep them under control during the data analysis process;
3. The cut-off distance ("B" label on the graph) that corresponds to forcing a given number of clusters. The clusters are colored in different ways to help visualization;
4. The true data labels—on the right axis—thus the user can visually check the quality of the achieved partition and samples misclassifications;
5. The magnitude of the CPCC ("C" label in Figure 9) to numerically assess the merit of the HC.

Partitional Clustering

Partitional Clustering (PC) aims obtaining a single partition of the data and it is advantageous for large data sets when the use of HC is computationally prohibitive.

One of the most important factors of PC is the criterion (or cost) function that must be minimized. The sum of squared error function, for instance, led to the well known k-means algorithm (McQueen, 1967; Jain, 1999, section 5.2). The k-means is very simple and computationally convenient (its time complexity is $O(n)$), thus it is suitable for clustering large amounts of data. On the other hand, its drawbacks are well known (Xu & Wun-

sch, 2005): it works very well only for compact hyperspherical clusters; the recovered centroids vary with different initial random guesses, thus often converging towards sub-optimal solutions; it is sensitive to outliers and noise.

Since a dendrogram structure is not available for visually judging the clustering results one must resolve to produce projection plots of the data (e.g. PCA or Multidimensional Scaling [MDS]) using the cluster indices output from k-means for labeling the patterns.

To get an idea of how well separated the resulting clusters are, the user can use *silhouette plot* (Kaufman, 1990): this displays a measure of how close each point in one cluster is to points in the neighboring clusters. This measure ranges from +1, indicating points that are very distant from neighboring clusters (cluster core), through 0, indicating points that are not distinctly in one cluster or another (points on the cluster boundary), to -1, indicating points that are probably assigned to the wrong cluster (in case of strong clusters' overlap).

A graphical example for PC is provided in Figure 10.

The upper figure shows a project plot of k-means clustering results, in this case a PCA plot since the (squared) Euclidean distance was used to obtain the partition. The recovered clusters are displayed with different colors/labels and the position of the estimated cluster centroid is returned.

The lower figure reports the silhouette plot of the same data (cluster numbers are the same as in the PCA plot legend). Since the k-means was able to recover three not overlapping clusters, the silhouette values are all non-negative.

Cluster Validity Techniques

A relevant problem which arises in CA is the interpretation of clustering results. Most of current clustering algorithms do not provide any estimate of the significance of the returned results.

Figure 10. Visualization tools for partitional k-means clustering: projection plot (upper plot) and silhouette plot (lower plot). Data source: Falasconi (2007).

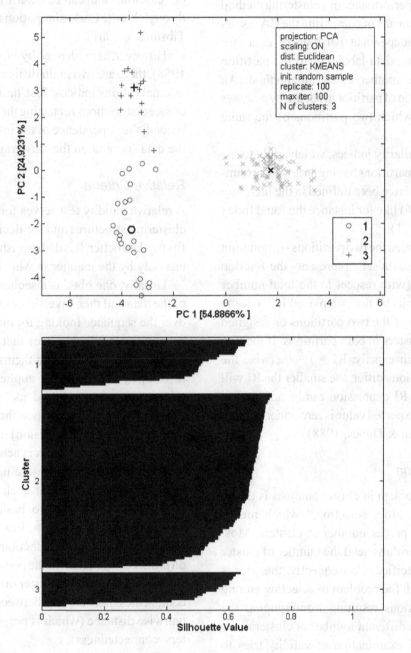

Moreover, it is well known that every clustering algorithm tends to produce clusters irrespectively of the data containing true clusters or not.

Cluster Validity (CV) methods have been developed to objectively and quantitatively assess the quality of the clustering results. For an overview

on this topic the reader can refer to the Jain's book (Jain and Dubes, 1988) or to more recent reviews (Handl, 2005; Halkidi, 2002).

CV procedure can be expressed in terms of three types of criteria: external, internal and relative.

External Criteria

Evaluating the performance of a clustering method requires some means of comparing the CA results to either an independent partition of data (for instance the true data labels) or to the partition resulting from another clustering method. An external criterion of partitional adequacy assesses the degree to which two partitions of the same data set agree.

Several similarity indices, which apply to the comparison of partitions having an arbitrary number of clusters, have been defined in the literature (Milligan, 1986) like for instance the Rand Index (RI) (Rand, 1971).

The RI between the two partitions - originating from the same data set - represents the fraction of point-pairs (with respect to the total number of pairs in n objects) that are placed in the same cluster in each of the two partitions or assigned to different clusters in both partitions. If the two partitions match exactly, RI = 1; otherwise the more the partitions differ, the smaller the RI will be. The above RI expression can be adjusted to ensure that its expected value is zero under random hypothesis (Jain & Dubes, 1988).

Internal Criteria

A recurrent problem in cluster analysis is the so called "model order selection," which means estimating the proper number of clusters. Most clustering algorithms need the number of cluster to be prior specified. Consequently, the user is confronted with the problem of selecting among different partitions resulting from running the algorithm with different number of clusters.

An internal examination of validity tries to determine if the clustering structure is intrinsically "appropriate" for the data by using only the information contained in the data themselves. Statistical test of hypothesis provides a framework for deciding how much appropriate it is (Jain & Dubes, 1988). Operatively, the result of cluster analysis is compared with the distribution of the results obtained under an appropriate null

hypothesis, also called "reference distribution" or "baseline" that can be determined for instance through Monte Carlo simulations (Halkidi, 2001; Tibshirani, 2001).

However, as evidenced by Jain (Jain & Dubes, 1988), there are two main difficulties in applying internal validity indices: first, the definition of reference distributions for testing the null hypothesis; second, the dependence of the internal indices on the data sets and on the clustering methodology.

Relative Criteria

A relative validity test serves for comparing two clustering structures and for deciding which one fits the data better. It is distinguished from internal test only by the manner in which it is applied.

Usually, one obtains a sequence of partitions of the data and then investigates the index values over the sequence looking for maxima (minima) or significant edges (knee) that may indicate a better fitting with the data themselves (Milligan & Cooper, 1985). When applied to HC, these criteria are often referred as "stopping rules" (Xu & Wunsch, 2005) since the program stops the amalgamation (or division) process when the "right" number of clusters is achieved.

By following the intuitive notion of cluster, most indices assume that a cluster is a group of patterns satisfying two basic requirements: compactness and isolation. For this reason, the corresponding objective functions are often based on proper combination of the pooled within cluster sum of squares around cluster means (to measure compactness) and the total between cluster-centers pairwise distance (which is proportional to clusters' connectedness).

Some of the mostly recognized indices are for instance the following: CH (Calinski & Harabasz, 1974); KL (Krzanowski & Lai, 1985); DB (Davies & Bouldin, 1979) and Gap statistics (Tibshirani, 2001). The reader shall refer to Falasconi et al. (Falasconi, 2007) for mathematical definitions and more extended illustration of the indices peculiarities.

Table 1. RI used as external CV index to compare the performance of relative CV criteria in predicting the "best" partition of the data set (modified from Falasconi, 2007)

Relative CV index	CA method	Predicted number of clusters	Average RI across CA methods
KL	SL	2	0.9309
	CL	3	
	AVE	3	
	Ward	3	
	k-means	3	
DB	SL	4	0.9193
	CL	3	
	AVE	7	
	Ward	3	
	k-means	3	

A practical example of both external and relative CV criteria application is provided here; it refers to previously published experiments (Falasconi, 2005) and clustering results (Falasconi, 2007).

The relative CV indices allowed to estimate the optimal number of clusters present in the data set. In our case, the best number of clusters K is equal to three; in fact, by combining the individual CV indices with different CA strategies, this value was recovered 11 times over 15 partitions (see Table 2 in Falasconi, 2007, an extract of this table is reported in Table 1).

Table 2. RI used as external CV index to confront the recovered "best" partition with the true labels of the data (modified from Falasconi, 2007)

		True data categories		
		Fumonisin production	Fungal species	Fungal strains
CA method	Best number of clusters	RI	RI	RI
SL	2	0.7952	0.3488	0.2890
CL	3	0.8257	0.2759	0.2378
AVE	3	0.9512	0.4493	0.3718
Ward	3	0.9512	0.3321	0.2461
k-means	3	0.9512	0.3321	0.2461

Although almost all relative indices predicted the same number of clusters, peculiar behaviors that depend of the combination between the CA algorithms and the CV rule can be observed.

The CL approach was the most consistent, being the predicted number of clusters K=3 in every case. SL clustering with CH and KL indices has the tendency to underestimate the number of clusters (K=2 was often predicted). On the contrary, the DB index was returning K=7 when combined with AVE link depending on the peculiarity of AVE link to be sensitive to isolated patterns.

Gap statistics returned K values comprised between K=2 (for SL) and K=5 (for Ward and k-means), thus its performance are not superior to those of other CV indices considered here.

It is worthy to note that, while CH, KL and DB indices cannot be used for testing the hypothesis of clusters absence the Gap statistics can, being defined also for no clusters. Yet, the main drawback of the Gap statistics lies in the complexity and computation cost of the reference distribution estimation that makes this task very difficult (Tibshirani, 2001).

As an external CV index, the RI was used in two different ways:

- First, to quantitatively compare the recovery performance of the relative CV criteria and assessing their consistency. To illustrate this, the comparison of CV results for two of such indices (KL and DB) is reported in Table 1. Although, the average RI (4th column of the table) is very high for both indices and (on average) the predicted number of clusters is three for both (col. 3 of the table), it is evident that KL index performs better than DB and is less sensitive to the combination with the clustering algorithms (col. 2 of the table).

- Second, to estimate the degree of fitness of the "best" cluster partition with the true data labels or to evaluate which of the different data labelings better represents the true structure of the data (Table 2). In fact, the RI provides a quantitative assessment to the fact that the data are clustered according to the "Fumonisin production" ability of the various fungal strains, as further confirmed in later works (Gobbi, 2011), while the other two variables ("Fungal species" and "Fungal strain") are not so relevant.

CURRENT ISSUES AND FUTURE RESEARCH DIRECTIONS

Exploratory data analysis encompasses a set of well established methodologies, where no particular controversy can be found.

An issue is mostly the imprecise application of the methods, possibly resulting in overstatements. An example, in the chemical sensing field, is the common use of drawing circles around sparse point clouds in PCA plots, where sometimes the circles partially superpose on each other, masking the fact that the intra-cluster dispersion is higher than inter-cluster distance and thereby conveying the false idea of class separation. For this reason, the complementary combination of PCA with CA/CV techniques can be beneficial for the user: the former provides a visual sketch of data allowing the user a fast qualitative judgment, while the latter will help to quantitatively assess the unsupervised classification results.

Even more important is the ever arising problem of clustering over-interpretation, e.g. where a pre-determined number of clusters is taken for given and no validation is hence performed. Validation is mainly important for CA, since it is known that any clustering algorithm tends to produce clusters irrespective of the data containing true clusters or not.

Moreover, clustering results are often unstable, so any clustering outcome should really be checked for stability by using some kind of repeated data subsampling (e.g. bootstrap); an example in this direction was recently proposed by the authors in the framework of fuzzy clustering (Falasconi, 2010).

Finally, different clustering algorithms do normally come to different clustering results, so that results from any single clustering algorithm should be taken with a grain of salt. In practice hypotheses validation with a new set of data is in order, at least for high dimensionality datasets, as is the usual case in genomics and nowadays for some new chemical sensing projects.

Unsupervised dimensionality reduction—beyond principal components—is an active research topic. For the types of data produced by sensors, Kernel approaches offer some potential (Schölkopf & Smola, 2001). In addition, alternative extensions to the basic multivariate techniques exist, such as principal curves where the data are projected onto a curve (Hastie & Stuetzle, 1989) and both the projection and curve need to be determined during the fitting stages. Of particular interest are extensions to the basic methods which take explicit account of the error structure of the data. Probabilistic PCA was proposed by Tipping and Bishop (1999), and comparable methods exist for Independent Components Analysis (ICA) and even for Factor Analysis (FA).

On the more practical side, these state of the art visualization methods will be enhanced by providing suitable color palettes. There are different color palettes already available in R. However, they have certain drawbacks, such as only generating palettes of certain lengths or not following a color space which equally captures each of the axes of human perception. Hence infrastructure for the convenient generation of arbitrary long color palettes which conform to certain quality criteria must be developed. In addition guidelines are needed for the most important visualization methods in sensor data analysis to help the user to choose appropriate color schemes which are able to increase the information in the statistical graphic and do not have distorting effects (Ihaka, 2003).

The current trend (impelling need) in the field of artificial olfaction is to enlarge both the size of data sets and the dimensionality of the feature space. A beautiful example of that is for instance the building of huge micro-machined sensor arrays made of many thousands sensors, which is a main goal of the NEUROCHEM project (www. neurochem-project.org) funded under the FP7 European program.

In the near future, this shall definitively originate challenging issues for data analysis and data mining, e.g. requiring more powerful clustering algorithms able to handle large volume of data as well as high-dimensional features with acceptable time and storage complexities. Adequate cluster visualization techniques shall be also adopted. Some powerful approached have been formerly developed in other frameworks (Xu & Wunsch, 2005) and might be successfully transferred to electronic noses.

Very large sensor arrays will also pose problems connected to variables redundancy. Therefore, a further relevant issue is the selection of appropriate and meaningful features, which can greatly reduce the burden of subsequent designs of classification/regression systems. Unsupervised feature selection is a very active research field since the advent of bioinformatics (Dy & Brodley, 2004) and shall be a promising topic for people working on machine olfaction.

CONCLUSION

The chapter provided full coverage of some of mostly used techniques for Exploratory Data Analysis (EDA) in the chemical sensing field. The techniques have been illustrated in some relevant case studies by emphasizing the advantages of graphical and interactive visualization of the experimental data.

EDA is one of the most important parts of the data analysis cycle and an essential step to check the quality of experimental data before embarking in subsequent training and test phases (e.g. for odour classification or regression). In particular, for artificial olfaction systems, due to the amount of measurements and their multivariate nature, more efficient tools are required to overcome the limits of conventional methods generally applied for characterizing gas sensors.

Regarding EDA tools, we have shown how the systematic application of the exploratory methodology, through the visual inspection of feature plots and box plots, allows to select the optimal working conditions, e.g. the more stable and sensitive sensors. On the other hand, the use of interactive PCA plots allows us to investigate and draw sound conclusions that explain the data variability.

We have also illustrated how CA and CV techniques might be combined to infer data structures and to objectively and quantitatively assess such structures. CA can be seen as a complementary tool to single and multiple variables display techniques, such as PCA, due to the possibility to properly validate the final results. Given the ability of human mind to imagine post hoc justifications, a proper validation of results it is clearly necessary. The proposed CV procedures can help solving two interrelated problems often encountered in the EN field: first, the need of an expert practitioner performing EDA through lengthy and user driven data inspection; second, the lack of objectivity in such a visual judgment of the data plots.

Current issues and future research trends have been also presented. Linear and non-linear transformations and projection pursuit methods are now becoming popular in the sensor field and shall represent useful ways for overcoming the limitations of classical tools, such as PCA. At the same time, the availability of very high dimensional data matrices will require to elaborate and implement more powerful EDA tools.

REFERENCES

Barkó, G., Abonyi, J., & Hlavay, J. (1999). Application of fuzzy clustering and piezoelectric chemical sensor array for investigation on organic compounds. *Analytica Chimica Acta, 398*, 219–222. doi:10.1016/S0003-2670(99)00377-3

Calinsky, T., & Harabasz, J. (1974). A dendrite method for cluster analysis. *Communications in Statistics, 3*, 1–27. doi:10.1080/03610927408827101

Chaudry, A. N., Hawkins, T. M., & Travers, P. J. (2000). A method for selecting an optimum sensor array. *Sensors and Actuators. B, Chemical, 69*, 236–242. doi:10.1016/S0925-4005(00)00498-6

Davies, D. L., & Bouldin, D. W. (1979). A cluster separation measure. *IEEE Transactions on Pattern Analysis and Machine Intelligence, 1*, 224–227. doi:10.1109/TPAMI.1979.4766909

Dubes, R., & Jain, A. (1979). Validity studies in clustering methodologies. *Pattern Recognition, 11*, 235–254. doi:10.1016/0031-3203(79)90034-7

Dy, J. G., & Brodley, C. E. (2004). Feature selection for unsupervised learning. *Journal of Machine Learning Research, 5*, 845–889.

Falasconi, M., Gobbi, E., Pardo, M., Della Torre, M., Bresciani, A., & Sberveglieri, G. (2005). Detection of toxigenic strains of fusarium verticillioides in corn by electronic olfactory system. *Sensors and Actuators. B, Chemical, 108*, 250–257. doi:10.1016/j.snb.2004.09.046

Falasconi, M., Gutierrez, A., Pardo, M., Sberveglieri, G., & Marco, S. (2010). A stability based validity method for fuzzy clustering. *Pattern Recognition, 43*, 1292–1305. doi:10.1016/j.patcog.2009.10.001

Falasconi, M., Pardo, M., Vezzoli, M., & Sberveglieri, G. (2007). Cluster validation for electronic nose data. *Sensors and Actuators. B, Chemical, 125*, 596–606. doi:10.1016/j.snb.2007.03.004

Fend, R., Bessant, C., Williams, A. J., & Woodman, A. C. (2004). Monitoring haemodialysis using electronic nose and chemometrics. *Biosensors & Bioelectronics, 19*, 1581–1590. doi:10.1016/j.bios.2003.12.010

Gardner, J. W. (1991). Detection of vapours and odours from a multisensor array using pattern recognition: Principal component and cluster analysis. *Sensors and Actuators. B, Chemical, 4*, 109–115. doi:10.1016/0925-4005(91)80185-M

Gobbi, E., Falasconi, M., Torelli, E., & Sberveglieri, G. (2011). Electronic nose predicts high and low fumonisins contamination in maize cultures. *Food Research International, 44*, 992–999. doi:10.1016/j.foodres.2011.02.041

Gordon, D. (1999). *Classification* (2nd ed.). London, UK: Chapman & Hall/CRC.

Gutierrez-Osuna, R. (2002). Pattern analysis for machine olfaction: A review. *IEEE Sensors Journal, 2*(3), 189–202. doi:10.1109/JSEN.2002.800688

Halkidi, M., Batistakis, Y., & Vazirgiannis, M. (2001). On clustering validation techniques. *Journal of Intelligent Information Systems, 17*(2/3), 107–145. doi:10.1023/A:1012801612483

Halkidi, M., Batistakis, Y., & Vazirgiannis, M. (2002). Clustering validity methods. *SIGMOD Record, 31*(2), 40–45. doi:10.1145/565117.565124

Handl, J., Knowles, J., & Kell, D. B. (2005). Computational cluster validation in post-genomic data analysis. *Bioinformatics (Oxford, England), 21*, 3201–3212. doi:10.1093/bioinformatics/bti517

Hastie, T. J., & Stuetzle, W. (1989). Principal curves. *Journal of the American Statistical Association, 84*, 502–516. doi:10.1080/01621459.1989.10478797

Hines, E. L., Llobet, E., & Gardner, J. W. (1999). Electronic noses: A review of signal processing techniques. *IEEE Proceedings-Circuits Devices and Systems, 146*(6), 297-310.

Holberg, M., Winquist, F., Ludström, I., Gardner, J. W., & Hines, E. L. (1995). Identification of paper quality using a hybrid electronic nose. *Sensors and Actuators. B, Chemical, 26-27*, 246–249. doi:10.1016/0925-4005(94)01595-9

Ihaka, R. (2003). Colour for presentation graphics. In K. Hornik, F. Leisch, & A. Zeileis (Eds.), *Proceedings of the 3rd International Workshop on Distributed Statistical Computing*. Vienna, Austria: IEEE.

Ionescu, R., Vancu, A., & Tomescu, A. (2000). Time-dependent humidity calibration for drift corrections in electronic noses equipped with sno2 gas sensors. *Sensors and Actuators. B, Chemical, 69*(3), 283–286. doi:10.1016/S0925-4005(00)00508-6

Jain, A. K., & Dubes, R. (1988). *Algorithms for clustering data*. Englewood Cliffs, NJ: Prentice Hall.

Jain, A. K., Murty, M. N., & Flynn, P. J. (1999). Data clustering: A review. *ACM Computing Surveys, 31*, 264–323. doi:10.1145/331499.331504

Jurs, P. C., Bakken, G. A., & McClelland, H. E. (2000). Computational methods for the analysis of chemical sensor array data from volatile analytes. *Chemical Reviews, 100*, 2649–2678. doi:10.1021/cr9800964

Kaufman, L., & Rousseeuw, P. J. (1990). *Finding groups in data: an introduction to cluster analysis*. New York, NY: Wiley. doi:10.1002/9780470316801

Keshri, G., & Magan, N. (2000). Detection and differentiation between mycotoxigenic and non-mycotoxigenic strains of two Fusarium spp. using volatile production profiles and hydrolytic enzymes. *Journal of Applied Microbiology, 89*, 825–833. doi:10.1046/j.1365-2672.2000.01185.x

Krzanowski, W. J., & Lai, Y. T. (1985). A criterion for determining the number of groups in a data set using sum-of-squares clustering. *Biometrika, 44*, 23–34.

Mao, J., & Jain, A. K. (1996). A self-organizing network for hyperellipsoidal clustering (HEC). *IEEE Transactions on Neural Networks, 7*, 16–29. doi:10.1109/72.478389

McQueen, J. (1967). Some methods for classification and analysis of multivariate observations. In *Proceedings of the Fifth Berkeley Symposium on Mathematical Statistics and Probability*, (Vol. 1, pp. 281-297). Berkeley, CA: University of California Press.

Milligan, G. W., & Cooper, M. C. (1985). An examination of procedures for determining the number of clusters in a data set. *Psychometrika, 50*, 159–179. doi:10.1007/BF02294245

Milligan, G. W., & Cooper, M. C. (1986). A study of the comparability of external criteria for hierarchical clustering. *Multivariate Behavioral Research, 21*, 441–458. doi:10.1207/s15327906mbr2104_5

Naraghi, K., Sahgal, N., Adriaans, B., Barr, H., & Magan, N. (2010). Use of volatile fingerprints for rapid screening of antifungal agents for efficacy against dermatophyte Trichophyton species. *Sensors and Actuators. B, Chemical, 146*, 521–526. doi:10.1016/j.snb.2009.12.031

Padilla, M., Perera, A., Montoliu, I., Chaudry, A., Persaud, K., & Marco, S. (2010). Drift compensation of gas sensor array data by orthogonal signal correction. *Chemometrics and Intelligent Laboratory Systems, 100*(1), 28–35. doi:10.1016/j.chemolab.2009.10.002

Pardo, M., Niederjaufner, G., Benussi, G., Comini, E., Faglia, G., & Sberveglieri, G. (2000). Data preprocessing enhances the classification of different brands of Espresso coffee with an electronic nose. *Sensors and Actuators. B, Chemical, 69*(3), 397–403. doi:10.1016/S0925-4005(00)00499-8

Pardo, M., & Sberveglieri, G. (2002). Learning from data: a tutorial with emphasis on modern pattern recognition methods. *IEEE Sensors Journal*, *2*, 203–217. doi:10.1109/JSEN.2002.800686

Pardo, M., & Sberveglieri, G. (2004). Electronic olfactory systems based on metal oxide semiconductor sensor arrays. *MRS Bulletin*, *29*(10), 703–708. doi:10.1557/mrs2004.206

Pardo, M., & Sberveglieri, G. (2007). Comparing the performance of different features in sensor arrays. *Sensors and Actuators. B, Chemical*, *123*, 437–443. doi:10.1016/j.snb.2006.09.041

Penza, M., Cassano, G., Tortorella, F., & Zaccaria, G. (2001). Classification of food, beverages and perfumes by WO3 thin-flm sensors array and pattern recognition techniques. *Sensors and Actuators. B, Chemical*, *73*, 76–87. doi:10.1016/S0925-4005(00)00687-0

Persaud, K. C., & Dodd, G. H. (1982). Analysis of discrimination mechanisms of the mammalian olfactory system using a model nose. *Nature*, *299*, 352–355. doi:10.1038/299352a0

Rand, W. M. (1971). Objective criteria for the evaluation of clustering methods. *Journal of the American Statistical Association*, *66*, 846–850. doi:10.1080/01621459.1971.10482356

Röck, F., Barsan, N., & Weimar, U. (2008). Electronic nose: Current status and future trends. *Chemical Reviews*, *108*, 705–725. doi:10.1021/cr068121q

Rohlf, F. J., & Fisher, D. L. (1968). Test for hierarchical structure in random data sets. *Systematic Zoology*, *17*, 407–412. doi:10.2307/2412038

Roussel, S., Forsberg, G., Steinmetz, V., Grenier, P., & Bellon-Maurel, V. (1998). Optimisation of electronic nose measurements: Methodology of output feature selection. *Journal of Food Engineering*, *37*, 207–222. doi:10.1016/S0260-8774(98)00081-8

Roussel, S., Forsberg, G., Steinmetz, V., Grenier, P., & Bellon-Maurel, V. (1999). Optimisation of electronic nose measurements: Influence of experimental parameters. *Journal of Food Engineering*, *39*, 9–15. doi:10.1016/S0260-8774(98)00137-X

Sahgal, N., & Magan, N. (2008). Fungal volatile fingerprints: Discrimination between dermatophyte species and strains by means of an electronic nose. *Sensors and Actuators. B, Chemical*, *131*, 117–120. doi:10.1016/j.snb.2007.12.019

Schölkopf, B., & Smola, A. (2001). *Learning with kernels*. Cambride, MA: MIT Press.

Šetkus, A., Olekas, A., Senulienė, D., Falasconi, M., Pardo, M., & Sberveglieri, G. (2010). Analysis of the dynamic features of metal oxide sensors in response to SPME fiber gas release. *Sensors and Actuators. B, Chemical*, *146*, 539–544. doi:10.1016/j.snb.2009.12.034

Sharma, R. K., Chan, P. C. H., Tang, Z., Yan, G., Hsing, I.-M., & Sin, J. K. O. (2001). Investigation of stability and reliability of tin oxide thin-film for integrated micro-machined gas sensor devices. *Sensors and Actuators. B, Chemical*, *81*(1), 9–16. doi:10.1016/S0925-4005(01)00920-0

Tibshirani, R., Walther, G., & Hastie, T. (2001). Estimating the number of clusters in a data set via the gap statistics. *Journal of the Royal Statistical Society. Series B. Methodological*, *63*, 411–423. doi:10.1111/1467-9868.00293

Tipping, M. E., & Bishop, C. M. (1999). Mixtures of probabilistic principal component analyzers. *Neural Computation*, *11*(2), 443–482. doi:10.1162/089976699300016728

Tukey, J. (1977). *Exploratory data analysis*. Reading, MA: Addison-Wesley.

Vezzoli, M., Ponzoni, A., Pardo, M., Falasconi, M., Faglia, G., & Sberveglieri, G. (2008). Exploratory data analysis for industrial safety application. *Sensors and Actuators. B, Chemical*, *131*(1), 100–109. doi:10.1016/j.snb.2007.12.047

Webb, A. (2002). *Statistical pattern recognition* (2nd ed.). West Sussex, UK: Wiley. doi:10.1002/0470854774

Xu, R., & Wunsch, D. II. (2005). Survey of clustering algorithms. *IEEE Transactions on Neural Networks*, *16*(3), 645–678. doi:10.1109/TNN.2005.845141

Zhang, Q., Zhang, S., Xie, C., Zenga, D., Fan, C., & Bai, Z. (2006). Characterization of Chinese vinegars by electronic nose. *Sensors and Actuators. B, Chemical*, *119*, 538–546. doi:10.1016/j.snb.2006.01.007

ADDITIONAL READING

Anderberg, M. (1973). *Cluster analysis for applications*. New York, NY: Academic Press.

Duda, R., Hart, P., & Stork, D. (2001). *Pattern classification* (2nd ed.). New York, NY: Wiley.

Duran, B., & Odell, P. (1974). *Cluster analysis: A survey*. New York, NY: Springer-Verlag.

Everitt, B., Landau, S., & Leese, M. (2001). *Cluster analysis*. London, UK: Arnold.

Hartigan, J. (1975). *Clustering algorithms*. New York, NY: Wiley.

Jolliffe, I. T. (2002). *Principal component analysis*. Berlin, Germany: Springer.

Lee, J. A. N., & Verleysen, M. (2007). *Nonlinear dimensionality reduction*. New York, NY: Springer. doi:10.1007/978-0-387-39351-3

Späth, H. (1980). *Cluster analysis algorithms*. Chichester, UK: Ellis Horwood.

KEY TERMS AND DEFINITIONS

Cluster Analysis (CA): Assignment of a set of observations into groups (called clusters) so that objects in the same cluster are similar in some pre-defined sense.

Cluster Validity (CV): Methods serving for objectively and quantitatively assess the quality of the clustering results.

Exploratory Data Analysis (EDA): Approach for data analysis with the purpose of visualizing the data, mining significant information and formulating hypotheses.

Principal Component Analysis (PCA): Mathematical procedure that uses an orthogonal transformation to convert a set of observations of possibly correlated variables into a set of values of uncorrelated variables called principal components.

Chapter 16

Bio–Inspired Background Suppression Technique and its Implementation into Digital Circuit

Takao Yamanaka
Sophia University, Japan

Yuta Munakata
Sophia University, Japan

ABSTRACT

Gas sensors have been widely used for various applications, such as gas leak detection, fire alarm systems, and odor-sensing systems. A problem of the gas sensors has been the selectivity to a target gas: background gases interfere with the measurement of the target gas. In the human olfaction, sensitivity to background odors is decreased by adaptation to the odors. Recently, several bio-inspired signal-processing methods mimicking the adaptation mechanism have been proposed for improving the selectivity of the gas sensors. In this chapter, the studies on the bio-inspired background suppression methods are reviewed. Furthermore, a case study of the bio-inspired background suppression is introduced. In the case study, a perceptron neural network with anti-Hebbian learning was used for realizing the adaptation to the background gas, and was implemented into a digital circuit for real-time gas sensing.

INTRODUCTION

Odor sensing systems have been developed in recent years (Nagle, Gutierrez-Osuna, & Schiffman, 1998), and are expected to be applied to practical applications such as gas leak detection, quality control in food industry, and environmental monitoring (Pearce, Schiffman, Nagle, & Gardner, 2003). The odor sensing systems can identify odors and quantify the concentration of the odors using odor sensors. The target odor samples are usually prepared in a small bottle and are measured under well-controlled temperature and humidity conditions.

DOI: 10.4018/978-1-4666-2521-1.ch016

Copyright © 2013, IGI Global. Copying or distributing in print or electronic forms without written permission of IGI Global is prohibited.

In practical applications, however, it is sometimes necessary to measure an odor in an open air, where the target odor is drifted with other background odors. These background odors can be interferences in the measurement of the target odor. The odor sensing systems have to compensate the influence of the interferences for realizing accurate identification and quantification of the target odor.

A simple compensation method would be to subtract the baseline response of the odor sensor (the response to the background odors) from the measured sensor response (the response to the mixture of the background and target odors). This method would be satisfactory when the concentration of the background odors is constant. However, since odors in an open air fluctuate due to a turbulent flow (Yamanaka, Ishida, Nakamoto, & Moriizumi, 1998), the simple compensation method will not work well. Therefore, a more sophisticated compensation method is required for the practical applications.

A method of the compensation (background suppression) has been proposed by mimicking the adaptation to an odor in biological olfaction (Gutierrez-Galvez & Gutierrez-Osuna, 2006; Gutierrez-Galvez, 2005). The method uses a neural model of biological olfaction (KIII model [Yao & Freeman, 1990]) with anti-hebbian learning (Principe, Euliano, & Lefebvre, 2000), and has been successfully applied to the background suppression (Gutierrez-Galvez, 2005). However, the KIII model, which has been developed for modeling the neural activity in the biological olfaction, is too complex to be used for the engineering purposes. In this chapter, a simplified bio-inspired method for the background suppression is introduced as a case study of bio-inspired background suppression methods (Ohba & Yamanaka, 2008). This algorithm was enough simple for the implementation into a digital circuit, which will lead to real-time gas sensing.

BACKGROUND

The adaptation is a common biological function in a sensory system, which allows the sensory system to reduce the sensitivity to previously detected stimuli, and then to improve the selectivity to a novel and interesting stimuli. In this chapter, we focus on the adaptation in the olfaction for developing bio-inspired signal processing methods for gas/odor sensing.

Neural computation models for olfactory adaptation or mixture segmentation have been proposed in various researchers (Figure 1). For example, Wang, Buhmann, and Malsburg (1990) proposed a neural model of pattern segmentation based on a neural network of associative memory, as shown in Figure 1 (a). They employed a neural network of oscillatory units linked with Hebbian connections to perform temporal segmentation of the stored patterns. Alternating bursts of activity induced by self-inhibition creates a spatio-temporal pattern that sequentially extracts the components of mixture.

Hendin, Horn, and Hopfield (1994) proposed models for the olfactory bulb which perform separation and decomposition of mixed odor inputs from different sources. Since the odors are unknown to the system, their model is considered as a blind-source separation problem. One of their models has hierarchical layers of neural network in Figure 1 (b), where each layer is inhibited by all previous layers. This network produces the different temporal fluctuations of the input odors.

Hoshino et al. have also proposed hierarchical models of odor-mixture recognition based on spatio-temporal encoding, shown in Figure 1 (c) (Hoshino, Kashimori, & Kambara, 1998; Oyamada, Kashimori, Hoshino, & Kambara, 2000). It models a neural mechanism for discrimination of different complex odors in the olfactory cortex based on the dynamical encoding scheme. Feedback signals from the bottom internuron layer

Figure 1. Neural computation models for olfactory adaptation or mixture segmentation. (a) Mutually connected oscillatory units (Wang, Buhmann, & Malsburg, 1990), (b) hierarchical layers of neural network (Hendin, Horn, & Hopfield, 1994), (c) hierarchical neural network model of olfactory cortex (Oyamada, Kashimori, Hoshino, & Kambara, 2000), (d) bulb-cortex model with feedforward and feedback paths (Li & Hertz, 2000), (e) KIII model (Yao & Freeman, 1990)

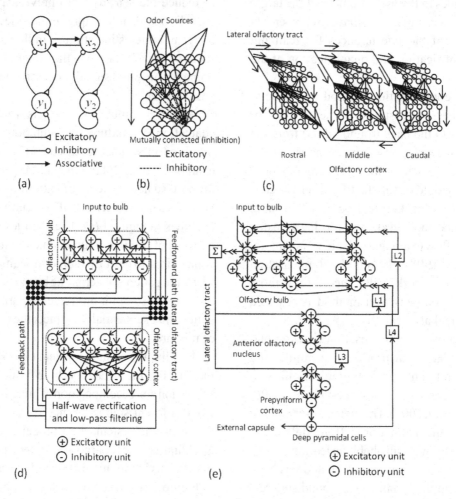

to the top layer inhibit the prominent pattern in the odor-mixture, leading to the itinerancy among the limit cycle attractors which represent components in the odor-mixture.

This kind of feedback signals was also used in the odor adaptation model in Figure 1 (d), proposed by Li and Hertz (2000). Although the feedback signals transmitted within the olfactory cortex in the Hoshino's model, the Li and Hertz model uses the feedback signals from the olfactory cortex to the olfactory bulb. When a background

odor is input to the model, the feedback signal corresponding to the background pattern was fed back to the olfactory bulb, which inhibits the neural activity in the olfactory bulb. Therefore, the activities in both the olfactory bulb and cortex decrease for the background odor. When the target odor is added to the background odor, the pattern corresponding to the target odor is observed by removing the background pattern.

The adaptation model based on the feedback signal has been applied to the signal processing for gas sensors (Gutierrez-Osuna & Powar, 2003). This model was successfully applied to binary mixtures for detecting a target odor from the mixture. Furthermore, they have also proposed a statistical pattern recognition approach for the background suppression based on Fisher's Linear Discriminant Analysis (Gutierrez-Osuna & Raman, 2004). Although the latter approach does not use the neural model of the olfactory adaptation, the adaptation mechanism in the olfaction has been referred in the concept level.

Other bio-inspired adaptation models have also been applied to gas sensing systems. Gutierrez-Osuna and Gutierrez-Galvez (2003) have proposed an adaptation model based on the KIII model in Figure 1 (e) (Yao & Freeman, 1990), where the connection weights from mitral nodes onto other neuron populations in the olfactory bulb follow an exponential decay. From the experimental results, it was confirmed that the target pattern was able to be extracted from the binary mixture pattern. Gutierrez-Galvez (2005) has also proposed another adaptation model based on the KIII model, where the connection weights for periglomerular lateral connections in the olfactory bulb were learned by the anti-hebbian learning. Raman and Gutierrez-Osuna (2005) have proposed the model of mixture segmentation and background suppression based on the hebbian and anti-hebbian learning on the feedback-connection weights from the olfactory cortex onto the olfactory bulb. The system behaves as a model of the mixture segmentation if the hebbian learning is applied, whereas the system behaves as a model of the background suppression (weaker-response suppression) if the anti-hebbian learning is applied.

As described above, the bio-inspired background suppression methods have successfully been applied to the gas/odor sensing systems. However, the neural models based on the biological olfaction tend to be too complex to be used in practical applications. If a neural model is implemented into a digital circuit, the circuit size may become quite large. Therefore, it would be desired

to develop a model simplified from the complex neural computation architecture. Therefore, in this chapter, we describe a bio-inspired model simple enough to be implemented into a digital circuit for real-time gas sensing.

PERCEPTRON MODEL WITH ANTI-HEBBIAN LEARNING

Model Description

The biological olfaction is known to have the property of adaptation, by which the sensitivity to a successive odor stimuli decreases so that the selectivity to novel odor stimuli can increase. By modeling this biological adaptation with a simple neural network, a method of suppressing the background odor effect was developed to detect target odor information.

The schematic of the biological olfactory pathway is shown in Figure 2(a). Odorant chemicals are captured in olfactory receptors, and those signals are transmitted to the olfactory bulb. The olfactory bulb is connected to the olfactory cortex in the brain where the odor impression is perceived. Since the adaptation of neural activities is observed in the olfactory cortex but not in the olfactory bulb (Kadohisa & Wilson, 2006), it can be hypothesized that the connection between the olfactory bulb and cortex has some role in the adaptation.

Based on such idea, a two-layer perceptron neural network in Figure 2(b) was used as an adaptation model, where the input and output layers correspond to the olfactory bulb and cortex, respectively. Each neuron on the input layer is connected to an odor sensor. When the connection weights between input and output layers are learned by anti-Hebbian learning, the outputs of the network become zero to the input pattern, whereas outputs to other patterns remain same (Principe, Euliano, & Lefebvre, 2000). Therefore, the adaptation to a background odor can be

Figure 2. Structure of olfactory adaptation model: (a) schematic of biological olfactory pathway, (b) perceptron neural network

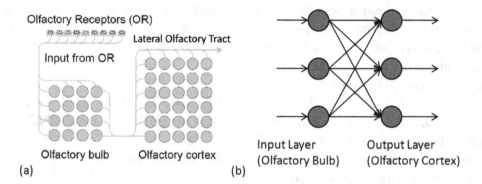

achieved by learning the weights with anti-Hebbian learning during the exposure of odor sensors to the background odor. The detailed analysis of the mechanism is described in the next section.

It should be noted that the neural model in Figure 2(b) does not have the lateral connections among neurons both in the input layer (olfactory bulb) and the output layer (cortex), whereas neural circuits in biological olfaction does have such connections. Furthermore, this model does not include the feedback connection from the cortex to the bulb, which might realize the adaptation in the biological olfaction. The reason why we did not include these connections is the simplification of the model for engineering applications. The usefulness of these connections needs to be further explored in future research.

Each neuron in the network is modeled by a delta-sigma modulator (Norsworthy, Schreier, & Temes, 1997), which has a similar property to the integrate-and-fire spiking neuron model (Shin, Lee, & Park, 1993). The anti-hebbian learning can be realized by the update rule of the connection weights formulated by the next equation:

$$w_{ij}(t + 1) = w_{ij}(t) - \alpha x_i(t)y_j(t) \qquad (1)$$

$w_{ij}(t)$ is the connection weight from an input neuron i to an output neuron j at time t, $x_i(t)$ and $y_j(t)$ are firing rates on the input and output layers, and α is a learning coefficient (a positive number).

Model Analysis

In this section, the mathematical analysis of the perceptron neural network with anti-Hebbian learning is described. The idea of this analysis partially comes from the reference (Matsuoka & Kawamoto, 1996). The network output y_j is represented by the following equation:

$$y_j = \mathbf{w}_j^T \mathbf{x} = \mathbf{x}^T \mathbf{w}_j , \qquad (2)$$

where $\mathbf{x}$ is an input vector of the network, and the weight vector $\mathbf{w}_j = [w_{1j}, w_{2j}, ..., w_{nj}]^T$. n is the number of network input (the dimension of the input vector). Equation 1 can be approximated to the next equation.

$$T \frac{\partial \mathbf{w}_j}{\partial t} \cong -\alpha \mathbf{x} y_j = -\alpha \mathbf{x} \mathbf{x}^T \mathbf{w}_j \qquad (3)$$

If the learning time constant T is enough large compared with the time constant of the input-signal change, $\mathbf{x}\mathbf{x}^T$ can be replaced by the ensemble mean $\mathbf{R} = \dfrac{1}{m}\sum \mathbf{x}\mathbf{x}^T$ (m is the number of input data).

$$T\frac{\partial \mathbf{w}_j}{\partial t} \cong -\alpha \mathbf{R}\mathbf{w}_j \qquad (4)$$

The *i*th eigen value and eigen vector are represented by λ_i and $\mathbf{u}_i$, respectively ($\lambda_1 > \lambda_2 > \cdots > \lambda_n$).

$$\mathbf{R}\mathbf{u}_i = \lambda_i \mathbf{u}_i \qquad (5)$$

When the weight vector $\mathbf{w}_j$ is expanded based on the eigen vectors,

$$\mathbf{w}_j = w_{u1}\mathbf{u}_1 + w_{u2}\mathbf{u}_2 + \cdots + w_{un}\mathbf{u}_n \qquad (6)$$

is obtained. Then,

$$\mathbf{R}\mathbf{w}_j = w_{u1}\mathbf{R}\mathbf{u}_1 + w_{u2}\mathbf{R}\mathbf{u}_2 + \cdots + w_{un}\mathbf{R}\mathbf{u}_n$$
$$= w_{u1}\lambda_1\mathbf{u}_1 + w_{u2}\lambda_2\mathbf{u}_2 + \cdots + w_{un}\lambda_n\mathbf{u}_n \qquad (7)$$

is obtained. Therefore, Equation 4 is transformed to

$$T\frac{\partial}{\partial t}\left(w_{u1}\mathbf{u}_1 + w_{u2}\mathbf{u}_2 + \cdots + w_{un}\mathbf{u}_n\right) \cong$$
$$-\alpha\left(w_{u1}\lambda_1\mathbf{u}_1 + w_{u2}\lambda_2\mathbf{u}_2 + \cdots + w_{un}\lambda_n\mathbf{u}_n\right) \qquad (8)$$

When the both sides of the equation are multiplied by $\mathbf{u}_i^T$ from left, the next differential equation is obtained.

$$T\frac{\partial}{\partial t}w_{ui} \cong -\alpha w_{ui}\lambda_i \qquad (9)$$

$$w_{ui} \cong w_{ui0}\exp\left(-\frac{\alpha\lambda_i}{T}t\right) \qquad (10)$$

w_{ui0} represents w_{ui} at $t = 0$ (The initial value of the weight vector). Therefore, the weight vector $\mathbf{w}_j$ is represented by the next equation.

$$\mathbf{w}_j \cong w_{u1}\mathbf{u}_1 + w_{u2}\mathbf{u}_2 + \cdots + w_{un}\mathbf{u}_n$$
$$= w_{u10}\exp\left(-\frac{\alpha\lambda_1}{T}t\right)\mathbf{u}_1 + \cdots \qquad (11)$$
$$+w_{un0}\exp\left(-\frac{\alpha\lambda_n}{T}t\right)\mathbf{u}_n$$

Therefore, the network output y_j is represented by the next equation.

$$y_j = \mathbf{x}^T\mathbf{w}_j$$
$$= w_{u10}\exp\left(-\frac{\alpha\lambda_1}{T}t\right)\mathbf{u}_1^T\mathbf{x} + \cdots \qquad (12)$$
$$+w_{un0}\exp\left(-\frac{\alpha\lambda_n}{T}t\right)\mathbf{u}_n^T\mathbf{x}$$

This equation represents that the network output becomes zero for the input vector of the $\mathbf{u}_1$ direction (the principal direction of the training data) after sufficiently large time of learning.

Let's consider the case that the initial weight matrix of the network is set to the unit matrix. In this case, $y_j = x_j$ at $t = 0$ ($\mathbf{y} = \mathbf{x}$). Therefore, from Equation 12,

$$y_j = w_{u10}\mathbf{u}_1^T\mathbf{x} + \cdots + w_{un0}\mathbf{u}_n^T\mathbf{x} = x_j \qquad (13)$$

is true for any input vector $\mathbf{x}$.

1. Input vector orthogonal to $\mathbf{u}_1$: $\mathbf{x}_\perp$

Since Equation 13 is true for any input vector $\mathbf{x}$,

$$w_{u10}\mathbf{u}_1^T\mathbf{x}_\perp + \cdots + w_{un0}\mathbf{u}_n^T\mathbf{x}_\perp = x_j \qquad (14)$$

is obtained. Since $\mathbf{u}_1^T \mathbf{x}_\perp = 0$,

$$w_{u20} \mathbf{u}_2^T \mathbf{x}_\perp + \cdots + w_{un0} \mathbf{u}_n^T \mathbf{x}_\perp = x_j. \qquad (15)$$

At time t, the network output y_j is represented by the following equation from Equation 12.

$$y_j = w_{u20} \exp\left(-\frac{\alpha \lambda_2}{T} t\right) \mathbf{u}_2^T \mathbf{x}_\perp + \cdots$$
$$+ w_{un0} \exp\left(-\frac{\alpha \lambda_n}{T} t\right) \mathbf{u}_n^T \mathbf{x}_\perp \qquad (16)$$

If the eigen values $\lambda_2, \cdots, \lambda_n$ are enough small so that the approximations

$$\exp\left(-\frac{\alpha \lambda_2}{T} t\right), \cdots, \exp\left(-\frac{\alpha \lambda_n}{T} t\right) \cong 1 \qquad (17)$$

are true,

$$y_j \cong w_{u20} \mathbf{u}_2^T \mathbf{x}_\perp + \cdots + w_{un0} \mathbf{u}_n^T \mathbf{x}_\perp = x_j \qquad (18)$$

is obtained from Equations 14 and 16. Therefore, the input vector $\mathbf{x}_\perp$ orthogonal to $\mathbf{u}_1$ passes through the network without attenuation.

2. Input vector parallel to $\mathbf{u}_1$: $\mathbf{x}_\parallel$

$$\mathbf{u}_2^T \mathbf{x}_\parallel = \mathbf{u}_3^T \mathbf{x}_\parallel = \cdots = \mathbf{u}_n^T \mathbf{x}_\parallel = 0 \qquad (19)$$

At time t, the network output y_j is represented by the following equation from Equation 12.

$$y_j = w_{u10} \exp\left(-\frac{\alpha \lambda_1}{T} t\right) \mathbf{u}_1^T \mathbf{x}_\parallel + \cdots$$
$$+ w_{un0} \exp\left(-\frac{\alpha \lambda_n}{T} t\right) \mathbf{u}_n^T \mathbf{x}_\parallel \qquad (20)$$
$$= w_{u10} \exp\left(-\frac{\alpha \lambda_1}{T} t\right) \mathbf{u}_1^T \mathbf{x}_\parallel$$

If the eigen values λ_1 is enough large so that the approximations

$$\exp\left(-\frac{\alpha \lambda_1}{T} t\right) \cong 0 \qquad (21)$$

is true,

$$y_j \cong 0 \qquad (22)$$

is obtained. Therefore, the network output becomes zero for the input pattern with the principal direction of the training data.

Form the analysis (1) and (2), the following condition should be satisfied so that the network output is zero for the trained pattern and is the same as the input for untrained patterns (orthogonal to the trained pattern).

$$\begin{cases} \exp\left(-\dfrac{\alpha \lambda_1}{T} t\right) \cong 0 \\ \exp\left(-\dfrac{\alpha \lambda_2}{T} t\right), \cdots, \exp\left(-\dfrac{\alpha \lambda_n}{T} t\right) \cong 1 \end{cases} \qquad (22)$$

That is,

$$\lambda_1 >> \lambda_2, \cdots, \lambda_n \qquad (23)$$

should be satisfied. When the training data include only the background pattern, the condition Equation 23 is usually satisfied since the matrix $\mathbf{R}$ is composed of the single pattern (ideally $\lambda_2, \cdots, \lambda_n = 0$).

Simulation Methods

The adaptation model based on the perceptron neural network with anti-Hebbian learning was evaluated with numerical simulations using both simulated and experimental data. In this section, the settings of these simulations are described.

Three simulations were performed: the simulation with the Gaussian input pattern, the simulation with the simulated sensor responses, and the simulation with the experimental data of gas sensors. It is assumed that a sensor array composed of 8 gas sensors is used for identifying a target gas mixed with a background gas. Eight neurons are also used on each layer (input/output layer) in the perceptron neural network. The initial weight matrix is set to the unit matrix.

In the first simulation, the sensor response patterns to the background and target gases were set to the Gaussian distributions with different peak positions and same variance. The concentration of gases was assumed to vary in the form of a sinusoidal wave.

In the second simulation, simulated sensor responses were used to evaluate the adaptation model. In order to produce the gas sensor responses, a sensor response model represented by a first-order difference equation (Yamanaka, Matsumoto, & Nakamoto, 2003) was used:

$$\mathbf{s}(k+1) = \mathbf{Fs}(k) + \mathbf{Gc}(k). \tag{24}$$

$\mathbf{s}(k)$ is the sensor response vector at time $k\Delta T$ (ΔT : sampling interval), $\mathbf{c}(k)$ is the concentration vector of gases from time $k\Delta T$ to $(k+1)\Delta T$, $\mathbf{F}$ and $\mathbf{G}$ are parameter matrices specific to the sensor array. These parameter matrices were obtained from the data in the reference (Yamanaka, Matsumoto, & Nakamoto, 2003). The sampling interval was 1 s. In the practical applications such as a measurement in the open air, the concentration of gases fluctuates due to a turbulent flow (Yamanaka, Ishida, Nakamoto, & Moriizumi, 1998). Therefore, the concentration in the sensor model in Equation 24 was set to a fluctuated time sequence. A Gaussian noise with the variance of 1.67% was added to the simulated sensor responses, which corresponds to the noise level in the actual gas sensors.

In the third simulation, the actual sensor responses were used to evaluate the adaptation

model. The sensor responses were obtained using the experimental setup in the reference (Yamanaka, Yoshikawa, & Nakamoto, 2004). In this setup, the odor samples were prepared in petri dishes in the liquid phase, and were placed under the inlet of the tube connected to the odor sensing system. The odorant chemicals evaporated from the samples were measured in open air with the odor sensing system. The distance between the petri dish and the inlet of the tube was 20 mm. The target and background odors were set to trans-2-hexenyl acetate and isobutyric acid, respectively. These odors are main components of an apple flavor. The gas sensors were 8 quartz crystal microbalance sensors coated with different types of sensing materials: cerebrosides, tricresyl phosphate (2 sensors), polyphenylether (2 sensors), free fatty acid polyester, polyethlylene glycol 1000, and Apiezon L. Although the sampling rate was 1 Hz in this experiment, the data was linearly interpolated at 50 Hz to increase the number of learning data for the neural network.

Simulation Results

The simulation results are described in this section. In the first simulation, the input pattern of the sensor array to the neural network was set to the Gaussian distribution. The wave forms of the neural-network outputs corresponding to the eight gas sensors are shown in Figure 3(a). The vertical axis represents the neuron outputs at the output layer of the neural network, whereas the lateral axis represents time. Since the initial weight matrix of the network was set to the unit matrix, each output neuron corresponds to each gas sensor. The simulation was performed during 18,000 steps. From 0 to 12,000th step, the background pattern was input to the neural network. The adaptation (anti-Hebbian learning) was OFF from 0 to 6,000, and ON from 6,001 to 12,000. During the adaptation ON, the network learned the input pattern of the background gas, so that the outputs to the pattern became zero. Then, the response pattern of the mixture of the background and target gases was input to the network from 12,001 to 18,000. Since the network learned the background pattern by the adaptation, the network outputs the pattern of the target gas, by removing the background pattern. It is noted that the target signals only exist during 12,001 – 18,000 (the period of Background + Target) as the mixture of background and target gases in this wave from. The output patterns calculated from Figure 3(a) are shown in Figure 4(a). The output pattern was calculated by averaging the output time sequence of the neural network during the period of the "adaptation off." The top, 2nd, and 3rd panels in

Figure 4(a) correspond to the output patterns for background, target, and mixture gases before the adaptation, respectively. The target and mixture patterns were obtained from the neural network outputs for the target and mixture inputs to the network with unit weight matrix, respectively (not shown in Figure 3[a]). The bottom panel represents the output pattern for the mixture gas after the adaptation (the period during [Background + Target] in Figure 3[a]), which is almost the same pattern as the target pattern. This indicates that the neural network remove the background pattern from the mixture pattern after the adaptation.

Figure 3. Outputs of adaptation neural network for background, target, and mixture gases: (a) simulation with Gaussian pattern, (b) simulated sensor responses, (c) experimental sensor responses

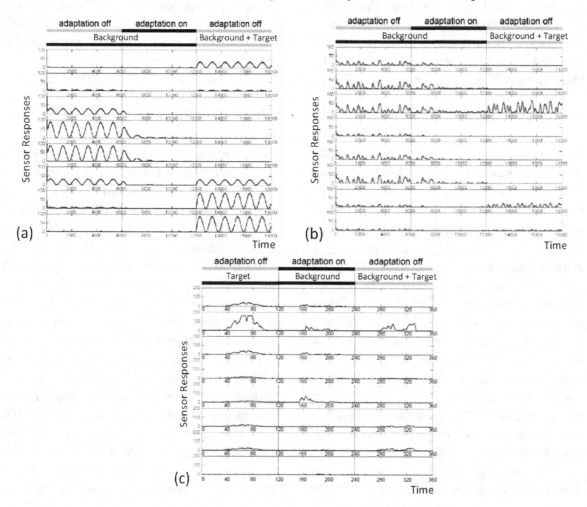

Figure 4. Output patterns of adaptation neural network for background (top), target (2nd), mixture gases (3rd) before adaptation, and mixture gases after adaptation (bottom): (a) simulation with Gaussian pattern, (b) simulated sensor responses, (c) experimental sensor responses

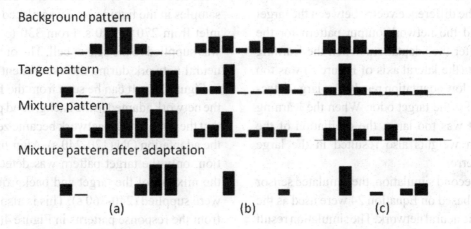

Background pattern

Target pattern

Mixture pattern

Mixture pattern after adaptation

(a)　(b)　(c)

The learning speed in the adaptation depends on the learning coefficient α in Equation 1. The larger the learning coefficient is, the faster the adaptation. However, when the learning coefficient is too large, the connection weights do not converge due to oscillation of the weights. Therefore, the learning coefficient has to be set to an

appropriate value. In the case study of this chapter, the learning coefficient was set to $\alpha = 10^{-7.3}$ so that the connection weights converged within the adaptation period (6,000 steps). The convergence property of the adaptation neural network with anti-habbian learning for the Gaussian input patterns is shown in Figure 5, where (a) represents

Figure 5. Convergence property of adaptation neural network with anti-Hebbian learning. The lateral axis represents the learning coefficient of the anti-Hebbian learning: (a) magnitude of output pattern after adaptation, (b) detection error after adaptation of 6,000 learning steps.

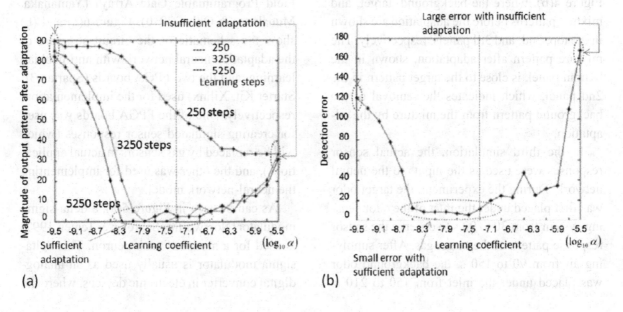

(a)

(b)

the magnitude of the adapted pattern during the adaptation, and (b) represents the detection error after the adaptation, which is defined as the magnitude of the difference vector between the target pattern and the network output pattern for the mixture after the adaptation. When the learning coefficient (the lateral axis of Figure 5) was too small, the slow adaptation resulted in large detection error for the target odor. When the learning coefficient was too large, the oscillation of the connection weights also resulted in the large detection error.

In the second simulation, the simulated sensor responses based on Equation 24 were used as the inputs to the neural network. The simulation result is shown in Figure 3(b). Similar to Figure 3(a), the sensor responses to the background gas were input to the network during 0-12,000. The adaptation was OFF from 0 to 6,000, and was ON from 6,001 to 12,000. The network learned the background response pattern during the period of the adaptation ON (6,001-12,000), as can be seen in Figure 3(b). Then, the sensor responses to the mixture of the background and target gases were input to the network. Since the network adapted to the background pattern, the target pattern was obtained at the output of the network. To see this more clearly, the response patterns are shown in Figure 4(b), where the background, target, and mixture patterns before the adaptation are shown in the top, 2nd, and 3rd panels, respectively. The mixture pattern after adaptation, shown in the bottom panel, is close to the target pattern in the 2nd panel, which indicates the removal of the background pattern from the mixture by the adaptation.

In the third simulation, the actual sensor responses were used as the inputs to the neural network. During the experiment, the target odor was first placed under the inlet of the odor sensing system from 30 to 90 s to observe the sensor response pattern of the target gas. After supplying air from 90 to 150 s, the background odor was placed under the inlet from 150 to 210 s.

During this period, the neural network adapted to the background pattern. After supplying air from 210 to 270 s, the mixture of the two odor samples in the liquid phase was placed under the inlet from 270 to 330 s. From 330 to 360 s, air was supplied to the sensor cell. The output of the neural network during the experiment is shown in Figure 3(c). It can be seen from the figure that the network adapted to the background pattern, so that the output of the network became zero during the adaptation ON (120-240 s). After the adaptation, only the target pattern was detected when the mixture of the target and background gases were supplied (240-360 s). This is also observed from the response patterns in Figure 4(c), where the output pattern after adaptation (bottom) was similar to the target pattern (2nd).

Implementation into Digital Circuit

In the practical applications of the odor sensing systems, it would be preferable to be used for real-time gas sensing. For this purpose, the signal-processing algorithms for the sensing systems are implemented into electronic circuits. In the case study introduced in this chapter, the adaptation model for the background suppression was implemented into a digital circuit (FPGA: Field Programmable Gate Array) (Yamanaka, Munakata, & Ohba, 2010). Figure 6(a) and (b) show the schematic of the circuit structure of the adaptation neural network with anti-hebbian learning, and the two FPGA boards (Spartan 3E Starter Kit, Xilinx) used for the implementation, respectively. One of the FPGA boards was used for creating simulated sensor responses (which will be replaced by gas sensors in actual applications), and the other was used for implementing the neural-network model.

As can be seen in Figure 6(a), a delta-sigma modulator (Norsworthy, Schreier, & Temes, 1997) is used for a model of each neuron. This delta-sigma modulator is usually used as an analog-digital converter in electronic devices, where the

Figure 6. Digital circuit implementation of adaptation neural network: (a) circuit structure of adaptation neural network with anti-hebbian learning (AHL), (b) picture of FPGA boards and logic analyzer used for the implementation

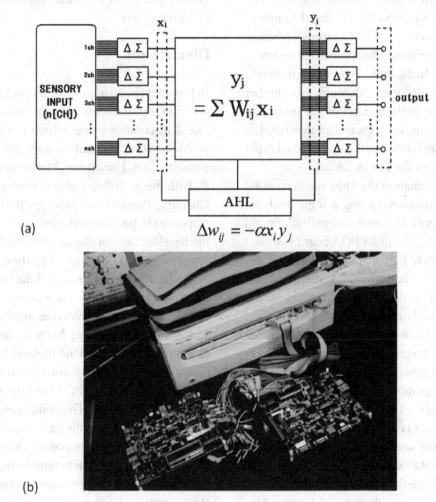

(a)

(b)

analog signal is represented in a single bit based on the over-sampling technique. In this circuit, x_i and y_j in Equation 1 are the output of the neuron in the input layer, and the input of the neuron in the output layer, respectively, as shown in Figure 6(a). Since the output of the delta-sigma modulator is a single bit, x_i is 0 or 1. Therefore, $\Delta w_{ij} = w_{ij}(t+1) - w_{ij}(t)$ is given by the next equation.

$$\Delta w_{ij} = -\alpha x_i y_j = \begin{cases} 0 & \text{for } x_i = 0 \\ -\alpha y_j & \text{for } x_i = 1 \end{cases} \quad (25)$$

If the learning coefficient α is limited to 2^{-a}, αy_j can be replaced by $y_j[\text{msb}:a]$, which represents the slice of bits from msb (most-significant-bit) to the ath bit.

$$\Delta w_{ij} = -\alpha x_i y_j = \begin{cases} 0 & \text{for } x_i = 0 \\ -y_j[\text{msb}:a] & \text{for } x_i = 1 \end{cases} \quad (26)$$

This means that the anti-hebbian learning can be realized without multiplication in the digital circuit, which leads to huge reduction of the circuit size. In our implementation of the circuit, y_j was set to the 34-bit signal (that is msb = 33), and a was set to 17. The former parameter was determined by the accuracy of weights (30 bits) and the number of output-layer neurons ($2^3 = 8$ neurons), whereas the latter was empirically determined for the learning coefficient. In the input layer of the network, 8 neurons were also used. Although this number is corresponding to the number of gas sensors in actual applications, our experiment described in this chapter was limited to the synthesized input signals created by the FPGA circuit.

The output signals of the implemented neural network were measured using a logic analyzer (1693AD, Agilent). The input pattern (background pattern) created in the first FPGA board is shown in the right panel of Figure 7(a). The input signals varying with time in the sinusoidal wave form, were converted to the single-bit signals by the delta-sigma modulators, as shown in the left panel of Figure 7(a). The input patterns and its time sequences for the target and mixture patterns were also shown in Figures 7(b) and (c), respectively. Before the adaptation, the output patterns and their time sequences for the background, target, and mixture patterns were the same as their input patterns and time sequences, as shown in Figure 7. After the adaptation to the background pattern, it can be seen from the right panel of Figure 8(a) that the output pattern of the network became zero for the background pattern. Correspondingly, the output signals for the background pattern were zero almost all of the time as seen in the time sequence of the output in Figure 8(a). On the contrary, the output pattern and time sequences were almost same as the input pattern and sequences for the target pattern in Figure 8(b). This agrees with the mathematical analysis of the network and the simulations described in the previous sections. The output pattern and time sequences for the mixture pattern were different from the input of the mixture, but same as those for the target pattern. It can be seen from these results that the

digital circuit of the adaptation neural network successfully performed the removal of the background gas effect from the response pattern for the mixture gas.

Discussion

In this chapter, an algorithm for background suppression is introduced. This is related to the baseline-drift compensation, which is a well-known problem in the chemical-sensors community (Artursson, Eklov, Lundstrom, Martensson, Sjostrom, & Holmberg, 2000; Padilla, Perera, Montoliu, Chaudry, Persaud, & Marco, 2010). If sensor responses to background odors are considered as the baseline drift of the sensors, the background suppression can be achieved by the methods proposed for the compensation of the baseline drift. An example of the drift-compensation methods is the component-correction method (Artursson, Eklov, Lundstrom, Martensson, Sjostrom, & Holmberg, 2000). This method has two versions: component corrections based on Principal Component Analysis (PCA) and based on Partial Least Squares (PLS). The component correction based on PCA extracts the baseline-drift direction using the principal-component direction of the sensor response patterns to remove the drift in this direction from the original sensor responses. On the contrary, the component correction based on PLS uses the PLS regression between the original sensor response pattern and the time variable, since the drift caused by aging effects often lies in one direction in the sensor response space as a function of time. PLS captures this direction as the baseline drift. Although these methods can compensate the time-varying baseline drift, it is limited to the direction with the most variance (based on PCA) or one-directional aging effect (based on PLS), whereas the method described in this chapter can capture any direction in the sensor response space based on the anti-hebbian learning of the background response pattern.

Figure 7. Output and input patterns of digital circuit for adaptation neural network before adaptation learning. Left: Time sequences measured with logic analyzer. Right: Output and input patterns calculated from observed pulses. (a) Background pattern, (b) target pattern, (c) mixture pattern.

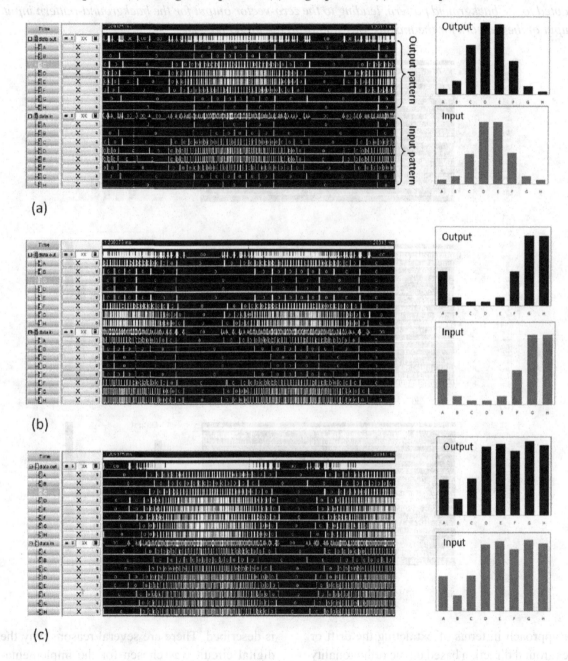

(a)

(b)

(c)

Another drift-compensation method is Orthogonal Signal Correction (OSC) applied to chemical sensors in the literature (Padilla, Perera, Montoliu, Chaudry, Persaud, & Marco, 2010). OSC removes extraneous variance from the original sensor responses that is unrelated to the target sensor responses by finding the directions in the sensor response space that describe large amounts of variance while being orthogonal to the target sensor responses. This method is similar to

Figure 8. Output and input patterns of digital circuit for adaptation neural network after adaptation learning. Left: Time sequences measured with logic analyzer. Right: Output and input patterns calculated from observed pulses. (a) Background pattern, (b) target pattern, (c) mixture pattern. The network was adapted to the background pattern, leading to the zero-vector output for the background-pattern input. Output of the network for the mixture was similar to the target pattern.

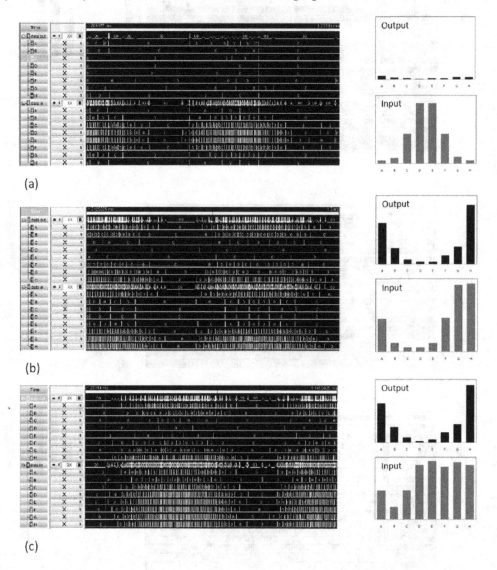

our approach in terms of extracting the drift or background direction based on the orthogonality of the sensor response patterns. The performance of our method should be compared with that of OSC in the future research.

In this chapter, the digital implementation of the proposed gas-sensing signal processing is described. There are several reasons why the digital circuit was chosen for the implementation platform. First, as mentioned before, the digital circuit enables us to realize a gas sensing system which can be used onsite. The system can be small with the digital circuit of the neural network. Second, the digital circuit is easy to be implemented compared with an analog circuit or a mixed-signal integrated circuit that has both analog circuits and digital circuits on a single semiconductor die. Although a microcontroller could also be used for the implementation platform, the digital circuit would have the benefits of working speed and device size. Third, the digital-circuit implementation would have similarity with the biological neural circuits. Most of the biological neurons represent the information with the spikes of the membrane potential. In out implementation in the digital circuit, the signals are represented with time sequences of single bit at each neuron by the delta-sigma modulator. This single bit signal (High/Low voltages) would correspond to the spikes at the biological neuron. This plausibility might be useful to extend our algorithm by mimicking the biological neural computation.

We want to discuss on the limitation of our method. First, based on the analysis described in the Model Analysis section, the target response pattern has to be orthogonal to the background pattern learned by the neural network. If they are not orthogonal, the neural network also suppresses the target response pattern in addition to the background pattern. This means that the odor sensor array used for this system needs to have good selectivity to target and background odors. Second, since this method uses a perceptron with linear connections, the patterns which can be suppressed by the neural network are limited to the linear combinations of the learned patterns. If the sensor responses have the properties of non-linearity on concentration changes and odorant mixing, the neural network needs to learn all the background patterns in various concentrations and possible background odorant mixtures (if the background odor is a mixture of multiple components). This limitation might be relaxed by applying a non-linear kernel function at neurons in the neural network and modifying network structure such as a multi-layer perceptron. These topics need to be explored in the future research.

FUTURE RESEARCH DIRECTIONS

In this chapter, a case study of the bio-inspired background suppression technique is introduced. It was confirmed in the simulation that the perceptron neural network with anti-Hebbian learning can detect the target pattern from the mixture pattern by suppressing the background pattern. Furthermore, the algorithm was implemented into a digital circuit for real-time gas sensing. The circuit was successfully applied to synthesized input signals.

There are several research topics which should be pursued in the future research. First, since the developed digital circuit of the adaptation model was evaluated only with the synthesized input signals, it would be necessary to evaluate the digital circuit with actual sensor signals. A typical actual gas sensor has less selectivity to gases than the synthesized signals used in the experiments. Moreover, the actual gas sensor tends to have non-linearity of the sensor response on gas concentration change and non-additivity of the sensor response on gas mixing, whereas the synthesized signals satisfy the linearity and additivity. Therefore, the evaluation of the actual sensors is essential in the future research. In theory, the algorithm proposed in this chapter can be applied to non-linear sensor signals, if the size of training data is enough large so that the training data include sensor responses on any possible concentration and combination of the mixture components. However, this increase of the training-data size would lead to the decrease of the detectable gas range, because the detectable gases are limited to those that have sensor response patterns orthogonal against the pattern in the training data set. Those problems should be tested on the actual sensor responses, which include various types of sensors such as metal oxide semiconductor sensors, conducting polymer sensors, quartz crystal microbalance sensors, and surface acoustic wave sensors.

Second, it would be nice if a system detects only a target pattern suppressing any other patterns by learning the target pattern, not the background pattern. The system proposed in this chapter has capability of suppressing only the learned background pattern. However, if the system learns a target pattern, it would be possible to develop the system, which responds only the target, and suppresses any other background patterns. This idea is similar to OSC discussed above, which suppresses the baseline drift by extracting the directions in the sensor response space orthogonal against the target response pattern (Padilla, Perera, Montoliu, Chaudry, Persaud, & Marco, 2010).

Last, it would be desired to apply this system to practical applications, such as gas leak detection, gas source localization, and environmental monitoring. Since this system can cancel the background effect, the application to the open air would be suitable to this system.

CONCLUSION

In the human olfaction, sensitivity to successive odors decreases due to the olfactory adaptation, causing the increase of the selectivity to novel odors. This chapter introduced the signal processing methods inspired by the adaptation phenomena in the olfaction.

The neural computation models for the olfactory adaptation or the mixture segmentation in the literature explain the adaptation or mixture segmentation phenomena with the excitatory and inhibitory coupling of the neurons and lateral connections with or without feedback signals from the cortex. Among them, neural models with feedback connections have been applied to gas-sensor signal processing (Gutierrez-Osuna & Powar, 2003; Gutierrez-Osuna & Gutierrez-Galvez, 2003; Gutierrez-Galvez, 2005; Raman & Gutierrez-Osuna, 2005).

Since the neural computation models which have been applied to the gas-sensor signal processing such as the KIII model are too complex to be used to real-time gas sensing, a simplified method based on a perceptron neural network with anti-Hebbian learning was proposed. Through the mathematical analysis, it was confirmed that the algorithm can be used for detecting the target pattern from the mixture removing the background pattern. It was clarified by the analysis that the target pattern to be detected should be orthogonal to the background pattern learned with the anti-Hebbian learning. It should be noted that the system described in this chapter is composed of linear connections, and therefore works well for linear sensor responses. Although the system would be able to be applied to the non-linear gas sensors if all the possible background patterns are learned, the detectable patterns for the target odors would decrease because the detectable patterns are orthogonal against the learned background patterns.

The proposed model was evaluated in the simulations using both the synthesized input signals and the experimental sensor signals. From these simulations, it was seen that the algorithm successfully performed the background suppression in the mixture response pattern. In addition, it was confirmed that the learning coefficient of the anti-Hebbian learning, a parameter of the algorithm, has to be appropriately adjusted. Otherwise, the output of the neural network oscillates for a too large learning coefficient, or takes long time to be converged for too small one. The algorithm was further implemented into a digital circuit for real-time gas sensing. It was possible to decrease the circuit size by avoiding the use of the multiplication. By using the synthesized input signals, it was confirmed that the circuit was able to detect the target pattern from the mixture pattern.

In the future research, it would be necessary to evaluate the digital circuit using the actual sensor signals. Furthermore, the evaluation on the robustness against non-linearity and non-additivity of gas sensors should be performed. These evaluations will lead to the applications of the proposed system to more practical situations.

REFERENCES

Artursson, T., Eklov, T., Lundstrom, I., Martensson, P., Sjostrom, M., & Holmberg, M. (2000). Drift correction for gas sensors using multivariate methods. *Journal of Chemometrics*, *14*, 711–723. doi:10.1002/1099-128X(200009/12)14:5/6<711::AID-CEM607>3.0.CO;2-4

Gutierrez-Galvez, A. (2005). *Coding and learning of chemosensor array patterns in a neurodynamics model of the olfactory system*. (Unpublished Ph.D. Dissertation) Texas A&M University. College Station, TX.

Gutierrez-Galvez, A., & Gutierrez-Osuna, R. (2006). Contrast enhancement and background suppression of chemosensor array patterns with the KIII model. *International Journal of Intelligent Systems*, *21*(9), 937–953. doi:10.1002/int.20170

Gutierrez-Osuna, R., & Gutierrez-Galvez, A. (2003). Habituation in the KIII olfactory model with chemical sensor arrays. *IEEE Transactions on Neural Networks*, *14*(6), 1565–1568. doi:10.1109/TNN.2003.820438

Gutierrez-Osuna, R., & Powar, N. U. (2003). Odor mixtures and chemosensory adaptation in gas sensor arrays. *International Journal of Artificial Intelligence Tools*, *12*(1), 1–16. doi:10.1142/S0218213003001083

Gutierrez-Osuna, R., & Raman, B. (2004). Cancellation of chemical backgrounds with generalized Fisher's linear discriminants. [). IEEE Press.]. *Proceedings of IEEE Sensors*, *3*, 1381–1384. doi:10.1109/ICSENS.2004.1426441

Hendin, O., Horn, D., & Hopfield, J. J. (1994). Decomposition of a mixture of signals in a model of the olfactory bulb. *Proceedings of the National Academy of Sciences of the United States of America*, *91*(13), 5942–5946. doi:10.1073/pnas.91.13.5942

Hoshino, O., Kashimori, Y., & Kambara, T. (1998). An olfactory recognition model based on spatio-temporal encoding of odor quality in the olfactory bulb. *Biological Cybernetics*, *79*(2), 109–120. doi:10.1007/s004220050463

Kadohisa, M., & Wilson, D. A. (2006). Olfactory cortical adaptation facilitates detection of odors against background. *Journal of Neurophysiology*, *95*(3), 1888–1896. doi:10.1152/jn.00812.2005

Li, Z., & Hertz, J. (2000). Odour recognition and segmentation by a model olfactory bulb and cortex. *Network (Bristol, England)*, *11*, 83–102. doi:10.1088/0954-898X/11/1/305

Matsuoka, K., & Kawamoto, M. (1996). The learning of linear neural nets with anti-hebbian rules. *Systems and Computers in Japan*, *27*(3), 84–93. doi:10.1002/scj.4690270308

Nagle, H. T., Gutierrez-Osuna, R., & Schiffman, S. S. (1998). The how and why of electronic noses. *IEEE Spectrum*, *35*(9), 22–31. doi:10.1109/6.715180

Norsworthy, S. R., Schreier, R., & Temes, G. C. (1997). *Delta-sigma data converters: Theory, design, and simulation*. Washington, DC: IEEE Press.

Ohba, T., & Yamanaka, T. (2008). Suppression of background odor effect in odor sensing system using olfactory adaptation model. *IEEJ Transactions on Sensors and Micromachines*, *128*(5), 240–245. doi:10.1541/ieejsmas.128.240

Oyamada, T., Kashimori, Y., Hoshino, O., & Kambara, T. (2000). A neural mechanism of hierarchical discrimination of odors in the olfactory cortex based on spatiotemporal encoding of odor information. *Biological Cybernetics, 83*(1), 21–33. doi:10.1007/s004229900139

Padilla, M., Perera, A., Montoliu, I., Chaudry, A., Persaud, K., & Marco, S. (2010). Drift compensation of gas sensor array data by orthogonal signal correction. *Chemometrics and Intelligent Laboratory Systems, 100*(1), 28–35. doi:10.1016/j.chemolab.2009.10.002

Pearce, T. C., Schiffman, S. S., Nagle, H. T., & Gardner, J. W. (Eds.). (2003). *Handbook of machine olfaction: Electronic nose technology.* New York, NY: WILEY-VCH.

Principe, J. C., Euliano, N. R., & Lefebvre, W. C. (2000). *Neural & adaptive systems.* New York, NY: Wiley.

Raman, B., & Gutierrez-Osuna, R. (2005). Mixture segmentation and background suppression in chemosensor arrays with a model of olfactory bulb-cortex interaction. In *Proceedings of IEEE International Joint Conference on Neural Networks,* (Vol. 1, pp. 131-136). IEEE Press.

Shin, J. H., Lee, K. R., & Park, S. B. (1993). Novel neural circuits based on stochastic pulse coding and noise feedback pulse coding. *International Journal of Electronics, 74*(3), 359–368. doi:10.1080/00207219308925840

Wang, D., Buhmann, J., & von der Malsburg, C. (1990). Pattern segmentation in associative memory. *Neural Computation, 2*(1), 94–106. doi:10.1162/neco.1990.2.1.94

Yamanaka, T., Ishida, H., Nakamoto, T., & Moriizumi, T. (1998). Analysis of gas sensor transient response by visualizing instantaneous gas concentration using smoke. *Sensors and Actuators. A, Physical, 69*(1), 77–81. doi:10.1016/S0924-4247(98)00045-4

Yamanaka, T., Matsumoto, R., & Nakamoto, T. (2003). Fundamental study of odor recorder for multi-component odor using recipe exploration method based on singular value decomposition. *IEEE Sensors Journal, 3*(4), 468–474. doi:10.1109/JSEN.2003.815778

Yamanaka, T., Munakata, Y., & Ohba, T. (2010). *Digital-circuit implementation of olfactory-adaptation neural network for gas sensing.* Paper presented at 13th International Meeting on Chemical Sensors. Perth, Australia.

Yamanaka, T., Yoshikawa, K., & Nakamoto, T. (2004). Improvement of odor-recorder capability for recording dynamical change in odor. *Sensors and Actuators. B, Chemical, 99*(2-3), 367–372. doi:10.1016/j.snb.2003.12.004

Yao, Y., & Freeman, W. J. (1990). Model of biological pattern recognition with spatially chaotic dynamics. *Neural Networks, 3,* 153–170. doi:10.1016/0893-6080(90)90086-Z

Chapter 17
Evaluating the Psychobiologic Effects of Fragrances through Salivary Biomarkers

Masaki Yamaguchi
Iwate University, Japan

Vivek Shetty
UCLA, USA

ABSTRACT

Olfactory stimulation by odorant molecules produces neurobiologic responses that manifest in the salivary proteome. This chapter highlights recent progress in the use of salivary biomarkers to augment conventional psychological assessments of the effects of fragrances and odors. New, low-cost, portable salivary biosensors enable point-of use measurements of physiological effects of fragrances in naturalistic settings. The ability to operationalize measurement of the sedative state induced by a fragrance will clarify the mechanistic underpinnings of olfactory stimulation and facilitate investigations of structure-odor relationships that are necessary for the synthesis of new odorant molecules.

INTRODUCTION

Considerable evidence links our sense of smell with the triggering of a range of psychological and physiological responses. As evident by the widespread use of fragrances to enhance an individual's sense of emotional well-being, the intake

of aroma molecules can act on the brain to enhance mood and create relaxing states. The reflectorial effect theory (Hirsch, 2001) suggests that odors perceived as positive may induce positive moods, and these mood changes may enhance both physical and psychological well-being. The capacity to engage olfaction in creating positive emotional

DOI: 10.4018/978-1-4666-2521-1.ch017

Copyright © 2013, IGI Global. Copying or distributing in print or electronic forms without written permission of IGI Global is prohibited.

states has led to the application of fragrances and essential oils in the treatment of depression, anxiety, dementia, insomnia, and stress-induced ailments (Buchbauer & Jirovetz, 1994; Ballard, et al., 2002). Given olfaction's role in the triggering of emotional responses, there is growing interest in exploring the linkages between smell and its biobehavioral outputs so that our sense of smell can be used to expand our sensory repertoire.

As Jellinek (1997) notes, the effects of fragrances on behavior and physiological response systems occurs through two principal mechanisms: (a) pharmacological where there is a direct interaction between odor molecules and olfactory receptors or nerve endings, and (b) psychological which involves the subjective experience of odor and involves memories and emotions. Correspondingly, efforts to assess the effects of olfactory stimulation on an activating-sedating (relaxing) dimension have involved subjective evaluations such as the use of questionnaires or self-reports (Lundström, et al., 2003) or the use of more objective physiological parameters including blood pressure (Haze, et al., 2002), heart rate (Romine, et al., 1999), and brain wave patterns (Diego, et al., 1998; Grosser, et al., 2000). However, most of these measurement approaches require laboratory-based investigations, involve the application of awkward recording device, and are burdensome to the subjects. Minimizing measurement reactivity and advancing the assessment of the psychological effect of fragrances under naturalistic conditions necessitates the development of alternative approaches to conventional assessment practices. Beyond clarifying the mechanistic underpinnings of olfactory stimulation, unobtrusive, objective, field-practical measurement techniques that produce unique "fingerprints" of the body's response to various fragrances and odors would be very useful in a variety of applications in medical, dental, food, pharmaceutical industries and environmental control fields.

SALIVARY MANIFESTATIONS OF OLFACTORY EFFECTS

Olfactory stimulation by fragrances or odors may be viewed as a stressor that produces either a state of eustress (good stress) or distress (bad stress). The neurobiologic responses to both types of stress responses manifest along common autonomic, endocrine, and immune pathways. Because the central changes in the brain are difficult to monitor, researchers have commonly utilized peripherally accessible biofluids, such as blood and urine, as a source for identifying accompanying neuroendocrine perturbations. However, the intrusive nature of biofluid collection (e.g. blood) alters the plasma profile of related biomarkers and raises concerns about the confounding impact of measurement reactivity. An attractive alternative is human saliva, which largely contains the range of proteins, hormones, antibodies, and other analytes normally measured in blood tests (Yan, et al., 2009). Sampling saliva has multiple advantages in that it is non-invasive, readily accepted by the subject, easily stored and transported and stable for longer periods.

Salivary indices of the individual stress response have included various components of the human salivary proteome including cortisol, dehydroepiandrosterone-sulphate (DHEA-S), testosterone, catecholamines, α-amylase, chromogranin A, and secretory immunoglobulin A (SIgA). Each of these putative stress biomarkers is considered reflective of the Sympathetic Nervous System (SNS), Hypothalamic-Pituitary-Adrenal axis (HPA) or the immune response system. Much of the attention has focused on salivary cortisol as an expression of HPA axis activation (Yehuda, 2005, 2006; Breslau, 2006). Cortisol is thought to enter saliva by passive diffusion and correlates closely with the free physiologically active serum cortisol fraction (Kirschbaum & Hellhammer, 1994). Unlike cortisol, conjugated steroid DHEA-S enters saliva via ultrafiltration through the tight junctions between acinar cells and has a serum-saliva correlation of 0.86 (Salimetrics assay). Stressors tend to decrease the testosterone levels, and this inverse relationship between stress and testosterone levels was substantiated independently by Opstad (1992) and Morgan and colleagues (Morgan, et al., 2000).

Since one objective of fragrances is to induce subjective calmness, testing for bioindicators of autonomic arousal are particularly useful. Salivary catecholamines are poorly correlated with plasma concentrations and as such are not considered as useful index of general sympathetic tone (Chiappin, et al., 2007). An attractive alternate biomarker of adrenergic stimulation is salivary α-amylase. Salivary Amylase activity (SAA) increases slightly with increased flow rates, and large increments in amylase concentration have been observed during sympathetic control by Speirs et al. (1974). Increased autonomic arousal is a major stimulus of amylase secretion and so, SAA is now considered as a useful index of plasma norepinephrine concentrations under a variety of stressful conditions (Jenkins, 1978; Ugolev, et al., 1979). Salivary chromogranin A, co-released with serum catecholamines, has also been investigated as an alternate indicator of the psychosomatic stress response (Nakane, et al., 2002). Yet other researchers have attempted to link salivary SIgA levels with the psychological reaction to stressors. It have shown that SIgA levels vary temporally with the stress response - high in the acute stress phase and decreased in the presence of chronic stress (Otsuki, et al., 2004). Linking these putative biomarkers to various olfaction-related conditions has the potential to provide mechanistic insights into the psychobiologic effects of fragrances and odors.

"POINT-OF–USE" MEASUREMENT OF SALIVARY INDICATORS

The promise of salivary stress biomarkers notwithstanding, their clinical utility has been restricted by the lack of appropriate technology platforms that allow near "real-time" detection and quantification of these biological response indicators. Typically, biological samples collected by human subjects are processed in centralized laboratories which results in extended reporting times and is fraught with several potential quality failure points. For example, the total process to deliver a salivary test result involves the multiple steps of sample acquisition, labeling, freezing, transportation, processing in the laboratory (centrifugation of the sample, sorting, aliquoting, loading into analyzer), analysis, and results reporting. The costs associated with expensive analytical equipment and testing supplies, sample acquisition and transport supplies, as well as all the labor costs incurred across the total process can be significant impediments. Finally, the relative stability of a biomarker can dramatically impact the measured levels over the collection-measurement-reporting cycle.

In contrast, the appeal of Point-Of-Care Testing (POCT) of saliva derives from the immediacy of the results reporting. The ability to readily measure salivary stress biomarkers in naturalistic settings renders the information provided more reflective of actual conditions and permits the information to inform decision making. Developments in biosensing technology by our research group now allow the fabrication of versatile biosensing platforms (Yamaguchi, et al., 2003) for low-cost, point-of-use devices that can measure and profile putative salivary correlates of the stress response (Takai, et al., 2004; Yamaguchi, et al., 2006b; Yamaguchi, et al., 2006c). Cheaper, smaller, faster, and smarter POCT devices have increased the use of POCT approaches by making it cost-effective and user-friendly. Embedded system software process measurable biochemical signals into simple digital feedback displays readily accessible to a wide range of end users (Yamaguchi, et al., 2004, 2006a).

Salivary Sensors for Quantification of Stress Response

The design challenge in developing low-cost, field-practical salivary biosensors is to create portable devices whose operation is simple and robust enough to deliver laboratory accuracy and reliability in locations far less well controlled than the laboratory. Because the early adrenergic response has been implicated in the stress, the authors have focused initially on the measurement of SAA that reflects Sympathetic Nervous System (SNS) activity. The SAA biosensor system (SAA monitor) design consists of two primary components: (a) hand-held reader (Figure 1) and (b) inexpensive ($\approx$ $1) disposable, plastic saliva collection strip. To initiate a measurement, the absorbent pad at the tip of the test strip is placed under the tongue, allowed to saturate with saliva ($\approx$ 10 s) and inserted

Figure 1. Handheld SAA biosensor system for measuring sympathetic nervous system activity (reader and test strip; Nipro Co., Japan)

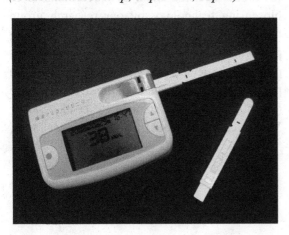

into the reader. This act activates the reader and initiates a transfer of the collected saliva onto the biosensing platform where the transcribed SAA metabolizes a chromogenic substrate to yield a colored product. The embedded microprocessor (MPU) notes the activation of the reader as the initiation of the reaction time ($t = 0$ s). At $t = 10$s, an alarm indicates the end of saliva transfer and the collector/strip is removed from the reader. At $t = 20$s, the reflectance of the product of the enzyme reaction is measured photometrically and the SAA levels reported on the display along with a date and time stamp.

The single use plastic strip, similar to the paper strips for glucose monitoring of diabetics, is based on dry reagents and allows considerable simplification of the analytical system and freedom from complex maintenance, calibration, and quality control procedures. Bioanalytical validation utilizing saliva samples from normal subjects indicates that, within the biosensor's linear range (10-230 kU/l), its accuracy (coefficient of multiple determination: $R^2 = 0.989$), precision (coefficient of variation: $CV < 9\%$), and measurement repeatability (range -3.1% to + 3.1%) approach more elaborate laboratory-based, clinical analyzers (Shetty *et al.*, 2010). The truncated sampling-reporting cycle (< 1 minute) and the excellent performance characteristics of the biosensor have potential testing application in a variety of settings.

EFFECTS OF FRAGRANCES ON SALIVARY BIOMARKER

In order to evaluate the olfactory stimulation produced by various fragrances, we set up a temperature-controlled, sensory isolation room that removed or minimized environmental triggers such as sights, sounds, and ambient smells. The olfactory evaluation apparatus comprised of an odor presentation dome on a movable arm, three sets of metal oxide semiconductor-type gas sensors (TGS2602; Figaro Engineering Inc., Japan), three sets of portable-type nebulizers to release the fragrances (NE-U22; Omron Co., Japan), the hand-held SAA monitor, a reclining chair, an A/D converter to convert the sensor signal into a digital one (NR-TH08; Keyence Co., Japan), and a personal computer for data collection (Figure 2; Yamaguchi, et al., 2008). Each subject is seated on the reclining chair and the dome positioned over the face. Then the dome is filled with a neutral chemical substance sprayed by the nebulizer. The nebulizer is calibrated by measurements made with the embedded gas sensors and adjusted to provide a known chemical concentration.

To investigate the utility of SAA as an indicator of decreased adrenergic arousal attributed to the calming/sedative effects of fragrances, we investigated the temporal changes in SAA levels before, during and after the inhalation of fragrance (Yamaguchi, et al., 2007). Twenty healthy female subjects in their late 30s were selected, since women at around this age may be thought as being very sensitive to fragrance. Four kinds of test samples were prepared as the fragrance including plant essential oil, which image Western pear (a), Woody (b), Fruity green (c), and Tropical sweet (d). All test samples were prepared by diluting the oil samples to 5% with dipropylene glycol

Figure 2. In order to evaluate olfactory stimulation produced by various fragrances, olfactory evaluation apparatus was set up in a temperature-controlled, sensory isolation room: (a) extension arm, (b) odor presentation dome, (c) neblizer for releasing fragrances, (d) hand-held SAA monitor, (e) reclining chair, (f) A/D converter for converting analog signals from the sensor into digital output, (g) personal computer for data collection, (#) gas sensor for measuring the concentration of odor samples

a Configuration

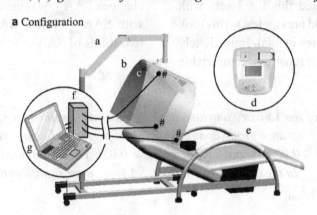

b View of setup

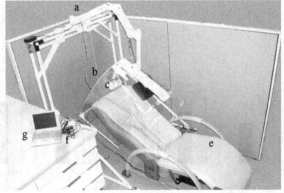

(odorless). Pure dipropylene glycol was used as the negative control. In order to prestress the subjects and induce adrenergic arousal, an uncomfortable cold pressor test was performed on the subject just prior to the inhalation of the test samples.

Saliva sampling was performed at an even interval, as far as possible, for the analysis of SAA, and repeated 7 times in total in order to evaluate the physiological effect. Initially, each subject took a sitting position for 15 min in order to measure the individual baseline of SAA. Next, in order to give the subjects a pre-stressor as a distress (uncomfortable stress) before the main stress, a cold pressor test was conducted on each subject as an uncomfortable distress task, prior to the inhalation of test samples (Light, et al., 1987). Each subject immersed one hand into an ice water for 5 s, then removed the hand from the ice water and rested for 10 s. This was defined as one set. The subject then repeated this for 3 sets with both hands (repeated cold pressor test). This took approximately 1.5 minutes in total. Immediately after, as the main stressor (eustress, comfortable stress), a cotton patch (20×50 mm^2), soaked in 0.4 ml of a test sample, was applied to the skin under the subject's nostril for 15 minutes as a procedure of inhalation of the fragrance, during which time the subject took a sitting position. Immediately after completion of the fragrance inhalation, the subject filled in the psychological state (Q_2) questionnaires. The values of post-score minus pre-score $(Q_2 - Q_1)$ were calculated for the 6 adjectives of the psychological state questionnaire in order to evaluate the psychological effect.

Comparison of the SAA in control between the baseline (SAA$_{base}$), task (SAA$_{task}$) and inhalation of test sample (SAA$_{sample}$) periods were 21.6 $\pm$ 17.1, 25.8 $\pm$ 23.0 and 22.4 $\pm$ 11.4 kU/l (Figure 3). There was no significant difference between SAA$_{task}$ and SAA$_{sample}$ in the control. In contrast, SAA$_{sample}$ were significantly reduced in samples A and C compared with SAA$_{task}$ ($P < 0.05$). In sample A, which exhibited the most marked changes, SAA$_{task}$ was increased by 40% compared with SAA$_{base}$, whilst SAA$_{sample}$ was reduced to two-thirds of SAA$_{task}$.

*Figure 3. Comparison of the salivary amylase activity between baseline, task, and inhalation of test sample periods. Within fragrance group comparisons were performed using paired t test. Values were expressed as ± SD. *: P < 0.05, NS: not significant (P > 0.05). There was no significant difference between SAA$_{task}$ and SAA$_{sample}$ in the control. In contrast, SAA$_{sample}$ were significantly reduced in samples A and C compared with SAA$_{task}$.*

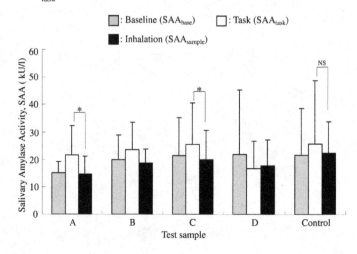

Correlations between the biomarker analysis and the subjective evaluations were statistically evaluated by using structural equation modeling (SEM, Jöreskog, 1978). A structural model of the factors influencing the acute psychological sedative effect of the test sample A (Western pear; 10 wt.% bergamot oil) is shown in Figure 4. $\Delta SAA_{task-sample}$ was determined by subtracting t SAA_{sample} from SAA_{task}. The Goodness of Fit Index (GFI) of the structural model was 0.90. The coefficient of multiple determination of R^2 of the unobserved variable was 0.59. The pass coefficient of relaxed (β_1), fun (β_2) and refreshed (β_4) exhibited positive values while anxious (β_3) stressed (β_5) and uplifted (β_6) exhibited negative values. The pass coefficient of relaxed (β_1) and refreshed (β_4) exhibited comparatively large values (0.63 and 0.64) when $\Delta SAA_{task-sample}$ (β_{SAA3}) exhibited

comparatively a large positive value (0.79). While the pass coefficient of fun (β_2), stressed (β_5) and uplifted (β_6) exhibited under 0.4. These results were consistent with the trend obtained from subjective evaluations. It was considered that the decrease in SAA_{sample} compared to SAA_{task} might be significantly involved in the differences in the score of subtract for the questions relating to relaxed and refreshed.

Our analysis of the biomarker and subjective evaluations indicate that (a) fragrances containing no chemical materials which could directly activate the central nervous system, significantly induced a sedative effect in women; (b) SAA can be a useful indicator for the evaluation of an acute, psychological sedative effect; and (c) *feel relaxed* and *refreshed* might be a appropriate question to

Figure 4. Structural equation model detailing the factors that influence acute sedative effect on sample A. The pass coefficient for the psychological state questionnaire ($\beta1_{-6}$), salivary amylase activities ($\beta SA_{A1-SAA3}$); $SAAba_{ses}$ hows the mean of salivary amylase activity during the baseline period, $SAAsa_{mples}$ hows the inhalation of test sample period, $\Delta SAAta_{sk-sample}$ s hows the subtract $SAAsa_{mplef}$ rom $SAAta_{sk;}$ disturbance variables (d), error variables (e) (N=20). The pass coefficient of relaxed ($\beta1$) a nd refreshed ($\beta4$) e xhibited comparatively large values (0.63 and 0.64) when $\Delta SAAtask_{-sample (\beta S}AA3)_{exh}$ ibited comparatively large positive value (0.79). While the pass coefficient of fun ($\beta2$), st ressed ($\beta5$), and uplifted ($\beta6$) exhib ited under 0.4.

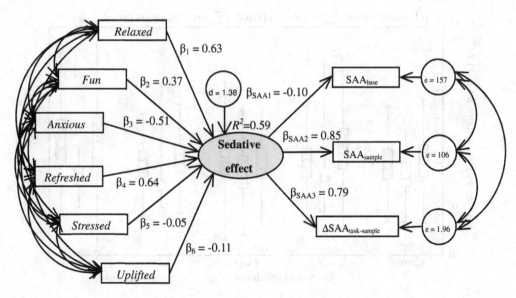

precisely describe the sedative state, rather than the questions *fun, stressed* or *uplifted.*

EFFECTS OF FRAGRANCE CONCENTRATION ON SALIVARY BIOMARKER

To investigate the influence of fragrance concentration on salivary biomarkers, we measured temporal changes in SAA (Yamaguchi, et al., 2009). Biomarkers levels were determined at baseline, inhalation and post-inhalation periods in a group of 15 young, healthy, adult females. Two traditional plant essential oils, *Lavandula officinalis* (Kido, 2002) and *Citrus aurantium* (Jäger, et al., 1992; Komori, et al., 1995) with reported sedative/relaxing effects were used as test samples. The test samples were prepared by diluting to 1 wt.% and 3 wt.% with distilled water. Distilled water was used as the negative control. After baseline SAA levels were established with the SAA biosensor, each subject was exposed to

the test sample for 10 mins and individual's SAA levels were recorded. SAA measurement was repeated in the post-inhalation period.

SAA were found to decrease on inhalation of both 1 wt.% test sample ($P < 0.05$, Figure 5). On the other hand, a significant difference was not observed between the baseline and the inhalation periods for the control (distilled water) and the 3 wt.% test sample. Additionally, the SAA level was slightly increased during the post-inhalation period for all of the test samples. The results of the intensity and subject's preference questionnaire agreed well with the decrease of SAA during the inhalation period in both 1 wt.% samples. This indicates that the intensity of fragrance is reflected in the emotional response and the SAA manifests the concomitant activation/deactivation of the sympathetic nervous system. It appears that olfactory stimulation by the inhalation of fragrances of varying concentrations is reflected by temporal changes in SAA levels. Additionally, the standard deviations showed comparatively large value. It

Figure 5. Effects of concentration of plant essential oils on salivary biomarkers. Mean ± standard deviation (SD) and standard error of mean (SE). P < 0.05. SAA were found to decrease upon inhalation of both 1 wt.% test sample. On the other hand, a significant difference was not observed between the baseline and inhalation periods for the control (distilled water) and 3 wt.% test sample.

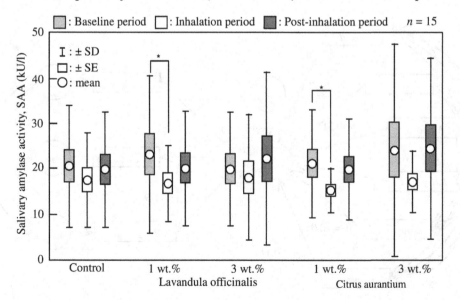

was suggested that there might be a large variation in the scale distribution for each individual.

Fragrances have been a classical domain for computer aided Structure-Odor Relationship (SOR) studies. However, this relation is hard to model, due to limited understanding of olfaction phenomena and the subjectivity of odor quantity and quality as stated in Rossitier's (1996) review. Olfactory research has long been challenged this relationship and it is the final frontier. Salivary biomarkers can be useful tool for the determination between olfaction phenomena and chemicals.

SUMMARY

The measurement of biomolecules presenting in saliva provide a window into the physiological and psychological reactions to fragrances and odors. New salivary biosensors can operationalize measurement of the sedative state induced by a fragrance contained in cosmetics, detergents, or household care products, as a measure of comfort or relaxation of the human body. Standardizing measurement of the neurobiologic effects of olfactory stimulation is critical to the investigation of structure-odor relationships necessary for the synthesis of new odorant molecules. Developed further, salivary expressions of olfactory effects will greatly enhance our limited understanding of olfaction phenomena and diminish the subjectivity that currently burdens assessments of odor quantity and quality.

REFERENCES

Ballard, C. G., O'Brien, J. T., Reichelt, K., & Perry, E. K. (2002). Aromatherapy as a safe and effective treatment for the management of agitation in severe dementia: The results of a double-blind, placebo-controlled trial with Melissa. *The Journal of Clinical Psychiatry*, *63*(7), 553–558. doi:10.4088/JCP.v63n0703

Breslau, N. (2006). Neurobiological research on sleep and stress hormones in epidemiological samples. *Annals of the New York Academy of Sciences*, *1071*, 221–230. doi:10.1196/annals.1364.017

Buchbauer, G., & Jirovetz, L. (1994). Aromatherapy-use of fragrances and essential oils as medicaments. *Flavour and Fragrance Journal*, *9*(5), 217–222. doi:10.1002/ffj.2730090503

Chiappin, S., Antonelli, G., Gatti, R., & De Palo, E. F. (2007). Saliva specimen: A new laboratory tool for diagnostic and basic investigation. *Clinica Chimica Acta*, *383*(1-2), 30–40. doi:10.1016/j.cca.2007.04.011

Diego, M. A., Jones, N. A., Field, T., Hernandez-Reif, M., Schanberg, S., & Kuhn, C. (1998). Aromatherapy positively affects mood, EEG patterns of alertness and math computations. *The International Journal of Neuroscience*, *96*(3-4), 217–224. doi:10.3109/00207459808986469

Grosser, B. I., Monti-Bloch, L., Jennings-White, C., & Berliner, D. L. (2000). Behavioral and electrophysiological effects of androstadienone, a human pheromone. *Psychoneuroendocrinology*, *25*(3), 289–299. doi:10.1016/S0306-4530(99)00056-6

Haze, S., Sakai, K., & Gozu, Y. (2002). Effects of fragrance inhalation on sympathetic activity in normal adults. *Japanese Journal of Pharmacology*, *90*(3), 247–253. doi:10.1254/jjp.90.247

Hirsch, A. R. (2001). Aromatherapy: Art, science, or myth? In Weintraub, M. I. (Ed.), *Alternative and Complementary Treatment in Neurologic Illness* (pp. 128–150). Philadelphia, PA: Churchill Livingstone.

Jäger, W., Buchbauer, G., Jirovetz, L., Dietrich, H., & Plank, C. (1992). Evidence of the sedative effect of neroli oil, citronellal and phenylethyl acetate on mice. *The Journal of Essential Oil Research, 4*, 387–394. doi:10.1080/10412905.1 992.9698090

Jellinek, J. S. (1997). Psychodynamic odor effects and their mechanisms. *Cosmetics & Toiletries, 112*, 61–71.

Jenkins, G. N. (1978). *The physiology and biochemistry of the mouth* (4th ed.). Oxford, UK: Blackwell Scientific Publications.

Jöreskog, K. G. (1978). Structural analysis of covariance and correlation matrices. *Psychometrika, 43*, 443–477. doi:10.1007/BF02293808

Kido, M. (2002). Physiological and psychological effects of fragrance. *Journal of International Society of Life Information Science, 20*(1), 148–151.

Kirschbaum, C., & Hellhammer, D. H. (1994). Salivary cortisol in psychoneuroendocrine research: Recent developments and applications. *Psychoneuroendocrinology, 19*(4), 313–333. doi:10.1016/0306-4530(94)90013-2

Komori, T., Fujiwara, R., Tanida, M., Nomura, J., & Yokoyama, M. M. (1995). Effects of citrus fragrance on immune function and depressive states. *Neuroimmunomodulation, 2*(3), 174–180. doi:10.1159/000096889

Light, K. C., Obrist, P. A., Sherwood, A., James, S. A., & Strogatz, D. S. (1987). Effects of race and marginally elevated blood pressure on responses to stress. *Hypertension, 10*(6), 555–563. doi:10.1161/01.HYP.10.6.555

Lundström, J. N., Goncalves, M., Esteves, F., & Olsson, M. J. (2003). Psychological effects of subthreshold exposure to the putative human pheromones 4,16-androstadien-3-one. *Hormones and Behavior, 44*(5), 395–401. doi:10.1016/j. yhbeh.2003.06.004

Morgan, C. A. III, Wang, S., Mason, J., Southwick, S. M., Fox, P., & Hazlett, G. (2000). Hormone profiles in humans experiencing military survival training. *Biological Psychiatry, 47*(10), 891–901. doi:10.1016/S0006-3223(99)00307-8

Nakane, H., Asami, O., Yamada, Y., & Ohira, H. (2002). Effect of negative air ions on computer operation, anxiety and salivary chromogranin A-like immunoreactivity. *International Journal of Psychophysiology, 46*(1), 85–89. doi:10.1016/ S0167-8760(02)00067-3

Opstad, P. K. (1992). Androgenic hormones during prolonged physical stress, sleep, and energy deficiency. *The Journal of Clinical Endocrinology and Metabolism, 74*(5), 1176–1183. doi:10.1210/ jc.74.5.1176

Otsuki, T., Sakaguchi, H., Hatayama, T., Takata, A., Hyodoh, F., & Tsujita, S. (2004). Secretory IgA in saliva and academic stress. *International Journal of Immunopathology and Pharmacology, 17*(2), 45–48.

Romine, I. J., Bush, A. M., & Geist, C. R. (1999). Lavender aromatherapy in recovery from exercise. *Perceptual and Motor Skills, 88*(3), 756–758. doi:10.2466/pms.1999.88.3.756

Rossiter, K. J. (1996). Structure-odor relationships. *Chemical Reviews, 96*(8), 3201–3240. doi:10.1021/cr950068a

Shetty, V., Zigler, C., Robles, T. F., Elashoff, D., & Yamaguchi, M. (2010). Developmental validation of a point-of-care, salivary α-amylase biosensor. *Psychoneuroendocrinology, 36*(2), 193–199. doi:10.1016/j.psyneuen.2010.07.008

Speirs, R. L., Herring, J., Cooper, W. D., Hardy, C. C., & Hind, C. R. (1974). The influence of sympathetic activity and isoprenaline on the secretion of amylase from the human parotid gland. *Archives of Oral Biology, 19*(9), 747–752. doi:10.1016/0003-9969(74)90161-7

Takai, N., Yamaguchi, M., Aragaki, T., Eto, K., Uchihashi, K., & Nishikawa, Y. (2004). Effect of psychological stress on the salivary cortisol and amylase levels in healthy young adults. *Archives of Oral Biology, 49*(12), 963–968. doi:10.1016/j.archoralbio.2004.06.007

Ugolev, A. M., De Laey, P., Iezuitova, N. N., Rakhimov, K. R., Timofeeva, N. M., & Stepanova, A. T. (1979). Membrane digestion and nutrient assimilation in early development. In *Proceedings of the Ciba Foundation Symposium*, (vol. 70, pp. 221-246). Ciba Foundation.

Yamaguchi, M., Deguchi, M., & Miyazaki, Y. (2006c). The effects of exercise in forest and urban environments on sympathetic nervous activity of normal young adults. *The Journal of International Medical Research, 34*(2), 152–159.

Yamaguchi, M., Deguchi, M., Wakasugi, J., Ono, S., Takai, N., Higashi, T., & Mizuno, Y. (2006a). Hand-held monitor of sympathetic nervous system using salivary amylase activity and its validation by driver fatigue assessment. *Biosensors & Bioelectronics, 21*(7), 1007–1014. doi:10.1016/j.bios.2005.03.014

Yamaguchi, M., Hanawa, N., Hamazaki, K., Sato, K., & Nakano, K. (2007). Evaluation of the acute sedative effect of fragrances based on a biochemical marker. *The Journal of Essential Oil Research, 19*(5), 470–476. doi:10.1080/10412905.2007.9699956

Yamaguchi, M., Kanemaru, M., Kanemori, T., & Mizuno, Y. (2003). Flow-injection-type biosensor system for salivary amylase activity. *Biosensors & Bioelectronics, 18*(5-6), 835–840. doi:10.1016/S0956-5663(03)00007-1

Yamaguchi, M., Kanemori, T., Kanemaru, M., Takai, N., Mizuno, Y., & Yoshida, H. (2004). Performance evaluation of salivary amylase activity monitor. *Biosensors & Bioelectronics, 20*(3), 491–497. doi:10.1016/j.bios.2004.02.012

Yamaguchi, M., Sakakima, J., Kosaka, S., & Nakabayashi, M. (2008). A method for evaluating the discomfort induced by odor using a biochemical marker. *Sensors and Actuators. B, Chemical, 131*, 143–147. doi:10.1016/j.snb.2007.12.009

Yamaguchi, M., Tahara, Y., & Kosaka, S. (2009). Influence of concentration of fragrances on salivary α-amylase. *International Journal of Cosmetic Science, 31*(5), 391–395. doi:10.1111/j.1468-2494.2009.00507.x

Yamaguchi, M., Takeda, K., Onishi, M., Deguchi, M., & Higashi, T. (2006b). Non-verbal communication method based on a biochemical marker for people with severe motor and intellectual disabilities. *The Journal of International Medical Research, 34*(1), 30–41.

Yan, W., Apweiler, R., Balgley, B. M., Boontheung, P., Bundy, J. L., & Cargile, B. J. (2009). Systematic comparison of the human saliva and plasma proteomes. *Proteomics. Clinical Applications, 3*(1), 116–134. doi:10.1002/prca.200800140

Yehuda, R. (2005). Neuroendocrine aspects of PTSD. *Handbook of Experimental Pharmacology, 169*, 371–403. doi:10.1007/3-540-28082-0_13

Yehuda, R. (2006). Advances in understanding neuroendocrine alterations in PTSD and their therapeutic implications. *Annals of the New York Academy of Sciences, 1071*, 137–166. doi:10.1196/annals.1364.012

Chapter 18
Measurement of Neocortical Responses to Odors using Optical Imaging

Akio Nakamura
T. Hasegawa Co., Ltd., Japan

ABSTRACT

Using multi-channel near-infrared spectroscopy, the authors sought to monitor cortical activity during the sensory evaluation period to evaluate the effect of flavorings on taste caused by central integration of olfactory and gustatory modalities. They noted that the neocortical response to a test solution showed adaptation by the conditional sugar solution, which was administered 60 seconds before the test solution. Sugar-sugar self adaptation was greater than sugar-artificial sweetener cross adaptation recorded at specific regions of the frontal and temporal cortex. The magnitude of sugar-flavored artificial sweetener cross adaptation tended to approach that of sugar-sugar self adaptation. Therefore, the similarity of the adaptation of cortical responses might be an important indicator in the screening of effective flavorings in order to improve taste.

INTRODUCTION

During food intake, flavor perception results from simultaneous stimulation of the gustatory, olfactory, and somatosensory systems. Flavor perception is one of the most complex human processes. It involves almost all of the senses, particularly the sense of smell, which is involved through odor images generated in the olfactory pathway.

DOI: 10.4018/978-1-4666-2521-1.ch018

Olfactory stimulation occurs mainly through the retronasal pathway, and the resulting perception is often interpreted as a taste perception (Shephard, 2006; Verhagen & Engelen, 2006). Retronasal stimulation occurs during food ingestion, when volatile molecules released from the food in the mouth are forced up into the nasal passages. Because the molecules arise from food in the mouth, the sensing of these molecules is referred to the mouth; that is, these molecules are perceived as if they are within the mouth (Bartoshuk, et al.,

Copyright © 2013, IGI Global. Copying or distributing in print or electronic forms without written permission of IGI Global is prohibited.

2004). This retronasal food-molecule-laden air is judged to be part of the 'taste' of the food (Murphy, et al., 1977). Our attention has been focused on the importance of the olfactory modality in sensing flavor. Perceptual taste caused by central integration is thought to be affected by olfactory stimulation by particular flavorings. To evaluate the effect of added flavorings on taste, we sought to monitor objective neocortical responses when subjects sensorily evaluated food quality. Until now, the major human brain mapping techniques used for olfaction-related functions have been Positron Emission Tomography (PET) (Dade, et al., 1998; Zald & Pardo, 2000; Savic & Gulyas, 2000), functional Magnetic Resonance Imaging (fMRI) (Levy, et al., 1999; Weismann, et al., 2001; Wang, et al., 2005), Magnetoencephalography (MEG) (Tonoike, et al., 1998; Walla, et al., 2002; Miyanari, et al., 2006; Boesbeldt, et al., 2009), and Electroencephalography (EEG) (Tateyama, et al., 1998; Laudien, et al., 2006, 2008). Although these methods have made important contributions to mapping of cerebral olfactory processing, they require participants to be restricted in their movements, and this feature does not allow them to perform tasting in a natural manner. In the present study, we used Near Infrared Spectroscopy (NIRS) to evaluate the effect of added flavorings on taste. Although NIRS measurements are limited to the cortical surface, several studies using NIRS reported olfactory-related activations (Ishimaru, et al., 2004a, 2004b; Harada, et al., 2006; Aoyama, et al., 2011; Takakura, et al., 2011; Kokan, et al., 2011), and taste-related activations (Okamoto, et al., 2006, 2009, 2011; Bembich, et al., 2010). The recording of the hemodynamic signals with NIRS enabled us to test subjects in a normal, seated position with minimal restriction of movement during drinking. We therefore used NIRS to record hemodynamic signals when subjects sensory evaluate food quality and the effect of the odor on taste.

BACKGROUND

NIRS Optical Imaging

NIRS is a non-invasive optical technique that continuously monitors cerebral hemodynamics (Jobsis, 1977) for the assessment of functional activity in the human brain (Chance, et al., 1993; Villringer, et al., 1993; Koizumi, et al., 1999; Hoshi, 2003; Obrig & Villringer, 2003; Plichta, et al., 2006). Changes in the concentration of oxygenated and deoxygenated hemoglobin in the cerebral vessels can be measured and taken as indicators for cortical activation. In the present study, NIRS optical imaging was conducted with an ETG-4000 Optical Topography System (Hitachi Medical Co., Japan) using a 3 × 11 optode set (consisting of 17 light-emitters and 16 photo-detectors), shown in Figure 1. The distance between pairs of source-detector probes was set at 3.0 cm, and each measuring area between pairs of source-detector probes was defined as one 'channel' (Figure 1). This separation enabled us to measure hemodynamic changes in the brain 2.5-3 cm deep from the head surface, which corresponds to the gray matter on the outer surface of the cerebral cortex (Fukui, et al., 2003). The optodes, which were mounted on a flexible cap, were carefully positioned on each subject's head so that the position was similar for all subjects. This configuration thus enabled us to detect signals simultaneously from the 52 channels, which covered a 60×300 mm^2 frontal area of the neocortex in both hemispheres. The 52 measurement areas were labeled CH 1–CH 52 from the right posterior to the left anterior (Figure 1). The holder was fixed with the lowest probes positioned along the T4-Fpz-T3 line based on the international 10–20 system (Jasper, 1958). Specifically, the optodes were set so that the midpoint of channels 47 and 48 fit Fpz, channels 43 to 52 were aligned on the T4 and T3 line, channels 37 to 16 were aligned on the Fpz to Fz line, resulting in the

Figure 1. Schematic illustration of the multi-channel array (52 channels, 3x11 grid) with location of photo-detectors, light emitters (sources), and measurement points (channels). Channels 1-52 are depicted as white squares and located between photo-detectors and light emitters, which are shown as gray and black circles, respectively.

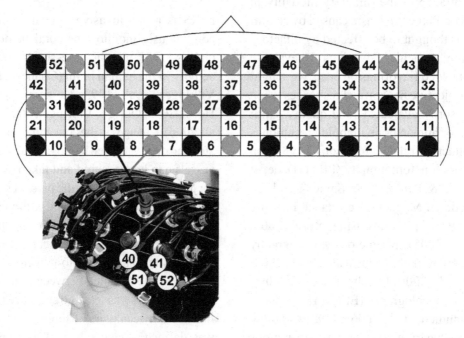

midpoint of channels 5 and 6 fitting around Fz, with channel 1/10 fitting around C4/C3. This arrangement of the probes can measure hemoglobin concentrations ([Hb]) from the bilateral prefrontal (approximately dorsolateral, ventrolateral, and frontopolar) and superior temporal cortical surface regions (Takizawa et al., 2009). Near-infrared laser diodes with two wavelengths (695 and 830 nm) were used as light emitters. Signals reflecting the relative changes in the oxygenated hemoglobin concentration ([oxyHb]) and deoxygenated hemoglobin concentration ([deoxyHb]) were recorded relative to the baseline.

Sugar-Like Flavorings

Among the types of flavorings we usually produce, we focused on the effect of added sugar-like flavorings on the taste of sweeteners. In response to recent markedly growing consumer demand for low-calorie/sugar-free food products containing

non-nutritive artificial sweeteners, such sweeteners are increasingly used as sugar substitutes (Lindley, 1999). However, it has been known for some time that, despite improvement, these sweeteners still differ in taste when compared with the preferred taste of sugar (Sprowl & Ehrcke, 1984; Horne, et al., 2002). This difference likely comes from complex multi-sensory modalities. For example, bitterness comes from the gustatory modality (Kuhn, et al., 2004). Astringency and the aftertaste might come from the somatosensory modality. Flavor is also an important factor to differentiate the taste of artificial sweeteners from that of sugar. Commercial granulated sugar has a specific taste and odor. Artificial sweeteners do not possess this sugar-like flavor. Here, our attention was focused on the importance of the olfactory modality in sensing sugar-like flavors. We sought to improve the taste of artificial sweeteners by applying sugar flavorings because of the continuing preference of many consumers for the taste of sugar. We hypothesized that adding particular flavorings might reduce the difference in taste between sugar and artificial sweeteners and thereby improve the taste of artificial sweeteners.

To evaluate the improvement and the difference in taste, we used two methods. The first method involved subjective sensory evaluation, and the second method involved optical imaging of cortical responses to sweeteners using Near-Infrared Spectroscopy (NIRS). In the current study, using multi-channel NIRS, we sought to monitor cortical activity during the sensory evaluation. Our first objective was to detect the difference between the neocortical responses to sugar and artificial sweeteners using the optical imaging method. Our second objective was to create flavorings that would minimize the sugar vs. artificial sweetener difference in neocortical responses and to minimize the difference found by the sensory evaluation. For this purpose, cortical responses to sweeteners with or without flavorings were recorded during the subjective sensory evaluation period.

DIFFERENCE IN CORTICAL RESPONSES

Self-Adaptation and Cross-Adaptation of Cortical Responses

To evaluate the difference in taste, we first tried to detect the difference between the neocortical responses to sugar and artificial sweeteners using an optical imaging method. In this experiment, a high sweetness sugar substitute, aspartame, was used for the artificial sweetener solution. The degree of sweetness was converted to sugar equivalence. Ten milliliters of 6% granulated sugar or 0.036% aspartame (Wako Pure Chemical Industries, Ltd, Japan) was given to subjects as a test sample using a disposable cup with a straw. After the optodes were placed on a subject's head, the subject was ready to start the task. At time 0 after resting for

60 seconds, we asked the resting subject to start the task. The subject would then pick up the cup and start to drink the first solution and then put back the cup on the desk. The subject would finish drinking by 5 seconds after starting the task and then concentrate on the sensation.

When a subject tasted a test solution, a distinctive increase in [oxyHb] and a decrease in [deoxyHb] were observed in specific regions of the frontal and temporal neocortices. The intensity of the changes was maximal in the lateral frontal portion of the measurable area in both left and right neocortical regions, with the middle area showing no clear increase or decrease. The left half of Figure 2 shows the time course of the typical change in [oxyHb]. [OxyHb] increased to a maximum level with a peak latency at about 20 seconds and then gradually returned to baseline. Each subject showed such cortical responses to various solutions. The regions evoked by the sensory evaluation task were quite similar for each solution. As a first step, we addressed the question of whether the amplitude of the cortical responses differed among sweetener solutions. Systematic analysis showed that there was no statistically significant difference in the amplitude of the cortical responses between sugar and aspartame. Furthermore, some subjects showed a greater response to aspartame in one experiment, whereas in another experiment the same subject showed a greater response to sugar. In these experiments, we measured cortical responses to sugar and aspartame in a sequential manner. Therefore, we hypothesized that the amplitude of the cortical response to a sample was influenced by the previous response.

When a subject drank a sugar solution and then 60 seconds later drank a second sugar solution, a significant reduction of the amplitude of the second response was noted. The amplitude of the response to the test sugar solution was apparently influenced by the previous response to the conditioning sugar solution, as shown in Figure 2. This is a self-adaptation of cortical responses

Figure 2. Typical responses to conditioning sugar-test sugar solutions and conditioning sugar-test aspartame solutions

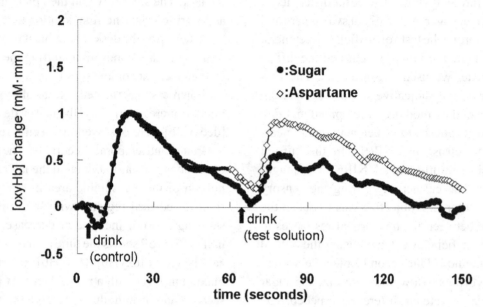

to sugar solutions. When the test solution was changed to aspartame, we noted that the conditioning sugar solution also reduced the amplitude of the response to the test aspartame solution. That is, the cortical response to an aspartame solution showed cross-adaptation in response to the conditioning sugar solution. It can be noted that the sugar-aspartame reduction was smaller than the sugar-sugar reduction as shown in Figure 2. This result raised the possibility that sugar-sugar self-adaptation of cortical responses might be greater than sugar-aspartame cross-adaptation of cortical responses. If this is the case, the comparison between cross and self-adaptation could be a useful tool to evaluate the difference between cortical responses to sugar and artificial sweeteners.

Sugar vs. Artificial Sweetener

In the previous experiment, each subject was asked to compare the taste of a second solution with that of the conditioning sugar solution, which he or she had tasted 60 seconds earlier, as

a sensory evaluation task. The subject knew that the first solution was a sugar solution, but did not know whether the second solution was the same sugar solution or an aspartame solution prior to drinking. We defined this experimental procedure as the control-unknown condition. We asked the following question: If the subject was provided information about both samples, can differences in the cortical responses between sugar and artificial sweetener solutions be detected? To verify the effect of the task, a similar experiment was done in which the subject was given information about both samples: that is, he/she knew that the first solution was a sugar solution and that the second solution was the same sugar solution or an aspartame solution prior to drinking (control-known condition). The amplitude of the response to the second sugar solution was influenced by the previous response to the conditioning sugar solution in both the control-known and the control-unknown conditions, as shown in Figure 3. However, the amplitude of the response to the conditioning sugar solution in the control-unknown condition seemed to be greater than that in the control-known

Figure 3. Averaged [oxyHb] changes of a subject in response to sugar-sugar solutions and sugar-aspartame solutions at a specific region in (a) the control-known condition and in (b) the control-unknown condition. (number of trials = 12)

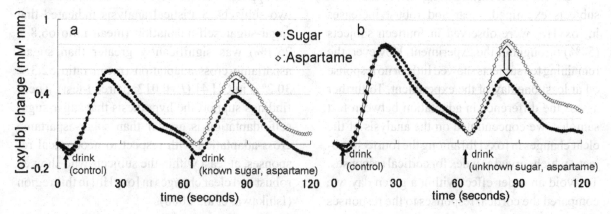

condition when these responses were compared in the same subject (Figure 3a). Moreover, the differences between sugar-aspartame cross-adaptation and sugar-sugar self-adaptation were greater in the control-unknown condition than in the control-known condition. The sensory evaluation task comprised two steps. The first step was a memorization step of the taste characteristics of the conditioning sugar solution; the second step was a comparison step, in which the taste of the second test solution was compared with that of the memorized taste of the conditioning sugar. These results suggested the possibility that sugar-sugar self-adaptation was greater than sugar-aspartame cross- adaptation in both conditions: however, both the memorization and the comparison steps performed without providing information about the second test solution are thought to be as important as the sensory evaluation task in determining the sugar vs. artificial sweetener differences in neocortical responses. Consequently, we used the control-unknown condition in the following experiments to evaluate the differences in adaptation.

Comparison between Self-Adaptation and Cross-Adaptation

We addressed the question of whether sugar-sugar self-adaptation was greater than sugar-aspartame

cross-adaptation with respect to cortical responses. To quantify these adaptations, the sugar solution was given to subjects as a conditioning solution before every test sample solution. We then compared the ratio of adaptations between test samples by calculating the ratio of the amplitudes of the responses to the test samples and those of the previous responses to the conditioning samples. Twenty-four healthy volunteers (fifteen male and nine female, mean age 35.6 ± 8.3 years) participated in this study. Written informed consent was obtained after a complete explanation of the study. To avoid any influence of environmental stress, each subject was seated comfortably in a room controlled for temperature, humidity, and brightness throughout the experiments. The subjects kept their eyes closed during the tasting and resting periods. At the beginning of the experiments, the session schedule was explained. Before measurement, subjects were trained to retain in their minds the taste characteristics of the sugar solution and of the artificial sweetener solution. Subjects were asked to compare the tastes of a test solution with that of the conditioning sugar solution, which had been ingested 60 seconds before the test solution, as a sensory evaluation task. After tasting the test solution for 30 seconds, subjects were asked to judge whether the taste of each test solution was similar to or different from the taste characteristics of the conditioning sugar solution and to identify their answer by raising one hand (left for similar or right for different). Among the twenty-four subjects examined, clear and robust increases in [oxyHb] were observed in fourteen subjects (58%) throughout the experiment. However, the remaining ten subjects showed little or no response on at least one day of the experiment. To further assess the difference in adaptation between test samples, we concentrated on the analysis of the clear changes in [oxyHb] among the fourteen subjects, which served as index for cortical responses. To avoid an order effect within a given day, we compared the cortical responses to the responses obtained for the first pair of conditioning and test solutions, although measurement of the cortical responses to the conditioning and test solutions was repeated four times in one day.

Figure 4 shows a comparison between sugar-sugar self-adaptation and sugar-aspartame cross-adaptation recorded at a specific region (CH 41). Among the fourteen subjects, twelve subjects showed clear and robust responses in this region throughout the experiment. The degree of adaptation differed among subjects, but in ten subjects of the twelve (83%), sugar-sugar self-adaptation was greater than sugar-aspartame cross-adaptation, and the opposite results were noted in the remaining two subjects. Statistical analysis indicated that sugar-sugar self-adaptation (mean ratio 66.8 ± 25.1%) was significantly greater than sugar-aspartame cross-adaptation (mean ratio 52.3 ± 30.2%) in CH 41 ($P=0.012$, paired t-test). These findings support the hypothesis that sugar-sugar self-adaptation is greater than sugar-aspartame cross-adaptation with respect to neocortical responses, at least within the subjects who showed robust and clear changes in [oxyHb] in this region (Ishikawa, et al., 2008).

The solid circle in Figure 5 indicates the region of interest (CH 41). In the surrounding regions of the left side of the brain and in some regions of the right side (dotted areas in Figure 5), sugar-sugar self-adaptation tended to be greater than sugar-aspartame cross-adaptation. However, the level of statistical significance was lower than that of CH 41 ($0.05<P<0.1$, paired t-test). The difference between neocortical responses to sugar and aspartame can thus be detected using the optical imaging.

Figure 4. Comparison between (a) conditioning sugar-test aspartame cross-adaptation and (b) conditioning sugar-test sugar self-adaptation in CH 41 using the average [oxyHb] changes of the twelve subjects. (c) Sugar-sugar self-adaptation is significantly greater than sugar-aspartame cross-adaptation.

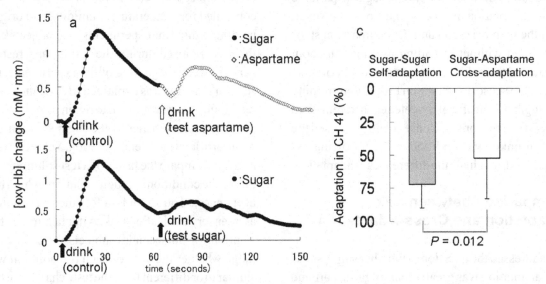

Figure 5. Sugar-sugar self adaptation was greater than sugar-aspartame cross-adaptation of cortical responses among the fourteen subjects in the specific regions shown in solid circle and dotted circles. The solid circle indicates the region of interest (CH 41).

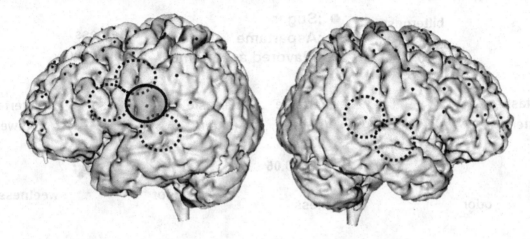

EVALUATION OF EFFECT OF ADDED FLAVORINGS

Sugar-Like Flavorings

The main objective of this research is to detect the effect of odor on neocortical responses to tastes. Does the olfactory modality in sensing volatile compounds trick the brain and change the perceptual taste? Can we monitor olfactory effect on taste using optical imaging based on the differences in neocortical responses to sweeteners? In order to evaluate the effect of added flavorings on taste, we used flavorings that would minimize the sugar vs. artificial sweetener difference in cortical responses and also minimize the difference found by the sensory evaluation. For this purpose, neocortical responses to sweeteners without or with flavorings were recorded during the sensory evaluation period. The flavoring contained volatile compounds based on analysis of raw cane sugar aroma constituents (Abe, et al., 1978). The subjects sensed granulated sugar-like sweet odor when they drank the flavored solution. The same twenty-four volunteers participated in this study. Other experimental setups were

the same as the previous experiment. Ten mL granulated sugar (6%) was given to the subjects as the conditional sugar solution, and the the sugar solution, aspartame (0.036%), or flavored aspartame solution was given to subjects as a test sample using a disposable cup with a straw. After each task, the subject filled out a sensory evaluation questionnaire for the given sample. Five descriptors were used, namely, sweetness, odor, bitterness/astringency, sweetness aftertaste, and bitterness aftertaste, with each being rate on a scale ranking from -3, indicating "much weaker" to +3, indicating "much stronger," with 0 as the same when compared to the corresponding conditional sugar solution.

Sensory Evaluation

In the sensory evaluations provided by all the twenty-four subjects who participated in this research, subjects reported that the bitterness/astringency, the sweetness aftertaste, and the bitterness aftertaste of aspartame were stronger than those of sugar. Subjects also reported that while a particular flavored aspartame had a profile which resembled aspartame, the bitterness/astringency

Figure 6. Spider-web-diagram resulting from tasting of sugar, aspartame, and flavored aspartame (a) in eight subjects who felt improvement in the taste of aspartame by the flavoring, (b) in six subjects who did not feel improvement

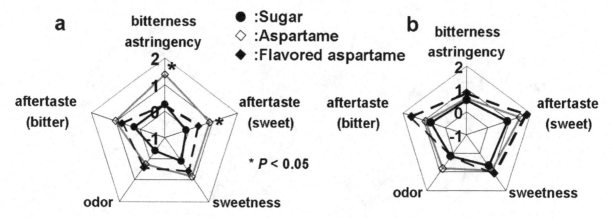

and the sweetness aftertaste of aspartame were significantly reduced by this flavoring ($P<0.05$, Wilcoxon's signed-ranked tests).

Figure 6 gives the summary of the sensory evaluations from the selected fourteen subjects. According to the results of the sensory evaluations of this particular flavored aspartame, the subjects were divided into two groups. Eight subjects reported that this flavoring effectively reduced the bitterness/astringency and the sweetness aftertaste of aspartame as shown in Figure 6a. These reductions were statistically significant ($P<0.05$, Wilcoxon's signed-ranked tests). On the other hand, the remaining six subjects reported that the bitterness/astringency, the bitterness aftertaste, and the sweetness aftertaste of this flavored aspartame were stronger than that of aspartame as shown in Figure 6b. Screening of additional flavorings for effectiveness or combined usage of non-volatile components was consequently necessary, because almost half of the subjects reported that such added flavoring did not effectively improve the taste of aspartame. Our aim became that all subjects and by extension, all customers would perceive improvement by using a particular flavoring. However, in this research, eight subjects felt the taste of this flavored aspartame came close to that

of sugar, whereas six subjects felt the taste was the same as that of aspartame.

Evaluation of Effect of Added Flavorings using Optical Imaging

The difference between neocortical responses to sugar and aspartame was detected, with likewise a different in sensory profile in aspartame vs. sugar being noted. In the sensory evaluations provided by all the twenty-four subjects examined, they reported that the bitterness/astringency, the sweetness aftertaste, and the bitterness aftertaste of aspartame were stronger than those of sugar. These findings may indicate that the difference in taste correlates with the difference in adaptations of neocortical responses. This raised the possibility that if the better tasting sample was found to resemble a sugar solution, sugar-sample cross adaptation would come closer to sugar-sugar self adaptation. The subjects also reported that while a particular flavored aspartame had a profile which resembled aspartame, the bitterness/astringency and the sweetness aftertaste of aspartame were significantly reduced by this flavoring ($P<0.05$, Wilcoxon's signed-ranked tests). The olfactory modality in sensing these volatile compounds might trick the brain and change the perceptual taste. Such improvement by this flavoring, however, was not always sensed by all subjects. For example, in the fourteen subjects who showed clear increases in [oxyHb], the subjects were divided into two groups. Eight subjects reported that this flavoring effectively reduced the bitterness/astringency and the sweetness aftertaste of aspartame. These reductions were statistically significant (*P*<0.05, Wilcoxon's signed-ranked tests). On the other hand, the remaining six subjects did not perceive such improvement. To further access the correlation between the difference in taste and the difference in adaptations of cortical responses, we compared sugar-flavored aspartame cross adaptation to sugar-aspartame cross adaptation in the two groups of the fourteen.

In the eight subjects who sensed improvement, statistically significant larger sugar-sugar self adaptation as compared to sugar-aspartame cross adaptation was confirmed (*P*<0.05, Dunnett's multiple comparison test) in regions including CH 41 (dotted areas in Figure 7). Sugar-flavored aspartame cross adaptation tended to be greater than sugar-aspartame cross adaptation (0.1<*P*<0.11, Dunnett's multiple comparison test) in the same

dotted areas in Figure 7 (Ishikawa et al., 2008). On the other hand, in the six subjects who did not sense improvement by addition of the flavoring, sugar-flavored aspartame cross adaptation differed further from sugar-sugar self adaptation. In all the fourteen subjects, there was no statistical difference between sugar-flavored aspartame cross adaptation and sugar-aspartame cross adaptation. Consequently, in the subjects who sensed that the taste of this flavored aspartame solution came close to that of a sugar solution by the flavoring, sugar-flavored aspartame cross adaptation tended to come closer to sugar-sugar self adaptation.

FUTURE RESEARCH DIRECTIONS

In the human brain, the perceptual systems are closely linked to systems for learning, memory, emotion, and language, so distributed neural mechanisms contribute to food preference and food cravings. The differences in subjective sensory evaluation affected the monitored differences in neocortical responses or information about samples also affected the monitored responses as shown in our research. These findings show that

Figure 7. Specific regions where the difference in adaptations of cortical responses might correlate with the difference in taste of sweetener solutions in the eight subjects who felt improvement by the flavoring. Sugar-flavored aspartame cross adaptation tended to be greater than sugar-aspartame cross adaptation in similar areas shown in Figure 5.

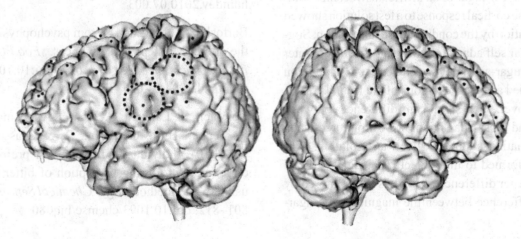

evaluating food quality during sensory evaluation influence the monitored cortical responses using the optical imaging. Greater recognition of the role of the brain's flavor system and its connection with eating behavior is needed for a deeper understanding. NIRS is a unique tool for monitoring cortical brain function. Improvement of the spatial resolution and development of whole brain scanning by increasing the number of the channels would increase the importance of this technique. However, we detected not only the differences in cortical responses between tastes, but also the influence caused by odors, suggesting that this technique is effective to detect the effect of odor on tastes caused by central integration of olfactory and gustatory modalities. How olfactory stimulation affect the cortical responses to tastes? In the future, the effect of odorants on cortical responses to tastants should be analyzed more precisely to understand the monitored differences in adaptations of cortical responses.

CONCLUSION

In order to evaluate the effectiveness of flavorings on taste caused by central integration of flavor, we recorded neocortical responses during sensory evaluation using multi-channel Near-Infrared Spectroscopy (NIRS). When a subject drank a conditional sugar solution, then after 60 seconds drank a test sugar or an artificial sweetener solution, the cortical response to a test solution showed adaptation by the conditional sugar solution. Sugar-sugar self adaptation was significantly greater than sugar-artificial sweetener cross adaptation recorded at specific regions of the frontal cortex. Moreover, such significant differences between self and cross-adaptations were monitored when information about the given test solutions was not informed to the subject. The sugar-artificial sweetener difference could thus be monitored by the difference between the magnitude of sugar-

sugar self adaptation and that of sugar-artificial sweetener cross adaptation of cortical responses. Sugar-flavored artificial sweetener cross adaptation tended to come close to sugar-sugar self adaptation in the subjects who felt improvement by the flavoring. Multi-channel NIRS was sensitive enough to detect the difference. In addition, the sugar-flavored artificial sweetener similarity in taste might be estimated by the difference in adaptations of cortical responses. Therefore, the similarity of the adaptation of cortical responses might be an important indicator for screening effective flavorings in order to improve taste.

It is still uncertain just how the brain functions in relation to the perception of sweetness. However, the method of recording neocortical responses to various foods with flavors may help improving the perceptual quality of the foods.

REFERENCES

Abe, E., Nakatani, Y., Yamanishi, T., & Muraki, S. (1978). Studies on the "sugary flavor" of raw cane sugar. *Proceedings of the Japanese Academy Series B*, *54*, 542–547. doi:10.2183/pjab.54.542

Aoyama, S., Toshima, T., Saito, Y., Konishi, N., Motoshige, K., & Ishikawa, N. (2010). Maternal breast milk odour induces frontal lobe activation in neonates: A NIRS study. *Early Human Development*, *86*, 541–545. doi:10.1016/j.earlhumdev.2010.07.003

Bartoshuk, L. M. (2004). From psychophysics to the clinic: Missteps and advances. *Food Quality and Preference*, *15*, 617–632. doi:10.1016/j.foodqual.2004.05.007

Bembich, S., Lanzara, C., Clarici, A., Demarini, S., Tepper, B. J., Gasparini, P., & Grasso, D. L. (2010). Individual differences in prefrontal cortex activity during perception of bitter taste using fNIRS methodology. *Chemical Senses*, *35*, 801–812. doi:10.1093/chemse/bjq080

Boesveldt, S., Stam, C. J., Knol, D. L., Verbunt, J. P., & Berendse, H. W. (2009). Advanced time-series analysis of MEG data as a method to explore olfactory function in healthy controls and Parkinson's disease patients. *Human Brain Mapping, 30*, 3020–3030. doi:10.1002/hbm.20726

Chance, B., & Zhuang, Z. UnAh, C., Alter, C., & Lipton, L. (1993). Cognition-activated low-frequency modulation of light absorption in human brain. *Proceedings of the National Academy of Science, 90*, 3770-3774.

Dade, L. A., Jones-Gotman, M., Zatorre, R. J., & Evans, A. C. (1998). Human brain function during odor encoding and recognition: A PET activation study. *Annals of the New York Academy of Sciences, 855*, 572–574. doi:10.1111/j.1749-6632.1998.tb10626.x

Fukui, Y., Ajichi, Y., & Okada, E. (2003). Monte Carlo prediction of near-infrared light propagation in realistic adult and neonatal head models. *Applied Optics, 42*, 2881–2887. doi:10.1364/AO.42.002881

Harada, H., Tanaka, M., & Kato, T. (2006). Brain olfactory activation measured by near-infrared spectroscopy in humans. *The Journal of Laryngology and Otology, 120*, 638–643. doi:10.1017/S002221510600123X

Horne, J., Lawless, H. T., Speirs, W., & Sposato, D. (2002). Bitter taste of saccharin and acesulfame-K. *Chemical Senses, 27*, 31–38. doi:10.1093/chemse/27.1.31

Hoshi, Y. (2003). Functional near-infrared optical imaging: Utility and limitations in human brain mapping. *Psychophysiology, 40*, 511–520. doi:10.1111/1469-8986.00053

Ishikawa, M., Nakamura, A., Fujiki, A., Ide, J., & Mori, K. (2008). Improving the taste of artificial sweeteners using flavors. In *Proceedings of Sweetness and Sweeteners: Biology, Chemistry and Psychophysics ACS Symposium,* (pp. 420-429). Washington, DC: ACS Press.

Ishimaru, T., Yata, T., & Hatanaka-Ikeno, S. (2004). Hemodynamic response of the frontal cortex elicited by intravenous thiamine propyldisulphide administration. *Chemical Senses, 29*, 247–251. doi:10.1093/chemse/bjh029

Ishimaru, T., Yata, T., Horikawa, K., & Hatanaka, S. (2004). Near-infrared spectroscopy of the adult human olfactory cortex. *Acta Oto-Laryngologica. Supplementum, 553*, 95–98. doi:10.1080/03655230410017751

Jasper, H. A. (1958). The ten–twenty system of the international federation. *Electroencephalography and Clinical Neurophysiology, 10*, 371–375.

Jobsis, F. F. (1977). Noninvasive, infrared monitoring of cerebral and myocardial oxygen sufficiency and circulatory parameters. *Science, 198*, 1264–1267. doi:10.1126/science.929199

Koizumi, H., Yamashita, Y., Maki, A., Yamamoto, T., Ito, Y., Itagaki, H., & Kennan, R. (1999). Higher-order brain function analysis by trans-cranial dynamic NIRS imaging. *Journal of Biomedical Optics, 4*, 403–413. doi:10.1117/1.429959

Kokan, N., Sakai, N., Doi, K., Fujio, H., Hasegawa, S., Tanimoto, H., & Nibu, K. (2011). Near-infrared spectroscopy of orbitofrontal cortex during odorant stimulation. *American Journal of Rhinology and Allergy, 25*, 163–165. doi:10.2500/ajra.2011.25.3634

Kuhn, C., Bufe, B., Winnig, M., Hofmann, T., Frank, O., & Behrens, M. (2004). Bitter taste receptors for saccharin and acesulfame K. *The Journal of Neuroscience, 24*, 10260–10265. doi:10.1523/JNEUROSCI.1225-04.2004

Laudien, J. H., Küster, D., Sojka, B., Ferstl, R., & Pause, B. M. (2006). Central odor processing in subjects experiencing helplessness. *Brain Research, 1120*, 141–150. doi:10.1016/j.brainres.2006.08.090

Laudien, J. H., Wencker, S., Ferstl, R., & Pause, B. M. (2008). Context effects on odor processing: An event-related potential study. *NeuroImage*, *41*, 1426–1436. doi:10.1016/j. neuroimage.2008.03.046

Levy, L. M., Henkin, R. J., Lin, C. S., & Finley, A. (1999). Rapid imaging of olfaction by functional MRI (fMRI): Identification of presence and type of hyposmia. *Journal of Computer Assisted Tomography*, *23*, 767–775. doi:10.1097/00004728-199909000-00026

Lindley, M. G. (1999). New developments in low-calorie sweeteners. *World Review of Nutrition and Dietetics*, *85*, 44–51. doi:10.1159/000059701

Miyanari, A., Kaneoke, Y., Ihara, A., Watanabe, S., Osaki, Y., & Kubo, T. (2006). Neuromagnetic changes of brain rhythm evoked by intravenous olfactory stimulation in humans. *Brain Topography*, *18*, 189–199. doi:10.1007/s10548-006-0268-3

Murphy, C., Cain, W. S., & Bartoshuk, L. M. (1977). Mutual action of taste and olfaction. *Sensory Processes*, *1*, 204–211.

Obrig, H., & Villringer, A. (2003). Beyond the visible--Imaging the human brain with light. *Journal of Cerebral Blood Flow and Metabolism*, *23*, 1–18. doi:10.1097/00004647-200301000-00001

Okamoto, M., Dan, H., Clowney, L., Yamaguchi, Y., & Dan, I. (2009). Activation in ventro-lateral prefrontal cortex during the act of tasting: An fNIRS study. *Neuroscience Letters*, *451*, 129–133. doi:10.1016/j.neulet.2008.12.016

Okamoto, M., Matsunami, M., Dan, H., Kohata, T., Kohyama, K., & Dan, I. (2006). Prefrontal activity during taste encoding: An fNIRS study. *NeuroImage*, *31*, 796–806. doi:10.1016/j.neuroimage.2005.12.021

Okamoto, M., Wada, Y., Yamaguchi, Y., Kyutoku, Y., Clowney, L., Singh, A. K., & Dan, I. (2011). Process-specific prefrontal contributions to episodic encoding and retrieval of tastes: A functional NIRS study. *NeuroImage*, *54*, 1578–1588. doi:10.1016/j.neuroimage.2010.08.016

Plichta, M. M., Herrmann, M. J., Baehne, C. G., Ehlis, A. C., Richter, M. M., Pauli, P., & Fallgatter, A. (2006). Event-related functional near-infrared spectroscopy (fNIRS): Are the measurements reliable? *NeuroImage*, *31*, 116–124. doi:10.1016/j.neuroimage.2005.12.008

Savic, I., & Gulyas, B. (2000). PET shows that odors are processed both ipsilaterally and contralaterally to the stimulated nostril. *Neuroreport*, *11*, 2861–2866. doi:10.1097/00001756-200009110-00007

Shepherd, G. M. (2006). Smell images and the flavour system in the human brain. *Nature*, *444*, 316–321. doi:10.1038/nature05405

Sprowl, D. J., & Ehrcke, L. A. (1984). Sweeteners: Consumer acceptance in tea. *Journal of the American Dietetic Association*, *84*, 1020–1022.

Takakura, H., Shojaku, H., Takamoto, K., Urakawa, S., Nishijo, H., & Watanabe, Y. (2011). Cortical hemodynamic responses to intravenous thiamine propyldisulphide administration detected by multichannel near infrared spectroscopy (NIRS) system. *Brain Topography*, *24*, 114–126. doi:10.1007/s10548-011-0179-9

Takizawa, R., Tochigi, M., Kawakubo, Y., Marumo, K., Sasaki, T., Fukuda, M., & Kasai, K. (2009). Association between catechol-O-methyltrasferase Val108/158Met genotype and prefrontal hemodynamic response in schizophrenia. *PLoS ONE*, *4*(5), e5495. doi:10.1371/journal.pone.0005495

Tateyama, T., Hummel, T., Roscher, S., Post, H., & Kobal, G. (1998). Relation of olfactory event-related potentials to changes in stimulus concentration. *Electroencephalography and Clinical Neurophysiology, 108,* 449–455. doi:10.1016/S0168-5597(98)00022-7

Tonoike, M., Yamaguchi, M., Kaetsu, I., Kida, H., Seo, R., & Koizuka, I. (1998). Ipsilateral dominance of human olfactory activated centers estimated from event-related magnetic fields measured by 122-channel whole-head neuromagnetometer using odorant stimuli synchronized with respirations. *Annals of the New York Academy of Sciences, 855,* 579–590. doi:10.1111/j.1749-6632.1998.tb10628.x

Verhagen, J. V., & Engelen, L. (2006). The neurocognitive bases of human multimodal food perception: Sensory integration. *Neuroscience and Biobehavioral Reviews, 30,* 613–650. doi:10.1016/j.neubiorev.2005.11.003

Villringer, A., Planck, J., Hock, C., Schleinkofer, L., & Dirnagl, U. (1993). Near infrared spectroscopy (NIRS): A new tool to study hemodynamic changes during activation of brain function in human adults. *Neuroscience Letters, 154,* 101–104. doi:10.1016/0304-3940(93)90181-J

Walla, P., Hufnagl, B., Lehrner, J., Mayer, D., Lindinger, G., Deecke, L., & Lang, W. (2002). Evidence of conscious and subconscious olfactory information processing during word encoding: A magnetoencephalographic (MEG) study. *Brain Research. Cognitive Brain Research, 14,* 309–316. doi:10.1016/S0926-6410(02)00121-0

Wang, J., Eslinger, P. J., Smith, M. B., & Yang, Q. X. (2005). Functional magnetic resonance imaging study of human olfaction and normal aging. *The Journals of Gerontology. Series A, Biological Sciences and Medical Sciences, 60,* 510–514. doi:10.1093/gerona/60.4.510

Weismann, M., Yousry, I., Heuberger, E., Nolte, A., Ilmberger, J., & Kobal, G. (2001). Functional magnetic resonance imaging of human olfaction. *Neuroimaging Clinics of North America, 11,* 237–250.

Zald, D. H., & Pardo, J. V. (2000). Functional neuroimaging of the olfactory system in humans. *International Journal of Psychophysiology, 36,* 165–181. doi:10.1016/S0167-8760(99)00110-5

Chapter 19
Aroma Chip Using a Functional Polymer Gel

Dong Wook Kim

National Institute of Information and Communications Technology, Japan

ABSTRACT

Conventionally, the controlled release of aroma molecules has been achieved by employing mechanical devices; however, it has not been possible to avoid the noise and gusts of air that devices emit prior to transmitting aroma information. Another problem is the adherence of odor components to the device structure, because the aroma source is located inside or at the bottom of the device. In this chapter, the authors focus on a chemical container of a functional polymer gel (temperature-responsive hydrogel) that features a reversible phase transition between sol and gel and the controlled release of aroma molecules using a Peltier module to control temperature. By this approach, they developed a soundless olfactory display based on an aroma chip and solved the problem of the adhesion of odor components by placing a card-based aroma source (aroma-chip array) on the top of the olfactory display.

INTRODUCTION

Human beings acquire information from the external world through five senses (sight, sound, smell, taste, and touch), but traditional media such as Television (TV) and Personal Computers (PC) provide only Audiovisual (AV) information. As a consequence, users do not have access to other information modalities. The use of olfactory information, for example, may effectively promote a more realistic experience and sense of presence by transmitting aromas associated with a particular location (Washburn, 2004). With this in mind, a variety of olfactory displays have been proposed (Kaye, 2001; Yamanaka, 2002; Yanagida, 2004; Yamada, 2006; Kim, 2006).

DOI: 10.4018/978-1-4666-2521-1.ch019

Copyright © 2013, IGI Global. Copying or distributing in print or electronic forms without written permission of IGI Global is prohibited.

Previous systems, however, have employed mechanical devices to control the release of aroma molecules, which implies that the noise and gusts of air associated with the operation of such devices cannot be avoided prior to each transmission of olfactory information. For example, solenoid valves and switching devices, which are used to generate aroma molecules, make noise with the result such that users could perceive auditory information prior to olfactory information. In addition, blowers, fans, air pumps, and air compressors generate air gusts (perceptible airflow) by the use of air streams to convey aroma molecules. Hence, users can also feel a breeze before the aroma reaches them.

In short, by employing mechanical devices, while olfactory information is usually received without auditory and tactile information, noise and gusts of air would precede the aroma. Moreover, because the aroma source in such systems is usually located inside or at the bottom of the device, odor components would adhere to the structure preventing the release of different aromas using the same device.

To solve these problems, we have been focusing our research on the next generation of biomedical Drug-Delivery System (DDS). A DDS is used to ensure that drugs enter the body and reach the target area. A functional polymer gel is widely used as a drug carrier material in the DDS field (Ulijn, 2007; You, 2010). This gel acts as a kind of a chemical container or chemical valve (Beebe, 2000; Yoshida, 2010), which might be promising for the controlled release of aroma molecules without the noise and gusts of air associated with mechanical devices.

In this study, we seek to develop an effective and soundless olfactory display for generating natural olfactory information. We also attempt to solve the problem of the adhesion of odor components by placing the aroma source (aroma-chip array in an aroma card) on the top of the olfactory display.

BACKGROUND

Controlled Release of Aroma Molecules

Information related to the physical senses of sight, sound, and touch can be conveyed by a Liquid-Crystal Display (LCD), loudspeaker, and haptic device (vibration motor), respectively. Information related to chemical senses of olfaction and gustation, on the other hand, can be conveyed by an olfactory display and gustatory device (unrealized), respectively, in which case, chemical (aroma) materials for the devices must be prepared in advance.

Since ancient times, aroma materials have been used in religious practices for sterilization and as antibiotics. More recently, aroma materials have come to be used for diverse purposes including aromatherapy (Cooke, 2000) and aromachology (Jellinek, 1994). The use of aroma materials now extends to many fields, including pharmacology, food and cosmetics, household products, and Virtual Reality (VR) (Tortell, 2007).

Owing to their physical properties, aroma materials are roughly classified into liquid- and solid-type (powder) materials, the former being more widely used (Calkin, 1994). However, liquid-type aroma materials evaporate easily and are nondurable, which means that they cannot provide a prolonged effect. To overcome this hindrance, gelatinization using natural polymers can be used to achieve the controlled release of aroma molecules. The natural polymer gels commonly used include gelatin, agar, konjac, and carrageenan. However, these gels tend to be weak; they can easily deteriorate by the effects of microbes. To solve this problem, we have been focusing on synthetic polymer gels in our research.

Synthetic polymer gels for gelatinization using various types of polymerizations have been investigated to achieve the controlled release of materials. In particular, a stimuli-responsive polymer gel has been used as one type of a gelatinizing agent in next-generation DDS research. The method primarily used to accomplish the controlled release of aroma materials has been incorporation of the materials within the stimuli-responsive polymer gel.

The stimuli-responsive polymer gel has two functions: it serves as a chemical container to retain aroma materials, and it serves as a chemical valve to release aroma molecules. The discharge of flexible quantities of chemicals at an appropriate time when stimulated by pH levels (Tanaka, 1978), ions (Kuhn, 1950), temperature (Harmon, 2003), and electricity (Kwon, 1991) has been investigated with the aim of achieving an ideal controlled release.

In our research, since aroma molecules are highly sensitive to temperature, we have focused on thermo-sensitive properties of gels. Therefore, we have used a temperature-responsive hydrogel known as "smart gel" that features a reversible phase transition between sol and gel by temperature stimuli. Aroma molecules become active in the sol form and are restrained in the gel form. A Peltier module was employed to drive the reversible conversion between electrical energy and heating (or cooling). Electrical signals control the temperature stimulus that induces the phase transition between the sol and gel forms. In short, a temperature-responsive hydrogel can be used to achieve a controlled release of aroma molecules by using a Peltier module to control temperature.

Olfactory Display

Research on communication and information technologies has been progressing rapidly toward the creation of real and virtual environments. Human-Computer Interaction (HCI) research including the five senses has also been expanding (Kaye, 2004) especially in the area of olfactory-information output devices. Several types of olfactory displays have actually been proposed

and developed. These include an odor-sensor and odor-blending system using solenoid valves and an air pump (Yamanaka, 2002), a system that tracks the user's nose to present scent using an air cannon system consisting of a mechanical shutter, valve, pump, and crank motor (Yanagida, 2004), a pulse-ejection system using a thermal Drop-On-Demand (DOD) inkjet and fan (bubble jet by Canon) (Sato, 2009), a wearable system using a check valve and air pump (Yamada, 2006), and a chemical capsule system using an artificial metal muscle and fan (Sakairi, 2009). Ultrasonic and piezoelectric DOD inkjets, aerosol and air compressors, Shape Memory Alloy (SMA), and polymer beads are also widely used (Kaye, 2004).

Essentially, olfactory information is like ambient information. Human beings normally acquire olfactory information from the external world without sound. However, most previously proposed and developed olfactory displays have employed mechanical devices. As a result, it has not been possible to avoid the noise associated with the operation of the device prior to each transmission of aroma information. In our research, we employ a chemical container of a temperature-responsive hydrogel to eliminate all complex mechanical or physical mechanisms. This approach also enables us to achieve miniaturization and natural delivery of olfactory information by ambient aroma convection.

MATERIALS AND METHODS

In this section, we perform two evaluations: one on materials and the other on an olfactory display system. First, we evaluate the controlled release of aroma molecules by using a temperature-responsive hydrogel by Differential Scanning Calorimetry (DSC) and Thermogravimetry (TG). Second, we evaluate the efficiency of an aroma-chip-based olfactory display system by sensory methods.

Material Preparation

A temperature-responsive hydrogel can also be used as a medical DDS because of its ability to spread drugs within the body in a uniform and continuous manner. In this study, we evaluated such physical and chemical properties for the controlled release of aroma molecules and the production of olfactory information. Based on the work of Kim et al., we used methoxy poly(ethylene glycol)-block-poly(ε-caprolactone) diblock copolymers (MPEG-PCL) (Kim, 2004) in this study.

MPEG-PCL powder was added to distilled water at concentration ratios of 10%–35% at 5% intervals to give six samples for testing the effect of the concentration ratio on gelation. After two weeks, the vials containing these samples were turned upside down to test the gelation process; it was found that gelation from sol to gel easily occurs by increasing the concentration ratio (%) of MPEG-PCL. Based on these results, the maximum solubility of MPEG-PCL, while 35%

in distilled water, becomes 30% when using solid-type (powder) aroma material. Thus, considering that we are using powder-type aroma material in this study, we decided to use 30% MPEG-PCL, which has excellent retention capability, for the controlled release of aroma molecules.

Using a temperature-responsive hydrogel of this density ratio, the sol-gel phase transition was demonstrated by simple temperature stimulation, as shown in Figure 1 (a).

As shown in Table 1, the mixture ratio of aroma material (vanilla by Hasegawa) to MPEG-PCL ranged from 5% to 50%. The aroma materials so generated were used to conduct a sensory evaluation of aroma intensity. In this evaluation, we assumed an environment similar to that of an average house. The subjects were three nonsmokers/nonrhinitis sufferers with good olfactory perception according to the conditions described in the Experimental Environment section below. Nine tests were conducted at a rate of three per day for three consecutive days.

Figure 1. (a) Reversible phase transition between sol and gel. (b) Determination of gel-to-sol phase transition (heating). (c) Determination of sol-to-gel phase transition (cooling). (d) Determination of aroma molecules release time.

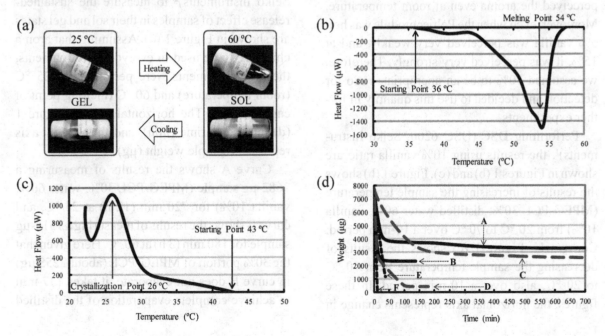

Table 1. Ratio of aroma material in MPEG-PCL

MPEG-PCL (%)	Distilled Water (%)	Aroma Material (Vanilla %)	Total
1.000 g (30%)	2.167 g (65%)	0.166 g (5%)	3.333 g
1.000 g (30%)	**2.000 g (60%)**	**0.333 g (10%)**	**3.333 g**
1.000 g (30%)	1,834 g (55%)	0.499 g (15%)	3.333 g
1.000 g (30%)	1.667 g (50%)	0.666 g (20%)	3.333 g
1.000 g (30%)	1.500 g (45%)	0.833 g (25%)	3.333 g
1.000 g (30%)	1.334 g (40%)	0.999 g (30%)	3.333 g
1.000 g (30%)	1.166 g (35%)	1.166 g (35%)	3.333 g
1.000 g (30%)	0.999 g (30%)	1.333 g (40%)	3.333 g
1.000 g (30%)	0.833 g (25%)	1.500 g (45%)	3.333 g
1.000 g (30%)	0.666 g (20%)	1.667 g (50%)	3.333 g

When the mixture ratio of vanilla used was 5% to 15%, participants perceived aroma only when the Peltier module was hot. When the mixture ratio used was 20% to 50%, all participants perceived the aroma even at room temperature. Moreover, even when the Peltier module was hot, 5% vanilla was perceived very weakly, and at 15%, it was perceived very strongly. Therefore, we assumed 10% to be an appropriate ratio for detection and decided to use this quantity in further experiments.

Performing DSC (DSC 6200, Seiko Instruments)[1], the results using 10% vanilla ratio are shown in Figures 1 (b) and (c). Figure 1 (b) shows the results of increasing the sample temperature (MPEG-PCL 30%, distilled water 60%, vanilla 10%) from 20 °C to 70 °C over a 10-min period. Conversely, Figure 1 (c) shows the results of decreasing the sample temperature from 70 °C to 20 °C, also over a 10-min period. In these figures, the horizontal axis represents change in

temperature (°C) over time, and the vertical axis represents heat flow (µW); that is, endothermic (or exothermic) energy.

On examining the curve in Figure 1 (b), it can be seen that an endothermic process begins at 36 °C, and that endothermic energy increases dramatically from 44 °C onwards. The increase in the endothermic energy peaks at 54 °C shows that a phase transition has occurred. In short, a phase transition in the temperature-responsive hydrogel used in this research begins at 36 °C, and the transition from gel to sol accelerates between 44 °C and 54 °C. Now, on examining the curve in Figure 1 (c), it can be seen that an exothermic process begins at 43 °C and that exothermic energy increases dramatically from 32 °C onwards, with a peak occurring at 26 °C showing that a phase transition has occurred. Thus, in the cooling process, a phase transition begins at 43 °C, and the transition from sol-to-gel accelerates between 32 °C and 26 °C. This difference in phase transition points between the above endothermic and exothermic processes is a phenomenon characteristic of polymers; that is, of a substance with high molecular weight.

The results of performing TG (TG/DTA 220, Seiko Instruments)[2] to measure the sustained-release effect of samples in their sol and gel states are shown in Figure 1 (d). Assuming that aroma chips are to be used in everyday environments, these measurements were performed at 25 °C (room temperature) and 60 °C (melting point of caprolactone). The horizontal axis in Figure 1 (d) represents time (min), and the vertical axis represents sample weight (µg).

Curve A shows the results of measuring a 7682-µg sample (MPEG-PCL 30%, water 60%, vanilla 10%) for 720 min (12 h) at 25 °C, and curve B shows the results of measuring a 7514-µg sample for 180 min (3 h) at 60 °C. Here given that the 30% portion of MPEG-PCL (about 2255 µg) in curve B does not evaporate, it takes 137 min to achieve complete evaporation of the distilled water and vanilla at 60 °C with the final residual amount being 2333 µg. However, in curve A for measurements conducted at 25 °C, there is no change in weight after the 595th min, and the residual amount after the 720th min is 3300 µg. Thus, excluding the 30% portion of MPEG-PCL (2305 µg) that does not evaporate, it is thought that 995 µg of distilled water and vanilla are retained by PCL crystallization.

Curve A, however, also shows that sample weight decreases rapidly in the first 30 min even without heating. To investigate this, we performed weight measurements again at 25 °C and 60 °C with a focus on the aroma material that occupies 10% of the samples created for this research. Curve C shows that a 7785-µg sample of the aroma material (vanilla 100%) gradually decreases in weight at 25 °C, eventually reaching a residual amount of 2558 µg after 720 min. Curve D, meanwhile, shows the results of heating a 7058-µg sample of the aroma material for 180 min at 60 °C. In this case, the residual amount decreased to 436 µg. Moreover, curve E shows that it took 38 min for 7402 µg of distilled water to completely evaporate at 25 °C, and curve F shows that it took only 12 min for 7209 µg of distilled water to completely evaporate when heated at 60 °C.

These measurement results reveal that most of the distilled water, which occupies 60% (about 4609 µg) of the sample, evaporates naturally within 30 min. Theoretically speaking, 85.7% of distilled water and 14.3% of vanilla should be retained in the final residual amount of 995 µg excluding the MPEG-PCL 30% portion (about 2255 µg) for the 7682-µg sample of curve A. In reality, however, distilled water, which has a low boiling point, evaporates more quickly, so it is thought that most of the 768 µg of vanilla making up 10% of the 7682-µg sample is retained in the final residual amount (995 µg).

The above results demonstrate that the aroma material can be retained for a long time by using a temperature-responsive hydrogel and that the controlled release of aroma molecules can be achieved by temperature stimulation. Furthermore, when dropping a 0.1 g sample consisting of 90% distilled water and 10% vanilla on a micro cover glass and letting the sample stand as such in a room, it was found that complete evaporation would occur in only 180 min. However, when the temperature-responsive hydrogel was added to the mixture, it was found that the sample was still functioning well even after three months.

Controlled-Release Mechanism

In this section, we describe the mechanism of the polymerization reaction and show that the sol-gel phase transition does not produce any noise or smoke.

We synthesized methoxy poly(ethylene glycol)-block-poly(ε-caprolactone) diblock copolymers (MPEG-PCL) by the living ring-opening polymerization of ε-caprolactone (ε-CL) via activated monomer cationic polymerization, based on the work of Kim et al. The polymerization of ε-CL (Mw = 114.14; 22 g, 192 mmol; Wako) was performed using MPEG (Mn = 2000; 16.24 g, 8 mmol; Sigma-Aldrich) in the presence of hydrogen chloride (1.0 M HCl solution in diethyl ether (Et$_2$O); 16 mL, 16 mmol; Sigma-Aldrich) in dichloromethane (CH$_2$Cl$_2$; 100 mL; Wako) at 25 °C for 48 h, as shown in Scheme 1.

As mentioned in the Material Preparation section, aqueous solutions of the MPEG-PCL diblock copolymers, which are assumed to be an aggregation of polymer chains, served as thermoresponsive materials. Hydrophilic segments of MPEG (transition temperature: 52 °C) are attracted to the charges within the water molecule by hydrophilic interaction. Meanwhile, hydrophobic segments of PCL (melting point: 58–60 °C) are associated toward other hydrophobic surfaces by hydrophobic interaction. Thereby, a temperature-responsive hydrogel forms a gel below the melting point and the polymer network acts as a kind

Scheme 1. Polymerization of MPEG-PCL

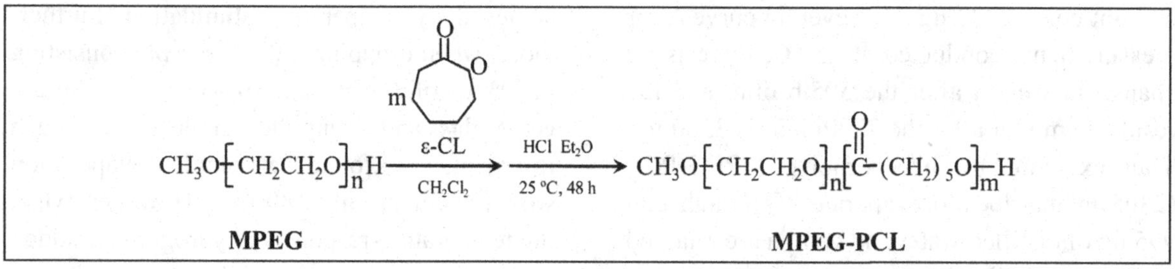

$$CH_3O\left[CH_2CH_2O\right]_n H \xrightarrow[\substack{CH_2Cl_2}]{\varepsilon\text{-CL}} \xrightarrow[\substack{25\,°C,\,48\,h}]{HCl\ Et_2O} CH_3O\left[CH_2CH_2O\right]_n\left[\overset{O}{\overset{\|}{C}}\text{-}(CH_2)_5O\right]_m H$$

MPEG   **MPEG-PCL**

of a chemical container by hydrophilic and hydrophobic interactions without noise. In fact, a temperature-responsive hydrogel has the ability to encapsulate both distilled water (boiling point: 100 °C) and the aroma material (vanilla) and can control the release profile by temperature.

In this work, we prepared the temperature-responsive hydrogel (MPEG-PCL 30%, distilled water 60%, vanilla 10%) with a phase transition at a melting point of 54 °C and crystallization point at 26 °C, and vanillin (4-hydroxy-3-methoxybenzaldehyde; melting point: 80–82 °C, boiling point: 285 °C), which is the most prominent principal flavor and aroma compound in vanilla. When heated to the melting temperature (60 °C) of PCL, the crystallization of MPEG-PCL will collapse and will start a phase transition from gel to sol. Thus, there is no smoke and no burnt smell, because the heating temperature (60 °C) does not affect the distilled water or the aroma material (vanilla).

Preparation of Experimental System

In this section, we describe the olfactory display using the temperature-responsive hydrogel described in the Material Preparation section. This display is controlled by Dual-Tone Multi-Frequency (DTMF) signals (Kim, 2006). The schematic block diagram of the experimental system is shown in Figure 2 (a).

The recording side is composed of a video camera, a DTMF tone generator, and a Video Tape Recorder (VTR) to edit visual images. The playback side consists of a VTR, a controller, which controls the aroma signals that are embedded as DTMF signals on the sound tracks of the video tape, and an olfactory display that controls the release of aroma molecules according to the aroma signals.

The embedded DTMF signals can be inputted into the controller not only from the sound tracks but also from the PC. These are the fundamental

Figure 2. (a) Schematic block diagram of experimental system, (b) Controller

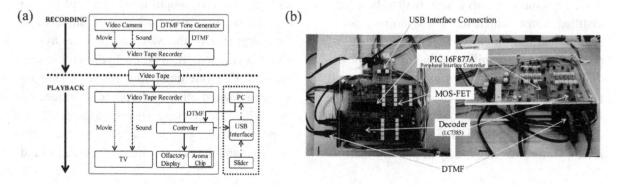

components of the olfactory display. In addition, to collect the sensory evaluation data from subjects, a slider, which is connected to a Universal Serial Bus (USB) interface, was prepared and combined with the experimental system. As shown in Figure 2 (a), the controller and slider are used collectively to input signals to the PC via the USB interface.

Controller

The signal that controls the olfactory display is synchronized with the AV content, which was produced beforehand. The olfactory information (signal) is embedded as sound data for one of the sound channels. Therefore, there is no need to reconstruct the existing AV equipment, and the olfactory display can be added as a set-up box. Moreover, because the synchronized information is merely sound information, it can be recorded and played back very easily, even in a home environment. The olfactory display controller uses DTMF signals.

Different signals can be used for different olfactory information; signals one to nine could correspond to nine different aroma sources. For example, at the place where the 2nd signal is recorded, the odor of the 2nd aroma chip could be released, and the signal numbered "0" could be used to suspend the release of all aroma sources. The signals used to release and suspend odors can be transmitted using one channel among five different channels, such as in 5.1 multi-channel systems. For the present experiment, a stereo channel was used to transmit aroma control signals, recorded on one of the two sound tracks. At the time of playback, the DTMF signals recorded on the sound track are not outputted to the speaker. Instead, they are inputted into the olfactory display controller.

The olfactory display controller decodes the DTMF signals and directs the olfactory display with the specified aroma source numbers. Figure 2 (a) shows the synchronization of the olfactory information, and Figure 2 (b) shows a photograph of the controller. The controller is composed of a peripheral interface controller (PIC 16F877A, Microchip) microcomputer and a metal–oxide–semiconductor field-effect transistor relay (G3VM-61BR, Omron) to drive each Peltier module according to the interpretation of results sent from the decoder (LC7385, Sanyo), which interprets the DTMF signals. In addition, a USB interface was used to collect sensory evaluation responses from the subjects participating in the experiment.

Aroma-Chip-Based Olfactory Display

A micro cover glass (18 × 18 × 0.17 mm, Matsunami 2) was used as an aroma chip. A temperature-responsive hydrogel mixed with the aroma material (MPEG-PCL 0.03 g, distilled water 0.06 g, vanilla 0.01 g) was placed in a microsyringe and was homogeneously applied with a similar thickness onto a 15 × 15 mm area on the micro cover glass. A photograph of the aroma chip is shown in Figure 3 (a). The reversible phase transition between sol and gel in the aroma chip, which can be applied to an olfactory display, is shown in Figure 3 (b). The gel state can be maintained at 25 °C (room temperature). The gel state changes to the sol state as current is applied to the Peltier module, and the temperature of the aroma chip side increases to 60 °C.

As shown in Figure 3 (c), the olfactory display consists of three different components: the Peltier module (30 × 30 × 3.8 mm, 12 V 5 A 44 W type, Akizuki Denshi Tsusho) that helps to drive the reversible conversion between electrical energy and heat; the heat sink (37 × 37 × 6 mm, Comon) that helps to output heat; and the rain pipe joint part (Bore 50 mmφ, National) that serves as a guard for the aroma chip. The main body of the olfactory display also incorporates a 40-mmφ-semicircular air conduit to magnify the role of the heat sink.

Figure 3. (a) Aroma chip, (b) phase transition of aroma chip, (c) olfactory display

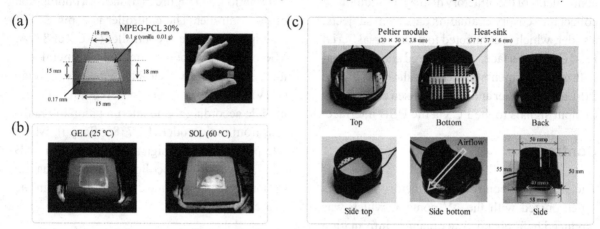

The olfactory display proposed in this research does not have any mechanical mechanisms, and thus is very stable and soundless.

Experimental Environment

The experiment was performed in a room equipped with an air conditioner (temperature 22 °C, humidity 26%). The experimental environment is shown in Figure 4 (a), and the USB interface slider used to measure the sensory evaluation of the aroma intensity by the subjects is shown in Figure 4 (b).

A USB interface slider was used to evaluate individual perception of sensory intensities of aroma by manipulating the slider (up and down) in accordance with the following conditions. The slider is operated only if the aroma in question is detected, and the slider is moved up and down according to the intensity of the aroma. If the intensity of the aroma is perceived to continue unchanged, the slider is maintained in the same

Figure 4. (a) Experimental environment, (b) USB interface slider, (c) temperature curve of the Peltier module

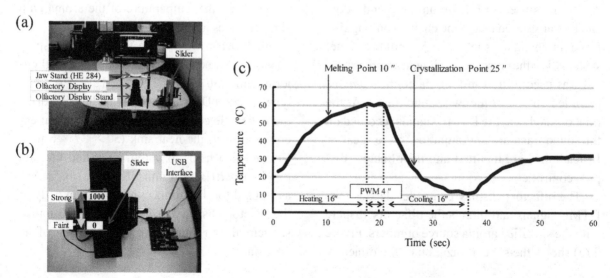

position. If the intensity of the aroma is perceived as decreasing, then the position of the slider is lowered. In short, subjects manipulate the position of the slider according to the intensity of the aroma. If the aroma is perceived to be strong, the position of the slider is increased but it is not necessary to move the slider to the extreme high position. However, if no aroma is perceived at all, the slider is moved to the extreme low position.

The output value of the slider changes continuously from 0 to 1000, and the data used by the controller to heat and cool the Peltier module are recorded on the PC via the USB interface (refer to Figure 2). The absolute values obtained from the movement of the slider for the sensory evaluation of the aroma intensity do not have any particular significance but relative transition values from individuals do have significance. To test the efficiency of the slider system, each subject was asked to operate the slider after a "START" instruction and to stop the operation after a "STOP" instruction.

The curve in Figure 4 (c) shows the change in temperature of the Peltier module, which was used in the sensory evaluation. The horizontal axis shows time (sec), and the vertical axis represents the temperature (°C).

As shown in Figure 4 (c), the temperature of the Peltier module was increased to 60 °C in 16 sec followed by the application of Pulse Width Modulation (PWM) for 4 sec. Then, after maintaining a constant temperature, the temperature of the Peltier module was decreased to 10 °C in 16 sec to solidify the temperature-responsive hydrogel. The rise in temperature after 36 sec shown in Figure 4 (c) was caused by room temperature after stopping the operation of the Peltier module.

The peaks for the phase transition (melting or crystallization point) of the temperature-responsive hydrogel into sol and back into gel are 54 °C and 26 °C, respectively. Therefore, if the temperature increases above 26 °C, the phase transition to sol does not occur again as long as

the temperature does not increase again to 54 °C. A rise in temperature to any point below 54 °C does not affect the state of the hydrogel, because the gel state is maintained below this point.

Sensory Evaluation

In this experiment, we evaluated the performance of the temperature-responsive hydrogel to achieve a controlled release of aroma molecules and conducted a sensory evaluation of the aroma intensity. The experimental setup is shown in Figure 5.

To design similar experimental conditions for all subjects in the experimental setup shown in Figures 4 (a) and 5 (a), the distance between the nose and olfactory display was set to be approximately 100 mm. To prevent subjects from moving their heads and maintain a constant distance, a jaw stand (Eye instrument HE 284, Handaya) was used. Furthermore, to prevent subjects from visually identifying the temperature-responsive hydrogel, we asked them to close their eyes while performing the test. Moreover, the temperature of the Peltier module was not controlled by playing the edited video tape but by sending DTMF signals directly from the PC to the controller.

The procedure for the experiment was as follows: 1) give the subject instructions regarding the experiment; 2) have the subject evaluate the aroma intensity by moving the slider up or down in accordance with the detected odor for 1 min; 3) have the subject fill out a questionnaire; and 4) conduct a sensory evaluation by an interview. The Peltier module was designed to start heating after 5 sec from the test start time. Other changes in the temperature of the Peltier module follow the curve in Figure 4 (c). To avoid the issue of aroma infiltration, enough ventilation was used to circulate fresh air in the test atmosphere after each test. In addition, all instruments used in the experiment were washed with ethanol and the aroma chip was changed for each subject.

Figure 5. (a) Sensory evaluation of aroma intensity, (b) normalization of sensory evaluation curves for 13 subjects, (c) average of sensory evaluation curve for 13 subjects

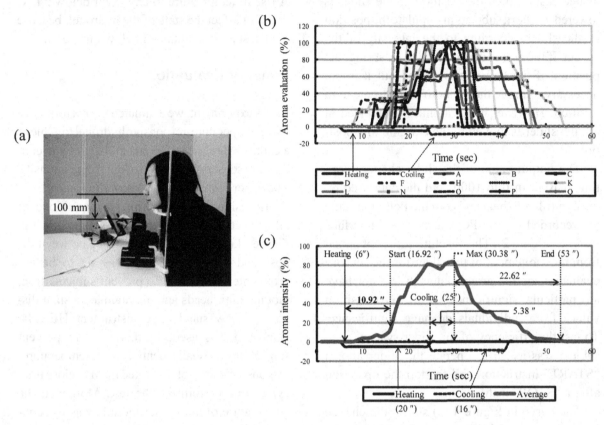

The experiment was performed by 17 subjects (7 males, 10 females; 11 participants in their 20s, 5 participants in their 30s, and one participant in his/her 40s). Two subjects were not able to sense the aroma at all, and two subjects reported sensing the aroma before the aroma was actually displayed, so the data from only 13 subjects were included in the subsequent analysis (6 males, 7 females; 9 in their 20s and 4 in their 30s). As previously described, the absolute value obtained from the slider movement does not have any particular significance, and the data were therefore normalized according to Equation 1.

$$I_{(t)norm} = I_{(t)} / I_{max} \times 100 \qquad (1)$$

Here $I_{(t)norm}$ is the normalized sensory evaluation value at time t, $I_{(t)}$ is the operation value of the slider at time t, and I_{max} is the maximum value of the slider manipulated by the participants. Figure 5 (b) shows the normalized value for all subjects, and Figure 5 (c) shows the average of 13 subjects.

The horizontal axis represents the time (sec), and the vertical axis represents the aroma intensity (%). Results confirmed that the perceived intensity of the aroma source is 100 mm away from the subjects. Accordingly, if we subtract the 10 sec required by the Peltier module to increase to 54 °C (melting point), it can be seen that the subjects would perceive the aroma within an average of 0.92 sec. This indicates that the proposed system can release aroma in a controlled and efficient way.

Next, in the questionnaire, a six-step category-rating method (Table 2.) was used for evaluating the aroma intensity, and a seven-step method (Table 3.) was used to evaluate aroma diffuse time.

Table 2. Aroma intensity (six-step method)

Step	Aroma Intensity
0	No odor
1	Very faint odor
2	Faint odor
3	Easily noticeable odor
4	Strong odor
5	Very strong odor

Table 3. Aroma diffuse time (seven-step method)

Step	Aroma Intensity
3	Very long-time odor
2	Long-time odor
1	Little long-time odor
0	Only diffuse odor
−1	Little short-time odor
−2	Short-time odor
−3	Very short-time odor

On tabulating the results of the questionnaire, on the basis of the six-step method, it was found that the aroma intensity was 2.31 (faint odor) on average when the intensity of the presented aroma was felt to be at its peak and that the aroma diffuse time on the basis of the seven-step method was −0.85 (little short-time odor) on average.

We next evaluated system performance when applying the system to video. In the experiment,

the jaw stand and olfactory display stand were removed to simulate an actual usage scenario, and the vertical distance between the nose and olfactory display was maintained at about 350 mm by adjusting the height of the subject's chair (Figure 6 [a]). As in the case of sensory evaluation, the subject operated the slider to evaluate the intensity while watching the video.

Figure 6. (a) Sensory evaluation of aroma intensity with movie, (b) normalization of sensory evaluation curves for 16 subjects, (c) average of sensory evaluation curve with movie for 16 subjects, (d) average of sensory evaluation curve comparison with temperature curve

(a)

(b)

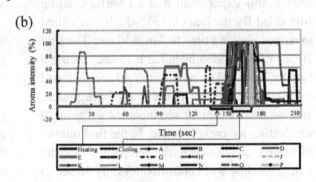

(c)

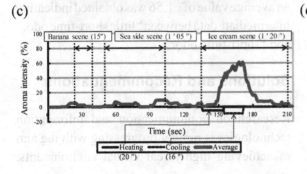

(d)

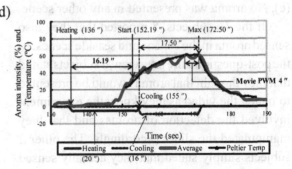

The procedure for the experiment was as follows: (1) give the subject instructions regarding the experiment; (2) have the subject evaluate the aroma intensity by manipulating the slider according to the way he or she senses the aroma while watching the video (running 3 min 30 sec); (3) have the subject fill out a questionnaire; and (4) conduct a sensory evaluation by an interview.

In this experiment, as in the system-performance evaluation experiment described above, the experimental environment was sufficiently ventilated to circulate fresh air, the olfactory display was cleaned with ethanol after each test, and the aroma chip was changed for each subject. A total of 16 subjects participated in the experiment (7 males and 9 females with 11 in their 20s, 4 in their 30s, and one in his/her 40s). The evaluation results of all subjects were also normalized (Figure 6 [b]) by the same procedure used in the performance experiment (Equation 1) and the average is shown in Figure 6 (c).

The horizontal axis in these figures represents time (sec), and the vertical axis represents the normalized value of sensory evaluation. The video used in this experiment was a Charlie Chaplin film titled By the Sea (1915), which was edited to reduce viewing time to 3 min 30 sec. The first 20 sec of this video included a 15 sec "eating a banana" scene. The next 1 min 40 sec included a 1 min 5 sec scene with the sea as background, and the final 1 min 30 sec included a 1 min 20 sec "eating ice cream" scene. In the first minute of the ice-cream scene, the temperature of the Peltier module was controlled for only 36 sec to present the vanilla aroma, the same as in Figure 4 (c). No aroma was presented in any other scene.

Of the 16 subjects, 5 reported that they also sensed aroma in the banana and seaside scenes. In the post-questionnaire interview, 3 subjects stated that they thought that aromas would be presented to match the video as they knew the experiment involved the detection of aromas and that they manipulated the slider accordingly. The other 2 subjects simply stated that they actually sensed odors in the banana and seaside scenes. Therefore, we considered the possibility that "olfactory illusions" in the sense of smell (similar to "optical illusions" in the sense of sight) affected those subjects who sensed aromas in the banana and seaside scenes in which no aromas were actually presented.

A close-up of the last minute in Figure 6 (c) corresponding to actual control of the Peltier module's temperature is shown in Figure 6 (d). It can be seen that a time delay in sensory evaluation occurs here similar to that in the performance experiment. In particular, because the vertical distance between the nose and aroma source was 350 mm in this experiment, it took an average of 6.19 sec for the subjects to sense the aroma after the gel-to-sol transition. On the other hand, the decrease in the aroma intensity started at 172.50 sec of 17.50 sec after the start of Peltier module cooling, which indicates that an aroma continues to be sensed even as it decreases. Furthermore, comparing the temperature curve of the Peltier module shown with the average-sensory curve in Figure 6 (d), it can be seen that there is a good agreement between them.

Results of the questionnaire for this experiment applying the system to video revealed the following. First, in the six-step method (Table 2.) for evaluating the aroma intensity at the point where the subject feels that the intensity of the presented aroma has reached its peak, an average value of 1.88 was obtained corresponding to "faint odor," the same value as in the performance experiment. Second, in the seven-step method (Table 3.), for evaluating the aroma diffuse time, an average value of −1.56 was obtained indicating intermediate data between "little short-time odor" and "short-time odor."

Solutions and Recommendations

Research on communication and information technologies is rapidly progressing with the aim of achieving highly real virtual environments.

In addition, research on multi-sensory communication including the five senses has increased. However, research related to the sense of smell and sense of taste that acknowledges the receptor organs of humans as well as research on related technology are still in the initial phase.

Light has three primary colors and taste has its own primary flavors, but unfortunately, smell does not have any primary odor. Developing an olfactory display that can transmit multiple smells is a challenging task. All olfactory displays developed to date have incorporated methods for replacing the aroma source. The complexity of exchanging the aroma source is the main hindrance in developing practical olfactory displays. In addition, appropriate mixtures of different aroma materials have to be prepared to achieve an olfactory display. Although the exchange of the aroma source is complex, different approaches have come into use; for example, cartridges consisting of liquid, sponge, or wax have been used for different materials that require frequent exchange. Other methods proposed include aroma enclosed in a microcapsule and slurry-type aroma materials printed on paper, both of which can be distributed very easily. As a result, the complexity in exchanging aroma sources has been reduced to some extent but olfactory displays still suffer from mechanical problems in the mechanism used for the controlled release of aroma molecules. To solve the noise problem, we decided to adopt a chemical container of a functional polymer gel and verified that the temperature-responsive hydrogel responds well and can be controlled effectively by using a Peltier module to control the temperature. With this approach, we eliminated all complex mechanical or physical mechanisms and achieved a soundless olfactory display. In addition, we were also able to achieve miniaturization and natural delivery of olfactory information by ambient aroma convection.

FUTURE RESEARCH DIRECTIONS

In this section, we propose a card-type olfactory display for practical use in home environments and suggest methods for distributing aroma sources (aroma cards).

Aroma-Card-Based Olfactory Display

The basic concept of the "aroma card" is that one card contains all aromas to be displayed for specific audiovisual content (Kim, 2008, 2009). The aroma card is positioned on the top of the Peltier module. This solves the adhesion problem[3], because the only part of the device that comes into contact with the aroma mixture is the aroma card itself. Moreover, because the aroma card is set on the very top of the device, aroma cards can be exchanged very easily when viewing different AV content. The prototype of an aroma-card-based olfactory display ($132 \times 92 \times 50$ mm) is shown in Figure 7 (a). The Peltier module ($15 \times 15 \times 3.1$ mm) has 15 sections for stimulating the temperature-responsive hydrogel. To achieve uniform heat distribution, a sheet of copper ($20 \times 20 \times 0.5$ mm) was installed on top of each Peltier module.

The new device employs a set of disk-shaped copper chips ("aroma chips") well known for their excellent heat-transfer properties (Figure 7 [b]). The upper disk of an aroma chip is 18 mmφ, with a hole of 10 mmφ at its center to allow the passage of the aroma component. The lower disk is 15 mmφ and the aroma mixture is painted on its upper surface. A column connects the upper and lower disks in the current version of the aroma chip. Here 0.3 g of the mixture is uniformly spread on the lower disk of each aroma chip. The aroma chips are placed inside a card-like transparent, acrylic board (1 mm in thickness)—the "aroma card"—that can contain up to 15 aroma chips on

Figure 7. (a) Prototype of a card-based olfactory display, (b) prototype of an aroma chip, (c) prototype of an aroma card, (d) aroma card set up on the olfactory display

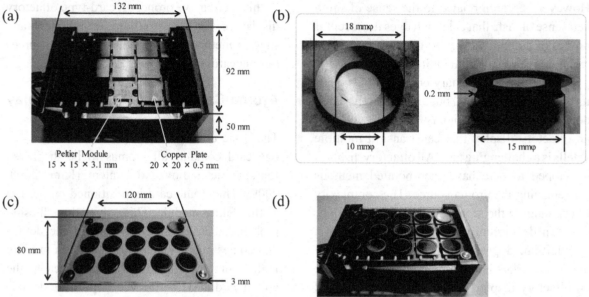

a 3 × 5 grid. The column in the aroma chip prevents it from shifting inside the aroma card. The size of the aroma card is 120 × 80 × 3 mm (Figure 7 [c]). Figure 7 (d) shows an aroma card set up on the top of the olfactory display.

Aroma cards created for particular AV content can be supplied to homes and elsewhere as an appendix to magazines and newspapers, TV programming, or as part of rental videos, CDs, DVDs. This approach would simplify the acquisition and exchange of aromas and make it easy for users to enjoy multimedia content with olfactory information from the comfort of their homes.

CONCLUSION

Olfactory displays in high-reality communication systems must be small, affordable, and effective. In addition, they must be silent and be able to serve different applications. In this research, we focused on a chemical container of a temperature-responsive hydrogel and the controlled release of aroma molecules by using a Peltier module to control the temperature. With this approach, we achieved a soundless olfactory display. We also solved the problem of adhesion of the aroma component by placing a card-based aroma source on the top of the olfactory display. The current experiment used only one "aroma chip," but it is possible that residual effects might be much stronger when using an "aroma card," which currently has space for 15 aroma chips. We plan to perform further experiments to analyze how the problem of the adhesion of the aroma component changes when using multi-chip aroma cards.

The olfactory display system that we developed does not rely on mechanical devices. Furthermore, the use of a chemical container in this system allows for the controlled release of aroma molecules by a small, affordable, soundless, and easy-to-maintain device. The proposed olfactory display can present olfactory information in a natural and accurate manner.

We hope that practical and useful olfactory displays will soon become accessible to a large number of people in a wide variety of applications.

REFERENCES

Beebe, D. J., Moore, J. S., Bauer, J. M., Yu, Q., Liu, R. H., Devadoss, C., & Jo, B. H. (2000). Functional hydrogel structures for autonomous flow control inside microfluidic channels. *Nature, 404*, 588–590. doi:10.1038/35007047

Calkin, R. R., & Jellinek, J. S. (1994). *Perfumery: Practice and principles*. Hoboken, NJ: John Wiley & Sons, Inc.

Cooke, B., & Ernst, E. (2000). Aromatherapy: A systematic review. *The British Journal of General Practice, 50*(455), 493–496.

Harmon, M. E., Tang, M., & Frank, C. W. (2003). A microfluidic actuator based on thermoresponsive hydrogels. *Polymer, 44*, 4547–4556. doi:10.1016/S0032-3861(03)00463-4

Jellinek, J. S. (1994). Aroma-chology: A status review. *Perfumer and Flavorist, 19*(5), 25–49.

Kaye, J. N. (2001). *Symbolic olfactory display*. (Master's Thesis). Massachusetts Institute of Technology Massachusetts. Cambridge, MA.

Kaye, J. N. (2004). Making scents: Aromatic output for HCI. *Interactions (New York, N.Y.), 11*(1), 48–61. doi:10.1145/962342.964333

Kim, D. W., Cho, Y. H., Nishimoto, K., Kawakami, Y., Kunifuji, S., & Ando, H. (2009). Development of aroma-card based soundless olfactory display. In *Proceedings of the IEEE International Conference on Electronics Circuits and Systems,* (pp. 703-706). IEEE Press.

Kim, D. W., Miura, M., Lee, D. W., Ryu, J. K., Nishimoto, K., Kawakami, Y., & Kunifuji, S. (2008). Developing an olfactory display using functional high-polymers application for video. *Journal of Information Processing Society of Japan, 49*(1), 160–175.

Kim, D. W., Nishimoto, K., & Kunifuji, S. (2006). An editing and displaying system of olfactory information for the home video. In *Proceedings of the Knowledge-Based & Intelligent Information & Engineering Systems International Conference,* (pp. 859-866). Berlin, Germany: Springer.

Kim, M. S., Seo, K. S., Khang, G., Cho, S. H., & Lee, H. B. (2004). Preparation of poly(ethylene glycol)-block-poly(caprolactone) copolymers and their applications as thermo-sensitive materials. *Journal of Biomedical Materials Research. Part A, 70A*(1), 154–158. doi:10.1002/jbm.a.30049

Kuhn, W., Hargitay, B., Katchalsky, A., & Eisenberg, H. (1950). Reversible dilation and contraction by changing the state of ionization of high-polymer acid networks. *Nature, 165*, 514–516. doi:10.1038/165514a0

Kwon, I. C., Bae, Y. H., & Kim, S. W. (1991). Electrically erodible polymer gel for controlled release of drugs. *Nature, 354*, 291–293. doi:10.1038/354291a0

Sakairi, M., Nishimura, A., & Suzuki, D. (2009). Olfaction presentation system using odor scanner and odor-emitting apparatus coupled with chemical capsules of alginic acid polymer. *IEICE Transactions on Fundamentals of Electronics, Communications and Computer Sciences. E (Norwalk, Conn.), 92A*(2), 618–629.

Sato, J., Ohtsu, K., Bannai, Y., & Okada, K. (2009). Effective presentation technique of scent using small ejection quantities of odor. In *Proceedings of the IEEE Virtual Reality Conference,* (pp. 151-158). IEEE Press.

Tanaka, T. (1978). Collapse of gels and the critical endpoint. *Physical Review Letters, 40*(12), 820–823. doi:10.1103/PhysRevLett.40.820

Tortell, R., Luigi, D. P., Dozois, A., Bouchard, S., Morie, J. F., & Ilan, D. (2007). The effects of scent and game play experience on memory of a virtual environment. *Virtual Reality (Waltham Cross), 11*(1), 61–68. doi:10.1007/s10055-006-0056-0

Ulijn, R. V., Bibi, N., Jayawarna, V., Thornton, P. D., Todd, S. J., & Mart, R. J. (2007). Bioresponsive hydrogels. *Materials Today, 10*(4), 40–48. doi:10.1016/S1369-7021(07)70049-4

Washburn, D. A., & Jones, L. M. (2004). Could olfactory displays improve data visualization? *Computing in Science & Engineering, 6*(6), 80–83. doi:10.1109/MCSE.2004.66

Yamada, T., Yokoyama, S., Tanikawa, T., Hirota, K., & Hirose, M. (2006). Wearable olfactory display: Using odor in outdoor environment. In *Proceedings of the IEEE Virtual Reality Conference,* (pp. 199-206). IEEE Press.

Yamanaka, T., Matsumoto, R., & Nakamoto, T. (2002). Study of odor blender using solenoid valves controlled by delta-sigma modulation method for odor recorder. *Sensors and Actuators. B, Chemical, 87*(3), 457–463. doi:10.1016/S0925-4005(02)00300-3

Yanagida, Y., Kwato, J., Noma, H., Tomono, A., & Tetsutani, N. (2004). Projection-based olfactory display with nose tracking. In *Proceedings of the IEEE Virtual Reality Conference,* (pp. 43-50). IEEE Press.

Yoshida, R. (2010). Design of self-oscillating gels and application to biomimetic actuators. *Sensors (Basel, Switzerland), 10*(3), 1810–1822. doi:10.3390/s100301810

You, J. O., Almeda, D., Ye, G. J., & Auguste, D. T. (2010). Bioresponsive matrices in drug delivery. *Journal of Biological Engineering, 4*(15), 1-12. Retrieved March 18, 2011, from http://www.jbioleng.org/content/4/1/15

ENDNOTES

[1] Differential Scanning Calorimetry (DSC): DSC was performed on a DSC 6200 (Seiko Instruments). The temperature was calibrated using indium and tin. The operating conditions in the open aluminum pan system were as follows: a sample weight of 25 µg, a heating rate of 10 °C/min, and a nitrogen gas flow rate of 100 mL/min.

[2] Thermogravimetry (TG): TG was performed on a TG/DTA 220 (Seiko Instruments). The operating conditions in the open aluminum pan system were as follows: a sample weight of 7440 µg on average, a heating rate of 10 °C/min, and an airflow rate of 250 mL/min.

[3] Most existing olfactory display systems have an "adhesion problem." Because the aroma source is arranged inside or under the device, substances released by the aroma source end up adhering to device components such as ejectors and switchgears, preventing different aromas from being displayed by the same device.

Chapter 20
Olfactory Display Based on Ink Jet Printer Mechanism and Its Presentation Techniques

Sayumi Sugimoto
Keio University, Japan

Kenichi Okada
Keio University, Japan

ABSTRACT

Considering the recent increase of interest in the transmission of olfactory information alongside audio/ visual information, the authors have developed an olfactory display, based on an inkjet printer mechanism, which emits scents for short periods of time and has high control and provides repeated stable pulse emissions of scents. By using pulse emission, the authors achieved chronological control for presentation of scents and were able to synchronize the pulse with human inspiration. Such synchronization is important because humans detect scents when they breathe in, inhaling scent molecules in the air. Applying pulse emission, the authors measured various human olfactory characteristics; furthermore, they developed scent presentation techniques to create perspective and to switch scents rapidly. This chapter introduces details about the olfactory display and scent presentation techniques using pulse ejection.

INTRODUCTION

Transmission of information via all five human senses is attracting much attention these days (Ministry of Posts and Telecommunications in Japan, 2007; Kim, et al., 2006). In particular, in-formation acquired via the olfactory organs largely affects humans, as this information is transmitted to the cerebral limbic system governing emotions and memories (Michael, et al., 2003). In addition, unlike words, olfactory information can directly present details with an environment about the

DOI: 10.4018/978-1-4666-2521-1.ch020

Copyright © 2013, IGI Global. Copying or distributing in print or electronic forms without written permission of IGI Global is prohibited.

atmosphere, presence of objects, a sense of the season, and can increase the sense of reality and understanding of contents.

However, it is difficult to synchronize scents with time-shifting information, such as movies and sounds, owing to scents lingering and olfactory adaptation. These problems are often caused by the method used for scent emission; existing techniques to emit scents present a greater than necessary volume of scent, over too long a time, in order to make detection easy. This excess in the amount and time of scent emission stimulates olfactory receptors continuously and causes olfactory adaptation. Moreover, emitted scents remain in the space and cause mixing of newly presented and lingering scents. Because of the use of excess scent, chronological control of scents has therefore been difficult.

In an effort to resolve this problem, we have developed an olfactory display based on the hypothesis that a small amount of ejected scent will present discrete and transient bursts of olfactory stimulation, thereby reducing the effect of adaptation. Utilizing an inkjet printer mechanism, this system emits scents for short periods of time and has high control such that it can provide repeated stable pulse emission of scents. By using this pulse emission, we achieved chronological control of scents, and can synchronize the mechanism with human inspiration, which is important due to humans detecting scents when they breathe in and inhale the molecules in the air.

Thus, this scent presentation technique has enabled temporal control over the scents, and by applying this pulse ejection system, we have been able to measure certain human olfactory characteristics. Furthermore, we have constructed scent presentation techniques: perspective creation by scents and rapid switching of scents.

In the following sections, we introduce a detailed description of both the olfactory display and scent presentation techniques using pulse ejection.

BACKGROUND

Research on the transmission of olfactory information together with audio/visual information is ongoing. Work first started in the 1950s with Heilig (1962) developing Sensorama, the first Virtual Reality (VR) system presenting olfactory and audio/visual information together. More recently, the virtual space system "Friend Park," developed by Tominaga *et al.* (2001), provides users with an increased sense of reality by generating the aroma of a virtual object or environment, where the aroma is defined as the area in which a scent can be perceived.

Kaye (2004) describes several systems that add scents to Web content, where computer-controlled olfactory displays, such as iSmell (Washburn, et al., 2004,) and Osmooze (2011), are utilized in these systems. Another type of display, the air cannon olfactory display (Yanagida, et al., 2003), has been proposed and generates toroidal vortices of a scent in order to present it within a restricted space.

Nakamoto *et al.* (2001) designed an odor blender device that presents scents of virtual objects remotely. The system first analyzes the odors to be transmitted and describes each odor by using a composition ratio of scent elements. By using the ratio found by the smell analysis, on the receiver side, the target smell is reproduced with a feedback control by emitting scent elements contained within the receiver. However, this system cannot be used to present a random scent.

A wearable olfactory display with position sensors has also been developed (Yamada, et al., 2006). This display can present spatiality of olfaction in an outdoor environment by controlling the density of odor molecules. The system for transmitting the olfactory information consists of the aforementioned display, a sensing unit with three gas sensors, and a matching database. Translating the obtained olfactory information, the user experiences a real sense of smell through the system. Another system, called AROMA (Bodnar, et al., 2004), attempts to introduce the olfactory modality as a potential alternative to visual and auditory modalities for messaging notification. Experimental results indicate that, while the olfactory modality is less effective in delivering notifications than other modalities, it has less of a disruptive effect on a user's engagement in a primary task.

Addition of scents to image media, such as movies, has been proposed by a number of researchers. Okada & Aiba measured viewers' brainwaves to assess their mental state, and analyzed the relationship between scents and the feelings of viewers watching a movie. In fact, movies with olfactory information included along with audiovisual information have been produced (Okada & Aiba, 2003), but because the synthetic fragrance did not match well with the images and the scent lingering in the air was not eliminated, the movies could not be widely distributed. Smell-o-vision, the aroma-emitting digital sign technology was also created (NTT Communications, 2007).

Finally, a mobile phone service, "scent communication mobile" (NTT Communications, 2008), delivers scent via the Internet to create so-called "scent communication."

Further, Ademoye *et al.* (2009) researched the effect on the sense of reality when scents are added to the part of movie, and Pornpanomchai *et al.* (2009) built the system that embed the information of scent to the movie. Gottfried *et al.* (2003) studied the effects of images on recognition of scents.

It is clear that the scent presentation techniques of previous works were designed merely to create the sense of experiencing a scent. To do this, higher densities and longer presentation times of scent than are actually necessary were used, and thus all of the techniques were hindered by the problem of olfactory adaptation due to scent lingering in the air.

CHARACTERISTICS OF OLFACTION

Olfactory Threshold

The olfactory threshold is the value used to express the strength and weakness of a scent (Odor Control Association of Japan, 2003). Generally, three kinds of values are used for the olfactory threshold, which are detection threshold, recognition threshold, and differential threshold. There values are expressed by the units of mol (concentration), and mass percentage.

- **Detection Threshold:** The smallest density at which scent can be detected and where the user does not need to recognize the kind of smell.
- **Recognition Threshold:** The smallest density at which the kind of scent can be recognized, and its value reflects the ability of the user to express quality and characteristics of the scent.
- **Differential Threshold:** The density at which the user can distinguish the strength of a scent, where its value reflects the ability of the user to detect changes in the stimulus and to quantify the change.

However, because the olfactory threshold is a measurement of the lowest olfactory stimulus intensity at which an individual can perceive scent, this value does not reflect the intensity of the scent perceived.

Olfactory Adaptation

Olfactory adaptation is the phenomenon where sensory nerve activity of olfactory receptor is decreased by continuous stimulation of odor molecules. The time takes to get adaptation and the time takes to recover from adaptation differ according to the kinds of scent. Adaptation is gradually strengthened over time, and it is restored for short time (3-5 minutes) by eliminating the scent (Saito, 2004). In addition, there are various patterns of adaptation and those are influenced by kinds of scents and recognition factors.

PULSE EJECTION OF SCENT

Difficulty in chronological control of scents is caused by olfactory adaptation and scents lingering in the air, resulting from excess amounts and times in scent emissions. Hence, to achieve chronological control of scent emission, it is important to reduce these excesses, and this is possible if small-volume, intermittent emission of scent can be achieved. Based upon this idea, the olfactory display described in next section has been constructed, which enables an emission of scent for a short period of time. We have named this emission "pulse ejection," which image is shown in Figure 1. Delta t represents the time of scent emission.

Olfactory Display

The developed olfactory display employs an inkjet mechanism to eject a jet broken into droplets from a small hole in the ink tank. In general, methods for emitting ink can be classified into thermal and piezo methods.

In the thermal method, a heater is installed in part of a narrow tube that is filled with ink. To emit the ink, bubbles are formed in the ink by instantaneous heating. This method is advantageous in terms of miniaturization as the structure is simple; however, it is difficult to stably control the ejection. Furthermore, there is the risk that the heat will degrade the ink.

In the piezo method, a piezoelectric element installed within the tube is energized to emit the ink. For this method, ejection control is comparatively simple, but miniaturization is difficult due to the mechanism containing the piezoelectric element being complex.

As a result, considering potential future miniaturization, the thermal method was selected for use in the developed olfactory display (Figure 2).

Looking at the display in more detail, it can set up a single scent-ejection head. This head is able to hold three small and one large tank, and hence the display can contain a maximum of four scents. There are 127 and 256 tiny holes in the heads connected to the small and 256 large tanks, respectively; moreover, the heads are adjustable and can emit scent from multiple holes at once. Thus, ejection can be from 0–127 holes for the small tanks and 0–256 holes for the large tank. An ejection heater is installed in the liquid route, which continues to the exit hole. The ejection

Figure 2. Olfactory display

Figure 1. Image of pulse ejection

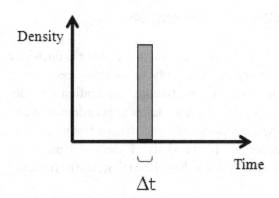

heater produces heat so that bubbles are generated in scent filled in the liquid route. By using the pressure generated by bubbling scent, the scent ejection head emits the scent from the exit hole. The liquid route is filled with scent that is loaded in liquid room, which is set backward. The scent in the liquid room is supplied along the supply route from the scent tank. We denote the average ejection quantity per hole as the "Unit Average Ejection Quantity" (UAEQ), and the number of holes emitting at one time as "the Number of Simultaneous Ejections" (NSE). The UAEQ from one hole in the heads on the small tanks is 4.7 pico-litters and 7.3 pico-litters for that on the large tank. Upon examination, it was confirmed that these values of UAEQ are approximately constant, independent of the residual quantity of ink. In addition, the user can set the number of ejection times in 100 ms from each hole to be from 1 to 150. We denote this as the "volume" and, by setting the volume, ejection control of 667 ms for a

unit is possible. In the experiments we conducted, which are described in later sections, we used the scents, which are diluted into 5% by adding water and ethanol.

Finally, the display is equipped with a fan, and there are 10 settings for the wind velocity control in the range of 0.8–1.8 m/s. Scents in the tanks are emitted from the gray-colored square in Figure 3 and ride on the wind from the fun. To avoid the users to feel the timing of scent ejection from the wind, it is set to run the fan for the whole time when the display is on.

Effectiveness of Pulse Ejection

Using continuous and intermittent ejection, an experiment comparing the detection thresholds before and after scent emission was conducted in order to validate the pulse ejection. The procedure was as follows.

Figure 3. Structural outline of olfactory display

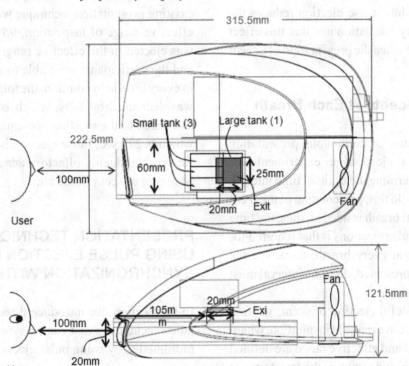

1. Before presenting the scents by continuous/
    intermittent ejection, measure the detection
    threshold for each participant.
2. After presenting the scent for 30 or 60 s by
    continuous or intermittent ejection, again
    measure the detection threshold for each
    participant.

For intermittent ejection, we used a breath sensor to determine the participant's inspiration rate and presented lavender in 0.3 s pulses. The breath sensor senses temperature change in air inhaled through the nose. The temperature detection element is the NTC (Negative Temperature Coefficient) thermistor which is widely used as a temperature detection element and has a negative temperature characteristic that resistance falls when temperature rises.

The result showed that, when the scents were presented for 30 s, the detection threshold increased 2.8 fold for continuous presentation and 1.5 fold for pulse ejection. Moreover, for the 60 s scent presentations, the threshold increased 3.5 fold for continuous presentation and 1.6 fold for pulse ejection. Thus, pulse ejection reduces the effect of olfactory adaptation and that this effect does not increase when the presentation of a scent is extended.

Presenting Scents at Each Breath

To provide a sense of continuous presentation when using pulse ejection, an experiment was conducted to determine the optimal time interval for the pulses. To do this, presentation of the scent at each individual breath is needed; thus, the time interval for the pulse ejections is that required for presenting scent at every breath; to reduce the amount of scent presented, the time interval must be as long as possible.

To avoid wasteful ejection of scent, we first measured the effective range in inspiration, where the limiting point and effective range are defined as follows. The limiting point is the latest time at which a user can still detect scent in the end phase of inspiration. The effective range is the time between the start of inspiration and limiting point.

It is well known that able-bodied people breathe approximately 12 times per minute at rest (Tanaka & Kakizaki, 2003). In breathing, the ratio of inspiration to expiration is 1:1.5, meaning that a person inhales for an average of 2 s at rest. Therefore, we measured the effective range for 10 participants when they were inhaling for 2 s, where breathing of the participants was regulated by sound cues to ensure that the inspiration period was 2 s.

This resulted in finding an average value for the limiting point of the participants of 1.5 s, and a minimum value of 1.3 s. These findings revealed that scent ejected in pulses from the start of inspiration until 1.3 s later was detected for all participants. The effective range is therefore from the start of inspiration to 1.3 s.

We verified this time interval by conducting a further experiment with 10 participants, comparing the existing presentation technique and scent pulse ejection at a time interval of 1.3 s. As a result, while the scents presented by using existing presentation technique was 100% in the effective range of inspiration, 98% of the scent was ejected in the effective range of inspiration and the participants were able to sense the scent in every breath. In addition, the total ejection time was decreased by 80%, which is 48 sec, when compared to the existing presentation technique which is 272 sec. Pulse ejection is, therefore, effective in reducing olfactory adaptation and the lingering of scent in the air.

PRESENTATION TECHNIQUES USING PULSE EJECTION FOR SYNCHRONIZATION WITH MEDIA

In this section, we introduce three scent presentation techniques that can be synchronized with multimedia, by using pulse ejection.

Presenting Two Different Scents at Once

In multimedia content, several objects having a scent frequently appear on the screen at the same time. For example, in a movie scene where someone eats an apple in a forest, both the apple and forest have distinctive scents. If both scents are presented at the same time, such that we can detect them both simultaneously, it should enhance the sense of reality because we can perceive, by olfaction, that there are two objects present. As mentioned previously, for an enhanced sense of realism it is also important to convey the relative distance between objects; thus, we would expect to perceive a strong scent of the apple in the foreground and a weak scent of the forest in the background. To this end, we have measured olfactory characteristics and constructed a presentation technique that is able to express the depth between foreground and background.

To create the technique, we measured the separable detection threshold of olfaction, that is, the minimum ejection time interval in which a participant could discriminate two individually emitted pulses.

An experiment was conducted with 20 participants. Scents were presented for a single breath in two patterns: two pulse ejections, and a single pulse ejection as a control. The gap between the two pulse ejections was set to be in the range of 0.1 and 1.5 s in 0.1 s intervals. The scent pattern was executed synchronously with inspiration, and the participants were asked to reveal the number of times that they noticed the scents. Here, we judged that the participant could separately detect two smells when their answer was correct for the two pulse ejection pattern. As a result, the average for the separable detection threshold was 1.2 s.

Using this result, we then constructed a scent presentation technique to express distance. However, to express a distance relation, it is necessary to alter the densities of the two scents presented in a single breath—highlighting the foreground scent by increasing its ejection quantity, while reducing the relative ejection quantity of the background scent. Therefore, to determine a suitable ejection quantity difference between the two scents and a suitable order of presentation to enable the user to experience the two scents and distance relation, we developed two methods of scent presentation within a single breath. Here, as the perceived intensity of a stimulus is proportional to the logarithm of the physical magnitude of stimulus, ejection levels were set where level 1 was the ejection quantity of the detection threshold and three further ejection levels were created by increasing stepwise logarithmically from level 1 to level 3.

The first method involved two pulse ejections, where the relative intensity of the stimuli was changed by varying the ejection amounts of the first and second pulses. This method is hereafter referred to as the "pulse mode" method. Figure 4 displays examples of this method by using the black-colored bar as a scent of closer object and gray-colored bar as a scent of further object, where (a) shows a pattern for presenting the higher ejection quantity scent first, and (b) and (c) show patterns for presenting the higher ejection quantity scent second. Note that (b) shows a large difference between the densities of the two scents, and (c) shows a smaller difference.

We considered that using the pulse mode may mean that the lower ejection quantity scent is only sensed slightly, and so developed a second presentation method—the "base mode" method—in which the presentation of the lower ejection quantity scent is over a long period and the higher ejection quantity scent is presented by pulse ejection (Figure 5). Here, we refer to the weaker scent with long presentation time as the "base scent," and the stronger scent presented by pulse ejection as the "single pulse." Additionally, the base scent had the lowest ejection quantity of the scents tested. Figure 5 shows patterns for the base mode method in which the base scent is presented either first (left) or second (right).

Figure 4. Image of pulse mode

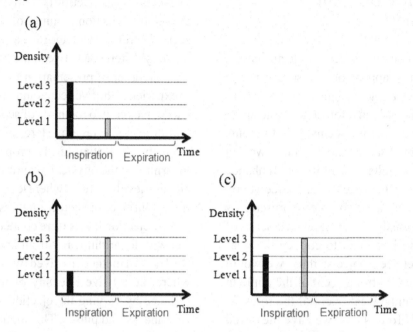

We began by examining a suitable technique for inferring a distance relation between two scents in a single breath. The experiment was conducted by presenting three scents, by pulse ejection, to 22 participants (18 men, 4 women), who were students in their 20s majoring in information technology. For the pattern using level 2 ejection quantity, since the standard deviation is large, the results showed large individual variation in the perception of scent; in other words, there is no correlation in the results when using level 2 ejection quantity. Further, when two scents were presented in one breath with only a single level of difference, due to a tendency for the difference in perceived distance to be assessed subjectively, this was not universally perceived by all of the participants. Thus, in order to best express distance relationships, it is necessary to present two scents with greater than fourfold stimulus difference (i.e., more than 2 levels of difference).

Moreover, the detection ratio results indicate that it was difficult to detect two scents when the high ejection quantity scent was presented first and the low ejection quantity scent was presented

Figure 5. Image of base mode

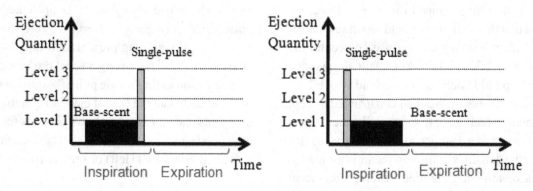

second, irrespective of whether the pulse mode or base mode method was used. It is thought that the second, weaker stimulus is difficult to detect due to the olfactory adaptation caused by the first, stronger scent. In addition, we had explained to the participants that stronger scents related to the foreground and weaker scents to the background.

We concluded that a scent presentation method which presents the first scent at level 1 ejection quantity and then the second scent at level 3 ejection quantity is suitable for expressing distance relations in a single breath cycle.

From this result, an experiment for consecutive breaths was conducted. In this experiment, we presented two scents in each breath, over six consecutive breaths, and measured the human olfactory characteristics related to this. The experiment was conducted by using pulse ejections of three scents with 20 participants (17 men, 3 women), who were also students in their 20s majoring in information technology. We used a pattern for the pulse mode method in which a level 1 pulse was presented first and level 3 pulse presented second, and a pattern for the base mode method in which the base scent was presented first and a single pulse presented second. We prepared two patterns in which the presentation frequency was changed: one in which the same pattern as used for the single breath experiments was presented 6 times consecutively (the ratio for the number of scent presentations for the first and second scent was 1:1), and another in which the second scent in each single breath was presented twice more than the first (i.e., with a ratio of 1:2). We found that the method which presents the scents by pulse mode with a ratio of 1:2 was most suitable for expressing foreground-background distance relations in multiple breath cycles.

Creating Dynamic Perspective

The perspective often changes in visual and audio information. For example, by using the zoom function of a camera and by adjusting the volume of an audio recording, we can create dynamic perspective easily. However, even if the transmitter in scent media presents scents using a similar method to those for images and sounds, the receiver does not actually sense this. Hence, we have developed a scent presentation technique, by using pulse ejection, to create dynamic perspective for a multimedia viewer.

To realize dynamic perspective using pulse ejection, we first measured the quantity of pulse ejection that would create static perspectives of distance and proximity, that is, "far" and "near." As the perceived intensity of a stimulus is proportional to the logarithm of the physical magnitude of stimulus, ejection levels were set where level 1 was the ejection quantity of the detection threshold and three further ejection levels were created by increasing stepwise logarithmically from level 1 to level 3.

Next, two different scents were presented with two pulse ejections in one inspiration. This pair of fragrances was used for all combinations of the three ejection levels—a total of 18 trials. Each participant was instructed to choose one of four images, which were most appropriate as to how the fragrances were perceived. The four images consisted of a sprig of lavender and a lemon that appeared to be either near or far. The order and the ejection level for the two scents were presented randomly.

20 participants took part in a total of 18 trials for each combination of order and ejection level of emitted scents. The results of this were that all of the participants chose the "far" image when they smelled a scent at ejection level 1, and chose the "near" image when they smelled a scent at ejection level 3. Thus, a scent presented at level 1 gives an impression of distance, while that presented at level 3 gives an impression of proximity. In contrast, at level 2, there was variation in the participants' choices, suggesting an impression of an intermediate distance.

Using these results, we then constructed a presentation technique to create dynamic perspec-

Figure 6. Method to create dynamic perspective using pulse ejection

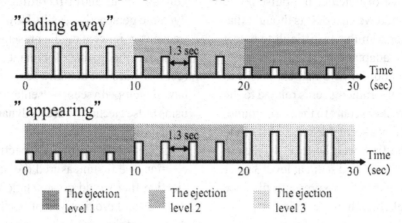

tive from scents by using pulse ejection shown in Figure 6. As discussed in the previous section, receivers can detect a scent at any timing of inspiration when scent is ejected in 1.3 s intervals. Again, it is well known that one breath cycle at rest in able-bodied people takes about 5 s. Therefore, in this experiment, to allow receivers to sense a fragrance for around six breath cycles, scent was ejected in 1.3 s intervals over a 30 s period. To narrow the changes in the intensity of the scents, ejection at level 2 was inserted between the ejections at level 1 and level 3. The result was then compared with that from an experiment using continuous presentation.

The findings showed that about 18 of the 20 participants felt a change in perspective when the scents were presented using pulse ejection. Conversely, for continuous ejection, even though the quantities of scents were precisely controlled, dynamic perspective was not expressed, once more due to olfactory adaptations and the lingering of scent in the air. Thus, a technique to represent dynamic perspective has been constructed.

Rapid Switching of Scents

Finally, visual/audio information often shifts from one subject to another chronologically. In movies in particular, scenes change from one

Figure 7 . Image of pulse ejection pattern for scent switch

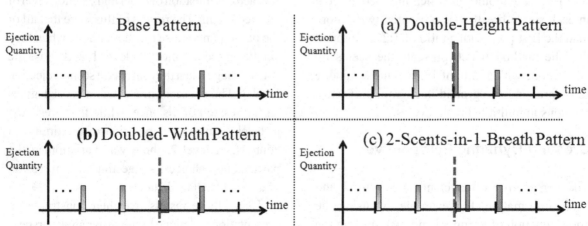

showing object with a particular scent to another showing a different object with a different scent. In this situation, changes in scent, in accordance with the shifts in scenes, deepen the viewer's sense of reality. Accordingly, we constructed a presentation technique that enables the switching of scents rapidly.

Initially, to find the most suitable technique to switch scents, we prepared an experiment with four patterns presented by pulse ejection and measured the time that the participants took to recognize the scent switch. The patterns, shown in Figure 7, were: "Base Pattern," in which the pulse ejection did not change when the scent altered; "Doubled-Height Pattern," where the height of the pulse doubled when the scent switched; "Doubled-Width Pattern," where the width of the pulse doubled when the scent changed; and "2-Scents-in-1-Breath Pattern," in which the previous and upcoming scent were presented within a single breath. Here, to avoid the effect such as participants notice the scent switch not from the olfactory information by from the visual information, we decided to avoid the use of images. The procedure for the experiment was as follows.

1. The scents were presented in synch with the participant's breathing for 6 inspirations.
2. The participants were asked to click a mouse when they sensed a switch in scent.
3. The time taken to recognize the switch was calculated from the difference between the actual time of the switch and the time that the participant sensed the switch.

The results from an experiment conducted with 20 participants showed that the time to recognize the switch of scent was minimal when the scents were presented using the "Doubled-Height Pattern."

To explore rapid switches in scent, we conducted another experiment to find the shortest period in which a scent could be changed when

using the "Doubled-Height Pattern." From this experiment, which used the same 20 participants, we found that the shortest period for recognition of a switch was around two breaths. We also measured the limit of continuous scent switching using the same "Doubled-Height Pattern" and minimum switching period. The results showed that sensing of a switch is still possible after more than 16 changes.

CONCLUSION AND FUTURE WORK

Many of the currently proposed presentation techniques for scents are at the level of either presenting the scents or not, and precise control has been difficult. However, for practical utilization of scents to express the atmosphere of environments, presence of objects, sense of the season, and an increase in the perception of reality and understanding of contents, precise control cannot be neglected.

In this research, to achieve precise control of scent presentation, we have developed an olfactory display that presents scents by pulse ejection. Using pulse ejection reduces the quantity of scents presented and due to problems, such as olfactory adaptations and scents lingering in the air, have been largely overcome. Applying this pulse ejection technique, we have constructed three scent presentation methods, all of which can be synchronized to multimedia, to express distance relations between foregrounds and backgrounds, to create dynamic perspectives, and to switch scents rapidly.

By further advancing the measurement of olfactory characteristics in the future, we will be able to use scents easily, and we are now focusing on measuring the effects of scents presented by pulse ejection in synch with movies. This technology brings us closer to being able to provide a greater sense of realism in multimedia environments.

ACKNOWLEDGMENT

This work is supported in part by a Grantin-Aid for Scientific Research (B), 2011, 23300049 from the Ministry of Education, Culture, Sport, Science, and Technology in Japan.

REFERENCES

Ademoye, O. A., & Ghinea, G. (2009). Synchronization of olfaction-enhanced multimedia. *IEEE Transactions on Multimedia, 11*(3), 561–565. doi:10.1109/TMM.2009.2012927

Bodnar, A., Corbett, R., & Nekrasovski, D. (2004). Aroma: Ambient awareness through olfaction in a messaging application. In *Proceedings of the ICMI 2004,* (pp. 183–190). ICMI.

Communications, N. T. T. (2007). *NTT com to test aroma-emitting digital signage.* Retrieved from http://www.ntt.com/release_e/news07/0010/1017.html

Communications, N. T. T. (2008). *NTT com to pilot test mobile fragrance communication service.* Retrieved from http://www.ntt.com/release_e/news08/0004/0407.html

Gottfried, J., & Dolan, R. (2003). The nose smells what the eye sees: Crossmodal visual facilitation of human olfactory perception. *Neuron, 39*(2), 375–386. doi:10.1016/S0896-6273(03)00392-1

Heilig, M. L. (1962). *US patent #3050870.* Washington, DC: United States Patent Office.

Kaye, J. (2004). Making scents: Aromatic output for hci. *Interaction, 11*, 48–61. doi:10.1145/962342.964333

Kim, J., Kim, D., Han, D., Byun, H., Ham, Y., & Jung, W. (2006). A proposal representation, digital coding and clustering of odor information. *Computational Intelligence and Security, 1*, 872–877.

Michael, G. A., Acquot, L., Millot, J.-L., & Brand, G. (2003). Ambient odors modulate visual attentional capture. *Neuroscience Letters, 352*, 221–225. doi:10.1016/j.neulet.2003.08.068

Ministry of Posts and Telecommunications in Japan. (2007). *Reports of the association for information and communications technology using five senses.* Tokyo, Japan: Ministry of Posts and Telecommunications in Japan.

Nakamoto, T., Nakahira, Y., Hiramatsu, H., & Moriizumi, T. (2001). Odor recorder using active odor sensing system. *Sensors and Actuators. B, Chemical, 2*, 465–469. doi:10.1016/S0925-4005(01)00587-1

Odor Control Association of Japan. (2003). *A term and a commentary of a odor.* Tokyo, Japan: Odor Control Association of Japan.

Okada, K., & Aiba, S. (2003). Toward the actualization of broadcasting service with smell information. *Institute of Image Information and Television Engineering of Japan Technical Report, 27*(64), 31–34.

Osmooze. (2012). *Website.* Retrieved from http://www.osmooze.com/

Pornpanomchai, C., Threekhunprapa, A., Pongrasamiroj, K., & Sukklay, P. (2009). Subsmell: Multimedia with a simple olfactory display. [PSIVT.]. *Proceedings of PSIVT, 2009*, 462–472.

Saito, S. (2004). Various time dependence of strength of sense for smell showed consecutively. *Japan Association on Odor Environment, 35*(1), 17–21. doi:10.2171/jao.35.17

Tanaka, K., & Kakizaki, F. (2003). *Theory and the technology of the respiratory movement medical treatment.* Tokyo, Japan: Medical View Co., Ltd.

Tominaga, K., Honda, S., Ohsawa, T., Shigeno, H., Okada, K., & Matsushita, Y. (2001). Friend park — Expression of the wind and the scent on virtual space. In *Proceedings of the Seventh International Conference on Virtual Systems and Multimedia,* (pp. 507-515). IEEE.

Washburn, D. A., Jones, L. M., Satya, R. V., Bowers, C. A., & Cortes, A. (2004). Olfactory use in virtual environment training. *Modeling and Simulation Magazine, 2*(3).

Yamada, T., Yokoyama, S., Tanikawa, T., Hirota, K., & Hirose, M. (2006). Wearable olfactory display: Using odor in outdoor environment. In *Proceedings of the IEEE Virtual Reality Conference,* (pp. 199 – 206). IEEE Press.

Yanagida, Y., Noma, H., Tetsutani, N., & Tomono, A. (2003). An unencumbering, localized olfactory display. In *CHI 2003 Extended Abstracts* (pp. 988–989). New York, NY: ACM Press. doi:10.1145/765891.766109

ADDITIONAL READING

Honma, T., & Wakamatsu, H. (2001). Telemedicine by the compact type of assist-respirator with a new ventilation pattern. *The Japanese Society of Clinical Physiology, 31*(6), 297–304.

Kadowaki, A., Noguchi, D., Sugimoto, S., Noguchi, D., Bannai, Y., & Okada, K. (2010). Development of a high-performance olfactory display and measurement of olfactory characteristics for pulse ejections. In *Proceedings of the 2010 10th Annual International Symposium on Applications and the Internet,* (pp. 1-6). IEEE.

Kadowaki, A., Sato, J., Bannai, Y., & Okada, K. (2007). Presentation technique of scent to avoid olfactory adaptation. In *Proceedings of the 17th International Conference on Arti☐cial Reality and Telexistence,* (pp. 97–104). IEEE.

Kadowaki, A., Sato, J., Bannai, Y., & Okada, K. (2008). Measurement and modeling of olfactory responses to pulse ejection of odors. *Japan Association on Odor Environment, 39*(1), 36–43. doi:10.2171/jao.39.36

Malnic, B., Hirono, J., Sato, T., & Buck, L. B. (1999). Combinatorial receptor codes for odors. *Cell, 96,* 713–723. doi:10.1016/S0092-8674(00)80581-4

Michael, G. A., Acquot, L., Millot, J.-L., & Brand, G. (2003). Ambient odors modulate visual attentional capture. *Neuroscience Letters, 352,* 221–225. doi:10.1016/j.neulet.2003.08.068

Miyashita, H., Segawa, R., Bannai, Y., & Okada, K. (2010). A control method of olfactory production with scents array. *TVRSJ, 15*(4), 523–530.

Noguchi, D., Ohtsu, K., Bannai, Y., & Okada, K. (2009). Scent presentation expressing two smells of different intensity simultaneously. In *Proceedings of the 2009 Joint Virtual Reality Conference of EGVE - ICAT – EuroVR,* (pp. 53-60). ICAT.

Noguchi, D., Sugimoto, S., Bannai, Y., & Okada, K. (2011). Time characteristics of olfaction in a single breath. In *Proceedings of the 2011 Annual Conference on Human Factors in Computing Systems,* (pp. 83-92). ACM Press.

Ohtsu, K., Sato, J., Bannai, Y., & Okada, K. (2009). Measurement of olfactory characteristics for two kinds of scent in a single breath. [IFIP.]. *Proceedings of IFIP INTERACT, 2009,* 306–318.

RS Components Ltd. (2012). *Website.* Retrieved from http://www.rswww.co.jp/cgibin/bv/home/Home.jsp?cacheID=jpie

Sato, J., Ohtsu, K., Bannai, Y., & Okada, K. (2008). Pulse ejection technique of scent to create dynamic perspective. [ICAT.]. *Proceedings of ICAT, 2008*, 167–174.

Sato, J., Ohtsu, K., Bannai, Y., & Okada, K. (2009). Effective presentation technique of scent using small ejection quantities of odor. [IEEE Press.]. *Proceedings of the IEEE, VR2009*, 151–158.

Shibuya, T., & Tonoike, T. (2002). *Odor receptors*. Tokyo, Japan: Fragrance Journal Ltd.

Sugimoto, S., Noguchi, D., Bannai, Y., & Okada, K. (2009). Ink jet olfactory display enabling instantaneous switches of scents. In *Proceeding of the ACM Multimedia 2010 International Conference*, (pp. 301-310). ACM Press.

Tanikawa, T., Hirota, K., Tomoya, Y., Yokoyama, S., & Hirose, M. (2006). Wearable olfactory display: Using odor in outdoor environment. [IEEE Press.]. *Proceedings of IEEE Virtual Reality, 2006*, 199–206.

Tonoike, T. (1968). Recording and analysis of olfactory evoked potentials on the human scalp. *Summaries of Reports of the Electrotechnical Laboratory, 863*, 1–76.

Tonoike, T., & Shibuya, T. (2003). *Smell and brain behavior*. Tokyo, Japan: Fragrance Journal Ltd.

Wada, M. (2005). *An approach to the study of brain waves induced by olfactory stimulation*. Tokyo, Japan: Fragrance Journal Ltd.

Washburn, D. A., Jones, L. M., Satya, R. V., Bowers, C. A., & Cortes, A. (2004). Olfactory use in virtual environment training. *Modeling and Simulation Magazine, 2*(3). Retrieved from http://www.modelingandsimulation.org/issue7/olfactory.html

Woodrow, H. F., & Karpman, B. (1917). A new olfactometric technique and some results. *Journal of Experimental Psychology, 31*, 447.

Yokoyama, S., Tanikawa, T., Hirota, K., & Hirose, M. (2004). Olfactory field simulation using wearable olfactory display. *Transactions of the Virtual Reality Society of Japan, 9*(3), 265–274. Retrieved from http://www.cyber.rcast.u-tokyo.ac.jp/project/nioi

KEY TERMS AND DEFINITIONS

Detection Threshold: The smallest density at which scent can be detected and where the user does not need to recognize the kind of smell.

Differential Threshold: The density at which the user can distinguish the strength of a scent, where its value reflects the ability of the user to detect changes in the stimulus and to quantify the change.

Number of Simultaneous Ejections (NSE): The number of holes emitting at one time.

Olfactory Adaptation: The phenomenon where sensory nerve activity of olfactory receptor is decreased by continuous stimulation of odor molecules.

Pulse Ejection: The emission of scents for a short period of time.

Recognition Threshold: The smallest density at which the kind of scent can be recognized, and its value reflects the ability of the user to express quality and characteristics of the scent.

Separable Detection Threshold of Olfaction: The minimum ejection time interval in which a participant could discriminate two individually emitted pulses.

Unit Average Ejection Quantity (UAEQ): Average ejection quantity per hole.

Chapter 21
Incorporating Fluid Dynamics Considerations into Olfactory Displays

Haruka Matsukura
Tokyo University of Agriculture and Technology, Japan

Hiroshi Ishida
Tokyo University of Agriculture and Technology, Japan

ABSTRACT

In this chapter, the authors describe fluid dynamics considerations regarding odor dispersal in real environments and their relationship with realistic odor presentation using an olfactory display. The authors propose the use of a Computational Fluid Dynamics (CFD) simulation in conjunction with the olfactory display. A CFD solver is employed to calculate the turbulent airflow field in a given environment and the dispersal of odor molecules from their source. The simulation result is used to reproduce realistic changes in the odor concentration with time and space at the nose. The results of sensory tests are presented as a demonstration of CFD-based odor presentation. The effect of body heat on odor dispersal in indoor environments and how it affects odor perception is also discussed.

INTRODUCTION

An olfactory display is a device that generates odors in the form of a gaseous vapor of odorous chemical molecules and presents them to the user. It can be used to add special effects to computer

games, for example, by creating a game with a "Press to Smell" button. Presenting a smell in response to a click on the button will provide the user of the game with a completely new experience that no traditional game machine can provide (Nakamoto, et al., 2008). The olfactory display

DOI: 10.4018/978-1-4666-2521-1.ch021

Copyright © 2013, IGI Global. Copying or distributing in print or electronic forms without written permission of IGI Global is prohibited.

should at least be able to generate a single type of odor associated with the button. However, most game machines can generate different sounds and images; therefore, it is natural to expect them to have multiple "Press to Smell" buttons. Thus, most research on olfactory displays so far has thus been devoted to the development of hardware devices capable of multiple odor generation and rapid on-off switching.

Practically any color can be generated by mixing three primary colors, i.e., red, green, and blue, because our eyes have only three types of color receptors. However, considering the complexity and diversity of olfactory receptor cells in mammalian noses (Buck & Axel, 1991), it is unlikely that an arbitrary smell can be generated simply by mixing a small set of primary odors. Therefore, in a typical olfactory display system, one ready-made mixture of odorous chemicals in liquid form is prepared for the generation of each specific smell to be presented to the user. The olfactory display system developed by Nakamoto and Yoshikawa (2006), for example, can hold up to eight bottles of solutions containing different mixtures of odorants. An odor vapor in the headspace of a selected bottle is delivered to the user's nose through tubing. The odor can be switched from one to another using computer-controlled solenoid valves. The intensity of the odor presented to the user can also be changed using the solenoid valves to dilute the odor vapor with clean air. An olfactory display system developed by Sato et al. (2008) uses ink jet devices to attain more precise control of odor concentrations and rapid switching between odors.

These sophisticated olfactory displays also allow attempts at realistic odor presentation. The concentrations of odorants reaching the nose in real environments vary with time and position. Therefore, it is expected that olfactory displays can provide users with a realistic experience if they reproduce the change in the odor concentration reaching the nose. For example, if the odors are intended to enhance the reality of a specific

scene in a movie, their concentrations should be carefully adjusted. The appropriate release rate of an odorant for a faint scent of flowers drifting in the air can be extremely different from that for a strong unpleasant odor sensed by the nose. If the scene is changed from a distant flower garden to a close-up view of roses, the release rate of the odorant should be increased accordingly.

To reproduce the change in the perceived odor intensity while walking through an environment, Yamada et al. (2006) assumed a mathematical model for odor distribution in a virtual world. They developed a wearable olfactory display system. In their experiments, each subject was asked to carry the wearable olfactory display and move around in the given space to find the position of a virtual odor source. The concentration of the odor released from the wearable olfactory display at the subject's nose was adjusted assuming isotropic diffusion of a gaseous chemical substance into the air. However, this assumption holds only in environments with extremely weak airflow (Murlis, et al., 1992). Moreover, the odor distribution in a given environment is affected by the presence of obstacles. Consider the scenes shown in Figure 1, for example. In Figure 1(A), a woman is reading a menu in an Indian curry restaurant. When the curry is ready to be served from the kitchen, as shown in Figure 1(B), the woman sitting at the table would perceive a faint smell of curry. When she walks toward the kitchen, as shown in Figure 1(C), the smell of curry would gradually become stronger. In Figure 1(D), the woman is looking into the kitchen over the counter. She would then sense a much stronger smell because most of the odorants evaporating from the curry pot are confined to the kitchen. Only a small portion of the odorants emerges from the opening above the counter and spreads throughout the restaurant.

Therefore, we proposed incorporating Computational Fluid Dynamics (CFD) simulations into odor presentation (Ishida, et al., 2008; Matsukura, et al., 2009). Various physics-based simulations have already been employed to make

Figure 1. Scenes in an Indian curry restaurant. (A) A woman is reading the menu. (B) A waitress is about to serve an Indian curry dish from the kitchen. (C) Closer view of the kitchen. A counter separates the kitchen from the dining space of the restaurant. (D) View of the kitchen from above the counter.

realistic computer graphics animations, but they have rarely been used for odor presentation. In the proposed odor presentation procedure, a physical model of the given virtual environment is prepared. Then a CFD simulation is conducted to determine the airflow field and odor concentration distribution in the model. The concentration of the odor vapor presented to the user is adjusted according to the user's assumed position in the virtual environment. The change in odor intensity that the user would sense in a real environment is thus reproduced in the virtual environment. However, during the course of our initial sensory test to determine the effectiveness of the proposed method, the method was not always successful. We found discrepancies between our olfactory sensations in real life and the experience of the CFD-based olfactory display. To identify the causes of these problems, we conducted further CFD simulations and sensory tests. Here we show some of the findings of these investigations.

BACKGROUND

All gas molecules at temperatures above absolute zero are in random thermal motion. When odor molecules are released into the air from their source, they gradually spread via the random thermal motion. This process is well known as molecular diffusion. However, it is a widespread misconception that the spatial distribution of the released odor molecules is fully determined by molecular diffusion. In reality, molecular diffusion is an extremely slow process. The typical diffusion constant of a volatile chemical such as ethanol in air is 0.2 cm^2/s (Dusenbery, 1992). The characteristic diffusion length of gas molecules in 1 h is calculated to be only 50 cm, which means that most of the gas molecules remain within a 50-cm radius of their source location even 1 h after being released from the source in air.

On the other hand, in almost all outdoor environments, the wind velocity overpowers this slow molecular diffusion. When we feel wind blowing on our faces, its velocity exceeds 20 cm/s. Odor molecules released into the air are immediately carried away from the source location by the wind. The transport of odor molecules by fluidic air motion also dominates molecular diffusion in most indoor environments. Even in a closed room, a small temperature variation causes convective air currents of the order of a few centimeters per second (Ishida, et al., 2008). Odor molecules released from their source are carried by this airflow and spread mostly in the downwind direction.

Another important factor that determines the odor distribution is the airflow's turbulence. Most flows we encounter are turbulent and contain a number of eddies of many different length scales (Murlis, et al., 1992). A puff of odor molecules released into air is therefore mixed with the surrounding air by these eddies while being transported by the main flow. As a result, odor molecules spread much faster in a turbulent flow field than in a laminar field. Odor dispersal in a given environment can thus be simulated by simulating the development of the airflow velocity field in that environment and calculating the advection/diffusion of odor molecules in that field. In a typical indoor environment, the main forces that generate air currents include spatial temperature variations and air conditioners. In biology, it is well known that various properties of the flow that carries odorant molecules affect animals' odor perception and olfactory-mediated behavior (Vickers, 2000).

CFD-BASED ODOR PRESENTATION

Odor Presentation with a Movie Clip

To test the idea of CFD-based odor presentation, we prepared a sample software application that presents an odor to the user with appropriate intensities synchronously with a movie clip. The

scenario modeled by the application is shown in Figure 2(A). The user is represented by a small animal, e.g., a rabbit that walks in a room along the path shown in Figure 2(A). Three teapots are placed in the room. Pot 1 is assumed to be full of peach-flavored tea, and the others are assumed to be empty. A vertical screen (90-cm wide, 180-cm high, and 4-cm deep) placed between pots 1 and 2 disturbs the distribution of the peach smell and therefore adds complexity to the modeled situation. The walking speed of the animal is assumed

Figure 2. (A) Room model with three teapots and a screen. A small animal such as a rabbit moves into this room and sniffs the teapots one by one. (B) Computational model of the room for CFD simulation.

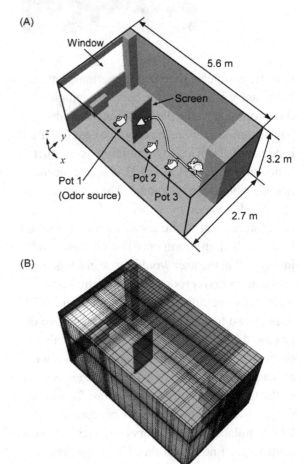

to be 10 cm/s. The animal makes a stop at each teapot for 10 s to check its smell. It takes 70 s for the animal to walk the complete path and finish checking the smell of all the teapots. During this 70-s period, a movie clip is played back on a computer, and images from the animal's point of view are presented on an LCD monitor, as shown in Figure 3(A). Snapshots captured from the movie clip are shown in Figures 3(B)–(E). These images were taken from points B–E in Figure 4(A), which shows a top view of the room. The path starts at point B, and the animal stops to check the smell of the teapots at points C–E.

While the animal moves in the room, the smell of peaches is presented to the user through tubing. The peach smell is generated using a multi-component odor blender, and its intensity is changed by mixing the peach-scented vapor with

clean air using solenoid valves. The technical details of the blender are given elsewhere (Nakamoto & Yoshikawa, 2006). The tube for odor delivery is attached to a headset such that its tip is fixed near the user's nose, as shown in Figure 3(A). The concentration of the peach-scented vapor released from the tube is adjusted according to the distribution of the smell in the room and the position of the animal. Data on the odor distribution and its changes with time were collected in advance by an offline CFD simulation. The animal's nose is assumed to be 20 cm above the floor; therefore, odor distribution at this height is used for the odor presentation.

Figure 3. Odor presentation with a movie clip. (A) Setup of odor blender, tube for odor release, and laptop computer. (B)–(E) Snapshots captured from the movie clip.

Figure 4. Results of CFD simulation. (A) Airflow field and odor distribution on the horizontal plane 20 cm above the floor. Airflow velocity vectors, indicated by white arrows, are in the range of 0–9 cm/s. Points B–E are the locations where the images shown in Figures 3(B)–(E) were taken. (B) Airflow field and odor distribution on the vertical plane including the odor source. The white arrows are in the range of 0–5 cm/s. The higher velocities shown in (A) were observed at a height slightly lower than the arrows in the bottom row.

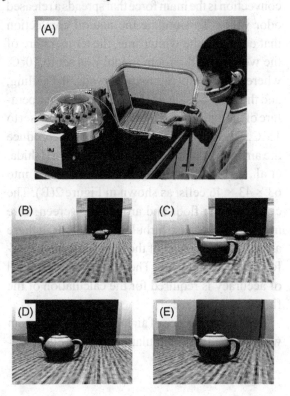

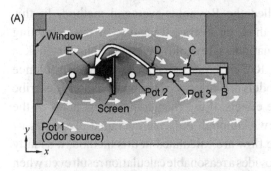

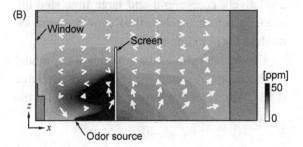

CFD Simulation

A CFD simulation was conducted to obtain data on the distribution of the odor vapor in the room shown in Figure 2(A) and its changes with time. There are three widely used approaches for numerical simulations of turbulent flows (Ferziger & Perić, 2002). In the most accurate approach called Direct Numerical Simulation (DNS), the Navier–Stokes equations that govern the motions of a viscous fluid are solved without averaging or approximation other than numerical discretizations. Turbulent flows contain fluctuations of a broad range of length and time scales. Therefore, the size of the spatial grid and the time step for solving the governing equations must be small enough to fully resolve the smallest fluctuations in the flow. For this reason, DNS is computationally expensive and is limited to flows with simple geometries, e.g., a flow in a round pipe. In the approach called Large Eddy Simulation (LES), the governing equations are solved only for the large-scale motions of the flow. Models are introduced to approximately describe the effects of the sub-grid scale motions of the flow, and thus, the computational cost is reduced. The least computationally demanding approach is called the Reynolds-averaged method. In this method, an averaged version of the governing equations (Reynolds-Averaged Navier–Stokes or RANS equations) are solved. Turbulence models are introduced to approximately describe the effects of the fluctuating components of the flow. Although only the averaged properties of the flow are calculated in this method, it usually provides a reasonable calculation result even when a relatively coarse grid and large time step are used. Therefore, we chose the Reynolds-averaged method for our simulation.

Figure 2(B) shows the computational model of the room. A commercial software package (CFD2000, Adaptive Research) was used for the simulation. The governing equations including the Navier–Stokes equations and the diffusion-convection equation were solved using the finite volume method. The velocity field as well as the distributions of odorant concentration and temperature was obtained such that the mass, momentum, and thermal energy were conserved in each cell of the grid shown in Figure 2(B). To simplify the simulation, the three teapots and the animal were not placed in the room model, although in reality their presence slightly disturbs the airflow field and odor distribution. Pot 1 was assumed to contain the peach-flavored tea; therefore, a 5 cm × 5 cm region releasing odor vapor was set on the floor as an odor source at the location of pot 1. In the simulation, odor vapor with a concentration of 50000 ppm was released from the odor source at a flow rate of 500 ml/min. The molecular diffusion coefficient of the odorant into air was set to 0.1 cm^2/s. For simplicity, other properties of the odorant, including its density and specific heat, were assumed to be the same as those of air.

In a closed unairconditioned room, natural convection is the main force that spreads a released odor vapor. To simulate the natural convection that occurs in the wintertime, the temperature of the window in the room model was set to 10°C, whereas the temperature of all walls, the ceiling, and the floor was set to 15°C. The initial temperature of the air inside the room model was also set to 15°C. These conditions were chosen to reproduce the airflow field developed in a real room (Ishida, et al., 2011). The room model was divided into 63 × 43 × 46 cells, as shown in Figure 2(B). The cells near the floor and around the screen were made small because turbulence develops in these areas, and the spread of the odor molecules is affected by its intensity. Therefore, a certain level of accuracy is required for the calculation of the flow in those places.

An initial absence of air movement in the room was assumed in the simulation. First, the development of a convective airflow field for 900 s was calculated. Odorant release was then initiated, and the development of the odor distribution for 360 s was calculated. All calculations used the standard k–ε turbulence model with a time step of 0.05 s. This is the most standard and most widely used turbulence model for the Reynolds-averaged method. The turbulent kinetic energy, k, is an index showing the magnitude of the flow velocity fluctuations. This turbulent kinetic energy is dissipated at a certain rate, ε, because the small-scale fluctuations of the flow are damped owing to the viscosity of the fluid. In the k–ε turbulence model, the effect of turbulent fluctuations on the mean flow is modeled using these two parameters. As mentioned earlier, only the time-averaged values of the airflow velocity and odorant concentration are calculated. The computational complexity is reduced by not reproducing high-frequency fluctuations in the airflow velocity and odorant concentration, which are characteristic features of the turbulent flow field. The airflow velocity and odor concentration were recorded on a hard drive at 1-s intervals. The total time required for the calculation of the 1260-s time period was approximately 42 h using a 2.66 GHz Celeron processor.

The results of the CFD simulation are presented in Figure 4, which shows the airflow field and odor distribution at 360 s after odor release began. The airflow field in the room model was generated by the temperature difference between the window and the rest of the room. Because the window was set to a lower temperature, the air temperature near the window decreased and the air descended to the floor. Then, as shown in Figure 4(A), the descended air spread to the wall on the opposite side of the room. As a result, a circulating airflow field was established in the room model. As shown in Figure 4(B), the airflow arriving at the screen was deflected upward. Because the odor vapor released from the odor source was carried primarily by the airflow, the resultant odor distribution corresponded well to the airflow field.

Sensory Tests

We first conducted a sensory test with 94 subjects. Each subject experienced odor presentation with the movie clip by using the application software described in a previous section. Before the start of the application, the scenario assumed in the movie clip was explained to the subject. The concentration of the peach smell presented to the subject was determined on the basis of the time-series data obtained from the CFD simulation. The values of the odor concentration were extracted along the animal's path assuming that the animal started moving from point B in Figure 4(A) after 290 s of odor release. The extracted time-series data are shown in Figure 5. In the odor blender, the concentration of the released odor was adjusted by diluting the odor vapor coming from a vial containing a liquid odor sample (Nakamoto & Yoshikawa, 2006). Therefore, the set point for the odor concentration was given to the odor blender in the form of a mixing ratio of the original odor vapor emerging from a vial and clean air. At a set point of 100%, the odor vapor was released without dilution with clean air. At a set point of 60%, the released odor vapor was a 60:40 mixture of the original odor vapor and clean air. The odor blender accepts a set point value from 0% to 100% at 1% intervals.

To make the best use of the maximum dynamic range of the odor blender, the concentration values extracted from the CFD simulation were normalized such that the maximum concentration on the animal's path, which was observed at point E, was 100%. The normalized values of the odor concentration at points B, C, and D were 8%, 13%, and 26%, respectively. The detection threshold of the released smell was 3–5%. As the animal moves from point B to point D, the odor concentration generally increases. However, when the animal makes a detour around the screen after leaving point D, the value of the odor concentration falls by approximately 5%. Then, the concentration rises rapidly as the animal approaches point E.

Figure 5. Variation in the odor concentration observed along the path shown in Figure 4(A). C–E are the time periods in which the animal stopped at points C–E in Figure 4(A). It should be noted that only the averaged concentration at each location was calculated in the Reynolds-averaged method. The random fluctuations in the odor concentration were not reproduced in the simulation. Therefore, the odor concentration remained at a constant level as long as the animal stayed in a same position.

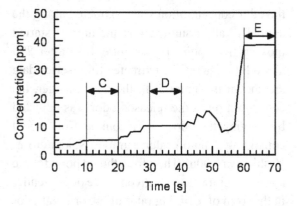

After each subject tried the application software, we asked each one which teapot contained the peach-flavored tea. The percentages of the subjects who chose pots 1, 2, and 3 were 47%, 22%, and 14%, respectively. In addition, 17% of the subjects answered "not sure." The most frequent answer was pot 1, as expected. However, more than half of the subjects gave wrong answers (pot 2, pot 3, and "not sure"). Most of the subjects who gave us wrong answers told us that they perceived the strongest peach smell at the pot they named in their answers, even though the odor at the highest concentration was presented in front of pot 1. This result motivated us to try almost the same sensory test but with certain modifications to increase the ratio of correct answers. In the first sensory test, presenting the odor with very high intensity to the subjects might have caused faster olfactory fatigue and/or saturation of the perceived odor intensity. Therefore, in the next sensory test, we decided to adjust the highest concentration of the presented odor according to individual variations in olfactory sensitivity.

The second sensory test, with adjusted odor intensities, was conducted with 123 subjects. The olfactory sensitivity of each subject was determined before the odor presentation. The peach smell at increasing concentrations (from 20% to 100% at intervals of 20%) was presented to the subject, and the subject determined the concentration level at which the peach smell was easily recognized but the smell intensity was not very strong. The maximum concentration of the odor released during the movie clip was set to this concentration level. For most subjects, the presented odor concentration was adjusted to lower values than that used in the initial sensory test (from 100% to 74% on an average). In this second sensory test, the percentages of the subjects who chose pots 1, 2, and 3 were 65%, 19%, and 11%, respectively. Only 5% of the subjects answered "not sure." The percentage of subjects giving the correct answer (pot 1) increased from 47% to 65%. The subjects who chose pot 1 for their answer told us that they indeed sensed the peach smell at the locations of pots 2 and 3 despite the reduced concentration but perceived a much stronger peach smell at pot 1. The results of this test suggest that the excessively high odor concentration in the initial test prevented the perception of contrast in the odor concentration.

EFFECT OF HUMAN BODY HEAT

CFD Simulation of Airflow around Human Body

In the sensory tests described in the previous section, an animal's motion in a room was modeled as it sniffed the teapots. The variations in the odor concentration at the height of the animal's nose were presented to the subjects. However, when the motion of an adult person was modeled, the odor presentation did not work well. In the CFD simulation result shown in Figure 4(B), the odor concentration at locations higher than 140 cm from the floor was extremely small. Therefore, no odor could be perceived at the height of the nose of an adult person walking in the room. In reality, we often sense an odor even if the source is located on the floor. To investigate the cause of this discrepancy between our initial CFD simulation and real environments, we conducted further CFD simulations.

The only reasonable explanation for the discrepancy that came to mind was the convection caused by body heat. To test this hypothesis, CFD simulations with and without a human body model were conducted. The room model used for these simulations was the same as that shown in Figure 2(B), but the screen was removed for simplicity. The parameters of the computational model, e.g., the position of the odor source, release rate of the odor vapor, and initial temperature distribution in the room, were set to the same values as in the initial simulation. A human body model, consisting of head and body parts, was prepared assuming a person of 160 cm in height. In the simulations both with and without the human body model, the development of a circulating convective airflow field in the room for 900 s was first calculated with no release of odor vapor. The release of the odorant was then initiated, and the development of the odor distribution with time was calculated. Figure 6 shows the odor concentration distributions and airflow fields at 90 s after odor release began.

In the simulation with the human body model, the temperature of the human model was not set at the beginning. It was assumed that no heat transfer occurred between the human model and the surrounding air until 60 s after odor release began. At that time, the temperatures of the head and body parts of the human model were set to 32°C and 27°C, respectively. These temperatures were determined using temperature measurements

made by a radiation thermometer for a person wearing clothes. This manipulation of temperature mimics the situation in which a person arrives at a location where the odor vapor had already spread along the floor.

As shown in Figure 6(A), upward air currents were generated around the human body model owing to the high body temperature. The maximum velocity of the airflow around the head part was approximately 25 cm/s. The velocity of the airflow caused by a human body was also experimentally validated by placing a hot-wire anemometer 20 cm above a human head. The maximum airflow velocity in a 1-min measurement was 23 cm/s, which agrees well with the simulation result. It should be noted that the detection threshold of airflow depends on its temperature. The detec-

Figure 6. Results of the CFD simulations (A) with and (B) without the human body model. The airflow velocities, indicated by white arrows, are in the range of 0–9 cm/s. The maximum airflow velocity, 25 cm/s, is not indicated by the arrows but is found around the head part of the human body model. The velocity of the air currents generated by the human body heat was even higher than the background airflow velocity.

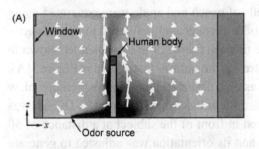

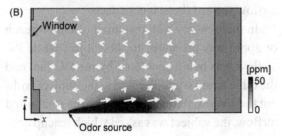

tion threshold velocity is lower for cold airflow and high for airflow having a temperature similar to human bodies. Therefore, we do not perceive the existence of upward air currents around our bodies. The odor concentration distribution in Figure 6(A) shows that the air currents generated around the human model carried the odor vapor spreading near the floor upward to the head part of the model. On the other hand, most of the odor vapor stayed near the floor in Figure 6(B). These simulation results showed that human body heat significantly affected the odor distribution. The air currents generated by human body heat appear to facilitate odor reception by bringing odor vapor drifting along the floor to nose level.

Effect of Airflow on Olfactory Perception

The results of the CFD simulations described in the previous section led us to conduct the following sensory test. In the test setup, shown in Figure 7, two empty teacups were used. One was handed to the subject and placed on the subject's lap. The other was placed on a desk approximately 1 m away from the subject. It was assumed that one of the two teacups contained peach-flavored tea and the other contained apple-flavored tea. The smells of peach and apple were generated using the odor blender and delivered to the subject's nose through tubing. The odor blender shown in Figure 7 is the same as that shown in Figure 3(A). It was also assumed that wind sometimes blew toward the subject from the front. A DC fan was placed in front of the subject at a distance of 50 cm, and its orientation was adjusted to generate airflow toward the subject's face.

In this sensory test, the smell of either peach or apple was presented to the subject while the airflow was being generated by the DC fan, and the other smell was presented to the subject without the airflow. After experiencing the smells and airflow, the subject was asked which teacup con-

Figure 7. Experimental setup for the sensory test to investigate the influence of airflow on the perceived location of the odor source. Each subject was asked to wear an eye mask during the test so that he or she received no visual clues.

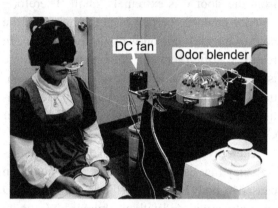

tained which tea. The airflow generated by the fan was used to provide the subject with a clue to distinguish the two different locations of the teacups. If the airflow is blowing from the direction of the teacup placed in front of the subject, the smell of the tea in the cup on the desk is brought to the subject's nose, as shown in Figure 8(A). We hypothesized that the presentation of the smell with the airflow would provide a sensation suggesting that the smell was coming from the direction of the airflow. If there is no perceptible airflow, the upward currents generated by body heat bring the smell to the subject's nose from the teacup held in the subject's hands, as shown in Figure 8(B). Odor presentation without airflow would therefore cause a sensation suggesting that the smell was coming from a nearby location.

The sensory test was conducted with 14 subjects. Before each subject experienced the smells and airflow, we explained that one of the two teacups was assumed to contain peach-flavored tea and the other was assumed to contain apple-flavored tea. We also told each subject that one of the two smells would be presented first followed by the other, and that wind would blow from time to time during the test. The concentrations of the

Figure 8. Scenarios assumed in the sensory test. (A) The smell of the tea in the cup on the desk is brought to the subject's nose when the wind is blowing from the front of the subject. (B) When the wind stops, the upward currents generated by body heat bring the smell to the subject's nose from the teacup held in the subject's hands.

(A)

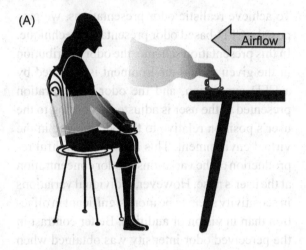

Airflow

(B)

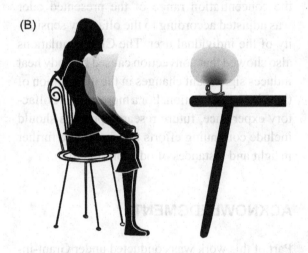

released peach-scented vapor and apple-scented vapor were adjusted for each subject to match the perceived odor intensities. Before the test, we also confirmed that each subject could easily distinguish the two smells.

After adjusting the presented smell intensities, two trials were conducted for each subject. In one of the two trials, the peach smell was first

presented to the subject for 30 s along with the airflow generated by the DC fan, and the apple smell was then presented for 30 s without the airflow. In the other trial, the peach smell was first presented for 30 s without the airflow, and the apple smell was then presented for 30 s with the airflow. The peach smell was presented first in both trials, although the subject was not told the order of presentation. In our preliminary test, we found that the change in the smells was barely perceived when the peach smell was presented after the apple smell. The order of the two trials was randomly changed for each subject. After each trial was conducted, the subject was asked the following four questions.

1. What was the smell you first perceived?
2. What was the second smell?
3. Which tea do you think was in the teacup on the desk?
4. Which tea do you think was in the teacup on your lap?

In 2 out of a total of 28 trials, the order of the presented smells was not correctly recognized. In the remaining 26 trials, the subjects correctly answered that they first sensed the smell of peach and then that of apple. In 24 out of these 26 trials, the subjects answered that the smell they sensed with the airflow was coming from the teacup on the desk, and the smell they sensed without the airflow was coming from the teacup on the subject's lap. The results of this sensory test suggest that the sensation of the location of the odor source was affected by the airflow. The odor presentation along with the airflow blowing from the front appears to induce a sensation suggesting that the source of the perceived odor is located in the front. An interesting open question is how the subjects judged the odor source location when the airflow from the DC fan was stopped. The velocity of the upward air currents generated by body heat is below our detection limit;

therefore, we cannot use them as a directional cue. Nevertheless, some subjects told us that they felt that the smell without airflow was coming from somewhere below. Our brains might instinctively know that an odor perceived in the absence of wind is carried upward from somewhere below the nose by the upward currents generated around our bodies. This hypothesis reasonably explains the subjects' sensation that the perceived smell was coming from the teacup on the lap when the airflow generation was stopped. However, there is no other evidence to support this claim, and it awaits further validation.

FUTURE RESEARCH DIRECTIONS

In photography, it is widely known that faithful reproduction of colors in a picture may not always results in a more realistic experience for viewers. In reality, the true color of cherry blossoms in full bloom is almost white; however, in our memory, the color of cherry blossoms is a lovely pink. Therefore, the sense of reality is often enhanced if some form of image processing is used to enhance the colors in a picture. We may have to think of similar effects in odor presentation.

Assume that you are looking down at a teapot placed on the floor. The teapot is assumed to contain peach-flavored tea. The peach smell would thus spread mostly in the downwind direction from the teapot. If you approach the teapot from the upwind side, you would perceive no smell. If this situation is reproduced using the olfactory display, a teapot appears on the computer screen, but no smell is presented. This situation obviously feels strange to the user, who generally expects to perceive the odor of the object shown on the computer screen. One potential solution to this issue would be to present airflow along with the odor. If the airflow is presented to the user from behind, the user could notice that he/she is standing on the upwind side. There are many open questions, and further investigations are required to establish techniques for realistic odor presentation.

CONCLUSION

To achieve realistic odor presentations, we proposed a CFD-based odor presentation technique. In this presentation scheme, the odor distribution in the given virtual environment is obtained by a CFD simulation, and the odor concentration presented to the user is adjusted according to the user's position relative to the odor source in the virtual environment. This allows for faithful reproduction of the variations in odor concentration at the user's nose. However, individual variations in sensitivity seem to be more significant in olfaction than in vision or audition. Better contrast in the perceived odor intensity was obtained when the concentration range of the presented odor was adjusted according to the olfactory sensitivity of the individual user. The CFD simulations also showed that convection caused by body heat induces significant changes in the distribution of the odor concentration. For a more realistic olfactory experience, future research projects should include continuing efforts to accumulate further insight and instances of odor presentation.

ACKNOWLEDGMENT

Part of this work was conducted under Grant-in-Aid for Scientific Research (B), No. 22300073, and Grant-in-Aid for JSPS Fellows, No. 22-8255, from the Japan Society for the Promotion of Science. The authors would like to thank Dr. Takamichi Nakamoto and two anonymous reviewers for the helpful comments. The authors would also like to thank Enago (www.enago.jp) for the English language review.

REFERENCES

Buck, L., & Axel, R. (1991). A novel multigene family may encode odorant receptors: A molecular basis for odor recognition. *Cell, 65*(1), 175–187. doi:10.1016/0092-8674(91)90418-X

Dusenbery, D. B. (1992). *Sensory ecology: How organisms acquire and respond to information.* New York, NY: W. H. Freeman and Company.

Ferziger, J. H., & Perić, M. (2002). *Computational methods for fluid dynamics* (3rd ed.). Berlin, Germany: Springer-Verlag. doi:10.1007/978-3-642-56026-2

Ishida, H., Matsukura, H., Yoshida, H., & Nakamoto, T. (2008). Application of computational fluid dynamics simulation to olfactory display. In *Proceedings of 18th International Conference on Artificial Reality and Telexistence*, (pp. 285–288). IEEE.

Ishida, H., Yoshida, H., & Nakamoto, T. (2011). Introducing computational fluid dynamics simulation into olfactory display. *Electrical Engineering in Japan, 177*(1), 65–72. doi:10.1002/eej.21087

Matsukura, H., Yoshida, H., Ishida, H., & Nakamoto, T. (2009). Interactive odor playback based on fluid dynamics simulation. In *Proceedings of the IEEE Virtual Reality Conference*, (pp. 255–256). IEEE Press.

Murlis, J., Elkinton, J. S., & Cardé, R. T. (1992). Odor plumes and how insects use them. *Annual Review of Entomology, 37*, 505–532. doi:10.1146/annurev.en.37.010192.002445

Nakamoto, T., Otaguro, S., Kinoshita, M., Nagahama, M., Ohinishi, K., & Ishida, T. (2008). Cooking up an interactive olfactory game display. *IEEE Computer Graphics and Applications, 28*(1), 75–78. doi:10.1109/MCG.2008.3

Nakamoto, T., & Yoshikawa, K. (2006). Movie with scents generated by olfactory display using solenoid valves. *IEICE Transactions on Fundamentals of Electronics, Communications and Computer Sciences. E (Norwalk, Conn.), 89A*(11), 3327–3332.

Sato, J., Ohtsu, K., Bannai, Y., & Okada, K. (2008). Pulse ejection technique of scent to create dynamic perspective. In *Proceedings of 18th International Conference on Artificial Reality and Telexistence*, (pp. 167–174). IEEE.

Vickers, N. J. (2000). Mechanisms of animal navigation in odor plumes. *The Biological Bulletin, 198*(2), 203–212. doi:10.2307/1542524

Yamada, T., Yokoyama, S., Tanikawa, T., Hirota, K., & Hirose, M. (2006). Wearable olfactory display: Using odor in outdoor environment. In *Proceedings of the IEEE Virtual Reality Conference*, (pp. 205–212). IEEE Press.

ADDITIONAL READING

Ishida, H., Matsukura, H., Yoshida, H., & Nakamoto, T. (2008). Odor playback based on computational fluid dynamics simulation. In *Proceedings of 18th International Conference on Artificial Reality and Telexistence*, (pp. 361–362). IEEE.

Matsukura, H., & Ishida, H. (2009). Olfactory display: Fluid dynamic considerations for realistic odor presentation. In *Proceedings of the Joint Virtual Reality Conference of EGVE – ICAT – EuroVR*, (pp. 61–64). ICAT.

Matsukura, H., Ohno, A., & Ishida, H. (2010). Fluid dynamic considerations for realistic odor presentation using olfactory display. *Presence (Cambridge, Mass.), 19*(6), 513–526. doi:10.1162/pres_a_00019

Matsukura, H., Ohno, A., & Ishida, H. (2010). On the effect of airflow on odor presentation. In *Proceedings of the IEEE Virtual Reality Conference*, (pp. 287–288). IEEE Press.

Matsukura, H., Yoshida, H., Ishida, H., Saitoh, A., & Nakamoto, T. (2009). Odor presentation with a vivid sense of reality: Incorporating fluid dynamics simulation into olfactory display. In *Proceedings of the IEEE Virtual Reality Conference*, (pp. 295–296). IEEE Press.

Matsukura, H., Yoshida, H., Nakamoto, T., & Ishida, H. (2010). Synchronized presentation of odor with airflow using olfactory display. *Journal of Mechanical Science and Technology*, 24(1), 253–256. doi:10.1007/s12206-009-1178-6

KEY TERMS AND DEFINITIONS

Computational Fluid Dynamics (CFD): A subdiscipline of fluid mechanics. The governing equations of fluid motion are numerically solved using computers to simulate various phenomena that involve fluid flows.

Convection: Transport of heat or mass by fluid motion. Convection also refers to such fluid motion itself especially when it is caused by an uneven temperature distribution. Hotter and therefore less dense fluid tends to rise while cooler and denser fluid sinks. The resultant fluid flow conveys heat and/or mass from one place to another.

Diffusion: A process of mass transport driven by random thermal motion of atoms or molecules, which is also referred to as "atomic diffusion" or "molecular diffusion." Atoms or molecules of chemical species migrate from regions of higher concentrations to those of lower concentrations as a result of their random thermal motion. Similarly, the term "turbulent diffusion" refers to a process through which chemical species spread by random swirling eddies in turbulent flow. Turbulent diffusion generally occurs much more rapidly than molecular diffusion.

k–ε Turbulence Model: A widely used turbulence model. The Reynolds stress term in the Reynolds-averaged Navier–Stokes equations is modeled as a function of turbulent kinetic energy, k, and turbulent dissipation, ε. The model also defines equations that describe how these two variables are transported in turbulent flow. k is the average of fluctuating kinetic energy per unit mass of the fluid. ε describes the rate at which the kinetic energy is dissipated by the viscous forces.

Navier–Stokes Equations: A set of equations that describe conservation of momentum at each point in fluid flow. The equations express the balance of momentum fluxes against viscous, pressure, and other types of forces acting on the fluid medium.

Reynolds-Averaged Navier–Stokes (RANS) Equations: A set of equations that describe the averaged behavior of turbulent flow. The derivation of the RANS equations starts with decomposing the variables in the original Navier–Stokes equations into mean and fluctuating parts. Turbulent fluctuations average out to zero. Taking either time average or ensemble average of the Navier–Stokes equations yields the RANS equations consisting only of the mean components of the variables and one additional term called the Reynolds stress, which describes the contributions of the fluctuating components to the mean flow. Some form of modeling is required for the Reynolds stress term to close the equations for solving.

Turbulent Flow: A type of fluid flow in which local velocities as well as other fluid properties fluctuate irregularly. Turbulent flows contain various scales of unsteady eddies, which facilitate dispersion of chemical substances released into the flows. Most flows we encounter in nature and in engineering applications are turbulent.

Chapter 22
Display Technology of Images with Scents and Its Psychological Evaluation

Akira Tomono
Tokai University, Japan

ABSTRACT

Scent is an important component of every individual's real life; it has many psychological and physical effects. Therefore, if a visual image is presented along with a matching scent, we expect it will possibly carry more detailed information and be perceived as a more realistic sensation than it would have on its own. In order to do so, it is necessary to solve some problems. First, the qualities for a device to be able to integrate a scent with an image are discussed. Second, a new method in which scents are emitted through a display screen in the direction of a viewer in order to enhance the reality of visual images is described. Third, the psychological effects on a viewer when scents are integrating with images are described. The authors investigated the viewing experiences and eye catching effects when applied to movies, a digital-signage, and virtual reality.

INTRODUCTION

Many researchers have studied high-intensity visual displays, such as large and high-definition screens, and the control of fields of sound. However, scent is also an important component of every individual's real life sensory experience,

and we know that scents have many psychological and physiological effects (Ayabe, et al., 2008). Therefore, if a visual image is presented along with a matching scent, we might expect that it will carry more detail and seem more realistic than it would have on its own. For instance, by presenting a picture of grass on a large screen,

DOI: 10.4018/978-1-4666-2521-1.ch022

Copyright © 2013, IGI Global. Copying or distributing in print or electronic forms without written permission of IGI Global is prohibited.

a real scent of grass comes to a viewer with the sound and the air of the wind. The viewer would be attracted to the picture on the screen and feel as if he or she was in the picture of the grass. In addition, by adding a scent to a commercial video, it will attract a viewer's eyes to the video, and a person will remember the contents displayed on the screen for a relatively long time. By doing so, the additional value from adding a scent will increase the value of the contents.

Such audiovisual images with scents are called KANSEI multimedia, and various applications have been researched recently (Nakamoto, et al., 2008). KANSEI is Japanese word that means sensibility and feeling. It is necessary to solve some of the following problems in order to employ scent manipulation for this purpose. First, in the development of a scent presentation device, the ability to switch the scent of a prescribed density at high speed corresponding to changes in the image and present it near the observers' nose is necessary. In short, it is expected to be able to present the scent at a pinpoint location, spatially and temporally. Moreover, it is preferable to use non-wearable equipment in order to appreciate the image for relaxation. Second, for the scent discharge control, it is necessary to select the image scene that should present the scent, prepare an appropriate scent, and link the scent to the image as if the scent were being discharged from the displayed object. Third, in the psychological evaluation of images with scents, it is required for KANSEI multimedia to select its effective application field and clarify its effects, and also to discuss the ways of presenting appropriate or inappropriate scents and its psychological effects. There are two methods for the evaluation of images with scents: (1) a psychological method of asking subjects for subjective judgment by questionnaire, and (2) an objective measurement method using a biological response measuring device. It is required to improve the assessment accuracy by combining both methods.

This chapter introduces the authors' approach to these problems as follows:

- The meaning of scent presentation with an image is described.
- New olfactory display method is explained which can present scents through a display screen so that an object with a scent can be expressed with realistic sensation.
- Experiments of examining the psychological effects (such as realistic sensation and eye-catching property) when a scent is presented together with a sentence or image is described.

BACKGROUND

The following approaches are known to the above-mentioned first and second problem. There are mainly two types of scent presentations, which are a wearable type and an unwearable type. Yamada *et al.* (2006) developed a wearable olfactory display in which various chemicals of scent are emitted into the nostril. By utilizing this technique along with the Head Mounted Display (HMD) system, it will be possible for this technique to collaborate scents with visual images on a screen. On the other hand, Kadowaki *et al.* (2007) developed an unwearable olfactory display in which pulse ejections are used to discharge scents. By using pulse ejections, they have developed scent presentation methods to avoid olfactory adaptations. Yanagida *et al.* (2004) developed air cannon systems to present scents. This system is able to emit air-rings through air cannons from a short distance away from a viewer. Matsukura *et al.* (2010) are proposing a display that emits airflow to viewers from the front of a display by colliding the generated airflows using two fans. The hoped characteristic of this device is to control the spatial distribution of the concentration of scent by mixing the scent with these airflows. It is preferable to be able to emit the scent from the vicinity of the visuals to viewer's position to display the visuals and the scent as a sense of unity. Also, Sawada *et al.* (2010) had proposed "A Wind Communication Interface" that utilized the symbiosis of the input/output of wind and graphics.

However, despite this research, to take control of discharging scent and relate it to various objects displayed on a large screen is a difficult technology.

Regarding the above-mentioned third problem, various research groups have studied the relationship between the simultaneous presentation of scents with visuals and the resulting brain activities such as memory and recognition (Chu, et al., 2000; Rasch, et al., 2007; Sobel, et al., 1998). However, there is not much research regarding the relationship between the presentation of images with scents and the biological reactions, such as the gaze movement, changes in the pupil diameter, and changes in skin conductance of the peripheral nervous system such as fingers.

MEANING OF SCENT PRESENTATION TO IMAGE

Is scent presentation necessary for the effective communication of the image? If so, how many kinds of scents are needed and for what kinds of

scenes? What changes occur if scents are included? These are questions that are still not given enough attention. However, they are important for the production of images tied to scents and for the design of olfactory displays. Thus, a variety of psychology evaluation experiments were performed for this purpose (Tomono, 2007).

Experiment Investigating the Necessity of Scent

Movie scenes that would benefit from the addition of scents were identified by a subjective experiment. The experiment set is shown in Figure 1. The movie was loaded onto a computer and then displayed on a large screen. We used a device of programmed control that detected the subjects' wish in real time by recording their presses of a button that was synchronized with the image. The subjects were directed to press the button whenever they imagined any scent and to stop pressing the button whenever they did not. They were also questioned about what kinds of scents were desirable.

Experimental Results

20 subjects evaluated about ten movies: dramas, animated cartoons, etc. Many subjects reacted

Figure 1. Set-up of experiment

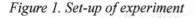

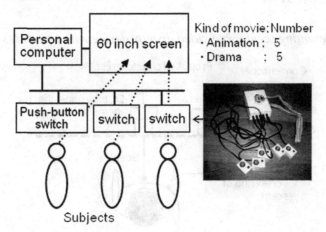

Kind of movie: Number
· Animation : 5
· Drama   : 5

Subjects

during scenes in which well-known scent objects appeared, and during scenes in which scent object important to the storyline appeared. On the other hand, their reactions varied during the scenes in which the scent objects appeared in the background.

They reported from several to about thirty different scenes, in each movie, that might enhance the realistic sensation from the addition of scents. For instance, scenes in places with water and steam, scenes in warm places, scenes of meals, etc. They answered that scenes that would have scents in the real world should have scents in order to be realistic when viewed. This is a natural and reasonable result. Viewers proposed from several to around ten different kinds of scents for each movie. They expressed a preference for a scent presentation time ranging from about 1/10 to 1/30 per screened time in a movie. It is about ten minutes from several minutes. Though scent objects appear in many scenes in every movie, it seems that the kinds and the time lengths of scents actually proposed by observers are considerably more limited.

These results are promising for the design of olfactory display devices for the following reasons: Based on the contents of the storyline of a movie, it is possible to prepare several kinds of scents before viewing. In addition, it seems that the design of the device will not become too complex if the number of necessary scents is limited to only around ten different types.

DISPLAY SYSTEM LINKING SCENTS TO IMAGES

The characteristic of linking a scent to an image object is expected in an olfactory display. Moreover, in order to promote realistic sensation, it is desirable to remit scents from the neighborhood of the targeted images. With the goal of delivering scents to viewers from a distance, we designed an olfactory display.

Concept of Presenting Scent through a Display Screen

Figure 2 shows the problem of the conventional olfactory display using an air cannon, and the concept of the proposed device to solve the problem. The olfactory display using an air cannon has the advantage of the scent being presented at a pinpoint location, both spatially and temporally. However, it is difficult to make the vortex ring flow straight when the distance to the user is far. Therefore, as it was placed to the side of the display screen at an oblique angle from the viewers, it was difficult to ensure that the vortex ring containing scents would be delivered precisely to the tips of their noses, as well as for the time of the release of these scents to coincide with their inhalations. The vortex ring may pass over the front of the user's nose when the direction of the flight shifts because the distance to the user is far. In this case, the user will not smell the scent.

Figure 2. Method of presenting scent using video display device with a porous screen

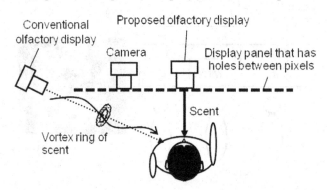

On the other hand, the scent-emitting video display system that author et al. are proposing can discharge the gas forward through a lot of minute holes installed in the screen, by raising the air pressure behind display screen by an air-pressure generating apparatus installed behind display screen (Tomono, et al., 2008). For the display device with the porous screen shown in Figure 2, a projector screen or a thin-type display panel using Light-Emitting Diodes (LEDs) as pixels can be used. According to the pattern of the air-pressure generating apparatus, two kinds of air flow can be generated: 1) a vortex ring of air can be emitted if the air pressure is raised instantaneously, and 2) air like wind can be emitted if it is raised continuously. These two kinds of flow generating systems are explained in the next section.

System Using an Air Cannon and Projector Screen

Structure of the System

(a) and (b) of Figure 3 show the structure and trial product of air cannon, respectively, and the cylinder of the cannon is attached to the screen (c) in the manner that its aperture area is pushed against the screen's reverse side. The cylinder of cannon is shaped so that from the middle part to the tip, its sectional area becomes smaller. The dimensions of the cylinder were 12 cm in length, 6.5 cm in diameter of middle part, 2.5 cm in the diameter of aperture area and 50° in inclination angle of the tip. A tube was fixed within the cylinder of the cannon to supply the scent to the direction of the air flow. If the air pressure within the cylinder of the cannon was raised instantaneously, the gas including the scent was emitted through multiple holes of the display, and those air particles formed a vortex ring by interfering with each other allowing the vortex ring moves ahead of the display screen. A method of driving a compression board by a program-controllable servomotor was used for the

mechanism of air compression (Tomono, et al., 2010). A link mechanism was fixed to the rotation axis of the motor, and its tip was connected to the compression board. This device was adjusted so that the movement of the compression board became approximately horizontal.

Figure 3. Display system linking scents to images using an air cannon and projector screen

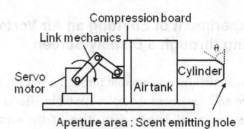

(A) Structure of air cannon with a servo motor in the air compression mechanism

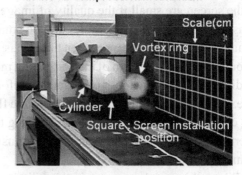

(B) Trial product of air cannon

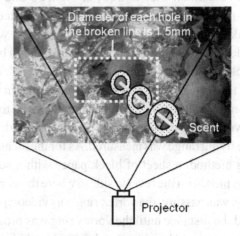

(C) Thin plate screen of 40-inch size with a lot of holes in central part.

The cannon cylinder could be moved anywhere within the square drawn with a broken line (20cm in width and 10cm in height) in Figure (c). If this method is used for presenting scent, the gap between the image and scent emitting position becomes less, the distance between viewers and the scent generating device becomes close, and the scent is presented from the front of image to the viewers so that a sense of unity between the image and scent can be obtained.

Experiment of Emitting an Air Vortex Ring through a Display Screen

When airflow was emitted through a screen, the size and density of the holes have big effects on the quality of image, formation of the vortex ring and its flying characteristics. It is desirable that the size and density of the holes provided in the screen are small if the quality of image is considered. However, if the holes are too small, it may increase the resistance when the air passes through them and the form of the vortex ring may be disturbed so that it does not fly far. Therefore, an experiment was conducted to examine the flying characteristics of vortex rings by varying the aperture ratio defined by the diameter and density of multiple holes.

First, white smoke was put in the cylinder of the air cannon shown in (b) of Figure 3 and the air-pressure generating apparatus was adjusted to make the flying range 70 cm. Then, a plate with holes (corresponding to the area surrounded by a broken line as shown in (c) of Figure 3 was placed on the square area shown by the solid line in the front of emitting hole of air cannon, and the form of vortex ring passing the plate was confirmed and the flying range was measured. As for the measuring method, a sheet of black paper with a scale was placed on the reverse side to where the vortex ring was passing, the vortex ring was videotaped, and the distance until the vortex ring was broken was measured by videotape being played in slow

motion. The experiment was made with screens of the ranges of 1.0-2.0 mm in thickness, 0.5-3.0 mm in diameter of holes and 1-4 mm intervals between holes. The flying range of the vortex ring was defined by the aperture ratio obtained from the diameter of holes and intervals between holes (total area ratio of air passing holes provided on the area where the cannon was installed on the reverse side of screen, corresponding to the dimension of the aperture area of the cannon) as parameters. The results are shown in Figure 4. The flying ranges of the vortex rings show the average values of 10 times' emissions. The ratio of flying range is the comparison of flying range through the screen with holes and that not through the screen.

From this experiment, it was learned that, although the flying range decreases when it is through the screen, the decreased amount is not so large if the aperture ratio is 20% or more, and the decreased amount can be compensated by a sufficient increase in the output of air-pressure generating apparatus. In the above experiment, the air compression force was set to low. However, it was known that the vortex ring can fly several meters while maintaining its form by the air compression force being increased. A projec-

Figure 4. The relationship between the aperture rate and the flying range of the vortex ring

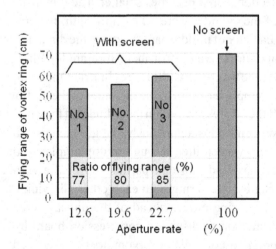

tor and screen were used as a display device this time, but it is possible to emit a vortex ring in the same manner with a thin-type LED display panel of 1-2 mm in thickness.

System Using Thin-Type LED Display Panel and Air Blower

Structure of the System

Figure 5 (a) and (b) shows a display system linking images and scents, with a thin-type display panel using LEDs which have a lot of minute air holes provided between the pixels and with a scent-emitting device installed on the reverse side of the display panel (Tomono, et al., 2011). A monitor camera was also placed behind this panel so that the scent was discharged through the holes to a person who was detected by the monitor. Therefore, it is possible for one to feel as if a scent flows from an object displayed on the

panel. Also, this system can express a consecutive current of air like the wind.

We used 1.6 mm thick FR-4 epoxy-glass for the panel. Holes, which had a diameter of 2.4 mm φ, were installed at intervals of four millimeters in spaces between the pixels in the display area of the panel. The driving circuits of the LEDs were made in both sides of the panel by using a printing technique, and then the LEDs were mounted at 4 mm intervals. The area of the holes accounted for 28 percent of the display screen. The scent-emitting device was composed of an air blower, an air controller box, and an air duct. Compressed air generated by the blower was carried to the air controller box by the air duct. The air controller box was tightly attached to a specific position on the reverse side of the screen. Therefore, the pressurized air in the box was smoothly emitted through the porous screen. By putting scents into the box, vaporized scents were discharged with the airflow.

Figure 5. Thin LED display panel with many holes in the screen and an experiment of airflow direction control

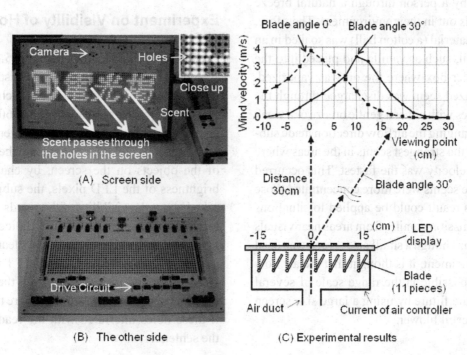

Blades were installed in the air controller. We thought that the air passed through in various directions through the holes on the screen by changing the angle of the blades because the display panel had a thin design.

Experiment of Controlling the Direction of Air Flow through the Screen

Then, the experiment that discharged the air through the screen into a prescribed direction was conducted. Figure5 (c) is one example of the experimental results, and shows the average velocity for ten seconds when the blades were adjusted to a right angle and then 30 degrees toward the display, with a distance of 30 cm between the display and each subject. This result indicates that adjusting the angle of the blades controls the airflow direction. From this experiment, it was revealed that the shape of holes, aperture ratio, and thickness of screen are important parameters for the control of the direction of air flow through a display screen.

In natural situations, scents are generally perceived by a person through a natural breeze that spreads out in their environment. Therefore, a porous material (a cotton ball) was soaked in an essential oil, such as vanilla and placed into the air controller box where the oil was vaporized. The vaporized scent was discharged through the porous holes with either a gentle breeze or a weak breeze. Changing the airflow direction made subjects smell the strongest scents in the areas where the wind velocity was the fastest. This occurred because the scents were more concentrated those areas. This result could be applied to situations of scent emission coming from areas near visuals on a screen. Though a small size screen was used in this experiment, it is thought that the air flow control is possible in the range scale of several meters in the future by using a large size screen and a powerful blower.

Discussion Concerning the Formation of Holes and Quality of Images

From the above experiment, it was learned that gas can be emitted through a display screen by using a thin-type display panel and, if the interval between pixels (pixel pitch) is approximately 4mm, it is possible by providing multiple holes with a diameter of 2-3 mm in this interval. A vortex ring of air can be emitted by air cannon being installed on the reverse side of a display screen and the direction of air flow can be continuously controlled by an air blowing mechanism being used.

However, when the image is presented on the display screen, if the holes can be clearly recognized by viewers, it will impair the quality of the image. Furthermore, if the pixel pitch is 4 mm and the size of the display screen is small, the images that can be presented may be limited. Therefore, the visibility of the holes when an image is presented on the above display screen was examined. Furthermore, the image that can be presented on a larger sized display screen and its application were discussed.

Experiment on Visibility of Holes

On the display panel shown in Figure 5, images of sentences in Japanese or English are displayed and run from right to left, and the size of each character that composes the sentences is 50 to 60 mm. The speed of the displayed sentence movement is 15 cm per second. In order to evaluate the visibility of the objects on the screen, by changing the brightness of the LED pixels, the subjects were asked about the visibility of the words. They had to choose between one of five choices ranging from "not really able to read," to "clearly able to read" and "comfortably able to read." The subjects were also asked if they recognized the holes on the screen and, if so, the subjects were then asked if these holes interfered with the readability of the sentences.

As a result of the experiment, although the holes could be recognized when an image was not presented on the display screen, they were hardly recognized the holes when the sentences were displayed, and, in particular, when it was observed from about a 2 m distance, the visibility of sentences was almost the same as that of a display panel without holes.

Application to Digital Signage

Recently, devices presenting advertising images called digital signage have become prevalent. If this device is installed with scent emitting mechanism and can present a product image combined with an appropriate scent, it will increase the added value of the advertising image (Sakaino, 2008). Therefore, the relationship between resolution and pixel pitch of the existent digital signage was examined and the possibility of application of a display panel that can emit a scent through the display screen, the sort of display panel used in the experiment described ahead, was discussed.

Resolution is usually expressed by the total number of vertical and horizontal pixels. The resolution required for a device that can display a TV image is approximately 648 (horizontal) x 486 (vertical) pixels by the NTSC (National Television System Committee) standard signal, and approximately 768 x 576 by PAL (Phase Alternating Line) (Musgrave, 2001). Recently, tri-color LED that can be used as pixels has been increasingly reduced in size, and pixels of 1-2 mm have been put on sale. If it is presumed to arrange the pixels in intervals of about 4 mm and present an image equivalent to that of one for TV, the width of the display device would be 2.6-3 m. As the display device that can correspond to High Definition Television (HDTV), a display device with a pixel pitch of 3mm and 1152x640 pixels and with the external dimensions of 3456 mm in width x 2471 mm in height has been developed and has been put on sale for digital signage. If the

image on this display device is viewed from about a 2m distance, the pixels can be easily ignored.

From the above, in the case of the digital signage with width of 3-4 m that can be often seen on the street, a resolution high enough for practical use can be obtained with a pixel pitch of 3-4 mm, and if holes or slits are provided between pixels, the display device possibly can remit scents to pedestrians. It is expected that images with scents can promote realistic sensation.

PSYCHOLOGICAL EFFECTS OF IMAGES WITH SCENTS

Though images with scents are expected in a wide range of fields such as movies, advertisements, simulations and games, because it is costly, it is necessary to evaluate its effectiveness. This section is to introduce psychological evaluation methods, with improvements of realistic sensation and eye catching property being the main focus.

Improvement of Realistic Sensation

Realistic sensation means "the feeling as if you are actually in the scene you are seeing." If the stimuli that humans' sensory organs can perceive at the real situation are presented as much as possible, humans' realistic sensation is considered to be promoted. Therefore, the improvement of realistic sensation when an olfactory stimulus is presented in addition to visual and auditory stimuli was investigated.

Subjective Assessment

Through an experiment that delivered scents concurrently with the image scenes for which scents had been requested, described ahead, we investigated the influence of these scents on the observer's understanding of the scenes, as well as on the reported realism of the scenes. The scents delivered were either suitable or unsuitable for the content of the image. The following opinions were reported in the introspective questionnaire by viewers who had experienced both kinds of image pairings:

When a suitable scent was delivered, it was described as: "I could more easily remember what the scene looked like," "The scene was very realistic," "It was very peaceful," "It made the content easier to understand," and so on.

When an unsuitable scent was delivered, it was described as: "It revolted me," "Because the scent was confusing, I could not concentrate on the image."

The questionnaires were psychologically analyzed using the Semantic Differential method (Osgood, et al., 1957; Heise, et al., 1970). When a scent suitable to the image was presented, the factor score showing harmony or distinctness was higher than when no scent was presented. When the scent of woody note was presented in the image of the mountain or the forest, the factor score that expressed the magnificent feeling or immersive feeling was high.

Moreover, in the experiment that shifted the timing of scent delivery away from the moment in which the scent object appeared, the sense of incompatibility was greater when the scent was delivered too late or too fast (Tomono, et al., 2008). We concluded that the timing of scent presentation has an important effect on the impression of the contents of a movie.

The result of the subjectivity evaluation experiment can be summarized now as follows:

1. When the scent is suitable for the content of the image, the improvement of the content understanding and the realistic sensation is remarkable.
2. When there is a mismatch in the content of the image and smell, an effect is not seen or a negative effect is seen.
3. When the scent is presented with a scene from which the scent is not so strongly considered, the difference is seen in the response to the sense among the subjects, and the risk is large.
4. As for the effect, even if a scent is presented for a long time, the effect is small, while presentation for a short time that synchronizes with the scene is more effective.

Measurement of Oculo-Pupillary Reflex

It is known that a subject's pupil size reflects not only ambient light conditions, but also his or her psychological condition. So far, most experiments performed on pupil size have been performed using still pictures. For instance, pupil dilation typically occurs when a sexual image of the opposite sex is viewed (Hess, 1965). This has been interpreted as a reflection of the feelings of the subjects. Keeping this interpretation in mind, we attempted to obtain results supporting the above-mentioned results of the subjective experiment by using the equipment as shown in Figure 3 (c). That is, we investigated whether or not any difference in the movement of the pupil occurred under the three following conditions: (a) presentation of a movie without scent, (b) presentation of a movie along with a scent suitable to its content, and (c) presentation of a movie along with a scent not suitable to its content.

To measure the pupillary reflex in these conditions, the device was composed of a small high-sensitivity camera, and a near-infrared lighting device was set up between the screen and the subject. The pupil could be clearly extracted by using brightness difference processing because the iris often reflects infrared light, so the iris appears bright, and the pupil appears dark. The pupil image was preserved along with the image that subjects were observing by a computer, the pupil was extracted after the experiments, and the change in the size was calculated.

Examples of adding scents to some scenes of a movie *The Girl Who Leapt through Time* are described (Tomono, et al., 2004). In the (a) condition, a scene where a heroine felt the smell of lavender was presented. In the (b) condition, the smell of lavender was presented in the scene. In the (c) condition, the smell of lavender was presented in the scene in which she took tea. The subjects were university student volunteers. Figure 6 shows the change in size of the pupils when a subject was observing the movie under (a) or (b) conditions. We found that, from the beginning of the scent presentation, the subjects' pupils grew for about 20 seconds more under the (b) condition than under the (a) condition. Moreover, the subjects reported that the images seemed more realistic under the (b) condition. On the other hand, a change like that of the (b) condition was not measured under the (c) condition in which the presented scent was not suitable to its contents, and the subjects reported feeling odd. From these results, it is considered that observers may be stimulated by empathy because their attention toward the images increases when the scents presented match their content. Pupil size after 20 seconds, similar under conditions (a) and (b), is shown in Figure 6. The reason for this similarity seems to be that the observer gradually adapts to the presence of a scent, which causes its stimulatory effects to weaken.

Measurement of Skin Conductance Change

It is well known that a person breaks a sweat with a psychological flutter when he or she gets nervous or excited. This sweating reflects the height of the sympathetic tone and the arousal level. SCR, Skin Conductance Response, is often used in experiments to analyze and measure one's psychological tension or emotional arousal (Khalfa, 2002). When the scent that relates to the visuals is presented, It is considered that SCR will change if subjects become strained or excited. Therefore, SCR was measured using the display device shown in Figure 5, and a comparison of SCR between the cases where the subjects were presented with advertising sentences as a visual stimulus together with the pertaining scent as an olfactory stimulus and where they were not presented with the scent was carried out. In addition, the relation between the improvement of realistic sensation and the SCR was investigated by being combined with the results of question-

Figure 6. Change in pupil size during movie presentation

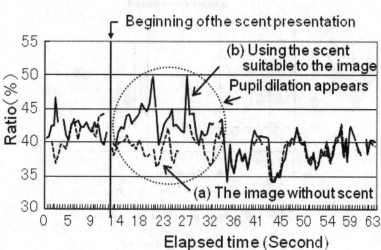

naires concerning realistic sensation performed after the experiment.

Figure 7 (a) shows the experimental environment. Active biological electrodes of a biological signal recording system (Polymate 2: TEAC CORPORATION) to measure skin conductance were mounted in two positions of a subject's left hand (index finger and middle finger). The distance from the subject to display was 60 - 100 cm. A simple picture and sentences that described the product flowed from left to right on the display. Seven kinds of products and the presented scents used for the experiment were as follows: Lemon juice: Essential oil of lemon (Palm Tree), Cookies: Real scents, Incense stick: Real scents, Cigarette:

Real scents (Seven Star), Apple pie: Essential oil of Vanilla (Palm Tree), Coffee: Real scents (Blue Mountain), Curry: Real curry spice. The scents were presented from inside the screen by mixing it into the current of air at a weak strength level as like breeze. The subjects were ten university students.

Figure 7 (b) shows the time variation of a subject's skin conductance. Disregarding the existence of scent, when the advertising visuals was presented, SCRs of all subjects were the same as those of rest time (normal time) or rose above them. Then, the parts that rose when a stimulus was presented were quantified based upon SCR values during rest time and the SCR values were

Figure 7. Experiment that discharges the scent with advertising messages

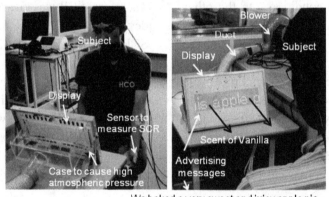

We baked a very sweet and juicy apple pie.
Would you like a piece of the pie?

(A) Experimental environment

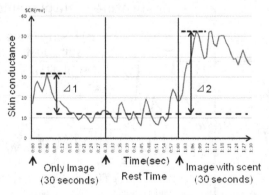

(Subject: 22 years old man / Product: Curry and rice)

(B) Example of Skin conductance

compared by the existence or non-existence of scent. As for the average value of the elevated values of 10 subjects, SCR values that rose when the scent was presented were larger in the cases of every product.

Large shifts regarding scents were also observed in the questionnaires. Presenting only visuals did not seem to influence one's critical thinking and mental image about the objects, though one could recognize and understand the meanings of the visuals. That is, a person's recognition and processing level did not seem to rise. On the other hand, by presenting scents, the impressions became more concrete and narrative. Some examples of this from the subjects included: "I imagined eating curry with rice in a curry restaurant when I was a child," "When I smelled the delicate fragrance of cookies, I became hungry," and "The scent of incense sticks reminded me of entering a temple when I participated in a memorial service this summer."

From the above elevated SCR values and the results of questionnaire, when a scent was presented, there is a possibility that their realistic sensation was promoted and they became strained or excited by the presentation of scent.

Improvement of Eye Catching Property

"Eye catching" is the working of the object in order to attract a person's eyes. So far, it is known that the important points include object brightness, a large object size, object movement, and object's proximity to the center of view. However, when the scent that relates to the object is presented, the gazing time of the object can be expected to become longer because the concern rises due to the scent, even if the eye catching of the above-mentioned item is small. For signboard advertisements, it is important to draw attention to the object, and to make the target product on the signboard stand out. As olfactory stimulation directly acts on humans'

memory and emotion, if an advertising image of a product with scent can act upon viewers' attention behavior, the value of the advertisement will rise. Therefore, the eye-catching property of the digital signage with scent mentioned ahead was investigated.

Measurement of Point of Gaze

According to the above-mentioned concept, the passer-by's eye movement when the scent was presented in a passageway where a lot of signboards were set up was analyzed (Tomono, et al., 2011). There are many restrictions in conducting experiments by installing a digital signage with scent in the street. Therefore, an experiment was conducted in a virtual town made with an Immersive Virtual Environment (IVE), where the eye movements of subjects were simulated. HoloStage™, a product of Christie, was used for IVE. Images were projected with three large-type screens interconnected with 10 high-brightness projectors. A virtual town of three-dimensional CG was made using 3dsMax Design. The gazing points of the subjects were measured using a cap-typed eye camera (EMR-8B) made by NAC Ltd. This device contained a view camera (viewing angle 44 degrees), and the gazing points in the camera image were detected. The gazed objects were estimated from the data of the gazing points, and the gazing time of each of the objects was measured.

Figure 8 (a) shows an example of the virtual town used for the experiment. The scale of the virtual space made by the virtual reality technology (VR) was equal to a real space, and the length of the passage was about 20m. Five digital sign boards were placed in a line on the left wall, and objects of the person type and the ornament, etc., were set up at the right of the passage. The digital signs for a cafe, roast meat (Japanese Yakitori), fruit, pizza, and flowers were queued up from this side sequentially on the left wall. The contents for each digital sign used animation.

The digital signs with scents were evaluated in two kinds of patterns. In the experiment for pattern A, when the target signboard (a roast meat shop's signboard or a flower shop's signboard) appeared, the roast meat scent or the rose scent was presented, respectively. In the experiment for pattern B, when a cafe's signboard or a fruits shop's signboard appeared, the coffee or apple scent was presented, respectively. Here, the subjects of each experiment of pattern A and B were different. In pattern A, they were nine men and one woman (in their twenties). In pattern B, they were seven men and three women (in their twenties). As the viewing angles were 100 degrees or more, there was a great feeling of immersion.

The procedure of the experiment was as follows. The subject advanced in the passage with the desire to take the moving sidewalk, because the experimenter drew the virtual space forward by the walking rate. The time to pass over the passage was about 40 seconds. The eye movement data of this time were accumulated, and the gaze at the objects was analyzed. The scents were presented so that they would not be noticed from the back of the subject for about 5-7 seconds with a scent atomizer when the subject approached the digital sign of the target. As the room was air-conditioned and a slight airflow was always flowing, most of the emitted scents disappeared before subjects came close to the next advertising

Figure 8. An experiment of the eye-catching property

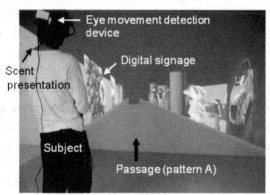

(A) Experimental environment

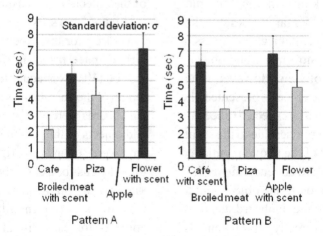

(B) Average gaze time of 10 subjects

displays. The subjects could not hear the driving sound of atomizer due to the driving sounds of the air conditioner and projector. The subjects could feel as if a scent was drifting from the street when coming close to an advertising board. The objects that were gazed at when the scent was or was not presented were compared. The subjects were questioned about their impression after the experiment ended.

Figure 8 (b) shows the relation between the kind of signboard and the average gaze time of ten of the subjects. Through these experiments, it seemed that the subjects gazed at the signboard with a scent at a higher frequency compared to those without a scent in both patterns (a) and (b). In addition, all subjects answered that he or she looked for the signboard when the scent was smelled, and were interested in it. The statistical hypothesis test about the difference in gaze time was conducted by using the gaze time data of subjects for about four targets of the café, broiled meat restaurant, fruit shop and flower shop. The results of this experiment rejected a null hypothesis of "there is no difference in gaze time due to existence or non-existence of scent," at a significance level of 0.05. Thus, it is understood that the sense of smell was stimulated by presenting a scent, and an advertising board with scent tends to be looked at longer. From the above, scent has certain effects to improve the eye catching properties of advertising boards.

CONCLUSION AND FUTURE WORK

In this chapter, a scent was defined as one of the multi-media senses like vision and sound, and a little portion of the technique to manage such an information system has been stated. In the field of visual display systems, larger and thinner displays will become more advanced in the near future. Regarding the presentation of a scent, techniques of analyzing its content, coding its information,

and controlling it by a computer are advanced enough to synthesize an optimal scent. In addition, techniques have been developed which can carry the information of scents through the Internet and present both visuals and scents at the same time (Tonoike, et al., 2007). Therefore, if a display system, which can simultaneously present both visuals and scents, is created by combining these technologies, various applications of this display will be expected. Our display system, which was introduced in this chapter, is also expected to be one of those applications; our display system presents both visuals and scents by blowing scents toward a viewer through holes in a display.

Scents can increase the qualities of visual content, for example improving realistic sensations and the understanding of its content etc. However, if emitted scents are not suitable to the visual scene, these scents cannot produce good psychological effects for the viewer, but rather give bad impressions like disturbing one's concentration on the visual contents. Therefore, a technique to evaluate one's mind will be necessary to produce visual images with scents, which are comfortable to a user. Also, scents produce various effects such as attracting one's interest to an object, improving one's memory and concentration, activating one's immune system, and decreasing one's psychological tension. Therefore, this technique of emitting scents can be applied not only for the improvement of visual images, but also in other fields such as advertisement, education, and lifetime.

REFERENCES

Ayabe, S., & Saitou, S. (2008). *Psychology of scent*. Tokyo, Japan: Fragrance Journal Ltd.

Chu, S., & Downes, J. (2000). Odour-evoked autobiographical memories: Psychological investigations of Proustian phenomena. *Chemical Senses*, 25(1), 111–116. doi:10.1093/chemse/25.1.111

Heise, D. (1970). The semantic differential and attitude research. In G. F. Summers (Ed.), *Attitude Measurement*, (pp. 235-253). Chicago, IL: Rand McNally. Retrieved from http://www.mendeley.com/research/semantic-differential-attitude-research/

Hess, E. H. (1965). Attitude and pupil size. *Scientific American, 212*(4), 46–54. Retrieved from http://hosting.udlap.mx/profesores/julioc.penagos/materias/fisiologia-conducta/archivos/files/lfc1.pdf doi:10.1038/scientificamerican0465-46

Kadowaki, A., Sato, J., Bannai, Y., & Okada, K. (2007). Presentation technique of sent to avoid olfactory adaptation. In *Proceedings of the 17th International Conference on Artificial Reality and Telexistence 2007*, (pp. 97-103). IEEE.

Khalfa, S., Isabelle, P., Blondin, J., & Manon, R. (2002). Event-related skin conductance responses to musical emotions in humans. *Neuroscience Letters, 328*, 145–149. doi:10.1016/S0304-3940(02)00462-7

Matsukura, H., Nihei, T., Ohno, A., & Ishida, H. (2010). Display for presenting spatial odor distribution and airflow field. *Transactions of the Virtual Reality Society of Japan, 15*(4), 563–570.

Musgrave, G. (2001). Very large-screen video displays. *Conception Associates*. Retrieved from http://www.conceptron.com/articles/!article_index.html

Nakamoto, T. (2008). *Olfactory display: Multimedia tool for presenting scents*. Tokyo, Japan: Fragrance Journal Ltd.

Osgood, C. E., Suci, G. J., & Tannenbaum, P. H. H. (1957). *The measurement of meaning*. Urbana, IL: University of Illinois Press.

Rasch, B., Buchel, C., Gais, S., & Born, J. J. (2007). Odor cues during slow-wave sleep prompt declarative memory consolidation. *Science, 315*, 1426–1429. doi:10.1126/science.1138581

Sakaino, A. (2008). The concept of sensitivity communication using aroma and a plan of demonstration experiment: The digital signage with fragrance communication. *Electronic Information Displays, 108*(291), 53-57. Retrieved from http://ci.nii.ac.jp/naid/110007124675/en/

Sawada, E., Ida, S., Awaji, T., Morishita, K., Aruga, T., & Takeichi, R. … Inami, M. (2007). BYU-BYU-view: A wind communication interface. *ACM SIGGRAPH 2007*. Retrieved from http://dl.acm.org/citation.cfm?id=1278282

Sobel, N., Prabhakaran, N., Desmond, J. E., Glover, G. H., Goode, R. L., Sullivan, E. V., & Gabrieli, J. D. (1998). Sniffing and smelling: Separate subsystem in the human olfactory cortex. *Nature, 392*, 282–286. doi:10.1038/32654

Tomono, A. (2007). Evaluation of hyper-realistic images using smells. In *Proceedings of International Display Workshops*, (vol. 2, pp. 1161-1164). JGlobal. Retrieved from http://jglobal.jst.go.jp/public/20090422/200902256709192830

Tomono, A., & Otake, S. (2010). The eye catching property of digital-signage with scent and a scent-emitting video display system. *IEEJ Transactions on Electronics. Information Systems, 130*(4), 668–675.

Tomono, A., & Tomono, K. (2008). *WIPO patent scope*. Retrieved from http://www.wipo.int/patentscope/search/en/detail.jsf?docId=WO2008093721

Tomono, A., Tomono, T., Fukiura, T., & Yamaguchi, H. (2008). Olfaction characteristics improvement of projection-based olfactory display. *The Journal of the Institute of Image Electronics Engineers of Japan, 37*(4), 444–451.

Tomono, A., Yamamoto, S., Utsunomiya, M., Ikei, D., Yanagida, Y., & Hosaka, K. (2004). The effect which visual media with scent exert on contents understanding. In *Proceedings of the Human Interface Symposium 2004*, (vol 1441, pp. 249-254). Human Interface. Retrieved from http://sciencelinks.jp/j-east/article/200510/0000 20051005A0295009.php

Tomono, K., Katsuyama, H., & Tomono, A. (2011). Scent-emitting display panel and its psychological effects. *The Journal of the Institute of Image Information and Television Engineers, 65*(10), 1411–1419. doi:10.3169/itej.65.1411

Tomono, K., Wakatsuki, H., Kumazawa, S., & Tomono, A. (2011). Display system for advertising image with scent and psychological effect. *Lecture Notes in Computer Science, 6781*, 110-119. Retrieved from http://www.springerlink.com/content/5j3165v5r1502v47/

Tonoike, M. (2007). *Information and communication technology of olfaction*. Tokyo, Japan: Fragrance Journal Ltd.

Yamada, T., Yokoyama, S., Tanikawa, T., Hirota, K., & Hirose, M. (2006). Wearable olfactory display: Using odor in outdoor environment. [IEEE Press.]. *Proceedings of IEEE Virtual Reality, 2006*, 205–212.

Yanagida, Y., Kawato, S., Noma, H., Tomono, A., & Tetsutani, N. (2004). Projection-based olfactory display with nose-tracking. In *Proceedings of IEEE Virtual Reality 2004*, (pp. 43-50). IEEE Press. http://www.computer.org/portal/web/csdl/doi/10.1109/VR.2004.1310054

KEY TERMS AND DEFINITIONS

Air Cannon: Device that discharges compress air as vortex ring.

Blade: Wing that changes current of air into prescribed direction.

Blower: Device that discharges compress air.

Digital Signage: Display device with thin large screen that presents advertising images.

Eye Catching Property: The working of the object in order to attract a person's eyes.

Immersive Virtual Environment: Virtual reality system that can experience existence in the virtual world by displaying three dimensional CG images in the space that encloses it on two or more screens.

KANSEI: Japanese word that means sensibility and feeling.

Oculo-Pupillary Reflex: Reaction that pupil is expanded or contracted by sensory stimulation.

Realistic Sensation: The feeling as if you are actually in the scene you are watching.

Skin Conductance Response: Phenomenon that electrical resistance in skin decreases by moisture or sweat of skin.

Chapter 23
Impact of Olfaction on Information Recall:
Perspectives from an Empirical Study

Gheorghita Ghinea
Brunel University, UK

Oluwakemi Ademoye
Brunel University, UK

ABSTRACT

Multimedia lies on an infotainment continuum, using multiple forms of information content to both inform and entertain users. In other words, multimedia applications are usually intended to add to the knowledge of the user, via its information content, as well as to keep the user entertained, i.e. interested or amused. In previous work, the authors have presented details of studies carried out to study the influence of using olfactory media content to augment multimedia applications on user perception and particularly focusing on users' enjoyment of the multimedia experience. Thus, in this respect, the authors have studied the influence of the use of olfaction in multimedia applications on entertaining users. Consequently, in this chapter, they focus their attention on the influence of using olfaction to augment multimedia applications with regards to the informational aspect of multimedia systems and applications.

INTRODUCTION

It is often the case that there is usually a predominance of either informational content or entertaining content in multimedia applications. Nonetheless, information processing and, to a

lesser degree, information recall is still required whether the intention of the multimedia application is to reach out to the user on an informational, entertainment or infotainment level. For example, multimedia gaming applications, which are strictly entertainment applications, the player is often

DOI: 10.4018/978-1-4666-2521-1.ch023

Copyright © 2013, IGI Global. Copying or distributing in print or electronic forms without written permission of IGI Global is prohibited.

required to recall certain elements and aspects of the game in order to play successfully. On an informational level, an example may be a multimedia training application where the main intention is for the user to process the information conveyed by the integrated media objects and to be able to recall this information as may be appropriate at some later time. In this chapter we focus on the effect that olfaction has on information recall when olfaction is used to augment multimedia applications.

OLFACTION, THE SENSE OF SMELL

Olfaction, the sense of smell, is the ability to use the nose to notice or discover the presence of an odorous substance in the air, that is, an odorant—a chemical compound that has a smell or odor. It works by transmitting the signals produced when the odorants perceived dissolve in the nasal mucous. These then bind with the cilia found on the olfactory neuron receptors projecting down from the olfactory epithelium into the mucous membrane. These neurons are responsible for transmitting the detected signals through their axons to the olfactory bulb, whose neurons in turn transmits the received signals to the olfactory part of the cortex. The olfactory information received in the olfactory cortex is then distributed to other areas of the brain, ultimately leading to the perceptions of odors and their emotional and physiological effects. At this point, odor signals are relayed to both the brain's higher cortex, which handles conscious thought processes, and to the limbic system, which generates emotional feelings

The majority of olfactory signals produced when smells are detected by the olfactory system travel in the way described above to the brain, that is, through what is called the orthonasal pathway. However, some smells also travel through a passage at the back of the mouth, experienced particularly when eating—flavour perception,

called the retronasal pathway (Kaye, 2001; Shepperd, 2006). For this reason, the olfactory system is sometimes described as being dual in nature, that is, it can sense odorous signals originating externally (orthonasal) and internally (retronasal) to the body. In the former case, orthonasal stimulation occurs when odorous substances are sniffed and travel through the nostrils or nasal cavities located in the external nares. In the latter case, however, retronasal stimulation is experienced during food ingestion when volatile molecules are released from the ingested food and are pumped from the back of the oral cavity up through the nasopharynx to the olfactory epithelium.

OLFACTION AND AUDIOVISUAL CONTENT

The first recorded attempt of combining artificially generated smell with audiovisual content dates back to 1906 when an audience was sprayed with the scent of roses while watching the screening of the Rose Bowl football game (Longino in Kaye, 2001), however, there is no mention of what the audience reaction to this was. The next significant development in the use of scented media in the film industry happened in 1943 (Kiger & Smith, 2006; Smith & Kiger, 2006), when Hans Laube, who had earlier discovered a technique for removing odors from an enclosed place, such as an auditorium, was also able to reverse this process to release selected odors into similar places at specific times and durations. Using his newly discovered technology, and with the help of his colleague, Robert Barth, they produced a 35 minute 'smell-o-drama' movie called Mein Traum in which 35 different odors were released to accompany the drama presentation. However, the technology behind the production of the emitted smells enjoyed more success than the scented drama presentation itself, with the audience agreeing that while the smells emitted were promptly released and subsequently removed, they smelled fake. Nonetheless, it was the success of Laube's technology for emitting smells that Michael Todd Jr was to rely on later in 1960 in his Smell-O-Vision Scent of Mystery film production (Kiger & Smith, 2006; Smith & Kiger, 2006).

In 1959, a year before the release of the afore-mentioned Michael Todd Jr.'s Smell-O-Vision Scent of Mystery film production, there was the AromaRama presentation, a documentary about Red China called Behind the Great Wall (ABC, 1999; Kaye, 2001; Kiger & Smith, 2006; Variety, 2001). Smells were emitted via the theatre's air-conditioning system to accompany the presentation of this documentary. Unfortunately, the producers had no way of knowing what a significant impact the characteristic nature of smell would have on their presentation, and they went all-out and had over 30 different smells released during the presentation. The reaction of the audience to this presentation is probably best described from the following extract from the review published back then by Time magazine (Kaye, 2001):

To begin with, most of the production's 31 odors will probably seem phoney, even to the average uneducated nose. A beautiful old pine grove in Peking, for instance, smells rather like a subway rest room on disinfectant day. Besides, the odors are strong enough to give a bloodhound a head-ache. What is more, the smells are not always removed as rapidly as the scene requires: at one point, the audience distinctly smells grass in the middle of the Gobi desert.

In the year following the AromaRama presentation, and hot on the heels of Laube's success with the technology used in the 'smell-o-drama' movie of 1943, there was another attempt at creating scented media for the film industry in a film production called Scent of Mystery (Kaye, 2001; Kiger & Smith, 2006; Smith & Kiger, 2006; Variety, 2001). This film production was a

murder mystery in which were synchronised with certain scenes of the film in order to scents aid in revealing the identity of the murderer. This time, the producers had done more research into the matter and of course had the added advantage of being able to refer to the AromaRama experience and of using technology that had proved reliable when it came to promptly releasing and subse-quently removing smells. Thus, they went ahead and also released as many as 30 smells during the film, as after all, the technology had proven that it could cope with this (Kiger & Smith, 2006; Smith & Kiger, 2006). Unfortunately, despite the better preparation and the better technology, this scented media production also fared badly and the Smell-O-Vision Scent of Mystery drama continues to live in infamy to date (ABC, 1999; Kaye, 2001; Kiger & Smith, 2006; Smith & Kiger, 2006; Variety, 2001). The audience complained that the scents emitted reached them seconds too late, were too faint resulting in them sniffing repeatedly to catch whiffs of the emitted smells and were accompanied by a hissing sound which they found distracting and the following comment was published in the New York Times then about the experience (Kaye, 2001):

If there is anything of lasting value to be learned from Michael Todd's Scent of Mystery it is that motion pictures and synthetic smells do not mix.

After these well publicised failures with the use of smell in the film industry, the production of scented films disappeared for a while, and though there have been a few more attempts to create scented media experiences for users since then, the idea still has not quite caught on to date. Some of the more popular of these later attempts at creating scented film productions include *Polyester* by John Waters in 1981 and *Love for Three Oranges* by the English National Opera Company in 1989, which both made use of the popular scratch 'n' sniff cards similar to those used in advertising perfumes in magazines (Kaye, 2001, 2004). In these productions, at specific intervals during the films, the audience had to scratch and sniff the smells on numbered cards they had been given prior to the start of the movie; one can only imagine how distracting that must have been as this cannot exactly be described as being advanced technology. More recently, in 2006, there was mention that audiences going to see the screening of the movie, The New World, in Japan will be treated to a scented movie experience (BBC, 2006; Heritage, 2006; NTT, 2006). However, whilst there were several reports advertising the 'smellovision' experience to-be, it is not quite clear if this actually happened and if it did what the audience's reaction to it was, as follow-up reports appear to be non-existent. It would definitely have been interesting to see how much the technology had improved since those earlier not so successful attempts at creating scented film productions, as well as if users are now more receptive towards the idea of scented films.

The predominant cause of these failed attempts at creating notable scented film experiences for users was the failure of the technology. Hence, with computing technology already well underway by the 70s, and enjoying considerable success, research started to look at ways of using computing technology to control the emission of scents in order to create an olfaction-enhanced experience for users. In the next section, we take a look at some of these efforts, focusing on the use of olfaction to aid information recall.

OLFACTION AND INFORMATION RECALL

There have been a number of research studies that involve our olfactory sense and information processing tasks and in the current chapter, we make reference to a number of these studies in two main areas: Olfactory Psychophysics and Multimedia

and Multimodal Computing. As the focus of this research is on the use of olfaction in multimedia applications, we summarise the findings from the studies carried out in the area of multimedia and multimodal computing only below:

- Olfactory cues are the least disruptive on a user's engagement of a task when compared to visual and audio cues, although they were also found to be the least effective in delivering notification system alerts to users (Bodnar, Corbett, & Nekrasovski, 2004).
- Odor memories have the potential to play a significant role in a multimedia content searching task (Brewster, McGookin, & Miller, 2006; Boyd, et al., 2006).
- Functional Magnetic Resonance Imaging (fMRI) showed that the subjective experience of the emotional potency of odor-evoked memory activates specific areas of the brain (Herz, et al., 2004); moreover, the presence of odor cues during a specific phase of a person's sleep helps consolidate declarative memories (Rasch, et al., 2007).
- The presence of ambient scent during only the learning phase of an information recall task in a virtual reality environment had the best effect on users' performance of an information recollection task when compared to the other cases investigated. The other cases in the study were ambient scent being present in both the learning and recall phase, unfamiliar ambient scent (unfamiliar in the sense that the scent was not present during the learning phase) was present in only the recall phase and ambient scent was absent from both phases of the task. In fact, the presence of unfamiliar ambient scent during the information recollection task proved to have the most detrimental impact on users' performance. Generally, however, the addition of scent

had a positive effect on subjects' recollection of the virtual reality environment (Tortell, et al., 2007).

The small number of studies highlighted above reflects the paucity of research studies relating to olfaction and information processing in multimedia systems and applications and further highlights the need for research in this area. The study by Bodnar, Corbett, and Nekrasovski (2004) concentrated on the impact olfaction has on disengaging a user from a task; while Brewster et al study concentrated on using odor memories to aid a user in a search task; and Tortell et al. focused on the influence of olfaction on a recollection task. Thus, of these three studies, the study carried out by Tortell et al. (2007) is the most similar to the study reported in this section. As such, we highlight the differences between the two approaches below:

- Tortell et al. (2007) in their study conducted their study in a virtual reality multimedia environment. Our study has not been conducted in a virtual reality environment.
- The multimedia system used by Tortell et al. (2007) for their study is predominantly an entertainment system, i.e. a multimedia virtual reality game, while in our study we use a mix of multimedia content aimed to engage the user on an informational, entertainment and infotainment level.
- The information recall task in the study by Tortell et al. (2007) is more of a 'recognition and identification task,' that is, did the player notice the virtual reality environment they were engaged in during the game play and subsequently become aware of its contents. On the other hand, the information recall task that participants in our study engage in is more of an information assimilation task, that is, where the users able to assimilate the information content and gain some knowledge from it.

EXPERIMENTAL METHODOLOGY

Experimental Goal

The main goal of the experiment reported in this study was to analyze the influence of olfaction on an information recall task in an olfaction-enhanced multimedia environment, specifically:

Does olfaction enhance user information recall in multimedia applications?

Procedure

We conducted two sets of experiments for this exploratory study, a control study and an experimental study. The two experiments involved participants watching a set of six multimedia video clips lasting for approximately 90 seconds. In the control study, clips were watched without the introduction of olfactory data, whilst in the experimental study, the video clips were augmented with olfactory media, i.e. computer generated scent. The olfactory data, which was emitted for about 30 seconds, was synchronized with appropriate audiovisual content of the multimedia videos in the two studies that involved the use of computer generated scent.

Furthermore, participants in both groups were required to complete a task at the end of each video clip viewed. The task required them to complete a set of questions based on the multimedia video they had just watched. For each video clip, questions were chosen to encompass the visual and aural aspects of the multimedia content. In addition, participants who watched the olfaction-enhanced videos, i.e. the experimental study group, were also required to complete a set of questions about their perception of the olfactory data content added to the multimedia videos. The multimedia video clips viewed by participants were 240 x 180 pixels in dimension and are described below:

- **Burnt:** Documentary on bush fires in Oklahoma (smell used: *burning wood*)
- **Flowery:** News broadcast featuring perfume launch (smell used: *wallflower*)
- **Foul:** Documentary about rotting fruits (smell used: *rubbish/acrid*)
- **Fruity:** Cookery show on how to make a fruit cocktail (smell used: *strawberry*)
- **Resinous:** Documentary on Spring allergies and cedar wood (smell used: *cedar wood*)
- **Spicy:** Cookery show on how to make chicken curry (smell used: *curry*)

Participants

30 participants (12 males, 18 females), recruited through a snowballing technique, were randomly allocated to either the control or the experimental group. Participants were between 18–41 years of age, and hailed from a wide variety of backgrounds, i.e. undergraduate and postgraduate students from different universities and departments, as well as both blue and white collar workers. Only two participants, across the two cohorts, said that they had had some smell recognition training.

After the purpose of the study had been explained to them and they had been informed that all data collected will be anonymized and treated in accordance with the UK Data Protection laws, participants signed a consent form. Participants were not offered any incentives to take part in any of the investigative studies and were also allowed to opt out of the experiment at any point in time during the course of the experiment without giving any reasons for so doing.

Olfactory Device

We have used Dale Air's Vortex Active scent dispensing system to generate computer controlled olfactory data for our experiment. This is a personal computer smell dispensing system, which uses miniature fans to propel the emitted smells in the

right direction. The Vortex Active connects to the computer via a USB port, and we used the USB fan controller application supplied with the device to control the synchronised release of olfactory data during the video playback.

MATERIAL

Notwithstanding the distinctive uniqueness associated with smell that makes it possible to detect its presence in the air, research has shown that it is easier for people to smell something than it is for them to identify what they have smelt, and more often than not people will try to identify a smell by associating it with a smell they are familiar with (Bodnar, Corbett, & Nekrasovski, 2004; Brewster, McGookin, & Miller, 2006; Kaye, 2001). Odor identification is also usually influenced by social and cultural factors (Saito, et al., 2006). For these reasons and also due to the lack of standard smell classification schemes (Chastrette, 2002; Issanchou, et al., 2002), it is advised that familiar smells be used for experiments involving the use of olfactory data (Kaye, 2001; Saito, et al., 2006). We finally opted for the six primary smells presented in the Hans Henning 'smell prism' (Chastrette, 2002; Kaye, 2001; Olfactory Types, 2007) as we felt it would not be too difficult to find at least one smell that is easily recognisable and identifiable within each of these 6 smell categories, which incidentally also has a fair distribution ratio between what can be termed as pleasant and unpleasant smell categories. The six smells categories used were *flowery, foul, fruity, burnt, resinous,* and *spicy*.

EXPERIMENT QUESTIONNAIRE

There were two different questionnaires used for the two cohorts involved in this investigation. The experimental study cohort included the set of questions about participants' perception of the olfactory data content added to the multimedia videos, as well as the questions relating to the content of the videos. For the control study, the questionnaire included the video content questions and excluded the questions based on participants' perception of the olfactory content. In addition, both sets of participants were asked about their enjoyment of the multimedia experience.

Keeping with previous research, a set of previously piloted questions was formulated for each clip viewed for the task performance exercise. These questions were chosen so that there were an equal number of questions targeting the first, second and last 30 seconds of each clip. Moreover, there was an equal distribution in respect of the number of questions targeting the video, audio, and textual components of the clip.

In keeping with the approach adopted by Ghinea and Thomas (1998) in their study of user perception and understanding of multimedia video clip, we measured the information assimilation of participants. In their approach, they measure the Quality of Perception (QoP), which they define as a measure which encompasses not only a user's satisfaction of a multimedia presentation, but also the user's ability to perceive, synthesize and analyse the informational content of such presentations. To this end, they analyse user perception and understanding of multimedia video clips by presenting participants with a variety of multimedia video clips (12 in this case) and immediately following each video clip viewing, participants are required to answer questions from all aspects of the information presented in the multimedia video, i.e. audio, visual or textual. There were other measures considered in their study, such as participants' rating of the quality of the video clips viewed, as they focused on investigating the interaction between QoP and the more traditional Quality of Service (QoS) and its implications from both a user perspective as well as from a networking angle. However, further reference to their study herein will only be related to the aspects of their study that deals with evaluation of information assimilation, as this is what is relevant to our study.

To measure information assimilation, we compute the score obtained in the performance task questions by each participant and express it as a percentage score.

RESULTS

The question we set out to answer in the study reported in this chapter, '*does olfaction enhance information recall for users in a multimedia application*' and we aim to use the results from our Control and Experimental study groups to find answers to this question. The results discussed in this chapter are based on participants responses to the content specific questions asked about each of the six videos watched, as well as their response to the question about their enjoyment of the multimedia experience.

As our experimental design was based on a 6 x 2 within-subjects, between-subjects design, we use the General Linear Model (GLM) repeated measures (repeated measures ANOVA) tests to analyse the results obtained in our study. The six video categories is our within-subjects factor, whilst the study group, dividing participants into the control and experimental subgroups, is our between-subjects factor. For our within-subjects factor, we measure the information assimilation of participants in each of the six video categories, as well as their enjoyment of the multimedia video clips. Using the GLM repeated measures test, we investigate and show the interactions between these factors, i.e. study group and video content, as well as the effects of the individual factors below.

INFORMATION ASSIMILATION

As mentioned above, we computed the scores obtained by participants in the performance task for each of the multimedia videos viewed and

Figure 1. Information assimilation percentage scores

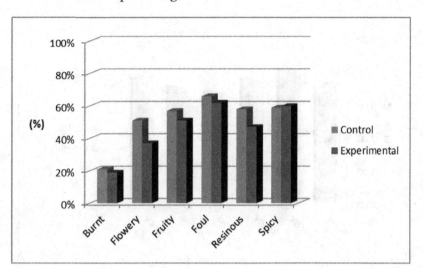

expressed it as a percentage to measure information assimilation. Results show that generally performance was better in the control study case, that is, for those participants who watched the videos without the presence of olfactory media. The only exception was in the case of the *Spicy* video, in which the mean score marks obtained are comparable between the two study groups. These results suggest that participants generally found it easier to assimilate the informational content of the multimedia videos in the absence of olfactory data, i.e. in the control case study, which further suggests that the presence of scented media proved to be somewhat of a distraction.

The scores obtained also show (Figure 1) that the difference in performance between the experimental study group and control study group was greatest for the *Flowery* video and least for the *Spicy* video. The lowest mean score was obtained in the experimental case for the *Burnt* video, although generally performance was also the worst for this video across both the experimental and control case studies. Performance was best in the *Fruity* video.

The repeated measures ANOVA test shows that there is a significant difference in performance across the six different video categories (F=32.179,

p=0.000). This is consistent with previous research studies (Chen, Ghinea, & Macredie, 2006; Ghinea & Thomas, 1998; Ghinea, Thomas, & Fish, 1999; Gulliver & Ghinea, 2006), which have also shown that content influences information assimilation. Moreover, although the performance mean scores mostly reflect that olfaction has a somewhat detrimental effect on information assimilation, the repeated measures ANOVA test (F=1.673, p=0.206) shows that the difference in performance between the control and experimental study groups is not statistically significant. However, the within-subjects by between-Subjects interaction effects (F=0.850, p=0.517) shows that there was no significant difference in performance between the two study groups across the six different video categories.

PERCEIVED ENJOYMENT OF THE MULTIMEDIA EXPERIENCE

Participants' perceived enjoyment of the multimedia experience for both study groups was measured on the popular 5-point Likert scale response categories reflecting disagreement and agreement. Generally, these results show (Figure

Figure 2. User-perceived enjoyment of the multimedia experience

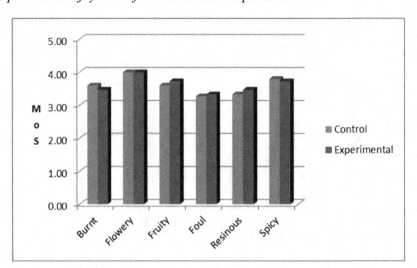

2) that with the exception of the *Foul* and *Resinous* videos, there was mostly a slight preference for the multimedia experience in the experimental study case, that is, the olfaction-enhanced multimedia experience. Moreover, the results also reflect that participants mostly enjoyed the multimedia experience or at the very least remained neutral in their opinion of the enjoyment of the experience across both study groups.

It is understandable that the olfaction-enhanced version of the *Foul* video clip generated a less enjoyable experience for participants (as manifested by the lower mean value)—because of the slightly unpleasant nature of the scent used to augment this video (rubbish acrid). In the case of the *Resinous* video, whilst the perceived degree of enjoyment is less in the experimental study group, the difference between the two study groups is not as pronounced as in the case of the *Foul* video and the results are in fact almost comparable.

Nonetheless, a repeated measures ANOVA test shows that the differences in participants' perception of enjoyment between the two exploratory study groups, as well as across the different video categories, are not statistically significant. However, the non-significance of our experiment results as manifested by the results from this test may be attributed to the small sample size used in this study. Moreover, we have obtained statistically significant results in a previous study involving a larger sample size that shows that indeed the addition of olfaction to multimedia applications does enhance the users' enjoyment of the experience.

CONCLUSION

Whilst the impact olfaction on information recall has been shown to be inconclusive, and further research is needed to explore this angle, in respect of the influence of an information recall task on user enjoyment and general perception of an olfaction-enhanced multimedia application, the results showed that generally there was no difference in the user-perceived experience as a result of the introduction of a performance task. Moreover, the results revealed that in some cases the addition of a performance task improved the understanding of the semantic relationship between olfaction and the audiovisual media objects. This can be quite beneficial in some instances, for example, in an olfaction-enhanced multimedia application designed to teach the user about characteristic smells associated with specific scenarios. Consequently, the addition of a performance task may help the user to further appreciate and understand the correlation between the characteristic odor(s) and the scenario under consideration. Having said that, some attention must also be paid to the other media objects that the olfactory data is to be integrated with in such applications, as our results also showed instances where the informational content of the audiovisual media the olfactory data was integrated with had a negative impact on user perception of the olfaction-enhanced multimedia experience.

REFERENCES

BBC. (2006). *Smellovision for Japan cinema*. Retrieved August 21 from http://news.bbc.co.uk/1/hi/entertainment/4903984.stm

Bodnar, A., Corbett, R., & Nekrasovski, D. (2004). AROMA: Ambient awareness through olfaction in a messaging application: Does olfactory notification make 'scents'? In *Proceedings of ICMI 2004 - Sixth International Conference on Multimodal Interfaces*, (p. 183). ICMI.

Boyd Davis, S., Davies, G., Haddad, R., & Lai, M. (2006). Smell me: Engaging with an interactive olfactory game. In *Proceedings of the Human Factors and Ergonomics Society 25th Annual Meeting*, (pp. 25-40). Human Factors and Ergonomics Society.

Brewster, S. A., McGookin, D. K., & Miller, C. A. (2006). Olfoto: Designing a smell-based interaction. In *Proceedings of CHI 2006: Conference on Human Factors in Computing Systems*, (p. 653). ACM Press.

Chastrette, M. (2002). Classification of odors and structure–odor relationships. In C. Rouby, B. Schall, d. Dubois, R. Gervais, & A. Holley (Eds.), *Olfaction, Taste, and Cognition,* (pp. 100-116). Cambridge, UK: Cambridge University Press.

Chen, S. Y., Ghinea, G., & Macredie, R. D. (2006). A cognitive approach to user perception of multimedia quality: An empirical investigation. *International Journal of Human-Computer Studies, 64*(12), 1200–1213. doi:10.1016/j.ijhcs.2006.08.010

Dale Air Limited Dispensers. (2007). *Vortex active*. Retrieved October 12, 2007 from http://www.daleair.com/acatalog/Dispensers.html

Dinh, H. Q., Walker, N., Hodges, L. F., Song, C., & Kobayashi, A. (1999). Evaluating the importance of multi-sensory input on memory and the sense of presence in virtual environments. In *Proceedings - Virtual Reality Annual International Symposium*, (pp. 222-228). IEEE.

Fragra. (2003). *IVRC*. Retrieved from http://chihara.aist-nara.ac.jp/ivrc2003/index.html

Ghinea, G., & Thomas, J. P. (1998). QoS impact on user perception and understanding of multimedia video clips. In *Proceedings of the Sixth ACM International Conference on Multimedia*, (pp. 49-54). New York, NY: ACM Press.

Ghinea, G., Thomas, J. P., & Fish, R. S. (1999). Multimedia, network protocols and users - Bridging the gap. In *Proceedings of the Seventh ACM International Conference on Multimedia*, (pp. 473-476). New York, NY: ACM Press.

Gulliver, S. R., & Ghinea, G. (2006). Defining user perception of distributed multimedia quality. *ACM Transactions on Multimedia Computing. Communications and Applications, 2*(4), 241–257.

Heritage, S. (2006). *The new Colin Farrell movie stinks in Japan*. Retrieved August 23, 2007 from http://www.hecklerspray.com/the-new-colin-farrell-movie-stinks-in-japan/20062756.php

Herz, R. S., Eliassen, J., Beland, S., & Souza, T. (2004). Neuroimaging evidence for the emotional potency of odor-evoked memory. *Neuropsychologia, 42*(3), 371–378. doi:10.1016/j.neuropsychologia.2003.08.009

Issanchou, S., Valentin, D., Sulmont, C., Degel, J., & Köster, E. P. (2002). Testing odor memory: Incidental versus intentional learning, implicit versus explicit memory. In C. Rouby, b. Schaal, D. Dubois, R. Gervais, & A. Holley (Eds.), *Olfaction, Taste, and Cognition*, (pp. 211-230). Cambridge, UK: Cambridge University Press.

Kaye, J. N. (2001). *Symbolic olfactory display*. (Master's Thesis). Massachusetts Institute of Technology. Cambridge, MA. Retrieved September 11, 2005 from http://www.media.mit.edu/~jofish/thesis/

Kaye, J. N. (2004). Making scents: Aromatic output for HCI. *Interaction*, *11*(1), 48–61. doi:10.1145/962342.964333

Kiger, P. J., & Smith, M. J. (2006). *Lesson #9 - Beware of unproven technologies the lingering reek of "smell-o-vision"*. New York, NY: HarperCollins. Retrieved August 21, 2007 from http://www.in70mm.com/news/2006/oops/index.htm

News, A. B. C. (1999). *Smell-o-vision coming to internet soon*. Retrieved August 21, 2007 from http://www.temple.edu/ispr/examples/ex99_10_20.html

Rasch, B., Büchel, C., Gais, S., & Born, J. (2007). Odor cues during slow-wave sleep prompt declarative memory consolidation. *Science*, *315*(5817), 1426–1429. doi:10.1126/science.1138581

Saito, S., Ayabe-Kanamura, S., Takashima, Y., Gotow, N., Naito, N., & Nozawa, T. (2006). Development of a smell identification test using a novel stick-type odor presentation kit. *Chemical Senses*, *31*(4), 379–391. doi:10.1093/chemse/bjj042

Shepherd, G. M. (2006). Smell images and the flavour system in the human brain. *Nature*, *444*, 316–321. doi:10.1038/nature05405

Smith, M. J., & Kiger, P. J. (2006). The lingering reek of smell-o-vision. *Los Angeles Times*. Retrieved August 21, 2007 from http://www.latimes.com/features/magazine/west/la-tm-oops-6feb05,1,2932206.story?coll=la-iraq-complete

Tortell, R., Luigi, D. P., Dozois, A., Bouchard, S., Morie, J. F., & Ilan, D. (2007). The effects of scent and game play experience on memory of a virtual environment. *Virtual Reality (Waltham Cross)*, *11*(1), 61–68. doi:10.1007/s10055-006-0056-0

Variety Staff. (2001). *Variety review of "scent of mystery"*. Retrieved August 21, 2007 from http://www.variety.com/review/VE1117794675?refcatid=31

Chapter 24
Odor Code Sensor and Odor Reproduction

Kenshi Hayashi
Kyushu University, Japan

ABSTRACT

In biological olfactory systems, odor receptors receive odor molecules by recognizing the molecular information. Humans can sense the odor by the signal from these activated receptors. The combination of the activated receptors is called "odor code," and the odor codes are expressed as an "odor cluster map" of glomeruli on the olfactory bulb surface. The odor code is essential information for qualitative and quantitative analyses of odor sensation. In this chapter, development of odor sensors based on the odor code concept and an attempt to extract the parameters for odor coding from molecular informatics are described. Application of the obtained odor code for odor reproduction is also presented.

INTRODUCTION

The methodology of artificial odor evaluation is mainly performed based on some assumed fundamental odorants in odor sensing systems, which are developed utilizing quartz-crystal odor microbalance, metal-oxide semiconductor, or conductive polymer sensor. However, there exists no obvious fundamental or elemental odor in olfaction; therefore, it cannot be said that this methodology is appropriate for the qualitative evaluation of general odor sensation.

Recent progressed research on biological olfaction reveals existence of hundreds number of odor receptors, receiving modality, and odor recognition mechanisms (Buck & Axel, 1991; Mori & Shepherd, 1994; Torinelli, et al., 2009). One receptor can recognize multiple odorants, and each odorant is recognized by multiple receptors in the olfactory system (Malnic, et al., 1999).

DOI: 10.4018/978-1-4666-2521-1.ch024

Copyright © 2013, IGI Global. Copying or distributing in print or electronic forms without written permission of IGI Global is prohibited.

This indicates that the olfactory system uses a combinatorial coding scheme. On the standpoint of molecular recognition, odor receptors recognize not whole chemical structures of odorants but their partial structures; i.e. odotope hypothesis (Araneda, et al., 2000; Malnic, et al., 1999). It can be said that a certain odorant activates several odor receptors and evokes combination of activated olfactory receptors; therefore, odor qualitative sensation depends on the combination of the molecular partial structures. Such combinatorial molecular information of odorants is "odor code" that can encode odor identity. Thus, receptors are able to recognize different features of molecules with flexible selectivity, and a particular odor compound may also consist of a number of these determinants that possess some of these features.

A first central nerve system connected to olfactory cells is an olfactory bulb, in which combinatorial coding information of activated olfactory receptors generates odor maps which are composed of activated glomeruli. The activated glomerulus points can be categorized into odor clusters, which respond to groups of odorants that has similar chemical properties (Matsumoto, 2010; Johnson, et al., 2010). Smell brought about natural stuffs forms a sparse pattern of odor cluster map (Lin, et al., 2006); therefore, odor information is not very complex compared with an image treated in biological sense of sight. Thus odor code can be expressed by the odor cluster map that has features of metric space, i.e. similar smell has similar spacial pattern of activated glomeruli in olfactory bulb space (Furudono, 2009). Consequently, similarity of odor qualitative sensation can be determined quantitatively through odor cluster maps.

The odor code is combinatorial information about odor molecules that consists of a substructure combination. Therefore, an odor sensor can be established based on the odor code concept; determinants of odor molecules, such as substructures of molecule, molecular size or functional group (Masunaga, et al., 2008; Izumi, et al., 2008) are target information to be detected by an odor sensing system that detects various volatile chemicals. In order to recognize molecular odor code information like the olfactory system, nanostructure on the sensor surface was developed to control the surface affinities that are attributed to molecular substructure (Masunaga, et al., 2005). Thus, design of nanostructures is important and necessary to detect a substructure of molecules, and such sensor technology may leads to an odor code sensor.

On the other hand, if the odor coding is successfully achieved, the code can be used to reproduce odor by elemental chemicals that represent each elemental odor code. The odor reproduction is very important aim also for sensor developments, because one of the most difficult problems to evaluate odor sensor ability is lack of reproducing way using developed odor sensor output. In other word, the problem of the odor sensor is lack of well-defined sensor output; no one can recognize the odor sensor output is proper or not. Odor code is based on distinct information of molecules; therefore, we can communicate sufficient information about odor using odor code. Consequently, odor sensing system and odor reproducing system can be developed on odor code information other than assumed fundamental odorants, and odor code concept can be a useful guiding principal for development of instruments treating odor (Figure 1).

In this chapter, odor code sensing system was developed to detect two essential information of the odor code; functional group type and molecular size of odor molecules. Various sensing techniques were introduced for the sensor, such as electrochemical impedance sensor and nanostructured surface.

Odor separating system using specific adsorbents was also developed to evaluate odorants as odor cluster maps. Artificial odor code calculation

Figure 1. Odor code and odor cluster map to measure odor information. Output information of the odor sensing system is limited to odor code. Estimation of impressional or emotional expression about odor is not the required function to the odor code sensor.

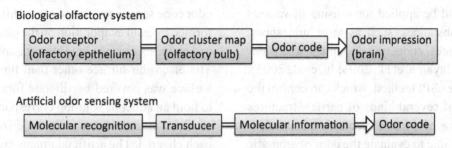

was also attempted through molecular informatics. The molecular parameters obtained by molecular modeling were examined for various odorants, for which parameters were several steric and electronic ones; e.g. cluster count, polar surface area, and dipole. A few extracted Principal Components (PCs) from molecular parameters were examined as parameters concerning to human olfactory sensation.

As an application of the odor code, odor reproduction was tried based on odor codes. Conceptual method to find elemental odorants that can synthesize natural odor on the standpoint of odor cluster map is proposed finally. As a conclusion, odor code can be used for odor qualitative evaluation, odor recording and olfactory displays.

INTEGRATED ODOR CODE SENSOR

In biological systems, odorants are received by a large number of receptors, which recognize not whole structures but partial structures of molecules. The system can be realized artificially by odor-sensing system with integrated multi-channel odor sensor, where the channels of the sensor for specific molecular partial structure were created by combining the surface polarization controlled sensor and the method with the surface modification technology such as Self-Assembled Monolayers (SAMs).

SAMs Electrode and cSPI Measurement for Substructure Recognition

As part of this approach, a sensor surface was developed to recognize a phenyl group within molecules. A phenyl group is one of the important substructures of aromatics. Preceding research revealed that electrochemical surface impedance of electrodes can be used for detections of various molecular substructures (Hayashi, et al., 2004); where the impedance was measured by cyclic Surface-Polarization Impedance (cSPI) method (Ju, et al., 2007; Masunaga, et al., 2005). The cSPI is a method to detect the adsorption of chemicals by measuring the electrode impedance depending upon Constant Phase Element (CPE) characteristics, with controlling the surface polarization of electrode potential dynamically. The CPE impedance characteristics are the particular behaviors of solid real electrodes. In an ideal electrode, the electrode-electrolyte interfacial impedance should be represented only as a capacitance by electric double layer in the case of no oxidation-reduction reaction with Faradaic current on the Electrochemical Impedance Spectroscopy (EIS) (Hayama, et al., 2002). The surface impedance of a real electrode, however, has a form corresponding to a 'frequency-dependent' capacitance. Thus, the interaction between odorants and the surface is altered through surface polarization, and information about adsorbing odorants can be obtained by measuring CPE impedance through EIS and dynamically controlled surface potential. The method could be applied for sensing of various chemical substances, such as taste substances, odor substances, endocrine disrupters, and water pollutants (Hayama, et al., 2003; Ju, et al., 2003).

Using the cSPI method, which can control the adsorption of several kinds of partial structures by regulating of surface electrode potential, it became possible to evaluate the odor of aromatic alcohol using the quantitative strength of alcoholic hydroxyl and aromatic ring (Hayashi, et al., 2004). The sensor is provided with thin water membrane on the electrode surface, which works as artificial mucus of olfactory system. On the other hand, the system had a problem that there were some odorants, which have a difficulty in discrimination with the others, because several odor molecules can be adsorbed to the electrode surface simultaneously. In order to improve the specificity to the aromatic ring, suitable adsorption site for it was designed. This was done by using surface modification such as Self-Assembled Monolayers (SAMs) with adsorption sites (Hayama, et al., 2003; Izumi, et al., 2008; Sasaki, et al., 2009).

Integrated Multi-Channel Odor Code Sensor

In the case of odor detection, an electrochemical method that requires a certain aqueous solution to connect electrodes electrically has some problems for odor detection because the water membrane is largely affected by room circumstances by drying of electrolytic solution. In addition, it was necessary for the sensor to prepare the electrode surface, including cleaning and SAM formation processes, every experiment; thus it took a long time for measurement-to-measurement. In order to improve the efficiency of odor measurements, an integrated multi-channel odor sensor was developed. In the multi-channel odor code sensor,

each electrode was designed corresponding to a certain property of the odor code.

Figure 2 shows the integrated multi-channel odor code sensor developed here. This sensor was formed by gold evaporation on the glass substrate and patterning using photolithography technique. The electrode surface other than functionalized surface was covered by silicone film with holes to hold an aqueous solution corresponding to the artificial mucus (water membrane covering) for each channel. The artificial mucus layer consists of 70% glycerin and KCl aqueous solution. Glycerin was used as a moist reagent, which kept concentration and property of the water membrane constant. The electrodes were covered with 10 μl of water membrane solution, and its thickness was approximately 800 μm.

Each channel of the sensor electrode is composed of electrochemical 3 electrodes, i.e. Working Electrode (WE), Reference Electrode (RE), and Counter Electrode (CE). WE, which detects the odor molecules, is located between RE and CE in each channel. In order to keep the electrode potential stable, RE was covered with platinum black, and CE was also covered with platinum black to keep the thickness of the water membrane even with their surface roughness. Pt black as a reference electrode indicates stable potential in this case because electrolytic compounds were constant in odor measurements.

Odor gases which are generated in gas washing bottles or by permeation tubes were introduced to the sensor and the cSPI measurement was performed by a potentiostat equipped with a frequency response analyzer (Izumi, et al., 2007).

In order to functionalize the electrode, design of the electrode surface was made using benzene-patterned SAM. Present multi-channel sensor utilized 1-octanethiol (OT) for the formation of SAM. As a first step, both benzene and OT were adsorbed to the well-cleaned electrode by immersing it into the 100 μM OT solution diluted by benzene for 30 minutes. Then, after

Figure 2. Integrated multi-channel odor sensor: (a) photograph of an electrode, (b) construction of electrode, (c) top view, (d) detailed composition of three electrochemical electrodes of each channel

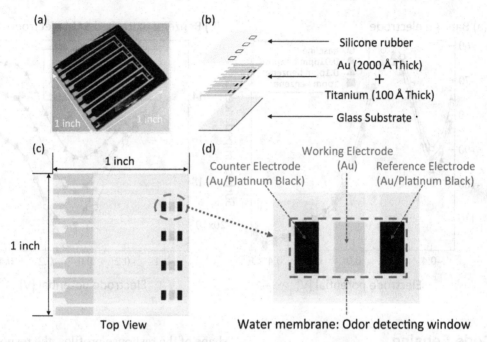

benzene and OT were adsorbed sufficiently, adsorbed benzene was removed by ethanol rinse and electrode potential sweep. The surface is expected to have the response specificity to the aromatic ring. Figure 3 shows the way of forming benzene-patterned SAM. The surface of benzene-patterned SAM was characterized using AFM, ellipsometry, electrochemical method (stripping voltammetry), and contact angle (Masunaga, et al., 2008). As a result, coverage and thickness of obtained benzene-patterned SAMs were about 90% compared with perfect SAMs. It means small

amount of defects in the SAM structure worked as benzene adsorbing sites.

The adsorption and detection of ethanol was interrupted by the water membrane, since glycerin has hydroxyl groups in its chemical structure. In order to avoid such interruption, cellulose phosphate (P cellulose) was combined into the water membrane. P cellulose is an ion-exchange resin, so it can be expected to avoid the influence by hydroxyl groups contained in glycerin. Thus functionalization of the electrode could be accomplished by the surface modification and composition of the water membrane.

Figure 3. Formation of benzene-patterned SAM (Masunaga, et al., 2008)

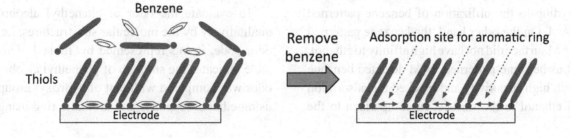

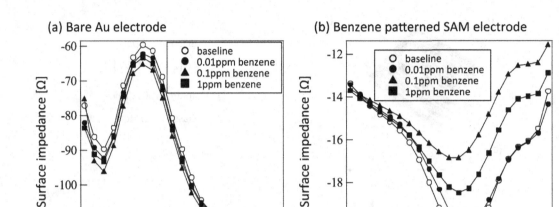

Figure 4. Responses to benzene of bare Au electrode and benzene-patterned SAM electrode. Reactances of the electrode impedance are displayed.

Odor Code Sensing

Present sensor for odor code, ethanol, benzene, and phenethyl alcohol, whose structures consist of hydroxyl, aromatic ring, or both, were measured as odorants. Figure 4 indicates typical response profiles of a bare Au electrode and the benzene-patterned SAM electrode. In this result, complex impedance values (reactance) were displayed. In Figure 4(b), the dependence on the benzene concentration change could be observed with benzene-patterned SAM, comparing to the response with bare gold electrode (Figure 4[a]) where the reactance is mainly determined only by surface electric double layer composed of cation or anion gathered onto the negatively or positively charged electrode surface. It is supposed that the affinity to the aromatic ring became higher according to the utilization of benzene-patterned SAM. On the other hand, the benzene patterned SAM surface did not have high affinity to ethanol. Thus benzene-patterned SAM detected benzene with high sensitivity and blocked the adsorption of ethanol to the surface. In comparison to the

shape of the response profiles, the response with benzene-patterned SAM is different from that with bare gold surface. Furthermore, addition of P cellulose to the glycerin membrane enhanced the ethanol detection and interfered with benzene detection. This result indicates that the information about the adsorbed odor molecules is different from each other.

Odor responses of the multi-channel sensor are shown in Figure 5 to compare the response characteristics with each channel. Phenethyl alcohol was detected with larger magnitude by both P cellulose and benzene patterned SAM channels, comparing to bare Au glycerin membrane. Therefore, the addition of P cellulose to the membrane and the formation of benzene-patterned SAM gave the response specificities depending on the substructure.

To evaluate the odor of phenethyl alcohol qualitatively by the molecular substructures, i.e. odor code, it was represented by Table 1. This table indicates the strength of phenethyl alcohol odor was compared with that of hydroxyl group using ethanol response and aromatic ring using

Figure 5. Responses of multi-channel odor code sensor. Unspecific channel is bare Au electrode covered with a simple water membrane that does not have specificity to odorants. Hydroxyl group is detected by P cellulose channel, and aromatic ring is detected by benzene patterned SAM channel.

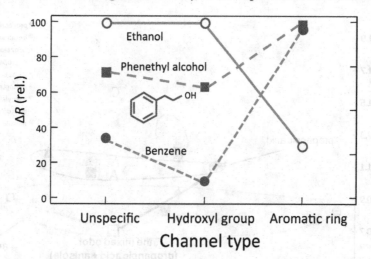

benzene response by two channels. Concentration dependencies of phenethyl alcohol responses altered odor code components, where the odor of phenethyl alcohol with lower concentration was mainly contributed by aromatic ring, and that with higher concentration was mainly contributed by hydroxyl group. According to human perception, the odor sensation was also changed by gas concentration, so this result can be acceptable. In this way, the odor sensation can be evaluated qualitatively and quantitatively with the molecular substructures. In conclusion, it can be said that this odor sensor recognizes the molecular partial structures, in similar way to odor recognition in biological system.

Table 1. Summarized odor code extracted from responses of hydroxyl group and aromatic ring channels in Figure 5

	Alcoholic	Aromatic
Ethanol	1.00	0.26
Benzene	0.08	1.00
Phenethyl alcohol	0.62	1.00

ODOR CODE SENSING BY ODOR SEPARATING SYSTEM

As described previous section, the odor code sensor directly detects substructure of odor molecules. The sensor with high molecular-recognition ability is a final goal for odor sensing system; however, it requires various kinds of nanostructured surfaces with high specificity and molecular-recognizing abilities to detect enormous numbers of odor molecules. On the other hand, there exist various kinds of adsorbents with various affinities to chemical compounds, e.g. column materials for Gas Chromatography (GC). Odor separating/sensing system was developed by using combination of adsorbent materials and an ordinal Metal Oxide (MOX) gas sensor. This is another approach that imitates the odor receptive mechanism of biological olfaction based on combination of conventional gas detecting methods (See chapter 5).

The developed odor separating system analyzes output information on the standpoint of odor clustering. Electronic nose technology has been researched, and the e-nose systems focused on odor discrimination using non-specific sensor

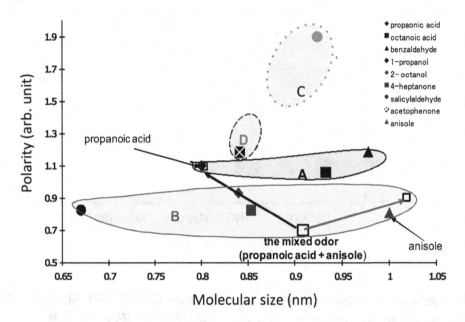

Figure 6. Odor map obtained experimentally by odor separating sensing system. The map corresponds to odor cluster map on biological olfactory bulb. Mixture of odors could be discriminated and decomposed into their elemental clusters by response data analysis.

array; however, previous sensors have not been used by appropriate evaluating methods like odor coding or odor clustering. Odor cluster map shown in Figure 1 and described in Introduction is convenient and effective way to evaluate odor code of odor substances because the odor cluster map has features of metric space and similarities and differences of the maps can be recognized easily by our sight of vision.

In order to realize the odor sensor system enabling odor clustering, the odor separating system makes it possible to detect and classify odorants by the difference in both molecular size and strength of polarity of molecules like the biological olfactory system (Imahashi, et al., 2011). The system mainly consists of adsorbing and separating cells that enable classification of measured odorants based on molecular size and polarity (dipole moment). Four micro ceramic heaters are attached in one adsorbing and separating cell and four kinds of zeolitic or carbon molecular sieves, or gas-chromatographic column

adsorbent materials are adhered on the surface of each heater. Gases from gas washing bottle filled with odorants were delivered through computer-controlled mass-flow controller and solenoid valve system (Imahashi, et al., 2011). On heating process, the trapped odorants desorb from the adsorbent are sent to the connected sensor cell and measured with the MOX gas sensor. Thus, it becomes roughly possible to detect and classify odorant by the difference of both the molecular size and the strength of polarity of molecules and to measure odor as time course patterns. In this development, representative odor materials of cluster A-D were measured and it was extracted odor information from time course patterns obtained. Then, with the obtained information, the artificial odor map close to the biological odor map was tried to make (Mori, 2006).

Here both the molecular size and the polarity of selected odorants were estimated from the responses caused by desorbed gases from adsorbent materials corresponding to specific size or

Figure 7. Scatter map of principal components obtained from molecular informatics

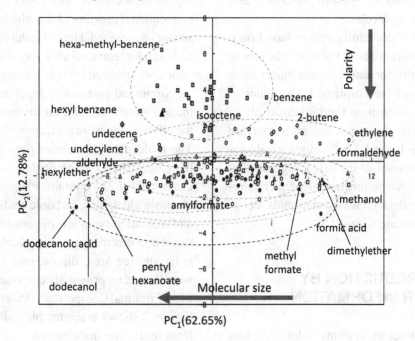

polarity obtained through the system. As a result, the correlation between molecular parameters of odorants was found and the molecular size and polarity could be estimated. Using the estimated odor information, the odor map was constructed that can classify odorants by their odor cluster at-

tributes (Figure 6). Thus, it was confirmed that the system enables measurement and discrimination of odorants by odor cluster map. In addition, mixed odors that consist of a couple of odor molecules from basis cluster were measured. Roughly, it was succeeded to divide odorants mixed two kinds of

Figure 8. Odor synthesis based on scatter map of principal components of molecular informatics. Cross (x) marks are the same points of scatter diagram shown in Figure 7.

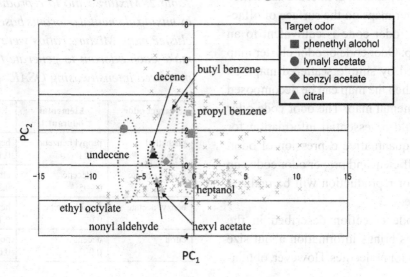

odor molecules into the appropriate cluster and constituent odor molecules.

Thus, the odor code information based on a newly defined notion about the odor clusters in olfactory bulb; an odor sensor system that enables odor clustering was accomplished. The obtained odor map close to map on the biological olfactory bulb, where the measured odorants are categorized into cluster A-D of the biological odor cluster map (Imahashi, et al., 2011), suggests that the system has basic performance to detect determinative factors through which mammals recognize and discriminate odor.

ODOR REPRODUCTION BY MOLECULAR INFORMATION

In biological olfactory systems, odor receptors receive odor molecules by recognizing the molecular information; where human can feel the odor by the combination of electric signals from the activated receptors induced by odor reception. The combination of the activated olfactory receptors is essential information of odor sensation (Malnic, et al., 1999), and the information is called as odor code in this article, where the coding is mainly depend on molecular sizes and electrical polarities. Signals from activated receptors are projected to corresponding glomeruli, and hence forms odor cluster maps on the surface of olfactory bulb. Thus, odor code is equivalent to an odor cluster map. Odor code or odor cluster map can be expressed by simple scattered maps on olfactory bulb, then the map can be decomposed into simple elemental map. The odor code/odor cluster map could be essential information for qualitative and quantitative expression of odor. Therefore, if sufficient and proper odor code can be obtained, odor reproduction will be realized by the odor code.

The odor-code detection described in the previous sections brings information about size and polarity of odor molecules. However, obtain-ing the odor code for any odorants is difficult by conventional instrumental methods or simple odor sensors developed. Here in order to examine odor code as odor reproduction information, an artificial odor code calculation was attempted.

Numerical parameters from molecular information were used, and multivariate analyses for the information were performed (Hayashi, 2009). The molecular informatics parameters obtained by ChemBio3D (Cambridge software) were examined for 211 odorants chosen from alkenes, alcohols, aldehydes, carbonic acids, ethers, esters, and aromatics. Numbers of parameters were 59 of steric and electric ones, for which cluster count, polar surface area, dipole, etc. The parameters were treated by principal component analysis and a few Principal Components (PCs) were obtained. Figure 7 shows a scatter plot of PCs extracted from molecular information.

PC1 was examined using quantification method type 3. As a result categorized qualitative value and PC1 had a correlation with human olfaction. Furthermore, odor intensity was evaluated quantitatively by PC1 and high correlation was confirmed. This odor code map shown in Figure 7 supposed to be another visual expression corresponding to an odor map appeared in a biological olfactory bulb, where odor molecules are

Table 2. Mixture ratio to reproduce target odor by mixing elemental odorants based on odor code cluster map. Mixture ratios were determined to make each odorant to generate the same odor-perceived intensity using QSAR.

Target odor	Elemental odorant 1	Elemental odorant 2
phenethyl alcohol	propyl benzene 0.024	heptanol 0.157
linalyl acetate	undecene 0.005	ethyl octylate 0.226
benzyl acetate	butyl benzene 0.006	hexyl acetate 0.157
citral	decene 0.002	nonyl aldehyde 0.042

scatter-mapped by the order of their functional groups and carbon chain lengths (Matsumoto, 2010; Johnson, et al., 2010). Thus, odor evaluation can be performed using the odor code by molecular information.

For an application of the odor code by molecular information, odor of chemicals, which have more than two functional groups, were decomposed into two elemental odorants based on the map shown in Figure 8, where a certain odorant is decomposed into two odorants that have similar sizes and different polarities. Structural information was also evaluated to determine the candidates. Mixture ratios, which were calculated using QSAR (quantitative structure-activity relationship) analysis, were shown in Table 2. Thus the odor could be expressed by the molecular information. The expression was sensory-evaluated using an odor synthesizer (Figure 9), which was developed by joint research of Kyushu University and Kansai Electric Power Co. Inc. (Hayashi, 2009). The synthesizer is composed of a nebulizer and fixed-quantity pumps. As a result, it was confirmed that the mixture of the chemicals evoked similar odor sensation to target odors

compared with each single elemental odorant in our olfactory sense. This preliminary fact suggests that qualitative regeneration of odor can be achieved using several odor molecules that belong to representative chemicals of various chemical structures corresponding to odor code or odor clusters. Consequently, odor code by molecular information can be used for odor qualitative evaluation, communication and recording of odor and olfactory displays.

CONCEPTUAL ODOR REPRODUCTION BY ODOR CLUSTER MAP

Odor code can be represented by odor map, which forms odor clusters as shown in Figures 6 and 7. The map contains sufficient information to reproduce odor sensation. As shown in Figure 8, a target odor to reproduce could be decomposed; however, the way of decomposition was obscure because the map was just a PCs scatter map and not odor cluster map. Figure 10 shows reproduction concept using the odor cluster map. In this

Figure 9. Odor synthesizer to mix elemental odor solution based on odor code

conceptual method, activated points on the olfactory bulb caused by a certain odor stimulus are decomposed into several activated patterns, which are produced by elemental odorants. This concept is equivalent to a color matching principle, in the case any color can be created by mixture of red, green, and blue in a human color vision sensation.

Candidates of elemental odorants can be chosen from simple chemical compounds appeared in principal component map (Figure 7). These chemicals have only two odor code information, size and functional group. Then odor map will be elemental, i.e. map will be composed of a few activated glomeruli. The fact that natural odor causes sparse cluster map means that complex image processing is not necessary in odor cluster map analysis (Lin, 2006). If database of basic cluster maps for these elemental chemicals were provided, it would not be difficult to find out composing odor chemicals for any natural odor.

CONCLUSION

Evaluation and reproduction of odor using odor code is discussed in this chapter. Odor code sensing based on multi-channel sensor chip and odor-separating apparatus are presented. Reproduction based on the odor code is also proposed. The odor code is based on biological olfactory sensation, in which odor chemicals are classified based on their chemical features and odor cluster map appeared in the olfactory bulb is essential information of odor. The map is composed of combinatorial code of activated receptors and glomeruli. Thus, odor code is bio-inspired coding method. As primary colors in human color vision are essential information to reconstruct various colors, the odor code could be essential information to evaluate and reproduce odor.

Figure 10. Conceptual method to synthesize odor based on odor cluster map. Star-shaped points correspond to activated glomeruli in olfactory bulb. The map is obtained by molecular informatics calculation and activated points are provisional ones. Activated glomeruli on olfactory bulb which form cluster map is decomposed into some elemental odorants C1, C2, C3, or C4, which activates a few glomeruli.

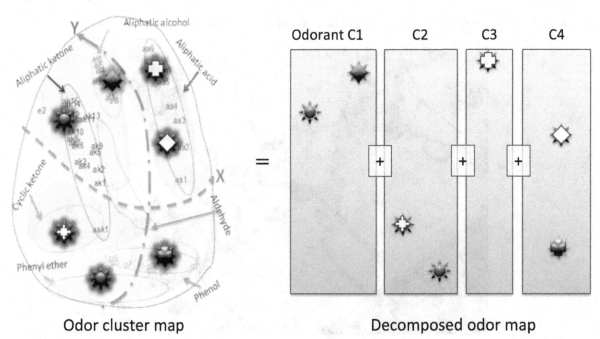

Odor cluster map   Decomposed odor map

REFERENCES

Araneda, R. C., Kini, A. D., & Firestein, S. (2000). The molecular receptive range of an odorant receptor. *Nature Neuroscience*, *3*(12), 1248–1255. doi:10.1038/81774

Buck, L., & Axel, R. (1991). A novel multigene family may encode odor recognition: A molecular basis for odor recognition. *Cell*, *65*(1), 175–187. doi:10.1016/0092-8674(91)90418-X

Furudono, Y., Sone, Y., Takizawa, K., Hirono, J., & Sato, T. (2009). Relationship between peripheral receptor code and perceived odor quality. *Chemical Senses*, *34*, 151–158. doi:10.1093/chemse/bjn071

Hayama, K., Hayashi, K., & Toko, K. (2003). Functionalization of gold surfaces using benzene-patterned self-assembled monolayers for surface-polarization controlling method. *Sensor Materials*, *15*, 403–412.

Hayama, K., Tanaka, H., Ju, M. J., Hayashi, K., & Toko, K. (2002). Fabrication of a flow cell for electrochemical impedance measurements. *Sensors and Materials*, *14*(8), 443–453.

Hayashi, K. (2009). Odor synthesis using odor code based on molecular informatics. In *Proceedings of the 26th Sensors Symposium*, (pp. 75-80). IEEE.

Hayashi, K., Hayama, K., Masunaga, K., Futagami, W., Lee, S. W., & Toko, K. (2004). Analysis of adsorbing molecules on pt surface using electrochemical impedance spectroscopy. *IEICE Transactions. E (Norwalk, Conn.)*, *87C*, 2087–2092.

Imahashi, M., Takamizawa, T., Miyagi, K., & Hayashi, K. (2011). Artificial odor map and discrimination of odorants using the odor separating system. In *Proceedings of the 14th International Symposium on Olfaction and Electronic Nose*, (vol. 1362, pp. 27-28). AIP.

Izumi, R., Abe, H., Hayashi, K., & Toko, K. (2007). Odor quantification of aromatic alcohols using artificial olfactory epithelium. *Sensors and Materials*, *19*, 299–307.

Izumi, R., Hayashi, K., & Toko, K. (2008). Odor sensor with water membrane using surface polarity controlling method and analysis of responses to partial structures of odor molecules. *Sensors and Actuators. B, Chemical*, *99*, 315–322. doi:10.1016/j.snb.2003.11.030

Johnson, B. A., Ong, J., & Leon, M. (2010). Glomerular activity patterns evoked by natural odor objects in the rat olfactory bulb are related to patterns evoked by major odorant components. *The Journal of Comparative Neurology*, *518*(9), 1542–1555. doi:10.1002/cne.22289

Ju, M. J., Hayama, K., Hayashi, K., & Toko, K. (2003). Discrimination of pungent-tasting substances using surface-polarity controlled sensor with indirect in situ modification. *Sensors and Actuators. B, Chemical*, *89*, 150–157. doi:10.1016/S0925-4005(02)00457-4

Ju, M. J., Yang, D. H., Lee, S. W., Kunitake, T., Hayashi, K., & Toko, K. (2007). Fabrication of TiO2/γ-CD films for nitro aromatic compounds and its sensing application via cyclic surface-polarization impedance (cSPI) spectroscopy. *Sensors and Actuators. B, Chemical*, *123*, 359–367. doi:10.1016/j.snb.2006.08.035

Lin, D. Y., Shea, S. D., & Katz, L. C. (2006). Representation of natural stimuli in the rodent main olfactory bulb. *Neuron*, *50*, 937–949. doi:10.1016/j.neuron.2006.03.021

Malnic, B., Hirono, J., Sato, T., & Buck, L. (1999). Combinatorial receptor codes for odors. *Cell*, *96*(5), 713–723. doi:10.1016/S0092-8674(00)80581-4

Masunaga, K., Hayama, K., Onodera, T., Hayashi, K., Miura, N., Matsumoto, K., & Toko, K. (2005). Detection of aromatic nitro compounds with electrode polarization controlling sensor. *Sensors and Actuators. B, Chemical*, *108*, 427–434. doi:10.1016/j.snb.2004.12.102

Masunaga, K., Michiwaki, S., Izumi, R., Ivarsson, P., Björefors, F., & Lundström, I. (2008). Development of sensor surface with recognition of molecular substructure. *Sensors and Actuators. B, Chemical*, *130*, 330–337. doi:10.1016/j.snb.2007.08.027

Matsumoto, H., Kobayakawa, K., Kobayakawa, R., Tashiro, T., Mori, K., Sakano, H., & Mori, K. (2010). Spatial arrangement of glomerular molecular-feature clusters in the odorant-receptor class domains of the mouse olfactory bulb. *Journal of Neurophysiology*, *103*(6), 3490–3500. doi:10.1152/jn.00035.2010

Mori, K., & Shepherd, G. M. (1994). Emerging principles of molecular signal processing by mitral/tufted cells in the olfactory bulb. *Seminars in Cell Biology*, *5*, 65–74. doi:10.1006/scel.1994.1009

Mori, K., Takahashi, Y. K., Igarashi, K., & Yamaguchi, M. (2006). Maps of odorant molecular features in the mammalian olfactory bulb. *Physiological Reviews*, *86*(2), 409–433. doi:10.1152/physrev.00021.2005

Sasaki, Y., Hayashi, K., & Toko, K. (2009). Fabrication of odor sensor surface recognizing substructure of odorant. *Sensors and Materials*, *21*(4), 191–199.

Tirindelli, R., Dibattista, M., Pifferi, S., & Menini, A. (2009). From pheromones to behavior. *Physiological Reviews*, *89*(3), 921–956. doi:10.1152/physrev.00037.2008

Compilation of References

(1971). InBeidler, L. M. (Ed.). Handbook of sensory physiology: *Vol. 4. Chemical senses: Part 1: Olfaction.* Berlin, Germany: Springer-Verlag.

Abaffy, T., Matsunami, H., & Luetje, C. W. (2006). Functional analysis of a mammalian odorant receptor subfamily. *Journal of Neurochemistry, 97,* 1506–1518. doi:10.1111/j.1471-4159.2006.03859.x

Abe, E., Nakatani, Y., Yamanishi, T., & Muraki, S. (1978). Studies on the "sugary flavor" of raw cane sugar. *Proceedings of the Japanese Academy Series B, 54,* 542–547. doi:10.2183/pjab.54.542

Abraham, M. H. (1994). New solute descriptors for linear free energy relationships and quantitative structure-activity relationships. In Politzer, P., & Murray, J. S. (Eds.), *Quantitative Treatments of Solute/Solvent Interactions.* Amsterdam, The Netherlands: Elsevier.

Abraham, M. H., Ibrahim, A., & Zissimos, A. M. (2004). Determination of sets of solute descriptors from chromatographic measurements. *Journal of Chromatography. A, 1037,* 29–47. doi:10.1016/j.chroma.2003.12.004

Ademoye, O. A., & Ghinea, G. (2009). Synchronization of olfaction-enhanced multimedia. *IEEE Transactions on Multimedia, 11*(3), 561–565. doi:10.1109/TMM.2009.2012927

Adrian, E. D. (1950). The electrical activity of the mammalian olfactory bulb. *Electroencephalography and Clinical Neurophysiology, 2,* 377–388. doi:10.1016/0013-4694(50)90075-7

Air Aroma. (2012). *Website.* Retrieved from http://www.air-aroma.com/Air/Q Whole Room Air Freshener. (2012). *Website.* Retrieved from http://www.airq.com/store/whole-room-air-freshener

Allison, A. C. (1953). The morphology of the olfactory system of vertebrates. *Biological Reviews of the Cambridge Philosophical Society, 28,* 195–244. doi:10.1111/j.1469-185X.1953.tb01376.x

Amoore, J. E. (1970). *Molecular basis of odor.* Springfield, IL: Charles C Thomas Publisher.

Amrani, M. E. H., Dowdeswell, R. M., Payne, P. A., & Persaud, K. C. (1997). An intelligent gas sensing system. *Sensors and Actuators. B, Chemical, 44,* 512–516. doi:10.1016/S0925-4005(97)00240-2

Ando, T., Akiyama, S., Shouge, N., & Shimizu, T. (2007). *Japanese unexamined patent application. Publication 2007-236400.* Tokyo, Japan: Patent Office.

Andrew, D. (1985). *Atlas of odor character profiles.* Philadelphia, PA: ASTM.

Antolin, S., Reisert, J., & Matthews, H. R. (2010). Olfactory response termination involves Ca^{2+}-ATPase in vertebrate olfactory receptor neuron cilia. *The Journal of General Physiology, 135,* 367–378. doi:10.1085/jgp.200910337

Aoyama, S., Toshima, T., Saito, Y., Konishi, N., Motoshige, K., & Ishikawa, N. (2010). Maternal breast milk odour induces frontal lobe activation in neonates: A NIRS study. *Early Human Development, 86,* 541–545. doi:10.1016/j.earlhumdev.2010.07.003

Apicella, A., Yuan, Q., Scanziani, M., & Isaacson, J. S. (2010). Pyramidal cells in piriform cortex receive convergent input from distinct olfactory bulb glomeruli. *The Journal of Neuroscience, 30,* 14255–14260. doi:10.1523/JNEUROSCI.2747-10.2010

Araneda, R. C., Kini, A. D., & Firestein, S. (2000). The molecular receptive range of an odorant receptor. *Nature Neuroscience*, *3*(12), 1248–1255. doi:10.1038/81774

Araneda, R. C., Peterlin, Z., Zhang, X., Chesler, A., & Firestein, S. (2004). A pharmacological profile of the aldehyde receptor repertoire in rat olfactory epithelium. *The Journal of Physiology*, *555*, 743–756. doi:10.1113/jphysiol.2003.058040

Ariyakul, Y., & Nakamoto, T. (2011). Improvement of olfactory display using electroosmotic pumps and a SAW device for VR application. In *Proceedings of International Conference on Artificial Reality and Telexistence (ICAT) 2011*, (pp. 15-21). Osaka, Japan: ICAT.

Armand, M., Endres, F., MacFarlane, D. R., Ohno, H., & Scrosati, B. (2009). Ionic-liquid materials for the electrochemical challenges of the future. *Nature Materials*, *8*, 621–629. doi:10.1038/nmat2448

AromaJet. (2012). *Website*. Retrieved from http://www.aromajet.com/

Arshak, K., Moore, E., Lyons, G. M., Harris, J., & Clifford, S. (2004). A review of gas sensors employed in electronic nose applications. *Sensor Review*, *24*(2), 181–198. doi:10.1108/02602280410525977

Artursson, T., Eklöv, T., Lundström, I., Mårtensson, P., Sjöström, M., & Holmberg, M. (2000). Drift correction for gas sensors using multivariate methods. *Journal of Chemometrics*, *14*(5-6), 711–723. doi:10.1002/1099-128X(200009/12)14:5/6<711::AID-CEM607>3.0.CO;2-4

Aungst, J. L., Heyward, P. M., Puche, A. C., Karnup, S. V., Hayar, A., & Szabo, G. (2003). Centre-surround inhibition among olfactory bulb glomeruli. *Nature*, *426*, 623–629. doi:10.1038/nature02185

Auvray, M., & Spence, C. (2008). The multisensory perception of flavor. *Consciousness and Cognition*, *17*, 1016–1031. doi:10.1016/j.concog.2007.06.005

Ayabe, S., & Saitou, S. (2008). *Psychology of scent*. Tokyo, Japan: Fragrance Journal Ltd.

Ayad, M. M., El-Hefnawey, G., & Torad, N. L. (2009). A sensor of alcohol vapours based on thin polyaniline base film and quartz crystal microbalance. *Journal of Hazardous Materials*, *168*, 85–88. doi:10.1016/j.jhazmat.2009.02.003

Ayad, M. M., & Torad, N. L. (2009). Alcohol vapours sensors based on thin polyaniline salt film and quartz microbalance. *Talanta*, *78*, 1280–1285. doi:10.1016/j.talanta.2009.01.053

Baimpos, T., Boutikos, P., Nikolakis, V., & Kouzoudis, D. (2010). A polymer-Metglas sensor used to detect volatile organic compounds. *Sensors and Actuators. A, Physical*, *158*, 249–253. doi:10.1016/j.sna.2010.01.020

Bakalyar, H. A., & Reed, R. R. (1990). Identification of a specialized adenylyl cyclase that may mediate odorant detection. *Science*, *250*, 1403–1406. doi:10.1126/science.2255909

Ballard, C. G., O'Brien, J. T., Reichelt, K., & Perry, E. K. (2002). Aromatherapy as a safe and effective treatment for the management of agitation in severe dementia: The results of a double-blind, placebo-controlled trial with Melissa. *The Journal of Clinical Psychiatry*, *63*(7), 553–558. doi:10.4088/JCP.v63n0703

Bao, Z., Bruening, M. L., & Baker, G. L. (2006). Rapid growth of polymer brushes from immobilized initiators. *Journal of the American Chemical Society*, *128*, 9056–9060. doi:10.1021/ja058743d

Barfield, W., & Danas, E. (1996). Comments on the use of olfactory displays for virtual environments. *Presence (Cambridge, Mass.)*, *5*(1), 109–121.

Bargmann, C. I. (2006). Chemosensation in C. elegans. *WormBook*. Retrieved from http://www.wormbook.org

Barié, N., Bücking, M., & Rapp, M. (2006). A novel electronic nose based on miniaturized SAW sensor arrays coupled with SPME enhanced headspace-analysis and its use for rapid determination of volatile organic compounds in food quality monitoring. *Sensors and Actuators. B, Chemical*, *114*(1), 482–488. doi:10.1016/j.snb.2005.06.051

Barkai, E., & Hasselmo, M. H. (1997). Acetylcholine and associative memory in the piriform cortex. *Molecular Neurobiology*, *15*, 17–29. doi:10.1007/BF02740613

Barkó, G., Abonyi, J., & Hlavay, J. (1999). Application of fuzzy clustering and piezoelectric chemical sensor array for investigation on organic compounds. *Analytica Chimica Acta*, *398*, 219–222. doi:10.1016/S0003-2670(99)00377-3

Barton, S. S., Evans, M. J. B., & Macdonald, J. A. F. (1998). Adsorption and immersion enthalpies on BPL carbon. *Carbon*, *36*(7-8), 969–972. doi:10.1016/S0008-6223(97)00224-8

Bartoshuk, L. M. (2004). From psychophysics to the clinic: Missteps and advances. *Food Quality and Preference*, *15*, 617–632. doi:10.1016/j.foodqual.2004.05.007

Bathellier, B., Margrie, T. W., & Larkum, M. E. (2009). Properties of piriform cortex pyramidal cell dendrites: Implications for olfactory circuit design. *The Journal of Neuroscience*, *29*, 12641–12652. doi:10.1523/JNEURO-SCI.1124-09.2009

Battiston, F. M., Ramseyer, J. P., Lang, H. P., Baller, M. K., Gerber, C., & Gimzewski, J. K. (2001). A chemical sensor based on a microfabricated cantilever array with simultaneous resonance-frequency and bending readout. *Sensors and Actuators. B, Chemical*, *77*, 122–131. doi:10.1016/S0925-4005(01)00683-9

BBC. (2006). *Smellovision for Japan cinema*. Retrieved August 21 from http://news.bbc.co.uk/1/hi/entertainment/4903984.stm

Becke, A. D. (1993). Density-functional thermochemistry 3: The role of exact exchange. *The Journal of Chemical Physics*, *98*, 5648–5652. doi:10.1063/1.464913

Becker, B., & Cooper, M. A. (2011). A survey of the 2006–2009 quartz crystal microbalance biosensor literature. *Journal of Molecular Recognition*, *24*, 754–787. doi:10.1002/jmr.1117

Bednarczyk, D., & DeWeerth, S. (1995). Smart chemical sensing arrays using tin oxide sensors and analog winner-take-all signal processing. *Sensors and Actuators. B, Chemical*, *27*(1-3), 271–274. doi:10.1016/0925-4005(94)01600-M

Beebe, D. J., Moore, J. S., Bauer, J. M., Yu, Q., Liu, R. H., Devadoss, C., & Jo, B. H. (2000). Functional hydrogel structures for autonomous flow control inside microfluidic channels. *Nature*, *404*, 588–590. doi:10.1038/35007047

Beebe, K. R., Pell, R. J., & Seasholz, M. B. (1998). *Chemomrtrics –Practical guide*. New York, NY: Wiley.

Belluscio, L., Gold, G. H., Nemes, A., & Axel, R. (1998). Mice deficient in G_{olf} are anosmic. *Neuron*, *20*, 69–81. doi:10.1016/S0896-6273(00)80435-3

Belmares, M., Blanco, M., & Goddard, W. A. (2004). Hildebrand and Hansen solubility parameters from molecular dynamics with applications to electronic nose polymer sensors. *Journal of Computational Chemistry*, *25*(15), 1814–1826. doi:10.1002/jcc.20098

Bembich, S., Lanzara, C., Clarici, A., Demarini, S., Tepper, B. J., Gasparini, P., & Grasso, D. L. (2010). Individual differences in prefrontal cortex activity during perception of bitter taste using fNIRS methodology. *Chemical Senses*, *35*, 801–812. doi:10.1093/chemse/bjq080

Ben Arie, N., Khen, M., & Lancet, D. (1993). Glutathione S-transferases in rat olfactory epithelium: Purification, molecular properties and odorant biotransformation. *Biochemical Journal*, *292*(2), 379–384.

Ben Chaim, Y., Cheng, M. M., & Yau, K. W. (2011). Unitary response of mouse olfactory receptor neurons. *Proceedings of the National Academy of Sciences of the United States of America*, *108*, 822–827. doi:10.1073/pnas.1017983108

Bender, F., Barie, N., Romoudis, G., Voigt, A., & Rapp, M. (2003). Development of a preconcentration unit for a SAW sensor micro array and its use for indoor air quality monitoring. *Sensors and Actuators. B, Chemical*, *93*, 135–141. doi:10.1016/S0925-4005(03)00239-9

Bensafi, M., & Rouby, C. (2007). Individual differences in odor imaging ability reflect differences in olfactory and emotional perception. *Chemical Senses*, *32*, 237–244. doi:10.1093/chemse/bjl051

Berna, A., Lammertyn, J., Saevels, S., Natale, C., & Nicolaï, B. M. (2004). Electronic nose systems to study shelf life and cultivar effect on tomato aroma pro□le. *Sensors and Actuators. B, Chemical*, *97*, 324–333. doi:10.1016/j.snb.2003.09.020

Best, A. R., & Wilson, D. A. (2004). Coordinate synaptic mechanisms contributing to olfactory cortical adaptation. *The Journal of Neuroscience*, *24*, 652–660. doi:10.1523/JNEUROSCI.4220-03.2004

Bhandawat, V., Reisert, J., & Yau, K. W. (2005). Elementary response of olfactory receptor neurons to odorants. *Science*, *308*, 1931–1934. doi:10.1126/science.1109886

Bhandawat, V., Reisert, J., & Yau, K. W. (2010). Signaling by olfactory receptor neurons near threshold. *Proceedings of the National Academy of Sciences of the United States of America, 107*, 18682–18687. doi:10.1073/pnas.1004571107

Billig, G. M., Pal, B., Fidzinski, P., & Jentsch, T. J. (2011). Ca^{2+}-activated Cl^- currents are dispensable for olfaction. *Nature Neuroscience, 14*(6), 763–769. doi:10.1038/nn.2821

Blanco, M., Shevade, A. V., & Ryan, M. A. (2009). Quantum mechanics and first-principles molecular dynamics selection of polymer sensing materials. In Ryan, M. A., Shevade, A. V., Taylor, C. J., Homer, M. L., Blanco, M., & Stetter, J. R. (Eds.), *Computational Methods for Sensor Material Selection*. New York, NY: Springer. doi:10.1007/978-0-387-73715-7_3

Blevins, R. D. (1979). *Formulas for natural frequency and mode shape*. Malabar, India: Krieger Publishing. doi:10.1115/1.3153712

Block, E., Putman, D., & Zhao, S. H. (1992). Allium chemistry: GC-MS analysis of thiosulfinates and related compounds from onion, leek, scallion, shallot, chive, and Chinese chive. *Journal of Agricultural and Food Chemistry, 40*, 2431–2438. doi:10.1021/jf00024a018

Bocca, E., Antonelli, A. R., & Mosciaro, O. (1965). Mechanical co-factors in olfactory stimulation. *Acta Oto-Laryngologica, 59*, 243–247. doi:10.3109/00016486509124558

Bodnar, A., Corbett, R., & Nekrasovski, D. (2004). AROMA: Ambient awareness through olfaction in a messaging application: Does olfactory notification make 'scents'? In *Proceedings of ICMI 2004 - Sixth International Conference on Multimodal Interfaces*, (p. 183). ICMI.

Boesveldt, S., Stam, C. J., Knol, D. L., Verbunt, J. P., & Berendse, H. W. (2009). Advanced time-series analysis of MEG data as a method to explore olfactory function in healthy controls and Parkinson's disease patients. *Human Brain Mapping, 30*, 3020–3030. doi:10.1002/hbm.20726

Bohbot, J., Pitts, R. J., Kwon, H. W., Rützler, M., Robertson, H. M., & Zwiebel, L. J. (2007). Molecular characterization of the Aedes aegypti odorant receptor gene family. *Insect Molecular Biology, 16*, 525–537.

Bohrer, F. I., Colesniuc, C. N., Park, J., Ruidiaz, M. E., Schuller, I. K., Kummel, A. C., & Trogler, W. C. (2008). Comparative gas sensing in cobalt, nickel, copper, zinc, and metal-free phthalocyanine chemiresistors. *Journal of the American Chemical Society, 131*, 478–485. doi:10.1021/ja803531r

Borysik, A. J., Briand, L., Taylor, A. J., & Scott, D. J. (2010). Rapid odorant release in mammalian odour binding proteins facilitates their temporal coupling to odorant signals. *Journal of Molecular Biology, 404*, 372–380. doi:10.1016/j.jmb.2010.09.019

Boyd Davis, S., Davies, G., Haddad, R., & Lai, M. (2006). Smell me: Engaging with an interactive olfactory game. In *Proceedings of the Human Factors and Ergonomics Society 25th Annual Meeting*, (pp. 25-40). Human Factors and Ergonomics Society.

Brennan, P. A., & Keverne, E. B. (2004). Something in the air? New insights into mammalian pheromones. *Current Biology, 14*, R81–R89. doi:10.1016/j.cub.2003.12.052

Breslau, N. (2006). Neurobiological research on sleep and stress hormones in epidemiological samples. *Annals of the New York Academy of Sciences, 1071*, 221–230. doi:10.1196/annals.1364.017

Brewster, S. A., McGookin, D. K., & Miller, C. A. (2006). Olfoto: Designing a smell-based interaction. In *Proceedings of CHI 2006: Conference on Human Factors in Computing Systems*, (p. 653). ACM Press.

Buchbauer, G., & Jirovetz, L. (1994). Aromatherapy-use of fragrances and essential oils as medicaments. *Flavour and Fragrance Journal, 9*(5), 217–222. doi:10.1002/ffj.2730090503

Buck, L., & Axel, R. (1991). A novel multigene family may encode odor recognition: A molecular basis for odor recognition. *Cell, 65*(1), 175–187. doi:10.1016/0092-8674(91)90418-X

Buck, L., & Axel, R. (1991). A novel multigene family may encode odorant receptors: a molecular basis for odor recognition. *Cell, 65*(1), 175–187. doi:10.1016/0092-8674(91)90418-X

Cain, W. S. (1979). To know with the nose: Keys to odor identification. *Science, 203*, 467–470. doi:10.1126/science.760202

Cai, X.-J., Block, E., Uden, P. C., Quimby, B. D., & Sullivan, J. J. (1995). Allium chemistry: Identification of natural abundance organoselenium compounds in human breath. *Journal of Agricultural and Food Chemistry, 43*, 1751–1753. doi:10.1021/jf00055a001

Cajal, S. R. Y. (1890). Origen y terminación de las fibras nerviosas olfatorias. *Gaceta Sanitaria de Barcelona, 3*, 133–139, 174–181, 206–212.

Calinsky, T., & Harabasz, J. (1974). A dendrite method for cluster analysis. *Communications in Statistics, 3*, 1–27. doi:10.1080/03610927408827101

Calkin, R. R., & Jellinek, J. S. (1994). *Perfumery: Practice and principles*. Hoboken, NJ: John Wiley & Sons, Inc.

Carey, R. M., Verhagen, J. V., Wesson, D. W., Pirez, N., & Wachowiak, M. (2009). Temporal structure of receptor neuron input to the olfactory bulb imaged in behaving rats. *Journal of Neurophysiology, 101*, 1073–1088. doi:10.1152/jn.90902.2008

Carey, W. P., Beebe, K. R., & Kowalski, B. R. (1987). Multicomponent analysis using an array of piezoelectric crystal sensors. *Analytical Chemistry, 59*, 1529–1534. doi:10.1021/ac00138a010

Carlson, G. C., Shipley, M. T., & Keller, A. (2000). Long-lasting depolarizations in mitral cells of the rat olfactory bulb. *The Journal of Neuroscience, 20*, 2011–2021.

Carmel1, L., & Harel, D. (2007). Mix-to-mimic odor synthesis for electronic noses. *Sensors and Actuators B, 125*, 635-643.

Castillo, P. E., Carleton, A., Vincent, J. D., & Lledo, P. M. (1999). Multiple and opposing roles of cholinergic transmission in the main olfactory bulb. *The Journal of Neuroscience, 19*, 9180–9191.

Ceyhan, T., Altmdal, A., Özkaya, A. R., Erbil, M. K., & Bekaroğlu, Ö. (2007). Synthesis, characterization, and electrochemical, electrical and gas sensing properties of a novel *tert*-butylcalix[4]arene bridged bis double-decker lutetium(III) phthalocyanine. *Polyhedron, 26*, 73–84. doi:10.1016/j.poly.2006.07.035

Chance, B., & Zhuang, Z. UnAh, C., Alter, C., & Lipton, L. (1993). Cognition-activated low-frequency modulation of light absorption in human brain. *Proceedings of the National Academy of Science, 90*, 3770-3774.

Chandrashekar, J., Hoon, M. A., Ryba, N. J., & Zuker, C. S. (2006). The receptors and cells for mammalian taste. *Nature, 444*, 288–294. doi:10.1038/nature05401

Chastrette, M. (2002). Classification of odors and structure–odor relationships. In C. Rouby, B. Schall, d. Dubois, R. Gervais, & A. Holley (Eds.), *Olfaction, Taste, and Cognition*, (pp. 100-116). Cambridge, UK: Cambridge University Press.

Chaudhury, D., Escanilla, O., & Linster, C. (2009). Bulbar acetylcholine enhances neural and perceptual odor discrimination. *The Journal of Neuroscience, 29*, 52–60. doi:10.1523/JNEUROSCI.4036-08.2009

Chaudhury, D., Manella, L., Arellanos, A., Escanilla, O., Cleland, T. A., & Linster, C. (2010). Olfactory bulb habituation to odor stimuli. *Behavioral Neuroscience, 124*, 490–499. doi:10.1037/a0020293

Chaudry, A. N., Hawkins, T. M., & Travers, P. J. (2000). A method for selecting an optimum sensor array. *Sensors and Actuators. B, Chemical, 69*, 236–242. doi:10.1016/S0925-4005(00)00498-6

Che Harun, F. K., Taylor, J. E., Covington, J., & Gardner, J. W. (2009). An electronic nose employing dual-channel odour separation columns with large chemosensor arrays for advanced odour discrimination. *Sensors and Actuators. B, Chemical, 141*(1), 134–140. doi:10.1016/j.snb.2009.05.036

Chen, G. Y., Thundat, T., Wachter, E. A., & Warmack, R. J. (1995). Dsorption-induced surface stress and its effects on resonance frequency of microcantilevers. *Journal of Applied Physics, 77*, 3618–3622. doi:10.1063/1.359562

Chen, S. Y., Ghinea, G., & Macredie, R. D. (2006). A cognitive approach to user perception of multimedia quality: An empirical investigation. *International Journal of Human-Computer Studies, 64*(12), 1200–1213. doi:10.1016/j.ijhcs.2006.08.010

Chen, T. Y., & Yau, K. W. (1994). Direct modulation by Ca^{2+}-calmodulin of cyclic nucleotide–activated channel of rat olfactory receptor neurons. *Nature, 368*, 545–548. doi:10.1038/368545a0

Chen, W. R., & Shepherd, G. M. (2005). The olfactory glomerulus: a cortical module with specific functions. *Journal of Neurocytology, 34*, 353–360. doi:10.1007/s11068-005-8362-0

Chen, Y., Getchell, M. L., Ding, X., & Getchell, T. V. (1992). Immunolocalization of two cytochrome P450 isozymes in rat nasal chemosensory tissue. *Neuroreport*, *3*, 749–752. doi:10.1097/00001756-199209000-00007

Chevallier, E., Scorsone, E., & Bergonzo, P. (2011). New sensitive coating based on modified diamond nanoparticles for chemical SAW sensors. *Sensors and Actuators. B, Chemical*, *154*(2), 238–244. doi:10.1016/j. snb.2010.01.042

Chiappin, S., Antonelli, G., Gatti, R., & De Palo, E. F. (2007). Saliva specimen: A new laboratory tool for diagnostic and basic investigation. *Clinica Chimica Acta*, *383*(1-2), 30–40. doi:10.1016/j.cca.2007.04.011

Christie, J. M., Bark, C., Hormuzdi, S. G., Helbig, I., Monyer, H., & Westbrook, G. L. (2005). Connexin36 mediates spike synchrony in olfactory bulb glomeruli. *Neuron*, *46*, 761–772. doi:10.1016/j.neuron.2005.04.030

Chu, S., & Downes, J. (2000). Odour-evoked autobiographical memories: Psychological investigations of Proustian phenomena. *Chemical Senses*, *25*(1), 111–116. doi:10.1093/chemse/25.1.111

Cichocki, A., Zdunek, R., Phan, A. H., & Amari, S. (2009). *Nonnegative matrix and tensor factorizations*. New York, NY: Wiley. doi:10.1002/9780470747278

Cleland, T. A., & Sethupathy, P. (2006). Non–topographical contrast enhancement in the olfactory bulb. *BMC Neuroscience*, *7*, 7. doi:10.1186/1471-2202-7-7

Communications, N. T. T. (2007). *NTT com to test aroma-emitting digital signage*. Retrieved from http://www.ntt. com/release_e/news07/0010/1017.html

Communications, N. T. T. (2008). *NTT com to pilot test mobile fragrance communication service*. Retrieved from http://www.ntt.com/release_e/news08/0004/0407.html

Concina, I., Falasconi, M., Gobbi, E., Bianchi, F., Musci, M., & Mattarozzi, M. (2009). Early detection of microbial contamination in processed tomatoes by electronic nose. *Food Control*, *20*, 873–880. doi:10.1016/j.foodcont.2008.11.006

Cooke, B., & Ernst, E. (2000). Aromatherapy: A systematic review. *The British Journal of General Practice*, *50*(455), 493–496.

Cox, J. P. (2008). Hydrodynamic aspects of fish olfaction. *Journal of the Royal Society, Interface*, *5*, 575–593. doi:10.1098/rsif.2007.1281

Curioni, P. M. G., & Bosset, J. O. (2002). Key odorants in various cheese types as determined by gas chromatography. *International Dairy Journal*, *12*, 959–984. doi:10.1016/S0958-6946(02)00124-3

Cury, K. M., & Uchida, N. (2010). Robust odor coding via inhalation-coupled transient activity in the mammalian olfactory bulb. *Neuron*, *68*, 570–585. doi:10.1016/j. neuron.2010.09.040

Cygnar, K. D., & Zhao, H. (2009). Phosphodiesterase 1C is dispensable for rapid response termination of olfactory sensory neurons. *Nature Neuroscience*, *12*, 454–462. doi:10.1038/nn.2289

Dade, L. A., Jones-Gotman, M., Zatorre, R. J., & Evans, A. C. (1998). Human brain function during odor encoding and recognition: A PET activation study. *Annals of the New York Academy of Sciences*, *855*, 572–574. doi:10.1111/j.1749-6632.1998.tb10626.x

Dale Air Limited Dispensers. (2007). *Vortex active*. Retrieved October 12, 2007 from http://www.daleair.com/acatalog/Dispensers.html

Davide, F., DiNatale, C., & D'Amico, A. (1994). Self-organizing multisensor systems for odour classi☐cation: Internal categorization, adaptation and drift rejection. *Sensors and Actuators. B, Chemical*, *18*, 244–258. doi:10.1016/0925-4005(94)87090-X

Davide, F., Holmberg, M., & Lundstrom, I. (2001). Virtual olfactory interfaces: electronic noses and olfactory displays. In Riva, G., & Davide, F. (Eds.), *Communications through Virtual Technologies* (pp. 193–220). Amsterdam, The Netherlands: IOS Press.

Davies, D. L., & Bouldin, D. W. (1979). A cluster separation measure. *IEEE Transactions on Pattern Analysis and Machine Intelligence*, *1*, 224–227. doi:10.1109/TPAMI.1979.4766909

Davison, I. G., & Ehlers, M. D. (2011). Neural circuit mechanisms for pattern detection and feature combination in olfactory cortex. *Neuron*, *70*, 82–94. doi:10.1016/j. neuron.2011.02.047

Dayhoff, J. (1990). *Neural network architecture*. London, UK: International Thomson Computer Press.

De Juan, A., & Tauler, R. (2001). Comparison of three-way resolution methods for non-trilinear chemical data sets. *Journal of Chemometrics*, *15*(10), 749–771. doi:10.1002/cem.662

De Juan, A., & Tauler, R. (2006). Multivariate curve resolution. In Gemperline, P. (Ed.), *Practical Guide to Chemometrics* (pp. 417–467). New York, NY: Taylor and Francis Group.

De Saint, J. D., Hirnet, D., Westbrook, G. L., & Charpak, S. (2009). External tufted cells drive the output of olfactory bulb glomeruli. *The Journal of Neuroscience*, *29*, 2043–2052. doi:10.1523/JNEUROSCI.5317-08.2009

De Vito, S., Massera, E., Piga, M., Martinotto, L., & De Francia, G. (2008). On field calibration of an electronic nose for benzene estimation in an urban pollution monitoring scenario. *Sensors and Actuators. B, Chemical*, *129*, 750–757. doi:10.1016/j.snb.2007.09.060

De Vito, S., Piga, M., Martinotto, L., & De Francia, G. (2009). CO, NO_2 and NOx urban pollution monitoring with on-field calibrated electronic nose by automatic bayesian regularization. *Sensors and Actuators. B, Chemical*, *143*, 182–191. doi:10.1016/j.snb.2009.08.041

Dejaegher, B., & Heyden, Y. (2007). Ruggedness and robustness testing. *Journal of Chromatography. A*, *1158*(1-2), 138–157. doi:10.1016/j.chroma.2007.02.086

Delage, F., Pre, P., & Cloirec, P. L. (2000). Mass transfer and warming during adsorption of high concentrations of VOCs on an activated carbon bed: Experimental and theoretical analysis. *Environmental Science & Technology*, *34*, 4816–4821. doi:10.1021/es001187x

Delley, R., & Friedrich, R. A. (1977). System CG 72 von bevorzugten trennflüssigkeiten für die gas-chromatographie. *Chromatographia*, *10*(10), 593–600. doi:10.1007/BF02265037

Delwiche, J. (2004). The impact of perceptual interactions on perceived flavor. *Food Quality and Preference*, *15*, 137–146. doi:10.1016/S0950-3293(03)00041-7

Desmaisons, D., Vincent, J. D., & Lledo, P. M. (1999). Control of action potential timing by intrinsic subthreshold oscillations in olfactory bulb output neurons. *The Journal of Neuroscience*, *19*, 10727–10737.

Dhawale, A. K., Hagiwara, A., Bhalla, U. S., Murthy, V. N., & Albeanu, D. F. (2010). Non-redundant odor coding by sister mitral cells revealed by light addressable glomeruli in the mouse. *Nature Neuroscience*, *13*, 1404–1412. doi:10.1038/nn.2673

Diego, M. A., Jones, N. A., Field, T., Hernandez-Reif, M., Schanberg, S., & Kuhn, C. (1998). Aromatherapy positively affects mood, EEG patterns of alertness and math computations. *The International Journal of Neuroscience*, *96*(3-4), 217–224. doi:10.3109/00207459808986469

Dillon, W. R., & Goldstein, M. (1983). *Multivariate analysis*. New York, NY: Wiley.

Dillon, W. R., & Goldstein, M. (1984). *Multivariate analysis methods analysis methods and applications*. New York, NY: John Wiley and Sons.

DiNatale, C., Martinelli, E., & D'Amico, A. (2002). Counteraction of environmental disturbances of electronic nose data by independent component analysis. *Sensors and Actuators. B, Chemical*, *82*(2-3), 158–165. doi:10.1016/S0925-4005(01)01001-2

Ding, S. X., Zhang, P., Naik, A., Ding, E. L., & Huang, B. (2009). Subspace method aided data-driven design of fault detection and isolation systems. *Journal of Process Control*, *19*, 1496–1510. doi:10.1016/j.jprocont.2009.07.005

Dinh, H. Q., Walker, N., Hodges, L. F., Song, C., & Kobayashi, A. (1999). Evaluating the importance of multi-sensory input on memory and the sense of presence in virtual environments. In *Proceedings - Virtual Reality Annual International Symposium*, (pp. 222-228). IEEE.

Dittman, B., Nitz, S., & Horner, G. (1998). A new chemical sensor on a mass spectrometric basis. *Advances in Food Science*, *30*, 115.

Dong, H. W., Hayar, A., Callaway, J., Yang, X. H., Nai, Q., & Ennis, M. (2009). Group I mGluR activation enhances Ca^{2+}-dependent nonselective cation currents and rhythmic bursting in main olfactory bulb external tufted cells. *The Journal of Neuroscience*, *29*, 11943–11953. doi:10.1523/JNEUROSCI.0206-09.2009

Dong, H. W., Hayar, A., & Ennis, M. (2007). Activation of group I metabotropic glutamate receptors on main olfactory bulb granule cells and periglomerular cells enhances synaptic inhibition of mitral cells. *The Journal of Neuroscience, 27,* 5654–5663. doi:10.1523/JNEURO-SCI.5495-06.2007

Dorman, F. L., Overton, E. B., Whiting, J. J., Cochran, J. W., & Gaedea-Torresdey, J. (2008). Gas chromatography. *Analytical Chemistry, 80,* 4487–4497. doi:10.1021/ac800714x

Doucette, W., Milder, J., & Restrepo, D. (2007). Adrenergic modulation of olfactory bulb circuitry affects odor discrimination. *Learning & Memory (Cold Spring Harbor, N.Y.), 14,* 539–547. doi:10.1101/lm.606407

Doucette, W., & Restrepo, D. (2008). Profound context-dependent plasticity of mitral cell responses in olfactory bulb. *PLoS Biology, 6,* e258. doi:10.1371/journal.pbio.0060258

Dubes, R., & Jain, A. (1979). Validity studies in clustering methodologies. *Pattern Recognition, 11,* 235–254. doi:10.1016/0031-3203(79)90034-7

Duchamp–Viret, P., Duchamp, A., & Chaput, M. A. (2003). Single olfactory sensory neurons simultaneously integrate the components of an odour mixture. *The European Journal of Neuroscience, 18,* 2690–2696. doi:10.1111/j.1460-9568.2003.03001.x

Duchamp-Viret, P., Duchamp, A., & Vigouroux, M. (1989). Amplifying role of convergence in olfactory system a comparative study of receptor cell and second-order neuron sensitivities. *Journal of Neurophysiology, 61,* 1085–1094.

Duda, D. O., Hart, P. E., & Stork, D. G. (2001). *Pattern classification.* New York, NY: John Wiley & Sons.

Dufour, I., & Fadel, L. (2003). Resonant microcantilever type chemical sensors: Analytical modeling in view of optimization. *Sensors and Actuators. B, Chemical, 91,* 353–361. doi:10.1016/S0925-4005(03)00110-2

Dulac, C., & Wagner, S. (2006). Genetic analysis of brain circuits underlying pheromone signaling. *Annual Review of Genetics, 40,* 449–467. doi:10.1146/annurev.genet.39.073003.093937

Dunia, R., Qin, S., Joe, E. T. F., & McAvoy, T. J. (1996). Use of principal component analysis for sensor fault identification. *Comprehensive Chemical Engineering, 20,* 713–718. doi:10.1016/0098-1354(96)00128-7

Dusenbery, D. B. (1992). *Sensory ecology: How organisms acquire and respond to information.* New York, NY: W. H. Freeman and Company.

Dutta, R., Hines, E., Gardner, J., & Kashwan, K. (2003). Tea quality prediction using a tin oxide-based electronic nose: An artiﬁcial intelligence approach. *Sensors and Actuators. B, Chemical, 94,* 228–237. doi:10.1016/S0925-4005(03)00367-8

Du, X., Wang, Z., Huang, J., Tao, S., Tang, X., & Jiang, Y. (2009). A new polysiloxane coating on QCM sensor for DMMP vapor detection. *Journal of Materials Science, 44,* 5872–5876. doi:10.1007/s10853-009-3829-5

Dy, J. G., & Brodley, C. E. (2004). Feature selection for unsupervised learning. *Journal of Machine Learning Research, 5,* 845–889.

Egger, V., Svoboda, K., & Mainen, Z. F. (2005). Dendro-dendritic synaptic signals in olfactory bulb granule cells: Local spine boost and global low-threshold spike. *The Journal of Neuroscience, 25,* 3521–3530. doi:10.1523/JNEUROSCI.4746-04.2005

Ema, K., Yokoyama, M., Nakamoto, T., & Moriizumi, T. (1989). Odour-sensing system using a quartz-resonator sensor array and neural-network pattern recognition. *Sensors and Actuators, 18*(3-4), 291–296. doi:10.1016/0250-6874(89)87036-2

Ennis, M., Zhou, F. M., Ciombor, K. J., Aroniadou–Anderjaska, V., Hayar, A., & Borrelli, E. (2001). Dopamine D2 receptor-mediated presynaptic inhibition of olfactory nerve terminals. *Journal of Neurophysiology, 86,* 2986–2997.

Escanilla, O., Arrellanos, A., Karnow, A., Ennis, M., & Linster, C. (2010). Noradrenergic modulation of behavioral odor detection and discrimination thresholds in the olfactory bulb. *The European Journal of Neuroscience, 32,* 458–468. doi:10.1111/j.1460-9568.2010.07297.x

Escanilla, O., Yuhas, C., Marzan, D., & Linster, C. (2009). Dopaminergic modulation of olfactory bulb processing affects odor discrimination learning in rats. *Behavioral Neuroscience, 123*, 828–833. doi:10.1037/a0015855

Eugene, F. (2007). *Columns for gas chromatography: Performance and selection.* New York, NY: Wiley-Interscience.

Eyre, M. D., Antal, M., & Nusser, Z. (2008). Distinct deep short-axon cell subtypes of the main olfactory bulb provide novel intrabulbar and extrabulbar GABAergic connections. *The Journal of Neuroscience, 28*, 8217–8229. doi:10.1523/JNEUROSCI.2490-08.2008

Falasconi, M., Gobbi, E., Pardo, M., Della Torre, M., Bresciani, A., & Sberveglieri, G. (2005). Detection of toxigenic strains of fusarium verticillioides in corn by electronic olfactory system. *Sensors and Actuators. B, Chemical, 108*, 250–257. doi:10.1016/j.snb.2004.09.046

Falasconi, M., Gutierrez, A., Pardo, M., Sberveglieri, G., & Marco, S. (2010). A stability based validity method for fuzzy clustering. *Pattern Recognition, 43*, 1292–1305. doi:10.1016/j.patcog.2009.10.001

Falasconi, M., Pardo, M., Vezzoli, M., & Sberveglieri, G. (2007). Cluster validation for electronic nose data. *Sensors and Actuators. B, Chemical, 125*, 596–606. doi:10.1016/j.snb.2007.03.004

Fantana, A. L., Soucy, E. R., & Meister, M. (2008). Rat olfactory bulb mitral cells receive sparse glomerular inputs. *Neuron, 59*, 802–814. doi:10.1016/j.neuron.2008.07.039

Fend, R., Bessant, C., Williams, A. J., & Woodman, A. C. (2004). Monitoring haemodialysis using electronic nose and chemometrics. *Biosensors & Bioelectronics, 19*, 1581–1590. doi:10.1016/j.bios.2003.12.010

Feng, R., Zhao, D., & Guo, Y. (2010). Revisiting characteristics of ionic liquids: A review for future application development. *Journal of Environmental Protection, 1*, 95–104. doi:10.4236/jep.2010.12012

Ferziger, J. H., & Perić, M. (2002). *Computational methods for fluid dynamics* (3rd ed.). Berlin, Germany: Springer-Verlag. doi:10.1007/978-3-642-56026-2

Fietzek, C., & Mack, H.-G. (2007). Influence of different transition metals in phthalocyanines on their interaction energies with volatile organic compounds: An experimental and computational study. *Journal of Molecular Modeling, 13*, 11–17. doi:10.1007/s00894-006-0118-y

Firestein, S. (2001). How the olfactory system makes sense of scents. *Nature, 413*, 211–218. doi:10.1038/35093026

Fischerauer, G., & Dickert, F. L. (2007). An analytic model of the dynamic response of mass-sensitive chemical sensors. *Sensors and Actuators. B, Chemical, 123*, 993–1001. doi:10.1016/j.snb.2006.11.002

Fragra. (2003). *IVRC.* Retrieved from http://chihara.aist-nara.ac.jp/ivrc2003/index.html

Franks, K. M., & Isaacson, J. S. (2006). Strong single-fiber sensory inputs to olfactory cortex: Implications for olfactory coding. *Neuron, 49*, 357–363. doi:10.1016/j.neuron.2005.12.026

Franks, K. M., Russo, M. J., Sosulski, D. L., Mulligan, A. A., Siegelbaum, S. A., & Axel, R. (2011). Recurrent circuitry dynamically shapes the activation of piriform cortex. *Neuron, 72*, 49–56. doi:10.1016/j.neuron.2011.08.020

Freeman, W. J., & Baird, B. (1987). Relation of olfactory EEG to behavior: Spatial analysis. *Behavioral Neuroscience, 101*, 393–408. doi:10.1037/0735-7044.101.3.393

Friedrich, J. E., & Acree, T. E. (2000). Issues in gas chromatography-olfactometry methodologies. In Rish & Ho (Eds.), *Flavor Chemistry,* (pp. 124-132). New York, NY: ACS Publications.

Friedrich, R. W., Yaksi, E., Judkewitz, B., & Wiechert, M. T. (2009). Processing of odor representations by neuronal circuits in the olfactory bulb. *Annals of the New York Academy of Sciences, 1170*, 293–297. doi:10.1111/j.1749-6632.2009.04010.x

Frings, S., Seifert, R., Godde, M., & Kaupp, U. B. (1995). Profoundly different calcium permeation and blockage determine the specific function of distinct cyclic nucleotide-gated channels. *Neuron, 15*, 169–179. doi:10.1016/0896-6273(95)90074-8

Fryder, M., Holmberg, M., Winquist, F., & Lundstrom, I. (1995). Calibration technique for an electronic nose. In *Proceedings of the 1995 8th International Conference on Solid-State Sensors and Actuators and Eurosensors,* (pp. 683-686). Stockholm, Sweden: IEEE.

Fukui, Y., Ajichi, Y., & Okada, E. (2003). Monte Carlo prediction of near-infrared light propagation in realistic adult and neonatal head models. *Applied Optics, 42,* 2881-2887. doi:10.1364/AO.42.002881

Funahashi, K. (1989). On the approximate realization of continuous mappings by neural networks. *Neural Networks, 2,* 183-192. doi:10.1016/0893-6080(89)90003-8

Furudono, Y., Sone, Y., Takizawa, K., Hirono, J., & Sato, T. (2009). Relationship between peripheral receptor code and perceived odor quality. *Chemical Senses, 34,* 151-158. doi:10.1093/chemse/bjn071

Gabrielsson, J., & Trygg, J. (2006). Recent developments in multivariate calibration. *Critical Reviews in Analytical Chemistry, 36*(3), 243-255. doi:10.1080/10408340600969924

Galan, R. F., Fourcaud–Trocme, N., Ermentrout, G. B., & Urban, N. N. (2006). Correlation-induced synchronization of oscillations in olfactory bulb neurons. *The Journal of Neuroscience, 26,* 3646-3655. doi:10.1523/JNEUROSCI.4605-05.2006

Gampp, H., Maeder, M., Meyer, C., & Zuberbuehler, A. (1987). Evolving factor analysis. *Comments on Inorganic Chemistry: A Journal of Critical Discussion of the Current Literature, 6*(1), 41-60.

Gamsjäger, H., Lorimer, J. W., Scharlin, P., & Shaw, D. G. (2008). Glossary of terms related to solubility. *Pure and Applied Chemistry, 80,* 233-276. doi:10.1351/pac200880020233

Gao, Y., & Strowbridge, B. W. (2009). Long–term plasticity of excitatory inputs to granule cells in the rat olfactory bulb. *Nature Neuroscience, 12,* 731-733. doi:10.1038/nn.2319

García-González, D., & Aparicio, R. (2002). Sensors: From biosensors to the electronic nose. *Grasas y Aceites-Sevilla, 53*(1), 96-114.

Gardner, J. W., Nadarajan, S., & Kimber, P. (2008). Modelling and measurement of odour transportation within the human naval cavity. In *Proceedings of the 6th IASTED International Conference on Biomedical Engineering,* (pp. 145-150). IASTED.

Gardner, J. W. (1991). Detection of vapours and odours from a multisensor array using pattern recognition: Principal component and cluster analysis. *Sensors and Actuators. B, Chemical, 4,* 109-115. doi:10.1016/0925-4005(91)80185-M

Gardner, J. W., & Bartlett, P. N. (1994). A brief history of electronic noses. *Sensors and Actuators. B, Chemical, 18,* 210. doi:10.1016/0925-4005(94)87085-3

Gardner, J. W., & Bartlett, P. N. (1999). *Electronic noses: Principles and application.* Oxford, UK: Oxford University Press.

Gardner, J. W., Covington, J., Tan, S. L., & Pearce, T. C. (2007). Towards an artificial olfactory mucosa for improved odour classification. *Proceedings of the Royal Society of London. Series A, 463,* 1713-1728. doi:10.1098/rspa.2007.1844

Gardner, J. W., & Taylor, J. E. (2009). Novel convolution-based signal processing techniques for an artificial olfactory mucosa. *IEEE Sensors Journal, 9,* 929-935. doi:10.1109/JSEN.2009.2024856

Geladi, P., & Kowalski, B. R. (1986). Partial least-squares regression: A tutorial. *Analytica Chimica Acta, 185,* 1-17. doi:10.1016/0003-2670(86)80028-9

Ghasemi-Varnamkhasti, M., Mohtasebi, S. S., & Siadat, M. (2010). Biomimetic-based odor and taste sensing systems to food quality and safety characterization: An overview on basic principles and recent achievements. *Journal of Food Engineering, 100,* 377-387. doi:10.1016/j.jfoodeng.2010.04.032

Ghinea, G., & Thomas, J. P. (1998). QoS impact on user perception and understanding of multimedia video clips. In *Proceedings of the Sixth ACM International Conference on Multimedia,* (pp. 49-54). New York, NY: ACM Press.

Ghinea, G., Thomas, J. P., & Fish, R. S. (1999). Multimedia, network protocols and users - Bridging the gap. In *Proceedings of the Seventh ACM International Conference on Multimedia,* (pp. 473-476). New York, NY: ACM Press.

Gilbert, A. (2008). *What the nose knows: The science of scent in everyday life*. New York, NY: Crown Publishing.

Gire, D. H., & Schoppa, N. E. (2009). Control of on/off glomerular signaling by a local GABAergic microcircuit in the olfactory bulb. *The Journal of Neuroscience, 29*, 13454–13464. doi:10.1523/JNEUROSCI.2368-09.2009

Gobbi, E., Falasconi, M., Torelli, E., & Sberveglieri, G. (2011). Electronic nose predicts high and low fumonisins contamination in maize cultures. *Food Research International, 44*, 992–999. doi:10.1016/j.foodres.2011.02.041

Godfrey, P. A., Malnic, B., & Buck, L. B. (2004). The mouse olfactory receptor gene family. *Proceedings of the National Academy of Sciences of the United States of America, 101*, 2156–2161. doi:10.1073/pnas.0308051100

Goicoechea, H., & Olivieri, A. (2001). A comparison of orthogonal signal correction and net analyte preprocessing methods: Theoretical and experimental study. *Chemometrics and Intelligent Laboratory Systems, 56*, 73–81. doi:10.1016/S0169-7439(01)00110-1

Goldsmith, B. R., Mitala, J. J., Josue, J., Castro, A., Lerner, M. B., & Bayburt, T. H. … Johnson, C.J. (2011). Biomimetic chemical sensors using nanoelectronic read out of olfactory receptor proteins. In *Proceeding of 14th International Symposium on Olfaction and Electronic Nose*. New York, NY: IEEE.

Golgi, C. (1875). Sulla fina struttura dei bulbi olfactorii. *Rivista Sperimentale diFreniatria e Medicina Legale, 1*, 405–425.

Gordon, D. (1999). *Classification* (2nd ed.). London, UK: Chapman & Hall/CRC.

Goto, H., Sakai, T., Mizoguchi, K., Tajima, Y., & Imai, M. (2010). *Odor generation alarm and method for informing unusual situation*. U. S. Patent Application 2010/0308995. Washington, DC: US Patent Office.

Gottfried, J., & Dolan, R. (2003). The nose smells what the eye sees: Crossmodal visual facilitation of human olfactory perception. *Neuron, 39*(2), 375–386. doi:10.1016/S0896-6273(03)00392-1

Gracia–Llanes, F. J., Blasco–Ibanez, J. M., Nacher, J., Varea, E., Liberia, T., & Martinez, P. (2010). Synaptic connectivity of serotonergic axons in the olfactory glomeruli of the rat olfactory bulb. *Neuroscience, 169*, 770–780. doi:10.1016/j.neuroscience.2010.05.034

Grate, J. W. (2000). Acoustic wave microsensor arrays for vapor sensing. *Chemical Reviews, 100*(7), 2627–2648. doi:10.1021/cr980094j

Grate, J. W., & Abraham, M. H. (1991). Solubility interactions and the design of chemically selective sorbent coatings for chemical sensors and arrays. *Sensors and Actuators. B, Chemical, 3*, 85–111. doi:10.1016/0925-4005(91)80202-U

Grate, J. W., Martin, S. J., & White, R. M. (1993). Acoustic wave microsensors. *Analytical Chemistry, 65*(22), 940A–948A.

Graziadei, P. P. (1971). The olfactory mucosa of vertebrates. In L. M. Beidler (Ed.), *Handbook of Sensory Physiology: Vol 4: Chemical Senses: 1 – Olfaction,* (pp. 27–58). New York, NY: Springer–Verlag.

Graziadei, P. P., & Monti–Graziadei, A. G. (1978). Continuous nerve cell renewal in the olfactory system. In M. Jacobson (Ed.), *Handbook of Sensory Physiology: Vol 9: Development of Sensory Systems,* (pp. 55–83). New York, NY: Springer–Verlag.

Grigor, J., Toller, S. V., Behan, J., & Richardson, A. (1999). The effect of odour priming on long latency visual evoked potentials of matching and mismatching objects. *Chemical Senses, 24*, 137–144. doi:10.1093/chemse/24.2.137

Grob, R. L., & Barry, E. F. (2004). *Modern practice of gas chromatography*. New York, NY: Wiley-Interscience. doi:10.1002/0471651141

Grosch, W. (1994). Determination of potent odorants in foods by aroma extract dilution analysis and calculation of odour activity values. *Flavour and Fragrance Journal, 9*, 147–158. doi:10.1002/ffj.2730090403

Grosser, B. I., Monti-Bloch, L., Jennings-White, C., & Berliner, D. L. (2000). Behavioral and electrophysiological effects of androstadienone, a human pheromone. *Psychoneuroendocrinology, 25*(3), 289–299. doi:10.1016/S0306-4530(99)00056-6

Groves, W. A., Zellersa, E. T., & Fryec, G. C. (1998). Analyzing organic vapors in exhaled breath using a surface acoustic wave sensor array with preconcentration: Selection and characterization of the preconcentrator adsorbent. *Analytica Chimica Acta*, *371*, 131–143. doi:10.1016/S0003-2670(98)00294-3

Guerin, D., Peace, S. T., Didier, A., Linster, C., & Cleland, T. A. (2008). Noradrenergic neuromodulation in the olfactory bulb modulates odor habituation and spontaneous discrimination. *Behavioral Neuroscience*, *122*, 816–826. doi:10.1037/a0012522

Gulliver, S. R., & Ghinea, G. (2006). Defining user perception of distributed multimedia quality. *ACM Transactions on Multimedia Computing. Communications and Applications*, *2*(4), 241–257.

Gutierrez-Galvez, A. (2005). *Coding and learning of chemosensor array patterns in a neurodynamics model of the olfactory system.* (Unpublished Ph.D. Dissertation) Texas A&M University. College Station, TX.

Gutierrez-Galvez, A., & Gutierrez-Osuna, R. (2006). Contrast enhancement and background suppression of chemosensor array patterns with the KIII model. *International Journal of Intelligent Systems*, *21*(9), 937–953. doi:10.1002/int.20170

Gutierrez–Mecinas, M., Crespo, C., Blasco–Ibanez, J. M., Gracia–Llanes, F. J., Marques–Mari, A. I., & Martinez–Guijarro, F. J. (2005). Soluble guanylyl cyclase appears in a specific subset of periglomerular cells in the olfactory bulb. *The European Journal of Neuroscience*, *21*, 1443–1448. doi:10.1111/j.1460-9568.2005.03960.x

Gutierrez-Osuna, R. (2000). Drift reduction for metal-oxide sensor arrays using canonical correlation regression and partial least squares. In *Proceedings of the 7th International Symposium on Olfaction and Electronic Nose.* Brighton, UK: IEEE.

Gutierrez-Osuna, R. (2002). Pattern analysis for machine olfaction: A review. *IEEE Sensors Journal*, *2*(3), 189–202. doi:10.1109/JSEN.2002.800688

Gutierrez-Osuna, R., & Gutierrez-Galvez, A. (2003). Habituation in the KIII olfactory model with chemical sensor arrays. *IEEE Transactions on Neural Networks*, *14*(6), 1565–1568. doi:10.1109/TNN.2003.820438

Gutierrez-Osuna, R., & Powar, N. U. (2003). Odor mixtures and chemosensory adaptation in gas sensor arrays. *International Journal of Artificial Intelligence Tools*, *12*(1), 1–16. doi:10.1142/S0218213003001083

Gutierrez-Osuna, R., & Raman, B. (2004). Cancellation of chemical backgrounds with generalized Fisher's linear discriminants. [). IEEE Press.]. *Proceedings of IEEE Sensors*, *3*, 1381–1384. doi:10.1109/ICSENS.2004.1426441

Haberly, L. B. (2001). Parallel-distributed processing in olfactory cortex: New insights from morphological and physiological analysis of neuronal circuitry. *Chemical Senses*, *26*, 551–576. doi:10.1093/chemse/26.5.551

Haberly, L. B., & Price, J. L. (1977). The axonal projection patterns of the mitral and tufted cells of the olfactory bulb in the rat. *Brain Research*, *129*, 152–157. doi:10.1016/0006-8993(77)90978-7

Haberly, L. B., & Price, J. L. (1978). Association and commissural fiber systems of the olfactory cortex of the rat. *The Journal of Comparative Neurology*, *178*, 711–740. doi:10.1002/cne.901780408

Halkidi, M., Batistakis, Y., & Vazirgiannis, M. (2001). On clustering validation techniques. *Journal of Intelligent Information Systems*, *17*(2/3), 107–145. doi:10.1023/A:1012801612483

Halkidi, M., Batistakis, Y., & Vazirgiannis, M. (2002). Clustering validity methods. *SIGMOD Record*, *31*(2), 40–45. doi:10.1145/565117.565124

Handl, J., Knowles, J., & Kell, D. B. (2005). Computational cluster validation in post-genomic data analysis. *Bioinformatics (Oxford, England)*, *21*, 3201–3212. doi:10.1093/bioinformatics/bti517

Haque, U. (2004). *Scents of space: An interactive smell system. ACM SIGGRAPH 2004 Sketches.* New York, NY: ACM Press.

Harada, H., Tanaka, M., & Kato, T. (2006). Brain olfactory activation measured by near-infrared spectroscopy in humans. *The Journal of Laryngology and Otology*, *120*, 638–643. doi:10.1017/S002221510600123X

Hardy, A., Palouzier–Paulignan, B., Duchamp, A., Royet, J. P., & Duchamp–Viret, P. (2005). 5-Hydroxytryptamine action in the rat olfactory bulb: In vitro electrophysiological patch–clamp recordings of juxtaglomerular and mitral cells. *Neuroscience*, *131*, 717–731. doi:10.1016/j. neuroscience.2004.10.034

Harkema, J. R., Carey, S. A., & Wagner, J. G. (2006). The nose revisited: A brief review of the comparative structure, function, and toxicologic pathology of the nasal epithelium. *Toxicologic Pathology*, *34*, 252–269. doi:10.1080/01926230600713475

Harmon, M. E., Tang, M., & Frank, C. W. (2003). A microfluidic actuator based on thermoresponsive hydrogels. *Polymer*, *44*, 4547–4556. doi:10.1016/S0032-3861(03)00463-4

Hashimoto, Y., Yamada, M., Suga, M., Kimura, K., Sakairi, M., & Tanaka, S. (2000). Online measurement of organic chlorides using an atmospheric-pressure chemical ionization ion-trap mass spectrometer. *Bunseki Kagaku*, *49*, 49–54. doi:10.2116/bunsekikagaku.49.49

Hastie, T. J., & Stuetzle, W. (1989). Principal curves. *Journal of the American Statistical Association*, *84*, 502–516. doi:10.1080/01621459.1989.10478797

Haugen, J., Tomic, O., & Kvaal, K. (2000). A calibration method for handling the temporal drift of solid state gas-sensors. *Analytica Chimica Acta*, *407*(1-2), 23–39. doi:10.1016/S0003-2670(99)00784-9

Hayama, K., Hayashi, K., & Toko, K. (2003). Functionalization of gold surfaces using benzene-patterned self-assembled monolayers for surface-polarization controlling method. *Sensor Materials*, *15*, 403–412.

Hayama, K., Tanaka, H., Ju, M. J., Hayashi, K., & Toko, K. (2002). Fabrication of a flow cell for electrochemical impedance measurements. *Sensors and Materials*, *14*(8), 443–453.

Hayar, A., Karnup, S., Ennis, M., & Shipley, M. T. (2004). External tufted cells: A major excitatory element that coordinates glomerular activity. *The Journal of Neuroscience*, *24*, 6676–6685. doi:10.1523/JNEUROSCI.1367-04.2004

Hayar, A., Karnup, S., Shipley, M. T., & Ennis, M. (2004). Olfactory bulb glomeruli: external tufted cells intrinsically burst at theta frequency and are entrained by patterned olfactory input. *The Journal of Neuroscience*, *24*, 1190–1199. doi:10.1523/JNEUROSCI.4714-03.2004

Hayashi, K. (2009). Odor synthesis using odor code based on molecular informatics. In *Proceedings of the 26th Sensors Symposium*, (pp. 75-80). IEEE.

Hayashi, K., Hayama, K., Masunaga, K., Futagami, W., Lee, S. W., & Toko, K. (2004). Analysis of adsorbing molecules on pt surface using electrochemical impedance spectroscopy. *IEICE Transactions. E (Norwalk, Conn.)*, *87C*, 2087–2092.

Haze, S., Sakai, K., & Gozu, Y. (2002). Effects of fragrance inhalation on sympathetic activity in normal adults. *Japanese Journal of Pharmacology*, *90*(3), 247–253. doi:10.1254/jjp.90.247

Heilig, M. L. (1962). *Sensorama simulator*. U. S. Patent 3,050,870. Washington, DC: US Patent Office.

Heilig, M. L. (1962). *US patent #3050870*. Washington, DC: United States Patent Office.

Heilig, M. L. (1992). El cine del futuro: The cinema of the future. *Presence (Cambridge, Mass.)*, *1*(3), 193–219.

Heinbockel, T., Heyward, P., Conquet, F., & Ennis, M. (2004). Regulation of main olfactory bulb mitral cell excitability by metabotropic glutamate receptor mGluR1. *Journal of Neurophysiology*, *92*, 3085–3096. doi:10.1152/jn.00349.2004

Heise, D. (1970). The semantic differential and attitude research. In G. F. Summers (Ed.), *Attitude Measurement*, (pp. 235-253). Chicago, IL: Rand McNally. Retrieved from http://www.mendeley.com/research/semantic-differential-attitude-research/

He, J., Wu, Y., Wu, J., Mao, X., Fu, L., & Qian, T. (2007). Study and application of a linear frequency-thickness relation for surface-initiated atom transfer radical polymerization in a quartz crystal microbalance. *Macromolecules*, *40*, 3090–3096. doi:10.1021/ma062613n

Henderson, M. J., Karger, B. A., & Wrenshall, G. A. (1952). Acetone in the breath: A study of acetone exhalation in diabetic and nondiabetic human subjects. *Diabetes*, *1*, 188–193.

Hendin, O., Horn, D., & Hopfield, J. J. (1994). Decomposition of a mixture of signals in a model of the olfactory bulb. *Proceedings of the National Academy of Sciences of the United States of America, 91*(13), 5942–5946. doi:10.1073/pnas.91.13.5942

Hengl, T., Kaneko, H., Dauner, K., Vocke, K., Frings, S., & Mohrlen, F. (2010). Molecular components of signal amplification in olfactory sensory cilia. *Proceedings of the National Academy of Sciences of the United States of America, 107*, 6052–6057. doi:10.1073/pnas.0909032107

Heritage, S. (2006). *The new Colin Farrell movie stinks in Japan*. Retrieved August 23, 2007 from http://www.hecklerspray.com/the-new-colin-farrell-movie-stinks-in-japan/20062756.php

Herz, R. S., & Cupchik, G. C. (1995). The emotional distinctiveness of odor–evoked memories. *Chemical Senses, 20*, 517–528. doi:10.1093/chemse/20.5.517

Herz, R. S., Eliassen, J., Beland, S., & Souza, T. (2004). Neuroimaging evidence for the emotional potency of odor-evoked memory. *Neuropsychologia, 42*(3), 371–378. doi:10.1016/j.neuropsychologia.2003.08.009

Herz, R. S., & von Clef, J. (2001). The influence of verbal labeling on the perception of odors: Evidence for olfactory illusion? *Perception, 30*, 381–391. doi:10.1068/p3179

Hess, E. H. (1965). Attitude and pupil size. *Scientific American, 212*(4), 46–54. Retrieved from http://hosting.udlap.mx/profesores/julioc.penagos/materias/fisiologia-conducta/archivos/files/lfc1.pdfdoi:10.1038/scientificamerican0465-46

Hierlemann, A., & Gutierrez-Osuna, R. (2008). Higher-order chemical sensing. *Chemical Reviews, 108*, 563–613. doi:10.1021/cr068116m

Hines, E. L., Llobet, E., & Gardner, J. W. (1999). Electronic noses: A review of signal processing techniques. *IEEE Proceedings-Circuits Devices and Systems, 146*(6), 297-310.

Hirose, H. (2002). Sensory info-communication technology and olfactory media. *Aroma Research, 10*, 60.

Hirsch, A. R. (2001). Aromatherapy: Art, science, or myth? In Weintraub, M. I. (Ed.), *Alternative and Complementary Treatment in Neurologic Illness* (pp. 128–150). Philadelphia, PA: Churchill Livingstone.

Holberg, M., Winquist, F., Ludström, I., Gardner, J. W., & Hines, E. L. (1995). Identification of paper quality using a hybrid electronic nose. *Sensors and Actuators. B, Chemical, 26-27*, 246–249. doi:10.1016/0925-4005(94)01595-9

Hollowell, C. D., & McLaughlin, R. D. (1973). Instrumentation for air pollution monitoring. *Environmental Science & Technology, 7*(11), 1011–1017. doi:10.1021/es60083a012

Holmberg, T. A. M. (2003). Drift compensation, standards, and calibration methods. In Pearce, T. C., Schiffman, S. S., Nagle, H. T., & Gardner, J. W. (Eds.), *Handbook of Machine Olfaction - Electronic Nose Technology* (pp. 325–346). Weinheim, Germany: WILEY-VCH.

Honda, K. (1994). *The world of ultrasound*. Tokyo, Japan: NHK Publishing Co., Ltd.

Honne, A., Schumann-Olsen, H., Kaspersen, K., Limero, T., Macatangay, A., et al. (2009). Evaluation of ANITA air monitoring on the international space station. In *Proceedings 39th International Conference on Environmental Systems*. Society of Automotive Engineers (SAE).

Hopfield, J. J., & Tank, D. W. (1986). Computing with neural circuits: A model. *Science, 233*, 625–633. doi:10.1126/science.3755256

Horne, J., Lawless, H. T., Speirs, W., & Sposato, D. (2002). Bitter taste of saccharin and acesulfame-K. *Chemical Senses, 27*, 31–38. doi:10.1093/chemse/27.1.31

Hoshino, O., Kashimori, Y., & Kambara, T. (1998). An olfactory recognition model based on spatio-temporal encoding of odor quality in the olfactory bulb. *Biological Cybernetics, 79*(2), 109–120. doi:10.1007/s004220050463

Hoshi, Y. (2003). Functional near-infrared optical imaging: Utility and limitations in human brain mapping. *Psychophysiology, 40*, 511–520. doi:10.1111/1469-8986.00053

Hsieh, C. T., & Chen, J. M. (2002). Adsorption energy distribution model for VOCs onto activated carbons. *Journal of Colloid and Interface Science, 255*, 248–253. doi:10.1006/jcis.2002.8668

Hubschmann, H. J. (2009). *Handbook of GC/MS: Fundamentals and applications*. New York, NY: Wiley-VCH.

Hui, D., Jun-Hua, L., & Zhong-Ru, S. (2003). Drift reduction of gas sensor by wavelet and principal component analysis. *Sensors and Actuators. B, Chemical, 96*, 354–363. doi:10.1016/S0925-4005(03)00569-0

Hu, J., Zhong, C., Ding, C., Chi, Q., Walz, A., & Mombaerts, P. (2007). Detection of near-atmospheric concentrations of CO_2 by an olfactory subsystem in the mouse. *Science, 317*, 953–957. doi:10.1126/science.1144233

Hussain, C. M. (2008). Carbon nanotubes as sorbents for the gas phase preconcentration of semivolatile organics in a microtrap. *Analyst (London), 133*, 1076–1082. doi:10.1039/b801415a

Ichinohe, S., Tanaka, H., & Konno, Y. (2007). Gas sensing by AT-cut quartz crystal oscillator coated with mixed-lipid film. *Sensors and Actuators. B, Chemical, 123*, 306–312. doi:10.1016/j.snb.2006.08.024

IFT. (1975, June 10). *Minutes of sensory evaluation*. Chicago, IL: IFT.

IFT. (1981). *Sensory evaluation guide for testing food & beverage products*. Chicago, IL: Sensory Evaluation Division of IFT.

Ihaka, R. (2003). Colour for presentation graphics. In K. Hornik, F. Leisch, & A. Zeileis (Eds.), *Proceedings of the 3rd International Workshop on Distributed Statistical Computing*. Vienna, Austria: IEEE.

Ikehara, T., Konno, M., Murakami, S., Fukawa, T., Kimura, M., & Mihara, T. (2011). Integration of p-n junction diode to cantilever mass sensor for frequency drift compensation due to temperature fluctuation. *Sensors and Materials, 23*, 381–396.

Ikehara, T., Lu, J., Konno, M., Maeda, R., & Mihara, T. (2007). High quality-factor silicon cantilever for high sensitive resonant mass sensor operated in air. *Journal of Micromechanics and Microengineering, 17*, 2491–2494. doi:10.1088/0960-1317/17/12/015

Imahashi, M., Takamizawa, T., Miyagi, K., & Hayashi, K. (2011). Artificial odor map and discrimination of odorants using the odor separating system. In *Proceedings of the 14th International Symposium on Olfaction and Electronic Nose*, (vol. 1362, pp. 27-28). AIP.

Imayoshi, I., & Sakamoto, M. (2008). Regenerating your senses: multiple roles for neurogenesis in the adult brain. *Nature Neuroscience, 11*, 1124–1126. doi:10.1038/nn1008-1124

Improbable Research. (2011). *Winners of the Ig Nobel prize*. Retrieved February 10, 2012 from http://www.improbable.com/ig/winners/

Ionescu, R., Vancu, A., & Tomescu, A. (2000). Time-dependent humidity calibration for drift corrections in electronic noses equipped with sno2 gas sensors. *Sensors and Actuators. B, Chemical, 69*(3), 283–286. doi:10.1016/S0925-4005(00)00508-6

Ippolito, S. J., Ponzoni, A., Kalantar-Zadeh, K., Wlodarski, W., Comini, E., Faglia, G., & Sberveglieri, G. (2006). Layered WO3/ZnO/36° LiTaO3 SAW gas sensor sensitive towards ethanol vapour and humidity. *Sensors and Actuators. B, Chemical, 117*(2), 442–450. doi:10.1016/j.snb.2005.12.050

Isaacson, J. S., & Strowbridge, B. W. (1998). Olfactory reciprocal synapses: Dendritic signaling in the CNS. *Neuron, 20*, 749–761. doi:10.1016/S0896-6273(00)81013-2

Ishida, H., Matsukura, H., Yoshida, H., & Nakamoto, T. (2008). Application of computational fluid dynamics simulation to olfactory display. In *Proceedings of 18th International Conference on Artificial Reality and Telexistence*, (pp. 285–288). IEEE.

Ishida, H., Yoshida, H., & Nakamoto, T. (2011). Introducing computational fluid dynamics simulation into olfactory display. *Electrical Engineering in Japan, 177*(1), 65–72. doi:10.1002/eej.21087

Ishikawa, M., Nakamura, A., Fujiki, A., Ide, J., & Mori, K. (2008). Improving the taste of artificial sweeteners using flavors. In *Proceedings of Sweetness and Sweeteners: Biology, Chemistry and Psychophysics ACS Symposium*, (pp. 420-429). Washington, DC: ACS Press.

Ishimaru, T., Yata, T., & Hatanaka-Ikeno, S. (2004). Hemodynamic response of the frontal cortex elicited by intravenous thiamine propyldisulphide administration. *Chemical Senses, 29*, 247–251. doi:10.1093/chemse/bjh029

Ishimaru, T., Yata, T., Horikawa, K., & Hatanaka, S. (2004). Near-infrared spectroscopy of the adult human olfactory cortex. *Acta Oto-Laryngologica. Supplementum, 553*, 95–98. doi:10.1080/03655230410017751

ISO. (2012). *International organization for standardization (ISO).* Retrieved from http://www.iso.org

Israelachvili, J. N. (1985). *Intermolecular and surface forces.* London, UK: Academic Press.

Issanchou, S., Valentin, D., Sulmont, C., Degel, J., & Köster, E. P. (2002). Testing odor memory: Incidental versus intentional learning, implicit versus explicit memory. In C. Rouby, b. Schaal, D. Dubois, R. Gervais, & A. Holley (Eds.), *Olfaction, Taste, and Cognition*, (pp. 211-230). Cambridge, UK: Cambridge University Press.

Ito, H., Doi, Y., Kameda, W., Shimoda, M., & Osajima, Y. (1991). Studies on characterization of odor-descriptive terms for food products, 6: Contribution of abstract terms to the characterization of concrete terms for odor-description. *Journal of the Japanese Society for Food Science and Technology, 38*(7), 588–594. doi:10.3136/nskkk1962.38.588

Iwasa, Y., Izumi, R., Hayahsi, K., & Toko, K. (2004). *Synthesis of odor based on substructures and physicochemical properties of odorants.* Retrieved from http://sciencelinks.jp/j-east/article/200507/000020050705A0243286.php

Iwata, H., Yano, H., Uemura, T., & Moriya, T. (2004). Food simulator: A haptic interface for biting. [IEEE Press.]. *Proceedings of IEEE Virtual Reality, 2004*, 51–57.

Izumi, R., Abe, H., Hayashi, K., & Toko, K. (2007). Odor quantification of aromatic alcohols using artificial olfactory epithelium. *Sensors and Materials, 19*, 299–307.

Izumi, R., Hayashi, K., & Toko, K. (2008). Odor sensor with water membrane using surface polarity controlling method and analysis of responses to partial structures of odor molecules. *Sensors and Actuators. B, Chemical, 99*, 315–322. doi:10.1016/j.snb.2003.11.030

Jäger, W., Buchbauer, G., Jirovetz, L., Dietrich, H., & Plank, C. (1992). Evidence of the sedative effect of neroli oil, citronellal and phenylethyl acetate on mice. *The Journal of Essential Oil Research, 4*, 387–394. doi:10.1080/10412905.1992.9698090

Jain, A. K., & Dubes, R. (1988). *Algorithms for clustering data.* Englewood Cliffs, NJ: Prentice Hall.

Jain, A. K., Murty, M. N., & Flynn, P. J. (1999). Data clustering: A review. *ACM Computing Surveys, 31*, 264–323. doi:10.1145/331499.331504

Janshoff, A., Galla, H.-J., & Steinem, C. (2000). Piezoelectric mass-sensing devices as biosensors-an alternative to optical biosensors? *Angewandte Chemie International Edition, 39*, 4004–4032. doi:10.1002/1521-3773(20001117)39:22<4004::AID-ANIE4004>3.0.CO;2-2

Japan Perfumery and Flavoring Association. (2001). *Encyclopedia of scent.* Tokyo, Japan: Asakura Publishing Co., Ltd.

Japanese Ministry of Health, Labor, and Welfare. (2000). *Guideline and standard evaluation method of the VOC indoor concentration in room.* Tokyo, Japan: Japanese Ministry of Health, Labor and Welfare.

Jasper, H. A. (1958). The ten–twenty system of the international federation. *Electroencephalography and Clinical Neurophysiology, 10*, 371–375.

Jellinek, J. S. (1994). Aroma-chology: A status review. *Perfumer and Flavorist, 19*(5), 25–49.

Jellinek, J. S. (1997). Psychodynamic odor effects and their mechanisms. *Cosmetics & Toiletries, 112*, 61–71.

Jenkins, G. N. (1978). *The physiology and biochemistry of the mouth* (4th ed.). Oxford, UK: Blackwell Scientific Publications.

Jinks, A., & Laing, D. G. (2001). The analysis of odor mixtures by humans: Evidence for a configurational process. *Physiology & Behavior, 72*, 51–63. doi:10.1016/S0031-9384(00)00407-8

Jin, X., Hung, Y., Mason, A., & Zeng, X. (2009). Multichannel monolithic quartz crystal microbalance gas sensor array. *Analytical Chemistry, 81*, 595–603. doi:10.1021/ac8018697

Jobsis, F. F. (1977). Noninvasive, infrared monitoring of cerebral and myocardial oxygen sufficiency and circulatory parameters. *Science, 198*, 1264–1267. doi:10.1126/science.929199

Johnson, B. A., & Leon, M. (2007). Chemotopic odorant coding in a mammalian olfactory system. *The Journal of Comparative Neurology, 503*, 1–34. doi:10.1002/cne.21396

Johnson, B. A., Ong, J., & Leon, M. (2010). Glomerular activity patterns evoked by natural odor objects in the rat olfactory bulb are related to patterns evoked by major odorant components. *The Journal of Comparative Neurology, 518*(9), 1542–1555. doi:10.1002/cne.22289

Johnson, B. A., Woo, C. C., & Leon, M. (1998). Spatial coding of odorant features in the glomerular layer of the rat olfactory bulb. *The Journal of Comparative Neurology, 393*, 457–471. doi:10.1002/(SICI)1096-9861(19980420)393:4<457::AID-CNE5>3.0.CO;2-#

Johnston, J., & Delaney, K. R. (2010). Synaptic activation of T-type Ca^{2+} channels via mGluR activation in the primary dendrite of mitral cells. *Journal of Neurophysiology, 103*, 2557–2569. doi:10.1152/jn.00796.2009

Jones, D. T., & Reed, R. R. (1989). G_{olf}: An olfactory neuron specific-G protein involved in odorant signal transduction. *Science, 244*, 790–795. doi:10.1126/science.2499043

Jordan, R., Ulman, A., Kang, J. F., Rafailovich, M. H., & Sokolov, J. (1999). Surface-initiated anionic polymerization of styrene by means of self-assembled monolayers. *Journal of the American Chemical Society, 121*, 1016–1022. doi:10.1021/ja981348l

Jöreskog, K. G. (1978). Structural analysis of covariance and correlation matrices. *Psychometrika, 43*, 443–477. doi:10.1007/BF02293808

Ju, J. F., Syu, M.-J., Teng, H.-S., Chou, S.-K., & Chang, Y.-S. (2008). Preparation and identification of β-cyclodextrin polymer thin film for quartz crystal microbalance sensing of benzene, toluene, and p-xylene. *Sensors and Actuators. B, Chemical, 132*, 319–326. doi:10.1016/j.snb.2008.01.052

Ju, M. J., Hayama, K., Hayashi, K., & Toko, K. (2003). Discrimination of pungent-tasting substances using surface-polarity controlled sensor with indirect in situ modification. *Sensors and Actuators. B, Chemical, 89*, 150–157. doi:10.1016/S0925-4005(02)00457-4

Ju, M. J., Yang, D. H., Lee, S. W., Kunitake, T., Hayashi, K., & Toko, K. (2007). Fabrication of TiO2/γ-CD films for nitro aromatic compounds and its sensing application via cyclic surface-polarization impedance (cSPI) spectroscopy. *Sensors and Actuators. B, Chemical, 123*, 359–367. doi:10.1016/j.snb.2006.08.035

Jurs, P. C., Bakken, G. A., & McClelland, H. E. (2000). Computational methods for the analysis of chemical sensor array data from volatile analytes. *Chemical Reviews, 100*, 2649–2678. doi:10.1021/cr9800964

Kadohisa, M., & Wilson, D. A. (2006). Olfactory cortical adaptation facilitates detection of odors against background. *Journal of Neurophysiology, 95*(3), 1888–1896. doi:10.1152/jn.00812.2005

Kadowaki, A., Sato, J., Bannai, Y., & Okada, K. (2007). Presentation technique of scent to avoid olfactory adaptation. In *Proceedings of 17th International Conference on Artificial Reality and Telexistence*, (pp. 97–104). IEEE.

Kaneko, H., Nakamura, T., & Lindemann, B. (2001). Noninvasive measurement of chloride concentration in rat olfactory receptor cells with use of a fluorescent dye. *American Journal of Physiology. Cell Physiology, 280*, C1387–C1393.

Kaneko, H., Putzier, I., Frings, S., Kaupp, U. B., & Gensch, T. (2004). Chloride accumulation in mammalian olfactory sensory neurons. *The Journal of Neuroscience, 24*, 7931–7938. doi:10.1523/JNEUROSCI.2115-04.2004

Kaneyasu, M., Ikegami, A., Arima, H., & Iwanaga, S. (1987). Smell identification using a thick-film hybrid gas sensor. *IEEE Transactions on Components. Hybrids and Manufacturing Technology, 10*, 267. doi:10.1109/TCHMT.1987.1134730

Karout, S., Racz, Z., Capurro, A., Cole, M., Gardner, J. W., & Pearce, T. C. (2011). Ratiometric chemical blend processing with a neuromorphic model of the insect macroglomerular complex. In *Proceedings of the AIP Conference*, (vol 1362, pp. 77-78). AIP.

Kasai, N., & Sugimoto, I. (1999). Effects of aging on radio frequency-sputtered polyethylene film. *Journal of Applied Polymer Science, 73*, 1869–1877. doi:10.1002/(SICI)1097-4628(19990906)73:10<1869::AID-APP6>3.0.CO;2-7

Katada, S., Hirokawa, T., Oka, Y., Suwa, M., & Touhara, K. (2005). Structural basis for a broad but selective ligand spectrum of a mouse olfactory receptor: Mapping the odorant-binding site. *The Journal of Neuroscience, 25*, 1806–1815. doi:10.1523/JNEUROSCI.4723-04.2005

Kaufman, L., & Rousseeuw, P. J. (1990). *Finding groups in data: an introduction to cluster analysis*. New York, NY: Wiley. doi:10.1002/9780470316801

Kaupp, U. B. (2011). Olfactory signalling in vertebrates and insects: differences and commonalities. *Nature Reviews. Neuroscience, 11*, 188–200.

Kawai, F. (1999). Odorant suppression of delayed rectifier potassium current in newt olfactory receptor cells. *Neuroscience Letters, 269*, 45–48. doi:10.1016/S0304-3940(99)00424-3

Kawai, F. (1999). Odorants suppress T- and L-type Ca^{2+} currents in olfactory receptor cells by shifting their inactivation curves to a negative voltage. *Neuroscience Research, 35*, 253–263. doi:10.1016/S0168-0102(99)00091-7

Kawai, F., Kurahashi, T., & Kaneko, A. (1997). Nonselective suppression of voltage–gated currents by odorants in the newt olfactory receptor cells. *The Journal of General Physiology, 109*, 265–272. doi:10.1085/jgp.109.2.265

Kawai, F., & Miyachi, E. (2001). Enhancement by T-type Ca^{2+} currents of odor sensitivity in olfactory receptor cells. *The Journal of Neuroscience, 21*, RC144.

Kawai, T., & Noro, K. (1996). Psychological effect of stereoscopic 3-D images with fragrances. *Ergonomics, 39*, 1364–1369. doi:10.1080/00140139608964556

Kaye, J. N. (2001). *Symbolic olfactory display*. (Master's Thesis). Massachusetts Institute of Technology Massachusetts. Cambridge, MA.

Kaye, J. (2004). Making scents: Aromatic output for hci. *Interaction, 11*, 48–61. doi:10.1145/962342.964333

Kaye, J. N. (2004). Making scents: Aromatic output for HCI. *Interactions (New York, N.Y.), 11*(1), 48–61. doi:10.1145/962342.964333

Keller, P. E., Kouzes, R. T., Kangas, L. J., & Hashem, S. (1995). Transmission of olfactory information for telemedicine. In Morgan, K., Satava, R. M., Sieburg, H. B., Matteus, R., & Christensen, J. P. (Eds.), *Interactive Technology and the New Paradigm for Healthcare* (pp. 168–172). Amsterdam, The Netherlands: IOS Press and Ohmsha.

Kelly, J. T., Prasad, A. K., & Wexler, A. S. (2000). Detailed flow patterns in the nasal cavity. *Journal of Applied Physiology, 89*(1), 323–337.

Kendrick, K. M., Guevara–Guzman, R., Zorrilla, J., Hinton, M. R., Broad, K. D., & Mimmack, M. (1997). Formation of olfactory memories mediated by nitric oxide. *Nature, 388*, 670–674. doi:10.1038/41765

Kermit, M., & Tomic, O. (2003). Independent component analysis applied on gas sensor array measurement data. *IEEE Sensors Journal, 3*(2), 218–228. doi:10.1109/JSEN.2002.807488

Keshri, G., & Magan, N. (2000). Detection and differentiation between mycotoxigenic and non-mycotoxigenic strains of two Fusarium spp. using volatile production profiles and hydrolytic enzymes. *Journal of Applied Microbiology, 89*, 825–833. doi:10.1046/j.1365-2672.2000.01185.x

Keskin, S., Kayrak-Talay, D., Akman, U., & Hortaçsu, Ö. (2007). A review of ionic liquids towards supercritical fluid applications. *The Journal of Supercritical Fluids, 43*, 150–180. doi:10.1016/j.supflu.2007.05.013

Khalfa, S., Isabelle, P., Blondin, J., & Manon, R. (2002). Event-related skin conductance responses to musical emotions in humans. *Neuroscience Letters, 328*, 145–149. doi:10.1016/S0304-3940(02)00462-7

Kido, M. (2002). Physiological and psychological effects of fragrance. *Journal of International Society of Life Information Science, 20*(1), 148–151.

Kiger, P. J., & Smith, M. J. (2006). *Lesson #9 - Beware of unproven technologies the lingering reek of "smell-o-vision"*. New York, NY: HarperCollins. Retrieved August 21, 2007 from http://www.in70mm.com/news/2006/oops/index.htm

Kikuchi, M., Tsuru, N., & Shiratori, S. (2006). Recognition of terpenes using molecular imprinted polymer coated quartz crystal microbalance in air phase. *Science and Technology of Advanced Materials*, *7*, 156–161. doi:10.1016/j.stam.2005.12.004

Kim, D. H., & Ando, H. (2010). Development of directional olfactory display. In *Proceedings of the 9th ACM SIGGRAPH Conference on Virtual-Reality Continuum and its Applications in Industry (VRCAI 2010)*, (pp. 143–144). ACM Press.

Kim, D. H., Cho, Y. H., Nishimoto, K., Kawakami, Y., Kunifuji, S., & Ando, H. (2009). Development of aroma-card based soundless olfactory display. In *Proceedings of 16th IEEE International Conference on Electronics, Circuits, and Systems (ICECS) 2009*, (pp. 703–706). IEEE Press.

Kim, D. W., Nishimoto, K., & Kunifuji, S. (2006). An editing and displaying system of olfactory information for the home video. In *Proceedings of the Knowledge-Based & Intelligent Information & Engineering Systems International Conference*, (pp. 859-866). Berlin, Germany: Springer.

Kim, B. H., Prins, F. E., Kern, D. P., Raible, S., & Weimar, U. (2001). Multicomponent analysis and prediction with a cantilever array based on gas sensor. *Sensors and Actuators. B, Chemical*, *78*, 12–18. doi:10.1016/S0925-4005(01)00785-7

Kim, D. W., Miura, M., Lee, D. W., Ryu, J. K., Nishimoto, K., Kawakami, Y., & Kunifuji, S. (2008). Developing an olfactory display using functional high-polymers application for video. *Journal of Information Processing Society of Japan*, *49*(1), 160–175.

Kim, J., Kim, D., Han, D., Byun, H., Ham, Y., & Jung, W. (2006). A proposal representation, digital coding and clustering of odor information. *Computational Intelligence and Security*, *1*, 872–877.

Kim, M. S., Seo, K. S., Khang, G., Cho, S. H., & Lee, H. B. (2004). Preparation of poly(ethylene glycol)-block-poly(caprolactone) copolymers and their applications as thermo-sensitive materials. *Journal of Biomedical Materials Research. Part A*, *70A*(1), 154–158. doi:10.1002/jbm.a.30049

Kimura, M., Liu, Y., Sakai, R., Sato, S., Hirai, T., Fukawa, T., & Mihara, T. (2011). Detection of volatile organic compounds by analyses of polymer-coated quartz crystal microbalance sensor arrays. *Sensors and Materials*, *23*, 359–368.

Kimura, M., Sakaguchi, A., Ohta, K., Hanabusa, K., Shirai, H., & Kobayashi, N. (2003). Selective ligation to sterically isolated metallophthalocyanines. *Inorganic Chemistry*, *42*, 2821–2823. doi:10.1021/ic026149o

Kirschbaum, C., & Hellhammer, D. H. (1994). Salivary cortisol in psychoneuroendocrine research: Recent developments and applications. *Psychoneuroendocrinology*, *19*(4), 313–333. doi:10.1016/0306-4530(94)90013-2

Kiyokage, E., Pan, Y. Z., Shao, Z., Kobayashi, K., Szabo, G., & Yanagawa, Y. (2010). Molecular identity of periglomerular and short axon cells. *The Journal of Neuroscience*, *30*, 1185–1196. doi:10.1523/JNEUROSCI.3497-09.2010

Kleene, S. J. (1993). Origin of the chloride current in olfactory transduction. *Neuron*, *11*, 123–132. doi:10.1016/0896-6273(93)90276-W

Kobari, K., Yamamoto, Y., Sakuma, M., Akao, S., & Yamanaka, K. (2009). Fabrication of thin sensitive film of ball surface acoustic wave sensor by off-axis spin-coating method. *Japanese Journal of Applied Physics*, *48*(7), 07GG13-1 – 07GG13-6.

Kobayakawa, K. (2007). Innate versus learned odour processing in the mouse olfactory bulb. *Nature*, *450*, 503–508. doi:10.1038/nature06281

Kobayakawa, K., Kobayakawa, R., Matsumoto, H., Oka, Y., Imai, T., & Ikawa, M. (2007). Innate versus learned odour processing in the mouse olfactory bulb. *Nature*, *450*, 503–508. doi:10.1038/nature06281

Kobayashi, A., Kagawa, S., Ishikawa, Y., Matsubara, H., Matsui, T., & Matsumoto, K. (2008). Identification of plastic off-odors from linear-low density polyethylene. *Journal of Packaging Science & Technology Japan*, *17*(6), 427–432.

Ko, H. J., Lee, S. H., Oh, E. H., & Park, T. H. (2010). Specificity of odorant-binding proteins: A factor influencing the sensitivity of olfactory receptor-based biosensors. *Bioprocess and Biosystems Engineering*, *33*, 55–62. doi:10.1007/s00449-009-0348-3

Kohonen, T. (1997). *Self-organizing maps*. Heidelberg, Germany: Springer. doi:10.1007/978-3-642-97966-8

Koizumi, H., Yamashita, Y., Maki, A., Yamamoto, T., Ito, Y., Itagaki, H., & Kennan, R. (1999). Higher-order brain function analysis by trans-cranial dynamic NIRS imaging. *Journal of Biomedical Optics*, *4*, 403–413. doi:10.1117/1.429959

Kojima, K., Sakairi, M., Takada, Y., & Nakamura, J. (2000). Vapor detection of TNT and RDX using atmospheric pressure chemical ionization mass spectrometry with counter-flow introduction (CFI). *Journal of Mass Spectrometry Society of Japan*, *48*, 360–362. doi:10.5702/massspec.48.360

Kokan, N., Sakai, N., Doi, K., Fujio, H., Hasegawa, S., Tanimoto, H., & Nibu, K. (2011). Near-infrared spectroscopy of orbitofrontal cortex during odorant stimulation. *American Journal of Rhinology and Allergy*, *25*, 163–165. doi:10.2500/ajra.2011.25.3634

Komori, T., Fujiwara, R., Tanida, M., Nomura, J., & Yokoyama, M. M. (1995). Effects of citrus fragrance on immune function and depressive states. *Neuroimmunomodulation*, *2*(3), 174–180. doi:10.1159/000096889

Kosaka, T., & Kosaka, K. (2007). Heterogeneity of nitric oxide synthase-containing neurons in the mouse main olfactory bulb. *Neuroscience Research*, *57*, 165–178. doi:10.1016/j.neures.2006.10.005

Kosaka, T., & Kosaka, K. (2011). "Interneurons" in the olfactory bulb revisited. *Neuroscience Research*, *69*, 93–99. doi:10.1016/j.neures.2010.10.002

Krasteva, N., Fogel, Y., Bauer, R. E., Müllen, K., Joseph, Y., & Matsuzawa, N. (2007). Vapor sorption and electrical response of Au-nanoparticle-dendrimer composites. *Advanced Functional Materials*, *17*, 881–888. doi:10.1002/adfm.200600598

Kruskal, J. B. (1964). Multidimensional scaling by optimizing goodness of fit to a nonmetric hypothesis. *Psychometrika*, *29*, 1–27. doi:10.1007/BF02289565

Krzanowski, W. J., & Lai, Y. T. (1985). A criterion for determining the number of groups in a data set using sum-of-squares clustering. *Biometrika*, *44*, 23–34.

Kuffler, S. W. (1953). Discharge patterns and functional organization of the mammalian retina. *Journal of Neurophysiology*, *16*, 37–68.

Kuhn, C., Bufe, B., Winnig, M., Hofmann, T., Frank, O., & Behrens, M. (2004). Bitter taste receptors for saccharin and acesulfame K. *The Journal of Neuroscience*, *24*, 10260–10265. doi:10.1523/JNEUROSCI.1225-04.2004

Kuhn, W., Hargitay, B., Katchalsky, A., & Eisenberg, H. (1950). Reversible dilation and contraction by changing the state of ionization of high-polymer acid networks. *Nature*, *165*, 514–516. doi:10.1038/165514a0

Kurahashi, T., Lowe, G., & Gold, G. H. (1994). Suppression of odorant responses by odorants in olfactory receptor cells. *Science*, *265*, 118–120. doi:10.1126/science.8016645

Kurahashi, T., & Menini, A. (1997). Mechanism of odorant adaptation in the olfactory receptor cell. *Nature*, *385*, 725–729. doi:10.1038/385725a0

Kurahashi, T., & Yau, K. W. (1993). Co-existence of cationic and chloride components in odorant–induced current of vertebrate olfactory receptor cells. *Nature*, *363*, 71–74. doi:10.1038/363071a0

Kurahashi, T., & Yau, K. W. (1994). Olfactory transduction: Tale of an unusual chloride current. *Current Biology*, *4*, 256–258. doi:10.1016/S0960-9822(00)00058-0

Kurahashi, T., & Yau, K.-W. (1993). Co-existence of cationic and chloride components in odorant-induced current of vertebrate olfactory receptor cells. *Nature*, *363*, 71–74. doi:10.1038/363071a0

Kuske, M., Padilla, M., Romain, A., Nicolas, J., Rubio, R., & Marco, S. (2006). Detection of diverse mould species growing on building materials by gas sensor arrays and pattern recognition. *Sensors and Actuators. B, Chemical*, *119*(1), 33–40. doi:10.1016/j.snb.2005.02.059

Kuske, M., Rubio, R., Romain, A., Nicolas, J., & Marco, S. (2005). Fuzzy k-nn applied to moulds detection. *Sensors and Actuators. B, Chemical*, *106*, 52–60. doi:10.1016/j.snb.2004.05.066

Ku, W., Storer, R., & Georgakis, C. (1995). Disturbance detection and isolation by dynamic principal component analysis. *Chemometrics and Intelligent Laboratory Systems*, *30*, 179–196. doi:10.1016/0169-7439(95)00076-3

Kwon, I. C., Bae, Y. H., & Kim, S. W. (1991). Electrically erodible polymer gel for controlled release of drugs. *Nature, 354,* 291–293. doi:10.1038/354291a0

Labreche, S., Bazzo, S., Cade, S., & Chanie, E. (2005). Shelf life determination by electronic nose: Application to milk. *Sensors and Actuators. B, Chemical, 106,* 199–206. doi:10.1016/j.snb.2004.06.027

Lange, D., Hagleitner, C., Hierlemann, A., Brand, O., & Baltes, H. (2002). Complementary metal oxide semiconductor cantilever arrays on a single chip: Mass-sensitive detection of volatile organic compounds. *Analytical Chemistry, 74,* 3084–3095. doi:10.1021/ac011269j

Lang, H. P., Baller, M. K., Berger, R., Gerber, C., Gimzewski, J. K., & Battiston, F. M. (1999). An artificial nose based on a micromechanical cantilever array. *Analytica Chimica Acta, 393,* 59–65. doi:10.1016/S0003-2670(99)00283-4

Laothawornkitkul, J., Moore, J. P., Taylor, J. E., Possell, M., Gibson, T. D., Hewitt, C. N., & Paul, N. D. (2008). Discrimination of plant volatile signatures by an electronic nose: A potential technology for plant pest and disease monitoring. *Environmental Science & Technology, 42*(22), 8433–8439. doi:10.1021/es801738s

Larmond, E. (1977). *Laboratory methods for sensory evaluation of food.* Ottawa, Canada: Agriculture Canada.

Laudien, J. H., Küster, D., Sojka, B., Ferstl, R., & Pause, B. M. (2006). Central odor processing in subjects experiencing helplessness. *Brain Research, 1120,* 141–150. doi:10.1016/j.brainres.2006.08.090

Laudien, J. H., Wencker, S., Ferstl, R., & Pause, B. M. (2008). Context effects on odor processing: An event-related potential study. *NeuroImage, 41,* 1426–1436. doi:10.1016/j.neuroimage.2008.03.046

Laurent, G. (2002). Olfactory network dynamics and the coding of multidimensional signals. *Nature Reviews. Neuroscience, 3,* 884–895. doi:10.1038/nrn964

Lawless, H. T. (1989). Exploration of fragrance categories and ambiguous odors using multidimensional scaling and cluster analysis. *Chemical Senses, 14*(3), 349–360. doi:10.1093/chemse/14.3.349

Lazarini, F., & Lledo, P. M. (2011). Is adult neurogenesis essential for olfaction? *Trends in Neurosciences, 34,* 20–30. doi:10.1016/j.tins.2010.09.006

Le Gros Clark, W. E. (1951). The projection of the olfactory epithelium on the olfactory bulb in the rabbit. *Journal of Neurology, Neurosurgery, and Psychiatry, 14,* 1–10. doi:10.1136/jnnp.14.1.1

LeDoux, J. (1996). *The emotional brain, the mysterious underpinnings of emotional life.* New York, NY: Simon & Schuster.

Lee, C. T., Yang, W. T., & Parr, R. G. (1998). Development of the Colle-Salvetti correlation-energy formula into a functional of the electron-density. *Physical Review B: Condensed Matter and Materials Physics, 37,* 785–789. doi:10.1103/PhysRevB.37.785

Lee, D. D., & Seung, H. S. (1999). Learning the parts of objects by non-negative matrix factorization. *Letters to Nature, 401*(21), 788–791.

Lee, F., Lee, M., Yang, F., & Bartle, K. (1984). *Open tubular column gas chromatography: Theory and practice.* Chichester, UK: John Wiley & Sons.

Lee, S. H., & Park, T. H. (2010). Recent advances in the development of bioelectronic nose. *Biotechnology and Bioprocess Engineering, 15,* 22–29. doi:10.1007/s12257-009-3077-1

Lee, S.-J., & Noble, A. (2003). Characterization of odor-active compounds in Californian chardonnay wines using GC-olfactometry and GC-mass spectrometry. *Journal of Agricultural and Food Chemistry, 51,* 8036–8044. doi:10.1021/jf034747v

Leinders–Zufall, T., Cockerham, R. E., Michalakis, S., Biel, M., Garbers, D. L., & Reed, R. R. (2007). Contribution of the receptor guanylyl cyclase GC-D to chemosensory function in the olfactory epithelium. *Proceedings of the National Academy of Sciences of the United States of America, 104,* 14507–14512. doi:10.1073/pnas.0704965104

Leinders–Zufall, T., Ma, M., & Zufall, F. (1999). Impaired odor adaptation in olfactory receptor neurons after inhibition of Ca^{2+}/calmodulin kinase II. *The Journal of Neuroscience, 19,* RC19.

Lepousez, G., Csaba, Z., Bernard, V., Loudes, C., Videau, C., & Lacombe, J. (2010). Somatostatin interneurons delineate the inner part of the external plexiform layer in the mouse main olfactory bulb. *The Journal of Comparative Neurology, 518,* 1976–1994. doi:10.1002/cne.22317

Levy, L. M., Henkin, R. J., Lin, C. S., & Finley, A. (1999). Rapid imaging of olfaction by functional MRI (fMRI): Identification of presence and type of hyposmia. *Journal of Computer Assisted Tomography, 23*, 767–775. doi:10.1097/00004728-199909000-00026

Liberles, S. D., & Buck, L. B. (2006). A second class of chemosensory receptors in the olfactory epithelium. *Nature, 442*, 645–650. doi:10.1038/nature05066

Light, K. C., Obrist, P. A., Sherwood, A., James, S. A., & Strogatz, D. S. (1987). Effects of race and marginally elevated blood pressure on responses to stress. *Hypertension, 10*(6), 555–563. doi:10.1161/01.HYP.10.6.555

Li, J. R. (2003). Carbon black/polystyrene composites as candidates for gas sensing materials. *Carbon, 41*(12), 2353–2360. doi:10.1016/S0008-6223(03)00273-2

Limero, T., Cheng, P., & Boyd, J. (2006). Evaluation of gas chromatography-differential mobility spectrometry for measurement of air contaminants in spacecraft. In *Proceedings 36th International Conference on Environmental Systems*. Society of Automotive Engineers (SAE).

Lin, D. Y., Shea, S. D., & Katz, L. C. (2006). Representation of natural stimuli in the rodent main olfactory bulb. *Neuron, 50*, 937–949. doi:10.1016/j.neuron.2006.03.021

Lindley, M. G. (1999). New developments in low-calorie sweeteners. *World Review of Nutrition and Dietetics, 85*, 44–51. doi:10.1159/000059701

Ling, S., Gao, T., Liu, J., Li, Y., Zhou, J., & Li, J. (2010). The fabrication of an olfactory receptor neuron chip based on planar multi-electrode array and its odor-response analysis. *Biosensors & Bioelectronics, 26*, 1124–1128. doi:10.1016/j.bios.2010.08.071

Liu, Y., Mihara, T., Kimura, M., Takasaki, M., & Hirai, T. (2007). Polymer film-coated quartz crystal microbalances sensor for volatile organic compounds sensing. In *Proceedings of the 24th Sensor Symposium Funabori*, (pp. 309-312). Tokyo, Japan: IEEJ.

Liu, S., & Shipley, M. T. (2008). Multiple conductances cooperatively regulate spontaneous bursting in mouse olfactory bulb external tufted cells. *The Journal of Neuroscience, 28*, 1625–1639. doi:10.1523/JNEUROSCI.3906-07.2008

Liu, W. L., & Shipley, M. T. (1994). Intrabulbar associational system in the rat olfactory bulb comprises cholecystokinin-containing tufted cells that synapse onto the dendrites of GABAergic granule cells. *The Journal of Comparative Neurology, 346*, 541–558. doi:10.1002/cne.903460407

Li, W., & Shah, S. (2002). Structured residual vector-based approach to sensor fault detection and isolation. *Journal of Process Control, 12*, 429–443. doi:10.1016/S0959-1524(01)00046-4

Li, Z., & Hertz, J. (2000). Odour recognition and segmentation by a model olfactory bulb and cortex. *Network (Bristol, England), 11*, 83–102. doi:10.1088/0954-898X/11/1/305

Lodovichi, C., Belluscio, L., & Katz, L. C. (2003). Functional topography of connections linking mirror–symmetric maps in the mouse olfactory bulb. *Neuron, 38*, 265–276. doi:10.1016/S0896-6273(03)00194-6

Lonergan, M. C. (1996). Array-based vapor sensing using chemically sensitive, carbon black polymer resistors. *Chemistry of Materials, 8*(9), 2298–2312. doi:10.1021/cm960036j

Lorig, T. S., Elmes, D. G., Zald, D. H., & Pardo, J. V. (1999). A computer-controlled olfactometer for fMRI and electrophysiological studies of olfaction. *Behavior Research Methods, 31*(2), 370–375.

Lowe, G. (2002). Inhibition of backpropagating action potentials in mitral cell secondary dendrites. *Journal of Neurophysiology, 88*, 64–85.

Lowe, G., & Gold, G. H. (1993). Nonlinear amplification by calcium-dependent chloride channels in olfactory receptor cells. *Nature, 366*, 283–286. doi:10.1038/366283a0

Lowe, G., & Gold, G. H. (1995). Olfactory transduction is intrinsically noisy. *Proceedings of the National Academy of Sciences of the United States of America, 92*, 7864–7868. doi:10.1073/pnas.92.17.7864

Lubbers, D. W., & Opitz, N. (1975). *Die pCO2-/pO2-Optode: Eine Neue pCO2-bzw. pO2-Messsonde zur. Meilgaard, M., Civille, G. V., & Thomas, B. (2006). Sensory evaluation techniques* (4th ed.). Boca Raton, FL: CRC Press.

Lucklum, R. (1997). Determination of polymer shear modulus with quartz crystal resonators. *Faraday Discussions, 107*, 123–140. doi:10.1039/a703127k

Lu, J., Ikehara, T., Zhang, Y., Maeda, R., & Mihara, T. (2006). Energy dissipation mechanisms in lead zirconate titanate thin film transduced micro cantilevers. *Japanese Journal of Applied Physics, 45*, 8795–8800. doi:10.1143/JJAP.45.8795

Lundström, J. N., Goncalves, M., Esteves, F., & Olsson, M. J. (2003). Psychological effects of subthreshold exposure to the putative human pheromones 4,16-androstadien-3-one. *Hormones and Behavior, 44*(5), 395–401. doi:10.1016/j.yhbeh.2003.06.004

Luo, M., & Katz, L. C. (2001). Response correlation maps of neurons in the Mammalian olfactory bulb. *Neuron, 32*, 1165–1179. doi:10.1016/S0896-6273(01)00537-2

Luskin, M. B., & Price, J. L. (1982). The distribution of axon collaterals from the olfactory bulb and the nucleus of the horizontal limb of the diagonal band to the olfactory cortex, demonstrated by double retrograde labeling techniques. *The Journal of Comparative Neurology, 209*, 249–263. doi:10.1002/cne.902090304

Maclean, P. D. (1952). Some psychiatric implications of physiological studies on frontotemporal portion of limbic system (visceral brain). *Electroencephalography and Clinical Neurophysiology, 4*, 407–418. doi:10.1016/0013-4694(52)90073-4

Mainland, J., & Sobel, N. (2006). The sniff is part of the olfactory percept. *Chemical Senses, 31*, 181–196. doi:10.1093/chemse/bjj012

Ma, J., & Lowe, G. (2007). Calcium permeable AMPA receptors and autoreceptors in external tufted cells of rat olfactory bulb. *Neuroscience, 144*, 1094–1108. doi:10.1016/j.neuroscience.2006.10.041

Ma, J., & Lowe, G. (2010). Correlated firing in tufted cells of mouse olfactory bulb. *Neuroscience, 169*, 1715–1738. doi:10.1016/j.neuroscience.2010.06.033

Malnic, B., Godfrey, P. A., & Buck, L. B. (2004). The human olfactory receptor gene family. *Proceedings of the National Academy of Sciences of the United States of America, 101*, 2584–2589. doi:10.1073/pnas.0307882100

Malnic, B., Hirono, J., Sato, T., & Buck, L. (1999). Combinatorial receptor codes for odors. *Cell, 96*(5), 713–723. doi:10.1016/S0092-8674(00)80581-4

Mamun, A. L., & Nakamoto, T. (2008). Recipe estimation using mass spectrometer and large-scale data. *Transactions of the Institute of Electrical Engineering of Japan, 128*, 467–471.

Mandairon, N., Didier, A., & Linster, C. (2008). Odor enrichment increases interneurons responsiveness in spatially defined regions of the olfactory bulb correlated with perception. *Neurobiology of Learning and Memory, 90*, 178–184. doi:10.1016/j.nlm.2008.02.008

Mandairon, N., Ferretti, C. J., Stack, C. M., Rubin, D. B., Cleland, T. A., & Linster, C. (2006). Cholinergic modulation in the olfactory bulb influences spontaneous olfactory discrimination in adult rats. *The European Journal of Neuroscience, 24*, 3234–3244. doi:10.1111/j.1460-9568.2006.05212.x

Mao, J., & Jain, A. K. (1996). A self-organizing network for hyperellipsoidal clustering (HEC). *IEEE Transactions on Neural Networks, 7*, 16–29. doi:10.1109/72.478389

Marco, S., Ortega, A., Pardo, A., & Samitier, J. (1998). Gas identification with tin oxide sensor array and self-organizing maps: Adaptive correction of sensor drifts. *IEEE Transactions on Instrumentation and Measurement, 47*(1), 316–321. doi:10.1109/19.728841

Maresh, A., Rodriguez, G. D., Whitman, M. C., & Greer, C. A. (2008). Principles of glomerular organization in the human olfactory bulb - Implications for odor processing. *PLoS ONE, 3*, e2640. doi:10.1371/journal.pone.0002640

Marsh, D., Bartucci, R., & Sportelli, L. (2003). Lipid membranes with grafted polymers: physicochemical aspects. *Biochimica et Biophysica Acta, 1615*(1-2), 33–59. doi:10.1016/S0005-2736(03)00197-4

Martinelli, E., Zampetti, E., Pantalei, S., Lo Castro, F., Santonico, M., & Pennazza, G. (2007). Design and test of an electronic nose for monitoring the air quality in the international space station. *Microgravity Science and Technology, 19*(2), 46–49.

Masunaga, K., Hayama, K., Onodera, T., Hayashi, K., Miura, N., Matsumoto, K., & Toko, K. (2005). Detection of aromatic nitro compounds with electrode polarization controlling sensor. *Sensors and Actuators. B, Chemical, 108*, 427–434. doi:10.1016/j.snb.2004.12.102

Masunaga, K., Michiwaki, S., Izumi, R., Ivarsson, P., Björefors, F., & Lundström, I. (2008). Development of sensor surface with recognition of molecular substructure. *Sensors and Actuators. B, Chemical, 130*, 330–337. doi:10.1016/j.snb.2007.08.027

Matsuguchi, M., & Ueno, T. (2006). Molecular imprinting strategy for solvent molecules and its application for QCM-based VOC vapor sensing. *Sensors and Actuators. B, Chemical, 113*, 94–99. doi:10.1016/j.snb.2005.02.028

Matsuguchi, M., Ueno, T., Aoki, T., & Yoshida, M. (2008). Chemically modified copolymer coatings for mass-sensitive toluene vapor sensors. *Sensors and Actuators. B, Chemical, 131*, 652–659. doi:10.1016/j.snb.2007.12.052

Matsukura, H., Yoshida, H., Ishida, H., & Nakamoto, T. (2009). Interactive odor playback based on fluid dynamics simulation. In *Proceedings of the IEEE Virtual Reality Conference*, (pp. 255–256). IEEE Press.

Matsukura, H., Nihei, T., & Ishida, H. (2011). Multisensorial field display: Presenting spatial distribution of airflow and odor. [IEEE Press.]. *Proceedings of IEEE Virtual Reality, 2011*, 119–122.

Matsukura, H., Nihei, T., Ohno, A., & Ishida, H. (2010). Display for presenting spatial odor distribution and airflow field. *Transactions of the Virtual Reality Society of Japan, 15*(4), 563–570.

Matsukura, H., Ohno, A., & Ishida, H. (2010). Fluid dynamic considerations for realistic odor presentation using olfactory display. *Presence (Cambridge, Mass.), 19*(6), 513–526. doi:10.1162/pres_a_00019

Matsukura, H., Yoshida, H., Saitoh, A., & Nakamoto, T. (2009). Odor presentation with a vivid sense of reality: Incorporating fluid dynamics simulation into olfactory display. [IEEE Press.]. *Proceedings of IEEE Virtual Reality, 2009*, 295–296.

Matsumoto, H., Kobayakawa, K., Kobayakawa, R., Tashiro, T., Mori, K., Sakano, H., & Mori, K. (2010). Spatial arrangement of glomerular molecular-feature clusters in the odorant-receptor class domains of the mouse olfactory bulb. *Journal of Neurophysiology, 103*(6), 3490–3500. doi:10.1152/jn.00035.2010

Matsuoka, K., & Kawamoto, M. (1996). The learning of linear neural nets with anti-hebbian rules. *Systems and Computers in Japan, 27*(3), 84–93. doi:10.1002/scj.4690270308

Matsushita, Y. (2002). A virtual space with aroma and wind. *Aroma Research, 3*, 42–49.

Matyjaszewski, K., Patten, T. E., & Xia, J. (1997). Controlled/"living" radical polymerization: Kinetics of the homogeneous atom transfer radical polymerization of styrene. *Journal of the American Chemical Society, 119*, 674–680. doi:10.1021/ja963361g

Maute, M., Raible, S., Prins, F. E., Kern, D. P., Ulmer, H., Weimar, U., & Goepel, W. (1998). Detection of volatile organic compounds (VOCs) with polymer-coated cantilevers. *Sensors and Actuators. B, Chemical, 58*, 505. doi:10.1016/S0925-4005(99)00110-0

Mayer, K. M., & Hafner, J. H. (2011). Localized surface plasmon resonance sensors. *Chemical Reviews, 111*(6), 3828–3857. doi:10.1021/cr100313v

Maynes-Aminzade, D. (2005). Edible bits: Seamless interfaces between people, data and food. In *ACM CHI 2005 Extended Abstracts*, (pp. 2207-2210). ACM Press.

McCarthy, R. E. (1986). *Scent-emitting systems*. U. S. Patent 4,603,030. Washington, DC: US Patent Office.

McNaughton, B. L., & Morris, R. G. M. (1987). Hippocampal synaptic enhancement and information storage within a distributed memory system. *Trends in Neurosciences, 10*, 408–415. doi:10.1016/0166-2236(87)90011-7

McQueen, J. (1967). Some methods for classification and analysis of multivariate observations. In *Proceedings of the Fifth Berkeley Symposium on Mathematical Statistics and Probability*, (Vol. 1, pp. 281-297). Berkeley, CA: University of California Press.

McReynolds, W. O. (1966). *Gas chromatographic retention data*. Niles, IL: Preston Publications Inc.

Mecea, V. M. (1994). Loaded vibrating quartz sensors. *Sensors and Actuators. A, Physical, 40*, 1–27. doi:10.1016/0924-4247(94)85026-7

Meister, M., & Bonhoeffer, T. (2001). Tuning and topography in an odor map on the rat olfactory bulb. *The Journal of Neuroscience, 21*, 1351–1360.

Messager, J. (2002). *The diffusion of fragrances in a multimedia environment*. Paper presented at the 3rd Aroma Science Forum. Tokyo, Japan.

Messager, J., & Takagi, S. (2003). The diffusion of fragrances in a multimedia environment. *Aroma Research, 14*, 69–73.

Michael, G. A., Acquot, L., Millot, J.-L., & Brand, G. (2003). Ambient odors modulate visual attentional capture. *Neuroscience Letters, 352*, 221–225. doi:10.1016/j.neulet.2003.08.068

Mihara, T., Ikehara, T., Lu, J., Maeda, R., Fukawa, T., & Kimura, M. (2009). High-sensitive chemical sensor system employing a higher-mode operative micro cantilever sensor and an adsorption tube. In *Proceedings of the 13th International Symposium on Olfaction and Electronic Nose*, (pp. 79-82). Brescia, Italy: American Institute of Physics.

Mihara, T., Ikehara, T., Lu, J., Maeda, R., Fukawa, T., & Kimura, M. ... Hirai, T. (2008). Integrated chemical sensor system employing micro cantilever and adsorption tube. In *Proceedings of the 12th International Meeting on Chemical Sensors*, (pp. 533-534). Columbus, OH: IEEE.

Mihara, T., Ikehara, T., Lu, J., Maeda, R., Fukawa, T., & Kimura, M. ... Hirai, T. (2008). Sensitivity improvement of a chemical sensor system employing a micro cantilever sensor and an adsorption tube. In *Proceedings of the 25th Sensor Symposium*, (pp. 591-594). Okinawa, Japan: IEEJ.

Mihara, T., Ikehara, T., Konno, M., Maeda, R., Kimura, M., & Fukawa, T. (2010). Design and fabrication of high-sensitive chemical sensor system with preconcentration and analysis functions employing a micro cantilever sensor. *IEEJ Transactions on SM, 130*, 275–282. doi:10.1541/ieejsmas.130.275

Mihara, T., Ikehara, T., Konno, M., Murakami, S., Maeda, R., Kimura, M., & Fukawa, T. (2011). Design, fabrication and evaluation of highly-sensitive compact chemical sensor system employing a microcantilever array and a preconcentrator. *Sensors and Materials, 23*, 397–417.

Milligan, G. W., & Cooper, M. C. (1985). An examination of procedures for determining the number of clusters in a data set. *Psychometrika, 50*, 159–179. doi:10.1007/BF02294245

Milligan, G. W., & Cooper, M. C. (1986). A study of the comparability of external criteria for hierarchical clustering. *Multivariate Behavioral Research, 21*, 441–458. doi:10.1207/s15327906mbr2104_5

Milner, S. T. (1991). Polymer brushes. *Science, 251*, 905–914. doi:10.1126/science.251.4996.905

Ministry of Posts and Telecommunications in Japan. (2007). *Reports of the association for information and communications technology using five senses*. Tokyo, Japan: Ministry of Posts and Telecommunications in Japan.

Miura, T., Nakamoto, T., & Moriizumi, T. (2003). Study of odor recorder using mass spectrometry. *Transactions of IEEJ, 456*, 513-518.

Miyamichi, K., Amat, F., Moussavi, F., Wang, C., Wickersham, I., & Wall, N. R. (2010). Cortical representations of olfactory input by trans-synaptic tracing. *Nature, 472*, 191–196. doi:10.1038/nature09714

Miyamoto, H., Kawato, M., Setoyama, T., & Suzuki, R. (1988). Feedback-error-learning neural network for trajectory control of a robotic manipulator. *Neural Networks, 1*, 251. doi:10.1016/0893-6080(88)90030-5

Miyanari, A., Kaneoke, Y., Ihara, A., Watanabe, S., Osaki, Y., & Kubo, T. (2006). Neuromagnetic changes of brain rhythm evoked by intravenous olfactory stimulation in humans. *Brain Topography, 18*, 189–199. doi:10.1007/s10548-006-0268-3

Miyazawa, N., Tomita, N., Kurobayasi, Y., Nakanishi, A., Ohkubo, Y., Maeda, T., & Fujita, A. (2009). Novel character impact compounds in yuzu. *Journal of Agricultural and Food Chemistry, 57*, 1990–1996. doi:10.1021/jf803257x

Mochizuki, A., Amada, T., Sawa, S., Takeda, T., Motoya-shiki, S., & Kohyama, K. … Chihara, K. (2004). Fragra: A visual-olfactory VR game. In *ACM SIGGRAPH 2004 Sketches*. New York, NY: ACM Press.

Mombaerts, P., Wang, F., Dulac, C., Chao, S. K., Nemes, A., & Mendelsohn, M. (1996). Visualizing an olfactory sensory map. *Cell*, *87*, 675–686. doi:10.1016/S0092-8674(00)81387-2

Montoliu, I., Tauler, R., Padilla, M., Pardo, A., & Marco, S. (2010). Multivariate curve resolution applied to tem-perature-modulated metal oxide gas sensors. *Sensors and Actuators. B, Chemical*, *145*(1), 464–473. doi:10.1016/j.snb.2009.12.051

Moreno, M. M., Linster, C., Escanilla, O., Sacquet, J., Didier, A., & Mandairon, N. (2009). Olfactory perceptual learning requires adult neurogenesis. *Proceedings of the National Academy of Sciences of the United States of America*, *106*, 17980–17985. doi:10.1073/pnas.0907063106

Morgan, C. A. III, Wang, S., Mason, J., Southwick, S. M., Fox, P., & Hazlett, G. (2000). Hormone profiles in humans experiencing military survival training. *Biological Psychiatry*, *47*(10), 891–901. doi:10.1016/S0006-3223(99)00307-8

Morie, J. F., Iyer, K., Valanejad, K., Sadek, R., Miraglia, D., & Milam, D. … Leshin, J. (2003). Sensory design for virtual environments. In *ACM SIGGRAPH 2003 Sketches*. New York, NY: ACM Press.

Mori, K., Imamamura, K., & Mataga, N. (1992). Differ-ential specificities of single mitral cells in rabbit olfactory bulb for a homologous series of fatty acid odor molecules. *Journal of Neurophysiology*, *67*, 786–789.

Mori, K., & Shepherd, G. M. (1994). Emerging principles of molecular signal processing by mitral/tufted cells in the olfactory bulb. *Seminars in Cell Biology*, *5*, 65–74. doi:10.1006/scel.1994.1009

Mori, K., Takahashi, Y. K., Igarashi, K. M., & Yamaguchi, M. (2006). Maps of odorant molecular features in the mammalian olfactory bulb. *Physiological Reviews*, *86*, 409–433. doi:10.1152/physrev.00021.2005

Mozell, M. M. (1974). Mechanisms underlying the analysis of odorant quality at the level of the olfac-tory mucosa I: Spatiotemporal sorption patterns. *An-nals of the New York Academy of Sciences*, *237*, 76–90. doi:10.1111/j.1749-6632.1974.tb49845.x

Mozell, M. M., & Jagodowicz, M. (1973). Chromato-graphic separation of odorants by the nose: Retention times measured across in vivo olfactory mucosa. *Science*, *181*, 1247–1249. doi:10.1126/science.181.4106.1247

Mumyakmaz, B., Özman, A., Ebeoğlu, M. A., Taşaltin, C., & Gürol, İ. (2010). A study on the development of a compensation method for humidity effect in QCM sen-sor responses. *Sensors and Actuators. B, Chemical*, *147*, 277–282. doi:10.1016/j.snb.2010.03.019

Munoz, S., Yoshino, A., Nakamoto, T., & Moriizumi, T. (2007). Odor approximation of fruit flavors using a QCM odor sensing system. *Sensors and Actuators. B, Chemical*, *123*, 1101–1106. doi:10.1016/j.snb.2006.11.025

Munro, J. C., & Frank, C. W. (2004). Adsorption of lipid-functionalized poly(ethylene glycol) to gold surfaces as a cushion for polymer-supported lipid bilayers. *Langmuir*, *20*(8), 3339–3349. doi:10.1021/la036062v

Murai, K., Serizawa, T., & Yanagida, Y. (2011). Localized scent presentation to a walking person by using scent projectors. In *Proceedings of the First International Symposium on Virtual Reality Innovation (ISVRI) 2011*, (pp. 67–70). Singapore, Singapore: ISVRI.

Murlis, J., Elkinton, J. S., & Cardé, R. T. (1992). Odor plumes and how insects use them. *Annual Review of Entomology*, *37*, 505–532. doi:10.1146/annurev.en.37.010192.002445

Murphy, C., Cain, W. S., & Bartoshuk, L. M. (1977). Mutual action of taste and olfaction. *Sensory Processes*, *1*, 204–211.

Musgrave, G. (2001). Very large-screen video displays. *Conception Associates*. Retrieved from http://www.conceptron.com/articles/!article_index.html

Nagashima, A., & Touhara, K. (2010). Enzymatic con-version of odorants in nasal mucus affects olfactory glomerular activation patterns and odor perception. *The Journal of Neuroscience*, *30*, 16391–16398. doi:10.1523/JNEUROSCI.2527-10.2010

Nagayama, S., Enerva, A., Fletcher, M. L., Masurkar, A. V., Igarashi, K. M., & Mori, K. (2010). Differential axonal projection of mitral and tufted cells in the mouse main olfactory system. *Frontiers in Neural Circuits, 4*, 1–8. doi:10.3389/fncir.2010.00120

Nagayama, S., Takahashi, Y. K., Yoshihara, Y., & Mori, K. (2004). Mitral and tufted cells differ in the decoding manner of odor maps in the rat olfactory bulb. *Journal of Neurophysiology, 91*, 2532–2540. doi:10.1152/jn.01266.2003

Nagle, H. T., Gutierrez-Osuna, R., & Schiffman, S. S. (1998). The how and why of electronic noses. *IEEE Spectrum, 35*(9), 22–31. doi:10.1109/6.715180

Nakagawa, T., & Voshall, L. B. (2009). Controversy and consensus: noncanonical signaling mechanisms in the insect olfactory system: Noncanonical signaling mechanisms in the insect olfactory system. *Current Opinion in Neurobiology, 19*, 284–292. doi:10.1016/j.conb.2009.07.015

Nakaizumi, F., Yanagida, Y., Noma, H., & Hosaka, K. (2006). SpotScents: A novel method of natural scent delivery using multiple scent projectors. [Alexandria, VA: IEEE Press.]. *Proceedings of IEEE Virtual Reality, 2006*, 213–218.

Nakaizumi, F., Yanagida, Y., Noma, H., & Hosaka, K. (2006). SpotScents: A novel method of natural scent delivery using multiple scent projectors. [IEEE Press.]. *Proceedings of IEEE Virtual Reality, 2006*, 207–212.

Nakamoto, T., & Dinh Minh, H. P. (2007). Improvement of olfactory display using solenoid valves. In *Proceeding of IEEE Virtual Reality*, (pp. 171-178). Charlotte, NC: IEEE Press.

Nakamoto, T., & Moriizumi, T. (1988). Odor sensor using quartz-resonator array and neural-network pattern recognition. In *Proceedings of the IEEE Ultrasonics Symposium*, (p. 613). Chicago, IL: IEEE Press.

Nakamoto, T., & Murakami, K. (2009). Selection method of odor components for olfactory display using mass spectrum database. In *Proceedings of IEEE Virtual Reality*, (pp. 159-162). Lafayette, LA: IEEE Press.

Nakamoto, T. (2005). Odor recorder. *Sensor Letters, 3*, 136–150. doi:10.1166/sl.2005.018

Nakamoto, T. (2008). Odor recorder using mass spectrometry. *Sensor Letters, 6*, 1–5. doi:10.1166/sl.2008.548

Nakamoto, T. (2008). *Olfactory display: Multimedia tool for presenting scents*. Tokyo, Japan: Fragrance Journal Ltd.

Nakamoto, T. (Ed.). (2008). *Olfactory display (multimedia tool for presenting scents)*. Tokyo, Japan: Fragrance Journal Ltd.

Nakamoto, T., Aoki, K., Ogi, T., Akao, S., & Nakaso, N. (2008). Odor sensing system using ball SAW devices. *Sensors and Actuators. B, Chemical, 130*(1), 386–390. doi:10.1016/j.snb.2007.09.022

Nakamoto, T., & Hiramatsu, H. (2002). Study of odor recorder for dynamical change of odor using QCM sensors and neural network. *Sensors and Actuators. B, Chemical, 85*, 263–269. doi:10.1016/S0925-4005(02)00130-2

Nakamoto, T., & Minh, H. P. D. (2007). Improvement of olfactory display using solenoid valves. [Charlotte, NC: IEEE Press.]. *Proceedings of IEEE Virtual Reality, 2007*, 179–186.

Nakamoto, T., & Moriizumi, T. (1990). A theory of a quartz crystal microbalance based upon a mason equivalent circuit. *Japanese Journal of Applied Physics, 29*(5), 963–969. doi:10.1143/JJAP.29.963

Nakamoto, T., Nakahira, Y., Hiramatsu, H., & Moriizumi, T. (2001). Odor recorder using active odor sensing system. *Sensors and Actuators. B, Chemical, 2*, 465–469. doi:10.1016/S0925-4005(01)00587-1

Nakamoto, T., Otaguro, S., Kinoshita, M., Nagahama, M., Ohinishi, K., & Ishida, T. (2008). Cooking up an interactive olfactory game display. *IEEE Computer Graphics and Applications, 28*(1), 75–78. doi:10.1109/MCG.2008.3

Nakamoto, T., Sukegawa, K., & Sumitomo, E. (2005). Higher order sensing using QCM sensor array and preconcentrator with variable temperature. *IEEE Sensors Journal, 5*, 68. doi:10.1109/JSEN.2004.839894

Nakamoto, T., Ustumi, S., Yamashita, N., Moriizumi, T., & Sonoda, Y. (1994). Active gas/odor sensing system using automatically controlled gas blender and numerical optimization technique. *Sensors and Actuators. B, Chemical, 20*(2-3), 131–137. doi:10.1016/0925-4005(93)01193-8

Nakamoto, T., & Yoshikawa, K. (2006). Movie with scents generated by olfactory display using solenoid valves. *IEICE Transactions on Fundamentals of Electronics, Communications and Computer Sciences. E (Norwalk, Conn.)*, *89A*(11), 3327–3332.

Nakamura, T., & Gold, G. H. (1987). A cyclic nucleotide-gated conductance in olfactory receptor cilia. *Nature*, *325*, 442–444. doi:10.1038/325442a0

Nakane, H., Asami, O., Yamada, Y., & Ohira, H. (2002). Effect of negative air ions on computer operation, anxiety and salivary chromogranin A-like immunoreactivity. *International Journal of Psychophysiology*, *46*(1), 85–89. doi:10.1016/S0167-8760(02)00067-3

Nakaso, N., Tsukahara, Y., Ishikawa, S., & Yamanaka, K. (2002). Diffraction-free propagation of collimated SAW around a quartz ball. In *Proceedings of the 2002 IEEE Ultrasonic Symposium*, (pp. 47–52). IEEE Press.

Nakazawa, C. (1998). *Japanese unexamined patent application publication H10-182398*. Tokyo, Japan: Patent Office.

Nakomoto, T., & Minh, H. P. D. (2007). Improvement of olfactory display using solenoid valves. [IEEE Press.]. *Proceedings of IEEE Virtual Reality*, *2007*, 179–186.

Nambu, A., Narumi, T., Nishimura, K., Tanikawa, T., & Hirose, M. (2008). A study of providing colors to change olfactory perception - Using "flavor of color". In Proceedings of ASIAGRAPH in Tokyo 2008, (vol 2, pp. 265-268). ASIAGRAPH.

Nambu, A., Narumi, T., Nishimura, K., Tanigawa, T., & Hirose, M. (2010). Visual-olfactory display using olfactory sensory map. [Waltham, MA: IEEE Press.]. *Proceedings of IEEE Virtual Reality*, *2010*, 39–42.

Nambu, A., Narumi, T., Nishimura, K., Tanikawa, T., & Hirose, M. (2008). Nioi cafe: Olfactory display system with visual feedback. In *SIGGRAPH Posters 2008* (p. 92). New York, NY: ACM Press.

Nambu, A., Narumi, T., Nishimura, K., Tanikawa, T., & Hirose, M. (2010). Visual-olfactory display using olfactory sensory map. [IEEE Press.]. *Proceedings of IEEE Virtual Reality*, *2010*, 39–42.

Nanto, H., & Stetter, J. R. (2003). Introduction to chemosensors. In Pearce, T. C. (Eds.), *Handbook of Machine Olfaction* (pp. 79–104). New York, NY: Wiley-VCH.

Naraghi, K., Sahgal, N., Adriaans, B., Barr, H., & Magan, N. (2010). Use of volatile fingerprints for rapid screening of antifungal agents for efficacy against dermatophyte Trichophyton species. *Sensors and Actuators. B, Chemical*, *146*, 521–526. doi:10.1016/j.snb.2009.12.031

Narumi, T., Nishizaka, S., Kajinami, T., Tanikawa, T., & Hirose, M. (2011). Augmented reality flavors: Gustatory display based on edible marker and cross-modal interaction. In *Proceedings of CHI 2011*, (pp. 93-102). ACM Press.

Narumi, T., Kajinami, T., Nishizaka, S., Tanikawa, T., & Hirose, M. (2011). Pseudo-gustatory display system based on cross-modal integration of vision, olfaction and gestation. [IEEE Press.]. *Proceedings of IEEE Virtual Reality*, *2011*, 127–130.

Narusuye, K., Kawai, F., & Miyachi, E. (2003). Spike encoding of olfactory receptor cells. *Neuroscience Research*, *46*, 407–413. doi:10.1016/S0168-0102(03)00131-7

News, A. B. C. (1999). *Smell-o-vision coming to internet soon*. Retrieved August 21, 2007 from http://www.temple.edu/ispr/examples/ex99_10_20.html

Nicolas, J., & Romain, A. (2004). Establishing the limit of detection and the resolution limits of odorous sources in the environment for an array of metal oxide gas sensors. *Sensors and Actuators. B, Chemical*, *99*, 384–392. doi:10.1016/j.snb.2003.11.036

Niimura, Y., & Nei, M. (2003). Evolution of olfactory receptor genes in the human genome. *Proceedings of the National Academy of Sciences of the United States of America*, *100*(21), 12235–12240. doi:10.1073/pnas.1635157100

Nimal, A. T., Mittal, U., Singh, M., Khaneja, M., Kannan, G. K., & Kapoor, J. C. (2009). Development of hand-held SAW vapor sensors for explosives and CW agents. *Sensors and Actuators. B, Chemical*, *135*(2), 399–410. doi:10.1016/j.snb.2008.08.040

Nishiguchi, M., Sakamoto, K., Nomura, S., Hirotomi, T., Shiwaku, K., & Hirakawa, M. (2010). Tabletop life review therapy system using olfactory display for presenting flavor. In *Proceedings of the International MultiConference of Engineers and Computer Scientists 2010*, (vol. 1). IEEE.

Nissant, A., Bardy, C., Katagiri, H., Murray, K., & Lledo, P. M. (2009). Adult neurogenesis promotes synaptic plasticity in the olfactory bulb. *Nature Neuroscience, 12*, 728–730. doi:10.1038/nn.2298

Noh, H., Hesketh, P., & Frye-Mason, G. (2002). Parylene gas chromatographic column for rapid thermal cycling. *Journal of Microelectromechanical Systems, 11*(6), 718–725. doi:10.1109/JMEMS.2002.805052

Nomura, E., Hosoda, A., Takagaki, M., Mori, H., Miyake, Y., Shibakami, M., & Taniguchi, H. (2010). Self-organized honeycomb-patterned microporous polystyrene thin films fabricated by Calix[4]arene derivatives. *Langmuir, 26*, 10266–10270. doi:10.1021/la100434b

Norsworthy, S. R., Schreier, R., & Temes, G. C. (1997). *Delta-sigma data converters: Theory, design, and simulation*. Washington, DC: IEEE Press.

Obrig, H., & Villringer, A. (2003). Beyond the visible--Imaging the human brain with light. *Journal of Cerebral Blood Flow and Metabolism, 23*, 1–18. doi:10.1097/00004647-200301000-00001

Odor Control Association of Japan. (2003). *A term and a commentary of a odor*. Tokyo, Japan: Odor Control Association of Japan.

Ohba, T., & Yamanaka, T. (2008). Suppression of background odor effect in odor sensing system using olfactory adaptation model. *IEEJ Transactions on Sensors and Micromachines, 128*(5), 240–245. doi:10.1541/ieejsmas.128.240

Ohno, M., Nihei, Y., & Nakamoto, T. (2011). Study of odor approximation by using mass spectrometer. In *Proceeding of 14th International Symposium on Olfaction and Electronic Nose*. New York, NY: IEEE.

Okada, K., & Aiba, S. (2003). Toward the actualization of broadcasting service with smell information. *Institute of Image Information and Television Engineering of Japan Technical Report, 27*(64), 31–34.

Okahata, Y., & Shimizu, O. (1987). Olfactory reception on a multibilayer-coated piezoelectric crystal in a gas phase. *Langmuir, 3*, 1171–1172. doi:10.1021/la00078a054

Okamoto, M., Dan, H., Clowney, L., Yamaguchi, Y., & Dan, I. (2009). Activation in ventro-lateral prefrontal cortex during the act of tasting: An fNIRS study. *Neuroscience Letters, 451*, 129–133. doi:10.1016/j.neulet.2008.12.016

Okamoto, M., Matsunami, M., Dan, H., Kohata, T., Kohyama, K., & Dan, I. (2006). Prefrontal activity during taste encoding: An fNIRS study. *NeuroImage, 31*, 796–806. doi:10.1016/j.neuroimage.2005.12.021

Okamoto, M., Wada, Y., Yamaguchi, Y., Kyutoku, Y., Clowney, L., Singh, A. K., & Dan, I. (2011). Process-specific prefrontal contributions to episodic encoding and retrieval of tastes: A functional NIRS study. *NeuroImage, 54*, 1578–1588. doi:10.1016/j.neuroimage.2010.08.016

Oka, Y., Omura, M., Kataoka, H., & Touhara, K. (2004). Olfactory receptor antagonism between odorants. *The EMBO Journal, 23*, 120–126. doi:10.1038/sj.emboj.7600032

Oka, Y., Takai, Y., & Touhara, K. (2009). Nasal airflow rate affects the sensitivity and pattern of glomerular odorant responses in the mouse olfactory bulb. *The Journal of Neuroscience, 29*, 12070–12078. doi:10.1523/JNEUROSCI.1415-09.2009

Okur, S., Kuş, M., Özel, F., & Yilmaz, M. (2010). Humidity adsorption kinetics of water soluble calix[4]arene derivatives measured using QCM technique. *Sensors and Actuators. B, Chemical, 145*, 93–97. doi:10.1016/j.snb.2009.11.040

Omatu, S., Marzuki, K., & Rubiyah, Y. (1996). *Neuro-control and its applications*. London, UK: Springer. doi:10.1007/978-1-4471-3058-1

Opstad, P. K. (1992). Androgenic hormones during prolonged physical stress, sleep, and energy deficiency. *The Journal of Clinical Endocrinology and Metabolism, 74*(5), 1176–1183. doi:10.1210/jc.74.5.1176

Osgood, C. E., Suci, G. J., & Tannenbaum, P. H. (1957). *The measurement of meaning*. Urbana, IL: University of Illinois Press.

Osmooze, S. A. (2012). *P@D diffusers*. Retrieved March 23, 2012, from http://www.osmooze.com/

Osmooze. (2012). *Website.* Retrieved from http://www.osmooze.com/

Otsuki, T., Sakaguchi, H., Hatayama, T., Takata, A., Hyodoh, F., & Tsujita, S. (2004). Secretory IgA in saliva and academic stress. *International Journal of Immunopathology and Pharmacology, 17*(2), 45–48.

Oyamada, T., Kashimori, Y., Hoshino, O., & Kambara, T. (2000). A neural mechanism of hierarchical discrimination of odors in the olfactory cortex based on spatiotemporal encoding of odor information. *Biological Cybernetics, 83*(1), 21–33. doi:10.1007/s004229900139

Padilla, M., Perera, A., Montoliu, I., Chaudry, A., Persaud, K., & Marco, S. (2007). Poisoning fault diagnosis in chemical gas sensor arrays using multivariate statistical signal processing and structured residuals generation. In *Proceedings of the IEEE International Symposium on Intelligent Signal Processing, WISP 2007.* IEEE Press.

Padilla, M., Perera, A., Montoliu, I., Chaudry, A., Persaud, K., & Marco, S. (2010). Fault detection, identication, and reconstruction of faulty chemical gas sensors under drift conditions, using principal component analysis and multiscale-PCA. In *Proceedings of the IEEE World Congress on Computational Intelligence, WCCI 2010.* IEEE Press.

Padilla, M., Montoliu, I., Pardo, A., Perera, A., & Marco, S. (2006). Feature extraction on three way enose signals. *Sensors and Actuators. B, Chemical, 116*(1-2), 145–150. doi:10.1016/j.snb.2006.03.011

Padilla, M., Perera, A., Montoliu, I., Chaudry, A., Persaud, K., & Marco, S. (2010). Drift compensation of gas sensor array data by orthogonal signal correction. *Chemometrics and Intelligent Laboratory Systems, 100*(1), 28–35. doi:10.1016/j.chemolab.2009.10.002

Pandipati, S., Gire, D. H., & Schoppa, N. E. (2010). Adrenergic receptor–mediated disinhibition of mitral cells triggers long-term enhancement of synchronized oscillations in the olfactory bulb. *Journal of Neurophysiology, 104*, 665–674. doi:10.1152/jn.00328.2010

Pardo, M., Faglia, G., Sberveglieri, G., & Corte, M. (2000). Monitoring reliability of sensors in an array by neural networks. *Sensors and Actuators. B, Chemical, 67*, 128–133. doi:10.1016/S0925-4005(00)00402-0

Pardo, M., Niederjaufner, G., Benussi, G., Comini, E., Faglia, G., & Sberveglieri, G. (2000). Data preprocessing enhances the classification of different brands of Espresso coffee with an electronic nose. *Sensors and Actuators. B, Chemical, 69*(3), 397–403. doi:10.1016/S0925-4005(00)00499-8

Pardo, M., & Sberveglieri, G. (2002). Learning from data: a tutorial with emphasis on modern pattern recognition methods. *IEEE Sensors Journal, 2*, 203–217. doi:10.1109/JSEN.2002.800686

Pardo, M., & Sberveglieri, G. (2004). Electronic olfactory systems based on metal oxide semiconductor sensor arrays. *MRS Bulletin, 29*(10), 703–708. doi:10.1557/mrs2004.206

Pardo, M., & Sberveglieri, G. (2007). Comparing the performance of different features in sensor arrays. *Sensors and Actuators. B, Chemical, 123*, 437–443. doi:10.1016/j.snb.2006.09.041

Pauca, V. P., Piper, J., & Plemmon, R. J. (2006). Nonnegative matrix factorization for spectral data analysis. *Linear Algebra and Its Applications, 416*, 29–47. doi:10.1016/j.laa.2005.06.025

Pawliszyn, J. (1997). *Solid phase microextraction, theory and practice.* New York, NY: Wiley-VCH.

Pearce, T. C. (1997). Computational parallels between the biological olfactory pathway and its analogue 'the electronic nose': Part I – Biological olfaction. *Bio Systems, 41*(2), 43–67. doi:10.1016/S0303-2647(96)01661-9

Pearce, T. C., Schiffman, S. S., Nagle, H. T., & Gardner, J. W. (2003). Applications and case studies. In Pearce, T. C., Schiffman, S. S., Nagle, H. T., & Gardner, J. W. (Eds.), *Handbook of Machine Olfaction - Electronic Nose Technology* (pp. 419–578). Weinheim, Germany: WILEY-VCH.

Pearce, T. C., Schiffman, S. S., Nagle, H. T., & Gardner, J. W. (Eds.). (2003). *Handbook of machine olfaction.* Weinheim, Germany: Wiley-VCH.

Pearce, T. C., Schiffman, S. S., Nagle, H. T., & Gardner, J. W. (Eds.). (2003). *Handbook of machine olfaction: Electronic nose technology.* New York, NY: WILEY-VCH.

Pearce, T. C., Schiffman, S. S., Nagle, H. T., & Gardner, J. W. (Eds.). (2003). *Handbook of Machine Olfaction - Electronic Nose Technology.* Berlin, Germany: WILEY-VCH.

Pearce, T. C., Schiffman, S., Nagle, H. T., & Gardner, J. W. (2003). *Handbook of machine olfaction*. Dordrecht, The Netherlands: Wiley-VCH.

Penza, M., Cassano, G., Tortorella, F., & Zaccaria, G. (2001). Classification of food, beverages and perfumes by WO3 thin-flm sensors array and pattern recognition techniques. *Sensors and Actuators. B, Chemical, 73*, 76–87. doi:10.1016/S0925-4005(00)00687-0

Perera, A., Papamichail, N., Barsan, N., Weimar, U., & Marco, S. (2006). On-line novelty detection by recursive dynamic principal component analysis and gas sensor arrays under drift conditions. *IEEE Sensors Journal, 6*(3), 770–783. doi:10.1109/JSEN.2006.874015

Persaud, K. C., & Dodd, G. H. (1982). Analysis of discrimination mechanisms of the mammalian olfactory system using a model nose. *Nature, 299*, 352–355. doi:10.1038/299352a0

Persaud, K. C., Pisanelli, A. M., Szyszko, S., Reichl, M., Horner, G., & Rakow, W. (1999). A smart gas sensor for monitoring environmental changes in closed systems: Results from the MIR space station. *Sensors and Actuators. B, Chemical, 55*, 118–126. doi:10.1016/S0925-4005(99)00168-9

Persaud, K., & Dodd, G. (1982). Analysis of discrimination mechanisms in the mammalian olfactory system using a model nose. *Nature, 299*, 352–355. doi:10.1038/299352a0

Peter, A. L., & Dickert, F. L. (2009). Chemosensors in environmental monitoring: Challenges in ruggedness and selectivity. *Analytical and Bioanalytical Chemistry, 393*, 467–472. doi:10.1007/s00216-008-2464-3

Petzold, G. C., Hagiwara, A., & Murthy, V. N. (2009). Serotonergic modulation of odor input to the mammalian olfactory bulb. *Nature Neuroscience, 12*, 784–791. doi:10.1038/nn.2335

Pillonel, L. (2002). Rapid preconcentration and enrichment techniques for the analysis of food volatiles: A review. *Lebensmittel-Wissenschaft + [i.e. Und] Technologie. Food Science + Technology. Science + Technologie Alimentaire, 35*, 1–14. doi:10.1006/fstl.2001.0804

Pirez, N., & Wachowiak, M. (2008). In vivo modulation of sensory input to the olfactory bulb by tonic and activity-dependent presynaptic inhibition of receptor neurons. *The Journal of Neuroscience, 28*, 6360–6371. doi:10.1523/JNEUROSCI.0793-08.2008

Plichta, M. M., Herrmann, M. J., Baehne, C. G., Ehlis, A. C., Richter, M. M., Pauli, P., & Fallgatter, A. (2006). Event-related functional near-infrared spectroscopy (fNIRS): Are the measurements reliable? *NeuroImage, 31*, 116–124. doi:10.1016/j.neuroimage.2005.12.008

Popescu, M., Joly, J. P., Carre, J., & Danatoiu, C. (2003). Dynamical adsorption and temperature-programmed desorption of VOCs (toluene, butyl acetate and butanol) on activated carbons. *Carbon, 41*, 739–748. doi:10.1016/S0008-6223(02)00391-3

Pornpanomchai, C., Threekhunprapa, A., Pongrasamiroj, K., & Sukklay, P. (2009). Subsmell: Multimedia with a simple olfactory display. [PSIVT.]. *Proceedings of PSIVT, 2009*, 462–472.

Pratt, K., & Williams, D. (1997). Self diagnostic gas sensitive resistors in sour gas applications. *Sensors and Actuators. B, Chemical, 45*(2), 147–153. doi:10.1016/S0925-4005(97)00288-8

Pressler, R. T., Inoue, T., & Strowbridge, B. W. (2007). Muscarinic receptor activation modulates granule cell excitability and potentiates inhibition onto mitral cells in the rat olfactory bulb. *The Journal of Neuroscience, 27*, 10969–10981. doi:10.1523/JNEUROSCI.2961-07.2007

Principe, J. C., Euliano, N. R., & Lefebvre, W. C. (2000). *Neural & adaptive systems*. New York, NY: Wiley.

Pybus, D. (2001). *Kodo: The way of incense*. Tokyo, Japan: Tuttle Publishing.

Qin, S. J., & Li, W. (1999). Detection, identification and reconstruction of faulty sensors with maximized sensitivity. *AIChE Journal. American Institute of Chemical Engineers, 45*(9), 1963–1976. doi:10.1002/aic.690450913

Raman, B., & Gutierrez-Osuna, R. (2005). Mixture segmentation and background suppression in chemosensor arrays with a model of olfactory bulb-cortex interaction. In *Proceedings of IEEE International Joint Conference on Neural Networks,* (Vol. 1, pp. 131-136). IEEE Press.

Rand, W. M. (1971). Objective criteria for the evaluation of clustering methods. *Journal of the American Statistical Association, 66*, 846–850. doi:10.1080/01621459.1971.10482356

Rasch, B., Büchel, C., Gais, S., & Born, J. (2007). Odor cues during slow-wave sleep prompt declarative memory consolidation. *Science, 315*(5817), 1426–1429. doi:10.1126/science.1138581

Rasch, B., Buchel, C., Gais, S., & Born, J. J. (2007). Odor cues during slow-wave sleep prompt declarative memory consolidation. *Science, 315*, 1426–1429. doi:10.1126/science.1138581

Redhead, P. A. (1962). Thermal desorption of gases. *Vacuum, 12*, 203–211. doi:10.1016/0042-207X(62)90978-8

Reidy, S. (2006). High-performance, static-coated silicon microfabricated columns for gas chromatography. *Analytical Chemistry, 78*(8), 2623–2630. doi:10.1021/ac051846u

Reisert, J., & Matthews, H. R. (2001). Response properties of isolated mouse olfactory receptor cells. *The Journal of Physiology, 530*, 113–122. doi:10.1111/j.1469-7793.2001.0113m.x

Ressler, K. J., Sullivan, S. L., & Buck, L. B. (1993). A zonal organization of odorant receptor gene expression in the olfactory epithelium. *Cell, 73*, 597–609. doi:10.1016/0092-8674(93)90145-G

Reston, R., & Kolesar, E. (1994). Silicon-micromachined gas chromatography system used to separate and detect ammonia and nitrogen dioxide: Design, fabrication, and integration of the gas chromatography system. *Journal of Microelectromechanical Systems, 3*(4), 134–146. doi:10.1109/84.338634

Reuter, D., Zierold, K., Schroder, W. H., & Frings, S. (1998). A depolarizing chloride current contributes to chemoelectrical transduction in olfactory sensory neurons in situ. *The Journal of Neuroscience, 18*, 6623–6630.

Rinberg, D., Koulakov, A., & Gelperin, A. (2006). Sparse odor coding in awake behaving mice. *The Journal of Neuroscience, 26*, 8857–8865. doi:10.1523/JNEUROSCI.0884-06.2006

Robertson, H. M., Warr, C. G., & Carlson, J. R. (2003). Molecular evolution of the insect chemoreceptor gene superfamily in Drosophila melanogaster. *Proceedings of the National Academy of Sciences of the United States of America, 100*(2), 14537–14542. doi:10.1073/pnas.2335847100

Röck, F., Barsan, N., & Weimar, U. (2008). Electronic nose: Current status and future trends. *Chemical Reviews, 108*(2), 705–725. doi:10.1021/cr068121q

Rohlf, F. J., & Fisher, D. L. (1968). Test for hierarchical structure in random data sets. *Systematic Zoology, 17*, 407–412. doi:10.2307/2412038

Rollmann, L. D., & Iwamoto, R. T. (1968). Electrochemistry, electron paramagnetic resonance, and visible spectra of cobalt, nickel, copper, and metal-free phthalocyanines in dimethyl sulfoxide. *Journal of the American Chemical Society, 90*, 1455–1463. doi:10.1021/ja01008a013

Rolls, E. T. (1996). The orbitofrontal cortex. *Philosophical Transactions of the Royal Society of London. Series B, Biological Sciences, 351*, 1433–1444. doi:10.1098/rstb.1996.0128

Romain, A., Andre, P., & Nicolas, J. (2002). Three years experiment with the same tin oxide sensor arrays for the identification of malodorous sources in the environment. *Sensors and Actuators. B, Chemical, 84*, 271–277. doi:10.1016/S0925-4005(02)00036-9

Romain, A., & Nicolas, J. (2009). Long term stability of metal oxide-based gas sensors for e-nose environmental applications: An overview. *AIP Conference Proceedings, 146*(2), 502–506.

Romine, I. J., Bush, A. M., & Geist, C. R. (1999). Lavender aromatherapy in recovery from exercise. *Perceptual and Motor Skills, 88*(3), 756–758. doi:10.2466/pms.1999.88.3.756

Rospars, J. P., Lansky, P., Chaput, M., & Duchamp-Viret, P. (2008). Competitive and noncompetitive odorant interactions in the early neural coding of odorant mixtures. *The Journal of Neuroscience, 28*, 2659–2666. doi:10.1523/JNEUROSCI.4670-07.2008

Rossiter, K. J. (1996). Structure-odor relationships. *Chemical Reviews, 96*(8), 3201–3240. doi:10.1021/cr950068a

Ross, P. W. (2001). Qualia and the senses. *The Philosophical Quarterly, 51,* 495–511. doi:10.1111/1467-9213.00243

Roussel, S., Forsberg, G., Steinmetz, V., Grenier, P., & Bellon-Maurel, V. (1998). Optimisation of electronic nose measurements: Methodology of output feature selection. *Journal of Food Engineering, 37,* 207–222. doi:10.1016/S0260-8774(98)00081-8

Roussel, S., Forsberg, G., Steinmetz, V., Grenier, P., & Bellon-Maurel, V. (1999). Optimisation of electronic nose measurements: Influence of experimental parameters. *Journal of Food Engineering, 39,* 9–15. doi:10.1016/S0260-8774(98)00137-X

Rozin, P. (1982). Taste-smell confusion and the duality of the olfactory sense. *Perception & Psychophysics, 31,* 397–401. doi:10.3758/BF03202667

Rubin, B. D., & Katz, L. C. (1999). Optical imaging of odorant representations in the mammalian olfactory bulb. *Neuron, 23,* 499–511. doi:10.1016/S0896-6273(00)80803-X

Rumelhart, D. E., & McClelland, J. L.PDP Research Group. (1986). *Parallel distributed processing.* Cambridge, MA: MIT Press.

Rutan, R. S. C., & de Juan, A. (2009). Introduction to multivariate curve resolution. In Brown, S. D., Tauler, R., & Walczak, B. (Eds.), *Comprehensive Chemometrics* (*Vol. 2,* pp. 249–258). London, UK: Elsevier. doi:10.1016/B978-044452701-1.00046-6

Ryan, M. A., Homer, M. L., Buehler, M. G., Manatt, K. S., Lau, B., Karmon, D., & Jackson, S. (1998). Monitoring space shuttle air for selected contaminants using an electronic nose. In *Proceedings 28th International Conference on Environmental Systems.* Society of Automotive Engineers (SAE).

Ryan, M. A., Homer, M. L., Buehler, M. G., Manatt, K. S., Zee, F., & Graf, J. (1997). Monitoring the air quality in a closed chamber using an electronic nose. In *Proceedings 27th International Conference on Environmental Systems.* Society of Automotive Engineers (SAE).

Ryan, M. A., Homer, M. L., Zhou, H., Manatt, K. S., Ryan, V. S., & Jackson, S. (2000). Operation of an electronic nose aboard the space shuttle and directions for research for a second generation device. In *Proceedings 30th International Conference on Environmental Systems.* Society of Automotive Engineers (SAE).

Ryan, M. A., Homer, M. L., Zhou, H., Manatt, K., & Manfreda, A. (2001). Toward a second generation electronic nose at JPL: Sensing film optimization studies. In *Proceedings 31st International Conference on Environmental Systems.* Society of Automotive Engineers (SAE).

Ryan, M. A., Homer, M. L., Zhou, H., Manatt, K., Manfreda, A., & Kisor, A. ... Yen, S. P. S. (2006). Expanding the capabilities of the JPL electronic nose for an international space station technology demonstration. In *Proceedings 36th International Conference on Environmental Systems.* Society of Automotive Engineers (SAE).

Ryan, M. A., Shevade, A. V., Kisor, A. K., Manatt, K. S., Homer, M. L., Lara, L. M., & Zhou, H. (2008). Ground validation of the third generation JPL electronic Nose. In *Proceedings 38th International Conference on Environmental Systems.* Society of Automotive Engineers (SAE).

Ryan, M. A., Shevade, A. V., Zhou, H., & Homer, M. L. (2004). Polymer-carbon-composite sensors for an electronic nose air quality monitor. *MRS Bulletin, 29,* 714. doi:10.1557/mrs2004.208

Ryan, M. A., Zhou, H., Buehler, M. G., Manatt, K. S., Mowrey, V. S., & Jackson, S. P. (2004). Monitoring space shuttle air quality using the JPL electronic nose. *IEEE Sensors Journal, 4,* 337. doi:10.1109/JSEN.2004.827275

Saevels, S., Lammertyn, J., Berna, A., Veraverbeke, E., Natale, C., & Nicolaï, B. (2004). An electronic nose and a mass spectrometry-based electronic nose for assessing apple quality during shelf life. *Postharvest Biology and Technology, 31,* 9–19. doi:10.1016/S0925-5214(03)00129-7

Sahgal, N., & Magan, N. (2008). Fungal volatile fingerprints: Discrimination between dermatophyte species and strains by means of an electronic nose. *Sensors and Actuators. B, Chemical, 131,* 117–120. doi:10.1016/j.snb.2007.12.019

Saito, S. (2004). Various time dependence of strength of sense for smell showed consecutively. *Japan Association on Odor Environment, 35*(1), 17–21. doi:10.2171/jao.35.17

Saito, S., Ayabe-Kanamura, S., Takashima, Y., Gotow, N., Naito, N., & Nozawa, T. (2006). Development of a smell identification test using a novel stick-type odor presentation kit. *Chemical Senses, 31*(4), 379–391. doi:10.1093/chemse/bjj042

Sakai, N., Imada, S., Saito, S., Kobayakawa, T., & Deguchi, Y. (2005). The effect of visual images on perception of odors. *Chemical Senses, 30*(1). doi:10.1093/chemse/bjh205

Sakaino, A. (2008). The concept of sensitivity communication using aroma and a plan of demonstration experiment: The digital signage with fragrance communication. *Electronic Information Displays, 108*(291), 53-57. Retrieved from http://ci.nii.ac.jp/naid/110007124675/en/

Sakaino, A. (2008). The concept of sensitivity communication using aroma and a plan of demonstration experiment: The digital signage with fragrance communication. *Technical Report of the Institute of Electronics. Information and Communication Engineers, 108*(291), 53–57.

Sakairi, M., Hashimoto, Y., Yamada, M., Suga, M., & Kojima, K. (2004). *Mass spectrometer, mass spectrometry, and monitoring system.* Patent US 6,686,592 B1. Washington, DC: US Patent Office.

Sakairi, M., Hashimoto, Y., Yamada, M., Suga, M., & Kojima, K. (2005). *Mass spectrometer, mass spectrometry, and monitoring system.* Patent US 6,838,664 B2. Washington, DC: US Patent Office.

Sakairi, M., Nakamura, H., & Nakamura, J. (1998). Highly sensitive vapor detection of nitro-compounds by atmospheric pressure chemical ionization mass spectrometry. In *Proceedings of 6th International Symposium on Analysis and Detection of Explosives.* IEEE.

Sakairi, M., Nishimura, A., & Suzuki, D. (2009). Olfaction presentation system using odor scanner and odor-emitting apparatus coupled with chemical capsules of alginic acid polymer. *IEICE Transactions on Fundamentals, E92*(A), 618-629.

Sakairi, M., & Kato, Y. (1998). Multi-atmospheric pressure ionization interface for liquid chromatography-mass spectrometry. *Journal of Chromatography. A, 794,* 391–406. doi:10.1016/S0021-9673(97)01220-X

Sakairi, M., Nishimura, A., & Suzuki, D. (2009). Olfaction presentation system using odor scanner and odor-emitting apparatus coupled with chemical capsules of alginic acid polymer. *IEICE Transactions on Fundamentals of Electronics, Communications and Computer Sciences. E (Norwalk, Conn.), 92A*(2), 618–629.

Salin, P. A., Lledo, P. M., Vincent, J. D., & Charpak, S. (2001). Dendritic glutamate autoreceptors modulate signal processing in rat mitral cells. *Journal of Neurophysiology, 85,* 1275–1282.

Salit, M., & Turk, G. (1998). A drift correction procedure. *Analytical Chemistry, 70,* 3184–3190. doi:10.1021/ac980095b

Sankaran, S., Mishra, A., Ehsani, R., & Davis, C. (2010). A review of advanced techniques for detecting plant diseases. *Computers and Electronics in Agriculture, 72*(1), 1–13. doi:10.1016/j.compag.2010.02.007

Sasaki, Y., Hayashi, K., & Toko, K. (2009). Fabrication of odor sensor surface recognizing substructure of odorant. *Sensors and Materials, 21*(4), 191–199.

Sato, J., Ohtsu, K., Bannai, Y., & Okada, K. (2008). Pulse ejection technique of scent to create dynamic perspective. In *Proceedings of 18th International Conference on Artificial Reality and Telexistence,* (pp. 167–174). IEEE.

Sato, J., Ohtsu, K., Bannai, Y., & Okada, K. (2008). Pulse ejection technique of scent to create dynamic perspective. In *Proceedings of the 18th International Conference on Artificial Reality and Telexistence,* (pp. 167-174). IEEE.

Sato, J., Ohtsu, K., Bannai, Y., & Okada, K. (2009). Effective presentation technique of scent using small ejection quantities of odor. In *Proceedings of the IEEE Virtual Reality Conference,* (pp. 151-158). IEEE Press.

Sato, K., Pellegrino, M., Nakagawa, T., Nakagawa, T., Vosshall, L. B., & Touhara, K. (2008). Insect olfactory receptors are heteromeric ligand–gated ion channels. *Nature, 452,* 1002–1006. doi:10.1038/nature06850

Sauerbrey, G. (1959). Verwendung von schwingquarzen zur wägung dünner schichten und zur mikrowägung. *Zeitschrift fur Physik, 155*(2), 206–222. doi:10.1007/BF01337937

Savic, I., & Gulyas, B. (2000). PET shows that odors are processed both ipsilaterally and contralaterally to the stimulated nostril. *Neuroreport, 11*, 2861–2866. doi:10.1097/00001756-200009110-00007

Sawada, E., Ida, S., Awaji, T., Morishita, K., Aruga, T., & Takeichi, R. … Inami, M. (2007). BYU-BYU-view: A wind communication interface. *ACM SIGGRAPH 2007*. Retrieved from http://dl.acm.org/citation.cfm?id=1278282

ScentAir. (2012). *Website.* Retrieved from http://www.scentair.com/

Scentcommunication. (2012). *Website.* Retrieved from http://www.scentcommunication.com/

Schaller, E., Bosset, J., & Escher, F. (1999). Practical experience with 'electronic nose' systems for monitoring the quality of dairy products. *CHIMIA International Journal for Chemistry, 53*, 98–102.

Schaller, E., Bosset, J., & Escher, F. (2000). Instability of conducting polymer sensors in an electronic nose system. *Analusis, 28*, 217–227. doi:10.1051/analusis:2000113

Schiffman, S., & Pearce, T. C. (2003). Introduction to olfaction: Perception, anatomy, physiology and molecular biology. In Nagle, H. T., Gardner, J. W., Schiffman, S. S., & Pearce, T. C. (Eds.), *Handbook of Machine Olfaction* (pp. 1–32). Weinheim, Germany: Wiley-VCH. doi:10.1002/3527601597.ch1

Schilling, B., Kaiser, R., Natsch, A., & Gautschi, M. (2010). Investigation of odors in the fragrance industry. *Chemoecology, 20*, 135–147. doi:10.1007/s00049-009-0035-5

Schlupp, M., Weil, T., Berresheim, A. J., Wiesler, U. M., Bargon, J., & Müllen, K. (2001). Polyphenylene dendrimers as sensitive and selective sensor layers. *Angewandt Chemie International Edition, 40*, 4011-4015.

Schoenfeld, T. A., & Cleland, T. A. (2006). Anatomical contributions to odorant sampling and representation in rodents: Zoning in on sniffing behavior. *Chemical Senses, 31*, 131–144. doi:10.1093/chemse/bjj015

Schoenfeld, T. A., Marchand, J. E., & Macrides, F. (1985). Topographic organization of tufted cell axonal projections in the hamster main olfactory bulb: An intrabulbar associational system. *The Journal of Comparative Neurology, 235*, 503–518. doi:10.1002/cne.902350408

Schölkopf, B., & Smola, A. (2001). *Learning with kernels.* Cambridge, MA: MIT Press.

Schoppa, N. E. (2006). Synchronization of olfactory bulb mitral cells by precisely timed inhibitory inputs. *Neuron, 49*, 271–283. doi:10.1016/j.neuron.2005.11.038

Schoppa, N. E., & Westbrook, G. L. (2002). AMPA autoreceptors drive correlated spiking in olfactory bulb glomeruli. *Nature Neuroscience, 5*, 1194–1202. doi:10.1038/nn953

Scott, J. W., McBride, R. L., & Schneider, S. P. (1980). The organization of projections from the olfactory bulb to the piriform cortex and olfactory tubercle in the rat. *The Journal of Comparative Neurology, 194*, 519–534. doi:10.1002/cne.901940304

Seiyama, T., Kato, A., Fujiishi, K., & Nagatani, M. (1962). A new detector for gaseous components using semiconductive thin films. *Analytical Chemistry, 34*, 1502–1503. doi:10.1021/ac60191a001

Sekhar, P. K., Brosha, E. L., Mukundan, R., & Garzon, F. H. (2010). Chemical sensors for environmental monitoring and homeland security. *Electrochemical Society Interface*. Retrieved from http://shinwa-cpc.co.jp/gc/product/needl.html and http://www2.shimadzu.com/applications/GC/G261.pdf

Sekine, M., Wyszynski, B., Nakamoto, T., Nakaso, N., & Noguchi, K. (2008). Sensitivity improvement of the odor sensors using Ball SAW device. *IEEJ Transactions on Sensors and Micromachines, 128-E*(12), 487–492. doi:10.1541/ieejsmas.128.487

Šetkus, A., Olekas, A., Senulienė, D., Falasconi, M., Pardo, M., & Sberveglieri, G. (2010). Analysis of the dynamic features of metal oxide sensors in response to SPME fiber gas release. *Sensors and Actuators. B, Chemical, 146*, 539–544. doi:10.1016/j.snb.2009.12.034

Severin, E. J., & Lewis, N. S. (2000). Relationships among resonant frequency changes on a coated quartz crystal microbalance, thickness changes, and resistance responses of polymer-carbon black composite chemiresistors. *Analytical Chemistry, 72*, 2008–2015. doi:10.1021/ac991026f

Seyama, M., Iwasaki, Y., Tate, A., & Sugimoto, I. (2006). Room-temperature ionic-liquid-incorporated plasma-deposited thin films for discriminative alcohol-vapor sensing. *Chemistry of Materials, 18*, 2656–2662. doi:10.1021/cm052088r

Shah, R. R., Merreceyes, D., Husemann, M., Rees, I., Abbott, N. L., Hawker, C. J., & Hedrick, J. L. (2000). Using atom transfer radical polymerization to amplify monolayers of initiators patterned by microcontact printing into polymer brushes for pattern transfer. *Macromolecules, 33*, 597–605. doi:10.1021/ma991264c

Sharaf, M. A., Illman, D. L., & Kowalski, B. R. (1986). *Chemometrics*. New York, MY: Wiley.

Sharma, R. K., Chan, P. C. H., Tang, Z., Yan, G., Hsing, I.-M., & Sin, J. K. O. (2001). Investigation of stability and reliability of tin oxide thin-film for integrated micro-machined gas sensor devices. *Sensors and Actuators. B, Chemical, 81*(1), 9–16. doi:10.1016/S0925-4005(01)00920-0

Shepherd, G. M. (1972). Synaptic organization of the mammalian olfactory bulb. *Physiological Reviews, 52*, 864–917.

Shepherd, G. M. (2004). The human sense of smell: are we better than we think? *PLoS Biology, 2*(5), 146. doi:10.1371/journal.pbio.0020146

Shepherd, G. M. (2006). Smell images and the flavour system in the human brain. *Nature, 444*, 316–321. doi:10.1038/nature05405

Shetty, V., Zigler, C., Robles, T. F., Elashoff, D., & Yamaguchi, M. (2010). Developmental validation of a point-of-care, salivary α-amylase biosensor. *Psychoneuroendocrinology, 36*(2), 193–199. doi:10.1016/j.psyneuen.2010.07.008

Shevade, A. V., Homer, M. L., Zhou, H., Jewell, A. D., Kisor, A. K., & Manatt, K. S. ... Ryan, M. A. (2007). Development of the third generation JPL electronic nose for international space station technology demonstration. *Journal of Aerospace*. Retrieved from http://enose.jpl.nasa.gov/publications/ICES-Amy-2007.pdf

Shevade, A. V., Ryan, M. A., Homer, M. L., Kisor, A. K., Lara, L. M., & Zhou, H. ... Gluck, S. (2010). Characterization of unknown events observed by the 3rd generation JPL electronic nose using sensor tesponse models. In *Proceedings 40th International Conference on Environmental Systems*. American Institute of Aeronautics and Astronautics (AIAA).

Shevade, A. V., Homer, M. L., Taylor, C. J., Zhou, H., Jewell, A. D., & Manatt, K. S. (2006). Correlating polymer-carbon composite sensor response with molecular descriptors. *Journal of the Electrochemical Society, 153*, 209–216. doi:10.1149/1.2337771

Shevade, A. V., Ryan, M. A., Homer, M. L., & Zhou, H. (2009). Chemical sensor array response modeling using quantitative structure-activity relationships. In Ryan, M. A., Shevade, A. V., Taylor, C. J., Homer, M. L., Blanco, M., & Stetter, J. R. (Eds.), *Computational Methods for Sensor Material Selection*. New York, NY: Springer. doi:10.1007/978-0-387-73715-7_8

Shimojo, S., & Shams, L. (2001). Sensory modalities are not separate modalities: Plasticity and interactions. *Current Opinion in Neurobiology, 11*(4), 505–509. doi:10.1016/S0959-4388(00)00241-5

Shin, J. H., Lee, K. R., & Park, S. B. (1993). Novel neural circuits based on stochastic pulse coding and noise feedback pulse coding. *International Journal of Electronics, 74*(3), 359–368. doi:10.1080/00207219308925840

Shusterman, R., Smear, M. C., Koulakov, A. A., & Rinberg, D. (2011). Precise olfactory responses tile the sniff cycle. *Nature Neuroscience, 14*, 1039–1044. doi:10.1038/nn.2877

Si, P., Mortensen, J., Komolov, A., Denborg, J., & Møller, P. J. (2007). Polymer coated quartz crystal microbalance sensors for detection of volatile organic compounds in gas mixture. *Analytica Chimica Acta, 597*, 223–230. doi:10.1016/j.aca.2007.06.050

Sisk, B., & Lewis, N. (2005). Comparison of analytical methods and calibration methods for correction of detector response drift in arrays of carbon black-polymer composite vapor detectors. *Sensors and Actuators. B, Chemical, 104*, 249–268. doi:10.1016/j.snb.2004.05.010

Skogestad, S., & Postlethwaite, I. (1996). *Multivariable feedback control*. Chichester, UK: Wiley.

Skov, T., & Bro, R. (2005). A new approach for modelling sensor based data. *Sensors and Actuators. B, Chemical, 106*, 719–729. doi:10.1016/j.snb.2004.09.023

Smear, M., Shusterman, R., O'Connor, R., Bozza, T., & Rinberg, D. (2011). Perception of sniff phase in mouse olfaction. *Nature, 479*, 397–400. doi:10.1038/nature10521

Smilde, A., & Rasmus, B. (Eds.). (2004). *Multi-way analysis with applications in the chemical sciences*. New York, NY: John Wiley & Sons. doi:10.1002/0470012110

Smith, M. J., & Kiger, P. J. (2006). The lingering reek of smell-o-vision. *Los Angeles Times*. Retrieved August 21, 2007 from http://www.latimes.com/features/magazine/west/la-tm-oops6feb05,1,2932206.story?coll=la-iraq-complete

Smith, A. (2007). The quartz crystal microbalance. In Brown, M., & Gallagher, P. (Eds.), *Handbook of Thermal Analysis and Calorimetry (Vol. 5)*. Amsterdam, The Netherlands: Elsevier Science.

Smith, R. G., D'Souza, N., & Nicklin, S. (2008). A review of biosensors and biologically-inspired systems for explosives detection. *Analyst (London), 133*, 571–584. doi:10.1039/b717933m

Snow, A. W., & Barger, W. R. (1989). Phthalocyanine films in chemical sensors. In Lezonoff, C. C., & Lever, A. B. P. (Eds.), *Phthalocyanines: Properties and Applications* (pp. 341–392). New York, NY: John Wiley and Sons.

Sobel, N. (1998). Sniffing and smelling: Separate subsystems in the human olfactory cortex. *Nature, 392*, 282–286. doi:10.1038/32654

Sobel, N., Prabhakaran, N., Desmond, J. E., Glover, G. H., Goode, R. L., Sullivan, E. V., & Gabrieli, J. D. (1998). Sniffing and smelling: Separate subsystem in the human olfactory cortex. *Nature, 392*, 282–286. doi:10.1038/32654

Somboon, P., Wyszynki, B., & Nakamoto, T. (2007). Realization of recording wide range of odor by utilizing both of transient and steady-state sensor responses in recording process. *Sensors and Actuators. B, Chemical, 124*, 557–563. doi:10.1016/j.snb.2007.01.030

Somboon, P., Wyszynski, B., & Nakamoto, T. (2007). Novel odor recorder for extending range of recordable odor. *Sensors and Actuators. B, Chemical, 121*, 583–589. doi:10.1016/j.snb.2006.04.105

Somboon, P., Wyszynski, B., & Nakamoto, T. (2009). Development of odor recorder with enhanced recording capabilities based on real-time mass spectrometry. *Sensors and Actuators. B, Chemical, 141*, 141–146. doi:10.1016/j.snb.2009.06.005

Song, Y., Cygnar, K. D., Sagdullaev, B., Valley, M., Hirsh, S., & Stephan, A. (2008). Olfactory CNG channel desensitization by Ca^{2+}/CaM via the B1b subunit affects response termination but not sensitivity to recurring stimulation. *Neuron, 58*, 374–386. doi:10.1016/j.neuron.2008.02.029

Sosulski, D. L., Lissitsyna, B. M., Cutforth, T., Axel, R., & Datta, S. R. (2011). Distinct representations of olfactory information in different cortical centres. *Nature, 472*(7342), 213–216. doi:10.1038/nature09868

Soucy, E. R., Albeanu, D. F., Fantana, A. L., Murthy, V. N., & Meister, M. (2009). Precision and diversity in an odor map on the olfactory bulb. *Nature Neuroscience, 12*, 210–220. doi:10.1038/nn.2262

Speirs, R. L., Herring, J., Cooper, W. D., Hardy, C. C., & Hind, C. R. (1974). The influence of sympathetic activity and isoprenaline on the secretion of amylase from the human parotid gland. *Archives of Oral Biology, 19*(9), 747–752. doi:10.1016/0003-9969(74)90161-7

Spence, C., Levitan, C., Shankar, M., & Zampini, M. (2010). Does food color influence taste and flavor perception in humans? *Chemosensory Perception, 3*(1), 68–84. doi:10.1007/s12078-010-9067-z

Spors, H., Wachowiak, M., Cohen, L. B., & Friedrich, R. W. (2006). Temporal dynamics and latency patterns of receptor neuron input to the olfactory bulb. *The Journal of Neuroscience, 26*, 1247–1259. doi:10.1523/JNEUROSCI.3100-05.2006

Sprowl, D. J., & Ehrcke, L. A. (1984). Sweeteners: Consumer acceptance in tea. *Journal of the American Dietetic Association, 84*, 1020–1022.

Steinhart, H., Stephan, A., & Bücking, M. (2000). Advances in flavor research. *Journal of High Resolution Chromatography, 23*(7-8), 489–496. doi:10.1002/1521-4168(20000801)23:7/8<489::AID-JHRC489>3.0.CO;2-O

Stephan, A. B., Shum, E. Y., Hirsh, S., Cygnar, K. D., Reisert, J., & Zhao, H. (2009). ANO2 is the cilial calcium-activated chloride channel that may mediate olfactory amplification. *Proceedings of the National Academy of Sciences of the United States of America, 106*, 11776–11781. doi:10.1073/pnas.0903304106

Stetter, J. R. (2008). Amperometric gas sensors - A review. *Chemical Reviews, 108*(2), 352–366. doi:10.1021/cr0681039

Stettler, D. D., & Axel, R. (2009). Representations of odor in the piriform cortex. *Neuron, 63*, 854–864. doi:10.1016/j.neuron.2009.09.005

Stevenson, R. J., Prescott, J., & Boakes, R. A. (1999). Confusing tastes and smells: How odours can influence the perception of sweet and sour tastes. *Chemical Senses, 24*(6), 627–635. doi:10.1093/chemse/24.6.627

Stevens, S. S. (1957). On the psychophysical law. *Psychological Review, 64*(3), 153–181. doi:10.1037/h0046162

Stewart, W. B., Kauer, J. S., & Shepherd, G. M. (1979). Functional organization of rat olfactory bulb analysed by the 2-deoxyglucose method. *The Journal of Comparative Neurology, 185*, 715–734. doi:10.1002/cne.901850407

Stillman, M. J., & Nyokong, T. (1989). Absorption and magnetic circular dichroism spectral properties of phthalocyanines part 1: Complexes of the dianion Pc(-2). In Lezonoff, C. C., & Lever, A. B. P. (Eds.), *Phthalocyanines: Properties and Applications* (pp. 133–290). New York, NY: John Wiley and Sons.

Stokes, C. C., & Isaacson, J. S. (2010). From dendrite to soma: dynamic routing of inhibition by complementary interneuron microcircuits in olfactory cortex. *Neuron, 67*, 452–465. doi:10.1016/j.neuron.2010.06.029

Stuffler, T., Mosebach, H., Kampf, D., Honne, A., Schumann-Olsen, H., & Kaspersen, K. ... Tan, G. (2008). ANITA air monitoring on the international space station part 1: The mission. In *Proceedings 38th International Conference on Environmental Systems*. Society of Automotive Engineers (SAE).

Sugimoto, I., Mitsui, K., Nakamura, M., & Seyama, M. (2011). Effects of surface water on gas sorption capacities of gravimetric sensing layers analyzed by molecular descriptors of organic adsorbates. *Analytical and Bioanalytical Chemistry, 399*, 1891–1899. doi:10.1007/s00216-010-4556-0

Sugimoto, I., Nagaoka, T., Seyama, M., Nakamura, M., & Takahashi, K. (2007). Classification and characterization of atmospheric VOCs based on sorption/desorption behaviors of plasma polymer films. *Sensors and Actuators. B, Chemical, 124*, 53–61. doi:10.1016/j.snb.2006.11.045

Sugimoto, I., Nakamura, M., & Muzunuma, M. (1999). Structures and VOC-sensing performance of high-sensitivity plasma-polymer films coated on quartz crystal resonator. *Sensors and Materials, 11*, 59–70.

Sugimoto, I., Nakamura, M., Seyama, M., Ogawa, S., & Katoh, T. (2000). Chiral-discriminative amino acid films prepared by vacuum vaporization and/or plasma processing. *Analyst (London), 125*, 169–174. doi:10.1039/a907149k

Sugimoto, I., Okamoto, M., Sone, K., & Takahashi, K. (2010). Structures and gas-sorption properties of carbonaceous film prepared by radio-frequency sputtering of polysaccharides pectin. *Polymer Degradation & Stability, 95*, 929–934. doi:10.1016/j.polymdegradstab.2010.03.023

Sugimoto, I., & Sekiguchi, H. (2010). Structure and N_2-sorption properties of carbonaceous films prepared by high-powered sputtering of D-phenylalanine. *Thin Solid Films, 518*, 2876–2882. doi:10.1016/j.tsf.2009.10.002

Sugiyama, H., Kanamura, A., & Kikuchi, T. (2006). Are olfactory images sensory in nature? *Perception, 35*, 1699–1708. doi:10.1068/p5453

Sugiyama, M., Hasegawa, H., & Hashimoto, Y. (2009). Mass-selective axial ejection from a linear ion trap with a direct current extraction field. *Rapid Communications in Mass Spectrometry, 23*, 2917–2922. doi:10.1002/rcm.4204

Sundgren, H., Winquist, F., & Lundstrom, I. (1991). Artifical neural networks and statistical pattern recognition improve MOSFET gas sensor array calibration. [IEEE.]. *Proceedings of the Technological Digest of Transducers, 1991*, 574–577.

Su, T., Bao, Z., Zhang, Q. Y., Smith, T. J., Hong, J. Y., & Ding, X. (2000). Human cytochrome P450 CYP2A13: Predominant expression in the respiratory tract and its high efficiency metabolic activation of a tobacco–specific carcinogen, 4-(methylnitrosamino)-1-(3-pyridyl)-1-butanone. *Cancer Research, 60*, 5074–5079.

Svensson, O., Kourti, T., & MacGregor, J. F. (2002). An investigation of orthogonal signal correction algorithms and their characteristics. *Journal of Chemometrics, 16*, 176–188. doi:10.1002/cem.700

Swanson, L. W., & Petrovich, G. D. (1998). What is the amygdala? *Trends in Neurosciences, 21*, 323–331. doi:10.1016/S0166-2236(98)01265-X

Swierenga, H., Weijer, A. D., & Wijk, R. V. (1999). Strategy for constructing robust multivariate calibration models. *Chemometrics and Intelligent Laboratory Systems, 49*, 1–17. doi:10.1016/S0169-7439(99)00028-3

Taguchi, N. (1962). Gas alarm device. *Japanese Pat., 45*(38200).

Takada, S., Nakai, K., Thurakitseree, T., Shiomi, J., Maruyama, S., & Takagi, H. (2010). Micro gas preconcentrator made of a film of single-walled carbon nanotubes. *IEEJ Transactions on Sensors and Micromachines, 130*(6), 207–211. doi:10.1541/ieejsmas.130.207

Takada, Y. (2007). Explosives trace detection by mass spectrometry. *Journal of the Mass Spectrometry Society of Japan, 55*, 91–94. doi:10.5702/massspec.55.91

Takada, Y. (2008). High-throughput walkthrough portal to detect improvised explosive devices. *Safety Engineering, 4*(8), 149.

Takada, Y., Nagano, H., Suga, M., Hashimoto, Y., Yamada, M., & Sakairi, M. (2002). Detection of military explosives by atmospheric pressure chemical ionization mass spectrometry with counter-flow introduction. *Propellants, Explosives. Pyrotechnics, 27*, 224–228. doi:10.1002/1521-4087(200209)27:4<224::AID-PREP224>3.0.CO;2-V

Takada, Y., Nagano, H., Suzuki, Y., Sugiyama, M., Nakajima, E., Hashimoto, Y., & Sakairi, M. (2011). Detection of military high-throughput detection of triacetone triperoxide (TATP) by atmospheric pressure chemical ionization ion trap mass spectrometry (APCI-ITMS). *Rapid Communications in Mass Spectrometry, 25*, 2448–2452. doi:10.1002/rcm.5147

Takagi, F. S. (1999). *Human olfaction*. Tokyo, Japan: University Tokyo Press.

Takagi, S. F. (1987). A standardized olfactometer in Japan. *Annals of the New York Academy of Sciences, 510*, 113–118. doi:10.1111/j.1749-6632.1987.tb43476.x

Takai, N., Yamaguchi, M., Aragaki, T., Eto, K., Uchihashi, K., & Nishikawa, Y. (2004). Effect of psychological stress on the salivary cortisol and amylase levels in healthy young adults. *Archives of Oral Biology, 49*(12), 963–968. doi:10.1016/j.archoralbio.2004.06.007

Takakura, H., Shojaku, H., Takamoto, K., Urakawa, S., Nishijo, H., & Watanabe, Y. (2011). Cortical hemodynamic responses to intravenous thiamine propyldisulphide administration detected by multichannel near infrared spectroscopy (NIRS) system. *Brain Topography, 24*, 114–126. doi:10.1007/s10548-011-0179-9

Takeuchi, H., Ishida, H., Hikichi, S., & Kurahashi, T. (2009). Mechanism of olfactory masking in the sensory cilia. *The Journal of General Physiology, 133*, 583–601. doi:10.1085/jgp.200810085

Takizawa, R., Tochigi, M., Kawakubo, Y., Marumo, K., Sasaki, T., Fukuda, M., & Kasai, K. (2009). Association between catechol-O-methyltrasferase Val108/158Met genotype and prefrontal hemodynamic response in schizophrenia. *PLoS ONE, 4*(5), e5495. doi:10.1371/journal.pone.0005495

Tanabe, T., Yarita, H., & Iino, M. (1975). An olfactory projection area in orbitofrontal cortex of the monkey. *Journal of Neurophysiology, 38*, 1269–1283.

Tanaka, K., & Kakizaki, F. (2003). *Theory and the technology of the respiratory movement medical treatment*. Tokyo, Japan: Medical View Co., Ltd.

Tanaka, T. (1978). Collapse of gels and the critical endpoint. *Physical Review Letters, 40*(12), 820–823. doi:10.1103/PhysRevLett.40.820

Tan, J., Savigner, A., Ma, M., & Luo, M. (2010). Odor information processing by the olfactory bulb analyzed in gene–targeted mice. *Neuron, 65,* 912–926. doi:10.1016/j.neuron.2010.02.011

Tateyama, T., Hummel, T., Roscher, S., Post, H., & Kobal, G. (1998). Relation of olfactory event-related potentials to changes in stimulus concentration. *Electroencephalography and Clinical Neurophysiology, 108,* 449–455. doi:10.1016/S0168-5597(98)00022-7

Taylor, J. E. (2010). *Novel convolution-based processing techniques for applicationn in chemical sensing.* (PhD Thesis). University of Warwick. Coventry, UK.

Teghtsoonian, R., Teghtsoonian, M., Berglund, B., & Berglund, U. (1978). Invariance of odor strength with sniff vigor: An olfactory analogue to size constancy. *Journal of Experimental Psychology. Human Perception and Performance, 4,* 144–152. doi:10.1037/0096-1523.4.1.144

Terry, S. C., Jerman, J. H., & Angell, J. B. (1979). A gas chromatographic air analyzer fabricated on a silicon wafer. *IEEE Transactions on Electron Devices, 26,* 1880–1886. doi:10.1109/T-ED.1979.19791

Terry, S., Jerman, J., & Angell, J. (1979). A gas chromatographic air analyzer fabricated on a silicon wafer. *IEEE Transactions on Electron Devices, 26*(12), 1880–1886. doi:10.1109/T-ED.1979.19791

Thaler, E. R., Kennedy, D. W., & Hanson, C. W. (2001). Medical applications of electronic nose technology: Review of current status. *American Journal of Rhinology, 15*(5), 291–295.

Tian, W.-C., Pang, S. W., Lu, C.-J., & Zellers, E. T. (2003). Microfabricated preconcentrator-focuser for a microscale gas chromatograph. *Journal of Microelectromechanical Systems, 12,* 264–272. doi:10.1109/JMEMS.2003.811748

Tibshirani, R., Walther, G., & Hastie, T. (2001). Estimating the number of clusters in a data set via the gap statistics. *Journal of the Royal Statistical Society. Series B. Methodological, 63,* 411–423. doi:10.1111/1467-9868.00293

Tipping, M. E., & Bishop, C. M. (1999). Mixtures of probabilistic principal component analyzers. *Neural Computation, 11*(2), 443–482. doi:10.1162/089976699300016728

Tirado-Rives, L., & Jorgensen, W. L. (2008). Performance of B3LYP density functional methods for a large set of organic molecules. *Journal of Chemical Theory and Computation, 4,* 297–306. doi:10.1021/ct700248k

Tirindelli, R., Dibattista, M., Pifferi, S., & Menini, A. (2009). From pheromones to behavior. *Physiological Reviews, 89*(3), 921–956. doi:10.1152/physrev.00037.2008

Toda, K. (1994). *Japanese unexamined patent application publication H6-7721.* Tokyo, Japan: Patent Office.

Toko, K., Matsuno, T., Yamafuji, K., Hayashi, K., Ikezaki, H., & Sato, K. (1994). Taste sensor using electric potential changes in lipid membranes. *Biosensors & Bioelectronics, 9,* 359–364. doi:10.1016/0956-5663(94)80036-7

Tomaru, A., & Kurahashi, T. (2005). Mechanisms determining the dynamic range of the bullfrog olfactory receptor cell. *Journal of Neurophysiology, 93,* 1880–1888. doi:10.1152/jn.00303.2004

Tomic, O., Ulmer, H., & Haugen, J. (2002). Standardization methods for handling instrument related signal shift in gas-sensor array measurement data. *Analytica Chimica Acta, 472*(1-2), 99–111. doi:10.1016/S0003-2670(02)00936-4

Tominaga, K., Honda, S., Ohsawa, T., Shigeno, H., Okada, K., & Matsushita, Y. (2001). Friend park — Expression of the wind and the scent on virtual space. In *Proceedings of the Seventh International Conference on Virtual Systems and Multimedia,* (pp. 507-515). IEEE.

Tomono, A. (2007). Evaluation of hyper-realistic images using smells. In *Proceedings of International Display Workshops,* (vol. 2, pp. 1161-1164). JGlobal. Retrieved from http://jglobal.jst.go.jp/public/20090422/200902256709192830

Tomono, A. (2008). *Gas discharger.* PCT Application, WO/2008/072744. Retrieved from http://patentscope.wipo.int/search/en/WO2008072744

Tomono, A., & Tomono, K. (2008). *WIPO patent scope.* Retrieved from http://www.wipo.int/patentscope/search/en/detail.jsf?docId=WO2008093721

Tomono, A., & Uehara, A. (2006). *Scent generator and scent generation device.* Japanese Patent Number 3874715. Tokyo, Japan: Patent Office.

Tomono, A., & Uehara, A. (2006). *Mist generator and mist emission rendering apparatus*. PCT Application, WO/2006/095816. Retrieved from http://patentscope. wipo.int/search/en/WO2006095816

Tomono, A., Yamamoto, S., Utsunomiya, M., Ikei, D., Yanagida, Y., & Hosaka, K. (2004). The effect which visual media with scent exert on contents understanding. In *Proceedings of the Human Interface Symposium 2004*, (vol 1441, pp. 249-254). Human Interface. Retrieved from http://sciencelinks.jp/j-east/article/200510/00002005100 5A0295009.php

Tomono, K., Wakatsuki, H., Kumazawa, S., & Tomono, A. (2011). Display system for advertising image with scent and psychological effect. *Lecture Notes in Computer Science, 6781*, 110-119. Retrieved from http://www. springerlink.com/content/5j3165v5r1502v47/

Tomono, A., Kanda, K., & Otake, S. (2008). Effect that smell presentation has on an individual in regards to eye catching and memory. *IEEJ Transactions on Sensors and Micromachines, 128*(12), 478–486. doi:10.1541/ ieejsmas.128.478

Tomono, A., & Otake, S. (2010). The eye catching property of digital-signage with scent and a scent-emitting video display system. *IEEJ Transactions on Electronics. Information Systems, 130*(4), 668–675.

Tomono, A., Tomono, T., Fukiura, T., & Yamaguchi, H. (2008). Olfaction characteristics improvement of projection-based olfactory display. *The Journal of the Institute of Image Electronics Engineers of Japan, 37*(4), 444–451.

Tomono, A., & Uehara, A. (2005). *Japanese unexamined patent application publication 2005-296540*. Tokyo, Japan: Patent Office.

Tomono, K., Katsuyama, H., & Tomono, A. (2011). Scent-emitting display panel and its psychological effects. *The Journal of the Institute of Image Information and Television Engineers, 65*(10), 1411–1419. doi:10.3169/itej.65.1411

Tonoike, M., et al. (1998). Article. In *Proceedings of 20th Annual International Conference IEEE/EMBS/1998*, (pp. 2213-2216). IEEE Press.

Tonoike, M., et al. (1998). Olfaction and taste XII. *New York Academy of Sciences, 855*, 579-590.

Tonoike, M., et al. (2004). Article. In *Proceedings of the 12th International Conference on Biomag2000*, (pp. 238-291). Biomag2000.

Tonoike, M., Miyamoto, K., Yokoo, Y., Toyofuku, T., Miwakeichi, F., & Uno, T. … Shintani, M. (2008). *Bio-magnetsim–Transdiciplinary research and exploration*. Sapporo, Japan: Hokkaido University Press.

Tonoike, M., Yamaguchi, M., & Hamada, T. (2001). Article. In *Proceedings of Biomag2000*, (pp. 288-291). Biomag2000.

Tonoike, M. (1996). Article. *Electroencephalography and Clinical Neurophysiology, 47*, 143–150.

Tonoike, M. (2003). Article. *Journal of Temperature Design and Environment, 3*, 43–53.

Tonoike, M. (2007). *Information and communication technology of olfaction*. Tokyo, Japan: Fragrance Journal Ltd.

Tonoike, M. (2011). The relation of human brain and olfaction. *Aroma Research, 46*, 121–128.

Tonoike, M., Uno, T., Yoshida, T., & Wang, L. Q. (2010). Article. *Electroencephalography and Clinical Neurophysiology, 121*, 217–218.

Tonoike, M., Yamaguchi, M., Kaetsu, I., Kida, H., Seo, R., & Koizuka, I. (1998). Ipsilateral dominance of human olfactory activated centers estimated from event-related magnetic fields measured by 122-channel whole-head neuromagnetometer using odorant stimuli synchronized with respirations. *Annals of the New York Academy of Sciences, 855*, 579–590. doi:10.1111/j.1749-6632.1998. tb10628.x

Tortell, R., Luigi, D. P., Dozois, A., Bouchard, S., Morie, J. F., & Ilan, D. (2007). The effects of scent and game play experience on memory of a virtual environment. *Virtual Reality (Waltham Cross), 11*(1), 61–68. doi:10.1007/ s10055-006-0056-0

Touhara, K., Sengoku, S., Inaki, K., Tsuboi, A., Hirono, J., & Sato, T. … Haga, T. (1999). Functional identification and reconstitution of an odorant receptor in single olfactory neurons. *Proceeding of the National Academy of Sciences, 96*(7), 4040–4045.

Toxicology Group. (1999). *Spacecraft maximum allowable concentrations for airborne contaminants.* Houston, TX: National Aeronautics and Space Administration (NASA).

Transportation Security Administration. (2012). *Homepage*. Retrieved from http://www.tsa.gov/

Trisenx. (2012). *Website.* Retrieved from http://www.trisenx.com/intro.html

Tsujii, T., Ohno, K., Yamamoto, S., Goto, A., & Fukuda, T. (2006). Structure and properties of high-density polymer brushes prepared by surface-initiated living radical polymerization. *Advances in Polymer Science, 197*, 1–46.

Tsuji, M., Takagi, S., Hirano, K., & Yoshihara, M. (2004). A new experiment in practical use of scent web. *Aroma Research, 20*, 34–39.

Tsujita, W., Yoshino, A., Ishida, H., & Moriizumi, T. (2005). Gas sensor network for air-pollution monitoring. *Sensors and Actuators. B, Chemical, 110*, 304–311. doi:10.1016/j.snb.2005.02.008

Tsuno, Y., Kashiwadani, H., & Mori, K. (2008). Behavioral state regulation of dendrodendritic synaptic inhibition in the olfactory bulb. *The Journal of Neuroscience, 28*, 9227–9238. doi:10.1523/JNEUROSCI.1576-08.2008

Tuantranont, A., Wisitsora-at, A., Sritongkham, P., & Jaruwongrungsee, K. (2011). A review of monolithic multichannel quartz crystal microbalance. *Analytica Chimica Acta, 687*, 114–128. doi:10.1016/j.aca.2010.12.022

Tukey, J. (1977). *Exploratory data analysis.* Reading, MA: Addison-Wesley.

Uchida, N., & Mainen, Z. F. (2003). Speed and accuracy of olfactory discrimination in the rat. *Nature Neuroscience, 6*, 1224–1229. doi:10.1038/nn1142

Uchida, N., Takahashi, Y. K., Tanifuji, M., & Mori, K. (2000). Odor maps in the mammalian olfactory bulb: Domain organization and odorant structural features. *Nature Neuroscience, 3*, 1035–1043. doi:10.1038/79857

Ugolev, A. M., De Laey, P., Iezuitova, N. N., Rakhimov, K. R., Timofeeva, N. M., & Stepanova, A. T. (1979). Membrane digestion and nutrient assimilation in early development. In *Proceedings of the Ciba Foundation Symposium,* (vol. 70, pp. 221-246). Ciba Foundation.

Ulijn, R. V., Bibi, N., Jayawarna, V., Thornton, P. D., Todd, S. J., & Mart, R. J. (2007). Bioresponsive hydrogels. *Materials Today, 10*(4), 40–48. doi:10.1016/S1369-7021(07)70049-4

USP. (2012). *United States pharmacopeial convention (USP).* Retrieved from http://www.usp.org

van Drongelen, W., Holley, A., & Doving, K. B. (1978). Convergence in the olfactory system: Quantitative aspects of odour sensitivity. *Journal of Theoretical Biology, 71*, 39–48. doi:10.1016/0022-5193(78)90212-6

Vandenburg, H. J., Clifford, A. A., Bartle, K. D., Carlson, R. E., Carroll, J., & Newton, I. D. (1999). A simple solvent selection method for accelerated solvent extraction of additives from polymers. *Analyst (London), 124*, 1707–1710. doi:10.1039/a904631c

Variety Staff. (2001). *Variety review of "scent of mystery".* Retrieved August 21, 2007 from http://www.variety.com/review/VE1117794675?refcatid=31

Verhagen, J. V., & Engelen, L. (2006). The neurocognitive bases of human multimodal food perception: Sensory integration. *Neuroscience and Biobehavioral Reviews, 30*, 613–650. doi:10.1016/j.neubiorev.2005.11.003

Verhagen, J. V., Wesson, D. W., Netoff, T. I., White, J. A., & Wachowiak, M. (2007). Sniffing controls an adaptive filter of sensory input to the olfactory bulb. *Nature Neuroscience, 10*, 631–639. doi:10.1038/nn1892

Vezzoli, M., Ponzoni, A., Pardo, M., Falasconi, M., Faglia, G., & Sberveglieri, G. (2008). Exploratory data analysis for industrial safety application. *Sensors and Actuators. B, Chemical, 131*(1), 100–109. doi:10.1016/j.snb.2007.12.047

Vickers, N. J. (2000). Mechanisms of animal navigation in odor plumes. *The Biological Bulletin, 198*(2), 203–212. doi:10.2307/1542524

Vickers, N. J. (2006). Winging it: Moth flight behavior and responses of olfactory neurons are shaped by pheromone plume dynamics. *Chemical Senses, 31*, 155–166. doi:10.1093/chemse/bjj011

Villringer, A., Planck, J., Hock, C., Schleinkofer, L., & Dirnagl, U. (1993). Near infrared spectroscopy (NIRS): A new tool to study hemodynamic changes during activation of brain function in human adults. *Neuroscience Letters, 154*, 101–104. doi:10.1016/0304-3940(93)90181-J

Vinaixa, M., Vergara, A., Duran, C., Llobet, E., Badia, C., & Brezmes, J. (2005). Fast detection of rancidity in potato crisps using e-noses based on mass spectrometry or gas sensors. *Sensors and Actuators. B, Chemical, 106*, 67–75. doi:10.1016/j.snb.2004.05.038

Vosshall, L. B., & Hansson, B. S. (2011). A unified nomenclature system for the insect olfactory coreceptor. *Chemical Senses, 36*, 497–498. doi:10.1093/chemse/bjr022

Vossmeyer, T., Guse, B., Besnard, I., Bauer, R. E., Müllen, K., & Yasuda, A. (2002). Gold nanoparticle/polyphenylene dendrimer compodite films: Preparation and vaporsensing properties. *Advanced Materials, 14*, 238–242. doi:10.1002/1521-4095(20020205)14:3<238::AID-ADMA238>3.0.CO;2-#

Wachowiak, M., & Cohen, L. B. (2001). Representation of odorants by receptor neuron input to the mouse olfactory bulb. *Neuron, 32*, 723–735. doi:10.1016/S0896-6273(01)00506-2

Wachowiak, M., & Shipley, M. T. (2006). Coding and synaptic processing of sensory information in the glomerular layer of the olfactory bulb. *Seminars in Cell & Developmental Biology, 17*, 411–423. doi:10.1016/j.semcdb.2006.04.007

Walla, P., Hufnagl, B., Lehrner, J., Mayer, D., Lindinger, G., Deecke, L., & Lang, W. (2002). Evidence of conscious and subconscious olfactory information processing during word encoding: A magnetoencephalographic (MEG) study. *Brain Research. Cognitive Brain Research, 14*, 309–316. doi:10.1016/S0926-6410(02)00121-0

Walsh, C. J., & Mandal, B. K. (2000). A novel method for the peripheral modification of phthalocyanines: Synthesis and third-order nonlinear optical absorption of β-teterakis(2,3,4,5,6-pentaphenylbenzene)phthalocyanine. *Chemistry of Materials, 12*, 287–289. doi:10.1021/cm9907662

Walt, D. R. (2010). Bead-based optical fiber arrays for artificial olfaction. *Current Opinion in Chemical Biology, 14*, 767–770. doi:10.1016/j.cbpa.2010.06.181

Wang, D., Buhmann, J., & von der Malsburg, C. (1990). Pattern segmentation in associative memory. *Neural Computation, 2*(1), 94–106. doi:10.1162/neco.1990.2.1.94

Wang, J., Eslinger, P. J., Smith, M. B., & Yang, Q. X. (2005). Functional magnetic resonance imaging study of human olfaction and normal aging. *The Journals of Gerontology. Series A, Biological Sciences and Medical Sciences, 60*, 510–514. doi:10.1093/gerona/60.4.510

Wang, X., Ding, B., Sun, M., Yu, J., & Sun, G. (2010). Nanofibrous polyethyleneimine membranes as sensitive coating for quartz crystal microbalance-based formaldehyde sensors. *Sensors and Actuators. B, Chemical, 144*, 11–17. doi:10.1016/j.snb.2009.08.023

Wang, Z., Hwang, J., & Kowalski, B. R. (1995). ChemNets: Theory and application. *Analytical Chemistry, 67*, 1497–1504. doi:10.1021/ac00105a003

Wang, Z., Isaksson, T., & Kowalski, B. R. (1994). New approach for distance measurement in locally weighted regression. *Analytical Chemistry, 66*, 249–260. doi:10.1021/ac00074a012

Washburn, D. A., Jones, L. M., Satya, R. V., Bowers, C. A., & Cortes, A. (2004). Olfactory use in virtual environment training. *Modeling and Simulation Magazine, 2*(3).

Washburn, D. A., & Jones, L. M. (2004). Could olfactory displays improve data visualization? *Computing in Science & Engineering, 6*(6), 80–83. doi:10.1109/MCSE.2004.66

Watkins, C. J. (2002). *Methods and apparatus for localized delivery of scented aerosols.* U. S. Patent 6,357,726. Washington, DC: US Patent Office.

Webb, A. (2002). *Statistical pattern recognition* (2nd ed.). West Sussex, UK: Wiley. doi:10.1002/0470854774

Wehr, M., & Laurent, G. (1996). Odour encoding by temporal sequences of firing in oscillating neural assemblies. *Nature, 384*, 162–166. doi:10.1038/384162a0

Wei, J., Zhao, A. Z., Chan, G. C., Baker, L. P., Impey, S., & Beavo, J. A. (1998). Phosphorylation and inhibition of olfactory adenylyl cyclase by CaM kinase II in Neurons: A mechanism for attenuation of olfactory signals. *Neuron, 21*, 495–504. doi:10.1016/S0896-6273(00)80561-9

Weismann, M., Yousry, I., Heuberger, E., Nolte, A., Ilmberger, J., & Kobal, G. (2001). Functional magnetic resonance imaging of human olfaction. *Neuroimaging Clinics of North America*, *11*, 237–250.

Welton, T. (1999). Room-temperature ionic liquids: Solvents for synthesis and catalysis. *Chemical Reviews*, *99*, 2071–2083. doi:10.1021/cr980032t

Wesson, D. W., Verhagen, J. V., & Wachowiak, M. (2009). Why sniff fast? The relationship between sniff frequency, odor discrimination, and receptor neuron activation in the rat. *Journal of Neurophysiology*, *101*, 1089–1102. doi:10.1152/jn.90981.2008

Wicher, D., Schäfer, R., Bauernfeind, R., Stensmyr, M. C., Heller, R., Heinemann, S. H., & Hansson, B. S. (2008). Drosophila odorant receptors are both ligand–gated and cyclic–nucleotide-activated cation channels. *Nature*, *452*, 1007–1011. doi:10.1038/nature06861

Willhite, D. C., Nguyen, K. T., Masurkar, A. V., Greer, C. A., Shepherd, G. M., & Chen, W. R. (2006). Viral tracing identifies distributed columnar organization in the olfactory bulb. *Proceedings of the National Academy of Sciences of the United States of America*, *103*, 12592–12597. doi:10.1073/pnas.0602032103

Willson, K. C., & Clifford, M. N. (1992). Aroma of green tea. In *Tea* (pp. 428–439). London, UK: Chapman & Hall. doi:10.1007/978-94-011-2326-6

Wilson, A. D., & Baietto, M. (2009). Applications and advances in electronic-nose technologies. *Sensors (Basel, Switzerland)*, *9*, 5099–5148. doi:10.3390/s90705099

Wilson, A. D., & Baietto, M. (2011). Advances in electronic-nose technologies developed for biomedical applications. *Sensors (Basel, Switzerland)*, *11*, 1105–1176. doi:10.3390/s110101105

Wilson, D. A. (1998). Habituation of odor responses in the rat anterior piriform cortex. *Journal of Neurophysiology*, *79*, 1425–1440.

Wilson, D. A. (2000). Odor specificity of habituation in the rat anterior piriform cortex. *Journal of Neurophysiology*, *83*, 139–145.

Wilson, D. A. (2001). Scopolamine enhances generalization between odor representations in rat olfactory cortex. *Learning & Memory (Cold Spring Harbor, N.Y.)*, *8*, 279–285. doi:10.1101/lm.42601

Wilson, D. A. (2003). Rapid, experience-induced enhancement in odorant discrimination by anterior piriform cortex neurons. *Journal of Neurophysiology*, *90*, 65–72. doi:10.1152/jn.00133.2003

Wilson, D. A. (2009). Pattern separation and completion in olfaction. *Annals of the New York Academy of Sciences*, *1170*, 306–312. doi:10.1111/j.1749-6632.2009.04017.x

Wilson, D. A., Kadohisa, M., & Fletcher, M. L. (2006). Cortical contributions to olfaction: Plasticity and perception. *Seminars in Cell & Developmental Biology*, *17*, 462–470. doi:10.1016/j.semcdb.2006.04.008

Wilson, D. A., & Stevenson, R. J. (2003). Olfactory perceptual learning: The critical role of memory in odor discrimination. *Neuroscience and Biobehavioral Reviews*, *27*, 307–328. doi:10.1016/S0149-7634(03)00050-2

Wilson, D. A., & Stevenson, R. J. (2003). The fundamental role of memory in olfactory perception. *Trends in Neurosciences*, *26*, 243–247. doi:10.1016/S0166-2236(03)00076-6

Wilson, D., & DeWeerth, S. (1995). Odor discrimination using steady-state and transient characteristics of tin-oxide sensors. *Sensors and Actuators. B, Chemical*, *28*(2), 123–128. doi:10.1016/0925-4005(95)80036-0

Windig, W., & Guilment, J. (1991). Interactive self-modeling mixture analysis. *Analytical Chemistry*, *63*, 1425–1432. doi:10.1021/ac00014a016

Wise, M. B., & Guerin, M. R. (1997). Direct sampling MS for environmental screening. *Analytical Chemistry*, *69*, 26A–32A. doi:10.1021/ac971504r

Wohltjen, H. (1984). Mechanism of operation and design considerations for surface acoustic wave device vapor sensors. *Sensors and Actuators. B, Chemical*, *5*(4), 307–325. doi:10.1016/0250-6874(84)85014-3

Wold, S., Antti, H., Lindgren, F., & Öhman, J. (1998). Orthogonal signal correction of near-infrared spectra. *Chemometrics and Intelligent Laboratory Systems*, *44*, 175–185. doi:10.1016/S0169-7439(98)00109-9

Wong, S. T., Trinh, K., Hacker, B., Chan, G. C., Lowe, G., & Gaggar, A. (2000). Disruption of the type III adenylyl cyclase gene leads to peripheral and behavioral anosmia in transgenic mice. *Neuron, 27,* 487–497. doi:10.1016/S0896-6273(00)00060-X

Wyszynski, B., & Nakamoto, T. (2010). Humidity-robust and highly-sensitive QCM odor sensors with amphiphilic GC-materials physisorbed overlipopolymer-protected nano-Au. In *Proceedings of the 27th Sensor Symposium,* (pp. 375-378). IEEE.

Wyszynski, B., Nakamoto, T., Akao, S., & Nakaso, N. (2010). Odor sensing system using ball SAW devices functionalized with self-assembled lipid-derivatives and GC materials. In *Proceedings of the 9th IEEE Conference on Sensors,* (pp. 342-345). IEEE Press.

Wyszynski, B., Gutierrez-Galvez, A., & Nakamoto, T. (2007). Improvement of ultrasonic atomizer method for deposition of gas-sensing film on QCM. *Sensors and Actuators. B, Chemical, 127*(1), 253–259. doi:10.1016/j.snb.2007.07.052

Wyszynski, B., Sekine, M., Nakamoto, T., Nakaso, N., & Noguchi, K. (2010). Spherical ball-SAW devices functionalized with self-assembled lipopolymers for odor-sensing. *Sensors and Actuators. B, Chemical, 144*(1), 247–254. doi:10.1016/j.snb.2009.10.059

Wyszynski, B., Somboon, P., & Nakamoto, T. (2009). Self-assembled lipopolymers with physisorbed amphiphilic GC materials for QCM odor sensors. *IEEJ Transactions on Sensors and Micromachines, 129*(9), 273–277. doi:10.1541/ieejsmas.129.273

Xiong, W., & Chen, W. R. (2002). Dynamic gating of spike propagation in the mitral cell lateral dendrites. *Neuron, 34,* 115–126. doi:10.1016/S0896-6273(02)00628-1

Xu, R., & Kwan, C. (2003). Robust isolation of sensor failures. *Asian Journal of Control, 5,* 12–23. doi:10.1111/j.1934-6093.2003.tb00093.x

Xu, R., & Wunsch, D. II. (2005). Survey of clustering algorithms. *IEEE Transactions on Neural Networks, 16*(3), 645–678. doi:10.1109/TNN.2005.845141

Xu, Z., Gu, A., & Fang, Z. (2007). Electric conductivity of PS/PA6/carbon black composites. *Journal of Applied Polymer Science, 103*(2), 1042–1047. doi:10.1002/app.25300

Yamada, T., Yokoyama, S., Tanikawa, T., Hirota, K., & Hirose, M. (2006). Wearable olfactory display: Using odor in outdoor environment. In *Proceedings of the IEEE Virtual Reality Conference,* (pp. 199 – 206). IEEE Press.

Yamada, M., Sakairi, M., Hashimoto, Y., Suga, M., Takada, Y., & Waki, I. (2001). On-line monitoring of dioxin precursors in flue gas. *Analytical Sciences, 17,* i559–i562.

Yamada, M., Waki, I., Sakairi, M., Sakamoto, M., & Imai, T. (2004). Real-time-monitored decrease of trichlorophenol as a dioxin surrogate in flue gas using iron oxide catalyst. *Chemosphere, 54,* 1475–1480. doi:10.1016/j.chemosphere.2003.10.031

Yamada, T., Yokoyama, S., Tanikawa, T., Hirota, K., & Hirose, M. (2006). Wearable olfactory display: Using odor in outdoor environment. [Alexandria, VA: IEEE Press.]. *Proceedings of IEEE Virtual Reality, 2006,* 205–212.

Yamaguchi, M., Deguchi, M., & Miyazaki, Y. (2006). The effects of exercise in forest and urban environments on sympathetic nervous activity of normal young adults. *The Journal of International Medical Research, 34*(2), 152–159.

Yamaguchi, M., Deguchi, M., Wakasugi, J., Ono, S., Takai, N., Higashi, T., & Mizuno, Y. (2006). Hand-held monitor of sympathetic nervous system using salivary amylase activity and its validation by driver fatigue assessment. *Biosensors & Bioelectronics, 21*(7), 1007–1014. doi:10.1016/j.bios.2005.03.014

Yamaguchi, M., Hanawa, N., Hamazaki, K., Sato, K., & Nakano, K. (2007). Evaluation of the acute sedative effect of fragrances based on a biochemical marker. *The Journal of Essential Oil Research, 19*(5), 470–476. doi:10.1080/10412905.2007.9699956

Yamaguchi, M., Kanemaru, M., Kanemori, T., & Mizuno, Y. (2003). Flow-injection-type biosensor system for salivary amylase activity. *Biosensors & Bioelectronics, 18*(5-6), 835–840. doi:10.1016/S0956-5663(03)00007-1

Yamaguchi, M., Kanemori, T., Kanemaru, M., Takai, N., Mizuno, Y., & Yoshida, H. (2004). Performance evaluation of salivary amylase activity monitor. *Biosensors & Bioelectronics, 20*(3), 491–497. doi:10.1016/j.bios.2004.02.012

Yamaguchi, M., Sakakima, J., Kosaka, S., & Nakabayashi, M. (2008). A method for evaluating the discomfort induced by odor using a biochemical marker. *Sensors and Actuators. B, Chemical, 131*, 143–147. doi:10.1016/j.snb.2007.12.009

Yamaguchi, M., Tahara, Y., & Kosaka, S. (2009). Influence of concentration of fragrances on salivary α-amylase. *International Journal of Cosmetic Science, 31*(5), 391–395. doi:10.1111/j.1468-2494.2009.00507.x

Yamaguchi, M., Takeda, K., Onishi, M., Deguchi, M., & Higashi, T. (2006). Non-verbal communication method based on a biochemical marker for people with severe motor and intellectual disabilities. *The Journal of International Medical Research, 34*(1), 30–41.

Yamanaka, K., Ishikawa, S., Nakaso, N., Takeda, N., Mihara, T., & Tsukuhara, Y. (2004). Ball SAW device for hydrogen gas sensor. In *Proceedings of the 2003 IEEE Ultrasonic Symposium,* (pp. 299-302). IEEE Press.

Yamanaka, T., Munakata, Y., & Ohba, T. (2010). *Digital-circuit implementation of olfactory-adaptation neural network for gas sensing.* Paper presented at 13th International Meeting on Chemical Sensors. Perth, Australia.

Yamanaka, K., Cho, H., & Tsukuhara, Y. (2000). Precise velocity measurement of surface acoustic waves on bearing ball. *Applied Physics Letters, 76*(19), 2797–2799. doi:10.1063/1.126481

Yamanaka, K., Ishikawa, S., Nakaso, N., Takeda, N., Sim, D. Y., & Mihara, T. (2006). Ultramultiple roundtrips of surface acoustic wave on sphere realizing innovation of gas sensors. *IEEE Transactions on UFFC, 53*(4), 793–801.

Yamanaka, T., Ishida, H., Nakamoto, T., & Moriizumi, T. (1998). Analysis of gas sensor transient response by visualizing instantaneous gas concentration using smoke. *Sensors and Actuators. A, Physical, 69*(1), 77–81. doi:10.1016/S0924-4247(98)00045-4

Yamanaka, T., Matsumoto, R., & Nakamoto, T. (2002). Study of odor blender using solenoid valves controlled by delta-sigma modulation method for odor recorder. *Sensors and Actuators. B, Chemical, 87*(3), 457–463. doi:10.1016/S0925-4005(02)00300-3

Yamanaka, T., Matsumoto, R., & Nakamoto, T. (2003). Article. *Sensors and Actuators. B, Chemical, 89*, 120–135. doi:10.1016/S0925-4005(02)00452-5

Yamanaka, T., Matsumoto, R., & Nakamoto, T. (2003). Fundamental study of odor recorder for multi-component odor using recipe exploration based on singular value decomposition. *IEEE Sensors Journal, 3*, 468–474. doi:10.1109/JSEN.2003.815778

Yamanaka, T., Matsumoto, R., & Nakamoto, T. (2003). Odor recorder for multi-component odor using two-level quantization method. *Sensors and Actuators. B, Chemical, 89*, 120–125. doi:10.1016/S0925-4005(02)00452-5

Yamanaka, T., Matsumoto, R., & Nakamoto, T. (2003). Study of recording apple flavor using odor recorder with five components. *Sensors and Actuators. B, Chemical, 89*, 112–119. doi:10.1016/S0925-4005(02)00451-3

Yamanaka, T., & Nakamoto, T. (2002). Improvement of odor-recorder robustness against environmental change using real-time reference method. *IEEJ Transactions on Sensors and Micromachines, 122*, 317.

Yamanaka, T., & Nakamoto, T. (2003). Real-time reference method in odor blender under environmental change. *Sensors and Actuators. B, Chemical, 93*, 51–56. doi:10.1016/S0925-4005(03)00202-8

Yamanaka, T., Yoshikawa, K., & Nakamoto, T. (2004). Improvement of odor-recoder capability for dynamical change of odor. *Sensors and Actuators. B, Chemical, 99*, 367. doi:10.1016/j.snb.2003.12.004

Yanagida, Y., Kawato, S., Noma, H., Tomono, A., & Tetsutani, N. (2004). Projection-based olfactory display with nose tracking. In *Proceedings of the IEEE Virtual Reality 2004,* (p. 43). Chicago, IL: IEEE Press.

Yanagida, Y., Kawato, S., Noma, H., Tomono, A., & Tetsutani, N. (2004). Projection-based olfactory display with nose tracking. [Chicago, IL: IEEE Press.]. *Proceedings of IEEE Virtual Reality, 2004*, 43–50.

Yanagida, Y., Noma, H., Tetsutani, N., & Tomono, A. (2003). An unencumbering, localized olfactory display. In *ACM CHI2003 Extended Abstracts* (pp. 988–989). New York, NY: ACM Press.

Yan, C., Zhao, A. Z., Bentley, J. K., Loughney, K., Ferguson, K., & Beavo, J. A. (1995). Molecular cloning and characterization of a calmodulin–dependent phosphodiesterase enriched in olfactory sensory neurons. *Proceedings of the National Academy of Sciences of the United States of America*, *92*, 9677–9681. doi:10.1073/pnas.92.21.9677

Yang, G. C., Scherer, P. W., Zhao, K., & Mozell, M. M. (2007). Numerical modeling of odorant uptake in the rat nasal cavity. *Chemical Senses*, *32*, 273–284. doi:10.1093/chemse/bjl056

Yan, W., Apweiler, R., Balgley, B. M., Boontheung, P., Bundy, J. L., & Cargile, B. J. (2009). Systematic comparison of the human saliva and plasma proteomes. *Proteomics. Clinical Applications*, *3*(1), 116–134. doi:10.1002/prca.200800140

Yan, Z., Tan, J., Qin, C., Lu, Y., Ding, C., & Luo, M. (2008). Precise circuitry links bilaterally symmetric olfactory maps. *Neuron*, *58*, 613–624. doi:10.1016/j.neuron.2008.03.012

Yao, Y., & Freeman, W. J. (1990). Model of biological pattern recognition with spatially chaotic dynamics. *Neural Networks*, *3*, 153–170. doi:10.1016/0893-6080(90)90086-Z

Yarita, H., Iino, M., & Tanabe, T. (1980). A transthalamic olfactory pathway to orbitofrontal cortex in the monkey. *Journal of Neurophysiology*, *43*, 69–85.

Yates, J., Chappell, M. J., & Gardner, J. W. (2007). Novel phenomena based dynamic model of carbon-black/composite vapour sensors. *Proceedings of the Royal Society of London. Series A*, *463*, 551–568. doi:10.1098/rspa.2006.1776

Yehuda, R. (2005). Neuroendocrine aspects of PTSD. *Handbook of Experimental Pharmacology*, *169*, 371–403. doi:10.1007/3-540-28082-0_13

Yehuda, R. (2006). Advances in understanding neuroendocrine alterations in PTSD and their therapeutic implications. *Annals of the New York Academy of Sciences*, *1071*, 137–166. doi:10.1196/annals.1364.012

Yokoi, M., Mori, K., & Nakanishi, S. (1995). Refinement of odor molecule tuning by dendrodendritic synaptic inhibition in the olfactory bulb. *Proceedings of the National Academy of Sciences of the United States of America*, *92*, 3371–3375. doi:10.1073/pnas.92.8.3371

Yoshida, R. (2010). Design of self-oscillating gels and application to biomimetic actuators. *Sensors (Basel, Switzerland)*, *10*(3), 1810–1822. doi:10.3390/s100301810

You, J. O., Almeda, D., Ye, G. J., & Auguste, D. T. (2010). Bioresponsive matrices in drug delivery. *Journal of Biological Engineering*, *4*(15), 1-12. Retrieved March 18, 2011, from http://www.jbioleng.org/content/4/1/15

Young, T. Y., & Fu, K. S. (1986). *Handbook of pattern recognition and image processing*. San Diego, CA: Academic Press.

Yuan, Q., & Knopfel, T. (2006). Olfactory nerve stimulation-evoked mGluR1 slow potentials, oscillations, and calcium signaling in mouse olfactory bulb mitral cells. *Journal of Neurophysiology*, *95*, 3097–3104. doi:10.1152/jn.00001.2006

Yu, F. D., Luo, L. A., & Grevillot, G. (2002). Adsorption isotherms of VOCs onto an activated carbon monolith: Experimental measurement and correlation with different models. *Journal of Chemical & Engineering Data*, *47*, 467–473. doi:10.1021/je010183k

Zald, D. H., & Pardo, J. V. (2000). Functional neuroimaging of the olfactory system in humans. *International Journal of Psychophysiology*, *36*, 165–181. doi:10.1016/S0167-8760(99)00110-5

Zampini, M., Wantling, E., Phillips, N., & Spence, C. (2008). Multisensory flavor perception: Assessing the influence of fruit acids and color cues on the perception of fruit flavored beverages. *Food Quality and Preference*, *18*, 335–343. doi:10.1016/j.foodqual.2007.11.001

Zatorre, R. (1992). Functional localization and lateralization of human olfactory cortex. *Nature*, *360*, 339–340. doi:10.1038/360339a0

Zeaiter, M., Roger, J., & Bellon-Maurel, V. (2005). Robustness of models developed by multivariate calibration: The inﬂuence of pre-processing methods. *Trends in Analytical Chemistry*, *24*(5), 437–445. doi:10.1016/j.trac.2004.11.023

Zeaiter, M., Roger, J., Bellon-Maurel, V., & Rutledge, D. (2004). Robustness of models developed by multivariate calibration: The assessment of robustness. *Trends in Analytical Chemistry*, *23*(2), 157–170. doi:10.1016/S0165-9936(04)00307-3

Zellers, E. T., Reidy, S., Veeneman, R. A., Gordenker, R., Steinecker, W. H., & Lambertus, G. R. ... Wise, K. D. (2007). An integrated micro-analytical system for complex vapor mixtures. In *Proceedings of the Technological Digest of Transducers 2007*, (pp. 1491-1494). IEEE.

Zellers, E. T., Batteman, S. A., Han, M., & Patrish, S. J. (1995). Optimal coating selection for the analysis of organic vapor mixtures with polymer-coated surface acoustic wave sensor arrays. *Analytical Chemistry*, *67*, 1092. doi:10.1021/ac00102a012

Zelles, T., Boyd, J. D., Hardy, A. B., & Delaney, K. R. (2006). Branch-specific Ca^{2+} influx from Na+-dependent dendritic spikes in olfactory granule cells. *The Journal of Neuroscience*, *26*, 30–40. doi:10.1523/JNEUROSCI.1419-05.2006

Zellner, D. A., & Kautz, M. A. (1990). Color affects perceived odor intensity. *Journal of Experimental Psychology. Human Perception and Performance*, *16*, 391–397. doi:10.1037/0096-1523.16.2.391

Zeng, H., Jiang, Y., Xie, G., & Yu, J. (2007). Polymer coated QCM sensor with modified electrode for the detection of DDVP. *Sensors and Actuators. B, Chemical*, *122*, 1–6. doi:10.1016/j.snb.2006.04.106

Zhan, C., & Luo, M. (2010). Diverse patterns of odor representation by neurons in the anterior piriform cortex of awake mice. *The Journal of Neuroscience*, *30*, 16662–16672. doi:10.1523/JNEUROSCI.4400-10.2010

Zhang, J. J., Okutani, F., Huang, G. Z., Taniguchi, M., Murata, Y., & Kaba, H. (2010). Common properties between synaptic plasticity in the main olfactory bulb and olfactory learning in young rats. *Neuroscience*, *170*, 259–267. doi:10.1016/j.neuroscience.2010.06.002

Zhang, Q., Zhang, S., Xie, C., Zenga, D., Fan, C., & Bai, Z. (2006). Characterization of Chinese vinegars by electronic nose. *Sensors and Actuators. B, Chemical*, *119*, 538–546. doi:10.1016/j.snb.2006.01.007

Zhang, X., & Firestein, S. (2002). The olfactory receptor gene superfamily of the mouse. *Nature Neuroscience*, *5*, 124–133.

Zhao, K., Dalton, P., Yang, G. C., & Scherer, P. W. (2006). Numerical modeling of turbulent and laminar airflow and odorant transport during sniffing in the human and rat nose. *Chemical Senses*, *31*, 107–118. doi:10.1093/chemse/bjj008

Zhou, H., Homer, M. L., Shevade, A. V., & Ryan, M. A. (2006). Nonlinear least-squares based method for identifying and quantifying single and mixed contaminants in air with an electronic nose. *Sensors (Basel, Switzerland)*, *6*, 1–18. doi:10.3390/s6010001

Ziyatdinov, A., Marco, S., Chaudry, A., Persaud, K., Caminal, P., & Perera, A. (2010). Drift compensation of gas sensor array data by common principal component analysis. *Sensors and Actuators. B, Chemical*, *146*, 460–465. doi:10.1016/j.snb.2009.11.034

Zuppa, M., Distante, C., Persaud, K., & Siciliano, P. (2007). Recovery of drifting sensor responses by means of DWT analysis. *Sensors and Actuators. B, Chemical*, *120*(2), 411–416. doi:10.1016/j.snb.2006.02.049

Zuppa, M., Distante, C., Siciliano, P., & Persaud, K. (2004). Drift counteraction with multiple self-organising maps for an electronic nose. *Sensors and Actuators. B, Chemical*, *98*, 305–317. doi:10.1016/j.snb.2003.10.029

Zybura, M., & Eskeland, G. A. (1999). *Olfaction for virtual reality. Quarter Project, Industrial Engineering 543*. Seattle, WA: University of Washington.

About the Contributors

Takamichi Nakamoto received his B.E. and M.E. degrees in 1982 and 1984, respectively, and his Ph.D. degree in Electrical and Electronic Engineering from Tokyo Institute of Technology, Tokyo, Japan. He worked for Hitachi in the area of VLSI design automation from 1984 to 1987. In 1987, he joined the Tokyo Institute of Technology as a Research Associate. In 1993, he became an Associate Professor with the Department of Electrical and Electronics Engineering, Tokyo Institute of Technology. From 1996 to 1997, he was a Visiting Scientist at Pacific Northwest Laboratories, Richland, WA, USA. He is currently an Associate Professor with the Department of Physical Electronics, Tokyo Institute of Technology. His research interests cover chemical sensing systems, acoustic wave sensors, neural networks, virtual reality, and ASIC design.

***

Oluwakemi Ademoye received a B.Sc. degree in Computer Science, in 1996, from the University of Benin, Nigeria. She then received a M.Sc. degree in Distributed Information Systems, and a Ph.D. degree in Information Systems and Computing from Brunel University, United Kingdom, in 2002 and 2008, respectively. Her field of research interest is focused on olfactory enhanced media and its use in virtual and augmented reality environments.

James Covington is an Associate Professor in the School of Engineering at the University of Warwick. He received his BEng in 1996 in Electronic Engineering and his PhD in 2000. His PhD was on the development of CMOS and SOI CMOS gas sensors for room temperature and high temperature operation. He worked as a research fellow for both Warwick University and Cambridge University on the development of gas and chemical sensors, and was appointed as a Lecturer in 2002, being promoted to Associate Professor in 2006. His current research interests focus on the development of silicon devices with novel materials using CMOS and SOI ASIC technology (nose-on-a-chip), and biologically inspired neuromorphic devices with applications based on environmental and biomedical engineering.

Jean-Jacques Delaunay was born on April 18, 1967. He received the Engineer degree from Strasbourg National School of Engineering and his Ph.D. degree from the University Louis Pasteur. He worked for NTT laboratories on various projects associated with the applications of new materials. He is currently an Associate Professor at the University of Tokyo. His research interests include the fabrication of sensors involving self-assembly (nanowires on film for water splitting, bridging nanowires for UV, cobalt-filled graphitic cages for storage) and the use of surface plasmons on subwavelength metallic structures for volatile molecule detection.

Matteo Falasconi received his degree in Physics (summa cum laude) in 2000 from the University of Pavia. In 2005, he obtained a PhD degree in Materials Engineering from the University of Brescia. At present, he is a member of the research staff of the SENSOR Lab at the University of Brescia. His research interests include chemical sensor devices and statistical data analysis for electronic noses. He is the author of 20 journal papers in the field of artificial olfaction and many contributions in topical conferences.

Jordi Fonollosa obtained the degrees in Physics (2002) and in Electronic Engineering (2007) and received his PhD in Engineering and Electronics Technologies (2009) from the University of Barcelona. His main areas of expertise include electronic instrumentation, sensors, and data processing for smart sensing.

Tadashi Fukawa graduated Bachelor of Engineering in 1995 from Osaka University and Master of Materials Science in 1997 from Japan Advanced Institute of Science and Technology. He has been a Researcher at Shinshu University since 2007, where he is working on the research and development of organic photovoltaic cell and organic nanomaterials for VOC sensor. He is also a Researcher at the Tokyo Institute of Technology.

Julian Gardner has received degrees from Birmingham University (BSc, First Class), Cambridge University (PhD in Electronics), and Warwick University (DSc in Engineering), UK. He is Professor of Electronic Engineering in the School of Engineering at Warwick University, UK. He is a Fellow of both the Institute of Engineering and Technology and the Royal Academy of Engineering, and has worked with more than 25 companies in the past 20 years developing CMOS gas sensors and electronic noses. He is an author of over 450 publications and more than 10 books. His is founder and head of the Warwick Microsensors and Bioelectronics Group within the School of Engineering. His research interests include the fields of smart sensors, biomimetic MEMS devices, and artificial olfaction. From 2009-2011, he was President of the International Society for Olfaction and Chemical Sensors.

Gheorghita Ghinea received the B.Sc. and B.Sc. (Hons) degrees in Computer Science and Mathematics in 1993 and 1994, respectively, and the M.Sc. degree in Computer Science in 1996, from the University of the Witwatersrand, Johannesburg, South Africa; he then received the Ph.D. degree in Computer Science from the University of Reading, United Kingdom, in 2000. He is a Reader in the School of Information Systems, Computing, and Mathematics at Brunel University, United Kingdom. Dr. Ghinea has over 100 refereed publications and currently leads a team of 8 research students in his fields of interest, which span perceptual multimedia, semantic media management, human computer interaction, and network security. He has co-edited four books including two on digital multimedia perception and design and multiple sensorial media advances and applications: new developments in mulsemedia.

Scott Gluck received a B.S. degree from the University of California at Santa Barbara and a M.S. degree from the University of Southern California, in 1985 and 1994, respectively, both in Computer Science. He has worked on numerous missions and received a number of NASA achievement awards while working at the Jet Propulsion Laboratory, Pasadena, CA, since joining in 1990. The projects he has contributed on include the ground data systems for the Electronic Nose, Tropospheric Emission Spectrometer (TES), Multi-angle Imaging Spectroradiometer (MISR), and the All Source Analysis System (ASAS) support processing. He is currently the system software engineer for the TES ground data system.

Fauzan Che Harun received his B.Eng degree in Electrical and Electronic Engineering from Universiti Teknologi Malaysia (UTM) in 2003. He then continued his studies in the area of Biomedical Electronic Engineering at University of Warwick, UK, where he was awarded an MSc in Advanced Electronic Engineering in 2005 and a PhD in Engineering in 2010. His research interests are mainly, but not restricted to, biomedical electronics, biologically-inspired micro-systems, biosensors, and MEMS/NEMS. Currently, he is Head of Department at the Therapy and Rehabilitation Department, Faculty of Health Science and Biomedical Engineering, UTM, and Researcher at the BioMedical and Instrumentation Electronics (bMIE), Infocomm Research Alliance, UTM.

Yuchiro Hashimoto was born in Gunma Prefecture, Japan, in 1972. He received the B.S., M.S., and Ph.D. degrees in Chemistry from the University of Tokyo. He has been a Chief Scientist of Mass Spectrometry Research Group in the Central Research Laboratory, Hitachi Ltd., since 2009. His research fields are mass spectrometry and its application researches such as forensic and medical applications.

Kenshi Hayashi was born in Fukuoka, Japan, and has received the B.E., M.E., and Ph.D. degrees in Electrical Engineering from Kyushu University, in 1984, 1986, and 1990, respectively. He is now a Professor at the Department of Electronics, School of Information Science and Electrical Engineering, Kyushu University. He belongs to graduate school of systems life sciences. His research interests are taste and odor sensors, odor imaging, nanomaterials, biometrics, electrochemical analysis, and surface science. Bio-inspired technologies are the basis of his research. Multichannel taste sensor, odor code sensor, odor clustering sensing, and odor image sensor depending on original transducer technologies have been invented through the research.

Michitaka Hirose is a Professor of Human Interface at the Graduate School of Information Science and Technology and Research Center for Advanced Science and Technology (RCAST), the University of Tokyo. His research interests include enhanced human interface, interactive computer graphics, wearable computer, and virtual reality. He received his B.E. degree in Mechanical Engineering and M.E. and Ph.D. degrees in Mechano-Informatics from the University of Tokyo.

Margie L. Homer is a Senior Technologist and currently the PI for the Rapid Analysis, Self-Calibrating Array Project at JPL. She was the co-investigator for the JPL ENose flight demonstration on the International Space Station. Her work on the ENose has included sensing film development, sensor design and testing, and data analysis. Work on sensing film development included optimization and testing of polymer-carbon composite films. She obtained a B.A. in Chemistry from Swarthmore College, Pennsylvania in 1985 and then a Ph.D. in Physical Chemistry from the University of California at Los Angeles in 1993.

Junichi Ide is the Principal Research Chemist with Technical Research Institute R&D Center of T. Hasegawa Co., Ltd., Kawasaki, Japan. He received the Master's degree from Department of Food Science and Technology, Faculty of Agriculture, Kyushu University, in 1977. His research interests are fusion of olfactory and visual information, sensory evaluation, and pattern analysis.

Tsuyoshi Ikehara received his MS and Ph.D. degrees in Physics from Tohoku University, Japan, in 1988 and 1993, respectively. From 1993 to 1999, he worked at the Micromachining Laboratory of Yokogawa Electric Corp., where he designed silicon pressure sensors and other microdevices. In 1999, he joined the National Institute of Advanced Industrial Science and Technology (AIST), where his current interests include the material property characterization of silicon and resonant type microsensors. Dr. Ikehara is a member of IEEE, the Institute of Electrical Engineers of Japan, and the Japan Society of Mechanical Engineers.

Hiroshi Ishida was born in Morgantown, WV, in 1970. He received the Master of Engineering and Doctor of Engineering degrees in Electrical and Electronic Engineering from the Tokyo Institute of Technology, Tokyo, Japan, in 1994 and 1997, respectively. From 1997 to 2004, he has been a Research Associate with the Department of Physical Electronics, Tokyo Institute of Technology. From 1998 to 2000, he was with Georgia Institute of Technology, Atlanta, as a Postdoctoral Fellow in the School of Chemistry and Biochemistry. In 2004, he joined the Department of Mechanical Systems Engineering, Tokyo University of Agriculture and Technology, as an Associate Professor, and currently holds the same position in Department of Bio-Applications and Systems Engineering. In 2007, he was a Visiting Researcher in the Centre for Applied Autonomous Sensor Systems, Örebro University, Sweden. His research interests are in biomimetic mechatronics with emphasis on chemical sensing systems and their applications in robotics.

Dong Wook Kim received the B.I.S. degree in Cultural Information Resources from Surugadai University, Saitama, Japan, in 2004, and the M.I.S. and Ph.D. degrees in Knowledge Science from Japan Advanced Institute of Science and Technology (JAIST), Ishikawa, Japan, in 2006 and 2009, respectively. From 2004 to 2009, he majored in olfactory display, focusing on the controlled release of aroma molecules. Since 2009, he has been an Expert Researcher with the National Institute of Information and Communications Technology (NICT), Kyoto, Japan. His current research interests include temporal and spatial control of aroma molecules for olfactory display, cross-modal perception, emotion and sensibility information processing, and multi-sensory interaction systems integrating four senses.

Mutsumi Kimura graduated Bachelor of Agriculture in 1990 and Master of Environmental Science in 1992, both from Tsukuba University. He completed his Doctor of Engineering in 1995 from Shinshu University. He became a Research Associate of Shinshu University in 1995 and has been an Associate Professor at Faculty of Textile Science and Technology, Shinshu University, since 2003. From 2002 to 2005, he was a PRESTO Researcher of JST. His research interests cover organic and inorganic nano-materials, functional polymer chemistry, self-organized soft materials, and smart textiles.

Adam K. Kisor received a B.A. in Cognitive Science and Visual Arts from the University of California, San Diego. Since coming to JPL in 1992, he has worked on advanced power conversion technologies and chemical sensor development. He is currently working on design, fabrication, and testing of fuel cell and electrolyzer devices.

Mitsuo Konno was born in Iwate, Japan, on October 15, 1943. He worked in the field of microwave research and developments at the Toshiba Corporation from 1970 to 2005. Since 2005, he is a Visiting Researcher at National Institute of Advanced Industrial Science and Technology (AIST). He worked in analysis and development of disk-type MEMS resonator for sensor application form 2005 to 2011. He received a Ph. D degree in Electrical Communication Engineering form Tohoku University in 1998.

Liana M. Lara received a BS in Fisheries from the University of Washington in 2000. On the JPL ENose project, she worked on fabricating and testing sensors, building and maintaining the gas delivery systems, collecting data, and troubleshooting instrumentation software. At JPL, she also worked with the Alkali Metal Thermal to Electric Converter (AMTEC) group, building and testing AMTECs. In 2010, she received a Masters in Business Administration from the California State University Los Angeles and is currently supporting the JPL Thermoelectrics group.

Graeme Lowe earned his PhD in Biophysics in 1987 at the California Institute of Technology, analyzing the mechanism of flagellar motility in the chemotactic behavior of bacterial cells. He engaged in postdoctoral studies at Yale University and the Monell Chemical Senses Center, focusing on the physiology of chemo-electrical transduction and the role of cyclic AMP in olfactory sensory neurons of amphibians and mammals. In 1998, he joined the faculty at Monell and established a laboratory to investigate signaling properties of dendrites and synapses of neurons in the mammalian olfactory bulb. His current research program is aimed at understanding basic mechanisms of a range of olfactory system functions, including neural synchronization, neuromodulation, plasticity, and odor mixture interactions, in the olfactory bulb.

Ryutaro Maeda, Doctor of Engineering, joined to Mechanical Engineering Laboratory, Agency of Advanced Science and Technology (AIST) in Tsukuba in 1980, after finishing Master course in Graduate School of Tokyo University. He is currently Director of UMEMSME (Research Centre of Ubiquitous MEMS and Micro Engineering) in AIST. He also works as Visiting Professor at Shanghai Jiaoton University since 2011. He has published more than 200 papers on MEMS and Nanoimprint, especially thin film actuators and 3D micro manufacturing, and his current research interest is application of wireless networked sensing for energy and safety management.

Kenneth S. Manatt received a B.S. degree in Earth Sciences from the University of California, Santa Cruz. Since coming to JPL in 1983, Ken has been involved in a number of flight projects as well as independent instrument development efforts. These missions include Voyager-Neptune, Cassini, Phoenix-MECA, Delta-183, and the Russian Mars 96 MOx instrument. He was the Lead Electronics Engineer on the JPL ENose team responsible for electronic design and fabrication. He has proved an asset to the project since the beginning, when he made significant contributions to the electronic design of the first and second generation instruments. He is currently helping to develop the PanFTS Mechanism thermal test system and develops custom electronic solutions for PanFTS's unique challenges.

Santiago Marco is Titular Professor at the Electronics Department in the University of Barcelona (UB) since 1995. He obtained his degree in and his PhD in Physics from the UB in 1988 and 1993, respectively. In 1994, he was a post-doc at the University of Rome "Tor Vergata" working on Data Processing for Artificial Olfaction. In 2004, he was in a sabbatical leave at the EADS-Corporate Research in Munich working in Ion Mobility Spectrometry.

Haruka Matsukura was born in Tochigi, Japan, in 1987. She received the Bachelor of Engineering and Master of Engineering degrees in Mechanical Systems Engineering from the Tokyo University of Agriculture and Technology, Tokyo, Japan, in 2009 and 2010, respectively. She is currently pursuing the Doctor of Engineering degree in the same institution. Her research interests are in olfactory displays and olfactory sensing systems for virtual reality applications.

Takashi Mihara received his MS degrees in Physics from Tokyo University of Science, Japan, in 1981. He worked on high-speed bipolar devices and ultra-high-speed ECL memories for super computer at Hitachi LSI system Corp. Since 1988, he worked on versatile BiCMOS with V-PNP, fatigue-free ferroelectric memories, and chemical sensor system using MEMS microcantilever in Olympus Corp. Now, he is a Director General of MEMS Industry Forum, PR and Promotion Dept., and MNOIC Strategy Planning Dept. Micromachine Center in Japan. He received the Ph.D. degree in Electrical Engineering in 1996.

Yuta Munakata received the Bachelor of Engineering in Electrical Engineering from Sophia University in 2010. He is currently a Master course student in Department of Information Science, Sophia University.

Sunao Murakami was born in Fukuoka, Japan, in 1978. He received the Ph. D. degree in Chemical Engineering from Kyushu University, Japan, in 2007. Since April 2008, he has been a Postdoctoral Fellow in the Advanced Manufacturing Research Institute (AMRI) and the Research Center for Ubiquitous MEMS and Micro Engineering (UMEMSME) of National Institute of Advanced Industrial Science and Technology (AIST), Tsukuba, Japan, in the research field of Microelectromechanical System (MEMS). His current main research interests are the areas of the MEMS including silicon microresonators and glass microchemical reactor systems.

Hisashi Nagano was born in Kumamoto Prefecture, Japan, in 1967. He graduated from Kumamoto Technical High School. He is a Senior Researcher of the Central Research Laboratory, Hitachi Ltd. His research fields are mass spectrometry and environmental monitoring. He managed the field test at train station.

Akio Nakamura is the Senior Food Technologist with Technical Research Institute R&D Center of T. Hasegawa Co., Ltd., Kawasaki, Japan. He received the Ph.D degree in Agricultural and Life Science at the University of Tokyo, Japan, in 2010. His research interests include physiological responses to flavors and aromas, chemosensory perception.

Noritaka Nakaso received BS degree in Materials Science from Hiroshima University, Hiroshima, Japan, in 1985, and the PhD degree in Electrical Engineering from Tohoku University, Sendai, Japan, in 1995. From 1985, he has been employed at Technical Research Institute of Toppan Printing Co., Ltd., Saitama, Japan, where he is currently a team leader. His current interests include study of ball SAW device from 2000. Dr. Nakaso received the 1989 Outstanding Paper Award of the IEEE Transaction on Ultrasonics, Ferroelectrics, and Frequency Control on a study of ultrasonic micro spectrometer, and he received the 2000 Best Paper Award of the Japanese Society for Non-Destructive Inspection.

Kenichi Okada received B.S., M.E., and Ph.D degrees in Instrumentation Engineering from Keio University, in 1973, 1975, and 1982, respectively. He is currently a Professor at the Department of Information and Computer Science at Keio University. His research interests include CSCW, group ware, human-computer interaction, and mobile computing. He is a member of IEEE, ACM, and IPSJ. He was a chairman of SIGGW, a chief editor of the IPSJ Journal, and an editor of *IEICE Transactions*. Dr. Okada received the IPSJ Best Paper Award in 1995, 2001, 2008, as well as the IPSJ 40th Anniversary Paper Award in 2000.

Sigeru Omatu, Professor, Department of Electronics, Information and Communication, Faculty of Engineering, Osaka Institute of Technology, Osaka, Japan. He received his Ph.D. in Electronic Engineering from Osaka Prefecture University and joined the faculty at University of Tokushima in 1969. He was Professor of University of Tokushima in 1988 and Professor of Osaka Prefecture University in 1995. He has been Professor of Osaka Institute of Technology since 2010. His honors and awards include the Best Paper Awards, IEE of Japan, 1991, SICE, Japan, 1995. Furthermore, he received Ichimura Distinguished Award for Intelligent Classification, New Technology Development Foundation, 1996, SICE Fellow and IEEJ Outstanding Achievement Award, 2005. He used to be the President of ISCIA (Institute of Systems, Control, and Information Association, Japan) in 2007 and President of Electronics, Information, and Systems Society, IEEJ, 2004-2006, Regional Editor of EAAI (IFAC Journal) for 1998-2001, Associate Editor of *IEEE Transactions on Neural Networks* for 1993-2003, and *IMA Journal of Mathematical Control and Information* (Oxford University Press) since 1991. His research area covers intelligent signal processing, pattern recognition, intelligent control, and adaptive control.

Marta Padilla received a degree in Physics from the University of La Laguna in 1999 and a degree in Electronic Engineering from University of Barcelona (UB) in 2003. Later, she joined the ISPlab (UB) and obtained her PhD in Engineering and Electronics Technologies in 2010.

Matteo Pardo received a degree in Physics (summa cum laude) in 1996 and a Ph.D. in Computer Engineering in 2000. Since 2002, he is a Researcher of the National Research Council (CNR). He was at the Max Planck Institute for Molecular Genetics in Berlin with a Von Humboldt Fellowship and was the Technical Chair of the International Symposium on Olfaction and Electronic Nose 2009. His research interest is data analysis and in particular the applications of pattern recognition techniques to artificial olfaction and genomics. Since 2011, he is the Scientific Attaché at the Italian Embassy in Berlin.

Margaret Amy Ryan holds a Ph.D. in Physical Chemistry from the University of Massachusetts at Amherst. Her work has included basic and applied research in the areas of electrochemical and photoelectrochemical energy conversion, thermal-to-electric energy conversion, and chemical sensing. At JPL, she was the Principal Investigator on the NASA Electronic Nose Technology Development and ISS Demonstration. She is retired from JPL.

Minoru Sakairi received his B.S., M.S., and Ph.D. degrees from The University of Tokyo in 1979, 1981, and 1989, respectively. During 1989-1990, he was a Guest Researcher at the National Institutes of Health (U.S.). He is Research Director of Life Science Research Laboratory, Central Research Laboratory, Hitachi, Ltd. He was awarded the Nikkei Global Environmental Technology Award (2000), the Okochi Memorial Technology Award (2000), the Ichimura Industrial Award (2007), and the Commendation for Science and Technology by the Minister of Education, Culture, Sports, Science, and Technology, Development Category (2008).

Giorgio Sberveglieri received his degree in Physics cum laude from the University of Parma (Italy), where in 1971 he started his research activities on the preparation of semiconductor thin film solar cells. In 1994, he was appointed Full Professor in Physics. He is Director of SENSOR Lab since its establishment in 1987 at the Department of Chemistry and Physics, University of Brescia. His work has had a significant impact at the international level in the field of metal oxide semiconductors, mainly for gas sensing and artificial olfaction applications. He is author of more than 380 publications (h-index: 39) cited more than 6,000 times, 9 patents, one book, and four book chapters.

Michiko Seyama received the B.S. and M.S. degrees in Applied Chemistry from Waseda University in 1995 and 1997, respectively. She entered NTT in 1997 and worked on sensor systems for environmental monitoring, odor sensing based on plasma-deposited organic films, and SPR sensors related with bio-molecules including G-protein coupled receptors and olfactory receptors. She also studies the microfluidic device combined with the SPR sensor for on-site biosensing. She received Ph.D degree from Waseda University in 2004. She is a member of the Japan Society of Applied Physics (JSAP) and the American Chemical Society (ACS).

Vivek Shetty is a Professor of Oral and Maxillofacial Surgery and Assistant Vice Chancellor for Research at the University of California, Los Angeles (UCLA). A clinician-scientist by training, his translational research program is defined by the significant burden of traumatic stress-related psychiatric sequelae in vulnerable population. His transdisciplinary collaborations focus on the synergistic application of emerging technologies to the development of decision support systems for screening, early detection, and management of mental health disorders. Professor Shetty's research has been supported by the National Institutes of Health for the past 18 years, and he serves as a scientific reviewer for several research agencies and specialty journals. Dr. Shetty graduated from the University of Bombay, completed his specialty training and research doctorate at the University of Regensburg, Germany, and his fellowship training at the Massachusetts General Hospital and UCLA, respectively.

Abhijit V. Shevade received his B.Chem.Eng. and M.Chem.Eng. degrees in Chemical Engineering from the University Department of Chemical Technology, University of Bombay, India, in 1993 and 1996, respectively. He received a Ph.D. in Chemical Engineering from Kansas State University, USA, in 2001. He was a Caltech Postdoctoral Scholar Resident at JPL from 2001-2003. On the JPL ENose project, he worked on the sensing materials selection and sensor response modeling aspects. His research interests include development and application of molecular/multiphysics modeling and simulation tools in combination with experimental approaches for design and characterization of materials, including: organic (e.g., polymers/polymer composites), inorganic (e.g., heterogeneous catalysts), biomimetic (e.g., self-assembly molecules, molecular imprinted materials). Applications include micro/nano chemical/biological sensors and energy generation and storage devices.

Iwao Sugimoto received B.S. and M.S. degrees in Synthetic Chemistry and Ph.D. degree in Molecular Engineering from Kyoto University, Kyoto, Japan, in 1983, 1985, and 1991, respectively. In 1985, he joined NTT (Nippon Telegraph and Telephone Corporation), where he was engaged in artificial olfaction in connection with sensor networks. He moved to Tokyo University of Technology in 2002. He is a Professor of School of Computer Science. His research activity focuses on the formation and properties of organic sensing layers for environmental monitoring. A range of vacuum and plasma techniques have been used to prepare sensing layers with interactive structures. His main interest is revealing the sorption-desorption behaviors of smell molecules based on quantitative structure property relationships.

Sayumi Sugimoto received her B.S. degree from the Department of Information and Computer Science at Keio University, Japan, in 2009. She is currently working toward an M.S. degree in Open and Environment Systems at Keio University. Her current research interests include olfactory information and its use in multimedia.

Masuyuki Sugiyama was born in Shizuoka Prefecture, Japan, in 1978. He received the B.S., M.S., and Ph.D. degrees in Chemistry from Tohoku University. He is a Researcher of the Central Research Laboratory, Hitachi Ltd. His research fields are mass spectrometry and its application. His current work is instrumentation development of the ion trap mass spectrometer.

Yasuaki Takada was born in Tochigi Prefecture, Japan, in 1965. He received the B.S. and M.S. degree in Physics from Shizuoka University and Kyushu University, respectively. He received the Ph.D. degree in Applied Chemistry from The University of Tokyo. He is a Senior Researcher of the Central Research Laboratory, Hitachi Ltd. His research fields are mass spectrometry and environmental monitoring. His current research is quick detection of explosives, illicit drugs, and chemical warfare agents by mass spectrometry. He was a research representative of the R&D program for the development of the walkthrough detection portal system operated by MEXT (Ministry of Education, Culture, Sports, Science, and Technology, Japan) in 2007-2009.

Tomohiro Tanikawa received his B.E. degree from the Department of Engineering Synthesis, the University of Tokyo in 1997, and M.E. and Ph.D. degrees from the Department of Mechano-Informatics, the University of Tokyo in 1999 and 2002, respectively. From 2002 to 2004, he worked as a Project Researcher for NICT (National Institute of Information and Communications Technology). He has been affiliated with the University of Tokyo since 2005, and he now is an Assistant Professor at the Graduate School of Information Science and Technology, the University of Tokyo. His research focuses on developing a high-level user interface using technologies of virtual reality, mixed reality, human-computer interaction, multimodal interface, and image-based rendering.

Akira Tomono received the B.E. and the M.E. degrees in Electronics Engineering from Yamanashi University, Japan, in 1974 and 1976, respectively, and the Dr. Eng. degree in Electrical Engineering from Tokyo Institute of Technology, Japan, in 1994. In 1976, he joined the Electrical Communication Laboratories of NTT, Japan. From 1987 to 1991, he was at Advanced Telecommunication Research Institute International (ATR), Kyoto, Japan. He has been a Professor at the Department of Information Media Technology, Tokai University, since 2000. His research interests include human interface, ergonomics, and virtual reality. Dr. Tomono is a member of the Institute of Electronics, Information, and Communication Engineers of Japan. He received the 1994 Best Paper Award from the Institute of Television Engineers and the 2003 Japan Society for Engineering Education Award.

Mitsuo Tonoike of Japan was born in Manchu in China in 1944. He graduated from Department of Physics, Faculty of Science, Shizuoka University, in Japan, in 1967. He acquired Doctor Degree of Engineering (Ph.D) from Osaka University in 1985. He has tried to apply the engineering techniques, physics, and artificial sensors to measure and analyze human sensing objectively in Electro-Technical Laboratory (ETL), in Ministry of International Trade and Industry (MITI) in Japan since about 1980. He started to study the bio-science fields, especially the research of human olfaction by using the techniques of a few non-invasive measurements (EEG, MEG, f-MRI, and so on) and an artificial odorant sensor system. Now, he belongs to Department of Medical Engineering, Faculty of Nursing and Rehabilitation, in Aino University, since in 2011 as a Professor, through a Professor of Faculty of Engineering and CFME Center in Chiba University from 2003 to 2010.

Bartosz Wyszynski received his ME and PhD degrees from Department of Chemical Technology and Engineering, Technical University of Szczecin, in 1997 and 2001, respectively. In 2001, he was a Research Assistant in Technical University of Szczecin. From 2005 to 2007, he was a Postdoctoral Researcher at Tokyo Institute of Technology under fellowship from Japan Society for the Promotion of Science. Currently, he is a Researcher in Tokyo Institute of Technology. His main research interests are psychophysiology of olfaction, artificial olfaction and chemical sensing, environmental impact of odors, and odor control policies.

Masuyoshi Yamada was born in Chiba Prefecture, Japan, in 1968. He received the B.Eng., M.Eng., and Ph.D. degrees in Mechanical Engineering from the University of Tokyo. He is a Senior Researcher of the Central Research Laboratory, Hitachi Ltd. His research fields are mass spectrometry and its application for forensic science and environmental monitoring.

Masaki Yamaguchi was born in Nagoya, Japan, in 1963. He received the B.S. and M.S. degrees in Engineering from Shinshu University, Japan, in 1985 and 1987. He joined the Research Laboratory of Brother Industries, Ltd., Japan, in 1987. He received the Doctoral degree in Engineering from Shinshu University in 1994. He started as an Assistant Professor at Tokyo University of Agriculture and Technology,

Japan, in 1995. Since 1999, he has been an Associate Professor in Faculty of Engineering at University of Toyama, Japan. He is currently working as a Professor in Graduate School of Engineering at Iwate University, Japan, since 2008. He coauthored 16 books, 93 refereed scientific and technical papers, and 11 US patents concerning electromagnetic actuators, medical sensors, robotics, and their applications. His primary research interests focus on the development of noninvasive medical sensors and robotics.

Takao Yamanaka received the Bachelor of Engineering, the Master of Engineering, and the Ph.D. in Engineering from Tokyo Institute of Technology in 1996, 1998, and 2004, respectively. He is currently an Associate Professor in the Department of Information and Communication Sciences, Sophia University, Japan. His research interests include sensory information processing, intelligent sensing systems, and pattern recognition.

Yasuyuki Yanagida is a Professor in the Department of Information Engineering, Faculty of Science and Technology, Meijo University, Nagoya, Japan. He received B.E., M.E., and Dr. Eng. degrees in Mathematical Engineering and Information Physics from the University of Tokyo in 1988, 1990, and 2000, respectively. Yanagida was a Research Associate at the University of Tokyo from 1990 to 2001 and a Senior Researcher at Advanced Telecommunication Research Institute International (ATR), Kyoto, Japan from 2001 to 2005. His research interests include virtual reality, telexistence, and interactive interfaces that make use of various sensory modalities.

Shiao-Ping S. Yen received a B.S. in Chemistry from National Taiwan Normal University (1954) and a M.S. in Polymer Chemistry from the University of Akron (1958). She was a Ph.D. candidate at the Case Institute of Technology (1958-1959) and a Fellow in the Fundamental Research Division at the Carnegie Mellon University (1959-1968). She received an Honorary D.Sc in Polymer Sciences from Pepperdine University, Malibu, California in 1985. Since 1969, she has been at JPL. For the JPL ENose project, she was responsible for synthesizing and formulating polymer based composite sensing films. Her research interests include: polymer synthesis and material characterization, high temperature polymers, anionic polymerization using organometallic initiator polyelectrolytes, electronic and ionic conductors, immuno-reagents, lithium battery electrolyte and electrodes, dielectric materials for high energy density capacitors, polymeric materials for microelectronics.

Hanying Zhou is a member of the JPL ENose team. She develops data analysis programs to deconvolute the patterns of the JPL ENose distributed response. She received her M. S. in Optical Engineering from Zhejiang University, China, in 1988, and a Ph.D. in Electrical Engineering from the Pennsylvania State University in 1995. Between 1988 and 1990, she was a Research Scientist at Shanghai Institute of Fine Optics and Mechanics, Academia Sinica. Since 1998, she has been with JPL, where her main research interests include optical pattern recognition and holographic memory.

Index